YOUR Window TO History

Reading
like a Historian

Historians use paintings, like this one from the golden throne of Tutankhamen, to help understand the past. As you study world history, you too will learn how to use different historical sources to **Read like a Historian.**

To find out more about reading like a historian and the historical sources that follow, visit

go.hrw.com
More Online
KEYWORD: HISTORIAN

By Frances Marie Gipson
Secondary Literacy Coordinator
Los Angeles Unified School District, Los Angeles, California

What Does It Mean to Read like a Historian?

In your history class you will be doing a lot of reading, thinking, and problem-solving. Much of your reading and thinking will center on different types of texts or materials. Since you are in a history class reading all sorts of things, a question to consider is, "What does it mean to think, read, and solve problems like a historian?"

Historians work with different types of sources to understand and learn from history. Two categories of sources are **primary** and **secondary** sources.

Primary Sources are historical documents, written accounts by a firsthand witness, or objects that have survived from the past. A study of primary sources might include letters, government documents, diaries, photographs, art objects, stamps, coins, and even clothing.

Secondary Sources are accounts of past events created by people some time after the events happened. This textbook and other books written about historical events are examples of secondary sources.

As you learn more about your work as a historian, you will begin to ask questions and analyze historical materials. You will be working as a detective, digging into history to create a richer understanding of the mysteries of the past.

How to Analyze an Artifact

Artifacts, such as this bronze food vessel from China's Shang dynasty, take many forms. They might be coins, stone tools, pieces of clothing, or even items found in your backpack. As you study artifacts in this textbook, ask yourself questions like the ones below.

- Why was this object created?

- When and where would it have been used?

- Who used the artifact?

- What does the artifact tell me about the technology available at the time it was created?

- What can it tell me about the life and times of the people who used it?

- How does the artifact help to make sense of the time period?

How to Analyze Written Sources

Code of Hammurabi

196. If a man put out the eye of another man, his eye shall be put out.

197. If he break another man's bone, his bone shall be broken.

198. If he put out the eye of a freed man, or break the bone of a freed man, he shall pay one gold mina.

199. If he put out the eye of a man's slave, or break the bone of a man's slave, he shall pay one-half of its value.

222. If he were a freed man he shall pay three shekels.

223. If he were a slave his owner shall pay the physician two shekels.

–Code of Hammurabi, translated by L. W. King

Asking questions can help you determine the relevance and importance of primary sources such as the Code of Hammurabi, the earliest known example of written laws. As you analyze the primary source above and the primary and secondary sources included in this textbook, ask questions like the ones below.

- Who created the source and why?
- Did the writer have firsthand knowledge of the event, or report what others saw or heard?
- Was the writer a neutral party, or did the author have opinions or interests that might have influenced what was recorded?
- Did the writer wish to inform or persuade others?
- Was the information recorded during the event, immediately after the event, or after some lapse of time?

The Military in Ancient Egypt

"The pharaohs began . . . leading large armies out of a land that had once known only small police forces and militia. The Egyptians quickly extended their military and commercial influence over an extensive region that included the rich provinces of Syria . . . and the numbers of Egyptian slaves grew swiftly."

–C. Warren Hollister, from *Roots of the Western Tradition*

When reading secondary sources, such as the description of the military in ancient Egypt above, historians ask additional questions to seek understanding. They try to source the text, build evidence, and interpret the message that is being conveyed. For historians, reading is a quest to find evidence to answer or challenge a historical problem. As you study secondary sources, ask questions like the ones below.

- Who is the author? What do I know about this author?
- Did the author have firsthand information? What is the author's relationship to the event?
- What might be the author's motivation in writing this piece?
- What type of evidence did the author look at?
- Are any assumptions or bias present?
- How does this document fit into the larger context of the events I am studying?
- What kind of source is it?
- Is the source an original?
- Is the content probable or reasonable?
- What does the date tell me about the event?
- What do I already know about this topic that will help me understand more of what I am reading?

How to Analyze a Historical Map

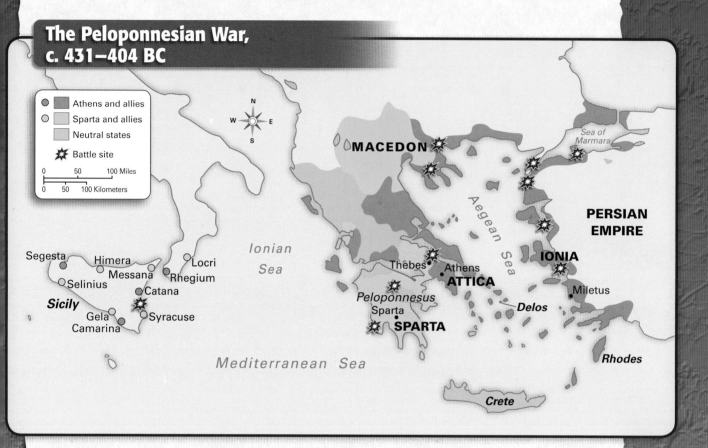

The Peloponnesian War, c. 431–404 BC

Legend:
- Athens and allies
- Sparta and allies
- Neutral states
- ✦ Battle site

0   50   100 Miles
0   50   100 Kilometers

MACEDON

Sea of Marmara

PERSIAN EMPIRE

Aegean Sea

IONIA

Ionian Sea

Thebes   Athens
ATTICA

Miletus

Peloponnesus
Sparta
SPARTA

Delos

Segesta
Himera   Locri
Messana   Rhegium
Selinius
Catana
Sicily
Gela   Syracuse
Camarina

Mediterranean Sea

Rhodes

Crete

Maps, such as the one above showing major allies in ancient Greece's Peloponnesian War, are symbolic representations of places shown in relation to one another. All maps necessarily include some details and leave out others. As you study maps in this textbook, ask questions like the ones below.

- What time period does the map show?
- What details has the mapmaker chosen to include (or exclude) on this map?
- Why was the map drawn?
- How can I determine if the map is accurate?
- How are maps used to analyze the past, present, and future?

How to Analyze **Art**

Art, like these 9,000-year-old rock paintings from Brazil, is another important source for historians. One way to study a piece of art is to write down everything that you think is important about it. Then divide the image into four sections and describe the important elements from each section. As you study art in this textbook, ask questions like the ones below.

- What is the setting for the art?
- When and where in the past was the art created?
- What is the subject of the art?
- What other details can I observe?
- What does the art reveal about its subject?
- How can I describe the artist's point of view?

How to Analyze an Infographic

Rulers of Kush

Like the Egyptians, the people of Kush considered their rulers to be gods. Kush's culture was similar to Egypt's, but there were also important differences.

Like the Egyptians, Kush's rulers built pyramids, but they were much smaller and the style was different.

Kush was ruled by a few different powerful queens. Queens seem to have been more important in Kush than in Egypt.

Stone carvings were made to commemorate important buildings and events, just like in Egypt. Kush's writing system was similar to Egyptian hieroglyphics, but scholars have been unable to understand most of it.

Infographics give you information in a visual format, using captions and call-out boxes to help explain the intent of the drawing. As you study infographics in this textbook, use the helpful tips and questions below.

- List the parts of the drawing and the importance of each part.
- Describe the focus or significance of the drawing.
- Do the captions and call-out boxes clarify the drawing's purpose?
- Does the drawing help me understand the information that I am studying in my textbook better?

HOLT

WORLD HISTORY

Ancient
Civilizations

Stanley M. Burstein

Richard Shek

HOLT, RINEHART AND WINSTON

A Harcourt Education Company

Orlando • **Austin** • New York • San Diego • Toronto • London

Authors

Dr. Stanley M. Burstein

Dr. Stanley M. Burstein is Professor Emeritus of Ancient History and former Chair of the Department of History at California State University, Los Angeles. Dr. Burstein received his B.A., M.A., and Ph.D. degrees from the University of California at Los Angeles and is the author of more than 100 books, articles, and chapters on ancient history. His specialties include ancient Greece, Greek and Roman Egypt, and Kush. Dr. Burstein has served as President of the Association of Ancient Historians and as a member of the California History–Social Science Standards/Course Models Project, the California Content Review Panel for History–Social Science, and the Content Review Panel for the California STAR test in history.

Dr. Richard Shek

Dr. Richard Shek is Professor of Humanities and Religious Studies at California State University, Sacramento. A native of China, Dr. Shek did his undergraduate work in Tokyo, Japan, and received his Ph.D. in history from the University of California at Berkeley. His specialties are East Asian cultural and religious history, and he has numerous publications on Confucianism, Daoism, Buddhism, and popular religion in China and Japan. Dr. Shek has served as a member of the California Content Review Panel for History–Social Science and is currently a member of the Content Review Panel for the California STAR test in history.

ISBN 0-03-073459-2

4 5 6 7 8 9 032 11 10 09 08 07 2007 Printing

Program Consultants

Contributing Author

Kylene Beers, Ed.D.
Senior Reading Researcher
School Development Program
Yale University
New Haven, Connecticut

General Editor

Frances Marie Gipson
Secondary Literacy
Los Angeles Unified School
    District
Los Angeles, California

Senior Literature and Writing Specialist

Carol Jago
English Department Chairperson
Santa Monica High School
Santa Monica, California

Consultants

John Ferguson, M.T.S., J.D.
Senior Religion Consultant
Assistant Professor
Political Science/Criminal Justice
Howard Payne University
Brownwood, Texas

Rabbi Gary M. Bretton-Granatoor
Religion Consultant
Director of Interfaith Affairs
Anti-Defamation League
New York, New York

J. Frank Malaret
Senior Consultant
Dean, Downtown and West
    Sacramento Outreach Centers
Sacramento City College
Sacramento, California

Kimberly A. Plummer, M.A.
Senior Consultant
History-Social Science Educator/
    Advisor
Holt, Rinehart and Winston
California Consultant Manager

Andrés Reséndez, Ph.D.
Senior Consultant
Assistant Professor
Department of History
University of California at Davis
Davis, California

California Specialists

Ann Cerny, M.A.
Middle School History Teacher
San Dieguito Union High School
    District
Solana Beach, California

Julie Chan, Ed.D.
Director, Literacy Instruction
Newport-Mesa Unified School
    District
Costa Mesa, California

Gary F. DeiRossi, Ed.D.
Assistant Superintendent
San Joaquin County Office of
    Education
Stockton, California

Fern M. Sheldon, M.Ed.
Curriculum Specialist
Rowland Unified School District
Rowland Heights, California

California Program Advisors

The California program consultants and reviewers included on these pages provided guidance throughout the development of Holt California Social Studies: *World History: Ancient Civilizations.* As the map below demonstrates, their valuable contributions represent the viewpoints of teachers throughout California.

Educational Reviewers

Sally Knudtson Adams
Garden Grove High School
Garden Grove, California

Anne Bjornson
A.P. Giannini Middle School
San Francisco, California

Anthony Braxton
Herbert H. Cruickshank
Middle School
Merced, California

Ann Cerny, M.A.
Middle School History Teacher
San Dieguito Union High
School District
Solana Beach, California

Julie Chan, Ed.D.
Director, Literacy Instruction
Newport-Mesa Unified School
District
Costa Mesa, California

Mary Demetrion
Patrick Henry Middle School
Los Angeles, California

Yolanda Espinoza
Walter Stiern Middle School
Bakersfield, California

Carla Freel
Hoover Middle School
Merced, California

Tim Gearhart
Daniel Lewis Middle School
Paso Robles, California

Frances Marie Gipson
Secondary Literacy
Los Angeles Unified School
District
Los Angeles, California

Carol Jago
English Department Chairperson
Santa Monica High School
Santa Monica, California

J. Frank Malaret
Senior Consultant
Dean, Downtown and West
Sacramento Outreach Centers
Sacramento City College
Sacramento, California

Kimberly A. Plummer, M.A.
Senior Consultant
History-Social Science Educator/
Advisor
Holt, Rinehart and Winston
California Consultant Manager

Andrés Reséndez, Ph.D.
Senior Consultant
Assistant Professor
Department of History
University of California at Davis
Davis, California

Fern M. Sheldon, M.Ed.
Curriculum Specialist
Rowland Unified School District
Rowland Heights, California

Robert Valdez
Pioneer Middle School
Tustin, California

Sheila Weiner
Gasparde Portola Middle School
San Diego, California

Field Test Teachers

Andy Alexander
Harvest Valley Elementary
Romoland, California

Harriette Bone
Pio Pico Middle School
Los Angeles, California

Christy King
Castle View Elementary
Riverside, California

Nancy Lamott
Tierra Del Sol Middle School
Lakeside, California

Tracy Leathers
Isabelle Jackson Elementary
Sacramento, California

Leigh Mauney
Isabelle Jackson Elementary
Sacramento, California

Susan Mitchell
Jefferson Middle School
Oceanside, California

James Nadler
Lennox Middle School
Lennox, California

Tisha Rugg
Thomas Coleman Middle School
Orangevale, California

JoAnn Wade
Lennox Middle School
Lennox, California

Sheila Weiner
Gasparde Portola Middle School
San Diego, California

Karen York
Mitchell Middle School
Rancho Cordova, California

Academic Reviewers

Jonathan Beecher, Ph.D.
Department of History
University of California, Santa Cruz

Jerry H. Bentley, Ph.D.
Department of History
University of Hawaii

Elizabeth Brumfiel, Ph.D.
Department of Anthropology
Northwestern University
Evanston, Illinois

Eugene Cruz-Uribe, Ph.D.
Department of History
Northern Arizona University

Toyin Falola, Ph.D.
Department of History
University of Texas

Sandy Freitag, Ph.D.
Director, Monterey Bay History and Cultures Project
University of California, Santa Cruz

Yasuhide Kawashima, Ph.D.
Department of History
University of Texas at El Paso

Robert J. Meier, Ph.D.
Department of Anthropology
Indiana University

Marc Van De Mieroop, Ph.D.
Department of History
Columbia University
New York, New York

M. Gwyn Morgan, Ph.D.
Department of History
University of Texas

Robert Schoch, Ph.D.
CGS Division of Natural Science
Boston University

David Shoenbrun, Ph.D.
Department of History
Northwestern University
Evanston, Illinois

Meet the Sikhs is a video that discusses the Sikh community in northern California. Starting with an annual Sikh celebration, the video provides an overview of the Sikh community, including the foundation of its religious beliefs and attire, immigration patterns, and the accomplishments of community members. The video can be downloaded for educational purposes only, and admission cannot be charged for any viewing of the piece. This video is available in QuickTime format at the KVIE Web site at http://www.kvie.org/education/outreachservices/.

Contents

UNIT 1 Early Humans and Societies 1

CHAPTER 1 Uncovering the Past 2

 California Standards

Analysis Skills
HI 5 Recognize that interpretations of history are subject to change as new information is uncovered.

 History's Impact Video Series
The Impact of Archaeology

California Standards

History–Social Science

6.1 Students describe what is known through archaeological studies of the early physical and cultural development of humankind from the Paleolithic era to the agricultural revolution.

Analysis Skills

CS 1 Explain how events are related in time.

HI 1 Explain central issues and problems from the past.

 History's Impact Video Series
The Impact of the Early Migrations to North America

California Standards

History–Social Science

6.5 Students analyze the geographic, political, economic, religious, and social structures of the early civilizations of India.

 History's Impact Video Series
The Impact of Buddhism as a World Religion

California Standards

History–Social Science
6.3 Students analyze the geographic, political, economic, religious, and social structures of the Ancient Hebrews.

Analysis Skills
HI 2 Understand and distinguish long- and short-term causal relations.
HR 2 Distinguish fact from opinion in historical narratives and stories.

History's Impact Video Series
The Impact of Judaism throughout the World

California Standards

History–Social Science
7.1 Students analyze the causes and effects of the vast expansion and ultimate disintegration of the Roman Empire.

Analysis Skills
HI 4 Recognize the role of chance, oversight, and error in history.

 History's Impact Video Series
The Impact of Ancient Rome on the World Today

California Standards

7.7 Students compare and contrast the geographic, political, economic, religious, and social structures of the Meso-American and Andean civilizations.

Analysis Skills
HR 3 Distinguish relevant from irrelevant, essential from incidental, and verifiable from unverifiable information.

 History's Impact Video Series
The Impact of Mayan Achievements on Math and Astronomy

References R1

Features

Justinian and Theodora

Charts, Graphics, and Time Lines

Analyze information presented visually to learn more about history.

Heavy mammoth bones were used as a frame for the shelter.

A mammoth house

Examine key facts and concepts quickly and easily with graphics.

Roman Society

Patricians	Plebeians
■ Wealthy, powerful citizens	■ Common people
■ Nobles	■ Peasants, crafts-people, traders, other workers
■ Small minority of the population	■ Majority of the population
■ Once controlled all aspects of government	■ Gained right to participate in government
■ After 218 BC, not allowed to participate in trade or commerce	■ Only Romans who could be traders, so many became wealthy

Reading Social Studies

Learn and practice skills that will help you read your social studies lessons.

Writing Workshop

Learn to write about history.

FOCUS ON WRITING

Use writing to study and reflect on the events and people who made history.

FOCUS ON SPEAKING

Use speaking skills to study and reflect on the events and people who made history.

Maps

Interpret maps to see where important events happened and analyze how geography has influenced history.

Primary Sources

Relive history through eyewitness accounts, literature, and documents.

Primary Source

BOOK

The Death of Socrates

*In 399 BC Socrates was arrested
and charged with corrupting the
young people of Athens and ignoring
religious traditions. He was sentenced
to die by drinking poison. Socrates
spent his last hours surrounded by
his students. One of them, Plato, later
described the event in detail.*

Socrates himself
does not protest
against his sentence
but willingly drinks
the poison.

The students and
friends who have vis-
ited Socrates, including
the narrator, are much
less calm than he is.

"Then raising the cup to his lips, quite
readily and cheerfully he drank off the poison. And hitherto most of us had been able
to control our sorrow; but now when we saw
him drinking . . . my own tears were flowing
fast; so that I covered my face and wept . . .
Socrates alone retained his calmness: What
is this strange outcry? he said . . . I have
been told that a man should die in peace.
Be quiet then, and have patience.**"**

–Plato, from *Phaedo*

Mapping the Earth

A **globe** is a scale model of the earth. It is useful for showing the entire earth or studying large areas of the earth's surface.

A pattern of lines circles the globe in east-west and north-south directions. It is called a **grid**. The intersection of these imaginary lines helps us find places on the earth.

The east-west lines in the grid are lines of **latitude**. Lines of latitude are called **parallels** because they are always parallel to each other. These imaginary lines measure distance north and south of the **equator**. The equator is an imaginary line that circles the globe halfway between the North and South Poles. Parallels measure distance from the equator in **degrees**. The symbol for degrees is °. Degrees are further divided into **minutes**. The symbol for minutes is ´. There are 60 minutes in a degree. Parallels north of the equator are labeled with an N. Those south of the equator are labeled with an S.

The north-south lines are lines of **longitude**. Lines of longitude are called **meridians**. These imaginary lines pass through the Poles. They measure distance east and west of the **prime meridian**. The prime meridian is an imaginary line that runs through Greenwich, England. It represents 0° longitude.

Lines of latitude range from 0°, for locations on the equator, to 90°N or 90°S, for locations at the Poles. Lines of longitude range from 0° on the prime meridian to 180° on a meridian in the mid-Pacific Ocean. Meridians west of the prime meridian to 180° are labeled with a W. Those east of the prime meridian to 180° are labeled with an E.

Lines of Latitude

Lines of Longitude

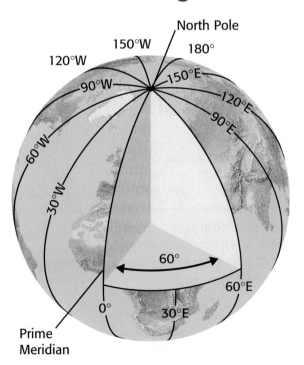

The equator divides the globe into two halves, called **hemispheres**. The half north of the equator is the Northern Hemisphere. The southern half is the Southern Hemisphere. The prime meridian and the 180° meridian divide the world into the Eastern Hemisphere and the Western Hemisphere. However, the prime meridian runs right through Europe and Africa. To avoid dividing these continents between two hemispheres, some mapmakers divide the Eastern and Western hemispheres at 20°W. This places all of Europe and Africa in the Eastern Hemisphere.

Our planet's land surface is divided into seven large landmasses, called **continents**. They are identified in the maps on this page. Landmasses smaller than continents and completely surrounded by water are called **islands**.

Geographers also organize Earth's water surface into parts. The largest is the world ocean. Geographers divide the world ocean into the Pacific Ocean, the Atlantic Ocean, the Indian Ocean, and the Arctic Ocean. Lakes and seas are smaller bodies of water.

Northern Hemisphere

Southern Hemisphere

Western Hemisphere

Eastern Hemisphere

Mapmaking

A **map** is a flat diagram of all or part of the earth's surface. Mapmakers have created different ways of showing our round planet on flat maps. These different ways are called **map projections**. Because the earth is round, there is no way to show it accurately in a flat map. All flat maps are distorted in some way. Mapmakers must choose the type of map projection that is best for their purposes. Many map projections are one of three kinds: cylindrical, conic, or flat-plane.

Paper cylinder

Cylindrical Projections

Cylindrical projections are based on a cylinder wrapped around the globe. The cylinder touches the globe only at the equator. The meridians are pulled apart and are parallel to each other instead of meeting at the Poles. This causes landmasses near the Poles to appear larger than they really are. The map below is a Mercator projection, one type of cylindrical projection. The Mercator projection is useful for navigators because it shows true direction and shape. However, it distorts the size of land areas near the Poles.

Mercator projection

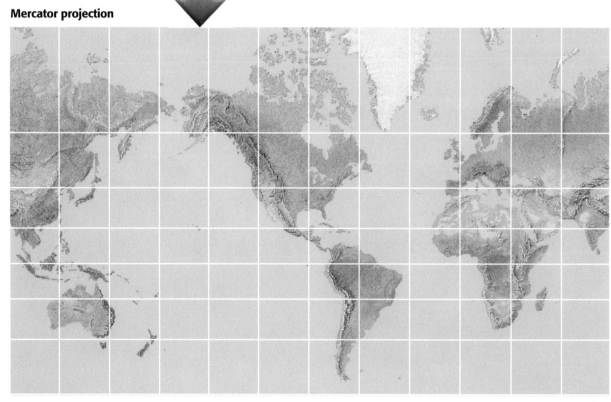

Conic Projections

Conic projections are based on a cone placed over the globe. A conic projection is most accurate along the lines of latitude where it touches the globe. It retains almost true shape and size. Conic projections are most useful for showing areas that have long east-west dimensions, such as the United States.

Paper cone

Conic projection

Flat-plane Projections

Flat-plane projections are based on a plane touching the globe at one point, such as at the North Pole or South Pole. A flat-plane projection is useful for showing true direction for airplane pilots and ship navigators. It also shows true area. However, it distorts the true shapes of landmasses.

Flat plane

Flat-plane projection

Map Essentials

Maps are like messages sent out in code. Mapmakers provide certain elements that help us translate these codes. These elements help us understand the message they are presenting about a particular part of the world. Of these elements, almost all maps have titles, directional indicators, scales, and legends. The map below has all four of these elements, plus a fifth—a locator map.

❶ Title

A map's **title** shows what the subject of the map is. The map title is usually the first thing you should look at when studying a map, because it tells you what the map is trying to show.

India: Physical

ELEVATION

Feet	Meters
13,120	4,000
6,560	2,000
1,640	500
656	200
(Sea level) 0	0 (Sea level)
Below sea level	Below sea level

0   250   500 Miles
0   250   500 Kilometers

Hindu Kush
Indus River
Thar Desert (Great Indian Desert)
Yamuna River
Ganges River
Ghaghara River
HIMALAYAS
Kanchenjunga 28,208 ft. (8,598 m)
Ganges R.
Jamuna R.
Brahmaputra River
Tropic of Cancer
Vindhya Range
Ganges Delta
20-N
Godavari
DECCAN PLATEAU
WESTERN GHATS
EASTERN GHATS
Arabian Sea
70 E
Bay of Bengal
Laccadive Islands
Malabar Coast
Coromandel Coast
GHATS
Andaman Islands
Andaman Sea
N W E S
INDIAN OCEAN
10-N

❷ Compass Rose

A directional indicator shows which way north, south, east, and west lie on the map. Some mapmakers use a "north arrow," which points toward the North Pole. Remember, "north" is not always at the top of a map. The way a map is drawn and the location of directions on that map depend on the perspective of the mapmaker. Most maps in this textbook indicate direction by using a compass rose. A **compass rose** has arrows that point to all four principal directions, as shown.

❸ Scale

Mapmakers use scales to represent the distances between points on a map. Scales may appear on maps in several different forms. The maps in this textbook provide a bar **scale**. Scales give distances in miles and kilometers.

To find the distance between two points on the map, place a piece of paper so that the edge connects the two points. Mark the location of each point on the paper with a line or dot. Then, compare the distance between the two dots with the map's bar scale. The number on the top of the scale gives the distance in miles. The number on the bottom gives the distance in kilometers. Because the distances are given in large intervals, you may have to approximate the actual distance on the scale.

❹ Legend

The **legend**, or key, explains what the symbols on the map represent. Point symbols are used to specify the location of things, such as cities, that do not take up much space on the map. Some legends, such as the one shown here, show colors that represent certain elevations. Other maps might have legends with symbols or colors that represent things such as roads. Legends can also show economic resources, land use, population density, and climate.

❺ Locator Map

A locator map shows where in the world the area on the map is located. The area shown on the main map is shown in red on the locator map. The locator map also shows surrounding areas so the map reader can see how the information on the map relates to neighboring lands.

Working with Maps

The Atlas at the back of this textbook includes both physical and political maps. Physical maps, like the one you just saw, show the major physical features in a region. These features include things like mountain ranges, rivers, oceans, islands, deserts, and plains. Political maps show the major political features of a region, such as countries and their borders, capitals, and other important cities.

Historical Map

In this textbook, most of the maps you will study are historical maps. Historical maps, such as this one, are maps that show information about the past. This information might be which lands an empire controlled, where a certain group of people lived, what large cities were located in a region, or how a place changed over time. Often colors are used to indicate the different things on the map. Be sure to look at the map title and map legend first to see what the map is showing. What does this map show?

The Roman Republic, 270-100 BC

Roman lands in 270 BC
Roman lands in 100 BC

Possible Routes of Abraham and Moses

HITTITE EMPIRE

• Haran

Euphrates River

ASSYRIA

Tigris River

Mediterranean
Sea

N
W — E
S

• Damascus

The Bible says that Abraham left Mesopotamia and settled in Canaan.

CANAAN

• Babylon

Jerusalem • • Jericho

MESOPOTAMIA

Dead Sea

Ramses •

• Ur

EGYPT

Moses led the Hebrews out of slavery in Egypt and into Canaan in a journey called the Exodus.

• Memphis

Nile River

Ezion-geber •

▲ Mt. Sinai

Pers
Gu

Possible route of Abraham
Possible route of Moses

0   100   200 Miles
0   100   200 Kilometers

Route Map

One special type of historical map is called a route map. A route map, like the one above, shows the route, or path, that someone or something followed. Route maps can show things like trade routes, invasion routes, or the journeys and travels of people. The routes on the map are usually shown with an arrow. If more than one route is shown, several arrows of different colors may be used. What does this route map show?

The maps in this textbook will help you study and understand history. By working with these maps, you will see where important events happened, where empires rose and fell, and where people moved. In studying these maps, you will learn how geography has influenced history.

Geographic Dictionary

OCEAN
a large body of water

CORAL REEF
an ocean ridge made up of
skeletal remains of tiny sea animals

GULF
a large part of
the ocean that
extends into land

PENINSULA
an area of land that sticks
out into a lake or ocean

BAY
part of a large
body of water
that is smaller
than a gulf

ISLAND
an area of land
surrounded entirely
by water

ISTHMUS
a narrow piece of land
connecting two larger
land areas

DELTA
an area where a
river deposits soil
into the ocean

STRAIT
a narrow body of
water connecting two
larger bodies of water

SINKHOLE
a circular depression
formed when the roof
of a cave collapses

WETLAND
an area of land
covered by
shallow water

RIVER
a natural flow of
water that runs
through the land

LAKE
an inland body
of water

FOREST
an area of densely
wooded land

COAST
an area of land
near the ocean

MOUNTAIN
an area of rugged
land that generally
rises higher than
2,000 feet

VALLEY
an area of low
land between
hills or mountains

GLACIER
a large area of
slow-moving ice

VOLCANO
an opening in Earth's crust
where lava, ash, and gases erupt

CANYON
a deep, narrow valley
with steep walls

HILL
a rounded, elevated
area of land smaller
than a mountain

PLAIN
a nearly
flat area

DUNE
a hill of sand
shaped by wind

OASIS
an area in the
desert with a
water source

DESERT
an extremely dry area with
little water and few plants

PLATEAU
a large, flat,
elevated
area of land

The Five Themes of Geography

Geography is the study of the world's people and places. As you can imagine, studying the entire world is a big job. To make the job easier, geographers have created the Five Themes of Geography. They are: **Location, Place, Human-Environment Interaction, Movement,** and **Region**. You can think of the Five Themes as five windows you can look through to study a place. If you looked at the same place through five different windows, you would have five different perspectives, or viewpoints, of the place. Using the Five Themes in this way will help you better understand the world's people and places.

1 **Location** The first thing to study about a place is its location. Where is it? Every place has an absolute location—its exact location on Earth. A place also has a relative location—its location in relation to other places. Use the theme of location to ask questions like, "Where is this place located, and how has its location affected it?"

2 **Place** Every place in the world is unique and has its own personality and character. Some things that can make a place unique include its weather, plants and animals, history, and the people that live there. Use the theme of place to ask questions like, "What are the unique features of this place, and how are they important?"

3 **Human-Environment Interaction** People interact with their environment in many ways. They use land to grow food and local materials to build houses. At the same time, a place's environment influences how people live. For example, if the weather is cold, people wear warm clothes. Use the theme of human-environment interaction to ask questions like, "What is this place's environment like, and how does it affect the people who live there?"

4 **Movement** The world is constantly changing, and places are affected by the movement of people, goods, ideas, and physical forces. For example, people come and go, new businesses begin, and rivers change their course. Use the theme of movement to ask questions like, "How is this place changing, and why?"

5 **Region** A region is an area that has one or more features that make it different from surrounding areas. A desert, a country, and a coastal area are all regions. Geographers use regions to break the world into smaller pieces that are easier to study. Use the theme of region to ask questions like "What common features does this area share, and how is it different from other areas?"

Canada

1

LOCATION

Most of the United States is located in the Western Hemisphere, north of Mexico and south of Canada. This location has good farmland, many resources, and many different natural environments.

4

5

United States

2

1

3

Mexico

2

PLACE

New York City is one of the most powerful cities in the world. The people of New York also make the city one of the most ethnically diverse places in the world.

3

HUMAN-ENVIRONMENT INTERACTION

People near Las Vegas, Nevada, transform the desert landscape by building new neighborhoods. Americans modify their environment in many other ways—by controlling rivers, building roads, and creating farmland.

5

REGION

The United States is a political region with one government. At the same time, smaller regions can be found inside the country, such as the Badlands in South Dakota.

4

MOVEMENT

People, goods, and ideas are constantly moving to and from places such as Seattle, Washington. As some places grow, others get smaller, but every place is always changing.

Become an Active Reader

by Dr. Kylene Beers

Did you ever think you would begin reading your social studies book by reading about reading? Actually, it makes better sense than you might think. You would probably make sure you learned some soccer skills and strategies before playing in a game. Similarly, you need to learn some reading skills and strategies before reading your social studies book. In other words, you need to make sure you know whatever you need to know in order to read this book successfully..

Tip #1

Use the Reading Social Studies Pages

Take advantage of the two pages on reading at the beginning of every chapter. Those pages introduce the chapter themes; explain a reading skill or strategy; and identify key terms, people, and academic vocabulary.

Themes

Why are themes important? They help our minds organize facts and information. For example, when we talk about baseball, we may talk about types of pitches. When we talk about movies, we may discuss animation.

Historians are no different. When they discuss history or social studies, they tend to think about some common themes: Economics, Geography, Religion, Politics, Society and Culture, and Science and Technology.

Reading Skill or Strategy

Good readers use a number of skills and strategies to make sure they understand what they are reading. These lessons will give you the tools you need to read and understand social studies.

Key Terms, People, and Academic Vocabulary

Before you read the chapter, review these words and think about them. Have you heard the word before? What do you already know about the people? Then watch for these words and their meanings as you read the chapter.

Gives you practice in the reading skill or strategy.

Tells which theme or themes are important in the chapter

Explains a skill or strategy good readers use

Identifies the important words in the chapter.

Tip #2
Read like a Skilled Reader

You will never get better at reading your social studies book—or any book for that matter—unless you spend some time thinking about how to be a better reader.

Skilled readers do the following:

- They preview what they are supposed to read before they actually begin reading. They look for vocabulary words, titles of sections, information in the margin, or maps or charts they should study.

- They divide their notebook paper into two columns. They title one column "Notes from the Chapter" and the other column "Questions or Comments I Have."

- They take notes in both columns as they read.

- They read like **active readers**. The Active Reading list below shows you what that means.

- They use clues in the text to help them figure out where the text is going. The best clues are called signal words.

  Chronological Order Signal Words: *first, second, third, before, after, later, next, following that, earlier, finally*

  Cause and Effect Signal Words: *because of, due to, as a result of, the reason for, therefore, consequently*

  Comparison/Contrast Signal Words: *likewise, also, as well as, similarly, on the other hand*

Active Reading

Successful readers are **active readers**. These readers know that it is up to them to figure out what the text means. Here are some steps you can take to become an active, and successful, reader.

Predict what will happen next based on what has already happened. When your predictions don't match what happens in the text, re-read the confusing parts.

Question what is happening as you read. Constantly ask yourself why things have happened, what things mean, and what caused certain events.

Summarize what you are reading frequently. Do not try to summarize the entire chapter! Read a bit and then summarize it. Then read on.

Connect what is happening in the part you're reading to what you have already read.

Clarify your understanding. Stop occasionally to ask yourself whether you are confused by anything. You may need to re-read to clarify, or you may need to read further and collect more information before you can understand.

Visualize what is happening in the text. Try to see the events or places in your mind by drawing maps, making charts, or jotting down notes about what you are reading.

Tip #3
Pay Attention to Vocabulary

It is no fun to read something when you don't know what the words mean, but you can't learn new words if you only use or read the words you already know. In this book, we know we have probably used some words you don't know. But, we have followed a pattern as we have used more difficult words.

Early Spread of Buddhism

GEOGRAPHY
SKILLS | **INTERPRETING MAPS**

Movement Buddhism spread to what island south of India?

Buddhism Spreads

Buddhism continued to attract followers after the Buddha's death. After spreading through India, the religion began to spread to other areas as well.

Buddhism Spreads in India

According to Buddhist tradition, 500 of the Buddha's followers gathered together shortly after he died. They wanted to make sure that the Buddha's teachings were remembered correctly.

In the years after this council, the Buddha's followers spread his teachings throughout India. The ideas spread very quickly, because Buddhist teachings were popular and easy to understand. Within 200 years of the Buddha's death, his teachings had spread through most of India.

Buddhism Spreads Beyond India

The spread of Buddhism increased after one of the most powerful kings in India, Asoka, became Buddhist in the 200s BC. Once he converted, he built Buddhist temples and schools throughout India. More importantly, though, he worked to spread Buddhism into areas outside of India. You will learn more about Asoka and his accomplishments in the next section.

Asoka sent Buddhist **missionaries**, or people who work to spread their religious beliefs, to other kingdoms in Asia. One group of these missionaries sailed to the island of Sri Lanka around 251 BC. Others followed trade routes east to what is now Myanmar and to other parts of Southeast Asia. Missionaries also went north to areas near the Himalayas.

160 CHAPTER 6

Key Terms and People

At the beginning of each section you will find a list of key terms or people that you will need to know. Be on the lookout for those words as you read through the section.

Asoka sent Buddhist **missionaries**, or people who work to spread their religious beliefs, to other kingdoms in Asia. One of these missionaries sailed to the

Trading Cultures

...ans and Mycenaens were ...ipbuilders and seafarers. ...ed throughout the eastern ...anean to trade.

...did the Minoans ...s use their ships?

The Minoans
The Minoans traded goods like this vase decorated with an octopus. Trade made the Minoans rich enough to build magnificent buildings. These are the ruins of a great palace in the Minoan city of Knossos, on the island of Crete.

ACADEMIC VOCABULARY

influence
change, or have an effect on

Academic Vocabulary

When we use a word that is important in all classes, not just social studies, we define it in the margin under the heading Academic Vocabulary. You will run into these academic words in other textbooks, so you should learn what they mean while reading this book.

ACADEMIC VOCABULARY
influence
change, or have an effect on

It's not surprising that the early Greeks used the sea as a source for food and as a way of trading with other communities.

The Greeks became skilled shipbuilders and sailors. Their ships sailed to Asia Minor, to Egypt, and to the islands of the Mediterranean and Aegean seas. As they traveled around these seas, they found sources of food and other products they needed. They also exchanged ideas with other cultures.

READING CHECK Drawing Conclusions
How did mountains affect the location of Greek settlements?

Trading Cultures Develop

Many cultures settled and developed in Greece. Two of the earliest were the Minoans (muh-NOH-uhnz) and the Mycenaens (my-suh-NEE-uhns). By 2000 BC the

Minoans had built an advanced society on the island of Crete. Crete lay south of the Aegean in the eastern Mediterranean. Later, the Mycenaeans built towns on the Greek mainland. These two civilizations **influenced** the entire Aegean region and helped shape later cultures in Greece.

The Minoans

Because they lived on an island, the Minoans spent much of their time at sea. They were among the best shipbuilders of their time. Minoan ships carried goods such as wood, olive oil, and pottery all around the eastern Mediterranean. They traded these goods for copper, gold, silver, and jewels.

Although Crete's location was excellent for Minoan traders, its geography had its dangers. Sometime in the 1600s BC a huge volcano erupted just north of Crete. This eruption created a giant wave that flooded much of Crete. In addition, the eruption

256 CHAPTER 9

Social Studies Vocabulary

We know that some words are special to this particular topic of social studies, world history. As you read this book, you will be more successful if you know the meaning of the words in the following list.

Social Studies Words to Know

Time

AD	refers to dates after Jesus's birth
BC	refers to dates before the birth of Jesus of Nazareth
BCE	refers to "Before Common Era," dates before the birth of Jesus of Nazareth
CE	refers to "Common Era," dates after Jesus's birth
century	a period of 100 years
decade	a period of 10 years
era	a period of time

The Earth and Its Resources

climate	the weather conditions in a certain area over a long period of time
geography	the study of the earth's physical and cultural features
landforms	the natural features of the land's surface
physical features	the features on the land's surface, such as mountains and rivers
region	an area with one or more features that make it different from surrounding areas
resources	materials found on the earth that people need and value

People and the Way They Live

civilization	the culture of a particular time or place
culture	the knowledge, beliefs, customs, and values of a group of people
custom	a repeated practice; tradition
economy	the system in which people make and exchange goods and services
politics	government
ritual	the regular form for a ceremony or observance
scholar	a person who has completed advanced study
society	a group of people who share common traditions
trade	the exchange of goods or services

Academic Words

If only ...
If only reading in school were like reading a letter from your best friend.
If only reading in History were like reading *Harry Potter.*
It can be . . .if you learn the language!

There is a reason that you might feel uncomfortable with reading academic textbooks. Common words in these books account for less than 2% of the words in your favorite novels. No wonder reading in school seems so different from reading for fun!

Academic vocabulary refers to words that are used in most of your school subjects. The Holt Social Studies program has identified Academic Words that will be highlighted throughout this textbook. The Holt program provides structured practice to help support and improve your knowledge of this specialized vocabulary.

Grade 6 Academic Words

acquire	to get
agreement	a decision reached by two or more people or groups
aspects	parts
authority	power, right to rule
cause	the reason something happens
classical	referring to the cultures of ancient Greece or Rome
contract	a binding legal agreement
development	creation
distribute	to divide among a group of people
effect	the results of an action or decision
establish	to set up or create
ideal	ideas or goals that people try to live up to
impact	effect, result
method	a way of doing something
neutral	unbiased, not favoring either side in a conflict
primary	main, most important
principle	basic belief, rule, or law
process	a series of steps by which a task is accomplished
purpose	the reason something is done
rebel	to fight against authority
role	a part or function
strategy	a plan for fighting a battle or war
vary	to be different

Grade 7 Academic Words

affect	to change or influence
aspects	parts
authority	power, right to rule
classical	referring to the cultures of ancient Greece or Rome
development	the process of growing or improving
efficient/ efficiency	productive and not wasteful
element	part
establish	to set up or create
features	characteristics
impact	effect, result
influence	change, or have an effect on
innovation	a new idea or way of doing something
logical	reasoned, well thought out
policy	rule, course of action
principle	basic belief, rule, or law
procedure	a series of steps taken to accomplish a task
process	a series of steps by which a task is accomplished
rebel	to fight against authority
role	assigned behavior
strategy	a plan for fighting a battle or war
structure	the way something is set up or organized
traditional	customary, time-honored
values	ideas that people hold dear and try to live by
various	of many types

abstract	expressing a quality or idea without reference to an actual thing
acquire	to get
advocate	to plead in favor of
agreement	a decision reached by two or more people or groups
aspects	parts
authority	power, right to rule
circumstances	surrounding situation
complex	difficult, not simple
concrete	specific, real
consequences	the effects of a particular event or events
contemporary	existing at the same time
criteria	rules for defining
develop/ development	the process of growing or improving
distinct	separate
efficient/ efficiency	productive and not wasteful
element	part
establish	to set up or create
execute	to perform, carry out
explicit	fully revealed without vagueness
facilitate	to bring about
factor	cause
function	use or purpose
implement	to put in place
implications	effects of a decision
implicit	understood though not clearly put into words
incentive	something that leads people to follow a certain course of action
influence	change, or have an effect on
innovation	a new idea or way of doing something
method	a way of doing something
motive	a reason for doing something
neutral	unbiased, not favoring either side in a conflict
policy	rule, course of action
primary	main, most important
principle	basic belief, rule, or law
procedure	a series of steps taken to accomplish a task
process	a series of steps by which a task is accomplished
reaction	a response
role	assigned behavior
strategy	a plan for fighting a battle or war
vary/various	of many types

History–Social Science Content Standards

Students in grade six expand their understanding of history by studying the people and events that ushered in the dawn of the major Western and non-Western ancient civilizations. Geography is of special significance in the development of the human story. Continued emphasis is placed on the everyday lives, problems, and accomplishments of people, their role in developing social, economic, and political structures, as well as in establishing and spreading ideas that helped transform the world forever. Students develop higher levels of critical thinking by considering why civilizations developed where and when they did, why they became dominant, and why they declined. Students analyze the interactions among the various cultures, emphasizing their enduring contributions and the link, despite time, between the contemporary and ancient worlds.

6.1 Students describe what is known through archaeological studies of the early physical and cultural development of humankind from the Paleolithic era to the agricultural revolution.

1. Describe the hunter-gatherer societies, including the development of tools and the use of fire.

2. Identify the locations of human communities that populated the major regions of the world and describe how humans adapted to a variety of environments.

3. Discuss the climatic changes and human modifications of the physical environment that gave rise to the domestication of plants and animals and new sources of clothing and shelter.

6.2 Students analyze the geographic, political, economic, religious, and social structures of the early civilizations of Mesopotamia, Egypt, and Kush.

1. Locate and describe the major river systems and discuss the physical settings that supported permanent settlement and early civilizations.

2. Trace the development of agricultural techniques that permitted the production of economic surplus and the emergence of cities as centers of culture and power.

3. Understand the relationship between religion and the social and political order in Mesopotamia and Egypt.

4. Know the significance of Hammurabi's Code.

5. Discuss the main features of Egyptian art and architecture.

6. Describe the role of Egyptian trade in the eastern Mediterranean and Nile valley.

7. Understand the significance of Queen Hatshepsut and Ramses the Great.

8. Identify the location of the Kush civilization and describe its political, commercial, and cultural relations with Egypt.

9. Trace the evolution of language and its written forms.

6.3 Students analyze the geographic, political, economic, religious, and social structures of the Ancient Hebrews.

1. Describe the origins and significance of Judaism as the first monotheistic religion based on the concept of one God who sets down moral laws for humanity.

2. Identify the sources of the ethical teachings and central beliefs of Judaism (the Hebrew Bible, the Commentaries): belief in God, observance of law, practice of the concepts of righteousness and justice, and importance of study; and describe how the ideas of the Hebrew traditions are reflected in the moral and ethical traditions of Western civilization.

3. Explain the significance of Abraham, Moses, Naomi, Ruth, David, and Yohanan ben Zaccai in the development of the Jewish religion.

4. Discuss the locations of the settlements and movements of Hebrew peoples, including the Exodus and their movement to and from Egypt, and outline the significance of the Exodus to the Jewish and other people.

5. Discuss how Judaism survived and developed despite the continuing dispersion of much of the Jewish population from Jerusalem and the rest of Israel after the destruction of the second Temple in AD 70.

6.4 Students analyze the geographic, political, economic, religious, and social structures of the early civilizations of Ancient Greece.

1. Discuss the connections between geography and the development of city-states in the region of the Aegean Sea, including patterns of trade and commerce among Greek city-states and within the wider Mediterranean region.

2. Trace the transition from tyranny and oligarchy to early democratic forms of government and back to dictatorship in ancient Greece, including the significance of the invention of the idea of citizenship (e.g., from *Pericles' Funeral Oration*).

3. State the key differences between Athenian, or direct, democracy and representative democracy.

4. Explain the significance of Greek mythology to the everyday life of people in the region and how Greek literature continues to permeate our literature and language today, drawing from Greek mythology and epics, such as Homer's *Iliad* and *Odyssey*, and from *Aesop's Fables*.

5. Outline the founding, expansion, and political organization of the Persian Empire.

6. Compare and contrast life in Athens and Sparta, with emphasis on their roles in the Persian and Peloponnesian Wars.

7. Trace the rise of Alexander the Great and the spread of Greek culture eastward and into Egypt.

8. Describe the enduring contributions of important Greek figures in the arts and sciences (e.g., Hypatia, Socrates, Plato, Aristotle, Euclid, Thucydides).

6.5 Students analyze the geographic, political, economic, religious, and social structures of the early civilizations of India.

1. Locate and describe the major river system and discuss the physical setting that supported the rise of this civilization.

2. Discuss the significance of the Aryan invasions.

3. Explain the major beliefs and practices of Brahmanism in India and how they evolved into early Hinduism.

4. Outline the social structure of the caste system.

5. Know the life and moral teachings of the Buddha and how Buddhism spread in India, Ceylon, and Central Asia.

6. Describe the growth of the Maurya empire and the political and moral achievements of the emperor Asoka.

7. Discuss important aesthetic and intellectual traditions (e.g., Sanskrit literature, including the *Bhagavad Gita*; medicine; metallurgy; and mathematics, including Hindu-Arabic numerals and the zero).

6.6 Students analyze the geographic, political, economic, religious, and social structures of the early civilizations of China.

1. Locate and describe the origins of Chinese civilization in the Huang-He Valley during the Shang Dynasty.

2. Explain the geographic features of China that made governance and the spread of ideas and goods difficult and served to isolate the country from the rest of the world.

3. Know about the life of Confucius and the fundamental teachings of Confucianism and Daoism.

4. Identify the political and cultural problems prevalent in the time of Confucius and how he sought to solve them.

5. List the policies and achievements of the emperor Shi Huangdi in unifying northern China under the Qin Dynasty.

6. Detail the political contributions of the Han Dynasty to the development of the imperial bureaucratic state and the expansion of the empire.

7. Cite the significance of the trans-Eurasian "silk roads" in the period of the Han Dynasty and Roman Empire and their locations.

8. Describe the diffusion of Buddhism northward to China during the Han Dynasty.

6.7 Students analyze the geographic, political, economic, religious, and social structures during the development of Rome.

1. Identify the location and describe the rise of the Roman Republic, including the importance of such mythical and historical figures as Aeneas, Romulus and Remus, Cincinnatus, Julius Caesar, and Cicero.

2. Describe the government of the Roman Republic and its significance (e.g., written constitution and tripartite government, checks and balances, civic duty).

3. Identify the location of and the political and geographic reasons for the growth of Roman territories and expansion of the empire, including how the empire fostered economic growth through the use of currency and trade routes.

4. Discuss the influence of Julius Caesar and Augustus in Rome's transition from republic to empire.

5. Trace the migration of Jews around the Mediterranean region and the effects of their conflict with the Romans, including the Romans' restrictions on their right to live in Jerusalem.

6. Note the origins of Christianity in the Jewish Messianic prophecies, the life and teachings of Jesus of Nazareth as described in the New Testament, and the contribution of St. Paul the Apostle to the definition and spread of Christian beliefs (e.g., belief in the Trinity, resurrection, salvation).

7. Describe the circumstances that led to the spread of Christianity in Europe and other Roman territories.

8. Discuss the legacies of Roman art and architecture, technology and science, literature, language, and law.

Historical and Social Sciences Analysis Skills

The intellectual skills noted below are to be learned through, and applied to, the content standards for grades six through eight. They are to be assessed *only in conjunction* with the content standards in grades six through eight.

In addition to the standards for grades six through eight, students demonstrate the following intellectual reasoning, reflection, and research skills:

Chronological and Spatial Thinking

1. Students explain how major events are related to one another in time.

2. Students construct various time lines of key events, people, and periods of the historical era they are studying.

3. Students use a variety of maps and documents to identify physical and cultural features of neighborhoods, cities, states, and countries and to explain the historical migration of people, expansion and disintegration of empires, and the growth of economic systems.

Research, Evidence, and Point of View

1. Students frame questions that can be answered by historical study and research.

2. Students distinguish fact from opinion in historical narratives and stories.

3. Students distinguish relevant from irrelevant information, essential from incidental information, and verifiable from unverifiable information in historical narratives and stories.

4. Students assess the credibility of primary and secondary sources and draw sound conclusions from them.

5. Students detect the different historical points of view on historical events and determine the context in which the historical statements were made (the questions asked, sources used, author's perspectives).

Historical Interpretation

1. Students explain the central issues and problems from the past, placing people and events in a matrix of time and place.

2. Students understand and distinguish cause, effect, sequence, and correlation in historical events, including the long- and short-term causal relations.

3. Students explain the sources of historical continuity and how the combination of ideas and events explains the emergence of new patterns.

4. Students recognize the role of chance, oversight, and error in history.

5. Students recognize that interpretations of history are subject to change as new information is uncovered.

6. Students interpret basic indicators of economic performance and conduct cost-benefit analyses of economic and political issues.

How to Make This Book Work for You

Studying history will be easy for you using this textbook. Take a few minutes to become familiar with the easy-to-use structure and special features of this history book. See how this textbook will make history come alive for you!

Unit

Each chapter of this textbook is part of a Unit of study focusing on a particular time period. Each unit opener provides an illustration showing a young person of the period and gives you an overview of the exciting topics that you will study in the unit.

Chapter

Each Chapter includes a chapter-opener introduction where the California History-Social Science Standards and Analysis Skills are listed out, a Social Studies Skills activity, Standards Review pages, and a Standards Assessment page.

Reading Social Studies These chapter level reading lessons give you skills and practice that you can use to help you read the text-book. Within each chapter there is a Focus on Reading note in the margin on the page where the reading skill is covered. There are also questions in the Standards Review activity to make sure that you understand the reading skill.

Social Studies Skills The Social Studies Skills lessons give you an opportunity to learn and use a skill that you will most likely use again. You will also be given a chance to make sure that you understand each skill by answering related questions in the Standards Review activity.

Section

The Section opener pages include Main Idea statements, an overarching big idea statement, and Key Terms and People. In addition, each section includes the following special features.

If You Were There . . . introductions begin each section with a situation for you to respond to, placing you in the time period and in a situation related to the content that you will be studying in the section.

Building Background sections connect what will be covered in this section with what you studied in the previous section.

Short sections of content organize the information in each section into small chunks of text that you shouldn't find too overwhelming.

The California History-Social Science Standards for 6th grade that are covered in each section are listed on the first page of each section of the textbook.

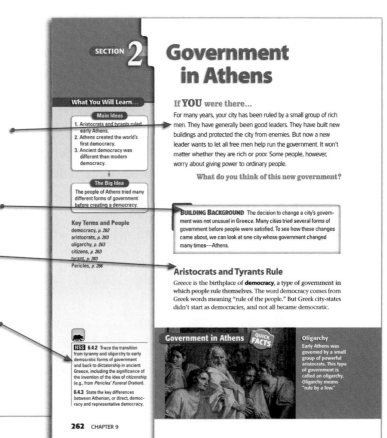

SECTION 2

Government in Athens

What You Will Learn...

Main Ideas
1. Aristocrats and tyrants ruled early Athens.
2. Athens created the world's first democracy.
3. Ancient democracy was different than modern democracy.

The Big Idea
The people of Athens tried many different forms of government before creating a democracy.

Key Terms and People
democracy, p. 262
aristocrats, p. 263
oligarchy, p. 263
citizens, p. 263
tyrant, p. 263
Pericles, p. 266

HSS **6.4.2** Trace the transition from tyranny and oligarchy to early democratic forms of government and back to dictatorship in ancient Greece, including the significance of the invention of the idea of citizenship (e.g., from Pericles' Funeral Oration).

6.4.3 State the key differences between Athenian, or direct, democracy and representative democracy.

262 CHAPTER 9

If YOU were there...
For many years, your city has been ruled by a small group of rich men. They have generally been good leaders. They have built new buildings and protected the city from enemies. But now a new leader wants to let all free men help run the government. It won't matter whether they are rich or poor. Some people, however, worry about giving power to ordinary people.

What do you think of this new government?

BUILDING BACKGROUND The decision to change a city's government was not unusual in Greece. Many cities tried several forms of government before people were satisfied. To see how these changes came about, we can look at one city whose government changed many times—Athens.

Aristocrats and Tyrants Rule
Greece is the birthplace of **democracy**, a type of government in which people rule themselves. The word democracy comes from Greek words meaning "rule of the people." But Greek city-states didn't start as democracies, and not all became democratic.

Government in Athens QUICK FACTS

Oligarchy
Early Athens was governed by a small group of powerful aristocrats. This type of government is called an oligarchy. Oligarchy means "rule by a few."

When the Assyrians invaded Egypt with their iron weapons, they forced Kush's rulers out of Egypt and south into Nubia.

The Kushite rulers of Egypt built temples to Egyptian gods and restored old ones. They also worked to preserve Egyptian writings. As a result, Egyptian culture thrived during the Kushite dynasty.

The Kushite Dynasty
After Piankhi died, his brother Shabaka (SHAB-uh-kuh) took control of the kingdom. Shabaka then declared himself pharaoh. This declaration began the Twenty-fifth, or Kushite, Dynasty in Egypt.

Shabaka and later rulers of his dynasty tried to restore old Egyptian cultural practices. Some of these practices had faded during Egypt's period of weakness. For example, Shabaka was buried in a pyramid. The Egyptians had stopped building pyramids for their rulers centuries before.

The End of Kushite Rule in Egypt
The Kushite dynasty remained strong in Egypt for about 40 years. In the 670s BC, however, the powerful army of the Assyrians from Mesopotamia invaded Egypt. The Assyrians' iron weapons were better than the Kushites' bronze weapons, and the Kushites were slowly pushed out of Egypt. In just 10 years the Assyrians had driven the Kushite forces completely out of Egypt.

READING CHECK Identifying Cause and Effect
How did internal problems in Egypt benefit Kush?

SUMMARY AND PREVIEW Kush was conquered by Egypt, but later the Kushites controlled Egypt. In the next section, you will learn how the civilization of Kush developed after the Kushites were forced out of Egypt by the Assyrians.

Section 1 Assessment

Reviewing Ideas, Terms, and People HSS 6.2.8
1. **a. Identify** On which river did Kush develop?
   b. Analyze How did Nubia's natural resources influence the early history of Kush?
2. **a. Describe** What is **ebony**?
   b. Analyze Why did people in Kush adopt some elements of Egyptian culture?
   c. Evaluate Why do you think Thutmose I destroyed the Kushite palace at Kerma?
3. **a. Describe** What territory did **Piankhi** conquer?
   b. Make Inferences Why is the Twenty-fifth Dynasty significant in the history of Egypt?
   c. Predict What might have happened in Kush and Egypt if Kush had developed iron weapons?

Critical Thinking
4. **Identifying Cause and Effect** Create a chart like the one here. For each cause listed, identify one effect.

Cause	Effect
Villages appear along the Nile.	
Kush trades with Egypt.	
Piankhi conquers Egypt.	
Assyrians use iron weapons.	

go.hrw.com
Online Quiz
KEYWORD: SQ6 HP5

FOCUS ON WRITING
5. **Characters and Plot** Make a chart with two columns labeled "Characters" and "Plot." In one column, take notes on the main characters and their interactions. In the other column, note major events and sources of conflict between the characters.

126 CHAPTER 5

Reading Check questions end each section of content so that you can test whether or not you understand what you have just studied.

Summary and Preview To connect what you have just studied in the section to what you will study in the next section, we include the Summary and Preview.

Section Assessments The section assessment boxes provide an opportunity for you to make sure that you understand the main ideas of the section. We also provide assessment practice online!

Places You Will Study

As you study world history, you will learn about many places around the world. You will discover the places where ancient civilizations began, how geography influenced early cultures, and how early cultures have helped shape the world today.

The maps that you see here show some of the main places you will study in this textbook. These are key places where ancient peoples created the first complex societies, cities, governments, and empires. You will learn much more about these places and the people who lived in them as you begin your study of ancient world history.

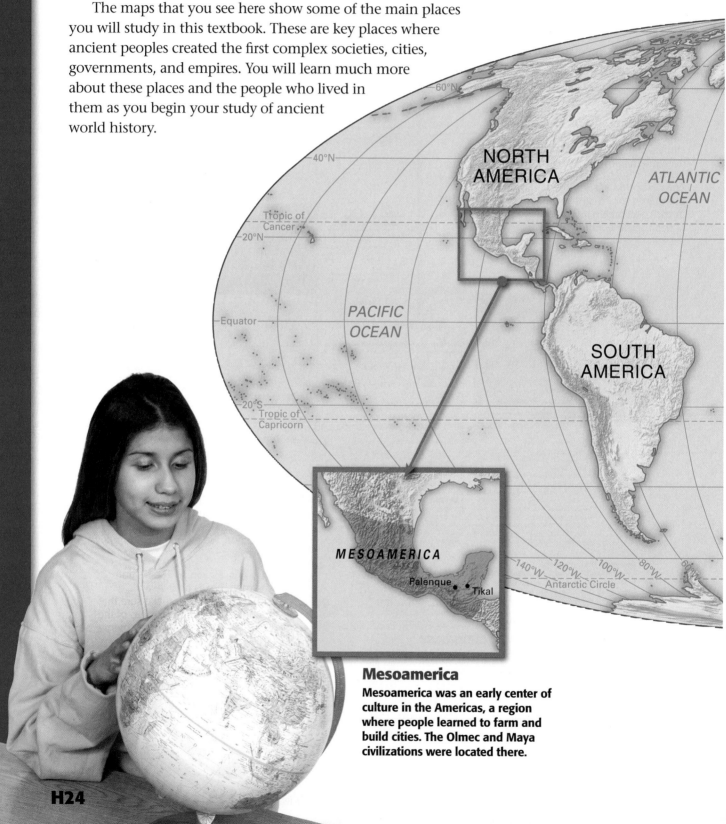

Mesoamerica

Mesoamerica was an early center of culture in the Americas, a region where people learned to farm and build cities. The Olmec and Maya civilizations were located there.

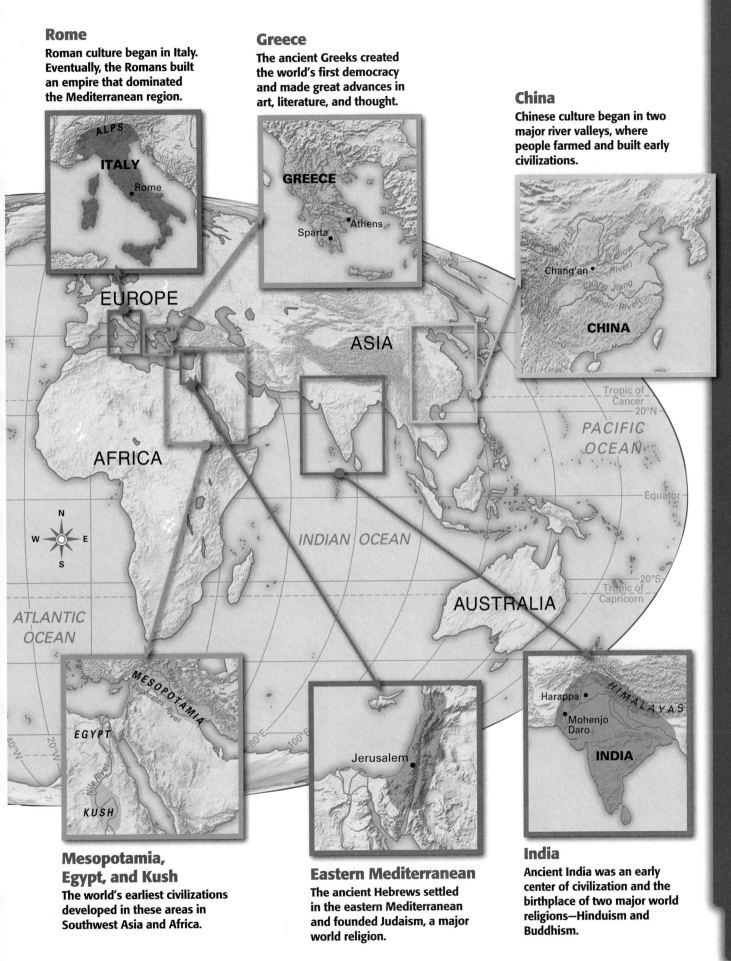

Rome

Roman culture began in Italy. Eventually, the Romans built an empire that dominated the Mediterranean region.

ALPS
ITALY
• Rome

Greece

The ancient Greeks created the world's first democracy and made great advances in art, literature, and thought.

GREECE
• Athens
Sparta •

China

Chinese culture began in two major river valleys, where people farmed and built early civilizations.

Huang He
Yellow River
Chang'an •
Chang Jiang
Yangzi River
CHINA

EUROPE

ASIA

Tropic of Cancer
20°N

PACIFIC OCEAN

AFRICA

Equator

INDIAN OCEAN

AUSTRALIA

20°S
Tropic of Capricorn

ATLANTIC OCEAN

N
W   E
S

MESOPOTAMIA
Euphrates River
EGYPT
Nile River
KUSH

Jerusalem •

HIMALAYAS
Harappa •
• Mohenjo Daro
Ganges River
INDIA

Mesopotamia, Egypt, and Kush

The world's earliest civilizations developed in these areas in Southwest Asia and Africa.

Eastern Mediterranean

The ancient Hebrews settled in the eastern Mediterranean and founded Judaism, a major world religion.

India

Ancient India was an early center of civilization and the birthplace of two major world religions—Hinduism and Buddhism.

Early Humans and Societies

History is the study of the past, and people who study history are called historians. Historians try to learn what life was like for people long ago in places around the world. To understand the people and places of the past, historians study clues and evidence.

Some historians study the earliest humans. Early people hunted animals, gathered plants, and learned how to make stone tools. Eventually, people learned to grow food and raise animals for themselves.

In the next two chapters, you will learn about the subject of history and about the world's earliest peoples.

Explore the Art

In this scene, young Maria de Sautuola discovers prehistoric cave paintings in Altamira, Spain, in 1879. What do these paintings say about the life of early people?

Uncovering the Past

California Standards

Analysis Skills

HI 5 Recognize that interpretations of history are subject to change as new information is uncovered.

English–Language Arts

Writing 6.2.2 Write expository compositions.

Reading 6.1.0 Students use their knowledge of word origins and word relationships, as well as historical and literary context clues, to determine the meaning of specialized vocabulary and to understand the precise meaning of grade-level-appropriate words.

FOCUS ON WRITING

A Job Description What is the job of a historian? an archaeologist? a geographer? In this chapter you will read about the work of people who study the past—its events, its people, and its places. Then you will write a job description to include in a career-planning guide.

HOLT

History's Impact
▶ **video series**
Watch the video to understand the impact of archaeology on what we have learned about the past.

What You Will Learn…

In this chapter you will learn how historians and geographers study the past. This photo shows clay warriors that were found in China. Finds like these teach us a lot about the history of ancient places.

Reading Social Studies

by Kylene Beers

Focus on Themes This chapter sets the stage for reading the rest of the book. In it you will learn the definitions of many important terms. You will learn how studying history helps you understand the past and the present. You will also read about the study of geography and learn how the world's physical features affected when and where civilization began. Finally, you will begin to think about how **society and culture** and **science and technology** have interacted throughout time.

Specialized Vocabulary of History

Focus on Reading Have you ever done a plié at the barre or sacked the quarterback? You probably haven't if you've never studied ballet or played football. In fact, you may not even have known what those words meant.

Specialized Vocabulary Plié, barre, sack, and quarterback are **specialized vocabulary**, words that are used in only one field. History has its own specialized vocabulary. The charts below list some terms often used in the study of history.

Terms that identify periods of time	
Decade	a period of 10 years
Century	a period of 100 years
Age	a long period of time marked by a single cultural feature
Era	a long period of time marked by great events, developments, or figures
Ancient	very old, or from a long time ago

Terms used with dates	
circa or **c.**	a word used to show that historians are not sure of an exact date; it means "about"
BC	a term used to identify dates that occurred long ago, before the birth of Jesus Christ, the founder of Christianity; it means "before Christ." As you can see on the time line below, BC dates get smaller as time passes, so the larger the number the earlier the date.
AD	a term used to identify dates that occurred after Jesus's birth; it comes from a Latin phrase that means "in the year of our Lord." Unlike BC dates, AD dates get larger as time passes, so the larger the number the later the date.
BCE	another way to refer to BC dates; it stands for "before the common era"
CE	another way to refer to AD dates; it stands for "common era"

300 BC	200 BC	100 BC	BC 1 AD	AD 100	AD 200	AD 300
300 BCE	200 BCE	100 BCE	BCE 1 CE	100 CE	200 CE	300 CE

You Try It!

As you read this textbook, you will find many examples of specialized vocabulary terms that historians use. Many of these terms will be highlighted in the text and defined for you as key terms. Others may not be highlighted, but they will still be defined. For some examples, read the passage below. Learning these words as you come across them will help you understand what you read later in the book. For your own reference, you may wish to keep a list of important terms in your notebook.

Learning Words through Context

We must rely on a variety of sources to learn history. For information on the very first humans, we have fossil remains. A **fossil** is a part or imprint of something that was once alive. Bones and footprints preserved in rock are examples of fossils.

As human beings learned to make things, by accident they also created more sources of information for us. They made what we call **artifacts**, objects created by and used by humans. Artifacts include coins, arrowheads, tools, toys, and pottery.

From Chapter 1, page 10

Answer the following questions about the specialized vocabulary of history.

1. What is a fossil? What is an artifact? How can you tell?

2. Were you born in a BC year or an AD year?

3. Put the following dates in order: AD 2000, 3100 BC, 15 BCE, AD 476, AD 3, CE 1215

4. If you saw that an event happened c. AD 1000, what would that mean?

Key Terms and People

Chapter 1

Section 1

Section 2

Academic Vocabulary

Success in school is related to knowing academic vocabulary—the words that are frequently used in school assignments and discussions. In this chapter, you will learn the following academic words:

As you read Chapter 1, keep a list in your notebook of specialized vocabulary words that you learn.

Studying History

What You Will Learn...

Main Ideas

1. History is the study of the past.
2. We can improve our understanding of people's actions and beliefs through the study of history.
3. Historians use clues from various sources to learn about the past.

The Big Idea

Historians use many kinds of clues to understand how people lived in the past.

Key Terms

history, *p. 6*
culture, *p. 7*
archaeology, *p. 7*
fossil, *p. 10*
artifacts, *p. 10*
primary source, *p. 10*
secondary source, *p. 10*

If YOU were there...

You are a student helping scholars uncover the remains of an ancient city. One exciting day you find a jar filled with bits of clay on which strange symbols have been carved. You recognize the marks as letters because for years you have studied the language of the city's people. This is your chance to put your skills to use!

What might you learn from the ancient writings?

BUILDING BACKGROUND Last year you learned about our country's past. Now you begin a study of world history, which started many centuries before the history of the United States. You will find that we learn about world history in many ways.

The Study of the Past

The people of the ancient world didn't build skyscrapers, invent the automobile, or send spaceships to Mars. But they did remarkable things. Among their amazing feats were building huge temples, inventing writing, and discovering planets. Every step we take—in technology, science, education, literature, and all other fields—builds on what people did long ago. We are who we are because of what people did in the past.

What Is History?

History is the study of the past. A battle that happened 5,000 years ago and an election that happened yesterday are both parts of history.

Historians are people who study history. Their main concern is human activity in the past. They want to know how people lived and why they did the things they did. They try to learn about the problems people faced and how they found solutions.

Historians are interested in how people lived their daily lives. How and where did they work, fight, trade, farm, and worship? What did they do in their free time? What games did they play? In other words, historians study the past to understand people's **culture**—the knowledge, beliefs, customs, and values of a group of people.

What Is Archaeology?

An important field that contributes much information about the past is **archaeology** (ahr-kee-AH-luh-jee). It is the study of the past based on what people left behind.

Archaeologists, or people who practice archaeology, explore places where people once lived, worked, or fought. The things that people left in these places may include jewelry, dishes, or weapons. They range from stone tools to computers.

Archaeologists examine the objects they find to learn what they can tell about the past. In many cases, the objects that people left behind are the only clues we have to how they lived.

READING CHECK **Comparing** How are the fields of history and archaeology similar?

Studying the Past
Historians and archaeologists study the people and places of the past. For example, by studying the remains of an ancient Egyptian temple (right), they can learn about the lives of the ancient Egyptians (left).

Understanding through History

There are many reasons why people study history. Understanding the past helps us to understand the world today. History can also provide us with a guide to making better decisions in the future.

ACADEMIC VOCABULARY

values ideas that people hold dear and try to live by

Knowing Yourself

History can teach you about yourself. What if you did not know your own past? You would not know which subjects you liked in school or which sports you enjoyed. You would not know what makes you proud or what mistakes not to repeat. Without your own personal history, you would not have an identity.

History is just as important for groups as it is for individuals. What would happen if countries had no record of their past? People would know nothing about how their governments came into being. They would not remember their nation's great triumphs or tragedies. History teaches us about the experiences we have been through as a people. It shapes our identity and teaches us the **values** that we share.

Knowing Others

Like today, the world in the past included many cultures. History teaches about the cultures that were unlike your own. You learn about other peoples, where they lived, and what was important to them. History teaches you how cultures were similar and how they were different.

History also helps you understand why other people think the way they do. You learn about the struggles people have faced. You also learn how these struggles have affected the way people view themselves and others.

Understanding the World

History can help us understand the world around us. For example, why do these buildings in San Francisco look the way they do? The answer is history. These buildings are in a neighborhood called Chinatown, where Chinese immigrants began settling in the 1800s.

Immigrants painted these houses bright colors like the houses in China. Chinese-style roofs and pillars were also added.

Chinese people who moved to California brought their language with them. By studying the languages spoken in a region, historians can learn who settled there.

For example, Native Americans, European settlers, enslaved Africans, and Asian immigrants all played vital roles in our country's history. But the descendants of each group have a different story to tell about their ancestors' contributions.

Learning these stories and others like them that make up history can help you see the viewpoints of other peoples. It can help teach you to respect and understand different opinions. This knowledge helps promote tolerance. History can also help you relate more easily to people of different backgrounds. In other words, knowing about the past can help build social harmony throughout the world today.

Knowing Your World

History can provide you with a better understanding of where you live. You are part of a culture that interacts with the outside world. Even events that happen in other parts of the world affect your culture. History helps you to understand how today's events are shaped by the events of the past. So knowing the past helps you figure out what is happening now.

History is concerned with the entire range of human activities. It is the record of humanity's combined efforts. So while you are studying history, you can also learn more about math, science, religion, government, and many other topics.

Studying the past will also help you develop mental skills. History encourages you to ask important questions. It forces you to analyze the facts you learn. Such analysis teaches you how to recognize which information is important and which is extra. This skill helps you to find the main facts when studying any topic.

History also promotes good decision-making skills. A famous, often repeated saying warns us that those who forget their past are doomed to repeat it. This means

that people who ignore the results of past decisions often make the same mistakes over and over again.

Individuals and countries both benefit from the wisdom that history can teach. Your own history may have taught you that studying for a test results in better grades. In a similar way, world history has taught that providing young people with education makes them more productive when they become adults.

Historians have been talking about the value of history for <u>centuries</u>. More than 2,000 years ago a great Greek historian named Polybius wrote:

"The purpose of history is not the reader's enjoyment at the moment of perusal [reading it], but the reformation [improvement] of the reader's soul, to save him from stumbling at the same stumbling block many times over."

–Polybius, from *The Histories, Book XXXVIII*

READING CHECK **Summarizing** What are some benefits of studying history?

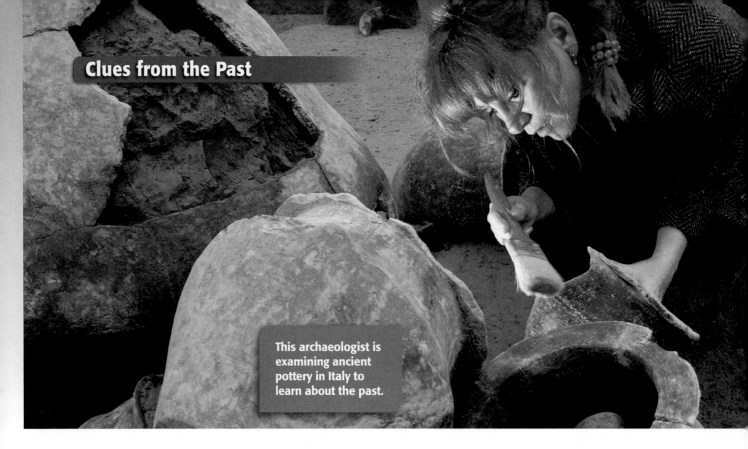

This archaeologist is examining ancient pottery in Italy to learn about the past.

Using Clues

We must rely on a variety of sources to learn history. For information on the very first humans, we have fossil remains. A **fossil** is a part or imprint of something that was once alive. Bones and footprints preserved in rock are examples of fossils.

As human beings learned to make things, by accident they also created more sources of information for us. They made what we call **artifacts**, objects created by and used by humans. Artifacts include coins, arrowheads, tools, toys, and pottery. Archaeologists examine artifacts and the places where the artifacts were found to learn about the past.

Sources of Information

About 5,000 years ago, people invented writing. They wrote laws, poems, speeches, battle plans, letters, contracts, and many other things. In these written sources, historians have found countless clues about how people lived. In addition, people have recorded their messages in many ways over the centuries. Historians have studied writing carved into stone pillars, stamped onto clay tablets, scribbled on turtle shells, typed with typewriters, and sent by computer.

Historical sources are of two types. A **primary source** is an account of an event created by someone who took part in or witnessed the event. Treaties, letters, diaries, laws, court documents, and royal commands are all primary sources. An audio or video recording of an event is also a primary source.

A **secondary source** is information gathered by someone who did not take part in or witness an event. Examples include history textbooks, journal articles, and encyclopedias. The textbook you are reading right now is a secondary source. The historians who wrote it did not take part in the events described. Instead, they gathered information about these events from different sources.

Written records, like this writing from a tomb in Egypt, are valuable sources of information about the past.

Sometimes, archaeologists must carefully reconstruct artifacts from hundreds of broken pieces, like they did with this statue of an Aztec bat god from Mexico.

Sources of Change

Writers of secondary sources don't always agree about the past. Historians form different opinions about the primary sources they study. As a result, historians may not interpret past events in the same way.

For example, one writer may say that a king was a brilliant military leader. Another may say that the king's armies only won their battles because they had better weapons than their enemies did. Sometimes new evidence leads to new conclusions. As historians review and reanalyze information, their interpretations can and do change.

READING CHECK Contrasting How are primary and secondary sources different?

SUMMARY AND PREVIEW We benefit from studying the past. Scholars use many clues to help them understand past events. In the next section you will learn how geography connects to history.

go.hrw.com
Online Quiz
KEYWORD: SQ6 HP1

Section 1 Assessment

Reviewing Ideas, Terms, and People

1. **a. Identify** What is **history**?
   b. Explain What kinds of things do historians try to discover about people who lived in the past?
   c. Predict What kinds of evidence will historians of the future study to learn about your **culture**?
2. **a. Describe** How does knowing its own history provide a group with a sense of unity?
   b. Elaborate Explain the meaning of the phrase, "Those who forget their past are doomed to repeat it."
3. **a. Identify** What is a **primary source**?
   b. Explain How did the invention of writing affect the sources on which historians rely?
   c. Elaborate Could a photograph be considered a primary source? Why or why not?

Critical Thinking

4. **Categorizing** Copy the diagram. In the empty circles, list the types of clues that historians and archaeologists use.

Historians and Archaeologists

FOCUS ON WRITING

5. **Understanding What Historians Do** What is the difference between a historian and an archaeologist? Take notes about the work these people do.

Studying Geography

If YOU were there...

Your parents are historians researching a city that disappeared long ago. You go with them to a library to help search for clues to the city's location and fate. While thumbing through a dusty old book, you find an ancient map stuck between two pages. Marked on the map are rivers, forests, mountains, and straight lines that look like roads. It is a map that shows the way to the lost city!

How can this map help you find the city?

What You Will Learn...

Main Ideas

1. Geography is the study of places and people.
2. Studying location is important to both physical and human geography.
3. Geography and history are closely connected.

The Big Idea

Physical geography and human geography contribute to the study of history.

Key Terms

geography, *p. 12*
landforms, *p. 12*
climate, *p. 12*
environment, *p. 13*
region, *p. 15*
resources, *p. 16*

Studying Places and People

When you hear about an event on the news, the first questions you ask may be, "Where did it happen?" and "Who was there?" Historians ask the same questions about events that happened in the past. That is why they need to study geography. **Geography** is the study of the earth's physical and cultural features. These features include mountains, rivers, people, cities, and countries.

Physical Geography

Physical geography is the study of the earth's land and features. People who work in this field are called physical geographers. They study **landforms**, the natural features of the land's surface. Mountains, valleys, plains, and other such places are landforms.

Physical geographers also study **climate**, the pattern of weather conditions in a certain area over a long period of time. Climate is not the same as weather. Weather is the conditions at a specific time and place. If you say that your city has cold winters, you are talking about climate. If you say it is below freezing and snowing today, you are talking about the weather.

Physical Geography

The study of the earth's physical features and processes, such as mountains, rivers, oceans, rainfall, and climate, including this section of California's coast

Human Geography

The study of the earth's people, including their way of life, homes and cities, beliefs, and travels, such as these members of the Dogon people in the country of Mali

Geography

The study of the earth's physical and cultural features

Climate affects many features of a region. For example, it affects plant life. Tropical rain forests require warm air and heavy rain, while a dry climate can create deserts. Climate also affects landforms. For example, constant wind can wear down mountains into flat plains.

Although climate affects landforms, landforms can also affect climate. For example, the Coast Ranges in northern California are mountains parallel to the Pacific coast. As air presses up against these mountains, it rises and cools. Any moisture that the air was carrying falls as rain. Meanwhile, on the opposite side of the range, the Central Valley stays dry. In this way, a mountain range creates two very different climates.

Landforms and climate are part of a place's environment. The **environment** includes all the living and nonliving things that affect life in an area. This includes the area's climate, land, water, plants, soil, animals, and other features.

Human Geography

The other branch of geography is human geography—the study of people and the places where they live. Specialists in human geography study many different things about people and their cultures. What kind of work do people do? How do they get their food? What are their homes like? What religions do they practice?

Human geography also deals with how the environment affects people. For example, how do people who live near rivers protect themselves from floods? How do people who live in deserts survive? Do different environments affect the size of families? Do people in certain environments live longer? Why do some diseases spread easily in some environments but not in others? As you can see, human geographers study many interesting questions about people and this planet.

READING CHECK **Summarizing** What are the two main branches of geography?

Studying Location

Both physical and human geographers study location. Location is the exact description of where something is. Every place on Earth has a specific location.

No two places in the world are exactly alike. Even small differences between places can lead to major differences in how people live. That is why geographers try to understand the effects that different locations have on human populations, or groups of people.

By comparing locations, geographers learn more about the factors that affected each of them. For example, they may study why a town grew in one location while a town nearby got smaller.

Learning from Maps

To study various locations, geographers use maps. A map is a drawing of an area. Some maps show physical **features**. Others show cities and the boundaries of states or countries. Most maps have symbols to show different things. For example, large dots often stand for cities. Blue lines show where rivers flow. Most maps also include a guide to show direction.

People have been making maps for more than 4,000 years. Maps help with many activities. Planning battles, looking for new lands, and designing new city parks all require good maps. On the first day of class, you may have used a map of your school to find your classrooms.

Studying Maps

By studying and comparing maps, you can see how a place's physical and human features are related.

California: Physical

1 What are some of California's main physical features? Where are the state's highest mountains?

California: Climates

2 What climates are found in California? How are the climate regions related to California's physical features?

Learning about Regions

Learning about regions is another key part of studying geography. A **region** is an area with one or more features that make it different from surrounding areas. These features may be physical, such as forests or grasslands. There may also be differences in climate. For example, a desert area is a type of region. Physical barriers such as mountains and rivers often form a region's boundaries.

Human features can also define regions. An area with many cities is one type of region. An area with only farms is another type. Some regions are identified by the language that people there speak. Other regions are identified by the religion their people practice.

READING CHECK **Categorizing** What are some types of features that can identify a region?

Primary Source

BOOK
What Geography Means

Some people think of geography as the ability to read maps or name state capitals. But as geographer Kenneth C. Davis explains, geography is much more. It is related to almost every branch of human knowledge.

❝Geography doesn't simply begin and end with maps showing the location of all the countries of the world. In fact, such maps don't necessarily tell us much. No—geography poses fascinating questions about who we are and how we got to be that way, and then provides clues to the answers. It is impossible to understand history, international politics, the world economy, religions, philosophy, or 'patterns of culture' without taking geography into account.❞

–Kenneth C. Davis, from *Don't Know Much About Geography*

ANALYSIS SKILL **ANALYZING PRIMARY SOURCES**
Why does the writer think that geography is important?

California: Population

One dot represents 25,000 people
⊛ State capital
0   75   150 Miles
0   75   150 Kilometers

OR
Sacramento
Oakland
San Francisco
San Jose
NV
Los Angeles
Long Beach
San Diego
PACIFIC OCEAN
AZ
MEXICO

3 Where are California's two main population centers? What kind of climate is found in these areas?

California: Roads

Interstate highways
Other highways
⊛ State capital
0   75   150 Miles
0   75   150 Kilometers

OR
Eureka
San Francisco
Sacramento
NV
Los Angeles
San Diego
PACIFIC OCEAN
AZ
MEXICO

4 How are California's roads related to its physical features? How are they related to its population centers?

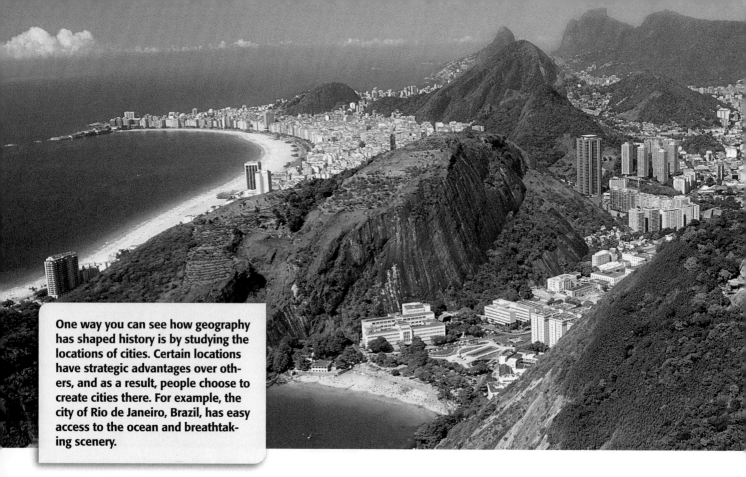

One way you can see how geography has shaped history is by studying the locations of cities. Certain locations have strategic advantages over others, and as a result, people choose to create cities there. For example, the city of Rio de Janeiro, Brazil, has easy access to the ocean and breathtaking scenery.

Geography and History

Geography gives us important clues about the people and places that came before us. Like detectives, we can piece together a great deal of information about ancient cultures by knowing where people lived and what the area was like.

Geography Affects Resources

An area's geography was critical to early settlements. People could survive only in areas where they could get enough food and water. Early people settled in places that were rich in **resources**, materials found in the earth that people need and value. All through history, people have used a variety of resources to meet their basic needs.

In early times, essential resources included water, animals, fertile land, and stones for tools. Over time, people learned to use other resources, including metals such as copper, gold, and iron.

Geography Shapes Cultures

Geography also influenced the early development of cultures. Early peoples, for example, developed vastly different cultures because of their environments. People who lived along rivers learned to make fishhooks and boats, while those far from rivers did not. People who lived near forests built homes from wood. In other areas, builders had to use mud or stone. Some people developed religious beliefs based on the geography of their area. For example, ancient Egyptians believed that the god Hapi controlled the Nile River.

Geography also played a role in the growth of civilizations. The world's first societies formed along rivers. Crops grown on the fertile land along these rivers fed large populations.

Some geographic features could also protect areas from invasion. A region surrounded by mountains or deserts, for example, was hard for attackers to reach.

environments in positive and negative ways. People have planted millions of trees. They have created new lakes in the middle of deserts. But people have also created wastelands where forests once grew and built dams that flooded ancient cities. This interaction between humans and their environment has been a major factor in history. It continues today.

READING CHECK **Describing** What are some ways geography has shaped human history?

SUMMARY AND PREVIEW The field of geography includes physical geography and human geography. Geography has had a major influence on history. In the next chapter you will learn how geography affected the first people.

Geography Influences History

Geography has helped shape history and has affected the growth of societies. People in areas with many natural resources could use their resources to get rich. They could build glorious cities and powerful armies. Features such as rivers also made trade easier. Many societies became rich by trading goods with other peoples.

On the other hand, geography has also caused problems. Floods, for example, have killed millions of people. Lack of rainfall has brought deadly food shortages. Storms have wrecked ships, and with them, the hopes of conquerors. In the 1200s, for example, a people known as the Mongols tried to invade Japan. However, most of the Mongol ships were destroyed by a powerful storm. Japanese history may have been very different if the storm had not occurred.

The relationship between geography and people has not been one-sided. For centuries, people have influenced their

Section 2 Assessment

go.hrw.com
Online Quiz
KEYWORD: SQ6 HP1

Reviewing Ideas, Terms, and People

1. **a. Define** What is **geography**?
   b. Summarize What are some of the topics included in human geography?
2. **a. Describe** Identify a **region** near where you live, and explain what sets it apart as a region.
   b. Predict How might a map of a city's **landforms** help an official who is planning a new city park?
3. **a. Recall** Where did early peoples tend to settle?
   b. Compare and Contrast How could a river be both a valuable **resource** and a problem for a region?

Critical Thinking

4. **Categorizing** Draw this chart. Under each heading, list the types of things that are studied in that branch of geography.

Geography	
Physical Geography	Human Geography

FOCUS ON WRITING

5. **Understanding What Geographers Do** In this section you learned how geographers contribute to the study of history. What is the difference between a physical geographer and a human geographer?

Mapping the Past

Maps are useful tools for historians. By creating a map of how a place used to be, historians can learn where things were located and what the place was like. In other words, by studying a place's geography, we can also learn something about its history.

This map shows the ancient city of Teotihuacán (tay-oh-tee-wah-KAHN) in central Mexico. Teotihuacán reached its height around AD 500. Study this map. What can it tell you about the history of the city?

Pyramid of the Moon

Teotihuacán, c. AD 500

Pyramid of the Moon

Pyramid of the Sun

Houses

San Juan River

Street of the Dead

Citadel

San Lorenzo River

| 0 | .25 | .50 Mile |
| 0 | .25 | .50 Kilometer |

Size and Importance As the map shows, Teotihuacán was a large city. It had many buildings and a large population. From this, you might conclude that the city was important, just as big cities are important today.

Religion The giant buildings that dominate the heart of the city, such as the Pyramid of the Sun, are religious temples. From this, you can conclude that religion was very important to the people of Teotihuacán.

Pyramid of the Sun

Citadel

Street of the Dead

San Juan River

Technology The map shows that this river turns at right angles, just like the city's streets. The people of Teotihuacán must have changed the course of this river. That tells you that they had advanced engineering skills and technology.

GEOGRAPHY SKILLS **INTERPRETING MAPS**

1. **Place** How does the map indicate that Teotihuacán was an important place?
2. **Location** What can you conclude from the fact that large religious buildings are located in the heart of the city?

19

Analysis | Critical Thinking | **Participation** | Study

Recognizing Personal Conviction and Bias

Understand the Skill

Everybody has *convictions*, or things that they strongly believe. However, if we form opinions about people or events based only on our beliefs, we may be showing bias. *Bias* is an idea about someone or something based solely on opinions, not facts.

There are many types of bias. Sometimes people form opinions about others based on the group to which that person belongs. For example, some people might believe that all teenagers are selfish or that all politicians are dishonest. These are examples of a type of bias called *stereotyping*. Holding negative opinions of people based on their race, religion, age, gender, or similar characteristics is known as *prejudice*.

We should always be on guard for the presence of personal biases. Such biases can slant how we view, judge, and provide information. Honest and accurate communication requires people to be as free of bias as possible.

Learn the Skill

As you read or write, watch out for biases. One way to identify a bias is to look for facts that support a statement. If a belief seems unreasonable when compared to the facts, it may be a sign of bias.

Another sign of bias is a person's unwillingness to question his or her belief if it is challenged by evidence. People sometimes cling to views that evidence proves are wrong. This is why bias is defined as a "fixed" idea about something. It also points out a good reason why we should try to avoid being biased. Our biases can keep us from considering new ideas and learning new things.

You will meet many peoples from the past as you study world history. Their beliefs, behaviors, and ways of life may seem different or strange to you. It is important to remain unbiased and to keep an open mind. Recognize that "different" does not mean "not as good."

Understand that early peoples did not have the technology or the accumulation of past knowledge that we have today. Be careful to not look down on them just because they were less advanced or might seem "simpler" than we are today. Remember that their struggles, learning, and achievements helped make us what we are today.

The following guidelines can help you to recognize and reduce your own biases. Keep them in mind as you study world history.

1 When discussing a topic, try to think of beliefs and experiences in your own background that might affect how you feel about the topic.

2 Try to not mix statements of fact with statements of opinion. Clearly separate and indicate what you *know* to be true from what you *believe* to be true.

3 Avoid using emotional, positive, or negative words when communicating factual information.

Practice and Apply the Skill

Professional historians try to be objective about the history they study and report. Being *objective* means not being influenced by personal feelings or opinions. Write a paragraph explaining why you think being objective is important in the study of history.

Standards Review

Visual Summary

Use the visual summary below to help you review the main ideas of the chapter.

QUICK FACTS

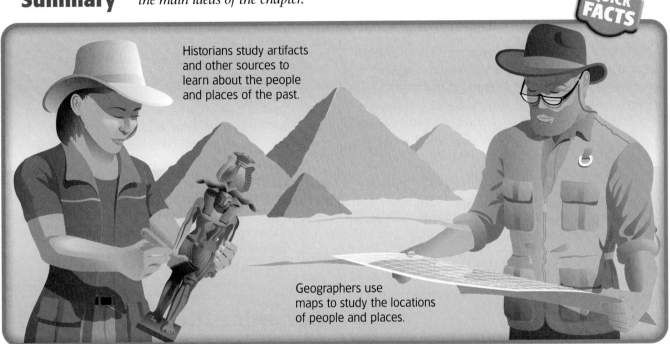

Historians study artifacts and other sources to learn about the people and places of the past.

Geographers use maps to study the locations of people and places.

Reviewing Vocabulary, Terms, and People

*For each statement below, write **T** if it is true or **F** if it is false. If the statement is false, write the correct term that would make the sentence a true statement.*

1. <u>History</u> is the study of the past based on what people left behind.

2. Knowledge, beliefs, customs, and values of a group of people are part of their <u>environment</u>.

3. A handwritten letter from a soldier to his family would be considered a <u>primary source</u>.

4. <u>Geography</u> is the study of the past, whether recent or long ago.

5. Your state probably has many different <u>landforms</u>, such as mountains, plains, and valleys.

6. Weather changes from day to day, but a location's <u>climate</u> does not change as often.

7. <u>Values</u> are ideas that people hold dear and try to live by.

Comprehension and Critical Thinking

SECTION 1 *(Pages 6–11)*

8. **a. Describe** What is history? What is archaeology? How do the two fields work together?

   b. Make Inferences Why may a historian who is still alive disagree with conclusions drawn by a historian who lived a hundred years ago?

   c. Evaluate Do you think primary sources or secondary sources are more valuable to modern historians? Why?

SECTION 2 *(Pages 12–17)*

9. **a. Identify** What are the two main branches of geography, and how does each contribute to our understanding of history?

   b. Analyze If you were asked to divide your state into regions, what features would you use to define those regions? Why?

   c. Predict How might a long period of severe heat or cold affect the history of a city or region?

Using the Internet

go.hrw.com
KEYWORD: SQ6 WH1

10. Activity: Describing Artifacts Archaeologists study the past based on what people have left behind. Enter the activity keyword and explore recent archaeological discoveries. Select one artifact that interests you and write a short article about it. Write your article as if it will be printed in a school magazine. Describe the artifact in detail: What is it? Who made it? Where was it found? What does the artifact tell archaeologists and historians about the society or culture that created it? You may want to create a chart like the one below to organize your information. If possible, include illustrations with your article.

Artifact	
What is it?	
Who made it?	
Where was it found?	
What does it tell us?	

Social Studies Skills

11. Developing Personal Participation Skills
Over the course of this year, your teacher will probably organize the class into groups to complete some assignments. Working in groups requires you to have certain skills. Those skills include being sensitive to the opinions of others, expressing your own opinions clearly and calmly, recognizing your personal biases or prejudices, and just being willing to participate.

Practice working in groups by examining objects in the classroom as if they were old artifacts left by an ancient civilization. Discuss with your classmates what these objects could tell later generations about education in the United States in the 2000s. Remember that you should be willing to express your ideas to the other members of your group. At the same time, you must be willing to listen to other people's thoughts, ideas, and opinions.

Reading Skills

12. Understanding the Specialized Language of History Read the following passage in which several words have been left blank. Fill in each of the blanks with the appropriate word that you learned in this chapter.

> "Although _____ is defined as the study of the past, it is much more. It is a key to understanding our _____, the ideas, languages, religions, and other traits that make us who we are. In the _____ left behind by ancient peoples we can see reflections of our own material goods: plates and dishes, toys, jewelry, and work objects. These objects show us that human _____ haven't changed that much. After all, people still hold many of the same ideas dear that they did years and years ago. In other words, studying the past can lead to a new _____ of the present as people re-examine and re-evaluate our lives and change how we view ourselves."

Reviewing Themes

13. Society and Culture How may a historian's description of a battle reveal information about his or her own society or culture?

14. Science and Technology If hundreds of years from now archaeologists study the things we leave behind, what may they conclude about the role of technology in American society? Explain your answer.

FOCUS ON WRITING

15. Writing Your Job Description Review your notes on the work of historians, archaeologists, and physical and human geographers. Choose one of these jobs and write a description of it. You should begin your description by explaining why the job is important. Then identify the job's tasks and responsibilities. Finally, tell what kind of person would do well in this job. For example, a historian may enjoy reading and an archaeologist may enjoy working outdoors. When you have finished your description, you may be able to add it to a class or school guide for career planning.

Standards Assessment

DIRECTIONS: Read each question, and write the letter of the best response.

1

The object with ancient writing that is shown in this photo is a

A primary source and a resource.

B primary source and an artifact.

C secondary source and a resource.

D secondary source and an artifact.

2 Which of the following is the *best* reason for studying history?

A We can learn the dates of important events.

B We can learn interesting facts about famous people.

C We can learn about ourselves and other people.

D We can hear stories about strange things.

3 The study of people and the places where they live is called

A archaeology.

B environmental science.

C human geography.

D history.

4 Which of the following subjects would interest a physical geographer the *least*?

A a place's climate

B a mountain range

C a river system

D a country's highways

5 The type of evidence that an archaeologist would find most useful is a(n)

A artifact.

B primary source.

C secondary source.

D landform.

Connecting with Past Learnings

6 Last year in Grade 5, you learned about American history from several different sources. Which of the following sources you might have studied is a secondary source?

A the Declaration of Independence

B the diary of a classmate's ancestor

C a chapter in your textbook

D a letter written by George Washington

7 Which of the following topics you studied in American History in Grade 5 is an example of a region?

A New England

B the Mayflower Compact

C the Iroquois people

D the slave trade

The Stone Ages and Early Cultures

California Standards

History–Social Science

6.1 Students describe what is known through archaeological studies of the early physical and cultural development of humankind from the Paleolithic era to the agricultural revolution.

Analysis Skills

CS 1 Understand how events are related in time.

HI 1 Explain central issues and problems from the past.

English–Language Arts

Writing 6.1.2 Conclude with a detailed summary linked to the purpose of the composition.

Reading 6.2.4 Clarify an understanding of texts by creating outlines, logical notes, summaries, or reports.

FOCUS ON WRITING

A Storyboard Prehistoric humans did not write. However, they did carve and paint images on cave walls. In the spirit of these images, you will create a storyboard that uses images to tell the story of prehistoric humans. Remember that a storyboard tells a story with simple sketches and short captions.

4–5 million
Early humanlike creatures called Australopithecus develop in Africa.

5 MILLION YEARS AGO

2.6 million
Hominids make the first stone tools.

HOLT

History's Impact

▶ **video series**
Watch the video to understand
the impact of the early human
migrations to North America.

What You Will Learn...

In this chapter you will learn about the earliest
people. You will see how they learned to make
tools, hunt, gather food, and even create art.
The cave painting above is in France and is more
than 15,000 years old!

500,000
By this time,
hominids live
all across Europe.

11,000
Humans occupy
all of the continents
except Antarctica.

8,500
More than 5,000
people live in
Çatal Hüyük, Turkey.

500,000 YEARS AGO	11,000 YEARS AGO	5,000 YEARS AGO

200,000
The first
modern humans
appear in Africa.

10,000
Ice ages end.
People begin
to develop
agriculture.

Reading Social Studies

by Kylene Beers

| Economics | Geography | Politics | Religion | Society and Culture | Science and Technology |

Focus on Themes In this chapter you will learn about the earliest humans and how they lived. You will read about scientists who work constantly to learn more about this mysterious time. As you read, you will see the beginnings of human society and culture—the making of tools, the use of fire, and the creation of language. You will also read about the **geography** of the world and how it shaped where and how early people lived.

Chronological Order

Focus on Reading History, just our like our lives, can be seen as a series of events in time. To understand history and events, we often need to see how they are related in time.

Understanding Chronological Order The word **chronological** means "related to time." Events discussed in this history book are discussed in **sequence**, in the order in which they happened. To understand history better, you can use a sequence chain to take notes about events in the order they happened.

Additional reading support can be found in the

Reader and Study Guide

Sequence Chain

A scientists goes to Africa and drives to a gorge to search for fossils.

⬇

She searches for several hours and finds a bone.

⬇

She calls another scientist to report what she found.

Writers sometimes signal chronological order, or sequence, by using words or phrases like these:

first, before, then, later, soon, after, before long, next, eventually, finally

HSS **Analysis CS 1** Understand how events are related in time.

ELA **Reading 6.2.4** Clarify an understanding of texts by creating outlines, logical notes, summaries, or reports.

You Try It!

The following passage is from the chapter you are about to read. Read the sentences carefully and think about order of events.

Scientists Study Remains

One archaeologist who made important discoveries about prehistory was Mary Leakey. In 1959 she found bones in East Africa that were more than 1.5 million years old. She and her husband, Louis Leakey, believed that the bones belonged to a hominid, an early ancestor of humans . . .

In 1974 anthropologist Donald Johanson found bones from another early ancestor . . . Johanson named his find Lucy. Tests showed that she lived more than 3 million years ago . . .

In 1994 anthropologist Tim White found even older remains. He believes that the hominid he found may have lived as long as 4.4 million years ago.

From Chapter 2, pages 28–29

After you read the sentences, answer the following questions.

1. Draw a three-part sequence chain on your own paper.

   a. What are the three dates that tell you the chronological order of the three discoveries?

   b. Where do the discoveries go in your sequence chain?

2. Study the sequence chain you've made. Leakey made her find in 1959. The bones she found were about 1.5 million years old. Johanson found bones in 1974 that were more than 3 million years old. White made his find in 1994 and the bones he found were 4.4 million years old. Why do you think that as time continued anthropologists were able to find older and older bones?

3. Create another sequence chain. Sequence the discoveries in the order of the age of the bones, oldest to youngest.

Key Terms and People

Chapter 2

Section 1
prehistory *(p. 28)*
hominid *(p. 28)*
ancestor *(p. 28)*
tool *(p. 30)*
Paleolithic Era *(p. 31)*
society *(p. 33)*
hunter-gatherers *(p. 33)*

Section 2
migrate *(p. 36)*
ice ages *(p. 36)*
land bridge *(p. 36)*
Mesolithic Era *(p. 38)*

Section 3
Neolithic Era *(p. 41)*
domestication *(p. 41)*
agriculture *(p. 42)*
megaliths *(p. 42)*

Academic Vocabulary

Success in school is related to knowing academic vocabulary— the words that are frequently used in school assignments and discussions. In this chapter, you will learn the following academic words:

distribute *(p. 33)*
development *(p. 42)*

As you read Chapter 2, look for words that indicate the order in which events occurred.

The First People

What You Will Learn...

Main Ideas

1. Scientists study the remains of early humans to learn about prehistory.
2. Hominids and early humans first appeared in East Africa millions of years ago.
3. Stone Age tools grew more complex as time passed.
4. Hunter-gatherer societies developed language, art, and religion.

The Big Idea

Prehistoric people learned to adapt to their environment, to make simple tools, to use fire, and to use language.

Key Terms

prehistory, *p. 28*
hominid, *p. 28*
ancestor, *p. 28*
tool, *p. 30*
Paleolithic Era, *p. 31*
society, *p. 33*
hunter-gatherers, *p. 33*

HSS 6.1.1 Describe the hunter-gatherer societies, including the development of tools and the use of fire.

If YOU were there...

You live 200,000 years ago, in a time known as the Stone Age. A local toolmaker has offered to teach you his skill. You watch carefully as he strikes two black rocks together. A small piece flakes off. You try to copy him, but the rocks just break. Finally you learn to strike the rock just right. You have made a sharp stone knife!

How will you use your new skill?

BUILDING BACKGROUND Over millions of years early people learned many new things. Making stone tools was one of the earliest and most valuable skills that they developed. Scientists who study early humans learn a lot about them from the tools and other objects that they made.

Scientists Study Remains

Although humans have lived on the earth for more than a million years, writing was not invented until about 5,000 years ago. Historians call the time before there was writing **prehistory**. To study prehistory, historians rely on the work of archaeologists and anthropologists.

One archaeologist who made important discoveries about prehistory was Mary Leakey. In 1959 she found bones in East Africa that were more than 1.5 million years old. She and her husband, Louis Leakey, believed that the bones belonged to an early **hominid** (HAH-muh-nuhd), an early ancestor of humans. An **ancestor** is a relative who lived in the past.

In fact, the bones belonged to an Australopithecus (aw-stray-loh-PI-thuh-kuhs), one of the earliest ancestors of humans. In 1974 anthropologist Donald Johanson (joh-HAN-suhn) found bones from another early ancestor. He described his discovery:

> "We reluctantly headed back toward camp ... I glanced over my right shoulder. Light glinted off a bone. I knelt down for a closer look ... Everywhere we looked on the slope around us we saw more bones lying on the surface."
>
> –Donald Johanson, from *Ancestors: In Search of Human Origins*

AFRICA

Nile River

Red Sea

White Nile

Blue Nile

Hadar

Gulf of Aden

ETHIOPIAN HIGHLANDS

Lake Turkana

INDIAN OCEAN

Congo River

Lake Victoria

Serengeti Plain — Olduvai Gorge

Lake Tanganyika

Lake Malawi

● Australopithecus remains found

0   300   600 Miles
0   300   600 Kilometers

Zambezi River

Madagascar

Limpopo River

Vaal River

Orange River

N
W   E
S

Donald Johanson discovered the bones of Lucy, an early hominid that lived more than 3 million years ago.

Mary Leakey found some of the earliest ancestors of humans in Olduvai Gorge.

GEOGRAPHY SKILLS **INTERPRETING MAPS**

Location On which continent are all of these sites located?

Johanson named his find Lucy. Tests showed that she lived more than 3 million years ago. Johanson could tell from her bones that she was small and had walked on two legs. The ability to walk on two legs was a key step in human development.

In 1994 anthropologist Tim White found even older remains. He believes that the hominid he found may have lived as long as 4.4 million years ago. But some scientists disagree with White's time estimate. Discoveries of ancient bones give us information about early humans and their ancestors, but not all scientists agree on the meaning of these discoveries.

READING CHECK **Drawing Inferences** What can ancient bones tell us about human ancestors?

Hominids and Early Humans

Later groups of hominids appeared about 3 million years ago. As time passed they became more like modern humans.

In the early 1960s Louis Leakey found hominid remains that he called *Homo habilis*, or "handy man." Leakey and his son Richard believed that *Homo habilis* was more closely related to modern humans than Lucy and had a larger brain.

Scientists believe that another group of hominids appeared in Africa about 1.5 million years ago. This group is called *Homo erectus*, or "upright man." Scientists think these people walked completely upright like modern people do.

Scientists believe that *Homo erectus* knew how to control fire. Once fire was started by natural causes, such as lightning, people used it to cook food. Fire also gave them heat and protection against animals.

Eventually hominids developed characteristics of modern humans. Scientists are not sure exactly when or where the first modern humans lived. Many think that they first appeared in Africa about 200,000 years ago. Scientists call these people *Homo sapiens*, or "wise man." Every person alive today belongs to this group.

READING CHECK **Contrasting** How was *Homo erectus* different from *Homo habilis*?

Stone Age Tools

The first humans and their ancestors lived during a long period of time called the Stone Age. To help in their studies, archaeologists divide the Stone Age into three periods based on the kinds of tools used at the time. To archaeologists, a **tool** is any handheld object that has been modified to help a person accomplish a task.

FOCUS ON READING

Dates in a text can help you keep events in order in your mind.

Early Hominids · QUICK FACTS

Four major groups of hominids appeared in Africa between 5 million and about 200,000 years ago. Each group was more advanced than the one before it and could use better tools.

Which early hominid learned to control fire and use the hand ax?

Australopithecus

- Name means "southern ape"
- Appeared in Africa about 4–5 million years ago
- Stood upright and walked on two legs
- Brain was about one-third the size of modern humans

Homo habilis

- Name means "handy man"
- Appeared in Africa about 2.4 million years ago
- Used early stone tools for chopping and scraping
- Brain was about half the size of modern humans

An early Stone Age chopper

The first part of the Stone Age is called the **Paleolithic** (pay-lee-uh-LI-thik) **Era**, or Old Stone Age. It lasted until about 10,000 years ago. During this time people used stone tools.

The First Tools

Scientists have found the oldest tools in Tanzania, a country in East Africa. These sharpened stones, about the size of an adult's fist, are about 2.6 million years old. Each stone had been struck with another rock to create a sharp, jagged edge along one side. This process left one unsharpened side that could be used as a handle.

Scientists think that these first tools were mostly used to process food. The sharp edge could be used to cut, chop, or scrape roots, bones, or meat. Tools like these, called choppers, were used for about 2 million years.

Later Tools

Over time people learned to make better tools. For example, they developed the hand ax. They often made this tool out of a mineral called flint. Flint is easy to shape, and tools made from it can be very sharp. People used hand axes to break tree limbs, to dig, and to cut animal hides.

People also learned to attach wooden handles to tools. By attaching a wooden shaft to a stone point, for example, they invented the spear. Because a spear could be thrown, hunters no longer had to stand close to animals they were hunting. As a result, people could hunt larger animals. Among the animals hunted by Stone Age people were deer, horses, bison, and elephantlike creatures called mammoths.

READING CHECK **Summarizing** How did tools improve during the Old Stone Age?

Homo erectus

- Name means "upright man"
- Appeared in Africa about 2–1.5 million years ago
- Used early stone tools like the hand ax
- Learned to control fire
- Migrated out of Africa to Asia and Europe

A hand ax

Homo sapiens

- Name means "wise man"
- Appeared in Africa about 200,000 years ago
- Migrated around the world
- Same species as modern human beings
- Learned to create fire and use a wide variety of tools
- Developed language

A flint knife

Hunter-Gatherers

Early people were hunter-gatherers. They hunted animals and gathered wild plants to survive. Life for these hunter-gatherers was difficult and dangerous. Still, people learned how to make tools, use fire, and even create art.

Hunting
Most hunting was done by men. They worked together to bring down large animals.

Art
People painted herds of animals on cave walls.

Gathering
Most gathering was done by women. They gathered food like wild plants, seeds, fruits, and nuts.

Fire
People learned to use fire to cook their food.

Tools
Early people learned to make tools such as this spear for hunting.

ANALYSIS SKILL **ANALYZING VISUALS**

What tools are people using in this picture?

Hunter-gatherer Societies

As early humans developed tools and new hunting techniques, they formed societies. A **society** is a community of people who share a common culture. These societies developed cultures with languages, religions, and art.

Society

Anthropologists believe that early humans lived in small groups. In bad weather they might have taken shelter in a cave if there was one nearby. When food or water became hard to find, groups of people would have to move to new areas.

The early humans of the Stone Age were **hunter-gatherers** —people who hunt animals and gather wild plants, seeds, fruits, and nuts to survive. Anthropologists believe that most Stone Age hunters were men. They hunted in groups, sometimes chasing entire herds of animals over cliffs. This method was both more productive and safer than hunting alone.

Women in hunter-gatherer societies probably took responsibility for collecting plants to eat. They likely stayed near camps and took care of children.

Language, Art, and Religion

The most important development of early Stone Age culture was language. Scientists have many theories about why language first developed. Some think it was to make hunting in groups easier. Others think it developed as a way for people to form relationships. Still others think language made it easier for people to resolve issues like how to **distribute** food.

Language wasn't the only way early people expressed themselves. They also created art. People carved figures out of stone, ivory, and bone. They painted and carved images of people and animals on cave walls. Scientists still aren't sure why people made art. Perhaps the cave paintings were used to teach people how to hunt, or maybe they had religious meanings.

ACADEMIC VOCABULARY

distribute to divide among a group of people

LINKING TO TODAY

Stone Tools

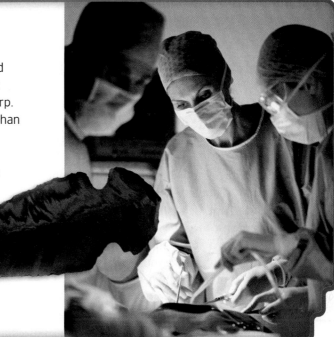

Did you know that Stone Age people's tools weren't as primitive as we might think? They made knife blades and arrowheads—like the one shown below—out of volcanic glass called obsidian. The obsidian blades were very sharp. In fact, they could be 100 times sharper and smoother than the steel blades used for surgery in modern hospitals.

Today some doctors are going back to using these Stone Age materials. They have found that blades made from obsidian are more precise than modern scalpels. Some doctors use obsidian blades for delicate surgery on the face because the stone tools leave "nicer-looking" scars.

ANALYSIS SKILL ANALYZING INFORMATION

How do you think modern obsidian blades are different from Stone Age ones?

Cave Paintings
Thousands of years ago, early people decorated cave walls with paintings like this one. No one knows for sure why people created cave paintings, but many historians think they were related to hunting.

Why do you think this cave painting may be connected to hunting?

Scholars know little about the religious beliefs of early people. Archaeologists have found graves that included food and artifacts. Many scientists think these discoveries are proof that the first human religions developed during the Stone Age.

READING CHECK **Analyzing** What was one possible reason for the development of language?

SUMMARY AND PREVIEW Scientists have discovered and studied the remains of hominids and early humans who lived in East Africa millions of years ago. These Stone Age people were hunter-gatherers who used fire, stone tools, and language. In the next section you will learn how early humans moved out of Africa and populated the world.

Section 1 Assessment

go.hrw.com
Online Quiz
KEYWORD: SQ6 HP2

Reviewing Ideas, Terms, and People HSS 6.1.1

1. a. Identify Who found the bones of Lucy?
  b. Explain Why do historians need archaeologists and anthropologists to study **prehistory**?
2. a. Recall What is the scientific name for modern humans?
  b. Make Inferences What might have been one advantage of walking completely upright?
3. a. Recall What kind of **tools** did people use during the **Paleolithic Era**?
  b. Design Design a stone and wood tool you could use to help you with your chores. Describe your tool in a sentence or two.
4. a. Define What is a **hunter-gatherer**?
  b. Rank In your opinion, what was the most important change brought by the development of language?

Critical Thinking

5. Evaluate Draw a graphic organizer like the one at right. Use it to rank the three most important advancements, such as the ability to control fire, made in the Paleolithic Era. Next to your organizer, write a sentence explaining why you ranked the advancements in that order.

1. → 2. → 3.

FOCUS ON WRITING

6. Listing Stone Age Achievements Look back through this section and make a list of important Stone Age achievements. Which of these will you include on your storyboard? How will you illustrate them?

The Iceman

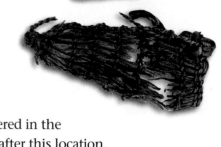

The Iceman's dagger and the scabbard, or case, he carried it in

Why was a Stone Age traveler in Europe's highest mountains?

When did he live? about 5,300 years ago

Where did he live? The frozen body of the Iceman was discovered in the snowy Ötztal Alps of Italy in 1991. Scientists nicknamed him Ötzi after this location.

What did he do? That question has been debated ever since Ötzi's body was found. Apparently, he was traveling. At first scientists thought he had frozen to death in a storm. But an arrowhead found in his shoulder suggests that his death was not so peaceful. After he died, his body was covered by glaciers and preserved for thousands of years.

Why is he important? Ötzi is the oldest mummified human ever found in such good condition. His body, clothing, and tools were extremely well preserved, telling us a lot about life during the Stone Ages. His outfit was made of three types of animal skin stitched together. He wore leather shoes padded with grass, a grass cape, a fur hat, and a sort of backpack. He carried an ax with a copper blade as well as a bow and arrows.

Drawing Conclusions Why do you think the Iceman was in the Alps?

Scientists examine the Iceman's body in 1991, before it was removed from the glacier.

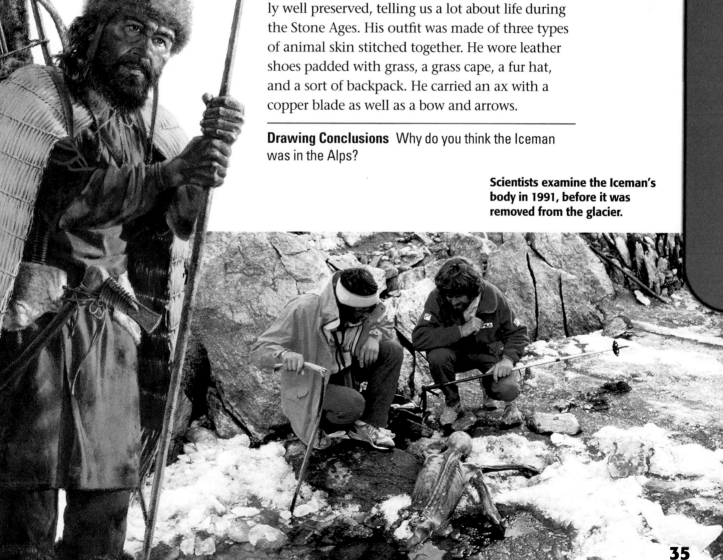

Early Human Migration

What You Will Learn...

Main Ideas

1. People moved out of Africa as the earth's climates changed.
2. People adapted to new environments by making clothing and new types of tools.

The Big Idea

As people migrated around the world they learned to adapt to new environments.

Key Terms

migrate, *p. 36*
ice ages, *p. 36*
land bridge, *p. 36*
Mesolithic Era, *p. 38*

HSS 6.1.2 Identify the locations of human communities that populated the major regions of the world and describe how humans adapted to a variety of environments.

If YOU were there...

Your tribe of hunter–gatherers has lived in this place for as long as anyone can remember. But now there are not enough animals to hunt. Whenever you find berries and roots, you have to share them with people from other tribes. Your leaders think it's time to find a new home in the lands far beyond the mountains. But no one has ever traveled there, and many people are afraid.

How do you feel about moving to a new home?

BUILDING BACKGROUND From their beginnings in East Africa, early humans moved in many directions. Eventually, they lived on almost every continent in the world. People probably had many reasons for moving. One reason was a change in the climate.

People Move Out of Africa

During the Old Stone Age, climate patterns around the world changed, transforming the earth's geography. In response to these changes, people began to **migrate**, or move, to new places.

The Ice Ages

Most scientists believe that about 1.6 million years ago, many places around the world began to experience long periods of freezing weather. These freezing times are called the **ice ages**. The ice ages ended about 10,000 years ago.

During the ice ages huge sheets of ice covered much of the earth's land. These ice sheets were formed from ocean water, leaving ocean levels lower than they are now. Many areas that are now underwater were dry land then. For example, a narrow body of water now separates Asia and North America. But scientists think that during the ice ages, the ocean level dropped and exposed a **land bridge**, a strip of land connecting two continents. Land bridges allowed Stone Age peoples to migrate around the world.

Early Human Migration

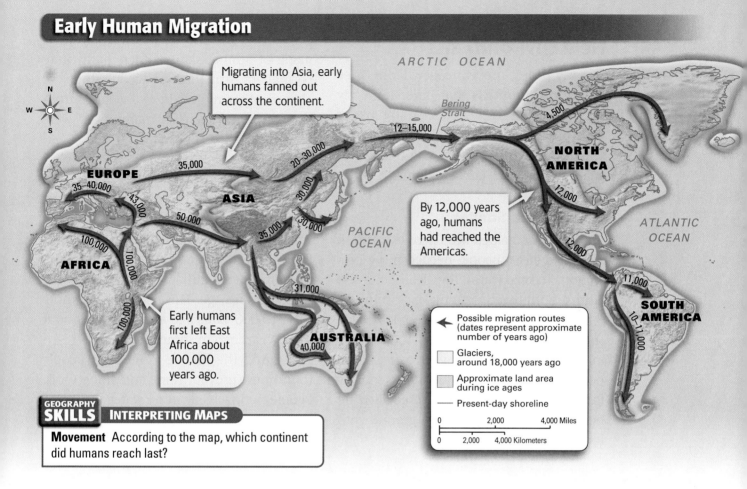

Migrating into Asia, early humans fanned out across the continent.

ARCTIC OCEAN

Bering Strait

12–15,000

4,500

NORTH AMERICA

35,000

20–30,000

EUROPE

35–40,000

43,000

50,000

ASIA

30,000

35,000

30,000

By 12,000 years ago, humans had reached the Americas.

12,000

ATLANTIC OCEAN

12,000

AFRICA

100,000

100,000

100,000

PACIFIC OCEAN

31,000

11,000

SOUTH AMERICA

10–11,000

Early humans first left East Africa about 100,000 years ago.

AUSTRALIA

40,000

← Possible migration routes (dates represent approximate number of years ago)

☐ Glaciers, around 18,000 years ago

☐ Approximate land area during ice ages

— Present-day shoreline

0   2,000   4,000 Miles

0   2,000   4,000 Kilometers

GEOGRAPHY SKILLS | **INTERPRETING MAPS**

Movement According to the map, which continent did humans reach last?

Settling New Lands

Scientists agree that migration around the world took hundreds of thousands of years. Early hominids, the ancestors of modern humans, migrated from Africa to Asia as early as 2 million years ago. From there, they spread to Southeast Asia and Europe.

Later, humans also began to migrate around the world, and earlier hominids died out. Look at the map to see the dates and routes of early human migration.

Humans began to migrate from East Africa to southern Africa and southwestern Asia around 100,000 years ago. From there, people moved east across southern Asia. They could then migrate to Australia. Scientists are not sure exactly how the first people reached Australia. Even though ocean levels were lower then, there was always open sea between Asia and Australia.

From southwestern Asia, humans also migrated north into Europe. Geographic features such as high mountains and cold temperatures delayed migration northward into northern Asia. Eventually, however, people from both Europe and southern Asia moved into that region.

From northern Asia, people moved into North America. Scientists disagree on when and how the first people arrived in North America. Most scholars think people must have crossed a land bridge from Asia to North America. Once in North America, these people moved south, following herds of animals and settling South America. By 9000 BC, humans lived on all continents of the world except Antarctica.

READING CHECK **Analyzing** How did the ice ages influence human migration?

THE STONE AGES AND EARLY CULTURES **37**

People Adapt to New Environments

As early people moved to new lands, they found environments that differed greatly from those in East Africa. Many places were much colder and had strange plants and animals. Early people had to learn to adapt to their new environments.

Clothing and Shelter

Although fire helped keep people warm in very cold areas, people needed more protection. To keep warm, they learned to sew animal skins together to make clothing.

In addition to clothing, people needed shelter to survive. At first they took shelter in caves. When they moved to areas with no caves, they built their own shelters. The first human-made shelters were called pit houses. They were pits in the ground with roofs of branches and leaves.

Later, people began to build homes above the ground. Some lived in tents made of animal skins. Others built more permanent structures of wood, stone, or clay or other materials. Even bones from large animals such as mammoths were used in building shelters.

New Tools and Technologies

People also adapted to new environments with new types of tools. These tools were smaller and more complex than tools from the Old Stone Age. They defined the **Mesolithic** (me-zuh-LI-thik) **Era**, or the Middle Stone Age. This period began more than 10,000 years ago and lasted to about 5,000 years ago in some places.

During the Middle Stone Age, people found new uses for bone and stone tools. People who lived near water invented hooks and fishing spears. Other groups invented the bow and arrow.

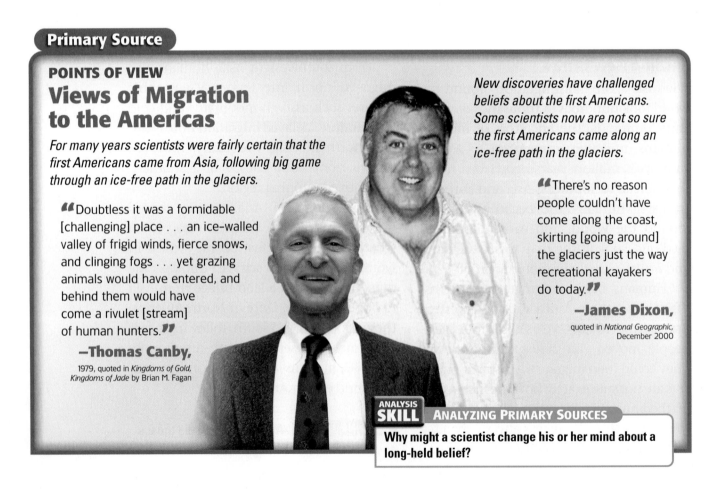

Primary Source

POINTS OF VIEW

Views of Migration to the Americas

For many years scientists were fairly certain that the first Americans came from Asia, following big game through an ice-free path in the glaciers.

❝Doubtless it was a formidable [challenging] place . . . an ice-walled valley of frigid winds, fierce snows, and clinging fogs . . . yet grazing animals would have entered, and behind them would have come a rivulet [stream] of human hunters.❞

—Thomas Canby,
1979, quoted in *Kingdoms of Gold, Kingdoms of Jade* by Brian M. Fagan

New discoveries have challenged beliefs about the first Americans. Some scientists now are not so sure the first Americans came along an ice-free path in the glaciers.

❝There's no reason people couldn't have come along the coast, skirting [going around] the glaciers just the way recreational kayakers do today.❞

—James Dixon,
quoted in *National Geographic*,
December 2000

ANALYSIS SKILL **ANALYZING PRIMARY SOURCES**

Why might a scientist change his or her mind about a long-held belief?

A Mammoth House

Early people used whatever was available to make shelters. In Central Asia, where wood was scarce, some early people made their homes from mammoth bones.

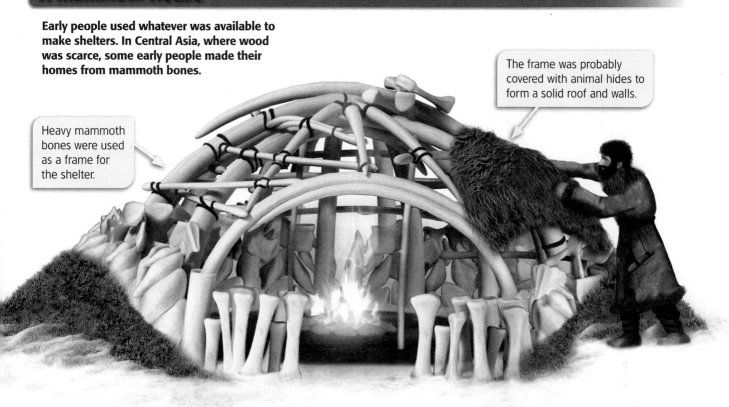

The frame was probably covered with animal hides to form a solid roof and walls.

Heavy mammoth bones were used as a frame for the shelter.

In addition to tools, people developed new technologies to improve their lives. For example, some learned to make canoes by hollowing out logs. They used the canoes to travel on rivers and lakes. They also began to make pottery. The first pets may also have appeared at this time. People kept dogs to help them hunt and for protection. Developments like these, in addition to clothing and shelter, allowed people to adapt to new environments.

READING CHECK Finding Main Ideas
What were two ways people adapted to new environments?

SUMMARY AND PREVIEW Early people adapted to new environments with new kinds of clothing, shelter, and tools. In Section 3 you will read about how Stone Age peoples developed farming.

go.hrw.com
Online Quiz
KEYWORD: SQ6 HP2

Section 2 Assessment

Reviewing Ideas, Terms, and People HSS 6.1.2

1. **a. Define** What is a **land bridge**?
   b. Analyze Why did it take so long for early people to reach South America?
2. **a. Recall** What did people use to make tools in the **Mesolithic Era**?
   b. Summarize Why did people have to learn to make clothes and build shelters?

Critical Thinking

3. **Sequencing** Draw the graphic organizer below. Complete it to show the order of human migration around the world.

FOCUS ON WRITING

4. **Illustrating** How will you illustrate early migration on your storyboard? Draw some sketches. How does this information relate to your ideas from Section 1?

Beginnings of Agriculture

What You Will Learn...

Main Ideas

1. The first farmers learned to grow plants and raise animals in the Stone Age.
2. Farming changed societies and the way people lived.

The Big Idea

The development of agriculture brought great changes to human society.

Key Terms

Neolithic Era, *p. 41*
domestication, *p. 41*
agriculture, *p. 42*
megaliths, *p. 42*

HSS 6.1.3 Discuss the climatic changes and human modifications of the physical environment that gave rise to the domestication of plants and animals and new sources of clothing and shelter.

If **YOU** were there...

As a gatherer, you know where to find the sweetest fruits. Every summer, you eat many of these fruits, dropping the seeds on the ground. One day you return to find new plants everywhere. You realize that the plants have grown from your dropped seeds.

How could this discovery change your way of life?

BUILDING BACKGROUND The discovery that plants grew from seeds was one of the major advances of the late Stone Age. Other similar advances led to great changes in the way people lived.

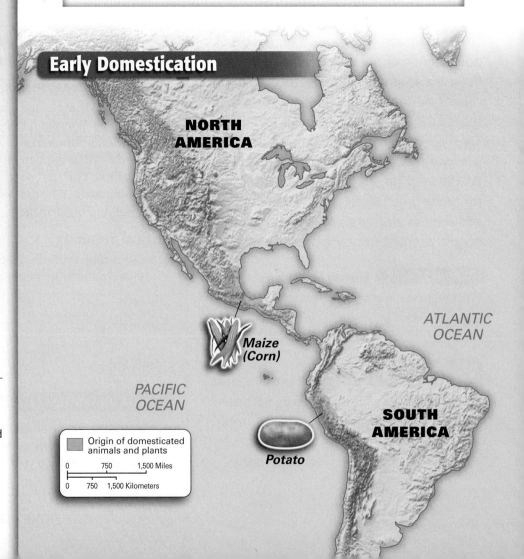

Early Domestication

NORTH AMERICA

Maize (Corn)

PACIFIC OCEAN

ATLANTIC OCEAN

SOUTH AMERICA

Potato

Origin of domesticated animals and plants

0   750   1,500 Miles

0   750   1,500 Kilometers

The First Farmers

After the Middle Stone Age came a period of time that scientists call the **Neolithic** (nee-uh-LI-thik) **Era**, or New Stone Age. It began as early as 10,000 years ago in Southwest Asia. In other places, this era began much later and lasted much longer than it did there.

During the New Stone Age people learned to polish stones to make tools like saws and drills. People also learned how to make fire. Before, they could only use fire that had been started by natural causes such as lightning.

The New Stone Age ended in Egypt and Southwest Asia about 5,000 years ago, when toolmakers began to make tools out of metal. But tools weren't the only major change that occurred during the Neolithic Era. In fact, the biggest changes came in how people produced food.

Plants

After a warming trend brought an end to the ice ages, new plants began to grow in some areas. For example, wild barley and wheat plants started to spread throughout Southwest Asia. Over time, people came to depend on these wild plants for food. They began to settle where grains grew.

People soon learned that they could plant seeds themselves to grow their own crops. Historians call the shift from food gathering to food producing the Neolithic Revolution. Most experts believe that this revolution, or change, first occurred in the societies of Southwest Asia.

Eventually, people learned to change plants to make them more useful. They planted only the largest grains or the sweetest fruits. The process of changing plants or animals to make them more useful to humans is called **domestication**.

GEOGRAPHY SKILLS **INTERPRETING MAPS**

1. **Location** Which animals were domesticated in Asia?
2. **Location** Where was corn first domesticated?

An Early Farming Society

The village of Çatal Hüyük in modern Turkey is one of the earliest farming villages discovered. Around 8,000 years ago, the village was home to about 5,000–6,000 people living in more than 1,000 houses. Villagers farmed, hunted and fished, traded with distant lands, and worshipped gods in special shrines.

Black Sea

TURKEY
Çatal
Hüyük•

Mediterranean Sea

Villagers used simple channels to move water to their fields.

Wheat, barley, and peas were some of the main crops grown outside the village.

ACADEMIC VOCABULARY

development
creation

The domestication of plants led to the **development** of **agriculture**, or farming. For the first time, people could produce their own food. This development changed human society forever.

Animals

Learning to produce food was a major accomplishment for early people. But learning how to use animals for their own purposes was almost equally important.

Hunters didn't have to follow wild herds anymore. Instead, farmers could keep sheep or goats for milk, food, and wool. Farmers could also use large animals like cattle to carry loads or to pull large tools used in farming. Using animals to help with farming greatly improved people's chances of surviving.

THE IMPACT TODAY

One famous megalith, Stonehenge in England, attracts millions of curious tourists and scholars each year.

READING CHECK Identifying Cause and Effect
What was one effect of the switch to farming?

Farming Changes Societies

The Neolithic Revolution brought huge changes to people's lives. With survival more certain, people could focus on activities other than finding food.

Domestication of plants and animals enabled people to use plant fibers to make cloth. The domestication of animals made it possible to use wool from goats and sheep and skins from horses for clothes.

People also began to build permanent settlements. As they started raising crops and animals, they needed to stay in one place. Then, once people were able to control their own food production, the world's population grew. In some areas farming communities developed into towns.

As populations grew, groups of people gathered to perform religious ceremonies. Some put up megaliths. **Megaliths** are huge stones used as monuments or as the sites for religious gatherings.

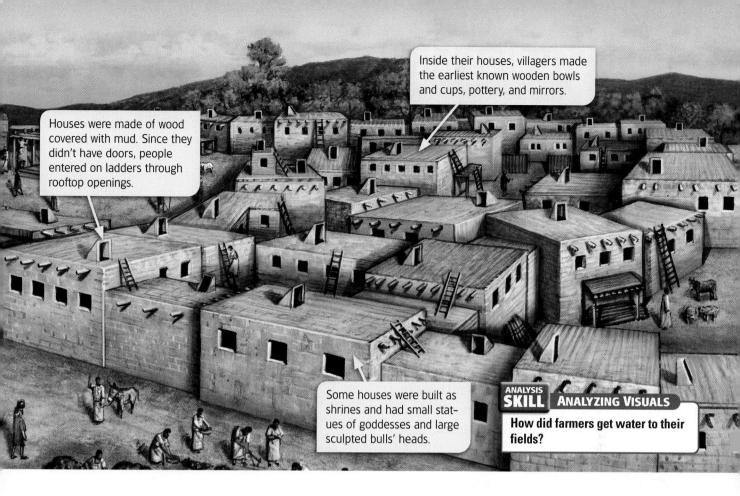

Houses were made of wood covered with mud. Since they didn't have doors, people entered on ladders through rooftop openings.

Inside their houses, villagers made the earliest known wooden bowls and cups, pottery, and mirrors.

Some houses were built as shrines and had small statues of goddesses and large sculpted bulls' heads.

ANALYSIS SKILL **ANALYZING VISUALS**

How did farmers get water to their fields?

Early people probably believed in gods and goddesses associated with the four elements—air, water, fire, and earth—or with animals. For example, one European group honored a thunder god, while another group worshipped bulls. Some scholars also believe that prehistoric peoples also prayed to their ancestors. People in some societies today still hold many of these same beliefs.

READING CHECK **Analyzing Information** How did farming contribute to the growth of towns?

SUMMARY AND PREVIEW Stone Age peoples adapted to new environments by domesticating plants and animals. These changes led to the development of religion and the growth of towns. In the next chapter you will learn more about early towns.

go.hrw.com
Online Quiz
KEYWORD: SQ6 HP2

Section 3 Assessment

Reviewing Ideas, Terms, and People **HSS** 6.1.3

1. **a. Define** What is **domestication** of a plant or animal?
   b. Make Generalizations How did early people use domesticated animals?
2. **a. Describe** What were gods and goddesses probably associated with in prehistoric religion?
   b. Explain How did domestication of plants and animals lead to the development of towns?

Critical Thinking

3. **Identifying Cause and Effect** Copy the graphic organizer at right. Use it to show one cause and three effects of the development of agriculture.

Cause

↓

Development of agriculture

↓

Effects

FOCUS ON WRITING

4. **Beginnings of Agriculture** Now that you've read about the birth of agriculture, you're ready to plan your storyboard. Look back through your notes from previous sections and the text of this one. Make a list of the events and ideas you will include on your storyboard. Then plan how you will arrange these items.

Social Studies Skills

Analysis	Critical Thinking	Participation	Study

Identifying Central Issues

Understand the Skill

Central issues are the main problems or topics that are related to an event. The issues behind a historical event can be varied and complicated. Central issues in world history usually involve political, social, economic, territorial, moral, or technological matters. The ability to identify the central issue in an event allows you to focus on information that is most important to understanding the event.

Learn the Skill

In this chapter you learned about prehistory. Some of the events you read about may not seem very important. It is hard for people in the computer age to appreciate the accomplishments of the Stone Age. For example, adding wooden handles to stone tools may seem like a simple thing to us. But it was a life-changing advance for people of that time.

This example points out something to remember when looking for central issues. Try not to use only modern-day values and standards to decide what is important about the past. Always think about the times in which people lived. Ask yourself what would have been important to people living then.

The following guidelines will help you to identify central issues. Use them to gain a better understanding of historical events.

1 Identify the subject of the information. What is the information about?

2 Determine the source of the information. Is it a primary source or a secondary source?

3 Determine the purpose of what you are reading. Why has the information been provided?

4 Find the strongest or most forceful statements in the information. These are often clues to issues or ideas the writer thinks are the most central or important.

5 Think about values, concerns, ways of life, and events that would have been important to the people of the times. Determine how the information might be connected to those larger issues.

Practice and Apply the Skill

Apply the guidelines to identify the central issue in the following passage. Then answer the questions.

"What distinguished the Neolithic Era from earlier ages was people's ability to shape stone tools by polishing and grinding. This allowed people to make more specialized tools. Even more important changes took place also. The development of agriculture changed the basic way people lived. Earlier people had been wanderers, who moved from place to place in search of food. Some people began settling in permanent villages. Exactly how they learned that seeds could be planted and made to grow year after year remains a mystery. However, the shift from food gathering to food producing was possibly the most important change ever in history."

1. What is the general subject of this passage?

2. What changes distinguished the Neolithic Era from earlier periods?

3. According to this writer, what is the central issue to understand about the Neolithic Era?

4. What statements in the passage help you to determine the central issue?

Standards Review

Visual Summary

Use the visual summary below to help you review the main ideas of the chapter.

QUICK FACTS

Hominids developed in Africa and learned how to use tools.

Early humans lived as hunter-gatherers.

Humans migrated around the world, adapting to new environments.

Eventually, people learned how to farm and raise animals.

Reviewing Vocabulary, Terms, and People

For each group of terms below, write a sentence that shows how all the terms in the group are related.

1. prehistory
   ancestor
   hominid

2. domestication
   Neolithic Era
   agriculture

3. Paleolithic Era
   tool
   hunter-gatherers
   develop

4. land bridge
   ice ages
   migrate

5. society
   megaliths
   Neolithic Era

Comprehension and Critical Thinking

SECTION 1 *(Pages 28–34)* HSS 6.1.1

6. **a. Recall** What does *Homo sapiens* mean? When may *Homo sapiens* have first appeared in Africa?

   b. Draw Conclusions If you were an archaeologist and found bead jewelry and stone chopping tools in an ancient woman's grave, what may you conclude?

   c. Elaborate How did stone tools change over time? Why do you think these changes took place so slowly?

SECTION 2 *(Pages 36–39)* HSS 6.1.2

7. **a. Describe** What new skills did people develop to help them survive?

   b. Analyze How did global climate change affect the migration of early people?

   c. Evaluate About 15,000 years ago, where do you think life would have been more difficult—in eastern Africa or northern Europe? Why?

8. a. Define What was the Neolithic Revolution?

b. Make Inferences How did domestication of plants and animals change early societies?

c. Predict Why do you think people of the Neolithic Era put up megaliths instead of some other kind of monuments?

Reviewing Themes

9. Geography What were three ways in which the environment affected Stone Age peoples?

10. Society and Culture How did the development of language change hunter-gatherer society?

Using the Internet

go.hrw.com
KEYWORD: SQ6 WH2

11. Activity: Creating a Skit In the beginning of the Paleolithic Era, or the Old Stone Age, early humans used modified stones as tools. As the Stone Age progressed, plants and animals became materials for tools too. Enter the activity keyword and research the development of tools and the use of fire. Then create a skit that tells about an early human society discovering fire, creating a new tool, or developing a new way of doing a task.

Reading and Analysis Skills

Understanding Chronological Order *Below are several lists of events. Arrange the events in each list in chronological order.*

12. Mesolithic Era begins.
Paleolithic Era begins.
Neolithic Era begins.

13. *Homo sapiens* appears.
Homo habilis appears.
Homo erectus appears.

14. People make stone tools.
People make metal tools.
People attach wooden handles to tools.

Social Studies Skills

Identifying Central Issues *Read the primary source passage below and then answer the questions that follow.*

"Almonds provide a striking example of bitter seeds and their change under domestication. Most wild almond seeds contain an intensely bitter chemical called amygdalin, which (as was already mentioned) breaks down to yield the poison cyanide. A snack of wild almonds can kill a person foolish enough to ignore the warning of the bitter taste. Since the first stage in unconscious domestication involves gathering seeds to eat, how on earth did domestication of wild almonds ever reach that first stage?"

–Jared Diamond, from *Guns, Germs, and Steel*

15. What is the main point of this passage?

16. What does the author suggest is the major issue he will address in the text?

FOCUS ON WRITING

17. Creating Your Storyboard Use the notes you have taken to plan your storyboard. What images will you include in each frame of the storyboard? How many frames will you need to tell the story of prehistoric people? How will you represent your ideas visually?

After you have sketched an outline for your storyboard, begin drawing it. Be sure to include all significant adaptations and developments made by prehistoric people, and don't worry if you can't draw that well. If you like, you might want to draw your storyboard in the simple style of prehistoric cave paintings. As the last frame in your storyboard, write a detailed summary to conclude your story.

Standards Assessment

DIRECTIONS: Read each question, and write the letter of the best response.

1 Use the map to answer the following question.

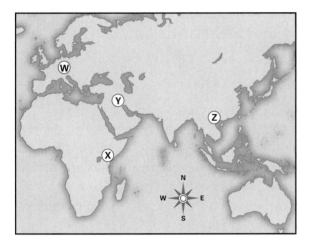

The region in which the first humans lived is shown on the map by the letter

A   W.

B   X.

C   Y.

D   Z.

2 The earliest humans lived

A   by hunting and gathering their food.

B   as herders of sheep and other livestock.

C   alone or in pairs.

D   in farming villages along rivers and streams.

3 The development of farming brought all of the following changes to the lives of early humans *except*

A   the first human-made shelters.

B   a larger supply of food.

C   the construction of permanent settlements.

D   new types of clothing.

4 The region of the world that was likely occupied *last* by early humans was

A   northern Asia.

B   southern Asia.

C   North America.

D   South America.

5 Hunter-gatherer societies in the Old Stone Age possessed all of the following *except*

A   fire.

B   art.

C   bone tools.

D   religious beliefs.

Connecting with Past Learnings

6 You know that history is the study of people and events from the past. To learn about prehistory, historians would likely study all of the following *except*

A   graves.

B   journals.

C   bones.

D   art.

7 Which of the following people that you studied in Grade 5 likely crossed a land bridge to get to the Americas?

A   Pilgrims

B   colonists

C   Native Americans

D   Christopher Columbus

Assignment

Write a paper comparing and contrasting two early human societies.

Comparing and Contrasting Societies

Comparing means finding likenesses between or among things. Contrasting means finding differences. You often compare and contrast things to understand them better and see how they are related.

TIP Using a Graphic Organizer

A Venn diagram can help you see ways that the two societies are similar and different.

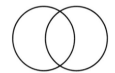

1. Prewrite

Getting Started

Unlike most essays, a compare and contrast paper has two subjects. However, it still has only one big idea, or thesis. For example, your idea may be to show how two societies dealt with the same problem or to show how two human societies changed over time.

Begin by choosing two subjects. Then identify specific points of similarities and differences between the two. Support each point with historical facts, examples, and details.

Organizing Your Information

Choose one of these two ways to organize your points of comparison.

- Present all the points about the first subject and then all the points about the second subject: AAABBB, or block style
- Alternate back and forth between the first subject and the second subject: ABABAB, or point-by-point style

2. Write

This framework will help you use your notes to write a first draft.

ELA Writing 6.2.2c Follow an organized pattern appropriate to the type of composition.

A Writer's Framework

Introduction

- Clearly identify your two subjects.
- Give background information readers will need in order to understand your points of comparison between the societies.
- State your big idea, or main purpose in comparing and contrasting these two societies.

Body

- Present your points of comparison in block style or point-by-point style.
- Compare the two societies in at least two ways, and contrast them in at least two ways.
- Use specific historical facts, details, and examples to support each of your points.

Conclusion

- Restate your big idea.
- Summarize the points you have made in your paper.
- Expand on your big idea, perhaps by relating it to your own life, to other societies, or to later historical events.

3. Evaluate and Revise

Evaluating

Use the following questions to discover ways to improve your paper.

Evaluation Questions for a Comparison/Contrast Paper

- Do you introduce both of your subjects in your first paragraph?
- Do you state your big idea, or thesis, at the end of your introduction?
- Do you present two or more similarities and two or more differences between the two societies?

- Do you use either the block style or point-by-point style of organization?
- Do you support your points of comparison with enough historical facts, details, and examples?
- Does your conclusion restate your big idea and summarize your main points?

TIP Help with Punctuation

Use the correct punctuation marks before and after clue words within sentences. Usually, a comma comes before *and, but, for, nor, or, so,* and *yet,* with no punctuation after the word. When they are in the middle of a sentence, clue words and phrases such as *however, similarly, in addition, in contrast,* and *on the other hand* usually have a comma before and after them.

Revising

When you are revising your paper, you may need to add comparison-contrast clue words. They will help your readers see the connections between ideas.

Clue Words for Similarities	Clue Words for Differences
also, another, both, in addition, just as, like, similarly, too	although, but, however, in contrast, instead, on the other hand, unlike

4. Proofread and Publish

Proofreading

Before sharing your paper, you will want to polish it by correcting any remaining errors. Look closely for mistakes in grammar, spelling, capitalization, and punctuation. To avoid two common grammar errors, make sure that you have used the correct form of *–er* or *more* and *–est* or *most* with adjectives and adverbs when making comparisons.

Publishing

One good way to share your paper is to exchange it with one or more classmates. After reading each other's papers, you can compare and contrast them. How are your papers similar? How do they differ? If possible, share papers with someone whose big idea is similar to yours.

● Practice and Apply

Use the steps and strategies outlined in this workshop to write your compare and contrast paper.

UNIT **2** 7000 BC–AD 350

Mesopotamia, Egypt, and Kush

50

The world's first civilizations developed in Asia and Africa after people learned how to farm. These civilizations began in river valleys, which were perfect places for people to grow crops.

With the development of farming, people no longer had to travel in search of food. Instead, they could settle down in one place. Eventually, people built the first towns and cities and invented government, writing, and the wheel. They also created huge buildings and temples and produced incredible works of art.

In the next three chapters, you will learn about the early civilizations of Mesopotamia, Egypt, and Kush.

Explore the Art

In this scene, the young King Tutankhamen of Egypt stands with his wife at the entrance to a temple. How does this scene show some of the features of Egyptian civilization?

Mesopotamia and the Fertile Crescent

California Standards

History–Social Science

6.2 Students analyze the geographic, political, economic, religious, and social structures of the early civilizations of Mesopotamia, Egypt, and Kush.

Analysis Skills

CS 3 Use maps to identify physical features.

English–Language Arts

Writing 6.1.2a Engage the interest of the reader and state a clear purpose.

Reading 6.2.3 Connect and clarify main ideas by identifying their relationships to other sources and related topics.

FOCUS ON WRITING

A Poster Most elementary school students have not read or heard much about ancient Mesopotamia. As you read this chapter, you can gather information about that land. Then you can create a colorful poster to share some of what you have learned with younger children.

CHAPTER EVENTS

c. 7000 BC
Agriculture first develops in Mesopotamia.

7000 BC

WORLD EVENTS

c. 3100 BC
Menes becomes the first pharaoh of Egypt.

HOLT
History's Impact
▶ video series
Watch the video to understand
the impact of a system of laws.

What You Will Learn...

In this chapter you will learn about the early
civilizations of Mesopotamia and the Fertile
Crescent. This photo shows the partially
reconstructed remains of an ancient temple
in Mesopotamia.

c. 2350–2330 BC
Sargon of Akkad
conquers Mesopotamia
and forms the world's
first empire.

c. 1770 BC
Hammurabi
of Babylon
issues a
written code
of laws.

c. 1000 BC
Phoenicians
trade all
around the
Mediterranean.

2750 BC	2000 BC	1250 BC	500 BC

c. 2300 BC
The Harappan
civilization rises
in the Indus Valley.

c. 1500 BC
The Shang
dynasty is
established
in China.

c. 965 BC
Solomon
becomes
king of
Israel.

53

Reading Social Studies

by Kylene Beers

| Economics | Geography | Politics | Religion | Society and Culture | Science and Technology |

Focus on Themes Chapter three introduces you to a region in southwest Asia called Mesopotamia, the home of the world's first civilization. You will read about what made this area one where civilizations could begin and grow. You will learn about one group of people—the Sumerians—and their great **technological** inventions. You will also read about other people who invaded Mesopotamia and brought their own rules of governing and **politics** to the area.

Main Ideas in Social Studies

Focus on Reading Have you ever set up a tent? If you have, you know that one pole provides structure and support for the whole tent. A paragraph has a similar structure. One idea—the **main idea**—provides support and structure for the whole paragraph.

Identifying Main Ideas Most paragraphs written about history include a main idea that is stated clearly in a sentence. At other times, the main idea is suggested, not stated. However, that idea still shapes the paragraph's content and the meaning of all of the facts and details in it.

Identifying Main Ideas
1. Read the paragraph. Ask yourself, "What is this paragraph mostly about, or its topic?"
2. List the important facts and details that relate to that topic.
3. Ask yourself, "What seems to be the most important point the writer is making about the topic?" Or ask, "If the writer could say only one thing about this paragraph, what would it be?" **This is the main idea of the paragraph.**

Having people available to work on different jobs meant that society could accomplish more. Large projects, such as constructing buildings and digging irrigation systems, required specialized workers, managers, and organization. To complete these projects, the Mesopotamians needed structure and rules. Structure and rules could be provided by laws and government.

Topic: The paragraph talks about people, jobs, and structure.

+

Facts and Details:
- People working on different jobs needed structure.
- Laws and government provided this structure.

=

Main Idea: Having people in a society work on many different jobs led to the creation of laws and government.

Additional reading support can be found in the

Inter active

Reader and Study Guide

You Try It!

The passage below is from the chapter you are about to read. Read it and then answer the questions below.

Technical Advances

From Chapter 3 p. 69

One of the Sumerians' most important developments was the wheel. They were the first people to build wheeled vehicles, including carts and wagons. Using the wheel, Sumerians invented a device that spins clay as a craftsperson shapes it into bowls. This device is called a potter's wheel.

The plow was another important Sumerian invention. Pulled by oxen, plows broke through the hard clay soil of Sumer to prepare it for planting. This technique greatly increased farm production. The Sumerians also invented a clock that used falling water to measure time.

Sumerian advances improved daily life in many ways. Sumerians built sewers under city streets. They learned to use bronze to make stronger tools and weapons. They even produced makeup and glass jewelry.

Answer the following questions about finding main ideas.

1. Reread the first paragraph. What is its main idea?

2. What is the main idea of the third paragraph? Reread the second paragraph. Is there a sentence that expresses the main idea of the paragraph? What is that main idea? Write a sentence to express it.

3. Which of the following best expresses the main idea of the entire passage?

   a. The wheel was an important invention.

   b. The Sumerians invented many helpful devices.

> **As you read Chapter 3,** find the main ideas of the paragraphs you are studying.

Key Terms and People

Chapter 3

Section 1
Fertile Crescent *(p. 57)*
silt *(p. 57)*
irrigation *(p. 58)*
canals *(p. 58)*
surplus *(p. 58)*
division of labor *(p. 58)*

Section 2
rural *(p. 62)*
urban *(p. 62)*
city-state *(p. 62)*
Gilgamesh *(p. 63)*
Sargon *(p. 63)*
empire *(p. 63)*
polytheism *(p. 64)*
priests *(p. 65)*
social hierarchy *(p. 65)*

Section 3
cuneiform *(p. 67)*
pictographs *(p. 68)*
scribe *(p. 68)*
epics *(p. 68)*
architecture *(p. 70)*
ziggurat *(p. 70)*

Section 4
monarch *(p. 74)*
Hammurabi's Code *(p. 75)*
chariot *(p. 76)*
Nebuchadnezzar *(p. 77)*
alphabet *(p. 79)*

Academic Vocabulary

Success in school is related to knowing academic vocabulary—the words that are frequently used in school assignments and discussions. In this chapter, you will learn the following academic words:

role *(p. 64)*
impact *(p. 65)*

Geography of the Fertile Crescent

What You Will Learn...

Main Ideas

1. The rivers of Southwest Asia supported the growth of civilization.
2. New farming techniques led to the growth of cities.

The Big Idea

The valleys of the Tigris and Euphrates rivers were the site of the world's first civilizations.

Key Terms

Fertile Crescent, *p. 57*
silt, *p. 57*
irrigation, *p. 58*
canals, *p. 58*
surplus, *p. 58*
division of labor, *p. 58*

HSS **6.2.1** Locate and describe the major river systems and discuss the physical settings that supported permanent settlement and early civilization.

6.2.2 Trace the development of agricultural techniques that permitted the production of economic surplus and the emergence of cities as centers of culture and power.

If YOU were there...

You are a farmer in Southwest Asia about 6,000 years ago. You live near a slow-moving river, with many shallow lakes and marshes. The river makes the land in the valley rich and fertile, so you can grow wheat and dates. But in the spring, raging floods spill over the riverbanks, destroying your fields. In the hot summers, you are often short of water.

How can you control the waters of the river?

BUILDING BACKGROUND In several parts of the world, bands of hunter-gatherers began to settle down in farming settlements. They domesticated plants and animals. Gradually their cultures became more complex. Most early civilizations grew up along rivers, where people learned to work together to control floods.

Rivers Support the Growth of Civilization

Early peoples settled where crops would grow. Crops usually grew well near rivers, where water was available and regular floods made the soil rich. One region in Southwest Asia was especially well suited for farming. It lay between two rivers.

The Land Between the Rivers

The Tigris and Euphrates rivers are the most important physical features of the region sometimes known as Mesopotamia (mes-uh-puh-TAY-mee-uh). Mesopotamia means "between the rivers" in Greek.

As you can see on the map, the region called Mesopotamia lies between Asia Minor and the Persian Gulf. The region is part of a larger area called the **Fertile Crescent**, a large arc of rich, or fertile, farmland. The Fertile Crescent extends from the Persian Gulf to the Mediterranean Sea.

In ancient times, Mesopotamia was actually made of two parts. Northern Mesopotamia was a plateau bordered on the north and the east by mountains. Southern Mesopotamia was a flat plain. The Tigris and Euphrates rivers flowed down from the hills into this low-lying plain.

The Rise of Civilization

Hunter-gatherer groups first settled in Mesopotamia more than 12,000 years ago. Over time, these people learned how to plant crops to grow their own food. Every year, floods on the Tigris and Euphrates rivers brought **silt**, a mixture of rich soil and tiny rocks, to the land. The fertile silt made the land ideal for farming.

The first farm settlements formed in Mesopotamia as early as 7000 BC. Farmers grew wheat, barley, and other types of grain. Livestock, birds, and fish were also good sources of food. Plentiful food led to population growth, and villages formed. Eventually, these early villages developed into the world's first civilization.

READING CHECK **Summarizing** What made civilization possible in Mesopotamia?

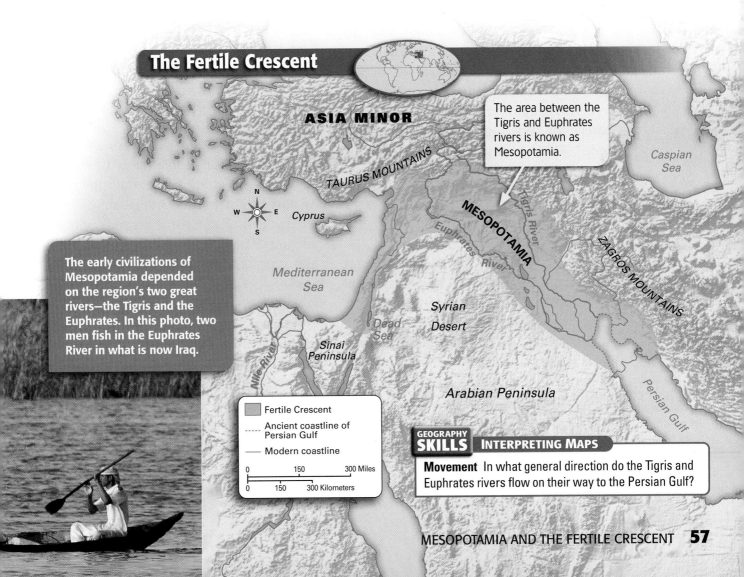

The Fertile Crescent

ASIA MINOR

The area between the Tigris and Euphrates rivers is known as Mesopotamia.

Caspian Sea

TAURUS MOUNTAINS

Cyprus

MESOPOTAMIA

Tigris River

Euphrates River

ZAGROS MOUNTAINS

Mediterranean Sea

The early civilizations of Mesopotamia depended on the region's two great rivers—the Tigris and the Euphrates. In this photo, two men fish in the Euphrates River in what is now Iraq.

Syrian Desert

Dead Sea

Nile River

Sinai Peninsula

Arabian Peninsula

Persian Gulf

Fertile Crescent

---- Ancient coastline of Persian Gulf

—— Modern coastline

0   150   300 Miles
0   150   300 Kilometers

GEOGRAPHY SKILLS **INTERPRETING MAPS**

Movement In what general direction do the Tigris and Euphrates rivers flow on their way to the Persian Gulf?

Early farmers faced the challenge of learning how to control the flow of river water to their fields in both rainy and dry seasons.

1 Early settlements in Mesopotamia were located near rivers. Water was not controlled, and flooding was a major problem.

2 Later, people built canals to protect houses from flooding and move water to their fields.

Farming and Cities

Although Mesopotamia had fertile soil, farming wasn't easy there. The region received little rain. This meant that the water levels in the Tigris and Euphrates rivers depended on how much rain fell in eastern Asia Minor where the two rivers began. When a great amount of rain fell there, water levels got very high. Flooding destroyed crops, killed livestock, and washed away homes. When water levels were too low, crops dried up. Farmers knew they needed a way to control the rivers' flow.

Controlling Water

To solve their problems, Mesopotamians used **irrigation**, a way of supplying water to an area of land. To irrigate their land, they dug out large storage basins to hold water supplies. Then they dug **canals**, human-made waterways, that connected these basins to a network of ditches. These ditches brought water to the fields. To protect their fields from flooding, farmers built up the banks of the Tigris and Euphrates. These built-up banks held back floodwaters even when river levels were high.

THE IMPACT TODAY

People still build dikes, or earthen walls along rivers or shorelines, to hold back water.

Food Surpluses

Irrigation increased the amount of food farmers were able to grow. In fact, farmers could produce a food **surplus**, or more than they needed. Farmers also used irrigation to water grazing areas for cattle and sheep. As a result, Mesopotamians ate a variety of foods. Fish, meat, wheat, barley, and dates were plentiful.

Because irrigation made farmers more productive, fewer people needed to farm. Some people became free to do other jobs. As a result, new occupations developed. For the first time, people became crafters, religious leaders, and government workers. The type of arrangement in which each worker specializes in a particular task or job is called a **division of labor**.

Having people available to work on different jobs meant that society could accomplish more. Large projects, such as constructing buildings and digging irrigation systems, required specialized workers, managers, and organization. To complete these projects, the Mesopotamians needed structure and rules. Structure and rules could be provided by laws and government.

3 With irrigation, the people of Mesopotamia were able to grow more food.

4 Food surpluses allowed some people to stop farming and concentrate on other jobs, like making clay pots or tools.

The Appearance of Cities

Over time, Mesopotamian settlements grew in size and complexity. They gradually developed into cities between 4000 and 3000 BC.

Despite the growth of cities, society in Mesopotamia was still based on agriculture. Most people still worked in farming jobs. However, cities were becoming important places. People traded goods there, and cities provided leaders with power bases.

They were the political, religious, cultural, and economic centers of civilization.

READING CHECK **Analyzing** Why did the Mesopotamians create irrigation systems?

SUMMARY AND PREVIEW Mesopotamia's rich, fertile lands supported productive farming, which led to the development of cities. In Section 2 you will learn about some of the first city builders.

Section 1 Assessment

Reviewing Ideas, Terms, and People HSS 6.2.1, 6.2.2

1. **a. Identify** Where was Mesopotamia?
   b. Explain How did the **Fertile Crescent** get its name?
   c. Evaluate What was the most important factor in making Mesopotamia's farmland fertile?
2. **a. Describe** Why did farmers need to develop a system to control their water supply?
   b. Explain In what ways did a **division of labor** contribute to the growth of Mesopotamian civilization?
   c. Elaborate How might running large projects prepare people for running a government?

Critical Thinking

3. **Sequencing** Create a flowchart like this one. Use it to explain how farmers used the Tigris and Euphrates to irrigate fields.

| Water levels in rivers get too low. | → | | → | | → | Mesopotamians enjoy many foods. |

 FOCUS ON WRITING

4. **Understanding Geography** Make a list of the words you might use to help young students imagine the land and rivers. Then start to sketch out a picture or map you could use on your poster.

History and Geography

River Valley Civilizations

All of the world's earliest civilizations had something in common—they all arose in river valleys that were perfect locations for farming. Three key factors made river valleys good for farming. First, the fields that bordered the rivers were flat, which made it easier for farmers to plant crops. Second, the soils were nourished by flood deposits and silt, which made them very fertile. Finally, the river provided the water farmers needed for irrigation.

Natural Highways River travel allowed early civilizations to trade goods and ideas. These people are traveling on the Euphrates River, one of the two main rivers of ancient Mesopotamia.

Caspian Sea

Mediterranean Sea

MESOPOTAMIA

Tigris River

Euphrates River

AFRICA

Memphis

EGYPT

Ur

Red Sea

Nile River

ARABIAN
PENINSULA

From Village to City With the development of agriculture, people settled into farming villages. Over time, some of these villages grew into large cities. These ancient ruins are near Memphis, Egypt.

ASIA

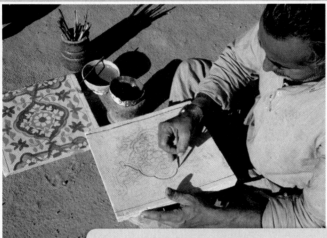

Gift of the River River water was key to farming in early civilizations. This farmer is using water from the Huang He (Yellow River) in China to water her crops.

New Activities Food surpluses allowed people to pursue other activities, like crafts, art, and writing. This tile designer lives in the Indus Valley.

Huang He (Yellow River)

CHINA

Harappa

H I M A L A Y A S

Indus River

Chang Jiang (Yangzi River)

Mohenjo Daro

INDUS VALLEY

Ganges River

INDIA

Arabian Sea

Bay of Bengal

N
W   E
S

| 0 | 500 | 1,000 Miles |
| 0 | 500 | 1,000 Kilometers |

GEOGRAPHY SKILLS   **INTERPRETING MAPS**

1. **Human-Environment Interaction** Why did the first civilizations all develop in river valleys?
2. **Location** Where were the four earliest river valley civilizations located?

INDIAN OCEAN

MESOPOTAMIA AND THE FERTILE CRESCENT   **61**

The Rise of Sumer

If YOU were there...

You are a crafter living in one of the cities of Sumer. Thick walls surround and protect your city, so you feel safe from the armies of other city-states. But you and your neighbors are fearful of other beings—the many gods and spirits that you believe are everywhere. They can bring illness or sandstorms or bad luck.

How might you protect yourself from gods and spirits?

BUILDING BACKGROUND As civilizations developed along rivers, their societies and governments became more advanced. Religion became a main characteristic of these ancient cultures. Kings claimed to rule with the approval of the gods, and ordinary people wore charms and performed rituals to avoid bad luck.

An Advanced Society

In southern Mesopotamia, a people known as the Sumerians (soo-MER-ee-unz) developed the world's first civilization. No one knows where they came from or when they moved into the region. However, by 3000 BC, several hundred thousand Sumerians had settled in Mesopotamia, in a land they called Sumer (SOO-muhr). There they created an advanced society.

The City-States of Sumer

Most people in Sumer were farmers. They lived mainly in **rural**, or countryside, areas. The centers of Sumerian society, however, were the **urban**, or city, areas. The first cities in Sumer had about 10,000 residents. Over time, the cities grew. Historians think that by 2000 BC, some of Sumer's cities had more than 100,000 residents.

As a result, the basic political unit of Sumer combined the two parts. This unit was called a city-state. A **city-state** consisted of a city and all the countryside around it. The amount of countryside controlled by each city-state depended on its military strength. Stronger city-states controlled larger areas.

Sargon's Empire, c. 2330 BC

Legend:
- Empire of Sargon
- Sumer
- Ancient coastline of Persian Gulf

0   100   200 Miles
0   100   200 Kilometers

ASIA MINOR

Tarsus
Harran
Halab
Nineveh
Cyprus
Euphrates R.
Ashur
Tigris R.
Mediterranean Sea
Byblos
Mari
Akkad
Syrian Desert
Kish
Babylon
Susa
Uruk
Lagash
Sinai Peninsula
Ur
Persian Gulf
Red Sea

GEOGRAPHY SKILLS | INTERPRETING MAPS

Location How far west did Sargon's empire stretch?

City-states in Sumer fought each other to gain more farmland. As a result of these conflicts, the city-states built up strong armies. Sumerians also built strong, thick walls around their cities for protection.

Individual city-states gained and lost power over time. By 3500 BC, a city-state known as Kish had become quite powerful. Over the next 1,000 years, the city-states of Uruk and Ur fought for dominance. One of Uruk's kings, known as **Gilgamesh**, became a legendary figure in Sumerian literature.

Rise of the Akkadian Empire

In time, another society developed along the Tigris and Euphrates. It was created by the Akkadians (uh-KAY-dee-uhns). They lived just north of Sumer, but they were not Sumerians. They even spoke a different language than the Sumerians. In spite of their differences, however, the Akkadians and the Sumerians lived in peace for many years.

That peace was broken in the 2300s BC when **Sargon** sought to extend Akkadian territory. He built a new capital, Akkad (A-kad), on the Euphrates River, near what is now the city of Baghdad. Sargon was the first ruler to have a permanent army. He used that army to launch a series of wars against neighboring kingdoms.

Sargon's soldiers defeated all the city-states of Sumer. They also conquered northern Mesopotamia, finally bringing the entire region under his rule. With these conquests, Sargon established the world's first **empire**, or land with different territories and peoples under a single rule. The Akkadian Empire stretched from the Persian Gulf to the Mediterranean Sea.

ACADEMIC VOCABULARY
role a part or function

Sargon was emperor, or ruler of his empire, for more than 50 years. However, the empire lasted only a century after his death. Later rulers could not keep the empire safe from invaders. Hostile tribes from the east raided and captured Akkad. A century of chaos followed.

Eventually, however, the Sumerian city-state of Ur rebuilt its strength and conquered the rest of Mesopotamia. Political stability was restored. The Sumerians once again became the most powerful civilization in the region.

READING CHECK Summarizing How did Sargon build an empire?

Religion Shapes Society

Religion was very important in Sumerian society. In fact, it played a **role** in nearly every aspect of public and private life. In many ways, religion was the basis for all of Sumerian society.

Sumerian Religion

The Sumerians practiced **polytheism**, the worship of many gods. Among the gods they worshipped were Enlil, the lord of the air; Enki, god of wisdom; and Inanna, goddess of love and war. The sun and moon were represented by the gods Utu and Nanna. Each city-state considered one god to be its special protector.

Most of the city was filled with a maze of houses and shops.

History Close-up

The City-State of Ur

Ur was one of the earliest and largest cities of ancient Mesopotamia. This great trading center and port was home to roughly 30,000 people. Located on the Euphrates River near the Persian Gulf, Ur carried on a rich trade with merchants from distant lands like India. This illustration shows what Ur may have looked like around 2000 BC.

Massive walls protected Ur from attack.

The Sumerians believed that their gods had enormous powers. Gods could bring a good harvest or a disastrous flood. They could bring illness, or they could bring good health and wealth. The Sumerians believed that success in every area of life depended on pleasing the gods. Every Sumerian had a duty to serve and to worship the gods.

Priests, people who performed religious ceremonies, had great status in Sumer. People relied on them to help gain the gods' favor. Priests interpreted the wishes of the gods and made offerings to them. These offerings were made in temples, special buildings where priests performed their religious ceremonies.

Sumerian Social Order

Because of their status, priests occupied a high level in Sumer's **social hierarchy**, the division of society by rank or class. In fact, priests were just below kings. The kings of Sumer claimed that they had been chosen by the gods to rule.

Below the priests were Sumer's skilled craftspeople, merchants, and traders. Trade had a great <u>impact</u> on Sumerian society. Traders traveled to faraway places and exchanged grain for gold, silver, copper, lumber, and precious stones.

Below traders, farmers and laborers made up the large working class. Slaves were at the bottom of the social order.

ACADEMIC VOCABULARY

impact effect, result

A giant temple dedicated to the moon god Nanna and his wife Ningal dominated the city.

Farmers grew crops like wheat and barley outside the city's walls.

Canals connected Ur to the nearby Euphrates River.

Inside the city's walls was another canal and a large harbor, where foreigners docked their boats while they traded with Ur's merchants.

ANALYSIS SKILL ANALYZING VISUALS

What can you see in this illustration that shows Ur was an advanced city?

Sumerian society was divided into different groups. This ancient artifact shows Sumerian leaders celebrating a military victory while a musician plays his instrument.

Men and Women in Sumer

Sumerian men and women had different roles. In general, men held political power and made laws, while women took care of the home and children. Education was usually reserved for men, but some upper-class women were educated as well.

Some educated women were priestesses in Sumer's temples. Some priestesses helped shape Sumerian culture. One, Enheduanna, the daughter of Sargon, wrote hymns to the goddess Inanna. She is the first known female writer in history.

READING CHECK Analyzing How did trade affect Sumerian society?

SUMMARY AND PREVIEW In this section you learned about Sumerian city-states, religion, and society. In Section 3, you will read about the Sumerians' achievements.

go.hrw.com
Online Quiz
KEYWORD: SQ6 HP3

Section 2 Assessment

Reviewing Ideas, Terms, and People HSS 6.2.3

1. **a. Recall** What was the basic political unit of Sumer?
   b. Explain What steps did **city-states** take to protect themselves from their rivals?
   c. Elaborate How do you think Sargon's creation of an **empire** changed the history of Mesopotamia? Defend your answer.
2. **a. Identify** What is **polytheism**?
   b. Draw Conclusions Why do you think **priests** were so influential in ancient Sumerian society?
   c. Elaborate Why would rulers benefit if they claimed to be chosen by the gods?

Critical Thinking

3. **Sequencing** Draw a diagram like the one shown. Then place the following events in the order that they occurred: Akkadian Empire forms. Sumerian city-states develop. City of Akkad is built. Farming villages appear.

FOCUS ON WRITING

4. **Gathering Information about Sumer** What aspects of Sumerian society will you include on your poster? What important people, religious beliefs, or social developments do you think the students should learn?

Sumerian Achievements

If **YOU** were there...

You are a student at a school for scribes in Sumer. Learning all the symbols for writing is very hard. Your teacher assigns you lessons to write on your clay tablet, but you can't help making mistakes. Then you have to smooth out the surface and try again. Still, being a scribe can lead to important jobs for the king. You could make your family proud.

Why would you want to be a scribe?

BUILDING BACKGROUND Sumerian society was advanced in terms of religion and government organization. The Sumerians were responsible for many other achievements, which were passed down to later civilizations.

The Invention of Writing

The Sumerians made one of the greatest cultural advances in history. They developed **cuneiform** (kyoo-NEE-uh-fohrm), the world's first system of writing. But Sumerians did not have pencils, pens, or paper. Instead, they used sharp tools called styluses to make wedge-shaped symbols on clay tablets.

Sumerians wrote on clay tablets with a special tool called a stylus.

What You Will Learn...

Main Ideas

1. The Sumerians invented the world's first writing system.
2. Advances and inventions changed Sumerian lives.
3. Many types of art developed in Sumer.

The Big Idea

The Sumerians made many advances that helped their society develop.

Key Terms and People

cuneiform, *p. 67*
pictographs, *p. 68*
scribe, *p. 68*
epics, *p. 68*
architecture, *p. 70*
ziggurat, *p. 70*

HSS **6.2.9** Trace the evolution of language in its written forms.

Development of Writing				
	3300 BC	2800 BC	2400 BC	1800 BC
Heaven				
Grain				
Fish				
Bird				
Water				

Sumerian writing developed from early symbols called pictographs. Writers used clay tablets to record business deals, like this tablet that describes a number of sheep and goats.

Earlier written communication had used **pictographs**, or picture symbols. Each pictograph represented an object, such as a tree or an animal. But in cuneiform, symbols could also represent syllables, or basic parts of words. As a result, Sumerian writers could combine symbols to express more complex ideas such as "joy" or "powerful."

Sumerians first used cuneiform to keep business records. A **scribe**, or writer, would be hired to keep track of the items people traded. Government officials and temples also hired scribes to keep their records. Becoming a scribe was a way to move up in social class.

Sumerian students went to school to learn to read and write. But, like today, some students did not want to study. A Sumerian story tells of a father who urged his son to do his schoolwork:

"Go to school, stand before your 'school-father,' recite your assignment, open your schoolbag, write your tablet . . . After you have finished your assignment and reported to your monitor [teacher], come to me, and do not wander about in the street."

–Sumerian essay quoted in *History Begins at Sumer*, by Samuel Noah Kramer

In time, Sumerians put their writing skills to new uses. They wrote works on history, law, grammar, and math. They also created works of literature. Sumerians wrote stories, proverbs, and songs. They wrote poems about the gods and about military victories. Some of these were **epics**, long poems that tell the stories of heroes. Later, people used some of these poems to create *The Epic of Gilgamesh*, the story of a legendary Sumerian king.

READING CHECK **Generalizing** How was cuneiform first used in Sumer?

Advances and Inventions

Writing was not the only great Sumerian invention. These early people made many other advances and discoveries.

Technical Advances

One of the Sumerians' most important developments was the wheel. They were the first people to build wheeled vehicles, including carts and wagons. Using the wheel, Sumerians invented a device that spins clay as a craftsperson shapes it into bowls. This device is called a potter's wheel.

The plow was another important Sumerian invention. Pulled by oxen, plows broke through the hard clay soil of Sumer to prepare it for planting. This technique greatly increased farm production. The Sumerians also invented a clock that used falling water to measure time.

Sumerian advances improved daily life in many ways. Sumerians built sewers under city streets. They learned to use bronze to make stronger tools and weapons. They even produced makeup and glass jewelry.

Math and Sciences

Another area in which Sumerians excelled was math. In fact, they developed a math system based on the number 60. Based on this system, they divided a circle into 360 degrees. Dividing a year into 12 months—a factor of 60—was another Sumerian idea. Sumerians also calculated the areas of rectangles and triangles.

Sumerian scholars studied science, too. They wrote long lists to record their study of the natural world. These tablets included the names of thousands of animals, plants, and minerals.

The Sumerians also made advances in medicine. They used ingredients from animals, plants, and minerals to produce healing drugs. Items used in these medicines included milk, turtle shells, figs, and salt. The Sumerians even catalogued their medical knowledge, listing treatments according to symptoms and body parts.

READING CHECK **Categorizing** What areas of life were improved by Sumerian inventions?

THE IMPACT TODAY

Like the Sumerians we use a base-60 system when we talk about 60 seconds in a minute and 60 minutes in an hour.

LINKING TO TODAY

The Wheel

Do you realize how much the achievements of ancient Sumer affect your life today—and every day? For instance, try to imagine life without the wheel. How would you get around? Look at the streets outside. The cars, trucks, and buses you see are all modern versions of Sumerian wheeled vehicles. Wheelchairs, bicycles, and in-line skates all depend on wheels as well. Even modern air travel owes a large debt to the Sumerians. As impressive as jets are, they could never get off the ground without their wheels!

ANALYSIS SKILL **ANALYZING INFORMATION**

Generalizing Why is the wheel so important to modern society?

The Sumerians' artistic achievements included beautiful works of gold, wood, and stone.

This stringed musical instrument is called a lyre. It features a cow's head and is made of silver decorated with shell and stone.

Cylinder seals like this one were carved into round stones and then rolled over clay to leave their mark.

The Arts of Sumer

The Sumerians' skills in the fields of art, metalwork, and **architecture**—the science of building—are well known to us. The ruins of great buildings and fine works of art have provided us wonderful examples of the Sumerians' creativity.

Architecture

Most Sumerian rulers lived in large palaces. Other rich Sumerians had two-story homes with as many as a dozen rooms. Most people, however, lived in smaller, one-story houses. These homes had six or seven rooms arranged around a small courtyard. Large and small houses stood side by side along the narrow, unpaved streets of the city. Bricks made of mud were the houses' main building blocks.

City centers were dominated by their temples, the largest and most impressive buildings in Sumer. A **ziggurat**, a pyramid-shaped temple tower, rose above each city. Outdoor staircases led to a platform and a shrine at the top. Some architects added columns to make the temples more attractive.

The Arts

Sumerian sculptors produced many fine works. Among them are the statues of gods created for temples. Sumerian artists also sculpted small objects out of ivory and rare woods. Sumerian pottery is known more for its quantity than quality. Potters turned out many items, but few were works of beauty.

Jewelry was a popular item in Sumer. The jewelers of the region made many beautiful works out of imported gold, silver, and gems. Earrings and other items found in the region show that Sumerian jewelers knew advanced methods for putting gold pieces together.

Cylinder seals are perhaps Sumer's most famous works of art. These small objects were stone cylinders engraved with designs. When rolled over clay, the designs would leave behind their imprint. Each seal left its own distinct imprint. As a result, a person could show ownership of a container by rolling a cylinder over the container's wet clay surface. People could also use cylinder seals to "sign" documents or to decorate other clay objects.

The Sumerians were the first people in Mesopotamia to build large temples called ziggurats.

This gold dagger was found in a royal tomb. The bull's head is made of gold and silver.

ANALYSIS SKILL **ANALYZING VISUALS**

What animal is shown in two of these works?

Some seals showed battle scenes. Others displayed worship rituals. Some were highly decorative, with hundreds of carefully cut gems. They required great skill to make.

The Sumerians also enjoyed music. Kings and temples hired musicians to play on special occasions. Sumerian musicians played reed pipes, drums, tambourines, and stringed instruments called lyres. Children learned songs in school. People sang hymns to gods and kings. Music and dance provided entertainment in marketplaces and homes.

READING CHECK **Drawing Inferences** What might historians learn from cylinder seals?

SUMMARY AND PREVIEW The Sumerians greatly enriched their society. Next you will learn about the later peoples who lived in Mesopotamia.

---

go.hrw.com
Online Quiz
KEYWORD: SQ6 HP3

Section 3 Assessment

Reviewing Ideas, Terms, and People **HSS** 6.2.9

1. **a. Identify** What is **cuneiform**?
   b. Analyze Why do you think writing is one of history's most important cultural advances?
   c. Elaborate What current leader would you choose to write an **epic** about, and why?
2. **a. Recall** What were two early uses of the wheel?
   b. Explain Why do you think the invention of the plow was so important to the Sumerians?
3. **a. Describe** What was the basic Sumerian building material?
   b. Make Inferences Why do you think cylinder seals developed into works of art?

Critical Thinking

4. **Identifying Cause and Effect** Draw a diagram like the one at right. List the effect of each invention on Sumerian life.

	Effect
Writing	
Wheel	
Plow	

FOCUS ON WRITING

5. **Evaluating Information** Review the Sumerian achievements you just read about. Then create a bulleted list of Sumerian achievements for your poster. Would this list replace some of the information you collected in Section 2?

MESOPOTAMIA AND THE FERTILE CRESCENT **71**

from The Epic of Gilgamesh

translated by N. K. Sandars

GUIDED READING

WORD HELP

menacing threatening

succor help

tempest storm

felled cut down

❶ Shamash, the sun-god, supports Gilgamesh.

What human emotion seems to seize Gilgamesh here? How can you tell?

❷ *What stops Humbaba in his tracks?*

❸ Gilgamesh tries to speak and act bravely, but he is terrified by Humbaba's evil glare.

ELA Reading 6.3.2 Analyze the effect of the qualities of the character (e.g., courage or cowardice, ambition or laziness) on the plot and the resolution of the conflict.

About the Reading The Epic of Gilgamesh *is the world's oldest epic, first recorded—carved on stone tablets—in about 2000 BC. The actual Gilgamesh, ruler of the city of Uruk, had lived about 700 years earlier. Over time, stories about this legendary king had grown and changed. In this story, Gilgamesh and his friend Enkidu seek to slay the monster Humbaba, keeper of a distant forest. In addition to his tremendous size and terrible appearance, Humbaba possesses seven splendors, or powers, one of which is fire. Gilgamesh hopes to claim these powers for himself.*

AS YOU READ Notice both the human qualities and the godly qualities of Gilgamesh.

Humbaba came from his strong house of cedar. He nodded his head and shook it, menacing Gilgamesh; and on him he fastened his eye, the eye of death. Then Gilgamesh called to Shamash and his tears were flowing, "O glorious Shamash, I have followed the road you commanded but now if you send no succor how shall I escape?" ❶ Glorious Shamash heard his prayer and he summoned the great wind, the north wind, the whirlwind, the storm and the icy wind, the tempest and the scorching wind; they came like dragons, like a scorching fire, like a serpent that freezes the heart, a destroying flood and the lightning's fork. The eight winds rose up against Humbaba, they beat against his eyes; he was gripped, unable to go forward or back. ❷ Gilgamesh shouted, "By the life of Ninsun my mother and divine Lugulbanda my father . . . my weak arms and my small weapons I have brought to this Land against you, and now I will enter your house." ❸

So he felled the first cedar and they cut the branches and laid them at the foot of the mountain. At the first stroke Humbaba blazed out, but still they advanced. They felled seven cedars and cut and bound the branches and laid them at the foot of the mountain, and seven times Humbaba loosed his glory on them. As the seventh blaze died out they reached his lair. He slapped his thigh in scorn. He approached like a noble wild bull roped on the mountain, a warrior whose elbows were bound together. The tears started to his eyes and he was pale, "Gilgamesh, let me speak. I have never known a mother, no, nor a father who reared me. I was born of the mountain, he reared me, and Enlil made me the keeper of this forest. Let me go free, Gilgamesh, and I will be your servant, you shall be my lord; all the trees of the forest that I tended on the mountain shall be yours. I will cut them down and build you a palace." ... ❹

Enkidu said, "Do not listen, Gilgamesh: this Humbaba must die. Kill Humbaba first and his servants after." But Gilgamesh said, "If we touch him the blaze and the glory of light will be put out in confusion, the glory and glamour will vanish, its rays will be quenched." Enkidu said to Gilgamesh, "Not so, my friend. First entrap the bird, and where shall the chicks run then? Afterwards we can search out the glory and the glamour, when the chicks run distracted through the grass."

Gilgamesh listened to the word of his companion, he took the ax in his hand, he drew the sword from his belt, and he struck Humbaba with a thrust of the sword to the neck, and Enkidu his comrade struck the second blow. At the third blow Humbaba fell. Then there followed confusion for this was the guardian of the forest whom they had felled to the ground ...

When he saw the head of Humbaba, Enlil raged at them. "Why did you do this thing? From henceforth may the fire be on your faces, may it eat the bread that you eat, may it drink where you drink." Then Enlil took again the blaze and the seven splendors that had been Humbaba's: he gave the first to the river, and he gave to the lion, to the stone of execration, to the mountain ... ❺

O Gilgamesh, king and conqueror of the dreadful blaze; wild bull who plunders the mountain, who crosses the sea, glory to him.

GUIDED READING

execration a cursing
plunders takes by force

❹ *What effect does Humbaba hope his words will have on Gilgamesh?*

❺ The angry air-god Enlil curses the heroes for slaying Humbaba. He takes back the monster's powers and gives them to other creatures and elements of nature.

In your opinion, is Gilgamesh more or less heroic for slaying Humbaba and angering Enlil?

Archaeologists think this statue from the 700s BC represents Gilgamesh.

CONNECTING LITERATURE TO HISTORY

1. **Analyzing** In Sumerian culture, the gods' powers were thought to be enormous. According to this story, what roles do gods play in people's lives?

2. **Making Inferences** Violence was common in Sumerian society. How does the character of Gilgamesh suggest that Sumerian society could be violent?

Later Peoples of the Fertile Crescent

If YOU were there...

You are a noble in ancient Babylon, an advisor to the great king Hammurabi. One of your duties is to collect all the laws of the kingdom. They will be carved on a tall block of black stone and placed in the temple. The king asks your opinion about the punishments for certain crimes. For instance, should common people be punished more harshly than nobles?

How will you advise the king?

BUILDING BACKGROUND Many peoples invaded Mesopotamia. A series of kings conquered the lands between the rivers. Each new culture inherited the earlier achievements of the Sumerians. Some of the later invasions of the region also introduced skills and ideas that still influence civilization today, such as a written law code.

The Babylonians Conquer Mesopotamia

Although Ur rose to glory after the death of Sargon, repeated foreign attacks drained its strength. By 2000 BC, Ur lay in ruins. With Ur's power gone, several waves of invaders battled to gain control of Mesopotamia.

The Rise of Babylon

Babylon was home to one such group. That city was located on the Euphrates River near what is today Baghdad, Iraq. Babylon had once been a Sumerian town. By 1800 BC, however, it was home to a powerful government of its own. In 1792 BC, Hammurabi (ham-uh-RAHB-ee) became Babylon's king. He would become the city's greatest **monarch** (MAH-nark), a ruler of a kingdom or empire.

Hammurabi's Code

Hammurabi was a brilliant war leader. His armies fought many battles to expand his power. Eventually, he brought all of Mesopotamia into his empire, called the Babylonian Empire, after his capital.

Hammurabi's skills were not limited to the battlefield, though. He was also an able ruler who could govern a huge empire. He oversaw many building and irrigation projects and improved Babylon's tax collection system to help pay for them. He also brought much prosperity through increased trade. Hammurabi, however, is most famous for his code of laws.

Hammurabi's Code was a set of 282 laws that dealt with almost every part of daily life. There were laws on everything from trade, loans, and theft to marriage, injury, and murder. It contained some ideas that are still found in laws today. Specific crimes brought specific penalties. However, social class did matter. For instance, injuring a rich man brought a greater penalty than injuring a poor man.

Hammurabi's Code was important not only for how thorough it was, but also because it was written down for all to see. People all over the empire could read exactly what was against the law.

Hammurabi ruled for 42 years. During his reign, Babylon became the most important city in Mesopotamia. However, after his death, Babylonian power declined. The kings that followed faced invasions from people Hammurabi had conquered. Before long, the Babylonian Empire came to an end.

READING CHECK **Analyzing** What was Hammurabi's most important accomplishment?

Primary Source

QUICK FACTS

HISTORIC DOCUMENT
Hammurabi's Code

The Babylonian ruler Hammurabi is credited with putting together the earliest known written collection of laws. The code set down rules for both criminal and civil law, and informed citizens what was expected of them.

196. If a man put out the eye of another man, his eye shall be put out.

197. If he break another man's bone, his bone shall be broken.

198. If he put out the eye of a freed man, or break the bone of a freed man, he shall pay one gold mina.

199. If he put out the eye of a man's slave, or break the bone of a man's slave, he shall pay one-half of its value.

221. If a physican heal the broken bone or diseased soft part of a man, the patient shall pay the physician five shekels in money.

222. If he were a freed man he shall pay three shekels.

223. If he were a slave his owner shall pay the physician two shekels.

–Hammurabi, from the Code of Hammurabi, translated by L. W. King

ANALYSIS SKILL **ANALYZING PRIMARY SOURCES**

How do you think Hammurabi's code of laws affected citizens of that time?

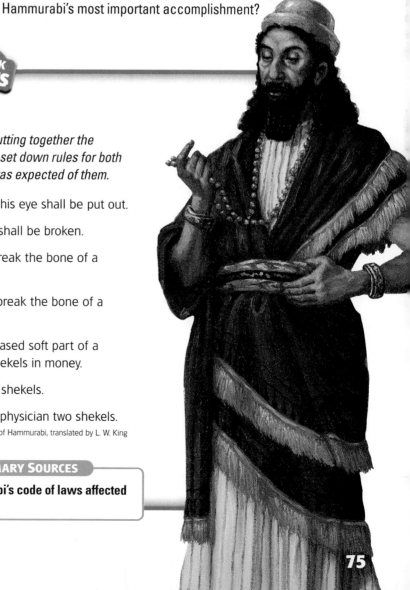

Invasions of Mesopotamia

Several other civilizations also developed in and around the Fertile Crescent. As their armies battled each other for fertile land, control of the region passed from one empire to another.

The Hittites and Kassites

A people known as the Hittites built a strong kingdom in Asia Minor, in what is today Turkey. Their success came, in part, from two key military advantages they had over rivals. First, the Hittites were among the first people to master ironworking. This meant that they could make the strongest weapons of the time. Second, the Hittites skillfully used the **chariot**, a wheeled, horse-drawn cart used in battle. The chariots allowed Hittite soldiers to move quickly around a battlefield and fire arrows at their enemy. Using these advantages, Hittite forces captured Babylon around 1595 BC.

Hittite rule did not last long, however. Soon after taking Babylon, the Hittite king was killed by an assassin. The kingdom plunged into chaos. The Kassites, a people who lived north of Babylon, captured the city and ruled for almost 400 years.

The Assyrians

Later, in the 1200s BC, the Assyrians (uh-SIR-ee-unz) from northern Mesopotamia briefly gained control of Babylon. However, their empire was soon overrun by invaders. After this defeat, the Assyrians took about 300 years to recover their strength. Then, starting about 900 BC, they began to conquer all of the Fertile Crescent. They even took over parts of Asia Minor and Egypt.

Babylonian and Assyrian Empires

Black Sea

ASIA MINOR

Cyprus

Mediterranean Sea

Byblos

Jerusalem

Memphis

EGYPT

Sinai Peninsula

Nile R.

Red Sea

Harran

Euphrates R.

Tigris R.

Ashur

Nineveh

Mari

Damascus

Babylon Kish

Nippur   Susa

Uruk   Lagash

Ur

Syrian Desert

Persian Gulf

Babylonian Empire, c. 1750 BC

Assyrian Empire, c. 650 BC

Ancient coastline of Persian Gulf

0   100   200 Miles

0   100   200 Kilometers

GEOGRAPHY SKILLS INTERPRETING MAPS

Place What region in the southwest did the Assyrian Empire include?

The key to the Assyrians' success was their strong army. Like the Hittites, the Assyrians used iron weapons and chariots. The army was very well organized, and every soldier knew his role.

The Assyrians were fierce in battle. Before attacking, they spread terror by looting villages and burning crops. Anyone who still dared to resist them was killed.

After conquering Mesopotamia, the Assyrians ruled from Nineveh (NI-nuh-vuh). They demanded heavy taxes from across the empire. Areas that resisted these demands were harshly punished.

Assyrian kings ruled their large empire through local leaders. Each governed a small area, collected taxes, enforced laws, and raised troops for the army. Roads were built to link distant parts of the empire. Messengers on horseback were sent to deliver orders to faraway officials.

The Chaldeans

In 652 BC a series of wars broke out in the Assyrian Empire over who should rule. These wars greatly weakened the empire.

Sensing this weakness, the Chaldeans (kal-DEE-uhnz), a group from the Syrian Desert, led other peoples in an attack on the Assyrians. In 612 BC, they destroyed Nineveh and the Assyrian Empire.

In its place, the Chaldeans set up a new empire of their own. **Nebuchadnezzar** (neb-uh-kuhd-NEZ-uhr), the most famous Chaldean king, rebuilt Babylon into a beautiful city. According to legend, his grand palace featured the famous Hanging Gardens. Trees and flowers grew on its terraces and roofs. From the ground the gardens seemed to hang in the air.

The Chaldeans admired Sumerian culture. They studied the Sumerian language and built temples to Sumerian gods.

At the same time, Babylon became a center for astronomy. Chaldeans charted the positions of the stars and kept track of economic, political, and weather events. They also created a calendar and solved complex problems of geometry.

READING CHECK **Sequencing** List in order the peoples who ruled Mesopotamia.

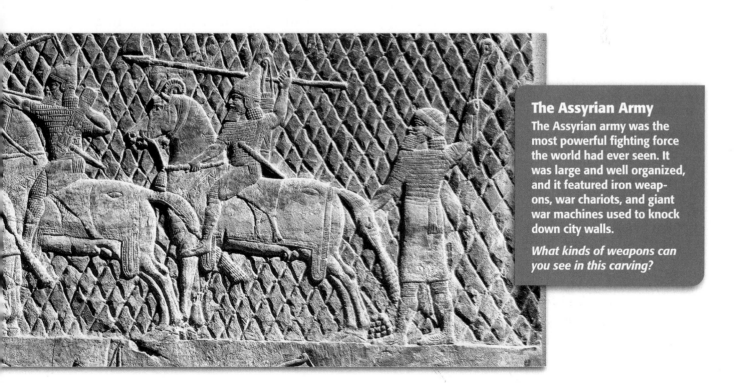

The Assyrian Army
The Assyrian army was the most powerful fighting force the world had ever seen. It was large and well organized, and it featured iron weapons, war chariots, and giant war machines used to knock down city walls.

What kinds of weapons can you see in this carving?

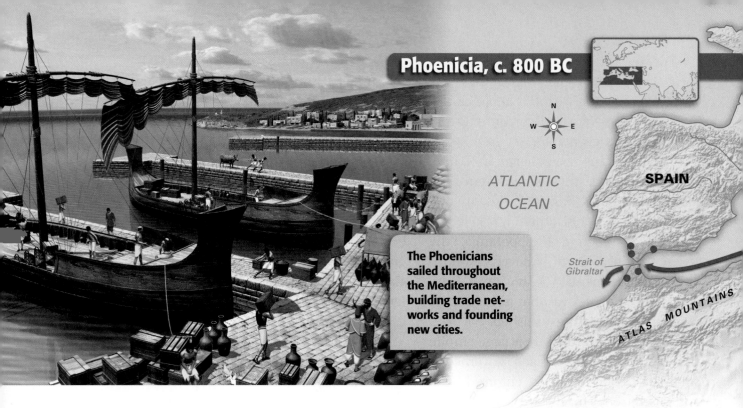

ATLANTIC OCEAN

SPAIN

The Phoenicians sailed throughout the Mediterranean, building trade networks and founding new cities.

Strait of Gibraltar

ATLAS MOUNTAINS

The Phoenicians

At the western end of the Fertile Crescent, along the Mediterranean Sea, was a land known as Phoenicia (fi-NI-shuh). It was not home to a great military power and was often ruled by foreign governments. Nevertheless, the Phoenicians created a wealthy trading society.

The Geography of Phoenicia

Today the nation of Lebanon occupies most of what was once Phoenicia. Mountains border the region to the north and east. The western border is the Mediterranean.

Phoenicia had few resources. One thing it did have, however, was cedar. Cedar trees were prized for their timber, a valuable trade item. But Phoenicia's overland trade routes were blocked by mountains and hostile neighbors. Phoenicians had to look to the sea for a way to trade.

The Expansion of Trade

Motivated by a desire for trade, the people of Phoenicia became expert sailors. They built one of the world's finest harbors at the city of Tyre. Fleets of fast Phoenician trading ships sailed to ports all around the Mediterranean Sea. Traders traveled to Egypt, Greece, Italy, Sicily, and Spain. They even passed through the Strait of Gibraltar to reach the Atlantic Ocean.

The Phoenicians founded several new colonies along their trade routes. Carthage (KAHR-thij), located on the northern coast of Africa, was the most famous of these. It later became one of the most powerful cities on the Mediterranean.

Phoenicia grew wealthy from its trade. Besides lumber, the Phoenicians traded silverwork, ivory carvings, and slaves. Beautiful glass objects also became valuable trade items after crafters invented glassblowing—the art of heating and shaping glass. In addition, the Phoenicians made purple dye from a type of shellfish. They then traded cloth dyed with this purple color. Phoenician purple fabric was very popular with rich people.

The Phoenicians' most important achievement, however, wasn't a trade good. To record their activities, Phoenician

THE IMPACT TODAY

Because so many cedar trees have been cut down in Lebanon's forests over the years, very few trees remain.

| Phoenicia |
| ● Phoenician colony |
| Area of Phoenician settlement |
| → Trade route |

0   150   300 Miles
0   150   300 Kilometers

ITALY

Corsica
Sardinia

Danube River

Black Sea

GREECE

Athens

LYDIA

TAURUS MOUNTAINS

Carthage

Sicily

Mediterranean Sea

Crete

Cyprus

PHOENICIA

Byblos

Tyre • Sidon

Tigris River

Euphrates River

Tripolis

Jerusalem

A F R I C A

Memphis

EGYPT

Nile River

GEOGRAPHY SKILLS **INTERPRETING MAPS**

Location Where was Phoenicia located?

traders developed one of the world's first alphabets. An **alphabet** is a set of letters that can be combined to form words. This development made writing much easier. It had a major impact on the ancient world and on our own. In fact, the alphabet we use for the English language is based on the Phoenicians', as modified by later civilizations. Later civilizations, including our own, benefited from the innovations passed along by Phoenician traders.

READING CHECK **Finding Main Ideas** What were the main achievements of the Phoenicians?

SUMMARY AND PREVIEW Many different peoples ruled in the Fertile Crescent after the Sumerians. Some made important contributions that are still valued today. In the next chapter you will learn about another people that created a remarkable civilization—the Egyptians.

Section 4 Assessment

go.hrw.com
Online Quiz
KEYWORD: SQ6 HP3

Reviewing Ideas, Terms, and People   **HSS** 6.2.4

1. **a. Identify** Where was Babylon located?
   b. Analyze What does **Hammurabi's Code** reveal about Babylonian society?
2. **a. Describe** What two advantages did Hittite soldiers have over their opponents?
   b. Rank Which empire discussed in this section do you feel contributed the most to modern-day society? Why?
3. **a. Identify** For what trade goods were the Phoenicians known? For what else were they known?
   b. Analyze How did Phoenicia grow wealthy?

Critical Thinking

4. **Categorizing** Draw a diagram like the one at right. In each circle, list one of the empires of the Fertile Crescent, as well as the empire's most famous leader or major city.

Fertile Crescent Empires

FOCUS ON WRITING

5. **Gathering Information about Later Peoples** Several different peoples contributed to civilization in the Fertile Crescent after the Sumerians. Which ones, if any, will you mention on your poster? What will you say?

Social Studies Skills

 HSS Analysis CS 3 Use maps to identify physical features.

Interpreting Physical Maps

Understand the Skill

A *physical map* is a map that shows the natural features and landscape, or *topography*, of an area. It shows the location and size of such features as rivers and mountain ranges. Physical maps also often show an area's *elevation*, or how high above sea level the land is. Topography and elevation often influence human activities. For example, people will live where they can find water and defend themselves. Therefore, being able to interpret a physical map can help you better understand how the history of an area unfolded.

Learn the Skill

Follow these steps to interpret a physical map.

❶ Read the map's title, distance scale, and legend. These will provide basic information about the map's contents.

❷ Note the colors used to show elevation. Use the legend to connect colors on the map to elevations of specific places.

❸ Note the shapes of the features, such as how high a mountain range is, how far it stretches, and how long a river is. Note where each feature is in relation to others.

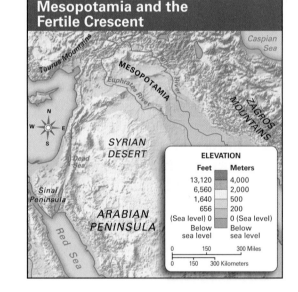

❹ Use information from the map to draw conclusions about the effect of the region's topography on settlement and economic activities.

Practice and Apply the Skill

Use the guidelines to answer these questions about the map above.

1. What is the elevation of the western half of the Arabian Peninsula?

2. Describe the topography of Mesopotamia. Why would settlement have occurred here before other places on the map?

3. What feature might have stopped invasions of Mesopotamia?

Standards Review

Visual Summary

Use the visual summary below to help you review the main ideas of the chapter.

QUICK FACTS

The early Mesopotamians developed irrigation to grow food.

Food production in Mesopotamia led to the world's first civilization.

Sumerian advances included ziggurats, the wheel, and the first writing system.

Later peoples developed the first written laws and the first empires.

Reviewing Vocabulary, Terms, and People

Using your own paper, complete the sentences below by providing the correct term for each blank.

1. Mesopotamian farmers built _____ to irrigate their fields.

2. While city dwellers were urban, farmers lived in _____ areas.

3. The people of Sumer practiced _____, the worship of many gods.

4. Instead of using pictographs, Sumerians developed a type of writing called _____.

5. Horse-drawn _____ gave the Hittites an advantage during battle.

6. The Babylonian king _____ is famous for his code of laws.

7. Another word for effect is _____.

8. Sumerian society was organized in _____, which consisted of a city and the surrounding lands.

Comprehension and Critical Thinking

SECTION 1 *(Pages 56–59)* HSS 6.2.1, 6.2.2

9. **a. Describe** Where was Mesopotamia, and what does the name mean?

   b. Analyze How did Mesopotamian irrigation systems allow civilization to develop?

   c. Elaborate Do you think a division of labor is necessary for civilization to develop? Why or why not?

SECTION 2 *(Pages 62–66)* HSS 6.2.3

10. **a. Identify** Who built the world's first empire, and what did that empire include?

    b. Analyze Politically, how was early Sumerian society organized? How did that organization affect society?

    c. Elaborate Why did the Sumerians consider it everyone's responsibility to keep the gods happy?

SECTION 3 *(Pages 67–71)* **HSS** 6.2.9

11. a. Identify What was the Sumerian writing system called, and why is it so significant?

b. Compare and Contrast What were two ways in which Sumerian society was similar to our society today? What were two ways in which it was different?

c. Evaluate Other than writing and the wheel, which Sumerian invention do you think is most important? Why?

SECTION 4 *(Pages 74–79)* **HSS** 6.2.4

12. a. Describe What were two important developments of the Phoenicians?

b. Draw Conclusions Why do you think several peoples banded together to fight the Assyrians?

c. Evaluate Do you think Hammurabi was more effective as a ruler or as a military leader? Why?

Reviewing Themes

13. Science and Technology Which of the ancient Sumerians' technological achievements do you think has been most influential in history? Why?

14. Politics Why do you think Hammurabi is so honored for his code of laws?

Reading Skills

Identifying Main Ideas *For each passage, choose the letter that corresponds to the main idea sentence.*

15. (A) Sumerians believed that their gods had enormous powers. (B) Gods could bring a good harvest or a disastrous flood. (C) They could bring illness or they could bring good health and wealth.

16. (A) The wheel was not the Sumerians' only great development. (B) They developed cuneiform, the world's first system of writing. (C) But Sumerians did not have pencils, pens, or paper. (D) Instead, they used sharp reeds to make wedge-shaped symbols on clay tablets.

Using the Internet

go.hrw.com
KEYWORD: SQ6 WH3

17. Activity: Looking at Writing The Sumerians made one of the greatest cultural advances in history by developing cuneiform. This was the world's first system of writing. Enter the activity keyword and research the evolution of language and its written forms. Look at one of the newest methods of writing: text messaging. Then write a paragraph explaining how and why writing was developed and why it was important using text-messaging abbreviations, words, and symbols.

Social Studies Skills

Using Physical Maps *Could you use a physical map to answer the questions below? For each question, answer yes or no.*

18. Are there mountains or hills in a certain region?

19. What languages do people speak in that region?

20. How many people live in the region?

21. What kinds of water features such as rivers or lakes would you find there?

FOCUS ON WRITING

22. Creating Your Poster Use the notes you have taken to create a plan for your poster. Work it out on a piece of paper before transferring it to poster board. Limit yourself to two or three main points. Remember that you will need to print the words on your poster and use large letters. You won't have room for many words.

Create a title for your poster and center it at the top. Write your main points in one color and your sub-points in another color. Plan where you'll place your map or picture of the Fertile Crescent. It should support the written ideas, not interfere with them. As a last touch for your poster, you might want to add a decorative border or an image that suggests the Fertile Crescent.

Standards Assessment

DIRECTIONS: Read each question, and write the letter of the best response.

1 Use the map to answer the following question.

The region known as Mesopotamia is indicated on the map by the letter

A W.

B X.

C Y.

D Z.

2 All of the following ancient civilizations developed in Mesopotamia *except* the

A Akkadians.

B Babylonians.

C Egyptians.

D Sumerians.

3 Which of the following is *not* true of the first writing system?

A It was developed by the Babylonians.

B It began with the use of pictures to represent syllables and objects.

C It was recorded on tablets made of clay.

D It was first used to keep business records.

4 In Sumerian society, people's social class or rank depended on their wealth and their

A appearance.

B religion.

C location.

D occupation.

5 Hammurabi's Code is important in world history because it was an early

A form of writing that could be used to record important events.

B written list of laws that controlled people's daily life and behavior.

C record-keeping system that enabled the Phoenicians to become great traders.

D set of symbols that allowed the Sumerians to communicate with other peoples.

6 What was the most important contribution of the Phoenicians to our civilization?

A purple dye

B their alphabet

C founding of Carthage

D sailing ships

Connecting with Past Learnings

7 In Grade 5 you studied a group of people in American history that placed great importance on religion. Religion was also at the center of Sumerian society. With which American group did the Sumerians share a strong emphasis on religion?

A the Dutch

B the Tories

C the Loyalists

D the Puritans

Ancient Egypt

California Standards

History–Social Science

6.2 Students analyze the geographic, political, economic, religious, and social structures of the early civilizations of Mesopotamia, Egypt, and Kush.

Analysis Skills

HR 4 Assess the credibility of primary and secondary sources.

English–Language Arts

Writing 6.2.2c Follow an organizational pattern appropriate to the type of content.

Reading 6.2.6 Determine the adequacy and appropriateness of the evidence for an author's conclusions.

FOCUS ON WRITING

A Riddle In this chapter you will read about the fascinating civilization of ancient Egypt. In ancient times a sphinx, an imaginary creature like the one whose sculpture is in Egypt, was supposed to have demanded the answer to a riddle. People died if they didn't answer the riddle correctly. After you read this chapter, you will write a riddle. The answer to your riddle will be "Egypt."

CHAPTER EVENTS

c. 4500 BC
Agricultural communities develop in Egypt.

4500 BC

WORLD EVENTS

c. 4500 BC
People in Europe begin using copper tools.

HOLT

History's Impact

▶ **video series**
Watch the video to understand the impact of the Egyptian pyramids.

What You Will Learn...

In this chapter you will learn about the civilization of ancient Egypt and how it developed along the Nile River. This photo shows an ancient temple of Ramses II, one of Egypt's most powerful rulers.

c. 3100 BC
Menes unites Upper and Lower Egypt, establishing the first dynasty.

2500s BC
Egyptians build the Great Pyramid of Khufu at Giza.

c. 1237 BC
Ramses the Great dies.

3500 BC	2750 BC	2000 BC	1250 BC	500 BC

c. 3100 BC
Sumerians create the world's first writing system.

c. 1200 BC
The Olmec form the first urban civilization in the Americas.

c. 1027 BC
The Zhou dynasty begins in China.

Reading Social Studies
by Kylene Beers

Focus on Themes In this chapter you will read about the development of the fascinating civilization of Egypt. You will learn how the Nile River, nearby deserts, and other **geographic** features shaped early Egyptian society. You will learn about the ancient Egyptians' **religious** beliefs and learn how those beliefs shaped everything from their daily lives to the art they created. Of course, you will also read about the pyramids, mummies, and pharaohs that made Egypt famous.

Drawing Conclusions about the Past

Focus on Reading Have you ever read a mystery story in which a detective puts together various clues to solve a puzzling crime? In other words, he combines various bits of information to reach a conclusion.

Drawing Conclusions A **conclusion** is a judgment someone makes by combining information. When you read, you can put together various bits of information from what you are reading to figure out new information that isn't stated exactly in the text.

Additional reading support can be found in the

Inter active

Reader and Study Guide

Burial Practices

The Egyptians developed a method called embalming to preserve bodies and keep them from decaying. The Egyptians preserved bodies as mummies, specially treated bodies wrapped in cloth. Embalming preserves a dead body for many, many years. A body that was not embalmed would decay quickly in a tomb . . .

Only royalty and other members of Egypt's elite, or people of wealth and power, could afford to have mummies made.

→ The Egyptians preserved dead bodies as mummies.

→ Only mummies could survive for thousands of years in tombs.

→ Embalming was expensive and so it was limited to kings and other rich people.

↓

Conclusion: The mummies that historians have found are the bodies of Egyptian kings and rich people

ELA Reading 6.2.6 Determine the adequacy and appropriateness of the evidence for an author's conclusions.

You Try It!

The following passage is from the chapter you are getting ready to read. As you read the passage, look for the facts about pyramids.

The Pyramids

From Chapter 4 p. 98

The Egyptians believed that burial sites, especially royal tombs, were very important. As a result, they built spectacular monuments in which to bury their rulers. The most spectacular of all were the pyramids—huge, stone tombs with four triangle-shaped sides that met in a point on top.

The Egyptians first built pyramids during the Old Kingdom. Some of the largest pyramids ever constructed were built during this time. Many of these huge pyramids are still standing. The largest is the Great Pyramid of Khufu near the town of Giza. It covers more than 13 acres at its base and stands 481 feet high. This single pyramid took thousands of workers and more than 2 million limestone blocks to build.

After you have finished the passage, answer the questions below, drawing conclusions about what you have read.

1. Based on their function, do you think pyramids were hollow or solid inside? Why?

2. Considering why the Egyptians built the pyramids, who do you think Khufu was? What makes you think this?

3. Do you think pyramids were first built early in Egypt's history, or late? Why?

4. Think about pictures of the pyramids you have seen. What do you think the landscape near Giza is like?

> **As you read Chapter 4,** think about what you already know about Egypt and draw conclusions to fill gaps in what you are reading.

Key Terms and People

Academic Vocabulary

Success in school is related to knowing academic vocabulary—the words that are frequently used in school assignments and discussions. In this chapter, you will learn the following academic words:

Geography and Early Egypt

If YOU were there...

Your family farms in the Nile Valley. Each year when the river's floodwaters spread rich soil on the land, you help your father plant barley. When you are not in the fields, you spin fine linen thread from flax you have grown. Sometimes you and your friends hunt birds in the tall grasses along the river banks.

Why do you like living in the Nile Valley?

BUILDING BACKGROUND Like the rivers of Mesopotamia, the narrow valley of the Nile River in Egypt also provided fertile land that drew people to live there. The culture that developed in ancient Egypt was more stable and long-lasting than those in Mesopotamia.

The Gift of the Nile

Geography played a key role in the development of Egyptian civilization. The Nile River brought life to Egypt and allowed it to thrive. The river was so important to people in this region that a Greek historian named Herodotus (hi-RAHD-uh-tuhs) called Egypt the gift of the Nile.

Location and Physical Features

The Nile is the longest river in the world. It begins in central Africa and runs north through Egypt to the Mediterranean Sea, a distance of over 4,000 miles. The civilization of ancient Egypt developed along a 750-mile stretch of the Nile.

Ancient Egypt included two regions, a southern region and a northern region. The southern region was called Upper Egypt. It was so named because it was located upriver in relation to the Nile's flow. Lower Egypt, the northern region, was located downriver. The Nile sliced through the desert of Upper Egypt. There, it created a fertile river valley about 13 miles wide. On either side of the Nile lay hundreds of miles of bleak desert sands.

As you can see on the map, the Nile flowed through rocky, hilly land south of Egypt. At several points, this rough terrain caused **cataracts**, or rapids, to form. The first cataract, located 720 miles south of the Mediterranean Sea, marked the southern border of Upper Egypt. Five more cataracts lay farther south. These cataracts made sailing on that portion of the Nile very difficult.

In Lower Egypt, the Nile divided into several branches that fanned out and flowed into the Mediterranean Sea. These branches formed a **delta**, a triangle-shaped area of land made from soil deposited by a river. In ancient times, swamps and marshes covered much of the Nile Delta. Some two-thirds of Egypt's fertile farmland was located in the Nile Delta.

The Floods of the Nile

Because little rain fell in the region, most of Egypt was desert. Each year, however, rainfall far to the south of Egypt in the highlands of East Africa caused the Nile to flood. The Nile's floods were easier to predict than those of the Tigris and Euphrates rivers in Mesopotamia. Almost every year, the Nile flooded Upper Egypt in mid-summer and Lower Egypt in the fall.

The Nile's flooding coated the land around it with a rich silt. As in Mesopotamia, the silt made the soil ideal for farming. The silt also made the land a dark color. That is why Egyptians called their country the black land. They called the dry, lifeless desert beyond the river valley the red land. Each year, Egyptians eagerly awaited the flooding of the Nile. For them, the river's floods were a life-giving miracle. Without the floods, people never could have farmed in Egypt.

READING CHECK Summarizing Why was Egypt called the gift of the Nile?

Ancient Egypt

GEOGRAPHY SKILLS INTERPRETING MAPS

1. **Place** What bodies of water can you see on the map?
2. **Location** Where are Upper Egypt and Lower Egypt located?

Civilization Develops in Egypt

The Nile provided both water and fertile soil for farming. Over time, scattered farms grew into villages and then cities. Eventually, an Egyptian civilization developed.

Increased Food Production

Hunter-gatherers first moved into the Nile Valley more than 12,000 years ago. They found plants, wild animals, and fish there to eat. In time, these people learned how to farm, and they settled along the Nile. By 4500 BC, farmers living in small villages grew wheat and barley.

As in Mesopotamia, farmers in Egypt developed an irrigation system. Unlike farmers in Mesopotamia, however, Egyptian farmers did not need to build basins for storing water. The Egyptians simply built a series of canals to direct the river's flow and carry water to their fields.

The Nile provided Egyptian farmers with an abundance of food. In addition to watering their crops, the Nile allowed farmers to raise animals. Farmers in Egypt grew wheat, barley, fruits, and vegetables. They also raised cattle and sheep. The river provided many types of fish, and hunters trapped wild geese and ducks along its banks. Like the Mesopotamians, the Egyptians enjoyed a varied diet.

Two Kingdoms

In addition to a stable food supply, Egypt's location offered another advantage. It had natural barriers that made it hard to invade Egypt. The desert to the west was too big and harsh to cross. To the north, the

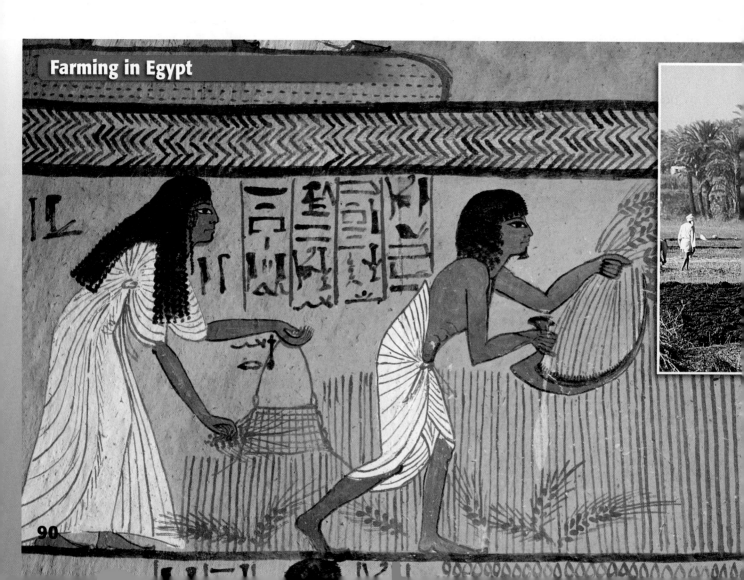

Farming in Egypt

Mediterranean Sea kept many enemies away. More desert lands and the Red Sea to the east provided protection against invasion as well. In addition, cataracts in the Nile made it difficult for invaders to sail in from the south.

Protected from invaders, the villages of Egypt grew. Wealthy farmers emerged as village leaders, and strong leaders gained control over several villages. By 3200 BC, the villages had grown, banded together, and developed into two kingdoms. One kingdom was called Lower Egypt, and the other was called Upper Egypt.

Each kingdom had its own capital city where its ruler was based. The capital of Lower Egypt was located in the northwest Nile Delta at a town called Pe. There, wearing the red crown that symbolized his authority, the king of Lower Egypt ruled.

Farmers in ancient Egypt learned how to grow wheat and barley. This tomb painting shows a couple harvesting their crop (left). Farmers in Egypt still use the fertile lands along the Nile River to grow food (above).

The capital city of Upper Egypt was called Nekhen. It was located on the west bank of the Nile. In this southern kingdom, the king wore a cone-shaped white crown. For centuries, Egyptians referred to their country as the two lands.

READING CHECK **Summarizing** What attracted early settlers to the Nile Valley?

Kings Unify Egypt

According to tradition, around 3100 BC **Menes** (MEE-neez) rose to power in Upper Egypt. Some historians think Menes is a myth and that his accomplishments were really those of other ancient kings named Aha, Scorpion, or Narmer.

Menes wanted to unify Upper and Lower Egypt. His armies invaded and took control of Lower Egypt. He then married a princess from Lower Egypt to strengthen his control over the newly unified country. Menes wore both the white crown of Upper Egypt and the red crown of Lower Egypt to symbolize his leadership over the two kingdoms. Later, he combined the two crowns into a double crown.

Many historians consider Menes to be Egypt's first **pharaoh** (FEHR-oh), the title used by the rulers of Egypt. The title *pharaoh* means "great house." Menes also founded Egypt's first **dynasty**, or series of rulers from the same family.

Menes built a new capital city at the southern tip of the Nile Delta. The city was later named Memphis. For centuries, Memphis was the political and cultural center of Egypt. Many government offices were located there, and the city bustled with artistic activity.

The First Dynasty lasted for about 200 years. Rulers who came after Menes also wore the double crown to symbolize their rule over Upper and Lower Egypt.

FOCUS ON READING
What can you conclude about the evidence we have for Menes's accomplishments?

The pharaoh Menes combined the white crown of Upper Egypt and the red crown of Lower Egypt as a symbol of his rule of Egypt as one kingdom.

They extended Egyptian territory southward along the Nile and into Southwest Asia. Eventually, however, rivals arose to challenge the First Dynasty for power. These challengers took over Egypt and established the Second Dynasty.

READING CHECK **Drawing Inferences** Why do you think Menes wanted to rule over both kingdoms?

SUMMARY AND PREVIEW As you have read, ancient Egypt began in the fertile Nile River Valley. Two kingdoms developed. The two kingdoms were later united under one ruler and Egyptian territory grew. In the next section you will learn how Egypt continued to grow and change under later rulers in a period known as the Old Kingdom.

Section 1 Assessment

go.hrw.com
Online Quiz
KEYWORD: SQ6 HP4

Reviewing Ideas, Terms, and People **HSS** 6.2.1, 6.2.2

1. **a. Identify** Where was Lower Egypt located?
   b. Analyze Why was the Nile Delta well suited for settlement?
   c. Predict How might the Nile's **cataracts** have both helped and hurt Egypt?
2. **a. Describe** What foods did the Egyptians eat?
   b. Analyze What role did the Nile play in supplying Egyptians with the foods they ate?
   c. Elaborate How did the desert on both sides of the Nile help ancient Egypt?
3. **a. Identify** Who was the first **pharaoh** of Egypt?
   b. Draw Conclusions Why did the pharaohs of the First Dynasty wear a double crown?

Critical Thinking

4. **Comparing and Contrasting** Draw a diagram like the one here. Use it to show the differences and similarities between the Nile River in Egypt and the Tigris and Euphrates rivers in Mesopotamia.

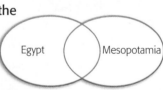

FOCUS ON WRITING

5. **Thinking about Geography and Early History** In this section you read about Egypt's geography and early history. What could you put in your riddle about the geography and historical events that would be a clue to the answer?

The Old Kingdom

If **YOU** were there...

You are a farmer in ancient Egypt. To you, the pharaoh is the god Horus as well as your ruler. You depend on his strength and wisdom. For part of the year, you are busy planting crops in your fields. But at other times of the year, you work for the pharaoh. You are helping to build a great tomb so that your pharaoh will be comfortable in the afterlife.

How do you feel about working for the pharaoh?

BUILDING BACKGROUND As in other ancient cultures, Egyptian society was based on a strict order of social classes. A small group of royalty and nobles ruled Egypt. They depended on the rest of the population to supply food, crafts, and labor. Few people questioned this arrangement of society.

Life in the Old Kingdom

The First and Second Dynasties ruled Egypt for about four centuries. Around 2700 BC, though, a new dynasty rose to power in Egypt. Called the Third Dynasty, its rule began a period in Egyptian history known as the Old Kingdom.

Early Pharaohs

The **Old Kingdom** was a period in Egyptian history that lasted for about 500 years, from about 2700 to 2200 BC. During this time, the Egyptians continued to develop their political system. The system they developed was based on the belief that the pharaoh, the ruler of Egypt, was both a king and a god.

The ancient Egyptians believed that Egypt belonged to the gods. They believed that the pharaoh had come to earth in order to manage Egypt for the rest of the gods. As a result, he had absolute power over all land and people in Egypt.

But the pharaoh's status as both king and god came with many responsibilities. People blamed him if crops did not grow well or if disease struck. They also demanded that the pharaoh make trade profitable and prevent wars.

What You Will Learn...

Main Ideas

1. Life in the Old Kingdom was influenced by pharaohs, roles in society, and trade.
2. Religion shaped Egyptian life.
3. The pyramids were built as huge tombs for Egyptian pharaohs.

The Big Idea

Egyptian government and religion were closely connected during the Old Kingdom.

Key Terms and People

Old Kingdom, *p. 93*
Khufu, *p. 94*
nobles, *p. 94*
afterlife, *p. 96*
mummies, *p. 96*
elite, *p. 97*
pyramids, *p. 98*
engineering, *p. 98*

HSS **6.2.3** Understand the relationship between religion and the social and political order in Mesopotamia and Egypt.

Pharaoh
The pharaoh ruled
Egypt as a god.

Nobles
Officials and priests helped run
the government and temples.

Scribes and Craftspeople
Scribes and craftspeople wrote
and produced goods.

**Farmers, Servants,
and Slaves**
Most Egyptians were farmers,
servants, or slaves.

ANALYSIS SKILL **ANALYZING VISUALS**

Which group helped run the government and temples?

The most famous pharaoh of the Old Kingdom was **Khufu** (KOO-foo), who ruled in the 2500s BC. Even though he is famous, we know relatively little about Khufu's life. Egyptian legend says that he was cruel, but historical records tell us that the people who worked for him were well fed. Khufu is best known for the monuments that were built to him.

Society and Trade

ACADEMIC
VOCABULARY
acquire (uh-KWYR)
to get

By the end of the Old Kingdom, Egypt had about 2 million people. As the population grew, social classes appeared. The Egyptians believed that a well-ordered society would keep their kingdom strong.

At the top of Egyptian society was the pharaoh. Just below him were the upper classes, which included priests and key government officials. Many of these priests and officials were **nobles**, or people from rich and powerful families.

Next in society was the middle class. It included lesser government officials, scribes, and a few rich craftspeople.

The people in Egypt's lower class, more than 80 percent of the population, were mostly farmers. During flood season, when they could not work in the fields, farmers worked on the pharaoh's building projects. Servants and slaves also worked hard.

As society developed during the Old Kingdom, Egypt traded with some of its neighbors. Traders traveled south along the Nile to Nubia to **acquire** gold, copper, ivory, slaves, and stone for building. Trade with Syria provided Egypt with wood for building and for fire.

Egyptian society grew more complex during this time. It continued to be organized, disciplined, and highly religious.

READING CHECK **Generalizing** How was society structured in the Old Kingdom?

Religion and Egyptian Life

Worshipping the gods was a part of daily life in Egypt. But the Egyptian focus on religion extended beyond people's lives. Many customs focused on what happened after people died.

The Gods of Egypt

The Egyptians practiced polytheism. Before the First Dynasty, each village worshipped its own gods. During the Old Kingdom, however, Egyptian officials expected everyone to worship the same gods, though how they worshipped the gods might differ from place to place.

The Egyptians built temples to the gods all over the kingdom. Temples collected payments from both worshippers and the government. These payments allowed the temples to grow more influential.

Over time, certain cities became centers for the worship of certain gods. In the city of Memphis, for example, people prayed to Ptah, the creator of the world.

The Egyptians worshipped many gods besides Ptah. They had gods for nearly everything, including the sun, the sky, and the earth. Many gods mixed human and animal forms. For example, Anubis, the god of the dead, had a human body but a jackal's head. Other major gods included

- Re, or Amon-Re, the sun god
- Osiris, the god of the underworld
- Isis, the goddess of magic
- Horus, a sky god, god of the pharaohs
- Thoth, the god of wisdom
- Geb, the earth god

Egyptian families also worshipped household gods at shrines in their homes.

Egyptian Gods

Re, or Amon-Re, the sun god

Osiris, the god of the underworld

Isis, the goddess of magic

Horus, a sky god and the god of the pharaohs

Mummies and the Afterlife

Osiris, god of the underworld, waited to judge the dead person's soul.

The god Anubis weighed the dead person's heart against the feather of truth. If they weighed the same amount, the person was allowed into the underworld.

Emphasis on the Afterlife

Much of Egyptian religion focused on the **afterlife**, or life after death. The Egyptians believed that the afterlife was a happy place. Paintings from Egyptian tombs show the afterlife as an ideal world where all the people are young and healthy.

The Egyptian belief in the afterlife stemmed from their idea of *ka* (KAH), or a person's life force. When a person died, his or her *ka* left the body and became a spirit. The *ka* remained linked to the body and could not leave its burial site. However, it had all the same needs that the person had when he or she was living. It needed to eat, sleep, and be entertained.

To fulfill the *ka*'s needs, people filled tombs with objects for the afterlife. These objects included furniture, clothing, tools, jewelry, and weapons. Relatives of the dead were expected to bring food and beverages to their loved ones' tombs so the *ka* would not be hungry or thirsty.

ACADEMIC VOCABULARY

method a way of doing something

Burial Practices

Egyptian ideas about the afterlife shaped their burial practices. The Egyptians believed that a body had to be prepared for the afterlife before it could be placed in a tomb. This meant the body had to be preserved. If the body decayed, its spirit could not recognize it. That would break the link between the body and spirit. The *ka* would then be unable to receive the food and drink it needed.

To keep the *ka* from suffering, the Egyptians developed a **method** called embalming to preserve bodies and keep them from decaying. The Egyptians preserved bodies as **mummies**, specially treated bodies wrapped in cloth. Embalming preserves a dead body for many, many years. A body that was not embalmed would decay quickly in a tomb.

Embalming was a complex process that took several weeks to complete. In the first step, embalmers cut open the body

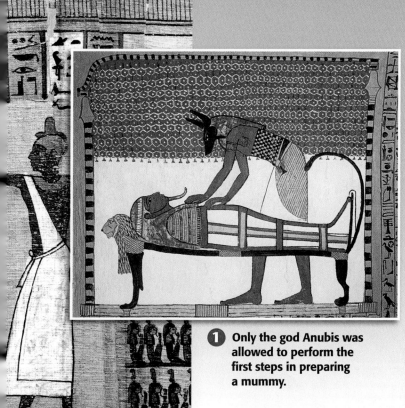

2 The body's organs were preserved in special jars and kept next to the mummy.

1 Only the god Anubis was allowed to perform the first steps in preparing a mummy.

and removed all the organs except for the heart. The removed organs were stored in special jars. Next, embalmers used a special substance to dry out the body and later applied some special oils. The embalmers then wrapped the dried-out body with linen cloths and bandages, often placing special charms inside the cloth wrappings. Wrapping the body was the last step in the mummy-making process. Once it was completely wrapped, a mummy was placed in a coffin.

Only royalty and other members of Egypt's **elite** (AY-leet), or people of wealth and power, could afford to have mummies made. Peasant families did not need the process, however. They buried their dead in shallow graves at the edge of the desert. The hot, dry sand of the desert preserved the bodies naturally.

3 The body was preserved as a mummy and kept in a case called a sarcophagus.

READING CHECK **Analyzing** How did religious beliefs affect Egyptian burial practices?

ANALYSIS SKILL **ANALYZING VISUALS**

How did gods participate in the afterlife?

The Pyramids

The Egyptians believed that burial sites, especially royal tombs, were very important. As a result, they built spectacular monuments in which to bury their rulers. The most spectacular of all were the **pyramids**—huge, stone tombs with four triangle-shaped sides that met in a point on top.

The Egyptians first built pyramids during the Old Kingdom. Some of the largest pyramids ever constructed were built during this time. Many of these huge pyramids are still standing. The largest is the Great Pyramid of Khufu near the town of Giza. It covers more than 13 acres at its base and stands 481 feet high. This single pyramid took thousands of workers and more than 2 million limestone blocks to build. Like all the pyramids, it is an amazing reminder of Egyptian **engineering**, the application of scientific knowledge for practical purposes.

History Close-up

Building the Pyramids

More than 4,000 years ago, workers near Giza, Egypt, built three massive pyramids as tombs for their rulers. The amount of work this job required is hard to imagine. Tens of thousands of people must have worked for decades to build these gigantic structures. In this illustration, men work to build the pharaoh Khafre's pyramid.

Giant ramps made of rubble were piled around the pyramid so workers could reach the top.

A statue called a sphinx was carved out of rock and left to guard Khafre's tomb.

Huge blocks of limestone were cut with copper and stone tools and taken by boat to the building site.

Building the Pyramids

The earliest pyramids did not have the smooth sides we usually imagine when we think of pyramids. The Egyptians began building the smooth-sided pyramids we usually see around 2700 BC. The steps of these pyramids were filled and covered with limestone. The burial chamber was deep inside the pyramid. After the pharaoh's burial, workers sealed the passages to this room with large blocks.

Historians are not sure how the Egyptians built the pyramids. What is certain is that such enormous projects required a huge labor force. As many as 100,000 workers may have been needed to build a single pyramid. The government kept records and paid the peasants for their work.

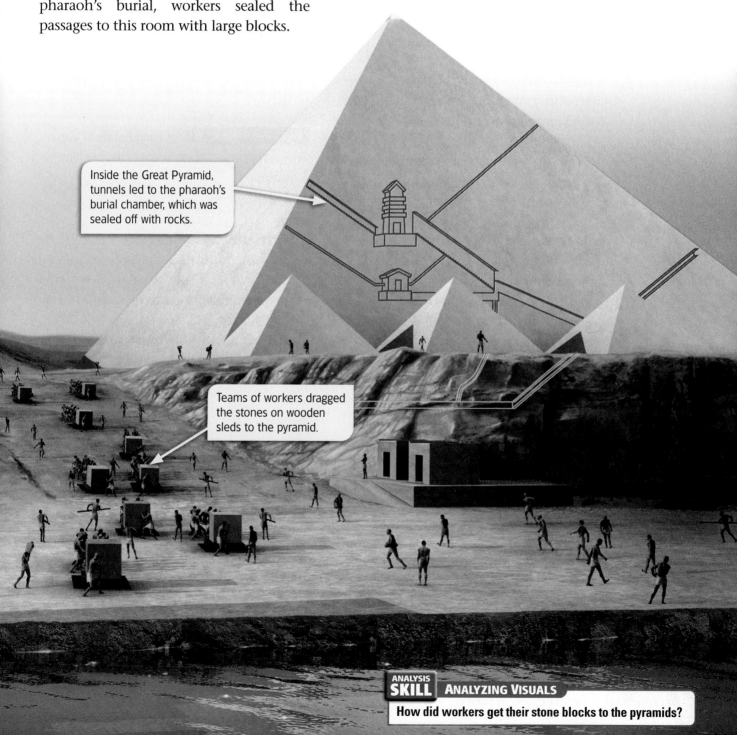

Inside the Great Pyramid, tunnels led to the pharaoh's burial chamber, which was sealed off with rocks.

Teams of workers dragged the stones on wooden sleds to the pyramid.

ANALYSIS SKILL **ANALYZING VISUALS**

How did workers get their stone blocks to the pyramids?

Wages for working on construction projects, however, were paid in goods such as grain instead of money.

For years, scholars have debated how the Egyptians moved the massive stones used to build the pyramids. Some believe that during the Nile's flooding, builders floated the stones downstream directly to the construction site. Most historians believe that workers used brick ramps and strong sleds to drag the stones up the pyramid once they reached the site.

Significance of the Pyramids

Burial in a pyramid demonstrated a pharaoh's importance. The size and shape of the pyramid were symbolic. Pointing to the skies, the pyramid symbolized the pharaoh's journey to the afterlife. The Egyptians wanted the pyramids to be spectacular because they believed that the pharaoh, as their link to the gods, controlled everyone's afterlife. Making the pharaoh's spirit happy was a way of ensuring one's own happy afterlife.

To ensure that pharaohs remained safe after their deaths, the Egyptians sometimes wrote magical spells and hymns on the pharaohs' tombs. Together, these spells and hymns are called Pyramid Texts. The first such text, addressed to Re, was carved into the pyramid of King Unas (OO-nuhs), a pharaoh of the Old Kingdom:

> "Re, this Unas comes to you,
> A spirit indestructible . . .
> Your son comes to you, this Unas . . .
> May you cross the sky united in the dark,
> May you rise in lightland, [where] you shine!"
> –from Pyramid Text, Utterance 217

The builders of Unas's pyramid wanted the god to look after their leader's spirit. Even after death, their pharaoh was important to them.

READING CHECK **Identifying Points of View** Why were pyramids important to the ancient Egyptians?

SUMMARY AND PREVIEW During the Old Kingdom, new political and social orders were created in Egypt. Religion was important, and many pyramids were built for the pharaohs. In Section 3 you will learn about life in later periods, the Middle and New Kingdoms.

go.hrw.com
Online Quiz
KEYWORD: SQ6 HP4

Section 2 Assessment

Reviewing Ideas, Terms, and People **HSS** 6.2.3

1. **a. Define** To what does the phrase **Old Kingdom** refer?
   b. Analyze Why was the pharaoh's authority never questioned?
   c. Elaborate Why do you think pharaohs might have wanted the support of **nobles**?
2. **a. Define** What did Egyptians mean by the **afterlife**?
   b. Analyze Why was embalming important to Egyptians?
3. **a. Describe** What is **engineering**?
   b. Elaborate What does the building of the **pyramids** tell us about Egyptian society?

Critical Thinking

4. **Categorizing** Draw a pyramid like the one here. In each level, write a sentence about the corresponding social class.

Pharaoh
Upper class
Middle class
Lower class

FOCUS ON WRITING

5. **Noting Characteristics of the Old Kingdom** The Old Kingdom has special characteristics of society and religion. Write down details about any of those characteristics you might want to include in your riddle.

The Middle and New Kingdoms

If **YOU** were there...

You are a servant to Hatshepsut, the ruler of Egypt. You admire her, but some people think a woman should not rule. She calls herself king and dresses like a pharaoh—even wearing a fake beard. That was your idea! But you want to help more.

What could Hatshepsut do to show her authority?

BUILDING BACKGROUND The power of the pharaohs expanded during the Old Kingdom. Society was orderly, based on great differences between social classes. But rulers and dynasties changed, and Egypt changed with them. In time, these changes led to new eras in Egyptian history, eras called the Middle and New Kingdoms.

The Middle Kingdom

At the end of the Old Kingdom, the wealth and power of the pharaohs declined. Building and maintaining pyramids cost a lot of money. Pharaohs could not collect enough taxes to keep up with their expenses. At the same time, ambitious nobles used their government positions to take power from pharaohs.

In time, nobles gained enough power to challenge the pharaohs. By about 2200 BC the Old Kingdom had fallen. For the next 160 years, local nobles ruled much of Egypt. The kingdom had no central ruler.

What You Will Learn...

Main Ideas

1. The Middle Kingdom was a period of stable government between periods of disorder.
2. The New Kingdom was the peak of Egyptian trade and military power, but their greatness did not last.
3. Work and daily life were different among Egypt's social classes.

The Big Idea

During the Middle and New Kingdoms, order and greatness were restored in Egypt.

Key Terms and People

Middle Kingdom, *p. 102*
New Kingdom, *p. 102*
trade routes, *p. 102*
Queen Hatshepsut, *p. 103*
Ramses the Great, *p. 103*

HSS **6.2.6** Describe the role of Egyptian trade in the eastern Mediterranean and Nile Valley.

6.2.7 Understand the significance of Queen Hatshepsut and Ramses the Great.

Time Line

Periods of Egyptian History

3000 BC	2000 BC	1000 BC
c. 2700–2200 BC Old Kingdom	**c. 2050–1750 BC** Middle Kingdom	**c. 1550–1050 BC** New Kingdom

Finally, around 2050 BC, a powerful pharaoh defeated his rivals, and once again all of Egypt was united. His rule began the **Middle Kingdom**, a period of order and stability which lasted to about 1750 BC. Toward the end of the Middle Kingdom, however, Egypt began to fall into disorder once more.

Around 1750 BC, a group from Southwest Asia called the Hyksos (HIK-sohs) invaded. They used horses, chariots, and advanced weapons to conquer Lower Egypt. The Hyksos ruled the region as pharaohs for 200 years.

The Egyptians eventually fought back, however. In the mid-1500s BC, Ahmose (AHM-ohs) of Thebes declared himself king and drove the Hyksos out of Egypt. Ahmose then ruled all of Egypt.

READING CHECK **Summarizing** What caused the end of the Middle Kingdom?

BIOGRAPHY

Queen Hatshepsut
Ruled c. 1503–1482 BC

Hatshepsut was married to the pharaoh Thutmose II, her half-brother. He died young, leaving the throne to Thutmose III, his son by another woman. Because Thutmose III was still very young, Hatshepsut took over power. Many people did not think women should rule, but Hatshepsut dressed as a man and called herself king. After she died, her stepson took back power and vandalized all the monuments she had built.

Identifying Cause and Effect
What do you think caused Hatshepsut to dress like a man?

The New Kingdom

Ahmose's rise to power marked the beginning of Egypt's eighteenth dynasty. More importantly, it was the beginning of the **New Kingdom**, the period during which Egypt reached the height of its power and glory. During the New Kingdom, which lasted from about 1550 to 1050 BC, conquest and trade brought wealth to the pharaohs.

Building an Empire
After battling the Hyksos, Egypt's leaders feared future invasions. To prevent such invasions from occurring, they decided to take control of all possible invasion routes into the kingdom. In the process, these leaders turned Egypt into an empire.

Egypt's first target was the homeland of the Hyksos. After taking over that area, the army continued north and conquered Syria. As you can see from the map, Egypt took over the entire eastern shore of the Mediterranean and the kingdom of Kush, south of Egypt. By the 1400s BC, Egypt was the leading military power in the region. Its empire extended from the Euphrates River to southern Nubia.

Military conquests made Egypt rich. The kingdoms it conquered regularly sent treasures to their Egyptian conquerors. For example, the kingdom of Kush in Nubia south of Egypt sent annual payments of gold, leopard skins, and precious stones to the pharaohs. In addition, Assyrian, Babylonian, and Hittite kings sent expensive gifts to Egypt in an effort to maintain good relations.

Growth and Effects of Trade
Conquest also brought Egyptian traders into contact with more distant lands. Egypt's trade expanded along with its empire. Profitable **trade routes**, or paths followed by traders, developed. Many of

the lands that Egypt took over also had valuable resources for trade. The Sinai Peninsula, for example, had large supplies of turquoise and copper.

One ruler who worked to increase Egyptian trade was **Queen Hatshepsut**. She sent Egyptian traders south to trade with the kingdom of Punt on the Red Sea and north to trade with people in Asia Minor and Greece.

Hatshepsut and later pharaohs used the money they gained from trade to support the arts and architecture. Hatshepsut especially is remembered for the many impressive monuments and temples built during her reign. The best known of these structures was a magnificent temple built for her near the city of Thebes.

Invasions of Egypt

Despite its great successes, Egypt's military might did not go unchallenged. In the 1200s BC the pharaoh Ramses (RAM-seez) II, or **Ramses the Great**, fought the Hittites, a group from Asia Minor. The two powers fought fiercely for years, but neither could defeat the other.

Egypt faced threats in other parts of its empire as well. To the west, a people known as the Tehenu invaded the Nile Delta. Ramses fought them off and built a series of forts to strengthen the western frontier. This proved to be a wise decision because the Tehenu invaded again a century later. Faced with Egypt's strengthened defenses, the Tehenu were defeated once again.

Soon after Ramses the Great died, invaders called the Sea Peoples sailed into Southwest Asia. Little is known about these people. Historians are not even sure who they were. All we know is that they were strong warriors who had crushed the Hittites and destroyed cities in Southwest Asia. Only after 50 years of fighting were the Egyptians able to turn them back.

Egyptian Trade, c. 1400 BC

GREECE
Hattusas
ASIA MINOR
Mycenae
Knossos
Enkomi Ugarit
Euphrates River
Kyrene
Mediterranean Sea
Byblos
Nile Delta
Memphis Timna
ARABIA
Akhetaton
Sawu
WESTERN DESERT
Thebes
Elephantine
New Kingdom, c. 1400 BC
Trade route
Gold
Copper
Timber
Oasis
Buhen
Nile River
NUBIAN DESERT
PUNT
KUSH
Red Sea
0   100   200 Miles
0   100   200 Kilometers
Napata

GEOGRAPHY SKILLS   INTERPRETING MAPS

Location Where was timber available?

Egypt survived, but its empire in Asia was gone. Shortly after the invasions of the Hittites and the Sea Peoples, the New Kingdom came to an end. Egypt fell into a period of violence and disorder. Egypt would never regain its power.

READING CHECK   **Identifying Cause and Effect**
What caused the growth of trade in the New Kingdom?

Work and Daily Life

Although Egyptian dynasties rose and fell, daily life for Egyptians did not change very much. But as the population grew, society became even more complex.

A complex society requires people to take on different jobs. In Egypt, these jobs were usually passed on within families. At a young age, boys started to learn their future jobs from their fathers.

Scribes

Other than priests and government officials, no one in Egypt was more honored than scribes. As members of the middle class, scribes worked for the government and the temples. They kept records and accounts for the state. Scribes also wrote and copied religious and literary texts, including stories and poems. Because they were so respected, scribes did not have to pay taxes, and many became wealthy.

Artisans, Artists, and Architects

Another group in society was made up of artisans whose jobs required advanced skills. Among the artisans who worked in Egypt were sculptors, builders, carpenters, jewelers, metalworkers, and leatherworkers. Most of Egypt's artisans worked for the government or for temples. They made statues, furniture, jewelry, pottery, shoes, and other items. Most artisans were paid fairly well for their work.

Architects and artists were also admired in Egypt. Architects designed the temples and royal tombs for which Egypt is famous. Talented architects could rise to become high government officials. Artists, often employed by the state or the

Daily Life in Egypt

Most Egyptians spent their days in the fields, plowing and harvesting their crops.

Queen Nefertiti, shown here, and other Egyptian queens wore makeup, jewelry, and perfume.

104

temples, produced many different works. Artists often worked in the deep burial chambers of the pharaohs' tombs painting detailed pictures.

Merchants and Traders

Although trade was important to Egypt, only a small group of Egyptians became merchants and traders. Some traveled long distances to buy and sell goods. Merchants were usually accompanied by soldiers, scribes, and laborers on their travels.

Soldiers

After the wars of the Middle Kingdom, Egypt created a professional army. The military offered people a chance to rise in social status. Soldiers received land as payment and could also keep any treasure they captured in war. Those who excelled could be promoted to officer positions.

Farmers and Other Peasants

As in Old Kingdom society, Egyptian farmers and other peasants were toward the bottom of Egypt's social scale. These hard-working people made up the vast majority of Egypt's population.

Farmers grew crops to support their families. Farmers depended on the Nile's regular floods to grow their crops. They used wooden hoes or plows pulled by cows to prepare the land before the flood. After the floodwaters had drained away, farmers planted seeds. They grew crops such as wheat and barley. At the end of the growing season, farmers worked together to gather the harvest.

Farmers had to give crops to the pharaoh as taxes. These taxes were intended to pay the pharaoh for using the land. Under Egyptian law, the pharoah controlled all land in the kingdom.

Servants worked for Egypt's rulers and nobles and did many jobs, like preparing food.

This jar probably held perfume, a valuable trade item.

ANALYSIS SKILL ANALYZING VISUALS

What were some luxury goods used by Egypt's queens and rulers?

All peasants, including farmers, were also subject to special duty. Under Egyptian law, the pharaoh could demand at any time that people work on projects, such as building pyramids, mining gold, or fighting in the army. The government paid the workers in grain.

ACADEMIC
VOCABULARY

contracts binding
legal agreements

Slaves

The few slaves in Egyptian society were considered lower than farmers. Many slaves were convicted criminals or prisoners captured in war. They worked on farms, on building projects, in workshops, and in private households. Unlike most slaves in history, however, slaves in Egypt had some legal rights. Also, in some cases, they could earn their freedom.

Family Life in Egypt

Family life was important in Egyptian society. Most Egyptian families lived in their own homes. Sometimes unmarried female relatives lived with them, but men were expected to marry young so that they could start having children.

Most Egyptian women were devoted to their homes and their families. Some, however, had jobs outside the home. A few served as priestesses, and some worked as royal officials, administrators, and artisans. Unlike most ancient women, Egyptian women had a number of legal rights. They could own property, make **contracts**, and divorce their husbands. They could even keep their property after a divorce.

Children's lives were not as structured as adults' lives were. They played with toys such as dolls, tops, and clay animal figurines. Children also played ballgames and hunted. Most children, boys and girls, received some education. At school they learned morals, writing, math, and sports. At age 14 most boys left school to enter their father's profession. At that time, they took their place in Egypt's social structure.

READING CHECK **Categorizing** What types of jobs existed in ancient Egypt?

SUMMARY AND PREVIEW Pharaohs faced many challenges to their rule. After defeating the Hyksos, the kingdom expanded in land and wealth. People in Egypt worked at many different jobs. In the next section you will learn about Egyptian achievements.

Section 3 Assessment

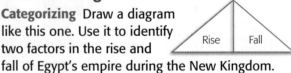
go.hrw.com
Online Quiz
KEYWORD: SQ6 HP4

Reviewing Ideas, Terms, and People   **HSS** 6.2.6, 6.2.7

1. **a. Define** What was the **Middle Kingdom**?
   b. Analyze How did Ahmose manage to become king of all Egypt?
2. **a. Identify** For what is **Ramses the Great** best known?
   b. Explain What did **Hatshepsut** do as pharaoh of Egypt?
3. **a. Identify** What job employed the most people in Egypt?
   b. Analyze What rights did Egyptian women have?
   c. Elaborate Why do you think scribes were so honored in Egyptian society?

Critical Thinking

4. **Categorizing** Draw a diagram like this one. Use it to identify two factors in the rise and fall of Egypt's empire during the New Kingdom.

   Rise | Fall

FOCUS ON WRITING

5. **Developing Key Ideas from the Middle and New Kingdoms** Your riddle should contain some information about the later pharaohs and daily life in Egypt. Decide which key ideas you should include in your riddle and add them to your list.

Ramses the Great

How could a ruler achieve fame that would last 3,000 years?

When did he live? late 1300s and early 1200s BC

Where did he live? As pharaoh, Ramses lived in a city he built on the Nile Delta. The city's name, Pi-Ramesse, means the "house of Ramses."

What did he do? From a young age, Ramses was trained as a ruler and a fighter. Made an army captain at age 10, he began military campaigns even before he became pharaoh. During his reign, Ramses greatly increased the size of his kingdom.

Why is he important? Many people consider Ramses the last great Egyptian pharaoh. He accomplished great things, but the pharaohs who followed could not maintain them. Both a great warrior and a great builder, he is known largely for the massive monuments he built. The temples at Karnak, Luxor, and Abu Simbel stand as 3,000-year-old symbols of the great pharaoh's power.

Drawing Conclusions Why do you think Ramses built monuments all over Egypt?

KEY IDEAS

Ramses had a poem praising him carved into the walls of five temples, including Karnak. One verse of the poem praises Ramses as a great warrior and the defender of Egypt.

"Gracious lord and bravest
    king, savior-guard
Of Egypt in the battle, be our
    ward;
Behold we stand alone, in the
    hostile Hittite ring,
Save for us the breath of life,
Give deliverance from the
    strife,
Oh! protect us Ramses Miamun!
Oh! save us, mighty king!"

–Pen-ta-ur, quoted in *The World's Story*, edited by Eva March Tappan

This copy of an ancient painting shows Ramses the Great on his chariot in battle against the Hittites.

Egyptian Achievements

HSS **6.2.5** Discuss the main features of Egyptian art and architecture.

6.2.9 Trace the evolution of language and its written forms.

If YOU were there...

You are an artist in ancient Egypt. A noble has hired you to decorate the walls of his family tomb. You are standing inside the new tomb, studying the bare, stone walls that you will decorate. No light reaches this chamber, but your servant holds a lantern high. You've met the noble only briefly but think that he is someone who loves his family, the gods, and Egypt.

What will you include in your painting?

BUILDING BACKGROUND The Egyptians had a rich and varied history, but most people today remember them for their cultural achievements, such as their unique writing system. In addition, Egyptian art, including the tomb paintings mentioned above, is admired by millions of tourists in museums around the world.

Egyptian Writing

If you were reading a book and saw pictures of folded cloth, a leg, a star, a bird, and a man holding a stick, would you know what it meant? You would if you were an ancient Egyptian. In the Egyptian writing system, or **hieroglyphics** (hy-ruh-GLIH-fiks), those five symbols together meant "to teach." Egyptian hieroglyphics were one of the world's first writing systems.

Writing in Ancient Egypt

The earliest known examples of Egyptian writing are from around 3300 BC. These early Egyptian writings were carved in stone or on other hard material. Later, the Egyptians learned how to make **papyrus** (puh-PY-ruhs), a long-lasting, paper-like material made from reeds. The Egyptians made papyrus by pressing layers of reeds together and pounding them into sheets. These sheets were tough and durable, yet easy to roll into scrolls. Scribes wrote on papyrus using brushes and ink.

Egyptian Writing

Egyptian hieroglyphics used picture symbols to represent sounds.

	Sound	Meaning
	Imn	Amon
	Tut	Image
	Ankh	Living

Translation—"Living image of Amon"

	Heka	Ruler
	Iunu	Heliopolis
	Resy	Southern

Translation—"Ruler of Southern Heliopolis"

ANALYSIS SKILL **ANALYZING VISUALS**

What does the symbol for ruler look like?

The hieroglyphic writing system used more than 600 symbols, mostly pictures of objects. Each symbol represented one or more sounds in the Egyptian language. For example, a picture of an owl represented the same sound as our letter M.

Hieroglyphics could be written either horizontally or vertically. They could be written from right to left or from left to right. These options made hieroglyphics flexible to write but difficult to read. The only way to tell which way a text is written is to look at individual symbols.

The Rosetta Stone

Historians and archaeologists have known about hieroglyphics for centuries, but for a long time they didn't know how to read it. In fact, it was not until 1799 when a lucky discovery by a French soldier gave historians the key they needed to read ancient Egyptian writing.

That key was the **Rosetta Stone**, a huge, stone slab inscribed with hieroglyphics. In addition to the hieroglyphics, the Rosetta Stone had text in Greek and a later form of Egyptian. Because the text in all three languages was the same, scholars who knew Greek were able to figure out what the hieroglyphics said.

Egyptian Texts

Because papyrus did not decay in Egypt's dry climate, many Egyptian texts still survive. Historians today can read Egyptian government records, historical records, science texts, and medical manuals. In addition, many literary works have survived. Some, such as *The Book of the Dead,* tell about the afterlife. Others tell stories about gods and kings.

READING CHECK **Comparing** How is our writing system similar to hieroglyphics?

THE IMPACT TODAY

An object that helps solve a difficult mystery is sometimes called a Rosetta Stone.

Egypt's Great Temples

In addition to their writing system, the Egyptians are famous today for their magnificent architecture. You have already read about the Egyptians' most famous structures, the pyramids. But the Egyptians also built massive temples. Those that survive are among the most spectacular sites in Egypt today.

The Egyptians believed that temples were the homes of the gods. People visited the temples to worship, offer the gods gifts, and ask for favors.

Many Egyptian temples shared some similar features. Rows of stone **sphinxes**—imaginary creatures with the bodies of lions and the heads of other animals or humans—lined the path leading to the entrance. That entrance itself was a huge, thick gate. On either side of the gate might stand an **obelisk** (AH-buh-lisk), a tall, four-sided pillar that is pointed on top.

Inside, the temples were lavishly decorated, as you can see in the drawing of the Temple of Karnak. Huge columns supported the temple's roof. In many cases, these columns were covered with paintings and hieroglyphics, as were the temple walls. Statues of gods and pharaohs often stood along the walls as well. The sanctuary, the most sacred part of the building, was at the far end of the temple.

The Temple of Karnak is only one of Egypt's great temples. Others were built by Ramses the Great at Abu Simbel and Luxor. The temple at Abu Simbel is especially known for the huge statues carved out of the sandstone cliffs at the temple's entrance. These 66-foot-tall statues show Ramses as pharaoh. Nearby are some smaller statues of his family.

READING CHECK **Generalizing** What were some features of Egyptian temples?

THE IMPACT TODAY

The Washington Monument, in Washington, DC, is an obelisk.

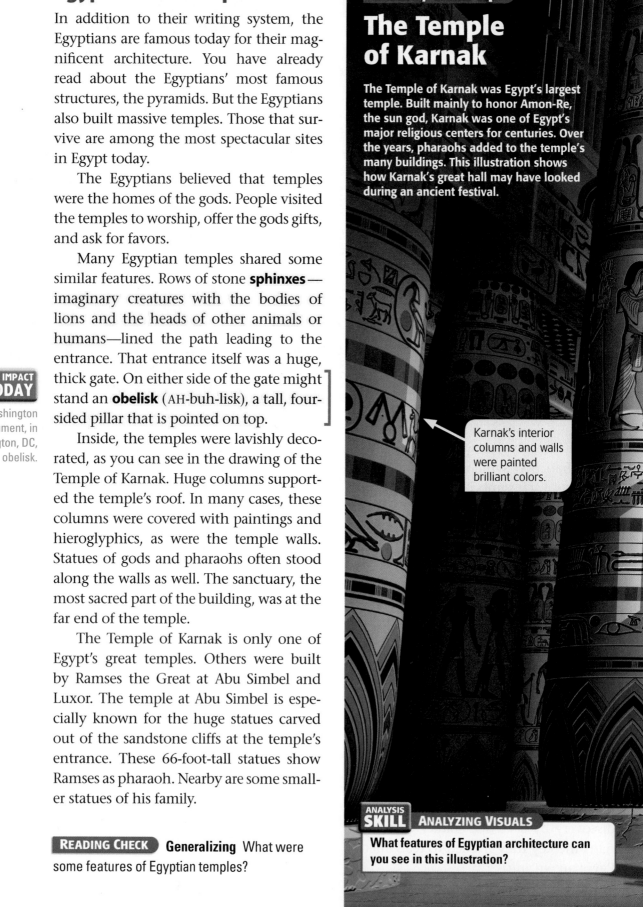

History Close-up

The Temple of Karnak

The Temple of Karnak was Egypt's largest temple. Built mainly to honor Amon-Re, the sun god, Karnak was one of Egypt's major religious centers for centuries. Over the years, pharaohs added to the temple's many buildings. This illustration shows how Karnak's great hall may have looked during an ancient festival.

Karnak's interior columns and walls were painted brilliant colors.

ANALYSIS SKILL **ANALYZING VISUALS**

What features of Egyptian architecture can you see in this illustration?

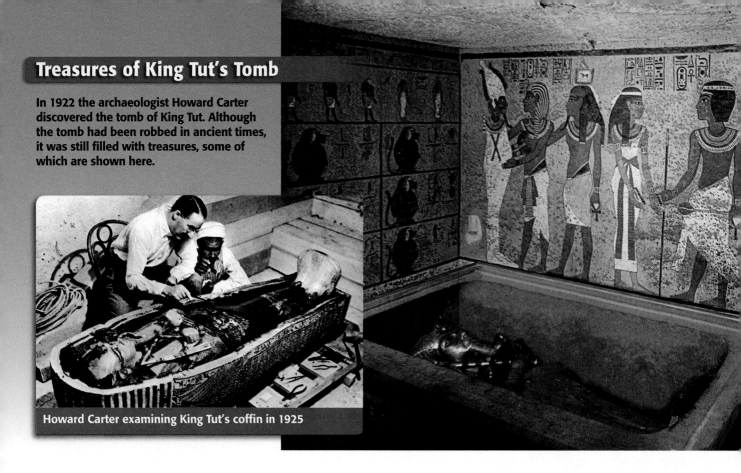

In 1922 the archaeologist Howard Carter discovered the tomb of King Tut. Although the tomb had been robbed in ancient times, it was still filled with treasures, some of which are shown here.

Howard Carter examining King Tut's coffin in 1925

Egyptian Art

One reason Egypt's temples are so popular with tourists is the art they contain. The ancient Egyptians were masterful artists. Many of their greatest works were created to fill the tombs of pharaohs and other nobles. The Egyptians took great care in making these items because they believed the dead could enjoy them in the afterlife.

Paintings

Egyptian art was filled with lively, colorful scenes. Detailed works covered the walls of temples and tombs. Artists also painted on canvas, papyrus, pottery, plaster, and wood. Most Egyptians, however, never saw these paintings. Only kings, priests, and important people could enter temples and tombs, and even they rarely entered the tombs.

The subjects of Egyptian paintings vary widely. Some paintings show important historical events, such as the crowning of kings and the founding of temples. Others illustrate major religious rituals. Still other paintings show scenes from everyday life, such as farming or hunting.

Egyptian painting has a distinctive style. People, for example, are drawn in a certain way. In Egyptian paintings, people's heads and legs are always seen from the side, but their upper bodies and shoulders are shown straight on. In addition, people do not all appear the same size. Important figures such as pharaohs appear huge in comparison to others, especially servants or conquered people. In contrast, Egyptian animals were usually drawn realistically.

Carvings and Jewelry

Painting was not the only art form Egyptians practiced. The Egyptians were also skilled stoneworkers. Many tombs included huge statues and detailed carvings.

The Egyptians also made beautiful objects out of gold and precious stones. They made jewelry for both women and men. This

The back of King Tut's chair was decorated with this image of the pharaoh and his wife.

ANALYSIS
SKILL **ANALYZING VISUALS**

What might archaeologists learn about ancient Egypt from these artifacts?

Gold mask

jewelry included necklaces, collars, and bracelets. The Egyptians also used gold to make burial items for their pharaohs.

Over the years, treasure hunters emptied many pharaohs' tombs. At least one tomb, however, was not disturbed. In 1922 some archaeologists found the tomb of **King Tutankhamen** (too-tang-KAHM-uhn), or King Tut. The tomb was filled with treasures, including boxes of jewelry, robes, a burial mask, and ivory statues. King Tut's treasures have taught us much about Egyptian burial practices and beliefs.

READING CHECK **Summarizing** What types of artwork were contained in Egyptian tombs?

SUMMARY AND PREVIEW Ancient Egyptians developed one of the best-known cultures of the ancient world. Next, you will learn about a culture that developed in the shadow of Egypt—Kush.

go.hrw.com
Online Quiz
KEYWORD: SQ6 HP4

Section 4 Assessment

Reviewing Ideas, Terms, and People HSS 6.2.5, 6.2.9

1. **a. Identify** What are **hieroglyphics**?
   b. Contrast How was hieroglyphic writing different from our writing today?
   c. Evaluate Why was finding the **Rosetta Stone** so important to scholars?
2. **a. Describe** What were two ways the Egyptians decorated their temples?
   b. Evaluate Why do you think pharaohs like Ramses the Great built huge temples?
3. **Recall** Why were tombs filled with art, jewelry, and other treasures?

Critical Thinking

4. **Summarize** Draw a chart like the one below. In each column, list two facts about the achievements of the ancient Egyptians.

Writing	Architecture	Art

FOCUS ON WRITING

5. **Considering Egyptian Achievements** Note some details about Egyptian achievements in writing, architecture, and art that make Egypt different from other places.

Social Studies Skills

| Analysis | Critical Thinking | Participation | Study |

Assessing Primary and Secondary Sources

Understand the Skill

Primary sources in history are materials created by people who lived during the times they describe. Examples include letters, diaries, and photographs. *Secondary sources* are accounts written later by someone who was not present. They are designed to teach about or discuss a historical topic. This textbook is an example of a secondary source.

Together, primary and secondary sources can present a good picture of a historical period or event. However, they must be used carefully to make sure that the picture they present is accurate.

Learn the Skill

Here are some questions to ask to help you judge the accuracy of primary and secondary sources.

1 What is it? Is it a firsthand account or is it based on information provided by others? In other words, is it primary or secondary?

2 Who wrote it? For a primary source, what was the author's connection to what he or she was writing about? For a secondary source, what makes the author an authority on this subject?

3 Who is the audience? Was the information meant for the public? Was it meant for a friend or for the writer alone? The intended audience can influence what the writer has to say.

4 What is the purpose? Authors of either primary or secondary sources can have reasons to exaggerate—or even lie—to suit their own goals or purposes. Look for evidence of emotion, opinion, or bias in the source. These might influence the accuracy of the account.

5 Does other evidence support the source? Look for other information that supports the source's account. Compare different sources whenever possible.

Practice and Apply the Skill

Below are two passages about the military in ancient Egypt. Read them both and use the guidelines to answer the questions that follow.

"The pharaohs began … leading large armies out of a land that had once known only small police forces and militia. The Egyptians quickly extended their military and commercial influence over an extensive region that included the rich provinces of Syria … and the numbers of Egyptian slaves grew swiftly."

–C. Warren Hollister, from *Roots of the Western Tradition*

"Let me tell you how the soldier fares … how he goes to Syria, and how he marches over the mountains. His bread and water are borne [carried] upon his shoulders like the load of [a donkey]; they make his neck bent as that of [a donkey], and the joints of his back are bowed [bent]. His drink is stinking water … When he reaches the enemy, he is trapped like a bird, and he has no strength in his limbs."

–from *Wings of the Falcon: Life and Thought of Ancient Egypt*, translated by Joseph Kaster

1. Which quote is a primary source, and which is a secondary source?

2. Is there evidence of opinion, emotion, or bias in the second quote? Explain why or why not.

3. Which information is more likely to be accurate on this subject? Explain your answer.

Visual Summary

Use the visual summary below to help you review the main ideas of the chapter.

QUICK FACTS

Egyptian civilization developed along the Nile River.

Egypt's kings were considered gods, and people built huge pyramids in their honor.

Egyptians developed a writing system and created beautiful art.

Reviewing Terms and People

Imagine these terms from the chapter are correct answers to items in a crossword puzzle. Write the clues for the answers. Then make the puzzle with some answers written down and some across.

1. cataract
2. Menes
3. pharaoh
4. nobles
5. mummy
6. elite
7. contract
8. Ramses
9. hieroglyphics
10. Tutankhamen

Comprehension and Critical Thinking

SECTION 1 *(Pages 88–92)* **HSS** 6.2.1, 6.2.2

11. **a. Identify** Where was most of Egypt's fertile land?

b. Make Inferences Why did Memphis become a political and social center of Egypt?

c. Predict How might history have been different if the Nile hadn't flooded every year?

SECTION 2 *(Pages 93–100)* **HSS** 6.2.3

12. **a. Describe** What responsibilities did pharaohs have?

b. Analyze How were beliefs about the **afterlife** linked to items placed in tombs?

c. Elaborate What challenges, in addition to moving stone blocks, do you think the pyramid builders faced?

SECTION 3 *(Pages 101–106)* **HSS** 6.2.6, 6.2.7

13. **a. Describe** What did a scribe do?

b. Analyze What two factors contributed to Egypt's wealth during the **New Kingdom**?

c. Evaluate **Ramses the Great** was a powerful pharaoh. Do you think his military successes or his building projects are more important to evaluating his greatness? Why?

SECTION 4 *(Pages 108–113)* **HSS** 6.2.5, 6.2.9

14. a. Describe For what was **papyrus** used?

b. Contrast How are the symbols in hieroglyphics different than the symbols used in our writing system?

c. Elaborate How does the Egyptian style of painting people reflect their society?

Social Studies Skills

Judging the Credibility of Sources *Each of the questions below lists two sources that a historian might consult to answer a question about ancient Egypt. For each question, decide which source is likely to be more accurate or believable and why.*

15. What were Egyptian beliefs about the afterlife?

a. tomb inscriptions

b. writings by a priest who visited Egypt in 1934

16. Why did the Nile flood every year?

a. songs of praise to the Nile written by Egyptian priests

b. a book about the rivers of Africa written by a modern geographer

17. What kinds of goods did the Egyptians trade?

a. government records of trade

b. an ancient Egyptian story about a trader

18. What kind of warrior was Ramses the Great?

a. a poem in praise of Ramses

b. a description of a battle written by an impartial observer

Internet Activity

go.hrw.com
KEYWORD: SQ6 WH4

19. Activity: Creating Egyptian Art The Egyptians developed an extraordinary artistic civilization. Their architecture included innovative pyramids and temples. Artisans created beautiful paintings, carvings, and jewelry. Enter the activity keyword and research the main features of Egyptian art and architecture. Then imagine you are an Egyptian artisan. Create a piece of art to place inside a pharaoh's tomb. Include hieroglyphics telling the pharaoh about your art.

Reviewing Themes

20. Geography Do you think that Egyptian society could have flourished in North Africa if the Nile had not existed? Why or why not?

21. Religion How did religious beliefs shape the rest of Egyptian culture?

Reading Skills

Drawing Conclusions from Sources *Read the following passage and answer the questions. If the passage does not provide enough information to answer the question, choose "d. not enough information."*

> *"* Hail to thee, O Nile! Who manifests thyself over this land, and comes to give life to Egypt! Mysterious is thy issuing forth from the darkness, on this day whereon it is celebrated! *"*
>
> —*Hymn to the Nile,* from *The Library of Original Sources,* edited by Oliver J. Thatcher

22. How do you think the Egyptians felt about the Nile?

a. They admired it.   **c.** They feared it.

b. They ignored it.   **d.** not enough information

23. Where did the Egyptians think the Nile's waters came from?

a. the highlands of Ethiopia

b. the Mediterranean

c. an unknown, mysterious location

d. not enough information

24. What does the name *Nile* mean in Egyptian?

a. inexhaustible   **c.** celebrated

b. mysterious   **d.** not enough information

FOCUS ON WRITING

25. Writing a Riddle Choose five details about Egypt. Then write a sentence about each detail. Each sentence of your riddle should be a statement ending with "me." For example, if you were writing about the United States, you might say, "People come from all over the world to join me." After you have written your five sentences, end your riddle with "Who am I?"

Standards Assessment

DIRECTIONS: Read each question, and write the letter of the best response.

1

> Oh great god and ruler, the gift of Amon-Re,
>   god of the Sun.
> Oh great protector of Egypt and its people.
> Great one who has saved us from the horrible
>   Tehenu.
> You, who have turned back the Hittites.
> You, who have fortified our western border to
>   forever protect us from our enemies.
> We bless you, oh great one.
> We worship and honor you, oh great pharaoh.

A tribute such as the one above would have been written in honor of which Egyptian ruler?

A Khufu

B Ramses the Great

C King Tutankhamen

D Queen Hatshepsut

2 The Nile helped civilization develop in Egypt in all of the following ways *except* by

A providing a source of food and water.

B allowing farming to develop.

C enriching the soil along its banks.

D protecting against invasion from the west.

3 The most fertile soil in Egypt was located in the

A Nile Delta.

B desert.

C cataracts.

D far south.

4 The high position priests held in Egyptian society shows that

A the pharaoh was a descendant of a god.

B government was large and powerful.

C religion was important in Egyptian life.

D the early Egyptians worshipped many gods.

5 The Egyptians are probably *best* known for building

A pyramids.

B irrigation canals.

C ziggurats.

D forts.

Connecting with Past Learnings

6 In this chapter you learned about hiero-glyphics, one of the world's first writing systems. In Chapter 3 you read about another ancient writing system called

A Sumerian.

B Hammurabi.

C ziggurat.

D cuneiform.

7 In Chapter 3 you read about Sargon I, who first united Mesopotamia under one rule. Which Egyptian ruler's accomplishments were *most* similar to Sargon's?

A Hyksos

B Khufu

C Menes

D Hatshepsut

Ancient Kush

California Standards

History–Social Science

6.2 Students analyze the geographic, political, economic, religious, and social structures of the early civilizations of Mesopotamia, Egypt, and Kush.

Analysis Skills

HI 2 Understand and distinguish cause and effect.

English–Language Arts

Writing 6.2.1b Include sensory details and concrete language to develop plot and character.

Reading 6.2.0 Students read and understand grade-level-appropriate material.

 FOCUS ON WRITING

A Fictional Narrative In this chapter you will read about events of the rise and fall of Kush. Then you will write a short story about fictional characters who lived through these events. The main character in your story will be from Kush; other main characters could be from Egypt, Assyria, or Aksum.

CHAPTER EVENTS

c. 2000 BC
The kingdom of Kush sets up its capital at Kerma.

2000 BC

WORLD EVENTS

2300 BC
The Harappan civilization rises in the Indus Valley.

HOLT

History's Impact
▶ video series
Watch the video to understand the impact of the Egyptian pyramids.

What You Will Learn...

In this chapter you will learn about the history and culture of Kush and its connections to Egypt. This photo shows ruins of the royal pyramids in Kush and some pyramids that have been reconstructed.

c. 750–700 BC Kush conquers Egypt.

c. 580 BC Meroë becomes capital of Kush.

c. AD 350 Aksum destroys Meroë.

1500 BC	1000 BC	500 BC	BC 1 AD	AD 500

c. 1550 BC The New Kingdom begins in Egypt.

c. 500 BC The Nok culture develops in West Africa.

AD 330 Constantinople becomes the capital of the Roman Empire.

119

Reading Social Studies

by Kylene Beers

Economics	Geography	Politics	Religion	Society and Culture	Science and Technology

Focus on Themes As you read this chapter, you will learn about an ancient kingdom called Kush that developed south of Egypt along the Nile River. You will see that the **geography** of the area helped this kingdom to develop. You will also learn how Egypt conquered and ruled Kush and then how Kush conquered and ruled Egypt. Finally, you will learn how the **economy** of Kush grew as it developed an iron industry and expanded its trade network.

Causes and Effects in History

Focus on Reading Have you heard the saying, "We have to understand the past to avoid repeating it."? That is one reason we look for causes and effects in history.

Identifying Causes and Effects A **cause** is something that makes another thing happen. An **effect** is the result of something else that happened. Most historical events have a number of causes as well as a number of effects. You can understand history better if you look for causes and effects of events.

Additional reading support can be found in the

Reader and Study Guide

1. *Because the Egyptians had captured the city of Kerma, the kings of Kush ruled from the city of Napata.* (p. 125)

Cause	Effect
Capture of Kerma	→ Kings ruled from Napata

Sometimes writers use words that signal a cause or an effect:

Cause—*reason, basis, because, motivated, as*

Effect—*therefore, as a result, for that reason, so*

2. *Piankhi fought the Egyptians because he believed that the gods wanted him to rule all of Egypt.* (p. 125)

Effect	Cause
Piankhi fought the Egyptians	← Believed gods wanted him to rule Egypt

HSS **Analysis HI 2** Distinguish cause and effect.
ELA **Reading 6.2.0** Read and understand grade-level-appropriate material.

You Try It!

The following selections are from the chapter you are about to read. As you read each, identify which phrase or sentence describes a cause and which describes an effect.

Finding Causes and Effects

1. "During the mid-1000s BC the New Kingdom in Egypt was ending. As the power of Egypt's pharaohs declined, Kushite leaders regained control of Kush. Kush once again became independent." (p. 124)
2. "A series of weak pharaohs left Egypt open to attack." (p. 125)
3. 'The Assyrians' iron weapons were better than the Kushites' bronze weapons, and the Kushites were slowly pushed out of Egypt." (p. 126)
4. "Because resources such as iron ore and wood for furnaces were easily available, the industry grew quickly." (p. 128)
5. "When the cows ate all the grass, there was nothing to hold the soil down. As a result, wind blew the soil away. Without this soil, farmers couldn't produce enough food for Kush's people." (p. 131)

After you read the sentences, answer the following questions.

1. In selection 1, is "Kush once again became independent" the cause of the Egyptians growing weaker or the effect?

2. In selection 2, what left Egypt open to attack? Is that the cause of why Egypt was easily attacked or the effect?

3. In selection 3, who is using the iron weapons, the Assyrians or the Kushites? What was the effect of using the weapons?

4. In selection 4, does the word *because* signal a cause or an effect?

5. Read selection 5 again. Decide which sentences identify causes and which identify effects. (Here's a hint: an event can be the effect of one thing and the cause of another.)

Key Terms and People

Chapter 5

Section 1
ebony (p. 124)
ivory (p. 124)
Piankhi (p. 125)

Section 2
trade network (p. 128)
merchants (p. 128)
exports (p. 128)
imports (p. 128)
Queen Shanakhdakheto (p. 129)
King Ezana (p. 131)

Academic Vocabulary

Success in school is related to knowing academic vocabulary—the words that are frequently used in school assignments and discussions. In this chapter, you will learn the following academic word:

authority (p. 129)

As you read **Chapter 5**, look for words that signal causes or effects. Make a chart to keep track of these causes and effects.

Kush and Egypt

If **YOU** were there...

You live along the Nile River, where it moves quickly through rapids. A few years ago, armies from the powerful kingdom of Egypt took over your country. Some Egyptians have moved to your town. They bring new customs, and many people are imitating them. Now your sister has a new baby and wants to give it an Egyptian name! This upsets many people in your family.

How do you feel about following Egyptian customs?

BUILDING BACKGROUND Egypt dominated the lands along the Nile, but it was not the only ancient culture to develop along the river. Another kingdom, called Kush, arose to the south of Egypt. Through trade, conquest, and political dealings, the histories of Egypt and Kush became closely tied together.

Geography and Early Kush

South of Egypt along the Nile, a group of people settled in the region we now call Nubia. These Africans established the first large kingdom in the interior of Africa. We know this kingdom by the name the ancient Egyptians gave it—Kush. Development of Kushite civilization was greatly influenced by the geography of Nubia.

The Land of Nubia

Nubia is a region in northeast Africa. It lies on the Nile River south of Egypt. Today desert covers much of Nubia, but in ancient times the region was more fertile than it is now. Heavy rainfall south of Nubia flooded the Nile every year. The floods provided a rich layer of fertile soil to nearby lands. The kingdom of Kush developed in this area.

In addition to having fertile soil, ancient Nubia was rich in valuable minerals such as gold, copper, and stone. These natural resources contributed to the region's wealth and played a major role in its history.

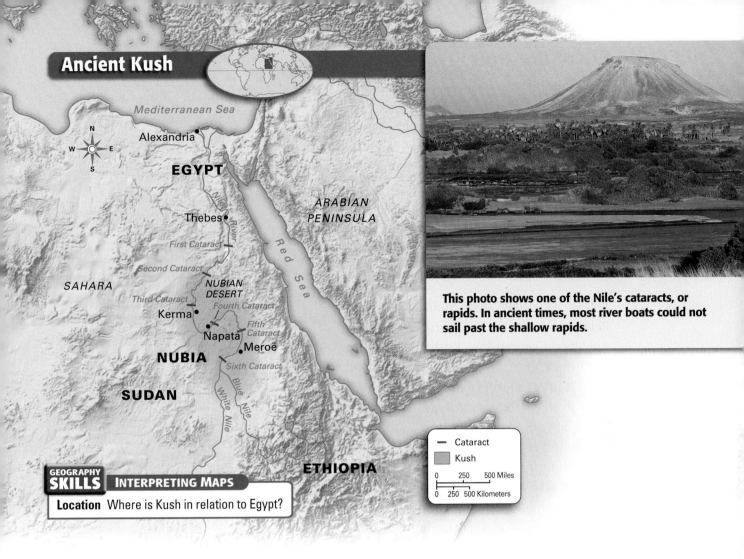

Ancient Kush

GEOGRAPHY
SKILLS | INTERPRETING MAPS

Location Where is Kush in relation to Egypt?

This photo shows one of the Nile's cataracts, or rapids. In ancient times, most river boats could not sail past the shallow rapids.

Cataract
Kush

0   250   500 Miles
0 250 500 Kilometers

Early Civilization in Nubia

Like all early civilizations, the people of Nubia depended on agriculture for their food. Fortunately for them, the Nile's floods allowed the Nubians to plant both summer and winter crops. Among the crops they grew were wheat, barley, and other grains. In addition to farmland, the banks of the river provided grazing land for cattle and other livestock. As a result, farming villages thrived all along the Nile by about 3500 BC.

Over time some farmers became richer and more successful than others. These farmers became leaders of their villages. Sometime around 2000 BC, one of these leaders took control of other villages and made himself king of the region. His new kingdom was called Kush.

The kings of Kush ruled from their capital at Kerma (KAR-muh). This city was located on the Nile just south of a cataract, or stretch of rapids. Because the Nile's cataracts made parts of the river hard to pass through, they were natural barriers against invaders. For many years the cataracts kept Kush safe from the more powerful Egyptian kingdom to the north.

As time passed, Kushite society grew more complex. In addition to farmers and herders, some people of Kush became priests or artisans. Early on, Kush was greatly influenced by civilizations to the south. Later, however, Egypt played a greater role in the kingdom's history.

FOCUS ON READING
What words on this page signal causes or effects?

READING CHECK **Finding Main Ideas** How did geography help civilization grow in Nubia?

ANCIENT KUSH   **123**

Egypt Controls Kush

Kush and Egypt were neighbors. Sometimes the neighbors lived in peace with each other and helped each other prosper. For example, Kush became a supplier of slaves and raw materials to Egypt. The Kushites sent materials such as gold, copper, and stone to Egypt. The Kushites also sent the Egyptians **ebony**, a type of dark, heavy wood, and **ivory**, a white material made from elephant tusks.

Egypt's Conquest of Kush

Relations between Kush and Egypt were not always peaceful. As Kush grew wealthy from trade, its army grew stronger as well. Egypt's rulers soon feared that Kush would grow even more powerful and could even attack Egypt.

To prevent such an attack from occurring, the pharaoh Thutmose I sent an army to take control of Kush around 1500 BC. The pharaoh's army conquered all of Nubia north of the Fifth Cataract. As a result, Kush became part of Egypt.

After his army's victory, the pharaoh destroyed the Kushite palace at Kerma. Later pharaohs—including Ramses the Great—built huge temples in what had been Kushite territory.

Effects of the Conquest

Kush remained an Egyptian territory for about 450 years. During that time, Egypt's influence over Kush grew tremendously. Many Egyptians settled in Kush, and Egyptian became the language of the region. Many Kushites used Egyptian names, and they wore Egyptian-style clothing. They also adopted Egyptian religious practices.

A Change in Power

During the mid-1000s BC the New Kingdom in Egypt was ending. As the power of Egypt's pharaohs declined, Kushite leaders regained control of Kush. Kush once again became independent.

READING CHECK **Identifying Cause and Effect** How did Egyptian rule change Kush?

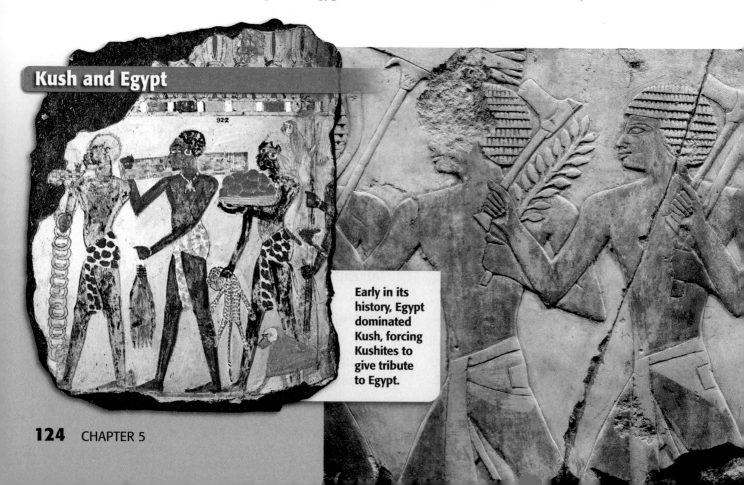

Kush and Egypt

Early in its history, Egypt dominated Kush, forcing Kushites to give tribute to Egypt.

Kush Rules Egypt

We know almost nothing about the history of the Kushites for about 200 years after they regained independence from Egypt. Kush is not mentioned in any historical records until the 700s BC, when armies from Kush swept into Egypt and conquered it.

The Conquest of Egypt

By around 850 BC, Kush had regained its strength. It was once again as strong as it had been before it had been conquered by Egypt. Because the Egyptians had captured the city of Kerma, the kings of Kush ruled from the city of Napata. Napata was located on the Nile, about 100 miles southeast of Kerma.

As Kush was growing stronger, Egypt was losing power. A series of weak pharaohs left Egypt open to attack. In the 700s BC a Kushite king, Kashta, took advantage of Egypt's weakness. Kashta attacked Egypt, and by about 751 BC he had conquered Upper Egypt. He then established relations with Lower Egypt.

BIOGRAPHY

Piankhi
c. 751–716 BC

Also known as Piye, Piankhi was among Kush's most successful military leaders. A fierce warrior on the battlefield, the king was also deeply religious. Piankhi's belief that he had the support of the gods fueled his passion for war against Egypt. His courage inspired his troops on the battlefield. Piankhi loved his horses and was buried with eight of them.

Drawing Conclusions How did Piankhi's belief that he was supported by the gods affect him in the war against Egypt?

After Kashta died, his son **Piankhi** (PYANG-kee) continued to attack Egypt. The armies of Kush captured many cities, including Egypt's ancient capital. Piankhi fought the Egyptians because he believed that the gods wanted him to rule all of Egypt. By the time he died in about 716 BC, Piankhi had accomplished this task. His kingdom extended north from Napata to the Nile Delta.

Later, as Kush's power increased, its warriors invaded and conquered Egypt. This photo shows Kushite and Egyptian warriors.

After conquering Egypt, Kush established a new dynasty. This photo shows one of Kush's pharaohs kneeling before an Egyptian god.

ANALYSIS SKILL **ANALYZING VISUALS**

What did Kushites give to Egypt as tribute?

When the Assyrians invaded Egypt with their iron weapons, they forced Kush's rulers out of Egypt and south into Nubia.

The Kushite rulers of Egypt built new temples to Egyptian gods and restored old ones. They also worked to preserve Egyptian writings. As a result, Egyptian culture thrived during the Kushite dynasty.

The End of Kushite Rule in Egypt

The Kushite dynasty remained strong in Egypt for about 40 years. In the 670s BC, however, the powerful army of the Assyrians from Mesopotamia invaded Egypt. The Assyrians' iron weapons were better than the Kushites' bronze weapons, and the Kushites were slowly pushed out of Egypt. In just 10 years the Assyrians had driven the Kushite forces completely out of Egypt.

READING CHECK Identifying Cause and Effect
How did internal problems in Egypt benefit Kush?

SUMMARY AND PREVIEW Kush was conquered by Egypt, but later the Kushites controlled Egypt. In the next section, you will learn how the civilization of Kush developed after the Kushites were forced out of Egypt by the Assyrians.

The Kushite Dynasty

After Piankhi died, his brother Shabaka (SHAB-uh-kuh) took control of the kingdom. Shabaka then declared himself pharaoh. This declaration began the Twenty-fifth, or Kushite, Dynasty in Egypt.

Shabaka and later rulers of his dynasty tried to restore old Egyptian cultural practices. Some of these practices had faded during Egypt's period of weakness. For example, Shabaka was buried in a pyramid. The Egyptians had stopped building pyramids for their rulers centuries before.

go.hrw.com
Online Quiz
KEYWORD: SQ6 HP5

Section 1 Assessment

Reviewing Ideas, Terms, and People HSS 6.2.8

1. **a. Identify** On which river did Kush develop?
   b. Analyze How did Nubia's natural resources influence the early history of Kush?

2. **a. Describe** What is **ebony**?
   b. Analyze Why did people in Kush adopt some elements of Egyptian culture?
   c. Evaluate Why do you think Thutmose I destroyed the Kushite palace at Kerma?

3. **a. Describe** What territory did **Piankhi** conquer?
   b. Make Inferences Why is the Twenty-fifth Dynasty significant in the history of Egypt?
   c. Predict What might have happened in Kush and Egypt if Kush had developed iron weapons?

Critical Thinking

4. **Identifying Cause and Effect** Create a chart like the one here. For each cause listed, identify one effect.

Cause	Effect
Villages appear along the Nile.	
Kush trades with Egypt.	
Piankhi conquers Egypt.	
Assyrians use iron weapons.	

FOCUS ON WRITING

5. **Characters and Plot** Make a chart with two columns labeled "Characters" and "Plot." In one column, take notes on the main characters and their interactions. In the other column, note major events and sources of conflict between the characters.

Later Kush

If YOU were there...

You live in Meroë, the capital of Kush, in 250 BC. Your father is a skilled ironworker. From him you've learned to shape iron tools and weapons. Everyone expects that you will carry on his work. If you do become an ironworker, you will likely make a good living. But you are restless. You'd like to travel down the Nile to see Egypt and the great sea beyond it. Now a neighbor who is a trader has asked you to join his next trading voyage.

Will you leave Meroë to travel? Why or why not?

BUILDING BACKGROUND The Assyrians drove the Kushites out of Egypt in the 600s BC, partly through their use of iron weapons. Although the Kushites lost control of Egypt, their kingdom did not disappear. In fact, they built up another empire in the African interior, based on trade and their own iron industry.

Kush's Economy Grows

After they lost control of Egypt, the people of Kush devoted themselves to increasing agriculture and trade, hoping to make their country rich again. Within a few centuries, Kush had indeed become a rich and powerful kingdom once more.

Kushite Metalwork
Kush's craftspeople made iron spearheads and gold jewelry like you see here.

PHOTOGRAPH © 2004
MUSEUM OF FINE ARTS, BOSTON

What You Will Learn...

Main Ideas

1. Kush's economy grew because of its iron industry and trade network.
2. Society and culture in Kush had elements borrowed from other cultures and elements unique to Kush.
3. The decline and defeat of Kush was caused by both internal and external factors.

The Big Idea

Kush developed an advanced civilization with a large trading network.

Key Terms and People
trade network, *p. 128*
merchants, *p. 128*
exports, *p. 128*
imports, *p. 128*
Queen Shanakhdakheto, *p. 129*
King Ezana, *p. 131*

HSS **6.2.8** Identify the location of the Kush civilization and describe its political, commercial, and cultural relations with Egypt.

Kush's Trade Network

Ancient Kush was at the center of a large trading network with connections to Europe, Africa, and Asia. Kush's location and production of iron goods helped make it a rich trading center.

Goods from the Mediterranean came to Kush through trade with Egypt.

In Meroë, workers made iron tools and weapons, jewelry, pottery, and other goods.

At ports on the Red Sea, merchants traded Kush's goods for luxury items like silk and glass.

Caravans from the south brought goods like leopard skins and ostrich eggs to Kush.

EGYPT

Giza

Luxor

Nubian Desert

KUSH

Meroë

Red Sea

Kush's Iron Industry

The economic center of Kush during this period was Meroë (MER-oh-wee), the kingdom's new capital. Meroë's location on the east bank of the Nile helped Kush's economy. Gold could be found nearby, as could forests of ebony and other wood. More importantly, the area around Meroë was full of iron ore deposits.

In this location the Kushites developed an iron industry. Because resources such as iron ore and wood for furnaces were easily available, the industry grew quickly.

Expansion of Trade

In time, Meroë became the center of a large **trade network**, a system of people in different lands who trade goods back and forth.

The Kushites sent goods down the Nile to Egypt. From there, Egyptian and Greek **merchants**, or traders, carried goods to ports on the Mediterranean and Red seas and to southern Africa. These goods may have eventually reached India and China.

Kush's **exports**—items sent to other regions for trade—included gold, pottery, iron tools, slaves, and ivory. Kushite merchants also exported leopard skins, ostrich feathers, and elephants. In return, the Kushites received **imports**—goods brought in from other regions—such as fine jewelry and luxury items from Egypt, Asia, and lands around the Mediterranean Sea.

READING CHECK **Drawing Inferences** What helped Kush's iron industry grow?

Society and Culture

As Kushite trade grew, merchants came into contact with people from other cultures. As a result, the people of Kush combined customs from other cultures with their own unique Kushite culture.

Kushite Culture

The most obvious influence on Kushite culture was Egypt. Many buildings in Meroë, especially temples, resembled those in Egypt. Many people in Kush worshipped Egyptian gods and wore Egyptian clothing. Like Egypt's rulers, the rulers of Kush used the title *pharaoh* and were buried in pyramids.

Many elements of Kushite culture were unique and not borrowed from anywhere else. For example, Kushite daily life and houses were different from those in other places. One Greek geographer noted some of these differences.

> "The houses in the cities are formed by interweaving split pieces of palm wood or of bricks . . . They hunt elephants, lions, and panthers. There are also serpents, which encounter elephants, and there are many other kinds of wild animals."
>
> –Strabo, from *The Geographies*

In addition to Egyptian gods, people of Kush worshipped their own gods. For example, they prayed to the lion-headed god Apedemek. Also, they developed their own written language, Meroitic. Unfortunately, historians are not able to understand this language.

Women in Kushite Society

Unlike the women of some other early societies, the women of Kush were expected to be active in their society. Like Kushite men, women worked long hours in the fields. They also raised children, cooked, and performed other household tasks. During times of war, many Kushite women fought alongside men.

Some Kushite women rose to positions of great **authority**, especially religious authority. For example, King Piankhi made his sister a powerful priestess. Later rulers followed his example and made other princesses priestesses as well. Other women from royal families led the ceremonies in which new kings were crowned.

Some Kushite women had even more power. These women served as co-rulers with their husbands or sons. A few Kushite women, such as **Queen Shanakhdakheto** (shah-nahk-dah-KEE-toh), even ruled the empire alone. Several other queens ruled Kush later, helping increase the strength and wealth of the kingdom. Throughout most of its history, however, Kush was ruled by kings.

READING CHECK **Contrasting** How was Kushite culture unlike Egyptian culture?

ACADEMIC VOCABULARY

authority power or influence

THE IMPACT TODAY

More than 50 ancient Kushite pyramids still stand near the ruins of Meroë.

BIOGRAPHY

Queen Shanakhdakheto
Ruled 170–150 BC

Historians believe Queen Shanakhdakheto was the first woman to rule Kush. But because we can't understand Meroitic writing, we know very little about Queen Shanakhdakheto. Most of what we know about her comes from carvings found in her tomb, one of the largest pyramids at Meroë. Based on these carvings, many historians think she probably gained power after her father or husband died.

Drawing Inferences What information do you think the carvings on the queen's tomb contained?

129

Rulers of Kush

Like the Egyptians, the people of Kush considered their rulers to be gods. Kush's culture was similar to Egypt's, but there were also important differences.

Like the Egyptians, Kush's rulers built pyramids, but they were much smaller and the style was different.

Kush was ruled by a few different powerful queens. Queens seem to have been more important in Kush than in Egypt.

Stone carvings were made to commemorate important buildings and events, just like in Egypt. Kush's writing system was similar to Egyptian hieroglyphics, but scholars have been unable to understand most of it.

ANALYSIS SKILL ANALYZING VISUALS

What can you see in the illustration that is similar to Egyptian culture?

Decline and Defeat

The Kushite kingdom centered at Meroë reached its height in the first century BC. Four centuries later, the empire had collapsed. Developments both inside and outside of Kush led to this downfall.

Loss of Resources

A series of problems within Kush weakened its economic power. One possible problem was that farmers allowed their cattle to overgraze the land. When the cows ate all the grass, there was nothing to hold the soil down. As a result, wind blew the soil away. Without this soil, farmers couldn't produce enough food for Kush's people.

In addition, ironmakers probably used up the forests near Meroë. As wood became scarce, furnaces shut down. Kush could no longer produce enough weapons or trade goods. As a result, Kush's military and economic power declined.

Trade Rivals

Kush was also weakened by a loss of trade. Foreign merchants set up new trade routes that went around Kush. For example, a new trade route bypassed Kush in favor of a nearby kingdom, Aksum (AHK-soom).

Rise of Aksum

Aksum was located southeast of Kush on the Red Sea, in present-day Ethiopia and Eritrea. In the first two centuries AD, Aksum grew wealthy from trade. But Aksum's wealth and power came at the expense of Kush. As Kush's power declined, Aksum became the most powerful state in the region.

By the AD 300s, Kush had lost much of its wealth and military might. Seeing that the Kushites were weak, the king of Aksum sent an army to conquer his former trade rival. In about AD 350, the Aksumite army of **King Ezana** (AY-zah-nah) destroyed Meroë and took over the kingdom of Kush.

In the late 300s, the rulers of Aksum became Christian. Their new religion reshaped culture throughout Nubia, and the last influences of Kush disappeared.

READING CHECK **Summarizing** Why did Kush's power decline?

THE IMPACT TODAY

Much of the population of Ethiopia, which includes what used to be Aksum, is still Christian.

SUMMARY AND PREVIEW From their capital at Meroë, the people of Kush controlled a powerful trading network. Next, you will learn about one of Kush's possible trading partners—India.

---

go.hrw.com
Online Quiz
KEYWORD: SQ6 HP5

Section 2 Assessment

Reviewing Ideas, Terms, and People HSS 6.2.8

1. **a. Recall** What city became Kush's third capital?
   b. Analyze Why was this capital in a good location?
2. **a. Identify** Who was **Queen Shanakhdakheto**?
   b. Compare How were Kushite and Egyptian cultures similar?
   c. Elaborate How does our inability to understand Meroitic affect our knowledge of Kush's culture?
3. **a. Identify** What kingdom conquered Kush in the AD 300s?
   b. Summarize What was the impact of new trade routes on Kush?

Critical Thinking

4. **Categorizing** Draw a diagram like this one in your notebook. Use it to list causes of the rise and causes of the fall of the Kushite kingdom centered at Meroë.

Causes of rise	Causes of fall

FOCUS ON WRITING

5. **Adding Details** Add details to your chart. What were your characters' lives like? What events caused Kush to change over time? Note events that your characters might take part in during your story.

Social Studies Skills

Analysis	Critical Thinking		Study
		Participation	

Participating in Groups

Understand the Skill

Making decisions can be difficult. It can be even harder if the decision is being made by a group. Organizing tasks and taking actions might be simpler if one person decided what to do, but that approach does not respect the desires and needs of the group's other members. Group participation is an important skill. A successful group depends on its members' ability to work together.

Learn the Skill

To be an effective part of an effective group, you and the other members need to behave in the following ways.

1 Be an active member of the group. Take part in setting the group's goals, making its decisions, planning, and taking action.

2 State your views and try to persuade others to accept them. However, be willing to listen to their views too. They have the same rights as you do. You have a duty to listen, even if you disagree.

3 Be willing to negotiate and compromise to settle differences.

Practice and Apply the Skill

You learned in Chapter 5 that trade caused Egypt to fear Kush's power. Imagine that you are a citizen of Kush. To prevent an invasion by Egypt, the king has named you to a council of merchants, farmers, craftspeople, and soldiers, a council represented by a group of your classmates. The council has been asked to create rules that will govern trade between Egypt and Kush and calm Egypt's fears. When your group has finished, answer the following questions.

1. Did the members of your group have differences of opinion about what to do? Explain. Evaluate your part in this discussion.

2. Did your group work well together to make decisions? Why or why not? Was compromise involved in your final decision? Explain.

Standards Review

Visual Summary

Use the visual summary below to help you review the main ideas of the chapter.

QUICK FACTS

Egypt dominated early Kush and forced the Kushites to pay tribute.

After Kush conquered Egypt, invaders forced the Kushites to move south to their ancient homeland.

Kush developed an advanced civilization that blended Egyptian culture with cultures from other parts of Africa.

Reviewing Terms and People

Match the words in the columns with the correct definitions listed below.

1. ebony
2. Piankhi
3. authority
4. merchant
5. export
6. import
7. Shanakhdakheto
8. trade network

a. item sent to other regions for trade

b. king who extended the Kushite empire into Egypt

c. a trader

d. dark, heavy wood

e. groups of people in different lands who trade goods back and forth

f. may have been the first woman to rule Kush by herself

g. item brought in for purchase from other regions

h. power or influence

Comprehension and Critical Thinking

SECTION 1 *(Pages 122–126)* **HSS** 6.2.8

9. a. Describe How did Nubia's physical features affect civilization in the region?

b. Analyze Why did the relationship between Kush and Egypt change more than once over the centuries?

c. Predict If an archaeologist found an artifact near the Fourth Cataract, why might he or she have difficulty deciding how to display it in a museum?

SECTION 2 *(Pages 127–131)* **HSS** 6.2.8

10. a. Identify Who was Queen Shanakhdakheto? Why don't we know more about her?

b. Compare and Contrast What are some features that Kushite and Egyptian cultures had in common? How were they different?

c. Evaluate How did two types of environmental damage contribute to the decline of Kush?

Using the Internet

go.hrw.com KEYWORD: SQ6 WH5

11. Activity: Researching Life in Ancient Nubia
Would you like to travel back in time to ancient Nubia and explore the wonders of that era? Enter the activity keyword. Then find out about the people, their customs, and their homes. Finally, imagine that you are a person living in ancient Nubia. Take notes about your imagined life and use a chart like the one below to organize your information. Write a journal entry to show what you have learned. In your journal entry, specify which parts of your life have Egyptian influences.

Activities	
Religion	
Homes	

Reading and Analysis Skills

Understanding Cause and Effect *Match each cause in List A with an effect from List B.*

List A

12. The army of Kush conquered Egypt.

13. The Nile flooded every year.

14. Meroë had large deposits of iron ore.

15. Kush and Aksum were trade rivals.

16. The Assyrians' iron weapons were better than the Kushites' bronze weapons.

List B

a. Kush developed an iron industry.

b. Aksum conquered Kush.

c. The Kushites were driven out of Egypt.

d. The soils of Nubia were very fertile.

e. The Kushite dynasty took power.

Reviewing Themes

17. Geography How did Kush's location on the Nile shape its early history?

18. Economics What led to the creation of Africa's first iron industry in Kush?

Social Studies Skills

19. Developing Group Interaction Skills Working with a small group of your classmates, imagine that you are the leaders of a small village located between Egypt and Kush. The rulers of the two countries have demanded that you choose which country you want to belong to. As a group, decide which country you will join. Remember to look at benefits and challenges associated with joining each country before you make your decision. You may want to use a chart like the one below to help your group organize your thoughts and make your decision.

	Benefits	Challenges
Egypt		
Kush		

FOCUS ON WRITING

20. Writing Your Story Use the notes you have taken to write your short story about a character from Kush. First, introduce your characters and describe them to readers. In your next paragraph, develop the plot of your story by telling about the conflicts that arise between the characters. In a final paragraph, describe how these conflicts come to a climax and eventually get resolved. Use as many concrete, descriptive details as possible to make your characters and your story come alive for your readers.

Standards Assessment

DIRECTIONS: *Read each question, and write the letter of the best response.*

1 Geography greatly influenced the development of Kushite society. Which of the following was *not* a benefit that geography provided for Kush?

  A fertile soil for farming

  B a port on the Red Sea

  C protection against invaders for many years

  D valuable gold, copper, and wood for trade

2 The ancient kingdom of Kush arose in what region?

  A Egypt

  B Nubia

  C Aksum

  D Mesopotamia

3 Which of the following statements about the relationship of Egypt and Kush is *not* true?

  A Egypt ruled Kush for many centuries.

  B Kush was an important trading partner of Egypt.

  C Egypt sent the first people to colonize Kush.

  D Kush ruled Egypt for a period of time.

4 How did Egypt influence Kush?

  A Egypt taught Kush how to raise cattle.

  B Kush adopted Christianity.

  C Egypt taught Kush to make iron products.

  D Kush learned about pyramids from Egypt.

5 The fall of the Kushite civilization resulted from all of the following events *except*

  A the conquest of Kush by Egypt.

  B Kush's exhaustion of its natural resources.

  C new trade routes that bypassed Kush.

  D the rise of a rival kingdom in the region.

Connecting with Past Learnings

6 You recently learned about the development of civilization in Sumer. Kush and Sumer had all of the following in common *except*

  A the importance of farming in their early civilization.

  B the rise of manufacturing and crafts.

  C involvement in trade.

  D the Meroitic writing system.

7 Kush, Egypt, and Sumer all share which of the following characteristics?

  A All developed along rivers.

  B All worshipped the same gods.

  C All used the same money.

  D All spoke the same language.

Assignment

Write a description of a place—a city, village, building, or monument—in ancient Mesopotamia or Africa.

TIP | **Organizing Details**

Organize the details you gather in one of these ways.

- **Spatial Order** Arrange details according to where they are. You can describe things from right to left, top to bottom, or faraway to close up.
- **Chronological Order** Arrange details in the order they occurred or in the order that you experienced them.
- **Order of Importance** Arrange details from the most to least important or vice versa.

ELA **Writing 6.2.0** Students write descriptive texts.

A Description of a Historical Place

If a picture is worth a thousand words, then a thousand words could add up to a good description. Writers turn to description when they want to explain what a place is like—what you would see if you were there, or what you might hear, smell, or touch.

1. Prewrite

Picking a Subject and a Main Idea

Think about the civilizations of ancient Mesopotamia and Africa. Which civilization seems most interesting to you? What villages, cities, or buildings seem interesting? Select one place and use this textbook, the Internet, or sources in your library to find out more about it.

You also need to decide on your point of view about your subject. For example, was this place scary, exciting, or overwhelming?

Choosing Details

As you conduct your research, look for details to show your readers what it would have been like to actually be in that place.

- **Sensory Details** What color(s) do you associate with your subject? What shape or shapes do you see? What sounds would you hear if you were there? What could you touch—rough walls, dry grass, a smooth, polished stone?
- **Factual Details** How big was this place? Where was it located? When did it exist? If people were there, what were they doing?

When you choose the details to use in your description, think about your point of view on this place. If it was exciting, choose details that will help you show that.

2. Write

This framework will help you use your notes to write a first draft.

A Writer's Framework

Introduction
- Identify your subject and your point of view on it.
- Give your readers any background information that they might need.

Body
- Describe your subject, using sensory and factual details.
- Follow a consistent and logical order.

Conclusion
- Briefly summarize the most important details about the place.
- Reveal your point of view about the place.

3. Evaluate and Revise

Evaluating

Use the following questions to discover ways to improve your paper.

Evaluation Questions for a Description of a Place

- Do you immediately catch the reader's interest?
- Do you use sensory and factual details that work together to create a vivid picture of your subject?
- Do you clearly state your point of view or most important idea?

- Is the information organized clearly?
- Do you end the description by summarizing the most important details?

TIP **Showing Location** When describing the physical appearance of something, make sure you use precise words and phrases to explain where a feature is located. Some useful words and phrases for explaining location are *below, beside, down, on top, over, next to, to the right,* and *to the left.*

Revising

We often help others understand or imagine something by making a comparison. Sometimes we compare two things that are really very much alike. For example, "The city grew like San Diego did. It spread along a protected harbor." At other times we compare two things that are not alike. These comparisons are called figures of speech, and they can help your readers see something in an interesting way.

- Similes compare two unlike things by using words such as *like* or *so.* **EXAMPLE** *The city center curved around the harbor like a crescent moon.*
- Metaphors compare two unlike things by saying one is the other. **EXAMPLE** *The city was the queen of the region.*

When you evaluate and revise your description, look for ways you can make your subject clearer by comparing it to something else.

4. Proofread and Publish

- Make sure you use commas correctly with a list of details. **EXAMPLE** *The temple was 67 feet high, 35 feet wide, and 40 feet deep.*
- Share your paper with students who wrote about a similar place. What details do your descriptions share? How are they different?
- Find or create a picture of the place you have described. Ask a classmate or a family member to read your description and compare it to the picture.

Practice and Apply

Use the steps and strategies outlined in this workshop to write your description of a place in ancient Mesopotamia or Africa.

Civilization in India and China

What You Will Learn...

Two of the earliest civilizations of the ancient world arose in India and in China. In both of these places, river valleys provided the setting for the development of civilization. The Indians and Chinese built large empires and made many advances in science, art, and learning.

These civilizations also gave rise to new spiritual traditions. Two of the world's major religions—Hinduism and Buddhism—began in India. In China, the scholars Confucius and Laozi developed ideas that influenced Chinese thinking and society for more than 2,000 years.

In the next two chapters, you will learn about the advanced civilizations and cultures of India and China.

Explore the Art

In this scene, the Chinese emperor Shi Huangdi oversees the building of a massive wall in 220 BC. Why do you think people might build such a giant barrier?

Ancient India

California Standards

History–Social Science

6.5 Students analyze the geographic, political, economic, religious, and social structures of the early civilizations of India.

English–Language Arts

Writing 6.1.0 Exhibit awareness of the audience and purpose.

Reading 6.2.0 Students read and understand grade-level-appropriate material.

FOCUS ON WRITING

An Illustrated Poster Ancient India was a fascinating place. It was the home of amazing cities, the site of strong empires, and the birthplace of major religions. As you read this chapter, think about how you could illustrate one aspect of Indian culture in a poster. When you finish the chapter, you will design such a poster, which will include captions that explain the illustrations you have drawn.

c. 2600 BC
Urban Harappan civilization reaches maturity.

CHAPTER EVENTS

2300 BC

WORLD EVENTS

2200 BC
The Old Kingdom ends in Egypt.

HOLT

History's Impact
▶ **video series**
Watch the video to understand the impact of Buddhism as a major world religion.

What You Will Learn...

In this chapter you will learn about the ancient civilization of India, the birthplace of two major world religions—Hinduism and Buddhism. In this photo, crowds of Hindus gather to bathe in the sacred Ganges River.

1500s BC
Aryans begin migrating into India.

c. 1250 BC
Central tenets of Hinduism take shape.

c. 563 BC
Prince Siddhartha Gautama, or the Buddha, is born in northern India.

c. AD 320
Chandragupta founds the Gupta Empire.

1500 BC	1000 BC	500 BC	BC 1 AD	AD 500

c. 1500 BC
The Shang Dynasty is established in China.

334 BC
Alexander the Great begins his conquests.

AD 391 All non-Christian religions are banned in the Roman Empire.

ANCIENT INDIA **141**

Reading Social Studies

by Kylene Beers

Economics	Geography	Politics	Religion	Society and Culture	Science and Technology

Focus on Themes This chapter outlines and describes the development of India. You will read about India's first civilization, called the Harappan civilization, so advanced that the people had indoor bathrooms and a writing system. You will also learn about the **society and culture** that restricted whom Indian people could talk with or marry. Finally, you will read about the **religions** and empires that united India and about the art and literature that the Indians created.

Inferences about History

Focus on Reading What's the difference between a good guess and a weak guess? A good guess is an *educated* guess. In other words, the guess is based on some knowledge or information. That's what an inference is, an educated guess.

Making Inferences About What You Read On pages 86 and 87, you practiced drawing conclusions. You use almost the same process to make an inference: combine information from your reading with what you already know, and make an educated guess about what it all means. Once you have made several inferences, you may be able to draw a conclusion that ties them all together.

Additional reading support can be found in the

Reader and Study Guide

Question **Why did Aryan priests have rules for performing sacrifices?**

Inside the Text	Outside the Text
• Sacred texts tell how to perform sacrifices. • Priests sacrificed animals in fire. • Sacrifices were offerings to the gods.	• Other religions have duties only priests can perform. • Many ancient societies believed sacrifices helped keep the gods happy.

Steps for Making Inferences

1. Ask a question.
2. Note information "Inside the Text."
3. Note information "Outside the Text."
4. **Use both sets of information to make an educated guess, or inference.**

Inference The Aryans believed that performing a sacrifice incorrectly might anger the gods.

You Try It!

The following passage is from the chapter you are about to read. Read the passage and then answer the questions that follow.

Harappan Achievements

Harappan civilization was very advanced. Most houses had bathrooms with indoor plumbing. Artisans made excellent pottery, jewelry, ivory objects, and cotton clothing. They used high-quality tools and developed a system of weights and measures.

From Chapter 6, p. 148

Harappans also developed India's first known writing system. However, scholars have not yet learned to read this language, so we know very little about Harappan society. Unlike Mesopotamia or Egypt, for example, there are no large religious monuments or palaces, so the relationship between the people and their government is less clear. On the other hand, the remarkable similarity of material culture from widely scattered Harappan sites suggests a high level of social control.

Harappan civilization ended by the early 1700s BC, but no one is sure why.

Answer the following questions to make inferences about Harappan society.

1. Do you think that the Harappan language was closely related to the languages spoken in India today? Consider the information inside the text and things you have learned outside the text to make an inference about the Harappan language.

2. What have you just learned about Harappan achievements? Think back to other civilizations you have studied that made similar achievements. What allowed those civilizations to make their achievements? From this, what can you infer about earlier Harappan society?

As you read Chapter 6, use the information you find in the text to make inferences about Indian society.

Key Terms and People

Chapter 6

Section 1
subcontinent *(p. 144)*
monsoons *(p. 145)*
Sanskrit *(p. 149)*

Section 2
caste system *(p. 151)*
Hinduism *(p. 153)*
reincarnation *(p. 153)*
karma *(p. 154)*
Jainism *(p. 155)*
nonviolence *(p. 155)*

Section 3
fasting *(p. 157)*
meditation *(p. 157)*
the Buddha *(p. 157)*
Buddhism *(p. 158)*
nirvana *(p. 158)*
missionaries *(p. 160)*

Section 4
Chandragupta Maurya *(p. 162)*
Asoka *(p. 163)*
Chandragupta II *(p. 164)*

Section 5
metallurgy *(p. 170)*
alloys *(p. 170)*
Hindu-Arabic numerals *(p. 170)*
inoculation *(p. 170)*
astronomy *(p. 171)*

Academic Vocabulary

Success in school is related to knowing academic vocabulary— the words that are frequently used in school assignments and discussions. In this chapter, you will learn the following academic words:

establish *(p. 164)*
process *(p. 170)*

Geography and Early India

What You Will Learn...

Main Ideas

1. The geography of India includes high mountains, great rivers, and heavy seasonal rain.
2. Harappan civilization developed along the Indus River.
3. The Aryan invasion of India changed the region's civilization.

The Big Idea

Indian civilization first developed on the Indus River.

Key Terms

subcontinent, *p. 144*
monsoons, *p. 145*
Sanskrit, *p. 149*

HSS **6.5.1** Locate and describe the major river system and discuss the physical setting that supported the rise of this civilization.

6.5.2 Discuss the significance of the Aryan invasions.

If YOU were there...

Your people are nomadic herders in southern Asia about 1200 BC. You live in a river valley with plenty of water and grass for your cattle. Besides looking after cattle, you spend time learning to recite sacred texts from the village elders. They say these words hold your people's history. One day, it will be your duty to teach them to your own children.

Why is it important to pass on these words?

BUILDING BACKGROUND Like Mesopotamia and Egypt, India was home to one of the world's first civilizations. Like other early civilizations, the one in India grew up in a river valley. But the society that eventually developed in India was very different from the ones that developed elsewhere.

Geography of India

Look at a map of Asia in the atlas of this book. Do you see the large, roughly triangular landmass that juts out from the center of the southern part of the continent? That is India. It was the location of one of the world's earliest civilizations.

Landforms and Rivers

India is huge. In fact, it is so big that many geographers call it a subcontinent. A **subcontinent** is a large landmass that is smaller than a continent. Subcontinents are usually separated from the rest of their continents by physical features. If you look at the map on the next page, for example, you can see that mountains largely separate India from the rest of Asia.

Among the mountains of northern India are the Himalayas, the highest mountains in the world. To the west are the Hindu Kush. Though these mountains made it hard to enter India, invaders have historically found a few paths through them.

The highest mountains in the world, the Himalayas, separate India from the rest of Asia.

Hindu Kush

HIMALAYAS

Kanchenjunga
28,208 ft.
(8,598 m)

Indus River

Thar Desert
(Great Indian Desert)

Yamuna River

Ganges River

Ghaghara River

Ganges R.

Jamuna R.

Brahmaputra River

Tropic of Cancer

India is a huge peninsula, so large it's called a subcontinent.

20° N

Vindhya Range

Ganges Delta

Godavari

Arabian
Sea

WESTERN GHATS

DECCAN
PLATEAU

EASTERN GHATS

70° E

Bay of
Bengal

ELEVATION

Feet	Meters
13,120	4,000
6,560	2,000
1,640	500
656	200
(Sea level) 0	0 (Sea level)
Below sea level	Below sea level

Laccadive
Islands

Malabar Coast

Coromandel Coast

Andaman
Islands

Andaman
Sea

INDIAN
OCEAN

10° N

10° N

N
W   E
S

← Dry monsoon air flow (Winter)

→ Wet monsoon air flow (Summer)

0   150   300 Miles
0   150   300 Kilometers

80° E

GEOGRAPHY SKILLS | **INTERPRETING MAPS**

1. Place When do the wet monsoons come to India?
2. Location What large plateau occupies the heart of India?

To the west of the Himalayas is a vast desert. Much of the rest of India is covered by fertile plains and rugged plateaus.

Several major rivers flow out of the Himalayas. The valleys and fertile plains of these rivers were the locations of India's early civilizations. The Indus is located in present-day Pakistan, west of India. When heavy snows in the Himalayas melted, the Indus flooded. As in Mesopotamia and Egypt, the flooding left behind a layer of fertile silt. The silt created ideal farmland for early settlers.

Climate

Most of India has a hot and humid climate. This climate is heavily influenced by India's **monsoons**, seasonal wind patterns that cause wet and dry seasons.

In the summer, monsoon winds blow into India from the Indian Ocean, bringing heavy rains that can cause terrible floods. Some parts of India receive as much as 100 or even 200 inches of rain during this time. In the winter, winds blow down from the mountains. This forces moisture out of India and creates warm, dry winters.

READING CHECK **Drawing Conclusions**
How do you think monsoons affected settlement in India?

Harappan Civilization

Historians call the civilization that grew up in the Indus River Valley the Harappan (huh-RA-puhn) civilization. Centered along the Indus, the civilization also controlled large areas on both sides of the river.

Like other ancient societies you have studied, the Harappan civilization grew as irrigation and agriculture improved. As farmers began to produce surpluses of food, towns and cities appeared in India.

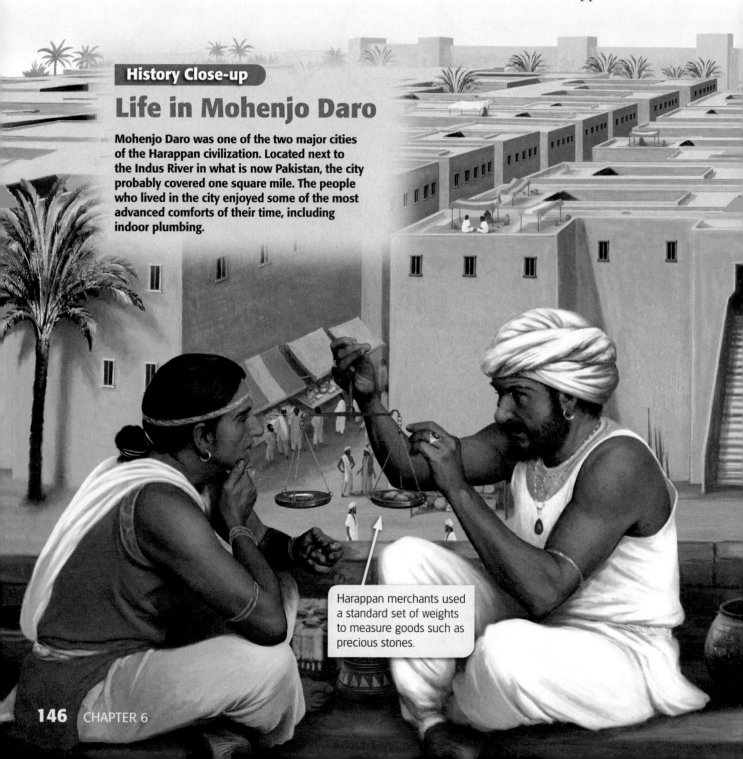

History Close-up

Life in Mohenjo Daro

Mohenjo Daro was one of the two major cities of the Harappan civilization. Located next to the Indus River in what is now Pakistan, the city probably covered one square mile. The people who lived in the city enjoyed some of the most advanced comforts of their time, including indoor plumbing.

Harappan merchants used a standard set of weights to measure goods such as precious stones.

India's Early Cities

The Harappan civilization was named after the modern city of Harappa (huh-RA-puh), Pakistan. It was near this city that ruins of the civilization were first discovered. From studying these ruins, archaeologists currently estimate that the civilization thrived between 2300 and 1700 BC.

The greatest sources of information we have about Harappan civilization are the ruins of two large cities, Harappa and Mohenjo Daro (mo-HEN-joh DAR-oh). The two cities lay more than 300 miles apart but were remarkably similar. More recent sources include the ruins discovered at Kalibangan, Dholavira, and the port of Lothal, in addition to the 2,600 rural settlements excavated in northwest India.

Both Harappa and Mohenjo Daro were well planned. Each stood near a towering fortress. From these fortresses, defenders could look down on the cities' brick streets, which crossed at right angles and were lined with storehouses, workshops, market stalls, and houses. In addition, both cities had many public wells.

Next to the city was a huge citadel, or fortress, to guard against invasions.

The houses of Mohenjo Daro had flat roofs. Many had staircases that allowed people to climb to the roof from the street.

The city's streets were paved and well drained. They met at right angles, creating a grid pattern.

Harappan Civilization

HIMALAYAS

Harappa

Mohenjo Daro

Thar Desert

Arabian Sea

N W E S

- Harappan civilization
- • Major settlement

0   100   200 Miles
0   100 200 Kilometers

ANALYSIS SKILL ANALYZING VISUALS

What in this picture suggests that Mohenjo Daro was a well-planned city?

Harappan Achievements

Harappan civilization was very advanced. Most houses had bathrooms with indoor plumbing. Artisans made excellent pottery, jewelry, ivory objects, and cotton clothing. They used high-quality tools and developed a system of weights and measures.

Harappans also developed India's first known writing system. However, scholars have not yet learned to read this language, so we know very little about Harappan society. Unlike Mesopotamia or Egypt, for example, there are no large religious monuments or palaces, so the relationship between the people and their government is less clear. On the other hand, the remarkable similarity of material culture from widely scattered Harappan sites suggests a high level of social control.

Harappan civilization ended by the early 1700s BC, but no one is sure why. Perhaps invaders destroyed the cities or natural disasters, like floods or earthquakes, caused the civilization to collapse.

READING CHECK Analyzing Why don't we know much about Harappan civilization?

Harappan Art

Like other ancient peoples, the Harappans made small seals like the one below that were used to stamp goods. They also used clay pots like the one at right decorated with a goat.

Aryan Invasion

Not long after the Harappan civilization crumbled, a new group took power in the Indus Valley. They were called the Aryans (AIR-ee-uhnz). Historians have long debated the origins of the Aryans. Some historians believe they came from Central Asia, but others disagree. Wherever the Aryans came from, some people think they may have helped end the Harappan civilization.

Invaders from the West

The Aryans were skilled warriors. Using chariots and advanced weapons, these invaders took new territory. By 1200 BC Aryan warriors had swept through the Hindu Kush and taken control of the entire Indus Valley. From there they moved east to the Ganges River Valley.

Much of what we know about Aryan society comes from religious writings known as the Vedas (VAY-duhs). These collections of poems, hymns, myths, and rituals were written by Aryan priests. You will read more about the Vedas later in this chapter.

Government and Society

As nomads, the Aryans took along their herds of animals as they moved. But over time, they settled in villages and began to farm. Unlike the Harappans, they did not build big cities.

The Aryan political system was also different from the Harappan system. The Aryans lived in small communities, based mostly on family ties. No single ruling authority existed. Instead, each group had its own leader, often a skilled warrior.

Aryan villages were governed by rajas (RAH-juhz). A raja was a leader who ruled a village and the land around it. Villagers farmed some of this land for the raja. They used other sections as pastures for their cows, horses, sheep, and goats.

Although many rajas were related, they didn't always get along. Sometimes rajas joined forces before fighting a common enemy. Other times, however, rajas went to war against each other. In fact, Aryan groups fought each other nearly as often as they fought outsiders.

Language

The first Aryan settlers did not read or write. Because of this, they had to memorize the sacred texts that were important in their culture, such as the Vedas. If people forgot these sacred texts, the works would be lost forever.

The language in which these Aryan sacred texts were composed was **Sanskrit**, the most important language of ancient India. At first, Sanskrit was only a spoken language. Eventually, however, people figured out how to write it down so they could keep records. These Sanskrit records are a major source of information about Aryan society. Sanskrit is no longer widely spoken today, but it is the root of many modern South Asian languages.

READING CHECK **Identifying** What source provides much of the information we have about the Aryans?

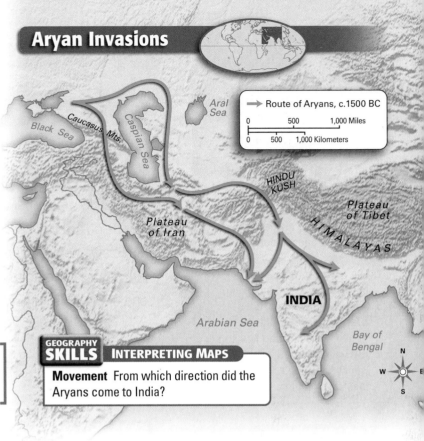

Aryan Invasions

→ Route of Aryans, c.1500 BC

0   500   1,000 Miles
0   500   1,000 Kilometers

GEOGRAPHY SKILLS **INTERPRETING MAPS**

Movement From which direction did the Aryans come to India?

SUMMARY AND PREVIEW The earliest civilizations in India were centered on the Indus Valley. First the Harappans and then the Aryans lived in this fertile valley. In the next section, you will learn about a new religion that developed in the Indus Valley after the Aryans settled there—Hinduism.

THE IMPACT TODAY

Hindi, the most widely spoken Indian language, is based on Sanskrit.

Section 1 Assessment

Reviewing Ideas, Terms, and People **HSS** 6.5.1, 6.5.2

1. **a. Define** What are **monsoons**?
   b. Contrast How does northern India differ from the rest of the region?
   c. Elaborate Why is India called a **subcontinent**?
2. **a. Recall** Where did Harappan civilization develop?
   b. Analyze What is one reason that scholars do not completely understand some important parts of Harappan society?
3. **a. Identify** Who were the Aryans?
   b. Contrast How was Aryan society different from Harappan society?

Critical Thinking

4. **Categorizing** Draw a diagram like this one. Use it to show how Indian society changed after the Aryan invasion.

India before the invasion → India after the invasion

FOCUS ON WRITING

5. **Illustrating Geography and Early Civilizations** This section described two possible topics for your poster: geography and early civilizations. Which of them is more interesting to you? Write down some ideas for a poster about your chosen topic.

Origins of Hinduism

If YOU were there...

Your family are skillful weavers who make beautiful cotton cloth. You belong to the class in Aryan society who are traders, farmers, and craftspeople. Often the raja of your town leads the warriors into battle. You admire their bravery but know you can never be one of them. To be an Aryan warrior, you must be born into that noble class. Instead, you have your own duty to carry out.

How do you feel about remaining a weaver?

BUILDING BACKGROUND As the Aryans moved into India, they developed a strict system of social classes. As the Aryans' influence spread through India, so did their class system. Before long, this class system was a key part of Indian society.

Indian Society Divides

As Aryan society became more complex, their society became divided into groups. For the most part, these groups were organized by people's occupations. Strict rules developed about how people of different groups could interact. As time passed, these rules became stricter and became central to Indian society.

The *Varnas*

According to the Vedas, there were four main *varnas*, or social divisions, in Aryan society. These *varnas* were:

- Brahmins (BRAH-muhns), or priests,
- Kshatriyas (KSHA-tree-uhs), or rulers and warriors,
- Vaisyas (VYSH-yuhs), or farmers, craftspeople, and traders, and
- Sudras (SOO-drahs), or laborers and non-Aryans.

The Brahmins were seen as the highest ranking because they performed rituals for the gods. This gave the Brahmins great influence over the other *varnas*.

The Brahmins were seen as the highest ranking because they performed rituals for the gods. This gave the Brahmins great influence over the other *varnas*.

The Caste System

As the rules of interaction between *varnas* got stricter, the Aryan social order became more complex. In time, each of the four *varnas* in Aryan society was further divided into many castes, or groups. This **caste system** divided Indian society into groups based on a person's birth, wealth, or occupation. At one time, some 3,000 separate castes existed in India.

The caste to which a person belonged determined his or her place in society. However, this ordering was by no means permanent. Over time, individual castes gained or lost favor in society as caste members gained wealth or power. On rare occasions, people could change caste.

Caste Rules

To keep their classes distinct, the Aryans developed sutras, or guides, which listed all the rules for the caste system. For example, people were not allowed to marry anyone from a different class. It was even forbidden for people from one class to eat with people from another. People who broke the caste rules could be banned from their homes and their castes, which would make them untouchables. Because of these rules, people spent almost all of their time with others in their same class.

READING CHECK Drawing Inferences How did a person become a member of a caste?

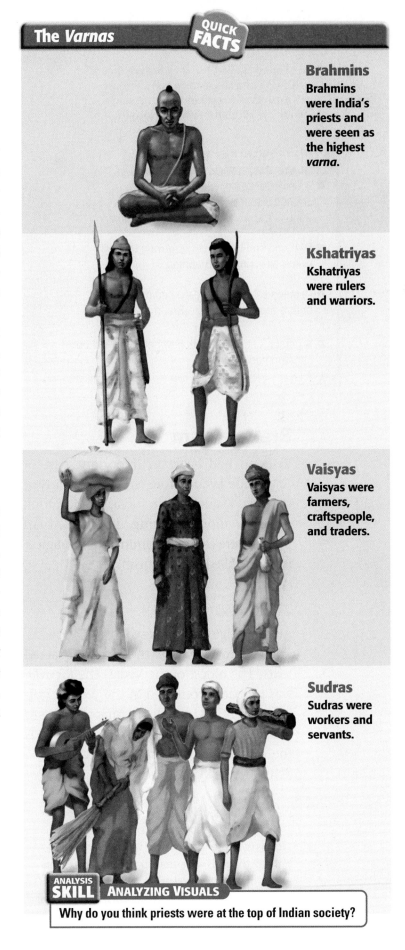

The *Varnas*

QUICK FACTS

Brahmins
Brahmins were India's priests and were seen as the highest *varna.*

Kshatriyas
Kshatriyas were rulers and warriors.

Vaisyas
Vaisyas were farmers, craftspeople, and traders.

Sudras
Sudras were workers and servants.

ANALYSIS SKILL **ANALYZING VISUALS**

Why do you think priests were at the top of Indian society?

Hindu Deities and Beliefs

Hindus believe in many deities, but they believe that all the deities are aspects of a single universal spirit called Brahman. Three aspects of Brahman are particularly important in Hinduism—Brahma, Siva, and Vishnu.

Major Beliefs of Hinduism

- A universal spirit called Brahman created the universe and everything in it. Everything in the world is just a part of Brahman.

- Every person has a soul or *atman* that will eventually join with Brahman.

- People's souls are reincarnated many times before they can join with Brahman.

- A person's karma affects how he or she will be reincarnated.

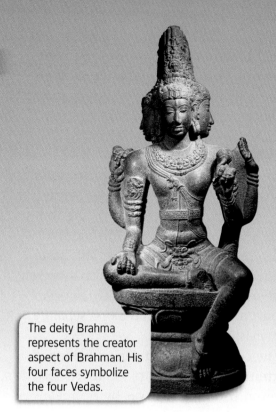

The deity Brahma represents the creator aspect of Brahman. His four faces symbolize the four Vedas.

Brahmanism

Religion had been an important part of Aryan life even before the Aryans moved to India. Eventually, in India, religion took on even more meaning. Because Aryan priests were called Brahmins, their religion is often called Brahmanism.

The Vedas

Aryan religion was based on the Vedas. There are four Vedas, each containing sacred texts. The oldest of the Vedas, the *Rigveda*, was probably compiled in the second millennium BC. It includes hymns of praise to many deities. This passage, for example, is the opening of a hymn praising Indra, a deity of the sky and war.

> "The one who is first and possessed of wisdom when born; the god who strove to protect the gods with strength; the one before whose force the two worlds were afraid because of the greatness of his virility [power]: he, O people, is Indra."
>
> –from the *Rigveda*, in *Reading about the World, Volume I*, edited by Paul Brians, et al

Vedic Texts

Over the centuries, Aryan Brahmins wrote down their thoughts about the Vedas. In time these thoughts were compiled into collections called Vedic texts.

One collection of Vedic texts describes Aryan religious rituals. For example, it describes how sacrifices should be performed. Priests placed animals, food, or drinks to be sacrificed in a fire. The Aryans believed that the fire would carry these offerings to the deities.

A second collection of Vedic texts describes secret rituals that only certain people could perform. In fact, the rituals were so secret that they had to be done in the forest, far from other people.

The final group of Vedic texts are the Upanishads (oo-PAHN-ee-shads), most of which were written by about 600 BC. These writings are reflections on the Vedas by religious students and teachers.

READING CHECK **Finding Main Ideas** What are the Vedic texts?

Siva, the destroyer aspect of Brahman, is usually shown with four arms and three eyes. Here he is shown dancing on the back of a demon he has defeated.

Vishnu is the preserver aspect of Brahman. In his four arms, he carries a conch shell, a mace, and a discus, symbols of his power and greatness.

Hinduism Develops

The Vedas, the Upanishads, and the other Vedic texts remained the basis of Indian religion for centuries. Eventually, however, the ideas of these sacred texts began to blend with ideas from other cultures. People from Persia and other kingdoms in Central Asia, for example, brought their ideas to India. In time, this blending of ideas created a religion called **Hinduism**, the largest religion in India today.

Hindu Beliefs

The Hindus believe in many deities. Among them are three major deities: Brahma the Creator, Siva the Destroyer, and Vishnu the Preserver. At the same time, however, Hindus believe that each deity is part of a single universal spirit called Brahman. They believe that Brahman created the world and preserves it. Deities like Brahma, Siva, and Vishnu represent different aspects of Brahman. In fact, Hindus believe that everything in the world is part of Brahman.

Life and Rebirth

According to Hindu teachings, everyone has a soul, or *atman*, inside them. This soul holds the person's personality, the qualities that make them who they are. Hindus believe that a person's ultimate goal should be to reunite that soul with Brahman, the universal spirit.

Hindus believe that their souls will eventually join Brahman because the world we live in is an illusion. Brahman is the only reality. The Upanishads taught that people must try to see through the illusion of the world. Since it is hard to see through illusions, it can take several lifetimes. That is why Hindus believe that souls are born and reborn many times, each time in a new body. This process of rebirth is called **reincarnation**.

Hinduism and the Caste System

According to the traditional Hindu view of reincarnation, a person who has died is reborn in a new physical form.

More than 800 million people in India practice Hinduism today.

The type of form depends upon his or her **karma**, the effects that good or bad actions have on a person's soul. Evil actions during one's life will build bad karma. A person with bad karma will be born into a lower caste or life form.

In contrast, good actions build good karma. People with good karma are born into a higher caste in their next lives. In time, good karma will bring salvation, or freedom from life's worries and the cycle of rebirth. This salvation is called *moksha*.

Hinduism taught that each person had a duty to accept his or her place in the world without complaint. This is called obeying one's *dharma*. People could build good karma by fulfilling the duties required of their specific caste. Through reincarnation, Hinduism offered rewards to those who lived good lives. Even untouchables could be reborn into a higher caste.

Hinduism was popular at all levels of Hindu society, through all four *varnas*. By teaching people to accept their places in life, Hinduism helped preserve the caste system in India.

READING CHECK **Summarizing** What determined how a person would be reborn?

LINKING TO TODAY

Nonviolence

In modern times, nonviolence has been a powerful tool for social protest. Mohandas Gandhi led a long nonviolent struggle against British rule in India. This movement helped India win its independence in 1947. About 10 years later, Martin Luther King Jr. adopted Gandhi's nonviolent methods in his struggle to win civil rights for African Americans. Then, in the 1960s, César Chávez organized a campaign of nonviolence to protest the treatment of farm workers in California. These three leaders proved that people can bring about social change without using violence. As Chávez once explained, "Nonviolence is not inaction. It is not for the timid or the weak. It is hard work. It is the patience to win."

Mohandas Gandhi (top), Martin Luther King Jr. (above), and César Chávez (right)

ANALYSIS SKILL **ANALYZING INFORMATION**

How did these three leaders prove that nonviolence is a powerful tool for social change?

Jains React to Hinduism

Although Hinduism was widely followed in India, not everyone agreed with its beliefs. Some unsatisfied people and groups looked for new religious ideas. One such group was the Jains (JYNZ), believers in a religion called Jainism (JY-ni-zuhm).

Jainism was based on the teachings of a man named Mahavira. Born into the Kshatriya *varna* around 599 BC, he was unhappy with the control of religion by the Brahmins, whom he thought put too much emphasis on rituals. Mahavira gave up his life of luxury, became a monk, and established the principles of Jainism.

The Jains try to live by four principles: injure no life, tell the truth, do not steal, and own no property. In their efforts not to injure anyone or anything, the Jains practice **nonviolence**, or the avoidance of violent actions. The Sanskrit word for this nonviolence is *ahimsa* (uh-HIM-sah). Many Hindus also practice *ahimsa*.

The Jains' emphasis on nonviolence comes from their belief that everything is alive and part of the cycle of rebirth. Jains are very serious about not injuring or killing any creature—humans, animals, insects, or even plants. They do not believe in animal sacrifice, like the ones the ancient Brahmins performed. Because they don't want to hurt living creatures, Jains are vegetarians. They do not eat any food that comes from animals.

READING CHECK Identifying Points of View
Why do Jains avoid eating meat?

SUMMARY AND PREVIEW You have learned about two religions that developed in India—Hinduism and Jainism. In Section 3, you will learn about another religion that began there—Buddhism.

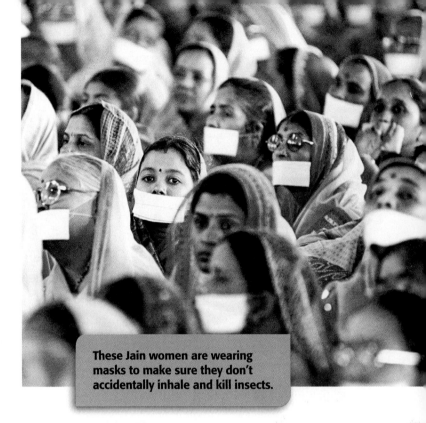

These Jain women are wearing masks to make sure they don't accidentally inhale and kill insects.

go.hrw.com
Online Quiz
KEYWORD: SQ6 HP6

Section 2 Assessment

Reviewing Ideas, Terms, and People HSS 6.5.3, 6.5.4

1. **a. Identify** What is the **caste system**?
   b. Explain Why did strict caste rules develop?
2. **a. Identify** What does the *Rigveda* include?
   b. Analyze What role did sacrifice play in Aryan society?
3. **a. Define** What is **karma**?
   b. Sequence How did Brahmanism develop into **Hinduism**?
   c. Elaborate How does Hinduism reinforce followers' willingness to remain within their castes?
4. **a. Recall** What are the four main teachings of **Jainism**?
   b. Predict How do you think the idea of **nonviolence** affected the daily lives of Jains in ancient India?

Critical Thinking

5. **Categorizing** Draw a graphic organizer like the one shown here. In each box, identify one of the four *varnas* of Aryan society. Below the name, list the people who belonged to that class.

FOCUS ON WRITING

6. **Illustrating Hinduism** Now you have a new possible topic for your poster. How might you explain a complex religion like Hinduism?

Origins of Buddhism

What You Will Learn...

Main Ideas

1. Siddhartha Gautama searched for wisdom in many ways.
2. The teachings of Buddhism deal with finding peace.
3. Buddhism spread far from where it began in India.

The Big Idea

Buddhism began in India and became a major religion.

Key Terms and People

fasting, *p. 157*
meditation, *p. 157*
the Buddha, *p. 157*
Buddhism, *p. 158*
nirvana, *p. 158*
missionaries, *p. 160*

HSS 6.5.5 Know the life and moral teachings of the Buddha and how Buddhism spread in India, Ceylon, and Central Asia.

If YOU were there...

You are a trader traveling in northern India in about 520 BC. As you pass through a town, you see a crowd of people sitting silently in the shade of a huge tree. A man sitting at the foot of the tree begins to speak about how one ought to live. His words are like nothing you have heard from the Hindu priests.

Will you stay to listen? Why or why not?

BUILDING BACKGROUND The Jains were not the only ones to break from Hinduism. In the 500s BC a young Indian prince attracted many people to his teachings about how people should live.

Siddhartha's Search for Wisdom

In the late 500s BC a restless young man, dissatisfied with the teachings of Hinduism, began to ask his own questions about life and religious matters. In time, he found answers. These answers attracted many followers, and the young man's ideas became the foundation of a major new religion in India.

The Quest for Answers

The restless young man was Siddhartha Gautama (si-DAHR-tuh GAU-tuh-muh). Born around 563 BC in northern India, near the Himalayas, Siddhartha was a prince who grew up in luxury. Born a Kshatriya, a member of the warrior class, Siddhartha never had to struggle with the problems that many people of his time faced. However, Siddhartha was not satisfied. He felt that something was missing in his life.

Siddhartha looked around him and saw how hard other people had to work and how much they suffered. He saw people grieving for lost loved ones and wondered why there was so much pain in the world. As a result, Siddhartha began to ask questions about the meaning of human life.

The Great Departure

In this painting, Prince Siddhartha leaves his palace to search for the true meaning of life, an event known as the Great Departure. Special helpers called *ganas* hold his horse's hooves so he won't awaken anyone.

Before Siddhartha reached age 30, he left his home and family to look for answers. His journey took him to many regions in India. Wherever he traveled, he had discussions with priests and people known for their wisdom. Yet no one could give convincing answers to Siddhartha's questions.

The Buddha Finds Enlightenment

Siddhartha did not give up. Instead, he became even more determined to find the answers he was seeking. For several years, he wandered in search of answers.

Siddhartha wanted to free his mind from daily concerns. For a while, he did not even wash himself. He also started **fasting**, or going without food. He devoted much of his time to **meditation**, the focusing of the mind on spiritual ideas.

According to legend, Siddhartha spent six years wandering throughout India. He eventually came to a place near the town of Gaya, close to the Ganges River. There, he sat down under a tree and meditated.

After seven weeks of deep meditation, he suddenly had the answers that he had been looking for. He realized that human suffering comes from three things:

- wanting what we like but do not have,
- wanting to keep what we like and already have, and
- not wanting what we dislike but have.

Siddhartha spent seven more weeks meditating under the tree, which his followers later named the Tree of Wisdom. He then described his new ideas to five of his former companions. His followers later called this talk the First Sermon.

Siddhartha Gautama was about 35 years old when he found enlightenment under the tree. From that point on, he would be called **the Buddha** (BOO-duh), or the "Enlightened One." The Buddha spent the rest of his life traveling across northern India and teaching people his ideas.

READING CHECK **Summarizing** What did the Buddha conclude about the cause of suffering?

THE IMPACT TODAY

Buddhists from all over the world still travel to India to visit the Tree of Wisdom and honor the Buddha.

Teachings of Buddhism

As he traveled, the Buddha gained many followers, especially among India's merchants and artisans. He even taught his views to a few kings. These followers were the first believers in **Buddhism**, a religion based on the teachings of the Buddha.

The Buddha was raised Hindu, and many of his teachings reflected Hindu ideas. Like Hindus, he believed that people should act morally and treat others well. In one of his sermons, he said:

> "Let a man overcome anger by love. Let him overcome the greedy by liberality [giving], the liar by truth. This is called progress in the discipline [training] of the Blessed."
>
> –The Buddha, quoted in *The History of Nations: India*

Four Noble Truths

At the heart of the Buddha's teachings were four guiding principles. These became known as the Four Noble Truths:

1. Suffering and unhappiness are a part of human life. No one can escape sorrow.

2. Suffering comes from our desires for pleasure and material goods. People cause their own misery because they want things they cannot have.

3. People can overcome desire and ignorance and reach **nirvana** (nir-VAH-nuh), a state of perfect peace. Reaching nirvana frees the soul from suffering and from the need for further reincarnation.

4. People can overcome ignorance and desire by following an eight-fold path that leads to wisdom, enlightenment, and salvation.

The chart on the next page shows the steps in the Eightfold Path. The Buddha believed that this path was a middle way between human desires and denying oneself any pleasure. He believed that people should overcome their desire for material goods. They should, however, be reasonable, and not starve their bodies or cause themselves unnecessary pain.

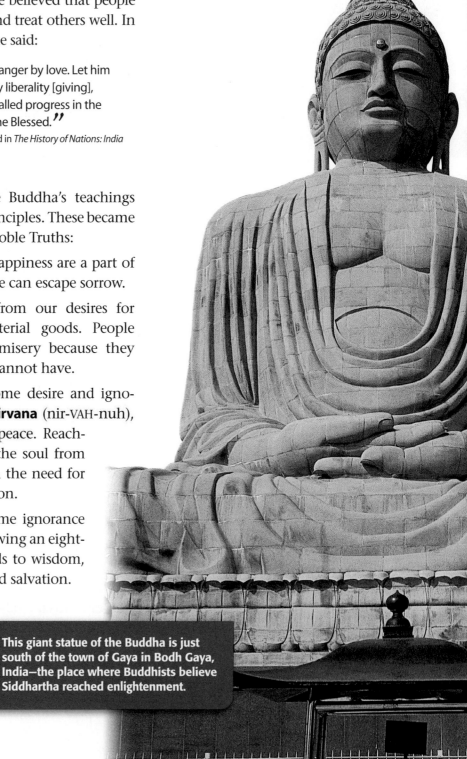

This giant statue of the Buddha is just south of the town of Gaya in Bodh Gaya, India—the place where Buddhists believe Siddhartha reached enlightenment.

The Eightfold Path

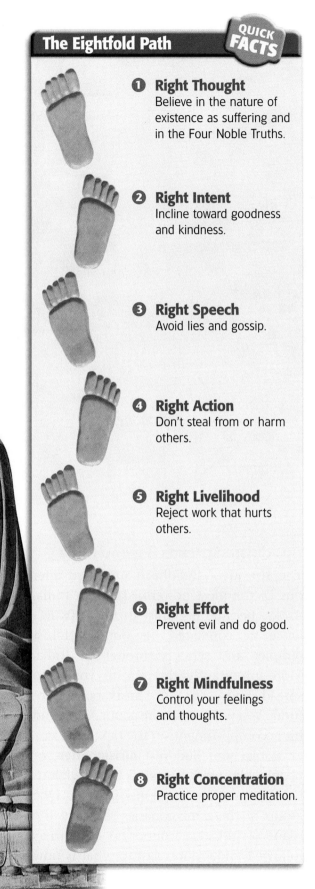

1 Right Thought
Believe in the nature of existence as suffering and in the Four Noble Truths.

2 Right Intent
Incline toward goodness and kindness.

3 Right Speech
Avoid lies and gossip.

4 Right Action
Don't steal from or harm others.

5 Right Livelihood
Reject work that hurts others.

6 Right Effort
Prevent evil and do good.

7 Right Mindfulness
Control your feelings and thoughts.

8 Right Concentration
Practice proper meditation.

Challenging Hindu Ideas

Some of the Buddha's teachings challenged traditional Hindu ideas. For example, the Buddha rejected many of the ideas contained in the Vedas, such as animal sacrifice. He told people that they did not have to follow these texts.

The Buddha challenged the authority of the Hindu priests, the Brahmins. He did not believe that they or their rituals were necessary for enlightenment. Instead, he taught that it was the responsibility of each individual to work for his or her own salvation. Priests could not help them. However, the Buddha did not reject the Hindu teaching of reincarnation. He taught that people who failed to reach nirvana would have to be reborn time and time again until they achieved it.

The Buddha was opposed to the caste system. He didn't think that people should be confined to a particular place in society. Everyone who followed the Eightfold Path properly, he said, would achieve nirvana. It didn't matter what *varna* or caste they had belonged to in life as long as they lived the way they should.

The Buddha's opposition to the caste system won him support from the masses. Many of India's herdsmen, farmers, artisans, and untouchables liked hearing that their low social rank would not be a barrier to enlightenment. Unlike Hinduism, Buddhism made them feel that they had the power to change their lives.

The Buddha also gained followers among the higher classes. Many rich and powerful Indians welcomed his ideas about avoiding extreme behavior while seeking salvation. By the time of his death around 483 BC, the Buddha's influence was spreading rapidly throughout India.

READING CHECK **Comparing** How did Buddha's teachings agree with Hinduism?

Early Spread of Buddhism

CENTRAL ASIA

PERSIA

CHINA

Yellow Sea

TIBET

NEPAL

Sarnath

Bodh Gaya

Sanchi

INDIAN OCEAN

INDIA

Bay of Bengal

SOUTHEAST ASIA

South China Sea

Early Buddhist area
Spread of Buddhism

0   250   500 Miles
0   250   500 Kilometers

CEYLON
(SRI LANKA)

N
W   E
S

Borneo

Sumatra

GEOGRAPHY SKILLS INTERPRETING MAPS

Movement Buddhism spread to what island south of India?

Buddhism Spreads

Buddhism continued to attract followers after the Buddha's death. After spreading through India, the religion began to spread to other areas as well.

Buddhism Spreads in India

According to Buddhist tradition, 500 of the Buddha's followers gathered together shortly after he died. They wanted to make sure that the Buddha's teachings were remembered correctly.

In the years after this council, the Buddha's followers spread his teachings throughout India. The ideas spread very quickly, because Buddhist teachings were popular and easy to understand. Within 200 years of the Buddha's death, his teachings had spread through most of India.

Buddhism Spreads Beyond India

The spread of Buddhism increased after one of the most powerful kings in India, Asoka, became Buddhist in the 200s BC. Once he converted, he built Buddhist temples and schools throughout India. More importantly, though, he worked to spread Buddhism into areas outside of India. You will learn more about Asoka and his accomplishments in the next section.

Asoka sent Buddhist **missionaries**, or people who work to spread their religious beliefs, to other kingdoms in Asia. One group of these missionaries sailed to the island of Sri Lanka around 251 BC. Others followed trade routes east to what is now Myanmar and to other parts of Southeast Asia. Missionaries also went north to areas near the Himalayas.

160 CHAPTER 6

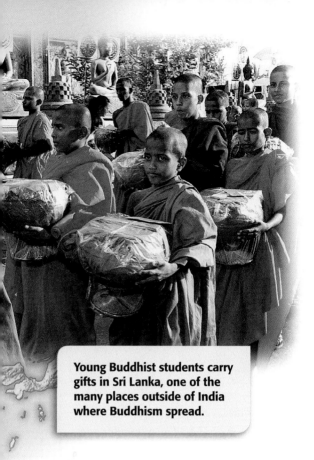

Young Buddhist students carry gifts in Sri Lanka, one of the many places outside of India where Buddhism spread.

Missionaries also introduced Buddhism to lands west of India. They founded Buddhist communities in Central Asia and Persia. They even taught about Buddhism as far away as Syria and Egypt.

Buddhism continued to grow over the centuries. Eventually it spread via the Silk Road into China, then Korea and Japan. Through their work, missionaries taught Buddhism to millions of people.

A Split within Buddhism

Even as Buddhism spread through Asia, however, it began to change. Not all Buddhists could agree on their beliefs and practices. Eventually disagreements between Buddhists led to a split within the religion. Two major branches of Buddhism were created—Theravada and Mahayana.

Members of the Theravada branch tried to follow the Buddha's teachings exactly as he had stated them. Mahayana Buddhists, though, believed that other people could interpret the Buddha's teachings to help people reach nirvana. Both branches have millions of believers today, but Mahayana is by far the larger branch.

READING CHECK **Sequencing** How did Buddhism spread from India to other parts of Asia?

SUMMARY AND PREVIEW Buddhism, one of India's major religions, grew more popular once it was adopted by rulers of India's great empires. You will learn more about those empires in the next section.

go.hrw.com
Online Quiz
KEYWORD: SQ6 HP6

Section 3 Assessment

Reviewing Ideas, Terms, and People HSS 6.5.5

1. **a. Identify** Who was **the Buddha**, and what does the term *Buddha* mean?
   b. Summarize How did Siddhartha Gautama free his mind and clarify his thinking as he searched for wisdom?
2. **a. Identify** What is **nirvana**?
   b. Contrast How are Buddhist teachings different from Hindu teachings?
   c. Elaborate Why do Buddhists believe that following the Eightfold Path leads to a better life?
3. **a. Describe** Into what lands did **Buddhism** spread?
   b. Summarize What role did **missionaries** play in spreading Buddhism?

Critical Thinking

4. **Summarizing** Draw a diagram like the one shown here. Use it to identify and describe the Four Noble Truths as taught by the Buddha.

1.	2.
3.	4.

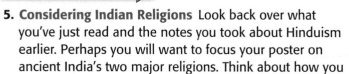

FOCUS ON WRITING

5. **Considering Indian Religions** Look back over what you've just read and the notes you took about Hinduism earlier. Perhaps you will want to focus your poster on ancient India's two major religions. Think about how you could design a poster around this theme.

Indian Empires

If YOU were there...

You are a merchant in India in about 240 BC. You travel from town to town on your donkey, carrying bolts of colorful cloth. In the heat of summer, you are grateful for the banyan trees along the road. They shelter you from the blazing sun. You stop at wells for cool drinks of water and rest houses for a break in your journey. You know these are all the work of your king, Asoka.

How do you feel about your king?

BUILDING BACKGROUND For centuries after the Aryan invasion, India was divided into small states. Each state had its own ruler and India had no central government. Then, in the 300s BC, a foreign conqueror, Alexander the Great, took over part of northwestern India. His armies soon left, but his influence continued to affect Indian society. Inspired by Alexander's example, a strong leader soon united India for the first time.

Mauryan Empire Unifies India

In the 320s BC a military leader named **Chandragupta Maurya** (kuhn-druh-GOOP-tuh MOUR-yuh) seized control of the entire northern part of India. By doing so, he founded the Mauryan Empire. Mauryan rule lasted for about 150 years.

The Mauryan Empire

Chandragupta Maurya ruled his empire with the help of a complex government. It included a network of spies and a huge army of some 600,000 soldiers. The army also had thousands of war elephants and thousands of chariots. In return for the army's protection, farmers paid a heavy tax to the government.

In 301 BC Chandragupta decided to become a Jainist monk. To do so, he had to give up his throne. He passed the throne to his son, who continued to expand the empire. Before long, the Mauryas ruled all of northern India and much of central India as well.

What You Will Learn...

Main Ideas

1. The Mauryan Empire unified most of India.
2. Gupta rulers promoted Hinduism in their empire.

The Big Idea

The Mauryas and the Guptas built great empires in India.

Key People

Chandragupta Maurya, *p. 162*
Asoka, *p. 163*
Chandragupta II, *p. 164*

HSS 6.5.6 Describe the growth of the Maurya Empire and the political and moral achievements of the emperor Asoka.

Asoka

Around 270 BC Chandragupta's grandson **Asoka** (uh-SOH-kuh) became king. Asoka was a strong ruler, the strongest of all the Mauryan emperors. He extended Mauryan rule over most of India. In conquering other kingdoms, Asoka made his own empire both stronger and richer.

For many years, Asoka watched his armies fight bloody battles against other peoples. A few years into his rule, however, Asoka converted to Buddhism. When he did, he swore that he would not launch any more wars of conquest.

After converting to Buddhism, Asoka had the time and resources to improve the lives of his people. He had wells dug and roads built throughout the empire. Along these roads, workers planted shade trees and built rest houses for weary travelers. He also encouraged the spread of Buddhism in India and the rest of Asia. As you read in the previous section, he sent missionaries to lands all over Asia.

Asoka died in 233 BC, and the empire began to fall apart soon afterward. His sons fought each other for power, and invaders threatened the empire. In 184 BC the last Mauryan king was killed by one of his own generals. India divided into smaller states once again.

FOCUS ON READING
What can you infer about the religious beliefs of Asoka's sons?

READING CHECK **Finding Main Ideas** How did the Mauryans gain control of most of India?

Mauryan Empire, c. 320–185 BC

Mauryan troops used war elephants in battle, striking fear in their enemies. As the elephants charged forward into battle, soldiers on top hurled spears at their enemies.

Hindu Kush
Karakoram Range
Taxila
Plateau of Tibet
HIMALAYAS
Indus River
Brahmaputra River
Thar Desert
Mathura
Ganges River
Pataliputra
Narmada River
Ajanta
Arabian Sea
DECCAN PLATEAU
Bay of Bengal
Ceylon (Sri Lanka)
INDIAN OCEAN

Mauryan Empire
0   200   400 Miles
0   200   400 Kilometers

GEOGRAPHY SKILLS **INTERPRETING MAPS**

Place Which cities were part of the Mauryan Empire?

Gupta Rulers Promote Hinduism

After the collapse of the Mauryan Empire, India remained divided for about 500 years. During that time, Buddhism continued to prosper and spread in India, and so the popularity of Hinduism declined.

A New Hindu Empire

ACADEMIC VOCABULARY
establish to set up or create

Eventually, however, a new dynasty was **established** in India. It was the Gupta (GOOP-tuh) Dynasty, which took over India around AD 320. Under the Guptas, India was once again united, and it once again became prosperous.

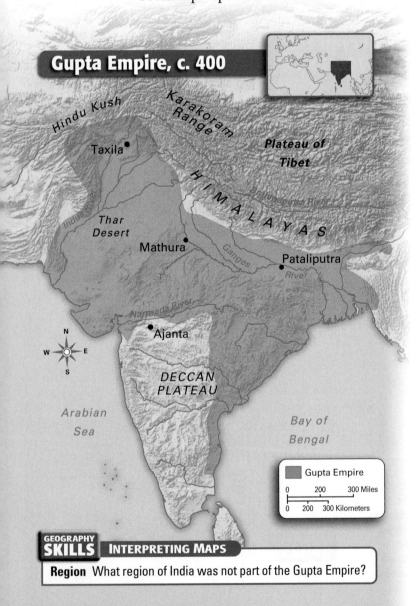

Gupta Empire, c. 400

Hindu Kush
Karakoram Range
Plateau of Tibet
Taxila
HIMALAYAS
Thar Desert
Mathura
Ganges River
Pataliputra
Narmada River
Ajanta
N W E S
DECCAN PLATEAU
Arabian Sea
Bay of Bengal

Gupta Empire
0   200   300 Miles
0   200   300 Kilometers

GEOGRAPHY SKILLS INTERPRETING MAPS

Region What region of India was not part of the Gupta Empire?

The first Gupta emperor was Chandragupta I. Although their names are similar, he was not related to Chandragupta Maurya. From his base in northern India, Chandragupta's armies invaded and conquered neighboring lands. Eventually he brought much of the northern part of India under his control.

Indian civilization flourished under the Gupta rulers. These rulers were Hindu, so Hinduism became India's major religion. The Gupta kings built many Hindu temples, some of which became models for later Indian architecture. They also promoted a revival of Hindu writings and worship practices.

Although they were Hindus, the Gupta rulers also supported the religious beliefs of Buddhism and Jainism. They promoted Buddhist art and built Buddhist temples. They also established a university at Nalanda that became one of Asia's greatest centers for Buddhist studies.

Gupta Society

In 375 Emperor **Chandragupta II** took the throne in India. Gupta society reached its high point during his rule. Under Chandragupta II, the empire continued to grow, eventually stretching all the way across northern India. At the same time, the empire's economy strengthened, and people prospered. They created fine works of art and literature. Outsiders admired the empire's wealth and beauty.

Gupta kings believed the social order of the Hindu caste system would strengthen their rule. They also thought it would keep the empire stable. As a result, the Guptas considered the caste system an important part of Indian society.

This was not good news for women, whose roles were limited by caste rules. Brahmins taught that a woman's role was to marry and have children. Women couldn't even choose their own husbands.

Gupta Art
This Gupta painting of a palace scene shows some of India's different castes. Gupta rulers supported Hinduism and the caste system.

Parents arranged all marriages. Once married, wives had few rights. They were expected to serve their husbands. Widows had an even lower social status than other women.

Gupta rule remained strong in India until the late 400s. At that time the Huns, a group from Central Asia, invaded India from the northwest. Their fierce attacks drained the Gupta Empire of its power and wealth. As the Hun armies marched farther into India, the Guptas lost hope.

By the middle of the 500s, Gupta rule had ended, and India had divided into small kingdoms yet again.

READING CHECK **Summarizing** What was the Gupta Dynasty's position on religion?

SUMMARY AND PREVIEW The Mauryas and Guptas united much of India in their empires. Next you will learn about their many achievements.

Section 4 Assessment

go.hrw.com
Online Quiz
KEYWORD: SQ6 HP6

Reviewing Ideas, Terms, and People HSS 6.5.6

1. **a. Identify** Who created the Mauryan Empire?
   b. Summarize What happened after **Asoka** became a Buddhist?
   c. Elaborate Why do you think many people consider Asoka the greatest of all Mauryan rulers?
2. **a. Recall** What religion did most of the Gupta rulers belong to?
   b. Compare and Contrast How were the rulers **Chandragupta Maurya** and Chandragupta I alike, and how were they different?
   c. Evaluate Do you think the Gupta enforcement of caste rules was a good thing? Why or why not?

Critical Thinking

3. **Categorizing** Draw a chart like this one. Fill it with information about India's rulers.

Ruler	Dynasty	Accomplishments

FOCUS ON WRITING

4. **Comparing Indian Empires** Another possible topic for your poster would be a comparison of the Maurya and Gupta empires. Make a chart in your notebook that shows such a comparison.

Asoka

How can one decision change a man's entire life?

When did he live? before 230 BC

Where did he live? Asoka's empire included much of northern and central India.

What did he do? After fighting many bloody wars to expand his empire, Asoka gave up violence and converted to Buddhism.

Why is he important? Asoka is one of the most respected rulers in Indian history and one of the most important figures in the history of Buddhism. As a devout Buddhist, Asoka worked to spread the Buddha's teachings. In addition to sending missionaries around Asia, he built huge columns carved with Buddhist teachings all over India. Largely through his efforts, Buddhism became one of Asia's main religions.

Generalizing How did Asoka's life change after he became Buddhist?

This Buddhist shrine, located in Sanchi, India, was built by Asoka.

KEY EVENTS

- **c. 270 BC** Asoka becomes the Mauryan emperor.

- **c. 261 BC** Asoka's empire reaches its greatest size.

- **c. 261 BC** Asoka becomes a Buddhist.

- **c. 251 BC** Asoka begins to send Buddhist missionaries to other parts of Asia.

Indian Achievements

If YOU were there...

You are a traveler in western India in the 300s. You are visiting a cave temple that is carved into a mountain cliff. Inside the cave it is cool and quiet. Huge columns rise all around you. You don't feel you're alone, for the walls and ceilings are covered with paintings. They are filled with lively scenes and figures. In the center is a large statue with calm, peaceful features.

How does this cave make you feel?

BUILDING BACKGROUND The Mauryan and Gupta empires united most of India politically. During these empires, Indian artists, writers, scholars, and scientists made great advances. Some of their works are still studied and admired today.

Religious Art

The Indians of the Maurya and Gupta periods created great works of art, many of them religious. Many of their paintings and sculptures illustrated either Hindu and Buddhist teachings. Magnificent temples—both Hindu and Buddhist—were built all around India. They remain some of the most beautiful buildings in the world today.

Temples

Early Hindu temples were small stone structures. They had flat roofs and contained only one or two rooms. In the Gupta period, though, temple architecture became more complex. Gupta temples were topped by huge towers and were covered with carvings of the god worshipped inside.

Buddhist temples of the Gupta period are also impressive. Some Buddhists carved entire temples out of mountainsides. The most famous such temple is at Ajanta. Its builders filled the caves with beautiful wall paintings and sculpture.

What You Will Learn...

Main Ideas

1. Indian artists created great works of religious art.
2. Sanskrit literature flourished during the Gupta period.
3. The Indians made scientific advances in metalworking, medicine, and other sciences.

The Big Idea

The people of ancient India made great contributions to the arts and sciences.

Key Terms

metallurgy, *p. 170*
alloys, *p. 170*
Hindu-Arabic numerals, *p. 170*
inoculation, *p. 170*
astronomy, *p. 171*

HSS 6.5.7 Discuss important aesthetic and intellectual traditions (e.g., Sanskrit literature, including the *Bhagavad Gita*; medicine; metallurgy; and mathematics, including Hindu-Arabic numerals and the zero).

This Hindu temple is covered with incredibly detailed carvings and decorations. Many individual sculptures are images of important Hindu deities, like the deity of Vishnu above.

Another type of Buddhist temple was the stupa. Stupas had domed roofs and were built to house sacred items from the life of the Buddha. Many of them were covered with detailed carvings.

Paintings and Sculpture

The Gupta period also saw the creation of great works of art, both paintings and statues. Painting was a greatly respected profession, and India was home to many skilled artists. However, we don't know the names of many artists from this period. Instead, we know the names of many rich and powerful members of Gupta society who paid artists to create works of beauty and significance.

Most Indian paintings from the Gupta period are clear and colorful. Some of them show graceful Indians wearing fine jewelry and stylish clothes. Such paintings offer us a glimpse of the Indians' daily and ceremonial lives.

Artists from both of India's major religions, Hinduism and Buddhism, drew on their beliefs to create their works. As a result, many of the finest paintings of ancient India are found in temples. Hindu painters drew hundreds of deities on temple walls and entrances. Buddhists covered the walls and ceilings of temples with scenes from the life of the Buddha.

Indian sculptors also created great works. Many of their statues were made for Buddhist cave temples. In addition to the temples' intricately carved columns, sculptors carved statues of kings and the Buddha. Some of these statues tower over the cave entrances. Hindu temples also featured impressive statues of their deities. In fact, the walls of some temples, such as the one pictured above, were completely covered with carvings and images.

READING CHECK Summarizing How did religion influence ancient Indian art?

Sanskrit Literature

As you read earlier, Sanskrit was the main language of the ancient Aryans. During the Maurya and Gupta periods, many works of Sanskrit literature were created. These works were later translated into many other languages.

Sacred Texts

The greatest of these Sanskrit writings are two sacred texts, the *Mahabharata* (muh-HAH-BAH-ruh-tuh) and the *Ramayana* (rah-MAH-yuh-nuh). Still popular in India, the *Mahabharata* is one of the world's longest sacred texts. It tells of the struggle between two families for control of a kingdom. Included within it are many long passages about Hindu beliefs. The most famous is called the *Bhagavad Gita* (BUG-uh-vuhd GEE-tah).

The *Ramayana*, according to Hindu tradition written prior to the *Mahabharata*, tells about a prince named Rama. In truth, the prince was the deity Vishnu in human form. He had become human so he could rid the world of demons. He also had to rescue his wife, a princess named Sita. For centuries, the characters of the *Ramayana* have been seen as models for how Indians should behave. For example, Rama is seen as the ideal ruler, and his relationship with Sita as the ideal marriage.

Other Works

Writers in the Gupta period also created plays, poetry, and other types of literature. One famous writer of this time was Kalidasa (kahl-ee-DAHS-uh). His work was so brilliant that Chandragupta II hired him to write plays for the royal court.

Sometime before 500, Indian writers also produced a book of stories called the *Panchatantra* (PUHN-chuh-TAHN-truh). The stories in this collection were intended to teach lessons. They praise people for cleverness and quick thinking. Each story ends with a message about winning friends, losing property, waging war, or some other idea. For example, the message below warns listeners to think about what they are doing before they act.

> " The good and bad of given schemes
> Wise thought must first reveal:
> The stupid heron saw his chicks
> Provide a mongoose meal. "
> –from the *Panchatantra*, translated
> by Arthur William Ryder

Eventually, translations of this collection spread throughout the world. It became popular even as far away as Europe.

READING CHECK **Categorizing** What types of literature did writers of ancient India create?

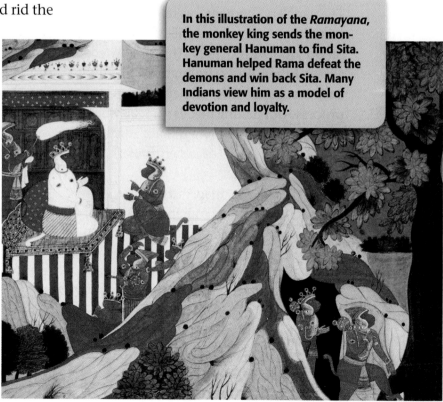

In this illustration of the *Ramayana*, the monkey king sends the monkey general Hanuman to find Sita. Hanuman helped Rama defeat the demons and win back Sita. Many Indians view him as a model of devotion and loyalty.

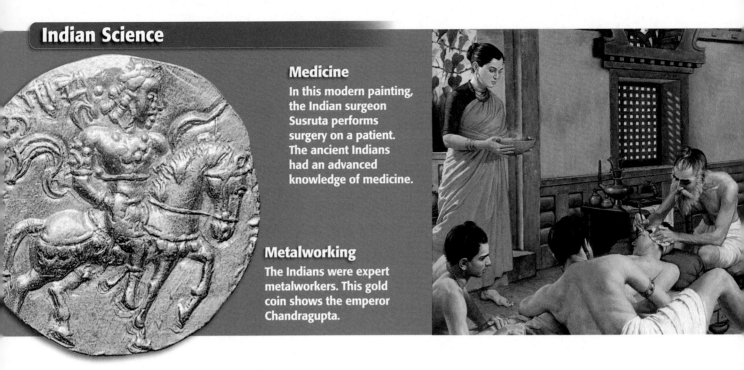

Indian Science

Medicine
In this modern painting, the Indian surgeon Susruta performs surgery on a patient. The ancient Indians had an advanced knowledge of medicine.

Metalworking
The Indians were expert metalworkers. This gold coin shows the emperor Chandragupta.

Scientific Advances

Indian achievements were not limited to art, architecture, and literature. Indian scholars also made important advances in metalworking, math, and the sciences.

Metalworking

The ancient Indians were pioneers of **metallurgy** (MET-uhl-uhr-jee), the science of working with metals. Their knowledge allowed them to create high-quality tools and weapons. The Indians also knew **processes** for mixing metals to create **alloys**, mixtures of two or more metals. Alloys are sometimes stronger or easier to work with than pure metals.

Metalworkers made their strongest products out of iron. Indian iron was very hard and pure. These features made the iron a valuable trade item.

During the Gupta Dynasty, metalworkers built the famous Iron Pillar near Delhi. Unlike most iron, which rusts easily, this pillar is very resistant to rust. The tall column still attracts crowds of visitors. Scholars study this column even today to learn the Indians' secrets.

THE IMPACT TODAY
People still get inoculations against many diseases.

Mathematics and Other Sciences

Gupta scholars also made advances in math and science. In fact, they were among the most advanced mathematicians of their day. They developed many elements of our modern math system. The very numbers we use today are called **Hindu-Arabic numerals** because they were created by Indian scholars and brought to Europe by Arabs. The Indians were also the first people to create the zero. Although it may seem like a small thing, modern math wouldn't be possible without the zero.

The ancient Indians were also very skilled in the medical sciences. As early as the AD 100s, doctors were writing their knowledge down in textbooks. Among the skills these books describe is making medicines from plants and minerals.

Besides curing people with medicines, Indian doctors knew how to protect people against disease. The Indians practiced **inoculation** (i-nah-kyuh-LAY-shuhn), or injecting a person with a small dose of a virus to help him or her build up defenses to a disease. By fighting off this small dose, the body learns to protect itself.

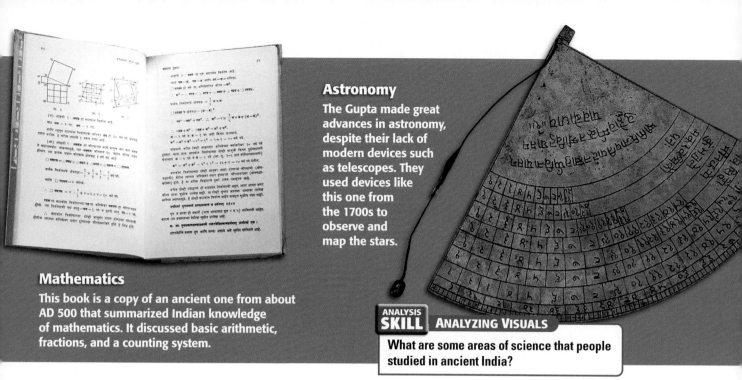

Astronomy

The Gupta made great advances in astronomy, despite their lack of modern devices such as telescopes. They used devices like this one from the 1700s to observe and map the stars.

Mathematics

This book is a copy of an ancient one from about AD 500 that summarized Indian knowledge of mathematics. It discussed basic arithmetic, fractions, and a counting system.

ANALYSIS SKILL **ANALYZING VISUALS**

What are some areas of science that people studied in ancient India?

For people who were injured, Indian doctors could perform surgery. Surgeons repaired broken bones, treated wounds, removed infected tonsils, reconstructed broken noses, and even reattached torn earlobes! If they could find no other cure for an illness, doctors would cast magic spells to help people recover.

Indian interest in **astronomy**, the study of stars and planets, dates back to early times as well. Indian astronomers knew of seven of the nine planets in our solar system. They knew that the sun was a star and that the planets revolved around it. They also knew that the earth was a sphere and that it rotated on its axis. In addition, they could predict eclipses of the sun and the moon.

READING CHECK **Finding Main Ideas** What were two Indian achievements in mathematics?

SUMMARY AND PREVIEW From a group of cities on the Indus River, India grew into a major empire whose people made great achievements. In the next chapter, you'll read about another civilization that experienced similar growth—China.

go.hrw.com
Online Quiz
KEYWORD: SQ6 HP6

Section 5 Assessment

Reviewing Ideas, Terms, and People **HSS** 6.5.7

1. **a. Describe** What did Hindu temples of the Gupta period look like?
   b. Analyze How can you tell that Indian artists were well respected?
   c. Evaluate Why do you think Hindu and Buddhist temples contained great works of art?
2. **a. Identify** What is the *Bhagavad Gita*?
   b. Explain Why were the stories of the *Panchatantra* written?
   c. Elaborate Why do you think people are still interested in ancient Sanskrit epics today?
3. **a. Define** What is **metallurgy**?
   b. Explain Why do we call the numbers we use today **Hindu-Arabic numerals**?

Critical Thinking

4. **Categorizing** Draw a chart like the one below. Use it to identify ancient Indian achievements in math and science.

Metallurgy	Math	Medicine	Astronomy

FOCUS ON WRITING

5. **Highlighting Indian Achievements** Make a list of Indian achievements that you could include on a poster. Now look back through your notes from this chapter. Which will you choose as the subject of your poster?

from the
Bhagavad Gita

translated by Barbara Stoler Miller

About the Reading *The* Bhagavad Gita, *one of Hinduism's most sacred texts, is part of the much longer epic called the* Mahabharata. *The title* Bhagavad Gita *is Sanskrit for "Song of the Lord." The lord to which the title refers is Krishna, who is the deity Vishnu in human form. The Gita, as the poem is sometimes known, is written as a conversation between Krishna and a prince named Arjuna. Faced with a battle in which he will have to fight many of his friends and family members, Arjuna turns to Krishna for advice. As part of his response, Krishna explains to Arjuna how a soul can find peace and eternal happiness.*

AS YOU READ **Think about the meaning behind Krishna's advice to Arjuna.**

From anger comes confusion;
from confusion memory lapses;
from broken memory understanding is lost;
from loss of understanding, he is ruined.

But a man of inner strength
whose senses experience objects
without attraction and hatred,
in self control, finds serenity. ❶

In serenity, all his sorrows
dissolve;
his reason becomes serene,
his understanding sure.

Without discipline,
he has no understanding or inner power;
without inner power, he has no peace;
and without peace where is joy?

If his mind submits to the play
of the senses,
they drive away insight,
as wind drives a ship on water. ❷

So, Great Warrior, when withdrawal
of the senses
from sense objects is complete,
discernment is firm.

When it is night for all creatures,
a master of restraint is awake;
when they are awake, it is night
for the sage who sees reality. ❸

As the mountainous depths
of the ocean
are unmoved when waters
rush into it,
so the man unmoved
when desires enter into him
attains a peace that eludes
the man of many desires. ❹

When he renounces all desires
and acts without craving,
possessiveness,
or individuality, he finds peace.

This is the place of the infinite spirit;
achieving it, one is freed from delusion;
abiding in it even at the time of death,
one finds the pure calm of infinity.

This painting from the 1700s shows Hindu women entering a forest on their way to meet Krishna.

GUIDED READING

WORD HELP

insight understanding; wisdom
discernment understanding
restraint holding back; self control
sage wise person
eludes escapes
renounces gives up
craving longing, wanting
delusion false belief

❷ Just as the wind pushes a ship along the water, Krishna says, the desire for objects pushes away peace and understanding of the world.

❸ Krishna says that people seeking peace should be more comfortable at night, because the senses are less active then than during the day.

❹ Just as the ocean doesn't change when water rushes into it, people shouldn't be changed by desires.

What does Krishna say will be the reward for people without many desires?

CONNECTING SACRED TEXTS TO HISTORY

1. **Analyzing** Hindus believe that the world is an illusion that people must see through to be united with Brahman. How is this idea supported by Krishna's discussion of how to find peace?

2. **Comparing** Krishna says the people who find peace will reach the "place of infinite spirit" and find the "pure calm of infinity." How does this idea compare to the Buddhist concept of nirvana?

Social Studies Skills

Analysis | Critical Thinking | Participation | **Study**

Interpreting Diagrams

Understand the Skill

Diagrams are drawings that illustrate or explain objects or ideas. Different types of diagrams have different purposes. The ability to interpret diagrams will help you to better understand historical objects, their functions, and how they worked.

Learn the Skill

Use these guidelines to interpret a diagram:

1. Read the diagram's title or caption to find out what it represents. If a legend is present, study it as well to understand any symbols and colors in the diagram.

2. Most diagrams include labels that identify the object's parts or explain relationships between them. Study these parts and labels carefully.

3. If any written information or explanation accompanies the diagram, compare it to the drawing as you read.

The diagram below is of the Great Stupa at Sanchi in India, which is thought to contain the Buddha's remains. Like most stupas, it was shaped like a dome.

The Sanchi stupa is surrounded by a stone railing with four gates called *torenas*. About halfway up the side of the mound is a second railing next to a walkway. Worshippers move along this walkway in a clockwise direction to honor the Buddha. The stupa is topped by a cube called the *harmika*. Rising from the harmika is a mast or spire. These parts and their shapes all have religious meaning for Buddhists.

Practice and Apply the Skill

Here is another diagram of the Sanchi stupa. Interpret both diagrams on this page to answer the questions that follow.

1. Which letter in this diagram labels the *torenas*?
2. What part of the stupa does the letter A label?
3. The walkway and railing are labeled by which letter?

Standards Review

Visual Summary

Use the visual summary below to help you review the main ideas of the chapter.

QUICK FACTS

The Harappan civilization began in the Indus River Valley.

Hinduism and Buddhism both developed in India.

Indians made great advances in art, literature, science, and other fields.

Reviewing Terms and People

Fill in the blanks with the correct term or name from this chapter.

1. _____ are winds that bring heavy rainfall.

2. A _____ is a division of people into groups based on birth, wealth, or occupation.

3. Hindus believe in _____, the belief that they will be reborn many times after death.

4. _____ founded the Mauryan Empire.

5. The focusing of the mind on spiritual things is called _____.

6. People who work to spread their religious beliefs are called _____.

7. People who practice _____ use only peaceful ways to achieve change.

8. _____ converted to Buddhism while he was ruler of the Mauryan Empire.

9. A mixture of metals is called an _____.

10. The study of the stars and planets is called _____.

Comprehension and Critical Thinking

SECTION 1 *(Pages 144–149)* HSS 6.5.1, 6.5.2

11. **a. Describe** What caused floods on the Indus River, and what was the result of those floods?

b. Contrast How was Aryan culture different from Harappan culture?

c. Elaborate Why is the Harappan culture considered a civilization?

SECTION 2 *(Pages 150–155)* HSS 6.5.3, 6.5.4

12. **a. Identify** Who were the Brahmins, and what role did they play in Aryan society?

b. Analyze How do Hindus believe karma affects reincarnation?

c. Elaborate Hinduism has been called both a polytheistic religion—one that worships many deities—and a monotheistic religion—one that worships only one. Why do you think this is so?

SECTION 3 (Pages 156–161) HSS 6.5.5

13. a. Describe What did the Buddha say caused human suffering?

b. Analyze How did Buddhism grow and change after the Buddha died?

c. Elaborate Why did the Buddha's teachings about nirvana appeal to many people of lower castes?

SECTION 4 (Pages 162–165) HSS 6.5.6

14. a. Identify What was Chandragupta Maurya's greatest accomplishment?

b. Compare and Contrast What was one similarity between the Mauryas and the Guptas? What was one difference between them?

c. Predict How might Indian history have been different if Asoka had not become a Buddhist?

SECTION 5 (Pages 167–171) HSS 6.5.7

15. a. Describe What kinds of religious art did the ancient Indians create?

b. Make Inferences Why do you think religious discussions are included in the *Mahabharata?*

c. Evaluate Which of the ancient Indians' achievements do you think is most impressive? Why?

Reviewing Themes

16. Religion What is one teaching that Buddhism and Hinduism share? What is one idea about which they differ?

17. Society and Culture How did the caste system affect the lives of most people in India?

Using the Internet

go.hrw.com
KEYWORD: SQ6 WH6

18. Activity: Making a Brochure In this chapter, you learned about India's diverse geographical features and the ways in which geography influenced India's history. Enter the activity keyword. Then research the geography and civilizations of India, taking notes as you go. Finally, use the interactive brochure template to present what you have found.

Reading Skills

19. Drawing Inferences Based on what you learned about the Gupta period, what inference can you draw about religious tolerance in ancient India? Draw a box like the one below to help you organize your thoughts.

Question:	
Inside the Text:	Outside the Text:
Inference:	

Social Studies Skills

20. Understanding Diagrams Look back over the diagram of the Buddhist temple in the skills activity at the end of this chapter. Using this diagram as a guide, draw a simple diagram of your house or school. Be sure to include labels of important features on your diagram. An example has been provided for you below.

Bedroom	Bathroom	Kitchen
Hallway		
Bedroom	Bedroom	Living Room

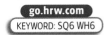

FOCUS ON WRITING

21. Designing Your Poster Now that you have chosen a topic for your poster, it's time to create it. On a large sheet of paper or poster board, write a title that identifies the subject of your poster. Then draw pictures, maps, or diagrams that illustrate your chosen topic.

Next to each picture, write a short caption. Each caption should be two sentences long. The first sentence should identify what the picture, map, or diagram shows. The second sentence should explain why the picture is important to the study of Indian history.

Standards Assessment

DIRECTIONS: Read each question, and write the letter of the best response.

1 Use the map to answer the following question.

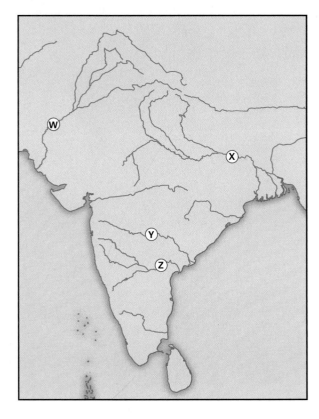

Civilization grew on the Indian subcontinent along the river marked on the map by the letter

A W.

B X.

C Y.

D Z.

2 The people of which *varna* in early India had the hardest lives?

A Brahmins

B Kshatriyas

C Sudras

D Vaisyas

3 What is the *main* goal of people who follow Buddhism as it was taught by the Buddha?

A wealth

B rebirth

C missionary work

D reaching nirvana

4 The Mauryan emperor Asoka is known for all of the following *except*

A expanding the empire across most of India.

B spreading Hinduism.

C working to improve his people's lives.

D practicing nonviolence.

5 Early India's contributions to world civilization included

A developing the world's first calendar.

B creating what is now called algebra.

C inventing the plow and the wheel.

D introducing zero to the number system.

Connecting with Past Learnings

6 In this chapter you learned about two sacred epics, the *Mahabharata* and the *Ramayana*. Which of the following is also an epic poem that you have studied?

A Hammurabi's Code

B the *Book of the Dead*

C *Gilgamesh*

D the Pyramid Texts

7 As you learned earlier in this course, the ancient Egyptians held elaborate religious rituals. Which of these Indian religions also involved many rituals, including sacrifices?

A Buddhism

B Brahmanism

C Jainism

D Mauryanism

Ancient China

California Standards

History–Social Science

6.6 Students analyze the geographic, political, economic, religious, and social structures of the early civilizations of China.

English–Language Arts

Speaking 6.2.2 Deliver informative presentations.

Reading 6.2.4 Clarify understanding by summarizing.

FOCUS ON SPEAKING

Oral Presentation In this chapter you will read about China's fascinating early years. Choose one person or event from that history. You will then tell your classmates why the person or event was important to the history of China.

CHAPTER EVENTS

c. 1500s BC
The Shang dynasty is established in China.

1600 BC

WORLD EVENTS

c. 1480 BC
Queen Hatshepsut rules Egypt.

What You Will Learn...

In this chapter you will learn about the geography, history, and culture of ancient China. China was one of the early centers of civilization. China's two major rivers played key roles in Chinese history and the development of Chinese society.

1100s BC
The Zhou dynasty begins.

1200 BC

551 BC
Confucius is born in China.

800 BC

c. 965 BC
Solomon becomes king of the Israelites.

c. 500 BC
Buddhism begins to emerge in India.

221 BC
Shi Huangdi unites China under the Qin dynasty.

400 BC

205 BC
The Han dynasty begins its rule of China.

BC 1 AD

c. 100 BC
The overland Silk Road connects China and Southwest Asia.

ANCIENT CHINA **179**

Focus on Themes This chapter will describe the early development of China—how Chinese civilization began and took shape under early dynasties. You will see how these dynasties controlled the government and **politics**. You will also see how the Chinese, influenced by the philosopher Confucius, established traditions such as the importance of families. They also encouraged art and learning, helping to shape the **society and culture** that would last for centuries in China.

Summarizing Historical Texts

Focus on Reading When you are reading a history book, how can you be sure that you understand everything? One way is to briefly restate what you've read in a summary.

Writing a Summary A summary is a short restatement of the most important ideas in a text. The example below shows three steps used in writing a summary. First identify important details. Then write a short summary of each paragraph. Finally, combine these paragraph summaries into a short summary of the whole passage.

Additional reading support can be found in the

Inter**active**

Reader and Study Guide

The first dynasty for which we have clear evidence is the Shang, which was firmly established by the 1500s BC. Strongest in the Huang He Valley, the Shang ruled a broad area of northern China. Shang rulers moved their capital several times, probably to avoid floods or attack by enemies.

The king was at the center of Shang political and religious life. Nobles served the king as advisors and helped him rule. Less important officials were also nobles. They performed specific governmental and religious duties.

→ **Summary of Paragraph 1**
China's first dynasty, the Shang, took power in northern China in the 1500s BC.

→ **Summary of Paragraph 2**
Shang politics and religion were run by the king and nobles.

Combined Summary
The Shang dynasty, which ruled northern China by the 1500s BC, was governed by a king and nobles.

ELA Reading 6.2.4 Clarify an understanding of texts by creating outlines, logical notes, summaries, or reports.

You Try It!

The following passage is from the chapter you are about to read. As you read it, think about what you would include in a summary.

Early Settlements

Archaeologists have found remains of early Chinese villages. One village site near the Huang He had more than 40 houses. Many of the houses were partly underground and may have had straw-covered roofs. The site also included animal pens, storage pits, and a cemetery.

From Chapter 7 p. 184

Some of the villages along the Huang He grew into large towns. Walls surrounded these towns to defend them against floods and hostile neighbors. In towns like these, the Chinese left many artifacts, such as arrowheads, fishhooks, tools, and pottery. Some village sites even contained pieces of cloth.

After you read the passage, answer the following questions.

1. Read the following summaries and decide which one is the better summary statement. Explain your answer.

a) Archaeologists have found out interesting things about the early settlements of China. For example, they have discovered that the Chinese had homes with straw-covered roofs, pens for their animals, and even cemeteries. Also, they have found that larger villages were surrounded by walls for defense. Finally, they have found tools like arrowheads and fishhooks.

b) Archaeologists have found remains of early Chinese villages, some of which grew into large walled settlements. Artifacts found there help us understand Chinese culture.

2. What should be included in a good summary?

Key Terms and People

Chapter 7

Section 1
jade *(p. 185)*
oracle *(p. 186)*

Section 2
lords *(p. 189)*
peasants *(p. 189)*
Confucius *(p. 191)*
ethics *(p. 191)*
Confucianism *(p. 191)*
Daoism *(p. 192)*
Laozi *(p. 192)*
Legalism *(p. 192)*

Section 3
Shi Huangdi *(p. 194)*
Great Wall *(p. 197)*

Section 4
sundial *(p. 204)*
seismograph *(p. 204)*
acupuncture *(p. 205)*

Section 5
silk *(p. 209)*
Silk Road *(p. 209)*
diffusion *(p. 211)*

Academic Vocabulary

Success in school is related to knowing academic vocabulary—the words that are frequently used in school assignments and discussions. In this chapter, you will learn the following academic words:

vary *(p. 183)*
structure *(p. 190)*
innovation *(p. 204)*
procedure *(p. 209)*

As you read Chapter 7, think about how you would summarize the material you are reading.

Geography and Early China

What You Will Learn...

Main Ideas

1. China's physical geography made farming possible but travel and communication difficult.
2. Civilization began in China along the Huang He and Chang Jiang rivers.
3. China's first dynasties helped Chinese society develop and made many other achievements.

The Big Idea

Chinese civilization began with the Shang dynasty along the Huang He.

Key Terms

jade, *p. 185*
oracle, *p. 186*

HSS 6.6.1 Locate and describe the origins of Chinese civilization in the Huang-He Valley during the Shang Dynasty.

6.6.2 Explain the geographic features of China that made governance and the spread of ideas and goods difficult and served to isolate the country from the rest of the world.

If YOU were there...

You live along a broad river in China in about 1400 BC. Your grandfather is a farmer. He tells you wonderful stories about an ancient king. Long ago, this legendary hero tamed the river's raging floods. He even created new rivers. Without him, no one could farm or live in this rich land.

Why is this legend important to your family?

BUILDING BACKGROUND Like other river civilizations, the Chinese people had to learn to control floods and irrigate their fields. China's geographical features divided the country into distinct regions.

China's Physical Geography

Geography played a major role in the development of Chinese civilization. China has many different geographical features. Some features separated groups of people within China. Others separated China from the rest of the world.

A Vast and Varied Land

China covers an area of nearly 4 million square miles, about the same size as the United States. One of the physical barriers that separates China from its neighbors is a harsh desert, the Gobi (GOH-bee). It spreads over much of China's north. East of the Gobi are low-lying plains. These plains, which cover most of eastern China, form one of the world's largest farming regions. The Pacific Ocean forms the country's eastern boundary.

More than 2,000 miles to the west, rugged mountains make up the western frontier. In the southwest the Plateau of Tibet has several mountain peaks that reach more than 26,000 feet. From the plateau, smaller mountain ranges spread eastward. The most important of these ranges is the Qinling Shandi (CHIN-LING shahn-DEE). It separates northern China from southern China.

China: Physical

ASIA

Amur River

Greater Khingan Range

Manchurian Plain

Tian Shan

GOBI DESERT

Taklimakan Desert

(Yellow River)

Shandong Peninsula

Kunlun Shan

Huang He

Qinling Shandi

North China Plain

Yellow Sea

Plateau of Tibet

HIMALAYAS

(Yangzi River)

East China Sea

Sea of Japan (East Sea)

140° E

Tropic of Cancer

Xi River

Taiwan

China's Size

The rivers and plains of eastern China have long been important farming areas.

ELEVATION

Feet		Meters
13,120		4,000
6,560		2,000
1,640		500
656		200
(Sea level) 0		0 (Sea level)
Below sea level		Below sea level

0   300   600 Miles
0   300   600 Kilometers

High mountains and dry plateaus dominate western China.

Hainan

South China Sea

110° E

PACIFIC OCEAN

GEOGRAPHY SKILLS **INTERPRETING MAPS**

Place What rivers can you see on the map?

Weather and temperature patterns **vary** widely across China. In the northeast, the climate is cold and dry. Winter temperatures drop well below 0°F. Rivers there are frozen for more than half of the year. In the northwest, the deserts are very dry. But on the eastern plains of China, heavy rains fall. The tropical southeast is the wettest region. Monsoons can bring 250 inches of rain each year. That's enough water to cover a two-story house!

The Rivers of China

Two great rivers flow from west to east in China. The Huang He, or Yellow River, stretches for nearly 3,000 miles across northern China. The river often floods, and the floods leave behind layers of silt

on the surrounding countryside. Because these floods can be very destructive, the river is sometimes called "China's Sorrow." Over the years, millions of people have died in Huang He floods.

To the south, the Chang Jiang, or Yangzi River, cuts through central China. It flows from the mountains of Tibet to the Pacific Ocean. The Chang Jiang is the longest river in Asia.

In early China, the two rivers helped link people in the eastern part of the country with those in the west. At the same time, the mountains between the rivers limited contact.

READING CHECK **Summarizing** What geographical features limited travel in China?

ACADEMIC VOCABULARY

vary to be different

Geography and Living

China is a large country with many different types of environments.

How do these photos show China's diverse geography?

1 In northern China, the Huang He, or Yellow River, has long been the center of civilization. The silt in the river gives it a yellow look.

Civilization Begins

Like other ancient peoples that you have studied, people in China first settled along rivers. There they farmed, built villages, and formed a civilization.

The Development of Farming

Farming in China started along the Huang He and Chang Jiang. The rivers' floods deposited fertile silt. These silt deposits made the land ideal for growing crops.

As early as 7000 BC farmers grew rice in the middle Chang Jiang Valley. North, along the Huang He, the land was better for growing cereals such as millet and wheat.

Along with farming, the early Chinese people increased their diets in other ways. They fished and hunted with bows and arrows. They also domesticated animals such as pigs and sheep. With more sources of food, the population grew.

Early Settlements

Archaeologists have found remains of early Chinese villages. One village site near the Huang He had more than 40 houses. Many of the houses were partly underground and may have had straw-covered roofs. The site also included animal pens, storage pits, and a cemetery.

Some of the villages along the Huang He grew into large towns. Walls surrounded these towns to defend them against floods and hostile neighbors. In towns like these, the Chinese left many artifacts, such as arrowheads, fishhooks, tools, and pottery. Some village sites even contained pieces of cloth.

Separate cultures developed in southern and northeastern China. These included the Sanxingdui (sahn-shing-DWAY) and Hongshan peoples. Little is known about them, however. As the major cultures along the Huang He and Chang Jiang grew, they absorbed these other cultures.

Over time, Chinese culture became more advanced. After 3000 BC people used potter's wheels to make more types of pottery. These people also learned to dig water wells. As populations grew, villages spread out over larger areas in both northern and southeastern China.

2 Southern China receives more rain than northern China, and farmers can grow several crops of rice a year.

3 Western China's high mountains and wide deserts make travel difficult and isolate China's population centers in the east.

Burial sites have provided information about the culture of this period. Like the Egyptians, the early Chinese filled their tombs with objects. Some tombs included containers of food, suggesting a belief in an afterlife. Some graves contained many more items than others. These differences show that a social order had developed. Often the graves of rich people held beautiful jewelry and other objects made from **jade**, a hard gemstone.

READING CHECK **Generalizing** What were some features of China's earliest settlements?

China's First Dynasties

Societies along the Huang He grew and became more complex. They eventually formed the first Chinese civilization.

The Xia Dynasty

According to ancient stories, a series of kings ruled early China. Around 2200 BC one of them, Yu the Great, is said to have founded the Xia (SHAH) dynasty.

Writers told of terrible floods during Yu's lifetime. According to these accounts, Yu dug channels to drain the water to the ocean. This labor took him more than 10 years and is said to have created the major waterways of north China.

Archaeologists have not yet found evidence that the tales about the Xia are true. However, the stories of Xia rulers were important to the ancient Chinese because they told of kings who helped people solve problems by working together. The stories also explained the geography that had such an impact on people's lives.

The Shang Dynasty

The first dynasty for which we have clear evidence is the Shang, which was firmly established by the 1500s BC. Strongest in the Huang He Valley, the Shang ruled a broad area of northern China. Shang rulers moved their capital several times, probably to avoid floods or attack by enemies.

The king was at the center of Shang political and religious life. Nobles served the king as advisors and helped him rule.

Less important officials were also nobles. They performed specific governmental and religious duties.

The social order became more organized under the Shang. The royal family and the nobles were at the highest level. Nobles owned much land, and they passed on their wealth and power to their sons. Warrior leaders from the far regions of the empire also had high rank in society. Most people in the Shang ruling classes lived in large homes in cities.

Artisans settled outside the city walls. They lived in groups based on what they made for a living. Some artisans made weapons. Other artisans made pottery, tools, or clothing. Artisans were at a middle level of importance in Shang society.

Farmers ranked below artisans in the social order. Farmers worked long hours but had little money. Taxes claimed much of what they earned. Slaves, who filled society's lowest rank, were an important source of labor during the Shang period.

The Shang made many advances, including China's first writing system. This system used more than 2,000 symbols to express words or ideas. Although the system has gone through changes over the years, the Chinese symbols used today are based on those of the Shang period.

Shang writing has been found on thousands of cattle bones and turtle shells. Priests had carved questions about the future on bones or shells, which were then heated, causing them to crack. The priests believed they could "read" these cracks to predict the future. The bones were called oracle bones because an **oracle** is a prediction.

In addition to writing, the Shang also made other achievements. Artisans made beautiful bronze containers for cooking and

Shang Dynasty, c. 1500–1050 BC

GOBI DESERT

ASIA

Huang He (Yellow River)

Anyang

Luoyang

Chang Jiang (Yangzi River)

Xi River

Yellow Sea

PACIFIC OCEAN

East China Sea

South China Sea

Shang dynasty

0   150   300 Miles
0   150   300 Kilometers

This bronze Shang container is shaped like a tigress.

GEOGRAPHY SKILLS INTERPRETING MAPS

Location What river flowed through the heart of Shang China?

Chinese Writing

	Writing from Shang Period	Current Chinese Writing
sun		
rain		
field		
moon		

Like other early forms of writing, Chinese writing developed from pictographs—symbols that look like what they represent. Over time, the symbols became more complex and looked less like real objects. Many examples of early Chinese writing are carved into bones like this turtle shell.

religious ceremonies. They also made axes, knives, and ornaments from jade. The military developed war chariots, powerful bows, and bronze body armor. Shang astrologers also made an important contribution. They developed a calendar based on the cycles of the moon.

READING CHECK **Contrasting** What is a major historical difference between the Xia and Shang dynasties?

SUMMARY AND PREVIEW China is a vast land with a diverse geography. Ancient Chinese civilization developed in the fertile valleys of the Huang He and Chang Jiang. Civilization there advanced under Shang rule. People developed a social order, a writing system, and made other achievements. In the next section you will learn about new ideas in China during the rule of the Zhou dynasty.

Section 1 Assessment

go.hrw.com
Online Quiz
KEYWORD: SQ6 HP7

Reviewing Ideas, Terms, and People **HSS** 6.6.1, 6.6.2

1. **a. Identify** Name China's two major rivers.
   b. Analyze How did China's geography affect its development?
2. **a. Identify** In which river valley did China's civilization begin?
   b. Explain What made China's river valleys ideal for farming?
   c. Elaborate What do Chinese artifacts reveal about China's early civilization?
3. **a. Describe** How do historians know about the Xia dynasty?
   b. Draw Conclusions What does the use of **oracle** bones tell us about the early Chinese?

Critical Thinking

4. **Comparing and Contrasting** Copy the diagram shown here. Use it to show similarities and differences in the geography of northern and southern China.

   Northern China   Southern China

FOCUS ON SPEAKING

5. **Thinking about Events** Look back over the section to note the important events of China's earliest times. Think about what it is that makes one event more important than another. Write down your ideas in your notebook.

The Zhou Dynasty and New Ideas

If YOU were there...

You are a student of the famous teacher Confucius. Like many older Chinese, he thinks that society has changed—and not for the better. He believes in old values and a strict social order. He is trying to teach you and your fellow students how to behave as gentlemen. You must respect those who are your superiors in society. You must set a good example for others.

How will these teachings affect your life?

BUILDING BACKGROUND The people of the Shang dynasty made many advances, including beautiful metalwork, a writing system, and a calendar. The next dynasty, the Zhou, established other Chinese traditions. Some of these traditions included the importance of family and social order. Later thinkers looked back with admiration to the values of the Zhou period.

The Zhou Dynasty

In the 1100s BC the leaders of a people who came to be known as the Zhou (JOH) ruled over a kingdom in China. They joined with other nearby tribes and attacked and overthrew the Shang dynasty. The Zhou dynasty lasted longer than any other dynasty in Chinese history.

Time Line

The Zhou Dynasty

1100s BC
The Zhou dynasty begins.

551 BC
Confucius is born.

1200 BC — 800 BC — 400 BC

771 BC
Invaders reach the Zhou capital.

481 BC
Civil war spreads across China during the Warring States period.

Zhou Dynasty, c. 1050–400 BC

GOBI DESERT

ASIA

Ji

Huang He (Yellow River)

Yellow Sea

Shangqiu

Luoyang

PACIFIC OCEAN

Hao

East China Sea

Chang Jiang (Yangzi River)

Xi River

Zhou dynasty

0   150   300 Miles
0   150   300 Kilometers

GEOGRAPHY SKILLS **INTERPRETING MAPS**

Region How far south did the Zhou dynasty reach?

Zhou Society

QUICK FACTS

King
The king led the government and gave land to lords.

Lords and Warriors
Lords paid taxes to the king and provided warriors to protect his lands.

Peasants
Peasants farmed the nobles' land.

The Zhou Political System

The Zhou kings claimed to possess the mandate of heaven. According to this idea, heaven gave power to the king or leader, and no one ruled without heaven's permission. If a king was found to be bad, heaven would support another leader.

The Zhou came from an area to the west of the Shang kingdom. Early Zhou rulers used the mandate of heaven to justify their rebellion against the Shang. Later Zhou rulers expanded their territory to the northwest and the east. Zhou soldiers then moved south, eventually expanding their rule to the Chang Jiang.

The Zhou established a new political order. They granted land to others in return for loyalty, military support, and other services. The Zhou king was at the highest level. He granted plots of land to **lords**, or people of high rank. Lords paid taxes and provided soldiers to the king as needed. **Peasants**, or farmers with small farms, were at the bottom of the order. Each peasant family received a small plot of land and had to farm additional land for the noble. The system was described in the *Book of Songs*:

" Everywhere under vast Heaven
There is no land that is not the king's
Within the borders of those lands
There are none who are not the king's servants. "
–from the Zhou *Book of Songs*

The Zhou system brought order to China. Ruling through lords helped the Zhou control distant areas and helped ensure loyalty to the king. Over time, however, the political order broke down. Lords passed their power to their sons, who were less loyal to the king. Local rulers gained power. They began to reject the authority of the Zhou kings.

The Decline of Zhou Power

As the lords' loyalty to the Zhou king lessened, many refused to fight against invasions. In 771 BC invaders reached the capital. According to legend, the king had been lighting warning fires to entertain a friend. Each time the fires were lit, the king's armies would rush to the capital gates to protect him. When the real attack came, the men thought the fires were just another joke, and no one came. The Zhou lost the battle, but the dynasty survived.

After this defeat the lords began to fight each other. By 481 BC, China had entered an era called the Warring States period, a time of many civil wars. Armies grew. Fighting became brutal and cruel as soldiers fought for territory, not honor.

Internal Problems

The decline of the Zhou took place along with important changes in the Chinese family **structure**. For many centuries the family had been the foundation of life in China. Large families of several generations formed powerful groups. When these families broke apart, they lost their power. Close relatives became rivals.

Bonds of loyalty even weakened within small families, especially among the upper classes. Sons plotted against each other over inheritances. A wealthy father sometimes tried to maintain peace by dividing his land among his sons. But this created new problems. Each son could build up his wealth and then challenge his brothers. Some sons even killed their own fathers. During the Warring States period, China lacked a strong government to stop the power struggles within the ruling-class families. Chinese society fell into a period of disorder.

READING CHECK **Identifying Cause and Effect** How did the Zhou's decline affect Chinese society?

The Warring States Period

During China's Warring States period, thousands of armies fought each other to gain territory. The armies used new weapons and battle techniques in the civil wars that lasted more than 200 years.

Iron weapons made warfare dangerous and bloody.

Horses were now ridden instead of just being used to pull chariots.

ANALYSIS SKILL **ANALYZING VISUALS**
What advantage did warriors gain by riding horses?

190

Confucius and Society

During the late Zhou period, thinkers came up with ideas about how to restore order to China. One such person, **Confucius**, became the most influential teacher in Chinese history. Confucius is a Western form of the Chinese title of "Master Kong" or "Kongfuzi."

Confucius felt that China was overrun with rude and dishonest people. Upset by the disorder and people's lack of decency, Confucius said that the Chinese needed to return to **ethics**, or moral values. The ideas of Confucius are known as **Confucianism**.

Confucius wanted China to return to ideas and practices from a time when people knew their proper roles in society. These are basic guidelines that Confucius thought would restore family order and social harmony:

- Fathers should display high moral values to inspire their families.
- Children should respect and obey their parents.
- All family members should be loyal to each other.

Confucius's ideas about government were similar to his ideas about family:

- Moral leadership, not laws, brought order to China.
- A king should lead by example, inspiring good behavior in all of his subjects.
- The lower classes would learn by following the example of their superiors. Confucius expressed this idea when he told kings:

“ Lead the people by means of government policies and regulate them through punishments, and they will be evasive and have no sense of shame. Lead them by means of virtue . . . and they will have a sense of shame and moreover have standards. ”

–Confucius, from *The Analects*

BIOGRAPHY

Confucius
551–479 BC

Confucius, whose Chinese title is Kongfuzi, grew up in extreme poverty. Confucius was a dedicated student into his teenage years. Little is known about how he received his formal education, but he mastered many subjects, including music, mathematics, poetry, and history. He served in minor government positions, then he became a teacher. He never knew his teachings would transform Chinese life and thought.

Drawing Inferences How do you think Confucius's government jobs helped shape his teachings?

As Confucius traveled to many different regions, he earned the reputation of a respected teacher. His ideas were passed down through his students and later compiled into a book called *The Analects*.

Because Confucianism focuses on morality, family, society, and government, people often think of it as a philosophy or way of thinking. But it is much more. Confucianism is a unique teaching that is both philosophical and religious. It has been a guiding force in human behavior and religious understanding in China.

Confucius believed that when people behaved well and acted morally, they were simply carrying out what heaven expected of them. Over the centuries Confucius's ideas about virtue, kindness, and learning became the dominant beliefs in China.

READING CHECK Identifying Points of View
What did Confucius believe about good behavior?

HISTORIC DOCUMENT
The Analects

The followers of Confucius placed their teacher's sayings together in a work called in Chinese the Lun Yü *and in English* The Analects. *The word* analects *means "writings that have been collected."*

❝Yu, shall I teach you what knowledge is? When you know a thing, say that you know it; when you do not know a thing, admit that you do not know it. That is knowledge.❞

❝Is there any one word that can serve as a principle for . . . life? Perhaps the word is reciprocity [fairness]: Do not do to others what you would not want others to do to you.❞

❝I do not enlighten anyone who is not eager to learn, nor encourage anyone who is not anxious to put his ideas into words.❞

–Confucius, from *The Analects*

 ANALYSIS SKILL ANALYZING PRIMARY SOURCES

What are some of the qualities that Confucius valued?

Daoism and Legalism

Other beliefs besides Confucianism influenced China during the Zhou period. Two in particular attracted many followers.

Daoism

Daoism (DOW-ih-zum) takes its name from *Dao*, meaning "the way." **Daoism** stressed living in harmony with the Dao, the guiding force of all reality. In Daoist teachings, the Dao gave birth to the universe and all things in it. Daoism developed in part as a reaction to Confucianism. Daoists didn't agree with the idea that active, involved leaders brought social harmony. Instead, they wanted the government to stay out of people's lives.

Daoists believed that people should avoid interfering with nature or each other. They should be like water and simply let things flow in a natural way. For Daoists,

 Main Ideas of Confucianism QUICK FACTS

- People should be respectful and loyal to their family members.

- Leaders should be kind and lead by example.

- Learning is a process that never ends.

- Heaven expects people to behave well and act morally.

the ideal ruler was a wise man who was in harmony with the Dao. He would govern so effortlessly that his people would not even know they were being governed.

Daoists taught that the universe is a balance of opposites: female and male, light and dark, low and high. In each case, opposing forces should be in harmony.

While Confucianism focused its followers' attention on the human world, Daoists paid more attention to the natural world. Daoists regarded humans as just a part of nature, not better than any other thing. In time the Dao, as represented by nature, became so important to the Daoists that they worshipped it.

Laozi (LOWD-zuh) was the most famous Daoist teacher. He taught that people should not try to gain wealth, nor should they seek power. Laozi is credited with writing the basic text of Daoism, *The Way and Its Power*. Later writers created many legends about Laozi's achievements.

Legalism

Legalism, the belief that people were bad by nature and needed to be controlled, contrasted with both Confucianism and Daoism. Unlike the other two beliefs, Legalism was a political philosophy without religious concerns. Instead, it dealt only with government and social control. Followers of Legalism disagreed with the moral preaching of Confucius. Legalists also rejected Daoism because it didn't stress respect for authority.

Legalists felt that society needed strict laws to keep people in line and that punishments should fit crimes. For example, they believed that citizens should be held responsible for each other's conduct. A guilty person's relatives and neighbors should also be punished. This way, everyone would obey the laws.

Unity and efficiency were also important to Legalists. They wanted appointed officials, not nobles, to run China. Legalists wanted the empire to continue to expand. Therefore, they urged the state to always be prepared for war.

Confucianism, Daoism, and Legalism competed for followers. All three beliefs became popular, but the Legalists were the first to put their ideas into practice throughout China.

READING CHECK **Contrasting** How did Daoism and Legalism differ in their theories about government?

BIOGRAPHY

Laozi
c. 500s or 400s BC

Scholars have found little reliable information about Laozi's life. Some believe that his book on Daoism was actually the work of several different authors. Most ancient sources of information about Laozi are myths. For example, one legend states that when Laozi was born, he was already an old man. In Chinese *Laozi* can mean "Old Baby." Over the years, many Daoists have worshipped Laozi as a supernatural being.

Drawing Inferences What do you think it meant to say Laozi was born "old"?

SUMMARY AND PREVIEW When the Zhou dynasty crumbled, political and social chaos erupted. In response, the new teachings of Confucianism, Daoism, and Legalism emerged. In the next section you will learn how the Qin dynasty applied the teachings of Legalism.

Section 2 Assessment

Reviewing Ideas, Terms, and People HSS 6.6.3, 6.6.4

1. **a. Identify** What is the mandate of heaven?
   b. Explain Describe the political order used by the Zhou kings to rule distant lands.
   c. Elaborate What happened when nobles began to reject the Zhou king's authority?
2. **a. Identify** Who was **Confucius**?
   b. Analyze Why did many of the teachings of Confucius focus on the family?
3. **a. Identify** Who was the most famous Daoist teacher?
   b. Summarize What were the main ideas of **Daoism**?
   c. Elaborate What might be some disadvantages of **Legalism**?

Critical Thinking

4. **Finding Main Ideas** Draw a chart like the one here. Use it to list two main ideas each about Confucianism, Daoism, and Legalism.

Confucianism	
Daoism	
Legalism	

FOCUS ON SPEAKING

5. **Exploring the Importance of Historical Figures** Many important people in history are rulers or conquerors. People who think and teach, however, have also played major roles in history. How did thinkers and teachers shape China's history? Write some ideas in your notebook.

The Qin Dynasty

If YOU were there...

You are a scholar living in China in about 210 BC. You have a large library of Chinese literature, poetry, and philosophy. The new emperor is a harsh ruler with no love for learning. He says you must burn all the books that disagree with his ideas. The idea horrifies you. But if you do not obey, the punishment may be severe.

Will you obey the order to burn your books? Why or why not?

BUILDING BACKGROUND Different dynasties held very different ideas about how to rule. As the Zhou period declined, putting new ideas into effect brought great changes.

The Qin Emperor's Strong Government

The Warring States period marked a time in China when several states battled each other for power. One state, the Qin (CHIN), built a strong army that defeated the armies of the rivaling states. Eventually, the Qin dynasty united the country under one government.

Shi Huangdi Takes the Throne

In 221 BC, the Qin king Ying Zheng succeeded in unifying China. He gave himself the title **Shi Huangdi** (SHEE hwahng-dee), which means "first emperor." Shi Huangdi followed Legalist political beliefs. He created a strong government with strict laws and harsh punishments.

HSS 6.6.5 List the policies and achievements of the emperor Shi Huangdi in unifying northern China under the Qin Dynasty.

Time Line

The Qin Dynasty

225 BC		215 BC		205 BC

c. 213 BC
Shi Huangdi orders book burnings.

c. 206 BC
The Qin dynasty collapses.

221 BC
Emperor Shi Huangdi unifies China, beginning the Qin dynasty.

210 BC
Shi Huangdi dies.

Qin Dynasty, c. 221–206 BC

GOBI DESERT

ASIA

YAN

ZHAO

QI

Huang He (Yellow River)

WEI
Luoyang • Xianyang

QIN   HAN   CHU   Wu •

SHU
Chengdu •

Chang Jiang (Yangzi River)

Yellow
Sea

PACIFIC
OCEAN

East
China
Sea

Xi River

South China
Sea

Qin dynasty

�519 Great Wall

WEI Warring state

0   150   300 Miles
0   150   300 Kilometers

Emperor Shi Huangdi — QUICK FACTS

Policies

■ Strong government with strict laws

■ Standard laws, writing system, money, and weights throughout China

Achievements

■ Unified China

■ Built network of roads and canals

■ Built irrigation system to improve farming

■ Built the Great Wall across northern China

GEOGRAPHY SKILLS INTERPRETING MAPS

Location Where was the Great Wall located during the Qin dynasty?

Shi Huangdi demanded that everyone follow his policies. He ordered the burning of all writings that did not agree with Legalism. The only other books that were saved dealt with farming, medicine, and predicting the future. Many scholars opposed the book burnings. The emperor responded to the opposition by burying 460 scholars alive.

Shi Huangdi also used his armies to expand the empire. First, they occupied the lands around both of China's major rivers. Then his soldiers turned north and advanced almost to the Gobi Desert. To the south, they invaded more lands and advanced as far as the Xi River.

Shi Huangdi ensured that there would not be any future revolts in his new territories. When his soldiers conquered a city, he had them destroy its walls and take all the weapons.

China under the Qin

Shi Huangdi changed China's old political system. He claimed all the power and did not share it with the lords. He even took land away from them and forced thousands of nobles to move with their families to the capital so he could keep an eye on them. He also forced thousands of commoners to work on government building projects. Workers faced years of hardship, danger, and often, death.

To control China, Shi Huangdi divided it into districts, each with its own governor. Districts were subdivided into counties that were governed by appointed officials. This organization helped the emperor enforce his tax system. It also helped the Qin enforce a strict chain of command.

READING CHECK **Summarizing** How did Shi Huangdi strengthen the government?

A Unified China

Qin rule brought other major changes to China. Under Shi Huangdi, new policies and achievements united the Chinese people.

Qin Policies

FOCUS ON READING

How might you summarize the new Qin policies?

As you read earlier, mountains and rivers divided China into distinct regions. Customs varied, and people in each area had their own money, writing styles, and laws. Shi Huangdi wanted all Chinese people to do things the same way.

Early in his reign, the emperor set up a uniform system of law. Rules and punishments were to be the same in all parts of the empire. Shi Huangdi also standardized the written language. People everywhere were required to write using the same set of symbols. People from different regions could now communicate with each other in writing. This gave them a sense of shared culture and a common identity.

Next, the emperor set up a new money system. Standardized gold and copper coins became the currency used in all of China. Weights and measures were also standardized. Even the axle width of carts had to be the same. With all these changes and the unified writing system, trade between different regions became much easier. The Qin government strictly enforced these new standards. Any citizen who disobeyed the laws would face severe punishment.

Guardians of Shi Huangdi's Tomb

In 1974 archaeologists found the tomb of Emperor Shi Huangdi near Xi'an and made an amazing discovery. Buried close to the emperor was an army of more than 6,000 life-size terra-cotta, or clay, soldiers. They were designed to be with Shi Huangdi in the afterlife. In other nearby chambers of the tomb there were another 1,400 clay figures of cavalry and chariots.

MONGOLIA

Huang He (Yellow River)

Xi'an • • Shi Huangdi's Tomb

CHINA

Chang Jiang (Yangzi River)

Qin Achievements

New, massive building projects also helped to unify the country. Under Shi Huangdi's rule, the Chinese built a network of roads that connected the capital to every part of the empire. These roads made travel easier for everyone. Each of these new roads was the same width, 50 paces wide. This design helped the army move quickly and easily to put down revolts in distant areas.

China's water system was also improved. Workers built canals to connect the country's rivers. Like the new roads, the canals improved transportation throughout the country. Using the new canals and rivers together made it easier and faster to ship goods from north to south. In addition, the Qin built an irrigation system to make more land good for farming. Parts of that system are still in use today.

Shi Huangdi also wanted to protect the country from invasion. Nomads from the north were fierce warriors, and they were a real threat to China. Hoping to stop them from invading, the emperor built the **Great Wall**, a barrier that linked earlier walls across China's northern frontier. The first section of the wall had been built in the 600s BC to keep invading groups out of China. The Qin connected earlier pieces of the wall to form a long, unbroken structure. Building the wall required years of labor from hundreds of thousands of workers. Many of them died building the wall.

THE IMPACT TODAY

The Great Wall is a major tourist attraction today.

Each terra-cotta soldier was different, with its own facial features, hairstyle, and unique expression. Here, a computer model shows what a soldier might have looked like when it was created.

The Great Wall has been added to and rebuilt many times since Shi Huangdi ruled China.

Rebel forces formed across the country. Each claimed to have received the mandate of heaven to replace the emperor. One of these groups attacked the Qin capital, and the new emperor surrendered. The palace was burned to the ground. Qin authority had disappeared. With no central government, the country fell into civil war.

READING CHECK **Recall** What massive building projects did Shi Huangdi order to unify China?

The Fall of the Qin

Shi Huangdi's policies unified China. However, his policies also stirred resentment. Many peasants, scholars, and nobles hated his harsh ways.

Still, Shi Huangdi was powerful enough to hold the country together. When he died in 210 BC China was unified, but that didn't last. Within a few years, the government began to fall apart.

SUMMARY AND PREVIEW Qin emperor Shi Huangdi's policies and achievements unified China, but his harsh rule led to resentment. After his death, the dynasty fell apart. In the next section you will learn about the Han dynasty that came to power after the end of the Qin.

Section 3 Assessment

Reviewing Ideas, Terms, and People HSS
6.6.5

1. **a. Identify** What does the title **Shi Huangdi** mean?
   b. Explain After unifying China, why did Shi Huangdi divide the country into military districts?
   c. Rate Which of the following acts do you think best showed how powerful Shi Huangdi was—burning books, forcing nobles to move, or forcing commoners to work on government projects? Explain your answer.
2. **a. Recall** Why was the **Great Wall** built?
   b. Summarize What actions did Shi Huangdi take to unify China and standardize things within the empire?
   c. Evaluate In your opinion, was Shi Huangdi a good ruler? Explain your answer.

Critical Thinking

3. **Analyzing** Draw a chart like the one here. Use it to show how each improvement helped the Qin dynasty.

Improvement	Advantage
1. Road system	
2. Canals	
3. Great Wall	

FOCUS ON SPEAKING

4. **Evaluating Contributions to History** When evaluating a person's contribution to history, it is important to consider both the person's good impact and bad impact. In what ways was Shi Huangdi great? What negative impact did he have on China? Write down your ideas.

Emperor Shi Huangdi

If you were a powerful ruler, how would you protect yourself?

When did he live? c. 259–210 BC

Where did he live? Shi Huangdi built a new capital city at Xianyang, now called Xi'an (SHEE-AHN), in eastern China.

What did he do? Shi Huangdi didn't trust people. Several attempts were made on his life, and the emperor lived in fear of more attacks. He was constantly seeking new ways to protect himself and extend his life. By the time Shi Huangdi died, he didn't even trust his own advisors. Even in death, he surrounded himself with protectors: the famous terra-cotta army.

Why is he important? Shi Huangdi was one of the most powerful rulers in Chinese history. The first ruler to unify all of China, he is also remembered for his building programs. He built roads and canals throughout China and expanded what would become the Great Wall.

Drawing Conclusions Why do you think Shi Huangdi feared for his life?

KEY EVENTS

246 BC Shi Huangdi becomes emperor. Because he is still young, a high official rules in his name.

238 BC He exiles the official, whom he suspects of plotting against him, and rules alone.

227 BC An assassination attempt adds fuel to the emperor's paranoia.

221 BC Shi Huangdi unites all of China under his rule.

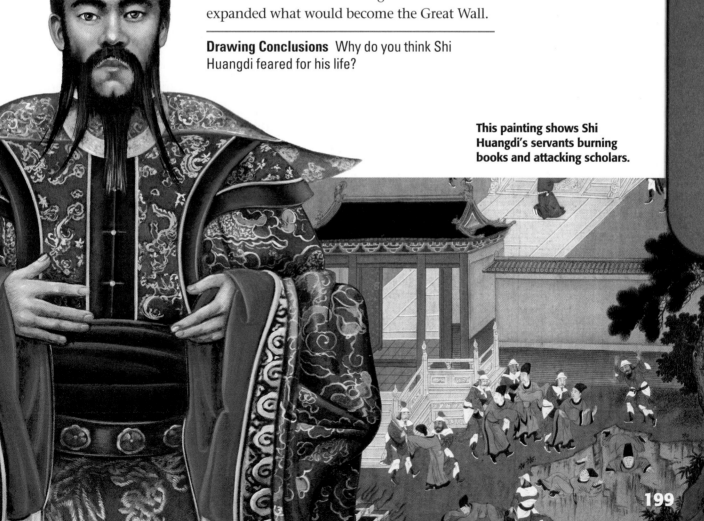

This painting shows Shi Huangdi's servants burning books and attacking scholars.

The Han Dynasty

What You Will Learn...

Main Ideas

1. Han dynasty government was based on the ideas of Confucius.
2. Family life was supported and strengthened in Han China.
3. The Han made many achievements in art, literature, and learning.

The Big Idea

The Han dynasty created a new form of government that valued family, art, and learning.

Key Terms

sundial, *p. 204*
seismograph, *p. 204*
acupuncture, *p. 205*

HSS 6.6.6 Detail the political contributions of the Han Dynasty to the development of the imperial bureaucratic state and the expansion of the empire.

If **YOU** were there...

You are a young Chinese student from a poor family. Your family has worked hard to give you a good education so that you can get a government job and have a great future. Your friends laugh at you. They say that only boys from wealthy families win the good jobs. They think it is better to join the army.

Will you take the exam or join the army? Why?

BUILDING BACKGROUND Though it was harsh, the rule of the first Qin emperor helped to unify northern China. With the building of the Great Wall, he strengthened defenses on the northern frontier. But his successor could not hold on to power. The Qin gave way to a remarkable new dynasty that would last for 400 years.

Han Dynasty Government

When the Qin dynasty collapsed in 207 BC, several different groups battled for power. After several years of fighting, an army led by Liu Bang (lee-oo bang) won control. Liu Bang became the first emperor of the Han dynasty. This Chinese dynasty lasted for more than 400 years.

The Rise of a New Dynasty

Liu Bang, a peasant, was able to become emperor in large part because of the Chinese belief in the mandate of heaven. He was the first common person to become emperor. He earned people's

Time Line

The Han Dynasty

206 BC
The Han dynasty begins.

200 BC

140 BC
Wudi becomes emperor and tries to strengthen China's government.

BC 1 AD

AD 25
The Han move their capital east to Luoyang.

AD 200

AD 220
The Han dynasty falls.

ASIA

GOBI DESERT

TIAN SHAN

TAKLIMAKAN DESERT

Dunhuang

Beijing

Yellow Sea

PACIFIC OCEAN

Huang He (Yellow River)

Luoyang

Chang'an

Chengdu

Yangzi River

Hefei

East China Sea

TIBET

HIMALAYAS

Chang Jiang

Xi River

Guangzhou

South China Sea

Han dynasty

Great Wall

0   150   300 Miles

0   150   300 Kilometers

GEOGRAPHY SKILLS **INTERPRETING MAPS**

Region What features marked the northern boundary of the Han dynasty?

loyalty and trust. In addition, he was well liked by both soldiers and peasants, which helped him to maintain control.

Liu Bang's rule was different from the strict Legalism of the Qin. He wanted to free people from harsh government policies. He lowered taxes for farmers and made punishments less severe. He gave large blocks of land to his supporters.

In addition to setting new policies, Liu Bang changed the way government worked. He set up a government structure that built on the foundation begun by the Qin. He also relied on educated officials to help him rule.

Wudi Creates a New Government

In 140 BC Emperor Wudi (woo-dee) took the throne. He wanted to create a stronger central government. To do that, he

took land from the lords, raised taxes, and placed the supply of grain under the control of the government.

Under Wudi, Confucianism became China's official government philosophy. Government officials were expected to practice Confucianism. Wudi even began a university to teach Confucian ideas.

If a person passed an exam on Confucian teachings, he could get a good position in the government. However, not just anyone could take the test. The exams were only open to people who had been recommended for government service already. As a result, wealthy or influential families continued to control the government.

READING CHECK **Analyzing** How was the Han government based on the ideas of Confucius?

Family Life

The Han period was a time of great social change in China. Class structure became more rigid. The family once again became important within Chinese society.

Social Classes

Based on the Confucian system, people were divided into four classes. The upper class was made up of the emperor, his court, and scholars who held government positions. The second class, the largest, was made up of the peasants. Next were artisans who produced items for daily life and some luxury goods. Merchants occupied the lowest class because they did not produce anything. They only bought and sold what others made. The military was not an official class in the Confucian system. Still, joining the army offered men a chance to rise in social status because the military was considered part of the government.

This Han artifact is an oil lamp held by a servant.

Lives of Rich and Poor

The classes only divided people into social rank. They did not indicate wealth or power. For instance, even though peasants made up the second highest class, they were poor. On the other hand, some merchants were wealthy and powerful despite being in the lowest class.

People's lifestyles varied according to wealth. The emperor and his court lived in a large palace. Less important officials lived in multilevel houses built around courtyards. Many of these wealthy families owned large estates and employed laborers to work the land. Some families even hired private armies to defend their estates.

The wealthy filled their homes with expensive decorations. These included paintings, pottery, bronze lamps, and jade figures. Rich families hired musicians for entertainment. Even the tombs of dead family members were filled with beautiful, expensive objects.

Most people in the Han dynasty, however, didn't live like the wealthy. Nearly 60 million people lived in China during the Han dynasty, and about 90 percent of them were peasants who lived in the countryside. Peasants put in long, tiring days working the land. Whether it was in the millet fields of the north or in the rice paddies of the south, the work was hard. In the winter, peasants were also forced to work on building projects for the government. Heavy taxes and bad weather forced many farmers to sell their land and work for rich landowners. By the last years of the Han dynasty, only a few farmers were independent.

Chinese peasants lived simple lives. They wore plain clothing made of fiber from a native plant. The main foods they ate were cooked grains like barley. Most peasants lived in small villages. Their small, wood-framed houses had walls made of mud or stamped earth.

The Importance of Family

Honoring one's family was an important duty in Han China. In this painting, people give thanks before their family shrine. Only the men participate. The women watch from inside the house.

How are these people giving thanks?

生十雨蒼天濟當年
與後人祭
欽天監五官
鴻臚寺序班
皆世

The Revival of the Family

Since Confucianism was the official government philosophy during Wudi's reign, Confucian teachings about the family were also honored. Children were taught from birth to respect their elders. Disobeying one's parents was a crime. Even emperors had a duty to respect their parents.

Confucius had taught that the father was the head of the family. Within the family, the father had absolute power. The Han taught that it was a woman's duty to obey her husband, and children had to obey their father.

Han officials believed that if the family was strong and people obeyed the father, then people would obey the emperor, too. Since the Han stressed strong family ties and respect for elders, some men even gained government jobs based on the respect they showed their parents.

Children were encouraged to serve their parents. They were also expected to honor dead parents with ceremonies and offerings. All family members were expected to care for family burial sites.

Chinese parents valued boys more highly than girls. This was because sons carried on the family line and took care of their parents when they were old. On the other hand, daughters became part of their husband's family. According to a Chinese proverb, "Raising daughters is like raising children for another family." Some women, however, still gained power. They could actually influence their sons' families. An older widow could even become the head of the family.

READING CHECK Identifying Cause and Effect
Why did the family take on such importance during the Han dynasty?

Han Achievements

During the Han dynasty, the Chinese made many advances in art and learning. Some of these advances are shown here.

Science
This is a model of an ancient Chinese seismograph. When an earthquake struck, a lever inside caused a ball to drop from a dragon's mouth into a toad's mouth, indicating the direction from which the earthquake had come.

Han Achievements

Han rule was a time of great accomplishments. Art and literature thrived, and inventors developed many useful devices.

Art and Literature

The Chinese of the Han period produced many works of art. They became experts at figure painting—a style of painting that includes portraits of people. Portraits often showed religious figures and Confucian scholars. Han artists also painted realistic scenes from everyday life. Their creations covered the walls of palaces and tombs.

In literature, Han China is known for its poetry. Poets developed new styles of verse, including the *fu* style which was the most popular. *Fu* poets combined prose and poetry to create long works of literature. Another style, called *shi*, featured short lines of verse that could be sung. Han rulers hired poets known for the beauty of their verse.

Han writers also produced important works of history. One historian by the name of Sima Qian wrote a complete history of all the dynasties through the early Han. His format and style became the model for later historical writings.

Inventions and Advances

The Han Chinese invented one item that we use every day—paper. They made it by grinding plant fibers, such as mulberry bark and hemp, into a paste. Then they let it dry in sheets. Chinese scholars produced "books" by pasting several pieces of paper together into a long sheet. Then they rolled the sheet into a scroll.

The Han also made other **innovations** in science. These included the sundial and the seismograph. A **sundial** uses the position of shadows cast by the sun to tell the time of day. The sundial was an early type of clock. A **seismograph** is a device that measures the strength of an earthquake. Han emperors were very interested

ACADEMIC VOCABULARY
innovation a new idea, method, or device

Medicine
Han doctors studied the human body and used acupuncture to heal people.

Art
This bronze horse is just one example of the beautiful objects made by Chinese artisans.

ANALYSIS SKILL **ANALYZING VISUALS**

How do these objects show the range of accomplishments in Han China?

in knowing about the movements of the earth. They believed that earthquakes were signs of future evil events.

Another Han innovation, acupuncture (AK-yoo-punk-cher), improved medicine. **Acupuncture** is the practice of inserting fine needles through the skin at specific points to cure disease or relieve pain. Many Han inventions in science and medicine are still used today.

READING CHECK Categorizing What advances did the Chinese make during the Han period?

SUMMARY AND PREVIEW Han rulers moved away from Legalism and based their government on Confucianism. This strengthened family bonds in Han China. In addition, art and learning thrived under Han rule. In the next section you will learn about China's contact beyond its borders.

go.hrw.com
Online Quiz
KEYWORD: SQ6 HP7

Section 4 Assessment

Reviewing Ideas, Terms, and People **HSS** 6.6.6

1. **a. Identify** Whose teachings were the foundation for government during the Han dynasty?
   b. Summarize How did Emperor Wudi create a strong central government?
   c. Evaluate Do you think that an exam system is the best way to make sure that people are fairly chosen for government jobs? Why or why not?
2. **a. Describe** What was the son's role in the family?
   b. Contrast How did living conditions for the wealthy differ from those of the peasants during the Han dynasty?
3. **Identify** What device did the Chinese invent to measure the strength of earthquakes?

Critical Thinking

4. **Categorizing** Copy the chart below. List the four classes of Chinese society and give at least two facts about each.

Class	Facts
1.	
2.	
3.	
4.	

FOCUS ON SPEAKING

5. **Analyzing Impact on History** Sometimes a ruler has the biggest impact on history. Other times, ideas that develop within a society have a greater impact. Which had a greater impact on Han China? Why?

from The Shiji

by Sima Qian

Translated by Burton Watson

About the Reading *The* Shiji, *also called the* Records of the Grand Historian, *is a history that describes more than two thousand years of Chinese culture. The author, Sima Qian (soo-MAH chee-EN), held the title Grand Historian under the Han emperor Wudi. He spent 18 years of his life writing the* Shiji. *His hard work paid off, and his history was well received. In fact, the* Shiji *was so respected that it served as the model for every later official history of China. This passage describes a man named Bu Shi, who attracted the emperor's attention through his generosity and good deeds. Eventually, the emperor invited him to live in the imperial palace.*

AS YOU READ Ask yourself why Sima Qian included Bu Shi in his history.

Bu Shi was a native of Henan, where his family made a living by farming and animal raising. ❶ When his parents died, Bu Shi left home, handing over the house, the lands, and all the family wealth to his younger brother, who by this time was full grown. For his own share, he took only a hundred or so of the sheep they had been raising, which he led off into the mountains to pasture. In the course of ten years or so, Bu Shi's sheep had increased to over a thousand and he had bought his own house and fields. His younger brother in the meantime had failed completely in the management of the farm, but Bu Shi promptly handed over to him a share of his own wealth. This happened several times. Just at that time the Han was sending its generals at frequent intervals to attack the Xiongnu. ❷ Bu Shi journeyed to the capital and submitted a letter to the throne, offering to turn over half of his wealth to the district officials to help in the defense of the border. The emperor dispatched an envoy to ask if Bu Shi wanted a post in the government. ❸

"From the time I was a child," Bu Shi replied, "I have been an animal raiser. I have had no experience in government and would certainly not want such a position" . . .

"If that is the case," said the envoy, "then what is your objective in making this offer?"

Bu Shi replied, "The Son of Heaven has sent out to punish the Xiongnu. ❹ In my humble opinion, every worthy man should be willing to fight to the death to defend the borders, and every person with wealth ought to contribute to the expense . . ."

The emperor discussed the matter with the chancellor, but the latter said, "The proposal is simply not in accord with human nature! ❺ Such eccentric people are of no use in guiding the populace, but only throw the laws into confusion. I beg Your Majesty not to accept his offer!"

For this reason the emperor put off answering Bu Shi for a long time, and finally after several years had passed, turned down the offer, whereupon Bu Shi went back to his fields and pastures . . .

The following year a number of poor people were transferred to other regions . . . At this point Bu Shi took two hundred thousand cash of his own and turned the sum over to the governor of Henan to assist the people who were emigrating to other regions . . . At this time the rich families were all scrambling to hide their wealth; only Bu Shi, unlike the others, had offered to contribute to the expenses of the government. ❻ The emperor decided that Bu Shi was really a man of exceptional worth after all . . . Because of his simple, unspoiled ways and his deep loyalty, the emperor finally appointed him grand tutor to his son Liu Hong, the king of Qi.

GUIDED READING

WORD HELP

objective goal
chancellor high official
accord agreement
eccentric someone who acts strangely
populace people
tutor private teacher

❹ The Chinese people believed that their emperor was the "Son of Heaven." They thought he received his power from heavenly ancestors.

❺ The "latter" means the one mentioned last. In this case, the latter is the chancellor.

❻ *What is Bu Shi's attitude toward his wealth? How is it different from the attitude of the rich families?*

In this painting from the 1600s, government officials deliver a letter.

CONNECTING LITERATURE TO HISTORY

1. **Drawing Conclusions** Like many Chinese historians, Sima Qian wanted to use history to teach lessons. What lessons could the story of Bu Shi be used to teach?

2. **Analyzing** The Emperor Wudi based his government on the teachings of Confucius. What elements of Confucianism can you see in this story?

Han Contacts with Other Cultures

What You Will Learn...

Main Ideas

1. Farming and manufacturing grew during the Han dynasty.
2. Trade routes linked China with the Middle East and Rome.
3. Buddhism came to China from India and gained many followers.

The Big Idea

Trade routes led to the exchange of new products and ideas among China, Rome, and other peoples.

Key Terms

silk, *p. 209*
Silk Road, *p. 209*
diffusion, *p. 211*

HSS **6.6.7** Cite the significance of the trans-Eurasian "silk roads" in the period of the Han Dynasty and Roman Empire and their locations.

6.6.8 Describe the diffusion of Buddhism northward to China during the Han Dynasty.

If YOU were there...

You are a trader traveling along the Silk Road to China. This is your first journey, but you have heard many stories about the country. You know the trip will be hard, through mountains and deserts and terrible weather. While you expect to make a good profit from silk, you are also curious about China and its people.

What do you expect to find in China?

BUILDING BACKGROUND During the Han dynasty Chinese society returned its focus to Confucian ideas, and new inventions were developed. In addition, increased trade allowed other countries to learn about the rich culture of China.

Farming and Manufacturing

Many advances in manufacturing took place during the Han dynasty. As a result, productivity increased and the empire prospered. These changes paved the way for China to make contact with people of other cultures.

Silk Production

By the Han period, the Chinese had become master ironworkers. They manufactured iron swords and armor that made the army more powerful.

Farmers also gained from advances in iron. The iron plow and the wheelbarrow, a single-wheeled cart, increased farm output. With a wheelbarrow a farmer could haul more than 300 pounds all by himself. With an iron plow, he could till more land and raise more food.

Another item that increased in production during the Han dynasty was **silk**, a soft, light, highly valued fabric. For centuries, Chinese women had known the complicated methods needed to raise silkworms, unwind the silk threads of their cocoons, and then prepare the threads for dyeing and weaving. The Chinese were determined to keep their **procedure** for making silk a secret. Revealing these secrets was punishable by death.

During the Han period, weavers used foot-powered looms to weave silk threads into beautiful fabric. Garments made from this silk were very expensive.

READING CHECK Finding Main Ideas How did advances in technology affect farming and silk production?

Trade Routes

Chinese goods, especially silk and fine pottery, were highly valued by people in other lands. During the Han period, the value of these goods to people outside China helped increase trade.

Expansion of Trade

Trade increased partly because Han armies conquered lands deep in Central Asia. Leaders there told the Han generals that people who lived still farther west wanted silk. At the same time, Emperor Wudi wanted strong, sturdy Central Asian horses for his army. China's leaders saw that they could make a profit by bringing silk to Central Asia and trading the cloth for the horses. The Central Asian peoples would then take the silk west and trade it for other products they wanted.

The Silk Road

Traders used a series of overland routes to take Chinese goods to distant buyers. The most famous trade route was known as the **Silk Road**. This 4,000-mile-long network of routes stretched westward from China across Asia's deserts and mountain ranges, through the Middle East, until it reached the Mediterranean Sea.

ACADEMIC VOCABULARY
procedure the way a task is accomplished

PHOTOGRAPH © 2004 MUSEUM OF FINE ARTS, BOSTON

The technique for making silk was a well-kept secret in ancient China, as silk was a valuable trade good in distant lands. Workers made silk from the cocoons of silkworms, just as they do today.

Chinese traders did not travel the entire Silk Road. Upon reaching Central Asia, they sold their goods to local traders who would take them the rest of the way.

Traveling the Silk Road was difficult. Hundreds of men and camels loaded down with valuable goods, including silks and jade, formed groups. They traveled the Silk Road together for protection. Armed guards were hired to protect traders from bandits who stole cargo and water, a precious necessity. Weather presented other dangers. Traders faced icy blizzards, desert heat, and blinding sandstorms.

Named after the most famous item transported along it, the Silk Road was worth its many risks. Silk was so popular in Rome, for example, that China grew wealthy from that trade relationship alone. Traders returned from Rome with silver, gold, precious stones, and horses.

READING CHECK **Summarizing** Why did Chinese trade expand under Han rule?

Buddhism Comes to China

When the Chinese people came into contact with other civilizations, they exchanged ideas along with trade goods. Among these ideas was a new religion. In the first century AD Buddhism spread from India to China along the Silk Road and other trade routes.

Arrival of a New Religion

Over time, the Han government became less stable. People ignored laws, and violence was common. As rebellions flared up, millions of peasants went hungry. Life became violent and uncertain. Many Chinese looked to Daoism or Confucianism to find out why they had to suffer so much, but they didn't find helpful answers.

Buddhism seemed to provide more hope than the traditional Chinese beliefs did. It offered rebirth and relief from suffering. This promise was a major reason the Chinese people embraced Buddhism.

The Silk Road

Rome
Antioch
Tyre
Ctesiphon
KUSHAN EMPIRE
Mathura
Kashgar
Hotan
Taklimakan Desert
Lake Balkhash
ASIA
Dunhuang
TIBET
HIMALAYAS
Shu
GOBI DESERT
Huang He (Yellow River)
Chang'an
Luoyang
Chang Jiang (Yangzi R.)
Guangzhou
PACIFIC OCEAN
Arabian Sea
INDIA
Bay of Bengal
Ceylon (Sri Lanka)
South China Sea
INDIAN OCEAN

Han China, c. AD 200
Silk Road
Other trade route
Great Wall

0   400   800 Miles
0   400   800 Kilometers

N W E S

GEOGRAPHY SKILLS **INTERPRETING MAPS**

Place Around what physical feature does the Silk Road split into two routes?

Impact on China

At first, Indian Buddhists had trouble explaining their religion to the Chinese. Then they used ideas found in Daoism to help describe Buddhist beliefs. Many people grew curious about Buddhism.

Before long, Buddhism caught on in China with both the poor and the upper classes. By AD 200, Buddhist altars stood in the emperor's palace.

Buddhism's introduction to China is an example of **diffusion**, the spread of ideas from one culture to another. Elements of Chinese culture changed in response to the new faith. For example, scholars translated Buddhist texts into Chinese. Many Chinese became Buddhist monks and nuns. Artists carved towering statues of Buddha into mountain walls.

READING CHECK **Finding Main Ideas** How did Chinese people learn of Buddhism?

SUMMARY AND PREVIEW Under the Han, trade brought new goods and ideas, including Buddhism, to China. In the next chapter you'll read about the religion of another people—the Jews.

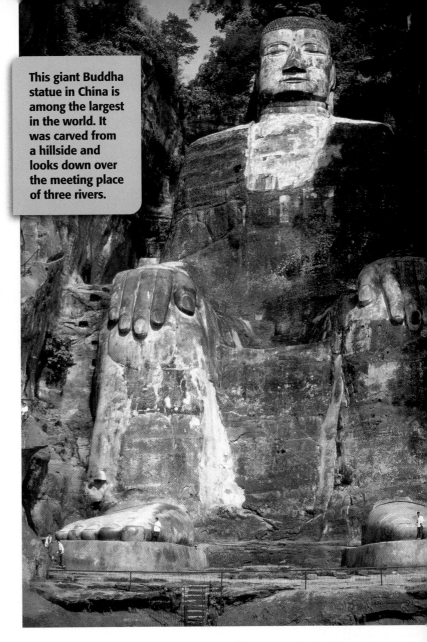

This giant Buddha statue in China is among the largest in the world. It was carved from a hillside and looks down over the meeting place of three rivers.

---

go.hrw.com
Online Quiz
KEYWORD: SQ6 HP7

Section 5 Assessment

Reviewing Ideas, Terms, and People **HSS** 6.6.7, 6.6.8

1. **a. Describe** How did wheelbarrows help farmers?
   b. Summarize How was **silk** made in ancient China?
   c. Elaborate Why did the Chinese keep silk-making methods a secret?
2. **a. Identify** Where did the **Silk Road** begin and end?
   b. Elaborate What information would you use to support the argument that the silk trade must have been very valuable?
3. **a. Identify** What is **diffusion**?
   b. Make Generalizations What Buddhist beliefs appealed to millions of Chinese peasants?

Critical Thinking

4. **Categorizing** Copy the chart here. Use it to show the goods and ideas that came into China and the goods that China sent to other countries along the Silk Road.

Goods into China

Trade Along the Silk Road

Goods out of China

FOCUS ON SPEAKING

5. **Evaluating the Importance of Events** Not all the important events in history are wars or invasions. What peaceful events in this section changed Chinese history? Write down some ideas.

The Silk Road

The Silk Road was a long trade route that stretched across the heart of Asia. Along this route, an active trade developed between China and Southwest Asia by about 100 BC. By AD 100, the Silk Road connected Han China in the east with the Roman Empire in the west.

The main goods traded along the Silk Road were luxury goods—ones that were small, light, and expensive. These included goods like silk, spices, and gold. Because they were small and valuable, merchants could carry these goods long distances and still sell them for a large profit. As a result, people in both the east and the west were able to buy luxury goods that were unavailable at home.

GAUL

SPAIN

E U R O P E

Rome

ROMAN EMPIRE

Black Sea

Byzantium

Carthage

GREECE

Asia Minor

Aral Sea

Caspian Sea

Merv

Antioch

Ecbatana

Ctesiphon

Babylon

Mediterranean Sea

Alexandria

Petra

PERSIA

Persepolis

A F R I C A

Goods from the West Roman merchants like this man grew rich from Silk Road trade. Merchants in the west traded goods like those you see here—wool, amber, and gold.

Aden

ASIA

Goods from the East Chinese merchants also got rich from Silk Road trade. Valuable Asian goods included silk cloth, jade objects, and spices like cinnamon, nutmeg, and ginger that didn't grow in Europe.

• Kaifeng

• Wuwei   Chang'an •

HAN EMPIRE

Chengdu •

TAKLIMAKAN DESERT

• Kashgar

HIMALAYAS

• Bagram

• Kandahar

A Network of Roads The Silk Road was actually a network of roads that linked trading centers in Asia. Most merchants only traveled a small part of the Silk Road, selling their goods along the way to other traders from distant lands.

South China Sea

India

N
W   E
S

—— Silk Road
—— Other trade routes
Han Empire
Roman Empire
Scale varies on this map.

GEOGRAPHY SKILLS INTERPRETING MAPS

1. **Place** What two empires did the Silk Road connect by AD 100?
2. **Movement** What were some goods traded along the Silk Road?

INDIAN OCEAN

Social Studies Skills

Conducting Internet Research

Understand the Skill

The Internet is a huge network of computers that are linked together. You can connect to this network from a personal computer or from a computer at a public library or school. Once connected, you can go to places called Web sites. Web sites consist of one or more Web pages. Each page contains information that you can view on the computer screen.

Governments, businesses, individuals, and many different types of organizations such as universities, news organizations, and libraries have Web sites. Most library Web sites allow users to search their card catalog electronically. Many libraries also have databases on their Web sites. A database is a large collection of related information that is organized by topic.

The Internet can be a very good reference source. It allows you to gather information on almost any topic without ever having to leave your chair. However, finding the information you need can sometimes be difficult. Having the skill to use the Internet efficiently increases its usefulness.

Learn the Skill

There are millions of Web sites on the Internet. This can make it hard to locate specific information. The following steps will help you in doing research on the Internet.

1 Use a search engine. This is a Web site that searches other sites. Type a word or phrase related to your topic into the search engine. It will list Web pages that might contain information on your topic. Clicking on an entry in this list will bring that page to your screen.

2 Study the Web page. Read the information to see if it is useful. You can print the page on the computer's printer or take notes. If you take notes, be sure to include the page's URL. This is its location or "address" on the Internet. You need this as the source of the information.

3 Use hyperlinks. Many Web pages have connections, called hyperlinks, to related information on the site or on other Web sites. Clicking on these links will take you to those pages. You can follow their links to even more pages, collecting information as you go.

4 Return to your results list. If the information or hyperlinks on a Web page are not useful, return to the list of pages that your search engine produced and repeat the process.

The Internet is a useful tool. But remember that information on the Internet is no different than printed resources. It must be evaluated with the same care and critical thinking as other resources.

Practice and Apply the Skill

Answer the following questions to apply the guidelines to Internet research on ancient China.

1. How would you begin if you wanted information about the Qin Dynasty from the Internet?

2. What words might you type into a search engine to find information about Confucianism?

3. Use a school computer to research the Great Wall of China. What kinds of pages did your search produce? Evaluate the usefulness of each type.

Visual Summary

Use the visual summary below to help you review the main ideas of the chapter.

QUICK FACTS

Chinese civilization began along the Huang He (Yellow River).

During the Zhou dynasty, armies fought for power, and the ideas of Confucius spread.

The Qin dynasty unified China with a strong government.

During the Han dynasty, China made advances in learning, and Buddhism spread.

Reviewing Vocabulary, Terms, and People

Match the "I" statement with the person or thing that might have made the statement. Not all of the choices will be used.

a. jade
b. innovation
c. lord
d. oracle
e. peasant
f. Confucius
g. Daoism
h. Shi Huangdi
i. seismograph
j. wheelbarrow
k. Great Wall
l. Legalism

1. "I stressed the importance of living in harmony with nature."

2. "I took a name that means 'first emperor.'"

3. "I stressed that people needed to be controlled with strict laws."

4. "I am a beautiful, hard gemstone that the Chinese made into many objects."

5. "I was built to keep invaders from attacking China."

6. "I can measure the strength of an earthquake."

7. "I am a person of high rank."

8. "I am a new idea, method, or device."

9. "I emphasized the importance of moral values and respect for the family."

10. "I am a farmer who tills a small plot of land."

Comprehension and Critical Thinking

SECTION 1 *(Pages 182–187)* HSS 6.6.1, 6.6.2

11. **a. Identify** In what region did the Shang dynasty develop?

b. Analyze How did China's geography contribute to the country's isolation?

c. Evaluate Considering the evidence, do you think the Xia dynasty was really China's first dynasty or a myth? Explain your answer.

SECTION 2 *(Pages 188–193)* **HSS** **6.6.3, 6.6.4**

12. a. Identify Which Chinese philosophy encouraged strict laws and severe punishments to keep order?

b. Analyze How would Confucianism benefit Chinese emperors?

c. Evaluate Would you be happier under a government influenced by Legalism or by Daoism? In which type of government would there be more order? Explain your answers.

SECTION 3 *(Pages 194–198)* **HSS** **6.6.5**

13. a. Describe What were the main reasons for the fall of the Qin dynasty?

b. Make Inferences Why did Shi Huangdi's armies destroy city walls and take weapons from people they conquered?

c. Evaluate Shi Huangdi was a powerful ruler. Was his rule good or bad for China? Why?

SECTION 4 *(Pages 200–205)* **HSS** **6.6.6**

14. a. Identify During the Han dynasty, who belonged to the first and second social groups?

b. Analyze What was the purpose of the exam system during Wudi's rule?

c. Elaborate What inventions show that the Chinese studied nature?

SECTION 5 *(Pages 208–211)* **HSS** **6.6.7, 6.6.8**

15. a. Identify What factors led to the growth of trade during the Han dynasty?

b. Draw Conclusions Who do you think wore silk garments in China?

c. Predict What might have happened if the Chinese had told foreign visitors how to make silk?

Reviewing Themes

16. Politics Why might historians differ in their views of Shi Huangdi's success as a ruler?

17. Society and Culture How did Confucianism affect people's roles in their family, in government, and in society?

Using the Internet

go.hrw.com KEYWORD SQ6 WH7

18. Activity: Solving Problems Confucius was one of the most influential teachers in Chinese history. His ideas suggested ways to restore order in Chinese society. Enter the activity keyword and research Confucianism. Take note of the political and cultural problems Confucianism tried to address. Then investigate some of the current political and cultural problems in the United States. Could Confucianism solve problems in the United States? Prepare a persuasive argument to support your answer.

Reading Skills

19. Summarizing From the chapter, choose a subsection under a blue headline. For each paragraph within that subsection, write a sentence that summarizes the paragraph's main idea. Continue with the other subsections under the blue heading to create a study guide.

Social Studies Skills

20. Retrieving and Analyzing Information Find a topic in the chapter about which you would like to know more. Use the Internet to explore your topic. Compare the sources you find to determine which seem most complete and reliable. Write a short paragraph about your results.

FOCUS ON SPEAKING

21. Giving Your Oral Presentation You have chosen a person or event and know why your choice was important to Chinese history. Now you must convince your classmates.

First, write a brief description of what the person did or what happened during the event. Then summarize why your person or event is important to Chinese history.

When you give your oral presentation, use vivid language to create pictures in your listeners' minds. Also, use a clear but lively tone of voice.

Standards Assessment

DIRECTIONS: Read each question, and write the letter of the best response.

1

> The connecting link between serving one's father and serving one's mother is love. The connecting link between serving one's father and serving one's prince is reverence [respect]. Thus the mother [brings forth] love, while the prince brings forth reverence. But to the father belong both—love and reverence . . . Likewise, to serve one's elders reverently paves the way for civic obedience.

The observation and advice in this passage *best* express the teachings of

A Buddhism.

B Confucianism.

C Daoism.

D Legalism.

2 Which feature of China's physical geography did *not* separate its early people from the rest of the world?

A the Gobi

B the Huang-He

C the Pacific Ocean

D the Tibetan Plateau

3 How did the Qin emperor Shi Huangdi unify and control China in the 200s BC?

A He created districts and counties that were governed by appointed officials.

B He gave land to China's nobles so that they would be loyal to him.

C He dissolved the army so that it could not be used against him by his enemies.

D He established the Silk Road to get goods from far away.

4 Which of the following developments in China is an example of diffusion?

A the growth of manufacturing and trade

B the building of the Great Wall

C the spread of Buddhism from India

D the use of inventions to improve farming

5 Which dynasty's rulers created a government based on the ideas of Confucius?

A the Shang dynasty

B the Zhou dynasty

C the Qin dynasty

D the Han dynasty

Connecting with Past Learnings

6 In your studies of ancient India, you learned about the Hindu belief in rebirth. Which belief system that influenced early China also emphasized rebirth?

A Buddhism

B Confucianism

C Daoism

D Legalism

7 What characteristic did early civilization in Mesopotamia share with early civilization in China?

A Both developed paper.

B Both were influenced by Buddhism.

C Both built ziggurats.

D Both first developed in river valleys.

Why Things Happen

Assignment

Write an expository essay explaining one of these topics:

- Why the Aryans developed the caste system
- Why Confucius is considered the most influential teacher in Chinese history

> **TIP** **Organizing Information**
>
> Essays that explain why should be written in a logical order. Consider using one of these:
>
> - **Chronological order**, the order in which things happened
> - **Order of importance**, the order of the least important reason to the most important, or vice versa.

ELA **Writing 6.2.2** Write expository compositions (for example, description, explanation, comparison and contrast, problem and solution).

Why do civilizations so often develop in river valleys? Why did early people migrate across continents? You learn about the forces that drive history when you ask why things happened. Then you can share what you learned by writing an expository essay, explaining why events turned out as they did.

1. Prewrite

Considering Topic and Audience

Choose one of the two topics in the assignment, and then start to think about your big idea. Your big-idea statement might start out like this:

- The Aryans developed the caste system to . . .
- Confucius is considered the most influential teacher in Chinese history because he . . .

Collecting and Organizing Information

You will need to collect information that answers the question *Why*. To begin, review the information in this unit of your textbook. You can find more information on your topic in the library or on the Internet.

You should not stop searching for information until you have at least two or three answers to the question *Why*. These answers will form the points to support your big idea. Then take another look at your big idea. You may need to revise it or add to it to reflect the information you have gathered.

2. Write

Here is a framework that can help you write your first draft.

A Writer's Framework

Introduction
- Start with an interesting fact or question.
- Identify your big idea.
- Include any important background information.

Body
- Include at least one paragraph for each point supporting your big idea.
- Include facts and details to explain and illustrate each point.
- Use chronological order or order of importance.

Conclusion
- Summarize your main points.
- Using different words, restate your big idea.

3. Evaluate and Revise

Evaluating

Effective explanations require clear, straightforward language. Use the following questions to discover ways to improve your draft.

Evaluation Questions for an Expository Essay

- Does your essay begin with an interesting fact or question?
- Does the introduction identify your big idea?
- Have you developed at least one paragraph to explain each point?
- Is each point supported with facts and details?

- Have you organized your points clearly and logically?
- Did you explain any unusual words?
- Does the conclusion summarize your main points?
- Does the conclusion restate your big idea in different words?

Revising

Reread your draft. See whether each point is connected logically to the main idea and the other points you are making. If needed, add transitions—words and phrases that show how ideas fit together.

To connect points and information in time, use words like *after*, *before*, *first*, *later*, *soon*, *eventually*, *over time*, *as time passed*, and *then*. To show order of importance, use transitional words and phrases like *first*, *last*, *mainly*, *to begin with*, and *more important*.

4. Proofread and Publish

Proofreading

If you create a bulleted or numbered list, be sure to capitalize and punctuate the list correctly.

- **Capitalization:** It is always acceptable to capitalize the first word of each item in the list.
- **Punctuation:** (1) If the items are sentences, put a period at the end of each. (See the list in the tip above.) (2) If the items are not complete sentences, you usually do not need any end punctuation.

Publishing

Share your explanation with students from another class. After they read it, ask them to summarize your explanation. How well did they undertand the points you wanted to make?

● Practice and Apply

Use the steps and strategies in this workshop to write your explanation.

TIP **Using Lists** To make an explanation easier to follow, look for information that can be presented in a list.

Sentence/Paragraph Form Confucius gave the Chinese people guidelines for behavior. He felt that fathers should display high moral values, and he thought it was important that women obey their husbands. Children were to be obedient and respectful.

List Form

Confucius gave the Chinese people guidelines for behavior:

- Fathers should display high moral values.
- Wives should obey their husbands.
- Children should obey and respect their parents.

Foundations of Western Ideas

The foundations of Western civilization can be traced back more than 2,000 years to the eastern Mediterranean region. There, the ancient Hebrews and Greeks developed many of the ideas and traditions that have shaped the world today.

The Hebrews' religion, Judaism, was based on a belief in one god and basic ideas about right and wrong. The ancient Greeks created the world's first democracy. The Greeks also revolutionized science and mathematics and created some of the world's most famous art and literature.

In the next three chapters, you will learn how the Hebrews and Greeks helped shape the world you live in today.

Explore the Art

In this scene, the daughter of a Greek king warns her father not to trust a general who needs help in a war. What does this scene show about life in ancient Greece?

The Hebrews and Judaism

California Standards

History-Social Science

6.3 Students analyze the geographic, political, economic, religious, and social structures of the Ancient Hebrews.

Analysis Skills

HI 2 Students understand and distinguish cause, effect, sequence, and correlation in historical events, including the long- and short-term causal relations.

HR 2 Students distinguish fact from opinion in historical narratives and stories.

English-Language Arts

Writing 6.1.3 Use a variety of effective and coherent organizational patterns.

Reading 6.2.0 Read and understand grade-level-appropriate material.

FOCUS ON WRITING

A Web Site Have you ever designed your own Web site? If not, here's your chance to create one. As you read this chapter, you'll gather information about Hebrew history, beliefs, values, and culture. Then you will write a description of how you would present this same information on a Web site.

CHAPTER EVENTS

c. 2000 BC Abraham leaves Mesopotamia.

2000 BC

WORLD EVENTS

c. 1750 BC Hammurabi issues his law code.

HOLT

History's Impact

▶ video series
Watch the video to understand the impact of Judaism throughout the world.

What You Will Learn...

In this chapter you will study the history and culture of the Jewish people. In this photo, hundreds of people pray at the Western Wall, the holiest site in the world of Judaism. The wall is about 2,000 years old.

c. 1200 BC
Moses leads the Hebrews out of Egypt during the Exodus.

586 BC
The Jews are enslaved in Babylon.

AD 70
The Romans destroy the Second Temple in Jerusalem.

1475 BC	950 BC	425 BC	AD 100

c. 1240–1224 BC
Ramses the Great rules Egypt.

c. 563 BC
The Buddha is born in India.

27 BC
Augustus becomes the first Roman emperor.

THE HEBREWS AND JUDAISM **223**

Reading Social Studies

by Kylene Beers

Focus on Themes In this chapter, you will read about the Hebrew people and the religion called Judaism. You will learn about Jewish beliefs, texts such as the Torah and the Dead Sea Scrolls, and leaders such as Abraham and Moses.

As you read, pay close attention to how the Hebrews' beliefs affected where and how they lived. In the process, you will discover that the lives of the early Hebrews were dominated by their **religious** beliefs and practices.

Facts, Opinions, and the Past

Focus on Reading Why is it important to know the difference between a fact and an opinion? Separating facts from opinions about historical events helps you know what really happened.

Identifying Facts and Opinions Something is a **fact** if there is a way to prove it or disprove it. For example, research can prove or disprove the following statement: "The ancient Jews recorded their laws." But research can't prove the following statement because it is just an **opinion**, or someone's belief: "Everyone should read the records of the ancient Jews."

Additional reading support can be found in the

Inter active

Reader and Study Guide

Use the process below to decide whether a statement is fact or opinion.

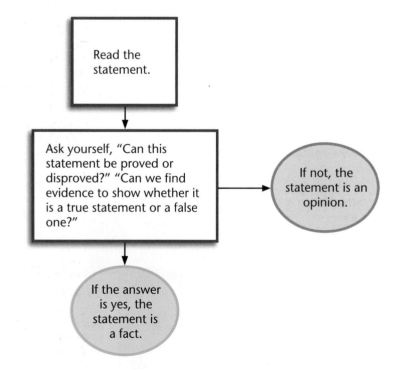

Read the statement.

Ask yourself, "Can this statement be proved or disproved?" "Can we find evidence to show whether it is a true statement or a false one?"

If not, the statement is an opinion.

If the answer is yes, the statement is a fact.

HSS Analysis HR 2 Distinguish fact from opinion
ELA Reading 6.2.0 Read and understand grade-level-appropriate material.

You Try It!

The following passage tells about boys who, years ago, found what came to be called the Dead Sea Scrolls. All the statements in this passage are facts. What makes them facts and not opinions?

Scrolls Reveal Past Beliefs

Until 1947 no one knew about the Dead Sea Scrolls. In that year, young boys looking for a lost goat near the Dead Sea found a small cave. One of the boys went in to explore and found several old jars filled with moldy scrolls.

From Chapter 8, pages 236–237

Scholars were very excited about the boy's find. Eager to find more scrolls, they began to search the desert. Over the next few decades, searchers found several more groups of scrolls.

Careful study revealed that most of the Dead Sea Scrolls were written between 100 BC and AD 50. The scrolls included prayers, commentaries, letters, and passages from the Hebrew Bible. These writings help historians learn about the lives of many Jews during this time.

Identify each of the following as a fact or an opinion and then explain your choice.

1. Boys discovered the Dead Sea Scrolls in 1947.

2. The discovery of the scrolls is one of the most important discoveries ever.

3. All religious leaders should study the Dead Sea Scrolls.

4. The Dead Sea Scrolls were written between 100 BC and AD 50.

Academic Vocabulary

Success in school is related to knowing academic vocabulary— the words that are frequently used in school assignments and discussions. In this chapter, you will learn the following academic word:

principles *(p. 234)*

As you read Chapter 8, look for clues that will help you determine which statements are facts.

The Early Hebrews

HSS **6.3.3** Explain the significance of Abraham, Moses, Naomi, Ruth, David, and Yohanan ben Zaccai in the development of the Jewish religion.

6.3.4 Discuss the locations of the settlements and movements of Hebrew peoples, including the Exodus and their movement to and from Egypt, and outline the significance of the Exodus to the Jewish and other people.

If YOU were there...

You and your family are herders, looking after large flocks of sheep. Your grandfather, the leader of your tribe, is very rich, so your life is easy. One day, your grandfather says that your whole family will be moving to a new country. The trip will be very long, and people there may not welcome you.

How do you feel about moving to a faraway land?

BUILDING BACKGROUND Like the family described above, the early Hebrews moved to new lands several times. From the beginning, the Hebrews were wanderers. According to Hebrew tradition, their history began with a search for a new home.

Abraham and Moses Lead the Hebrews

Sometime between 2000 and 1500 BC a new people appeared in Southwest Asia. They were the Hebrews (HEE-brooz). The early Hebrews were simple herders, but they developed a culture that became a major influence on later civilizations.

Most of what is known about early Hebrew history comes from the work of archaeologists and from accounts written by Hebrew scribes. These accounts describe the Hebrews' early history and the laws of their religion. In time these accounts became the Hebrew Bible. The Hebrew Bible is also part of the Christian Bible, which includes the New Testament as well.

The Beginnings in Canaan and Egypt

The Hebrew Bible traces the Hebrews back to a man named **Abraham**. One day, the Hebrew Bible says, God told Abraham to leave his home in Mesopotamia. He was to take his family on a long journey to the west. God promised to lead Abraham to a new land and make his descendants into a mighty nation.

Possible Routes of Abraham and Moses

HITTITE EMPIRE

Haran

Euphrates River

ASSYRIA

Tigris River

Mediterranean Sea

Damascus

The Hebrew Bible says that Abraham left Mesopotamia and settled in Canaan.

Babylon

CANAAN

Jerusalem • Jericho

MESOPOTAMIA

Dead Sea

Ramses

EGYPT

Memphis

Nile River

Ezion-geber

Moses led the Hebrews out of slavery in Egypt and into Canaan in a journey called the Exodus.

Ur

Persian Gulf

Mt. Sinai

Possible route of Abraham
Possible route of Moses

0   100   200 Miles
0   100   200 Kilometers

GEOGRAPHY SKILLS **INTERPRETING MAPS**

1. **Place** What natural features did Abraham and Moses follow on their long journeys?
2. **Movement** About how many miles was Abraham's journey from Ur to Canaan?

Abraham left Mesopotamia and settled in Canaan (KAY-nuhn), on the Mediterranean Sea. His descendants—the Hebrews—lived in Canaan for many years. Later, however, some Hebrews moved to Egypt, perhaps because of famine in Canaan.

The Hebrews lived well in Egypt, and their population grew. This growth worried Egypt's ruler, the pharaoh. He feared that the Hebrews might soon take over Egypt. To stop this from happening, the pharaoh made the Hebrews slaves.

The Exodus

According to the Hebrew Bible, a leader named **Moses** appeared among the Hebrews in Egypt. In the 1200s BC, God told Moses to lead the Hebrews out of Egypt. Moses went to the pharaoh and demanded that

the Hebrews be freed. The pharaoh refused. Soon afterward a series of terrible plagues, or disasters, struck Egypt.

The plagues frightened the pharaoh so much that he agreed to free the Hebrews. Overjoyed with the news of their release, Moses led his people out of Egypt in a journey called the **Exodus**. To the Hebrews, the release from slavery proved that God was protecting and watching over them. They believed that they had been set free because God loved them.

The Exodus is a major event in Hebrew history, but other people recognize its significance as well. Throughout history, for example, enslaved people have found hope in the story. Before the Civil War, American slaves sang about Moses to keep their hopes of freedom alive.

For many years after their release, the Hebrews wandered through the desert, trying to return to Canaan. During their wanderings they reached a mountain called Sinai. On that mountain, the Hebrew Bible says, God gave Moses two stone tablets. On the tablets was written a code of moral laws known as the **Ten Commandments**:

> " I am God your Lord, who brought you out of Egypt, from the place of slavery.
> Do not have any other gods before Me.
> Do not take the name of God your Lord in vain. God will not allow the one who takes his name in vain to go unpunished.
> Remember the Sabbath to keep it holy.
> Honor your father and mother. You will then live long on the land that God your Lord is giving you.
> Do not commit murder.
> Do not commit adultery.
> Do not steal.
> Do not testify as a false witness against your neighbor.
> Do not be envious of your neighbor's house.
> Do not be envious of your neighbor's wife . . . or anything else that is your neighbor's. "
>
> —Exodus 20:2–14, from *The Living Torah*

As you can see, by accepting the Ten Commandments, the Hebrews agreed to worship only God. They also agreed to value human life, self-control, and justice. Over time the commandments shaped the development of Hebrew society.

The Return to Canaan

According to the Hebrew Bible, the Hebrews wandered for 40 years before they reached Canaan. Once there, they had to fight to gain control of Canaan before they could settle. After they conquered Canaan and settled down, the Hebrews became known as the Israelites.

In Canaan, the Israelites lived in small, scattered communities. These communities had no central government. Instead, each community selected judges as leaders to enforce laws and settle disputes. Before long, though, a threat arose that called for a new kind of leadership.

READING CHECK Identifying Cause and Effect
Why did Abraham leave Mesopotamia?

Time Line

Early Hebrew History

c. 2000 BC
Abraham leaves Mesopotamia and goes to Canaan.

2100 BC

1300 BC

1200 BC

1200s BC
Moses leads the Hebrews on the Exodus out of slavery in Egypt.

Kings Unite the Israelites

The new threat to the Israelites came from the Philistines (FI-li-steenz), who lived along the Mediterranean coast. In the mid-1000s BC the Philistines invaded the Israelites' lands.

Frightened of these powerful invaders, the israelites banded together under a single ruler who could lead them in battle. That ruler was a man named Saul, who became the first king of Israel. Saul had some success as a military commander, but he wasn't a strong king. He never won the total support of tribal and religious leaders. They often fought against his decisions.

King David

After Saul died, a man once declared an outlaw became king. That king's name was **David**. As a young man, David had been a shepherd. The Hebrew Bible tells how David slew the Philistine giant Goliath, which brought him to the attention of the king. David was admired for his military skills and as a poet; many of the Psalms are attributed to him. He established the capital of Israel in Jerusalem. For many years, David lived in the desert, gathering support from local people. When Saul died, David used this support to become king.

Unlike Saul, David was well loved by the Israelites. He won the full support of Israel's tribal leaders. David was admired for his military skills and as a poet; many of the Psalms are attributed to him. He established the capital of Israel in Jerusalem.

King Solomon

David's son **Solomon** (SAHL-uh-muhn) took the throne in about 965 BC. Like his father, Solomon was a strong king. He expanded the kingdom and made nearby kingdoms, including Egypt and Phoenicia, his allies. Trade with these allies made Israel very rich. With these riches, Solomon built a great temple to God in Jerusalem. This temple became the center of the Israelites' religious life and a symbol of their faith.

FOCUS ON READING

Are the sentences in this paragraph facts or opinions? How can you tell?

READING CHECK Finding Main Ideas Why did the Israelites unite under a king?

mid-1000s BC
Saul becomes the first king of Israel.

c. 1000 BC
David becomes king of Israel.

c. 965 BC
David's son Solomon becomes king of Israel. Solomon builds a great temple in Jerusalem.

c. 930 BC
Solomon dies. His kingdom is split into the kingdoms of Judah and Israel.

1100 BC • 1000 BC • 900 BC • 800 BC

ANALYSIS SKILL **READING TIME LINES**

About how many years after Abraham settled in Canaan did Saul become the first king of Israel?

Invaders Conquer and Rule

After Solomon's death in about 930 BC, revolts broke out over who should be king. Within a year, conflict tore Israel apart. Israel split into two kingdoms called Israel and called Judah (JOO-duh). The people of Judah became known as Jews.

The two new kingdoms lasted for a few centuries. In the end, however, both were conquered. Israel fell to the Assyrians around 722 BC. As a result, the kingdom fell apart and most of its people scattered. Judah lasted longer, but before long it fell to the Chaldeans.

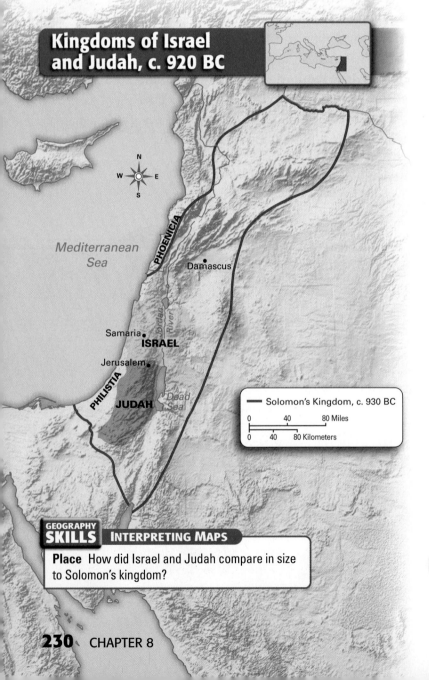

Kingdoms of Israel and Judah, c. 920 BC

Mediterranean Sea

PHOENICIA

Damascus

Samaria
ISRAEL
Jerusalem
PHILISTIA
JUDAH
Dead Sea

Jordan River

— Solomon's Kingdom, c. 930 BC

0   40   80 Miles
0   40   80 Kilometers

GEOGRAPHY SKILLS | INTERPRETING MAPS

Place How did Israel and Judah compare in size to Solomon's kingdom?

The Scattering of the Jews

The Chaldeans captured Jerusalem and destroyed Solomon's Temple in 586 BC. They marched thousands of Jews to their capital, Babylon, to work as slaves. The Jews called this enslavement the Babylonian Captivity. It lasted about 50 years.

In the 530s BC a people called the Persians conquered the Chaldeans and let the Jews return to Jerusalem. Despite this permission, many Jews never returned to Jerusalem. Instead, they moved to other parts of the Persian Empire. Scholars call the scattering of the Jews outside of Israel and Judah the **Diaspora** (dy-AS-pruh).

The rest of the Jews did return home to Jerusalem. There they rebuilt Solomon's Temple, which became known as the Second Temple. The Jews remained Persian subjects until the 330s BC, when the Persians were conquered by invaders.

Independence and Conquest

Tired of foreign rule, a Jewish family called the Maccabees (MA-kuh-beez) led a successful revolt in the 160s BC. For about 100 years, the Jews again ruled their own kingdom. Their independence, however, didn't last. In 63 BC the Jews were conquered again, this time by the Romans.

Although Jewish leaders added to the Second Temple under Roman rule, life was difficult. Heavy taxes burdened the people. The Romans were brutal masters who had no respect for the Jewish religion and way of life.

Some rulers tried to force the Jews to worship the Roman Emperor. The Roman rulers even appointed the high priests, the leaders of the Temple. This was more than the Jews could bear. They called on their people to rebel against the Romans.

READING CHECK **Summarizing** How did Roman rule affect Jewish society?

Women in Hebrew Society

Hebrew government and society were dominated by men, as were most ancient societies. Women had few rights. They had to obey their fathers and their husbands. A woman couldn't even choose her own husband. Instead, her husband was chosen by her father. A woman couldn't inherit property either, unless she had no brothers. If she did have a brother, all property went to him.

Some Hebrew women, however, made great contributions to their society. The Hebrew Bible describes them. Some were political and military leaders, such as Queen Esther and the judge Deborah. According to the Hebrew Bible, these women saved the Hebrew people from their enemies. Other women, such as Miriam, the sister of Moses, were spiritual leaders.

Some women in the Hebrew Bible were seen as examples of how Hebrew women should behave. For example, Ruth, who left her people to care for her mother-in-law, was seen as a model of devotion to one's family. The Hebrews told Ruth's story as an example of how people should treat their family members.

READING CHECK **Generalizing** What was life like for most Hebrew women?

Ruth and Naomi

The story of Ruth and Naomi comes from the Book of Ruth, one of the books of the Hebrew Bible. According to this account, Ruth was not a Hebrew, though her husband was. After he died, Ruth and her mother-in-law, Naomi, resettled in Israel. Inspired by Naomi's faith in God, Ruth joined Naomi's family and adopted her beliefs. She dedicated her life to supporting Naomi.

Drawing Inferences What lessons might the Hebrews have used the story of Ruth and Naomi to teach?

SUMMARY AND PREVIEW The history of the Hebrews and Judaism began some 3,500 to 4,000 years ago. The instructions that Jews believe God gave to the early Hebrews shaped their religion, Judaism. In the next section, you will learn about the main teachings of Judaism.

Section 1 Assessment

Reviewing Ideas, Terms, and People **HSS** 6.3.3, 6.3.4

1. **a. Identify** Who was **Abraham**?
   b. Evaluate Why was the **Exodus** a significant event in Hebrew history?
2. **Summarize** How did **David** and **Solomon** strengthen the kingdom of Israel?
3. **Describe** What happened during the Babylonian Captivity?
4. **a. Describe** Who had more rights in Hebrew society, men or women?
   b. Make Inferences How did Ruth and Naomi set an example for other Hebrews?

Critical Thinking

5. **Summarize** Draw a chart like the one here. In each row, list a key figure from Hebrew history and his or her contributions to Hebrew society. You may add more rows.

Key Figure	Contribution

FOCUS ON WRITING

6. **Taking Notes about Early Hebrew History** Make a list of events and people that played key roles in shaping Hebrew history. Look for ways to group your facts into features on your Web page.

Jewish Beliefs and Texts

What You Will Learn...

Main Ideas

1. Beliefs in God, education, justice, and obedience anchor Jewish society.
2. Jewish beliefs are listed in the Torah, the Hebrew Bible, and the Commentaries.
3. The Dead Sea Scrolls reveal many past Jewish beliefs.
4. The ideas of Judaism have helped shape later cultures.

The Big Idea

The central ideas and laws of Judaism are contained in sacred texts such as the Torah.

Key Terms

Judaism, *p. 232*
monotheism, *p. 232*
Torah, *p. 234*
synagogue, *p. 234*
prophets, *p. 235*
Talmud, *p. 236*
Dead Sea Scrolls, *p. 236*

HSS **6.3.1** Describe the origins and significance of Judaism as the first monotheistic religion based on the concept of one God who sets down moral laws for humanity.

6.3.2 Identify the sources of the ethical teachings and central beliefs of Judaism (the Hebrew Bible, the Commentaries): belief in God, observance of law, practice of the concepts of righteousness and justice, and importance of study; and describe how the ideas of the Hebrew traditions are reflected in the moral and ethical traditions of Western civilization.

If YOU were there...

You live in a small town in ancient Israel. Some people in your town treat strangers very badly. But you have been taught to be fair and kind to everyone, including strangers. One day, you tell one of your neighbors he should be kinder to strangers. He asks you why you feel that way.

How will you explain your belief in kindness?

BUILDING BACKGROUND The idea that people should be fair and kind to everyone in the community is an important Jewish teaching. Sometimes, their teachings set the Jews apart from other people in society. But at the same time, their shared beliefs tie all Jews together as a religious community.

Jewish Beliefs Anchor Their Society

Religion is the foundation upon which the Jews base their whole society. In fact, much of Jewish culture is based directly on Jewish beliefs. The central beliefs of **Judaism,** the Jewish religion, are beliefs in God, education, justice, and obedience.

Belief in One God

Most importantly, Jews believe in one God. The Hebrew name for God is YHWH, which is never pronounced by Jews, as it is considered too holy. The belief in only one God is called **monotheism**. Many people believe that Judaism was the world's first monotheistic religion. It is certainly the oldest such religion that is still widely practiced today.

In the ancient world where most people worshipped many gods, the Jews' worship of only God set them apart. This worship also shaped Jewish society. The Jews believed that they were God's chosen people. They believed that God had guided their history through his relationships with Abraham, Moses, and other leaders.

Moses and the Golden Calf
According to the Hebrew Bible, when Moses returned from Mount Sinai, he found the Hebrews worshipping a statue of a golden calf. They had become impatient waiting for Moses and wanted to worship a god they could see. Moses was furious that they were worshipping a statue instead of God. In this Italian painting from the 1600s, the Hebrews are destroying the golden calf.

How are the Hebrews destroying the golden calf?

Belief in Education

Another central element of Judaism is education and study. Teaching children the basics of Judaism has always been important in Jewish society. In ancient Jewish communities, older boys—but not girls—studied with professional teachers to learn their religion. Even today, education and study are central to Jewish life for children and adults.

Belief in Justice and Righteousness

Also central to the Jews' religion are the ideas of justice and righteousness. To Jews, justice means kindness and fairness in dealing with other people. Everyone deserves justice, even strangers and criminals. Jews are expected to give aid to those who need it, including the poor, the sick, and orphans. Jews are also expected to be fair in business dealings.

Righteousness refers to doing what is proper. Jews are supposed to behave properly, even if others around them do not. For the Jews, righteous behavior is more important than rituals, or ceremonies.

Belief in Obedience and Law

Closely related to the ideas of justice and righteousness is obedience to the law. Moral and religious laws have guided Jews through their history and continue to do so today. Jews believe that God gave them these laws to follow.

The most important Jewish laws are the Ten Commandments. The commandments, however, are only part of Jewish law. Jews believe that Moses recorded a whole system of laws that God had set down for them to obey. Named for Moses, this system is called Mosaic law.

Like the Ten Commandments, Mosaic laws guide many areas of Jews' daily lives. For example, Mosaic law governs how people pray and celebrate holy days. The laws prohibit Jews from working on holy days or on the Sabbath, the seventh day of each week. The Sabbath is a day of rest because, in Jewish tradition, God created the world in six days and rested on the seventh. As a result, Jews observe the Sabbath on Saturday, the seventh day of the week.

ACADEMIC VOCABULARY

principles
basic beliefs, rules, or laws

Among the Mosaic laws are rules about the foods that Jews can eat and rules that must be followed in preparing them. For example, the laws state that Jews cannot eat pork or shellfish, which are thought to be ritually unclean. Other laws say that meat has to be killed and prepared in a way that makes it acceptable for Jews to eat. Today foods that have been so prepared are called kosher (KOH-shuhr), or fit.

In many Jewish communities today, people still strictly follow Mosaic law. They are called Orthodox Jews. Other Jews choose not to follow many of the ancient laws. They are known as Reform Jews. A third group, the Conservative Jews, falls between the other two groups. These are the three largest groups of Jews in the world today.

READING CHECK **Generalizing** What are the most important beliefs of Judaism?

Texts List Jewish Beliefs

The laws and **principles** of Judaism are described in several sacred texts, or writings. Among the main texts are the Torah, the Hebrew Bible, and the Commentaries.

The Torah

The ancient Jews recorded most of their laws in five books. Together these books are called the **Torah**, the most sacred text of Judaism. In addition to laws, the Torah includes a history of the Jews until the death of Moses.

Readings from the Torah are central to Jewish religious services today. Nearly every **synagogue** (SI-nuh-gawg), or Jewish house of worship, has at least one Torah. Out of respect for the Torah, readers do not touch it. They use special pointers to mark their places in the text.

Hebrew Texts

The Torah

Using a special pointer called a *yad*, this girl is reading aloud from the Torah. The Torah is the most sacred of Hebrew writings. Jews believe its contents were revealed to Moses by God. The Torah plays a central role in many Jewish ceremonies, like this one.

The Hebrew Bible

The Torah is the first of three parts of a group of writings called the Hebrew Bible, or Tanach (tah-NAHK). The second part is made up of eight books that describe the messages of Hebrew prophets. **Prophets** are people who are said to receive messages from God to be taught to others.

The final part of the Hebrew Bible is 11 books of poetry, songs, stories, lessons, and history. For example, the Book of Daniel tells about a prophet named Daniel, who lived during the Babylonian Captivity. According to the book, Daniel angered the king who held the Hebrews as slaves. As punishment, the king had Daniel thrown into a den of lions. The story tells that Daniel's faith in God kept the lions from killing him, and he was released. Jews tell this story to show the power of faith.

Also in the final part of the Hebrew Bible are the Proverbs, short expressions of Hebrew wisdom. Many of these sayings are attributed to Hebrew leaders, especially King Solomon. For example, Solomon is supposed to have said, "A good name is to be chosen rather than great riches." In other words, it is better to be seen as a good person than to be rich and not respected.

The third part of the Hebrew Bible also includes the Book of Psalms. Psalms are poems or songs of praise to God. Many of these are attributed to King David. One of the most famous psalms is the Twenty-third Psalm. It includes lines often read today during times of difficulty:

> "The Lord is my shepherd, I shall not want [lack anything]. He makes me lie down in green pastures; He leads me beside still waters. He restores my soul [life]; He guides me in the paths of righteousness for His name's sake."
>
> —Psalms 23:1–3

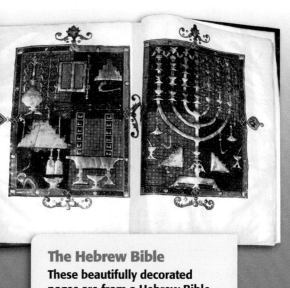

The Hebrew Bible
These beautifully decorated pages are from a Hebrew Bible. The Hebrew Bible, sometimes called the Tanach, includes the Torah and other ancient writings.

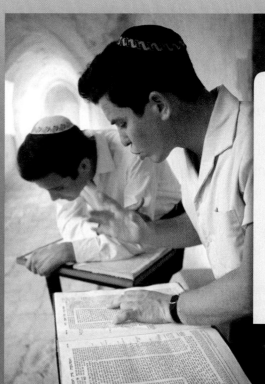

The Commentaries
The Talmud is a collection of laws, commentaries, and discussions about the Torah and the Hebrew Bible. The Talmud is a rich source of information for discussion and debate. Rabbis and religious scholars like these young men study the Talmud to learn about Jewish history and laws.

ANALYSIS
SKILL **ANALYZING VISUALS**

How does the Torah look different from the Hebrew Bible and the commentaries?

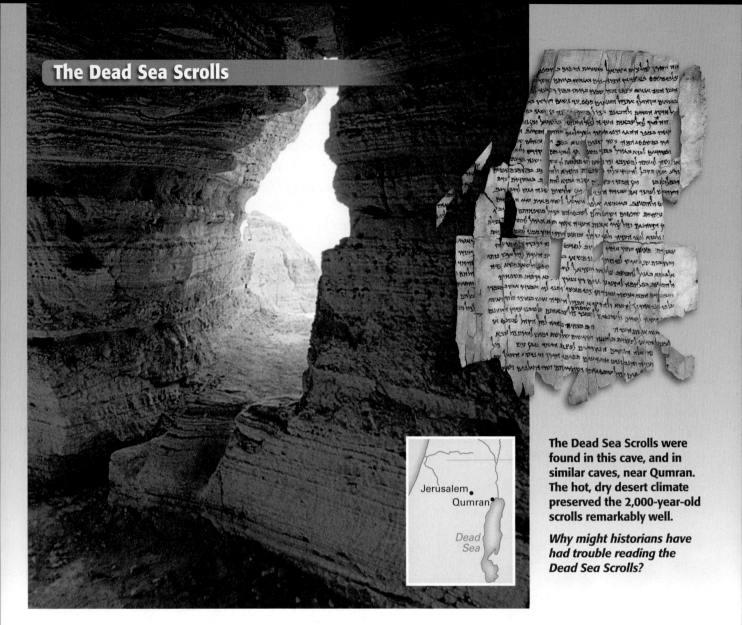

The Dead Sea Scrolls were found in this cave, and in similar caves, near Qumran. The hot, dry desert climate preserved the 2,000-year-old scrolls remarkably well.

Why might historians have had trouble reading the Dead Sea Scrolls?

Jerusalem
Qumran
Dead Sea

Commentaries

For centuries scholars have studied the Torah and Jewish laws. Because some laws are hard to understand, the scholars write commentaries to explain them.

Many of these commentaries are found in the **Talmud** (TAHL-moohd), a set of commentaries, stories, and folklore. The writings of the Talmud were produced between AD 200 and 600. Many Jews consider them second only to the Hebrew Bible in their significance to Judaism.

READING CHECK **Analyzing** What texts do Jews consider sacred?

Scrolls Reveal Past Beliefs

Besides the Torah, the Hebrew Bible, and the Commentaries, many other documents also explain ancient Jewish beliefs. Among the most important are the **Dead Sea Scrolls**, writings by Jews who lived about 2,000 years ago.

Until 1947 no one knew about the Dead Sea Scrolls. In that year, young boys looking for a lost goat near the Dead Sea found a small cave. One of the boys went in to explore and found several old jars filled with moldy scrolls.

Scholars were very excited about the boy's find. Eager to find more scrolls, they began to search the desert. Over the next few decades, searchers found several more groups of scrolls.

Careful study revealed that most of the Dead Sea Scrolls were written between 100 BC and AD 50. The scrolls included prayers, commentaries, letters, and passages from the Hebrew Bible. These writings help historians learn about the lives of many Jews during this time.

READING CHECK Finding Main Ideas What did the Dead Sea Scrolls contain?

Judaism and Later Cultures

For centuries, Jewish ideas have greatly influenced other cultures, especially those in Europe and the Americas. Historians call European and American cultures the Western world to distinguish them from the Asian cultures to the east of Europe.

Because Jews lived all over the Western world, people of many cultures learned of Jewish ideas. In addition, these ideas helped shape the largest religion of Western society today, Christianity. Jesus, whose teachings are the basis of Christianity, was Jewish, and many of his teachings reflected Jewish ideas. These ideas were carried forward into Western civilization by both Jews and Christians. Judaism also influenced the development of another major religion, Islam. The first people to adopt Islam believed that they, like the Hebrews, were descendants of Abraham.

How are Jewish ideas reflected in our society? Many people still look to the Ten Commandments as a guide to how they should live. For example, people are expected not to lie or cheat and to honor their parents, families, and neighbors. Although these ideas were not unique to Judaism, it was through the Jews that they entered Western culture.

Not all of the ideas adopted from Jewish teachings stem from the Ten Commandments. Other Jewish ideas can also be seen in how people live today. For example, many people do not work on weekends in honor of the Sabbath. In addition, people give money or items to charities to help the poor and needy. This concept of charity is based largely on Jewish teachings.

READING CHECK Summarizing How have Jewish ideas helped shape modern laws?

SUMMARY AND PREVIEW Judaism is based on the belief in and obedience to God as described in the Torah and other sacred texts. In the next section you will learn how religion helped unify Jews even when they were forced out of Jerusalem.

Section 2 Assessment

Reviewing Ideas, Terms, and People HSS 6.3.1, 6.3.2

1. **a. Define** What is **monotheism**?
   b. Explain What is the Jewish view of justice and righteousness?
2. **a. Identify** What are the main sacred texts of Judaism?
   b. Predict Why do you think the commentaries are so significant to many Jews?
3. **Recall** Why do historians study the Dead Sea Scrolls?
4. **Make Generalizations** How are Hebrew teachings reflected in Western society today?

Critical Thinking

5. **Explain** Redraw the diagram shown on a sheet of paper. Use it to identify and explain the basic teachings of Judaism.

Judaism

FOCUS ON WRITING

6. **Thinking about Basic Values and Teachings** While the information in Section 1 was mostly historical, this section has more different kinds of topics. As you write down this information, what links do you see between it and items already on your list?

from The Torah

Noah's Ark   Genesis 7:1–12 The Living Torah

About the Reading *The first book of the Torah is called the Book of Genesis, a Jewish account of the early history of the world. One of the most famous parts of Genesis is the story of Noah's ark.*

According to the Torah, God became angry with people for their wicked behavior. To punish the wicked people, he decided to cause a great flood that would destroy everything. But one man, Noah, was not wicked, and God did not want him to die. He told Noah to build an ark, a great ship, that would carry him and his family safely through the flood. In this passage, God tells Noah to bring animals onto the ark as well, so that they might be spared.

AS YOU READ Note who and what Noah brings onto the ark with him.

God said to Noah, "Come into the ark, you and your family. I have seen that you are righteous before me in this generation. Take seven pairs of every clean animal, each consisting of a male and its mate. Of every animal that is not clean, take two, a male and its mate. ❶ Of the birds of the heaven also take seven pairs, each consisting of a male and its mate. Let them keep seed alive on the face of all the earth, because in another seven days, I will bring rain on the earth for forty days and forty nights. I will obliterate every organism that I have made from the face of the earth."

Noah did all that God had commanded. Noah was 600 years old when the flood occurred; water was on the earth. ❷ Noah, along with his sons, his wife, and his sons' wives, came into the ark ahead of the waters of the flood. The clean animals, the animals which were not clean, the birds, and all that walked the earth came two by two to Noah, to the ark. They were male and female, as God had commanded Noah.

Seven days passed, and the flood waters were on the earth. It was in the 600th year of Noah's life, in the second month, on the 17th of the month. On that day all the wellsprings of the great deep burst forth and the floodgates of the heavens were opened. It would continue to rain on the earth for forty days and forty nights.

GUIDED READING

WORD HELP

righteous proper, free from wrongdoing

obliterate destroy completely

organism a living thing

wellsprings sources of water

floodgates gates that hold back water to prevent floods

❶ Clean animals were those the Hebrews considered ritually clean to eat, such as cows. Unclean animals were those they did not eat, such as pigs, camels, and rabbits.

❷ According to the Torah, Noah lived to be 950 years old.

How old was Noah when he built the ark?

ELA **Reading 6.2.7** Make reasonable assertions about a text through accurate, supporting citations.

The Tower of Babel Genesis 11:1–9 The Living Torah

About the Reading *The Book of Genesis also tells the story of the Tower of Babel. According to this story, everyone in the world once spoke the same language. In time, however, people became proud and tried to climb to heaven. To punish them for their pride, God scattered people throughout the world and changed their languages so that people could no longer understand one another.*

AS YOU READ Pay attention to the words that people and God speak. What do these words tell you about their moods and actions?

The entire earth had one language with uniform words. When [the people] migrated from the east, they found a valley in the land of Shinar, and they settled there. They said to one another, "Come, let us mold bricks and fire them." Then they had bricks to use as stone, and asphalt for mortar. They said, "Come, let us build ourselves a city, and a tower whose top shall reach the sky. Let us make ourselves a name, so that we will not be scattered all over the face of the earth." ❶

God descended to see the city and the tower that the sons of man had built. God said, "They are a single people, all having one language, and this is the first thing they do! Now nothing they plan to do will be unattainable for them! Come, let us descend and confuse their speech, so that one person will not understand another's speech." ❷

From that place, God scattered them all over the face of the earth, and they stopped building the city. He named it Babel, because this was the place where God confused the world's language. ❸ It was from there that God dispersed [humanity] over all the face of the earth.

The Tower of Babel, by Pieter Brueghel the Elder, 1563

GUIDED READING

WORD HELP

uniform the same
unattainable unreachable
dispersed scattered

❶ What did people do when they first arrived in the land of Shinar?

❷ The ancient Hebrews believed that God sometimes came to Earth to see what people were doing.

What was God's reaction when he saw what the people were building?

❸ In Hebrew, the word *Babel* means "confusion."

CONNECTING SACRED TEXTS TO HISTORY

1. **Analyzing** Jews believe that righteous behavior is very important. How is this belief reflected in the story of Noah's ark?

2. **Finding Main Ideas** Jews also believe that God plays an active role in world history. How does the Torah say God's actions changed the world in the story of the Tower of Babel?

Judaism over the Centuries

What You Will Learn...

Main Ideas

1. Revolt, defeat, and migration led to great changes in Jewish culture.
2. Because Jews settled in different parts of the world, two cultural traditions formed.
3. Jewish traditions and holy days celebrate their history and religion.

The Big Idea

Although they were forced out of Israel by the Romans, shared beliefs and customs helped Jews maintain their religion.

Key Terms

Zealots, *p. 240*
rabbis, *p. 242*
Passover, *p. 245*
High Holy Days, *p. 245*

HSS **6.3.5** Discuss how Judaism survived and developed despite the continuing dispersion of much of the Jewish population from Jerusalem and the rest of Israel after the destruction of the second Temple in AD 70.

If YOU were there...

Foreign soldiers have taken over your homeland and are forcing you to obey their laws. So, some people are urging you to stand up and fight for freedom. But your conquerors come from a huge, powerful empire. If your people revolt, you have little chance of winning.

Will you join the rebellion? Why or why not?

BUILDING BACKGROUND By about AD 60, many Jews in Jerusalem had to decide whether they would join a rebellion against their foreign conquerors. For a little over a century, Jerusalem had been ruled by Rome. The Romans had a strong army, but their disrespect for Jewish traditions angered many Jews.

Revolt, Defeat, and Migration

The teachings of Judaism helped unite the ancient Jews. After the conquest of Israel by the Romans, many events threatened to tear Jewish society apart.

One threat to Jewish society was foreign rule. By the beginning of the first century AD, many Jews in Jerusalem had grown tired of foreign rule. If they could regain their independence, these Jews thought they could re-create the kingdom of Israel.

Revolt against Rome

The most rebellious of these Jews were a group called the **Zealots** (ZE-luhts). This group didn't think that Jews should answer to anyone but God. As a result, they refused to obey Roman officials. The Zealots urged their fellow Jews to rise up against the Romans. Tensions between Jews and Romans increased. Finally, in AD 66, the Jews revolted. Led by the Zealots, they fought fiercely.

In the end, the Jews' revolt against the Romans was not successful. The revolt lasted four years and caused terrible damage. By the time the fighting ended, Jerusalem lay in ruins. The war had wrecked buildings and cost many lives. Even more devastating to the Jews was the fact that the Romans burned the Second Temple during the last days of fighting in AD 70:

" As the flames went upward, the Jews made a great clamor [shout], such as so mighty an affliction [ordeal] required, and ran together to prevent it; and now they spared not their lives any longer, nor suffered any thing to restrain their force, since that holy house was perishing. "

–Flavius Josephus, *The Wars of the Jews*

After the Temple was destroyed, most Jews lost their will to fight and surrendered. But a few refused to give up their fight. That small group of about 1,000 Zealots locked themselves in a mountain fortress called Masada (muh-SAH-duh).

Intent on smashing the revolt, the Romans sent 15,000 soldiers to capture these Zealots. However, Masada was hard to reach. The Romans had to build a huge ramp of earth and stones to get to it. For two years, the Zealots refused to surrender, as the ramp grew. Finally, as the Romans broke through Masada's walls, the Zealots took their own lives. They refused to become Roman slaves.

THE IMPACT TODAY

The western retaining wall of the Second Temple survived the fire and still stands. Thousands of Jews each year visit the wall.

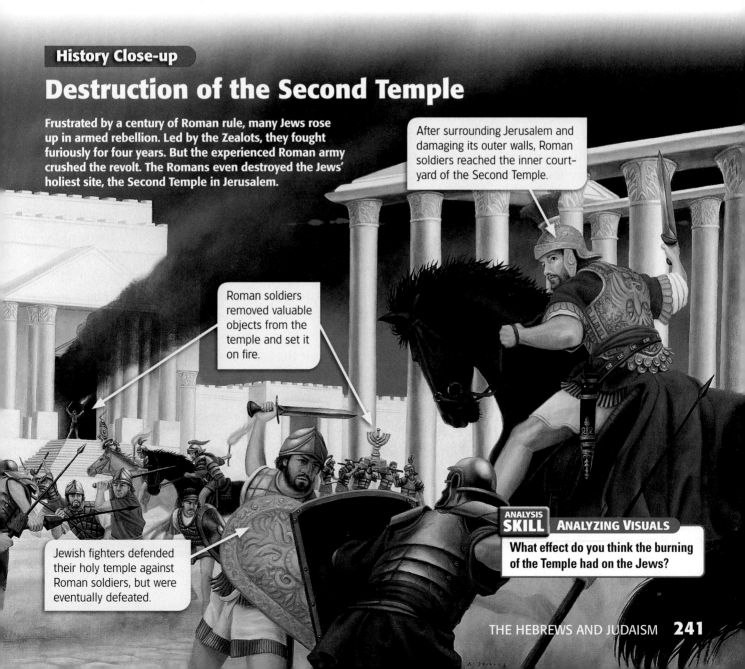

History Close-up

Destruction of the Second Temple

Frustrated by a century of Roman rule, many Jews rose up in armed rebellion. Led by the Zealots, they fought furiously for four years. But the experienced Roman army crushed the revolt. The Romans even destroyed the Jews' holiest site, the Second Temple in Jerusalem.

After surrounding Jerusalem and damaging its outer walls, Roman soldiers reached the inner courtyard of the Second Temple.

Roman soldiers removed valuable objects from the temple and set it on fire.

Jewish fighters defended their holy temple against Roman soldiers, but were eventually defeated.

ANALYSIS SKILL | **ANALYZING VISUALS**

What effect do you think the burning of the Temple had on the Jews?

THE HEBREWS AND JUDAISM **241**

Results of the Revolt

With the capture of Masada in AD 73, the Jewish revolt was over. As punishment for the Jews' rebellion, the Romans killed much of Jerusalem's population. They took many of the surviving Jews to Rome as slaves. The Romans dissolved the Jewish power structure and took over the city.

Besides those taken as slaves, thousands of Jews left Jerusalem after the destruction of the Second Temple. With the Temple destroyed, they didn't want to live in Jerusalem anymore. Many moved to Jewish communities in other parts of the Roman Empire. One common destination was Alexandria in Egypt, which had a large Jewish community. The populations of these Jewish communities grew after the Romans destroyed Jerusalem.

A Second Revolt

Some Jews, however, chose not to leave Jerusalem when the Romans conquered it. Some 60 years after the capture of Masada, these Jews, unhappy with Roman rule, began another revolt. Once again, however, the Roman army defeated the Jews. After this rebellion in the 130s the Romans banned all Jews from the city of Jerusalem. Roman officials declared that any Jew caught in or near the city would be killed. As a result, Jewish migration throughout the Mediterranean region increased.

Migration and Discrimination

For Jews not living in Jerusalem, the nature of Judaism changed. Because the Jews no longer had a single temple at which to worship, local synagogues became more important. At the same time, leaders called **rabbis** (RAB-yz), or religious teachers, took on a greater role in guiding Jews in their religious lives. Rabbis were responsible for interpreting the Torah and teaching.

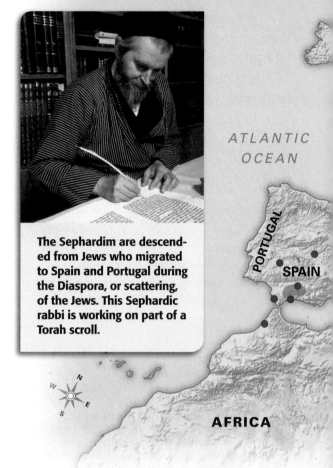

The Sephardim are descended from Jews who migrated to Spain and Portugal during the Diaspora, or scattering, of the Jews. This Sephardic rabbi is working on part of a Torah scroll.

This change was largely due to the actions of Yohanan ben Zaccai, a rabbi who founded a school at Yavneh, near Jerusalem. In this school, he taught people about Judaism and trained them to be rabbis. Influenced by Yohanan, rabbis' ideas shaped how Judaism was practiced for the next several centuries. Many rabbis also served as leaders of Jewish communities.

Over many centuries, Jews moved out of the Mediterranean region to other parts of the world. In many cases this movement was not voluntary. The Jews were forced to move by other religious groups who discriminated against them. This discrimination forced many Jews to leave their cities and find new places to live. As a result, some Jews settled in Asia, Russia, and much later, the United States.

READING CHECK Identifying Cause and Effect
Why did the Romans force Jews out of Jerusalem?

Jewish Migration After AD 70

The Ashkenazim are descended from Jews who moved to France, Germany, and Eastern Europe during the Diaspora. These Ashkenazi Jews are carrying a Torah before the Western Wall in Jerusalem.

GERMANY

EUROPE

FRANCE

ITALY

Rome

GREECE

ASIA MINOR

SYRIA

Mediterranean Sea

Jerusalem

Alexandria

EGYPT

Area of widespread Jewish settlement
● Jewish community
➤ Direction of Jewish migration

0   200   400 Miles
0   200 400 Kilometers

GEOGRAPHY SKILLS INTERPRETING MAPS

1. **Movement** What directions did the Jews migrate from their homeland?
2. **Region** Where are the largest areas of Jewish settlement?

Two Cultural Traditions

As you read earlier, the scattering of Jews around the world is called the Diaspora. It began after the Babylonian Captivity in the 500s BC. After that time, Jewish communities developed all around the world.

Jews everywhere shared the basic beliefs of Judaism. For example, all Jews still believed in one God and tried to obey God's law as set forth in the sacred texts. But communities in various parts of the world had different customs. As a result, the Jewish communities in different parts of the world began to develop their own languages, rituals, and cultures. These differences led to the creation of two main cultural traditions, both of which still exist today.

The Jews in Eastern Europe

One of the two traditions, the Ashkenazim (ahsh-kuh-NAH-zuhm), is made up of descendants of Jews who moved to France, Germany, and eastern Europe during the Diaspora. For the most part, these Jews had communities separate from their non-Jewish neighbors. Therefore, they developed their own customs that were unlike those of their neighbors. As an example, they developed their own language, Yiddish. Yiddish is similar to German but is written in the Hebrew alphabet.

The Jews in Spain and Portugal

Another Jewish cultural tradition developed during the Diaspora in what are now Spain and Portugal in Western Europe.

THE IMPACT TODAY

Some Yiddish words have entered the English language. For example, *schlep* means "to carry."

A Passover Meal

Passover honors the Exodus, one of the most important events in Hebrew history. In honor of this event from their past, Jews share a special meal called a seder. Each item in the seder symbolizes a part of the Exodus. For example, bitter herbs represent the Jews' bitter years of slavery in Egypt. Before eating the meal, everyone reads prayers from a book called the Haggadah (huh-GAH-duh). It tells the story of the Exodus and reminds everyone present of the Jews' history. The small picture shows a seder in a copy of the Haggadah from the 1300s.

ANALYSIS SKILL **ANALYZING INFORMATION**

How does the Passover seder reflect the importance of the Exodus in Hebrew history?

The descendants of the Jews there are called the Sephardim (suh-FAHR-duhm). They also have a language of their own—Ladino. It is a mix of Spanish, Hebrew, and Arabic. Unlike the Ashkenazim, the Sephardim mixed with the region's non-Jewish residents. As a result, Sephardic religious and cultural practices borrowed elements from other cultures. Known for their writings and their philosophies, the Sephardim produced a golden age of Jewish culture in the AD 1000s and 1100s. During this period, for example, Jewish poets wrote beautiful works in Hebrew and other languages. Hebrew scholars also made great advances in mathematics, astronomy, medicine, and philosophy.

READING CHECK **Summarizing** What were the two main Jewish cultural traditions?

Traditions and Holy Days

Jewish culture is one of the oldest in the world. Because their roots go back so far, many Jews feel a strong connection with the past. They also feel that understanding their history will help them better follow Jewish teachings. Their traditions and holy days help them understand and celebrate their history.

Hanukkah

One Jewish tradition is celebrated by Hanukkah, which falls in December. It honors the rededication of the Second Temple during the revolt of the Maccabees.

The Maccabees wanted to celebrate a great victory that had convinced their non-Jewish rulers to let them keep their religion. According to legend, though, the Maccabees didn't have enough lamp oil to perform the rededication ceremony. Miraculously, the oil they had—enough to burn for only one day—burned for eight full days.

Today Jews celebrate this event by lighting candles in a special candleholder called a menorah (muh-NOHR-uh). Its eight branches represent the eight days through which the oil burned. Many Jews also exchange gifts on each of the eight nights.

Passover

More important than Hanukkah to Jews, Passover is celebrated in March or April. **Passover** is a time for Jews to remember the Exodus, the journey of the Hebrews out of slavery in Egypt.

According to Jewish tradition, the Hebrews left Egypt so quickly that bakers didn't have time to let their bread rise. Therefore, during Passover Jews eat only matzo, a flat, unrisen bread. They also celebrate the holy day with ceremonies and a ritual meal called a seder (SAY-duhr). During the seder, participants recall and reflect upon the events of the Exodus.

High Holy Days

Ceremonies and rituals are also part of the **High Holy Days**, the two most sacred of all Jewish holy days. They take place each year in September or October. The first two days of the celebration, Rosh Hashanah (rahsh uh-SHAH-nuh), celebrate the beginning of a new year in the Jewish calendar.

On Yom Kippur (yohm ki-POOHR), which falls soon afterward, Jews ask God to forgive their sins. Jews consider Yom Kippur to be the holiest day of the entire year. Because it is so holy, Jews don't eat or drink anything for the entire day. Many of the ceremonies they perform for Yom Kippur date back to the days of the Second Temple. These ceremonies help many Jews feel more connected to their long past, to the days of Abraham and Moses.

READING CHECK Finding Main Ideas What name is given to the two most important Jewish holy days?

SUMMARY AND PREVIEW The Jewish culture is one of the oldest in the world. Over the course of their long history, the Jews' religion and customs have helped them maintain a sense of identity and community. This sense has helped the Jewish people endure many hardships. In the next chapter you will learn about another people who made major contributions to Western culture. These were the Greeks.

Section 3 Assessment

go.hrw.com
Online Quiz
KEYWORD: SQ6 HP8

Reviewing Ideas, Terms, and People HSS 6.3.5

1. **a. Recall** Who won the battle at Masada?
   b. Evaluate How did the defeat by the Romans affect Jewish history?
2. **a. Identify** What language developed in the Jewish communities of eastern Europe?
   b. Contrast How did communities of Ashkenazim differ from communities of Sephardim?
3. **Identify** What event does **Passover** celebrate?

Critical Thinking

4. **Compare and Contrast** Draw a diagram like the one shown here. In the left circle, write facts that describe life for the Jews before the second revolt against the Romans. In the right circle, write facts that describe life after the revolt.

FOCUS ON WRITING

5. **Organizing Your Information** Add notes about what you've just read to the notes you have already collected. Now that you have all your information, organize it into categories that will be windows, links, and other features on your Web page.

Social Studies Skills

 HSS Analysis HI 2 Students understand and distinguish the long- and short-term causal relations.

Analysis	Critical Thinking	Participation	Study

Identifying Short- and Long-Term Effects

Understand the Skill

Many events of the past are the result of other events that took place earlier. When something occurs as the result of things that happened earlier, it is an effect of those things.

Some events take place soon after the things that cause them. These events are short-term effects. Long-term effects can occur decades or even hundreds of years after the events that caused them. Recognizing cause-and-effect relationships will help you to better understand the connections between historical events.

Learn the Skill

As you learned in Chapter 5, "clue words" can reveal cause-and-effect connections between events. Often, however, no such words are present. Therefore, you should always be looking for what happened as a result of an action or event.

Short-term effects are usually fairly easy to identify. They are often closely linked to the event that caused them. Take this sentence, for example:

"After Solomon's death around 930 BC, revolts broke out over who should be king."

It is clear from this information that a short-term effect of Solomon's death was political unrest.

Now, consider this other passage:

"Some Hebrews . . . moved to Egypt . . . The Hebrews lived well in Egypt and their population grew. But this growing population worried Egypt's ruler, the pharaoh. He feared that the Hebrews would soon take over Egypt. To prevent this from happening, the pharaoh made the Hebrews slaves."

Look carefully at the information in the passage. No clue words exist. However, it shows that one effect of the Hebrews' move to Egypt was the growth of their population. It takes time for a population to increase, so this was a long-term effect of the Hebrews' move.

Recognizing long-term effects is not always easy, however, because they often occur well after the event that caused them. Therefore, the long-term effects of those events may not be discussed at the time. This is why you should always ask yourself why an event might have happened as you study it.

For example, many of our modern laws are a result of the Ten Commandments of the ancient Hebrews. Religion is a major force in history that makes things happen. Other such forces include economics, science and technology, geography, and the meeting of peoples with different cultures. Ask yourself if one of these forces is a part of the event you are studying. If so, the event may have long-term effects.

Practice and Apply the Skill

Review the information in Chapter 8 and answer the following questions.

1. What were the short-term effects of King Solomon's rule of the Hebrews? What long-term benefit resulted from his rule?

2. What was the short-term effect of the destruction of the temple at Jerusalem in AD 70? What effect has that event had on the world today?

Standards Review

Visual Summary

Use the visual summary below to help you review the main ideas of the chapter.

QUICK FACTS

The early Hebrews settled in Canaan.

In Canaan the Hebrews formed the kingdom of Israel and built a great temple to God.

The Romans destroyed the Second Temple in Jerusalem and forced the Jews to leave.

Jewish religion and traditions have united the Jews over the centuries.

Reviewing Vocabulary, Terms, and People

For each group of terms below, write a sentence that shows how the terms in the group are related.

1. Abraham
   Judaism

2. Moses
   Exodus

3. David
   Solomon

4. Torah
   Talmud

5. Passover
   High Holy Days

6. Moses
   Ten Commandments

7. Passover
   Exodus

8. monotheism
   Judaism

9. synagogues
   rabbis

10. principles
    Torah

Comprehension and Critical Thinking

SECTION 1 *(Pages 226–231)* HSS 6.3.3, 6.3.4

11. a. **Describe** How did Abraham and Moses shape the history of the Hebrew people?

    b. **Compare and Contrast** What did Saul, David, and Solomon have in common? How did they differ?

    c. **Evaluate** Of Esther, Deborah, Miriam, and Ruth, which do you think provided the best example of how people should treat their families? Explain your answer.

SECTION 2 *(Pages 232–237)* HSS 6.3.1, 6.3.2

12. a. **Identify** What are the basic beliefs of Judaism?

    b. **Analyze** What do the various sacred Jewish texts contribute to Judaism?

    c. **Elaborate** How are Jewish ideas reflected in modern Western society?

13. **a. Describe** What happened as a result of tensions between the Romans and the Jews?

b. Analyze What led to the creation of the two main Jewish cultural traditions?

c. Predict In the future, what role do you think holy days and other traditions will play in Judaism? Explain your answer.

Reading Skills

Identifying Fact and Opinion *Identify each of the following statements as a fact or an opinion.*

14. Much of what we know about Hebrew history comes from the work of archaeologists.

15. Archaeologists should spend more time studying Hebrew history.

16. The Exodus is one of the most fascinating events in world history.

17. Until 1947, scholars did not know about the Dead Sea Scrolls.

18. Hanukkah is a Jewish holy day that takes place every December.

Social Studies Skills

19. **Identifying Short- and Long-Term Effects** *Identify both the short-term and long-term effects of each of the following events.*

	Short-Term Effects	Long-Term Effects
the Exodus		
the Babylonian Captivity		
the expulsion of the Jews from Jerusalem		

Using the Internet

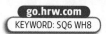
go.hrw.com
KEYWORD: SQ6 WH8

20. **Activity: Interpreting Maps** Migration and conflict were key factors shaping Jewish history and culture. The Exodus, the Babylonian Captivity, and the revolts against Rome forced the Jewish people to adapt their culture and settle in regions outside Israel. Enter the activity keyword. Then create an annotated map showing the birthplace of Judaism and the Jews' movements into other parts of the world. Your map should include a legend as well as labels to identify events and explain their impact on the Jewish people.

Reviewing Themes

21. **Religion** How did monotheism shape the history of the Hebrews?

22. **Religion** Do you agree or disagree with this statement: "The history of Judaism is also the history of the Hebrew people." Why?

23. **Religion** How does Mosaic law affect the daily lives of Jewish people?

FOCUS ON WRITING

24. **Designing Your Web Site** Look back at your notes and how you've organized them. Have you included all important facts and details? Will people be able to find information easily?

Write a description of your Web site. What is its name and Web address? What will you include on the home page? What will appear in menus or as hot links, and elsewhere on the page? What images will you include? Draw a rough diagram or sketch of your page. Be sure to label the parts of your page.

When you're finished, compare how the information is presented in your textbook with how you presented it on your Web site. Most of the information in the book is presented chronologically, by the year or era. How did you present the information?

Standards Assessment

DIRECTIONS: Read each question, and write the letter of the best response.

1 Use the map to answer the following question.

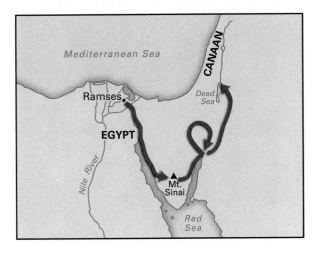

The map above illustrates

A the Babylonian Captivity.

B the Exodus.

C Abraham's migration to Canaan.

D the capture of Jerusalem by the Romans.

2 The Jews believe that the Ten Commandments were given by God to

A Moses.

B Abraham.

C King David.

D King Solomon.

3 The ancient Jews probably were the first people to

A conduct religious ceremonies.

B have a code of laws.

C practice monotheism.

D hold religious beliefs.

4 The basic teachings and laws that guide the Jewish people are found in the

A Talmud.

B Torah.

C Book of the Dead.

D Dead Sea Scrolls.

5 Which group was *most* responsible for the migration of Jews out of Jerusalem to other parts of the Mediterranean region?

A the Israelites

B the Philistines

C the Egyptians

D the Romans

Connecting with Past Learnings

6 In an earlier chapter, you learned about people of Mesopotamia who had a law code. Moses issued a set of laws for the Hebrew people to follow. What other ancient leader is famous for issuing laws?

A Gilgamesh

B Tutankhamen

C Asoka

D Hammurabi

7 Jewish teachings required people to honor and respect their parents. This was an idea also common in China. In his writings, who else encouraged people to respect their parents?

A Chandragupta Maurya

B Shi Huangdi

C Confucius

D Abraham

Ancient Greece

California Standards

History–Social Science

6.4 Students analyze the geographic, political, economic, religious, and social structures of the early civilizations of Ancient Greece.

Analysis Skills

HI 6 Conduct cost-benefit analyses of economic and political issues.

English–Language Arts

Writing 6.2.1a Establish and develop a plot and setting and present a point of view that is appropriate to the stories.

Reading 6.2.0 Read and understand grade-level-appropriate material.

FOCUS ON WRITING

A Myth Like most people, the Greeks enjoyed good stories. But they also took their stories seriously. They used stories called myths to explain everything from the creation of the world to details of everyday life. Reading this chapter will provide you with ideas you can use to create your own myth.

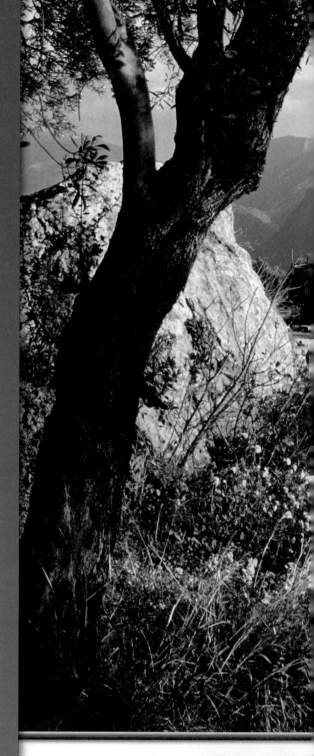

c. 2000 BC
The Minoan civilization prospers in Crete.

CHAPTER EVENTS

2000 BC

WORLD EVENTS

c. 2000 BC
The main part of Stonehenge is built in England.

HOLT

History's Impact
▶ **video series**
Watch the video to under-
stand the impact of democracy on the world today.

What You Will Learn...

In this chapter you will study Greece—home
to one of the great ancient civilizations. In
this photo you see the ruins of the temple at
Delphi. It was one of the most sacred places
in ancient Greece.

c. 1200 BC
The Greeks and
Trojans fight the
Trojan War.

c. 750 BC
The Greeks
begin to build
city-states.

c. 500 BC
Athens
becomes the
world's first
democracy.

| 1700 BC | 1400 BC | 1100 BC | 800 BC | 500 BC |

c. 1200 BC
The Olmec
civilization
develops in
the Americas.

c. 900 BC
The Phoenicians
dominate
trade in the
Mediterranean.

753 BC
According
to legend,
Rome is
founded.

ANCIENT GREECE **251**

Reading Social Studies

by Kylene Beers

| Economics | Geography | Politics | Religion | Society and Culture | Science and Technology |

Focus on Themes In this chapter, you will read about the civilizations of ancient Greece. Whether reading about the Minoans and Mycenaeans or the Spartans and Athenians, you will see that where the people lived affected how they lived.

You will also read how the government of these ancient people changed over the years. By the end of this chapter, you will have learned a great deal about the **geography** and the **politics** of the ancient Greeks.

Greek Word Origins

Focus on Reading Sometimes when you read an unusual word, you can figure out what it means by using the other words around it. Other times you might need to consult a dictionary. But sometimes, if you know what the word's root parts mean, you can figure out its meaning. The chart below shows you several English words that have Greek roots.

In this chapter you'll find...	which means...	and comes from the Greek root
1. geography, *p. 254* (jee-AH-gruh-fee)	the study of the earth's surface	*ge-*, which means "earth" *-graphy*, which means "writing about"
2. acropolis, *p. 258* (uh-KRAH-puh-luhs)	fortress of a Greek city up on a high hill	*acr-*, which means "top" *polis*, which means "city"
3. democracy, *p. 262* (di-MAH-kruh-see)	a form of government in which people hold power	*dem-*, which means "people" *-cracy*, which means "power"
4. tyrant, *p. 263* (TY-ruhnt)	a ruler [in modern times, a harsh ruler]	*tyrannos*, which means "master"
5. oligarchy, *p. 263* (AH-luh-gahr-kee)	rule by a few people	*olig-*, which means "few" *-archy*, which means "rule"
6. mythology, *p. 269* (mi-THAH-luh-jee)	a body of stories about gods and heroes	*mythos*, which means "stories about gods or heroes" *-ology*, which means "study of"

Additional reading support can be found in the

Inter active
Reader and Study Guide

You Try It!

Study each of the words below. Use the chart on the opposite page to find a Greek root or roots for each of them. How do the words' roots relate to their definitions?

Word	Definition
1. geology	a science that deals with the study of the makeup of the earth
2. police	the people who keep order in a city
3. Tyrannosaurus	one of the largest and fiercest dinosaurs
4. architect	the person in charge of designing buildings
5. acrophobia	the fear of heights
6. monarchy	rule by a single person
7. politics	the art or science of governing a city, state, or nation
8. demographer	a scientist who studies the growth of populations

Think about it.

1. How can studying Greek origins help you understand English?

2. Use the chart of roots on the previous page to answer this question. Where do you think a demagogue gets his or her power: the support of the people or a written constitution? Justify your answer.

3. Do you know words in other languages that help you understand English?

Key Terms and People

Chapter 9

Section 1
polis (p. 258)
classical (p. 258)
acropolis (p. 258)

Section 2
democracy (p. 262)
aristocrats (p. 263)
oligarchy (p. 263)
citizens (p. 263)
tyrant (p. 263)
Pericles (p. 266)

Section 3
mythology (p. 269)
Homer (p. 272)
Sappho (p. 273)
Aesop (p. 273)
fables (p. 273)

Academic Vocabulary

Success in school is related to knowing academic vocabulary—the words that are frequently used in school assignments and discussions. In this chapter, you will learn the following academic word:

influence (p. 256)

As you read Chapter 9, pay close attention to the highlighted words. Many of those words are Greek or come from Greek roots. Refer to the chart on the opposite page to help you understand what those words mean.

ANCIENT GREECE **253**

Geography and the Early Greeks

What You Will Learn...

Main Ideas

1. Geography helped shape early Greek civilization.
2. Trading cultures developed in the Minoan and Mycenaean civilizations.
3. The Greeks created city-states for protection and security.

The Big Idea

Greece's geography and its nearness to the sea strongly influenced the development of trade and the growth of city-states.

Key Terms

polis, *p. 258*
classical, *p. 258*
acropolis, *p. 258*

HSS 6.4.1 Discuss the connections between geography and the development of city-states in the region of the Aegean Sea, including patterns of trade and commerce among Greek city-states and within the wider Mediterranean region.

If YOU were there...

You live on the rocky coast of a bright blue sea. Across the water you can see dozens of islands and points of land jutting out into the sea. Rugged mountains rise steeply behind your village. It is hard to travel across the mountains in order to visit other villages or towns. Near your home on the coast is a sheltered cove where it's easy to anchor a boat.

What could you do to make a living here?

BUILDING BACKGROUND The paragraph you just read could be describing many parts of Greece, a peninsula in southern Europe. Greece's mountain ranges run right up to the coast in many places, making travel and farming difficult. Although it does not seem like the easiest place in the world to live, Greece was home to some of the ancient world's greatest civilizations.

Greece is a land of rugged mountains, rocky coastlines, and beautiful islands. The trees you see are olive trees. Olives were grown by the early Greeks for food and oil.

Geography Shapes Greek Civilization

The Greeks lived on rocky, mountainous lands surrounded by water. The mainland of Greece is a peninsula, an area of land that is surrounded on three sides by water. But the Greek peninsula is very irregular. It's one big peninsula made up of a series of smaller peninsulas. The land and sea intertwine like your hand and fingers in a bowl of water. In addition, there are many islands. Look at the map of Greece and notice the rugged coastline.

In your mind, picture those peninsulas and islands dominated by mountains that run almost to the sea. Just a few small valleys and coastal plains provide flat land for farming and villages. Now you have an image of Greece, a land where one of the world's greatest civilizations developed.

Mountains and Settlements

Because mountains cover much of Greece, there are few flat areas for farmland. People settled in those flat areas along the coast and in river valleys. They lived in villages and towns separated by mountains and seas.

Travel across the mountains and seas was difficult, so communities were isolated from one another. As a result, the people created their own governments and ways of life. Even though they spoke the same language, Greek communities saw themselves as separate countries.

Seas and Ships

Since travel inland across the rugged mountains was so difficult, the early Greeks turned to the seas. On the south was the huge Mediterranean Sea, to the west was the Ionian (eye-OH-nee-uhn) Sea, and to the east was the Aegean (ee-JEE-uhn) Sea.

Greece: Physical

Black Sea

PINDOS MOUNTAINS

Ionian Sea

GREECE

Gulf of Corinth

Peloponnesus

Mediterranean Sea

Aegean Sea

ASIA MINOR

Rhodes

Crete

ELEVATION

Feet	Meters
6,560	2,000
1,640	500
656	200
(Sea level) 0	0 (Sea level)

0   50   100 Miles
0   50   100 Kilometers

40° N

20° E   25° E   30° E

35° N

GEOGRAPHY SKILLS INTERPRETING MAPS

Location What bodies of water surround Greece?

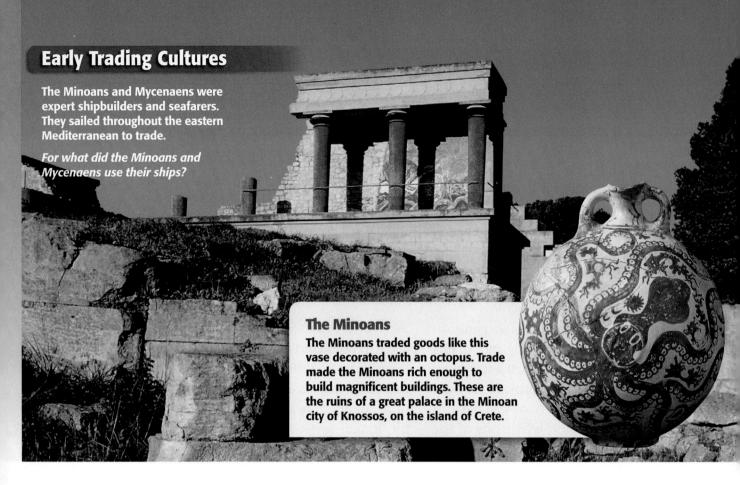

Early Trading Cultures

The Minoans and Mycenaens were expert shipbuilders and seafarers. They sailed throughout the eastern Mediterranean to trade.

For what did the Minoans and Mycenaens use their ships?

The Minoans

The Minoans traded goods like this vase decorated with an octopus. Trade made the Minoans rich enough to build magnificent buildings. These are the ruins of a great palace in the Minoan city of Knossos, on the island of Crete.

It's not surprising that the early Greeks used the sea as a source for food and as a way of trading with other communities.

The Greeks became skilled shipbuilders and sailors. Their ships sailed to Asia Minor, to Egypt, and to the islands of the Mediterranean and Aegean seas. As they traveled around these seas, they found sources of food and other products they needed. They also exchanged ideas with other cultures.

ACADEMIC VOCABULARY

influence
change, or have an effect on

READING CHECK Drawing Conclusions

How did mountains affect the location of Greek settlements?

Trading Cultures Develop

Many cultures settled and developed in Greece. Two of the earliest were the Minoans (muh-NOH-uhnz) and the Mycenaens (my-suh-NEE-uhns). By 2000 BC the Minoans had built an advanced society on the island of Crete. Crete lay south of the Aegean in the eastern Mediterranean. Later, the Mycenaeans built towns on the Greek mainland. These two civilizations **influenced** the entire Aegean region and helped shape later cultures in Greece.

The Minoans

Because they lived on an island, the Minoans spent much of their time at sea. They were among the best shipbuilders of their time. Minoan ships carried goods such as wood, olive oil, and pottery all around the eastern Mediterranean. They traded these goods for copper, gold, silver, and jewels.

Although Crete's location was excellent for Minoan traders, its geography had its dangers. Sometime in the 1600s BC a huge volcano erupted just north of Crete. This eruption created a giant wave that flooded much of Crete. In addition, the eruption

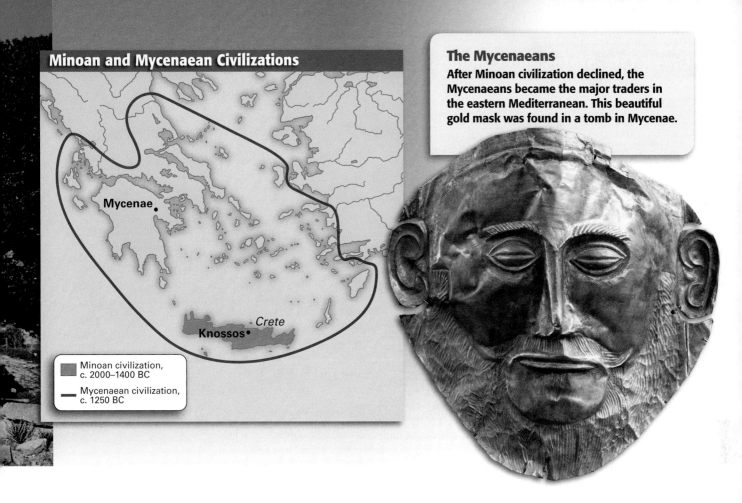

Minoan and Mycenaean Civilizations

Mycenae

Knossos *Crete*

Minoan civilization, c. 2000–1400 BC

Mycenaean civilization, c. 1250 BC

The Mycenaeans
After Minoan civilization declined, the Mycenaeans became the major traders in the eastern Mediterranean. This beautiful gold mask was found in a tomb in Mycenae.

threw up huge clouds of ash, ruining crops and burying cities. This eruption may have led to the end of Minoan civilization.

The Mycenaeans

Although they lived in what is now Greece and influenced Greek society, historians don't consider the Minoans to be Greek. This is because the Minoans didn't speak the Greek language. The first people to speak Greek, and therefore the first to be considered Greek, were the Mycenaeans.

While the Minoans were sailing the Mediterranean, the Mycenaeans were building fortresses all over the Greek mainland. The largest and most powerful fortress was Mycenae (my-SEE-nee), after which the Mycenaeans were named.

By the mid-1400s, Minoan society had declined. That decline allowed the Mycenaeans to take over Crete and become the major traders in the eastern Mediterranean.

They set up colonies in northern Greece and Italy from which they shipped goods to markets around the Mediterranean and Black seas.

The Mycenaeans didn't think trade had to be conducted peacefully. They often attacked other kingdoms. Some historians think the Mycenaeans attacked the city of Troy, possibly starting the legendary Trojan War, which is featured in many works of literature.

Mycenaean society began to fall apart in the 1200s BC when invaders from Europe swept into Greece. At the same time, earthquakes destroyed many cities. As Mycenaean civilization crumbled, Greece slid into a period of warfare and disorder, a period called the Dark Age.

READING CHECK **Finding Main Ideas**
To what regions did Minoan and Mycenaean traders travel?

Greek City-States and Colonies, c. 600 BC

ATLANTIC OCEAN

EUROPE

Massilia (Marseille)

ITALY

Adriatic Sea

Neapolis (Naples)

Mediterranean Sea

Corinth

GREECE

Athens

AFRICA

Byzantium (Istanbul)

Black Sea

ASIA MINOR

Cyrene

EGYPT

Area of Greek influence

● **Greek city-state or colony**

— **Trade route**

0   150   300 Miles
0   150   300 Kilometers

GEOGRAPHY SKILLS | **INTERPRETING MAPS**

Location Greek city-states and colonies were spread around the Mediterranean Sea and which other large sea?

Greeks Create City-States

The Greeks of the Dark Age left no written records. All that we know about the period comes from archaeological findings.

About 300 years after the Mycenaean civilization crumbled, the Greeks started to join together in small groups for protection and stability. Over time, these groups set up independent city-states. The Greek word for a city-state is **polis** (PAH-luhs). The creation of city-states marks the beginning of what is known as Greece's classical age. A **classical** age is one that is marked by great achievements.

Life in a City-State

A Greek city was usually built around a strong fortress. This fortress often stood on top of a high hill called the **acropolis** (uh-KRAH-puh-luhs). The town around the acropolis was surrounded by walls for added protection.

FOCUS ON READING

How do Greek roots give you clues to the meaning of acropolis?

Not everyone who lived in the city-state actually lived inside the city walls. Farmers, for example, usually lived near their fields outside the walls. In times of war, however, women, children, and elderly people all gathered inside the city walls for protection. As a result, they remained safe while the men of the polis formed an army to fight off its enemies.

Life in the city often focused on the marketplace, or agora (A-guh-ruh) in Greek. Farmers brought their crops to the market to trade for goods made by craftsmen in the town. Because it was a large open space, the market also served as a meeting place. People held both political and religious assemblies in the market. It often contained shops as well.

The city-state became the foundation of Greek civilization. Besides providing security for its people, the city gave them an identity. People thought of themselves as residents of a city, not as Greeks. Because the city-state was so central to their lives, the Greeks expected people to participate in its affairs, especially in its economy and its government.

City-States and Colonization

Life in Greece eventually became more settled. People no longer had to fear raiders swooping down on their cities. As a result, they were free to think about things other than defense. Some Greeks began to dream of becoming rich through trade. Others became curious about neighboring lands around the Mediterranean Sea. Some also worried about how to deal with Greece's growing population. Despite their different reasons, all these people eventually reached the same idea: the Greeks should establish colonies.

Before long, groups from city-states around Greece began to set up colonies in distant lands. After they were set up, Greek colonies became independent. In other words, each colony became a new polis. In fact, some cities that began as colonies began to create colonies of their own. Eventually Greek colonies spread all around the Mediterranean and Black seas. Many big cities around the Mediterranean today began as Greek colonies. Among them are Istanbul (is-tahn-BOOL) in Turkey, Marseille (mahr-SAY) in France, and Naples in Italy.

Patterns of Trade

Although the colonies were independent, they often traded with city-states on the mainland. The colonies sent metals such as copper and iron back to mainland Greece. In return, the Greek city-states sent wine, olive oil, and other products.

Trade made the city-states much richer. Because of their locations, some city-states became great trading centers. By 550 BC the Greeks had become the greatest traders in the whole Aegean region. Greek ships sailed to Egypt and cities around the Black Sea.

READING CHECK **Analyzing** Why did the Greeks develop city-states?

SUMMARY AND PREVIEW In this section you learned about the creation of city-states and how they affected Greek society. In the next section you will read about how the government of one city-state changed as people became more interested in how they were ruled.

go.hrw.com
Online Quiz
KEYWORD: SQ6 HP9

Section 1 Assessment

Reviewing Ideas, Terms, and People HSS 6.4.1

1. **a. Identify** What kinds of landforms are found in Greece?
   b. Interpret How did the sea help shape early Greek society?
   c. Predict How might the difficulty of mountain travel have been a benefit to the Greeks?
2. **a. Recall** What was the first major civilization to develop in Greece?
   b. Compare How were the Minoans and Mycenaeans similar?
3. **a. Define** What is a **polis**?
   b. Elaborate Why do you think the Greeks built their cities around a high **acropolis**?

Critical Thinking

4. **Summarize** Draw a diagram like the one here. Use it to identify three functions of the polis in early Greek society.

Polis

FOCUS ON WRITING

5. **Thinking About Geographical Features as Characters** Have you ever thought about physical features as having personalities? For example, you might describe a strong, blustery wind as angry. Think about the physical features of Greece you read about in this section. What kinds of personalities might they have? Write your ideas down in your notebook.

Natural Disaster!

Nature is a powerful force. Throughout history, great natural disasters have affected civilizations. One natural disaster was so devastating that it may have contributed to the destruction of the entire Minoan civilization.

In the 1600s BC a volcano on the Greek island of Thera erupted. The colossal explosion was one of the largest in history. It was so powerful that people could see and hear it from hundreds of miles away. In a moment of nature's fury, the history of the Mediterranean world was changed forever.

BLACK SEA

• Troy

A N A T O L I A

Mycenae •

PELOPONNESUS

Knossos
CRETE •

For centuries, the Minoans had thrived on the island of Crete. The Minoans were great sea traders who often sailed to the island of Thera, just 70 miles away.

The eruption of Thera produced fast-moving waves called tsunami (soo-NAH-mee) in the Mediterranean Sea. Scientists today estimate that the waves may have traveled at about 200 miles an hour.

M E D I T E R R A N E A N   S E A

N
W   E
S

L I B Y A

The ancient island of Thera is known as Santorini today. The huge gap on the island's western side and the water in the middle are evidence of the explosion more than 3,500 years ago.

Aleppo

CYPRUS

The explosion produced a massive cloud of ash that smothered crops, cities, and people. For years afterward, the ash dimmed the sunlight, making it difficult for farmers to grow their crops.

Jericho

Three Stages of Disaster

Stage 1

Warning Signs Following a series of earthquakes, the volcano begins to shoot ash into the sky. People flee the island in fear.

Stage 2

Explosion Ash and rock are flung into the air and sweep down the volcano's sides, destroying everything in their path. Cracks through the island rock begin to form from the powerful explosions.

Stage 3

Collapse The volcano collapses and falls into the sea, creating massive waves. The powerful waves slam into Crete, flooding coastal areas.

GEOGRAPHY SKILLS INTERPRETING MAPS

1. **Location** What direction did the ash cloud travel after the island's eruption?
2. **Human-Environment Interaction** How might the effects of the ash cloud have influenced Minoan civilization?

E G Y P T

Government in Athens

What You Will Learn...

Main Ideas

1. Aristocrats and tyrants ruled early Athens.
2. Athens created the world's first democracy.
3. Ancient democracy was different than modern democracy.

The Big Idea

The people of Athens tried many different forms of government before creating a democracy.

Key Terms and People

democracy, *p. 262*
aristocrats, *p. 263*
oligarchy, *p. 263*
citizens, *p. 263*
tyrant, *p. 263*
Pericles, *p. 266*

HSS **6.4.2** Trace the transition from tyranny and oligarchy to early democratic forms of government and back to dictatorship in ancient Greece, including the significance of the invention of the idea of citizenship (e.g., from *Pericles' Funeral Oration*).

6.4.3 State the key differences between Athenian, or direct, democracy and representative democracy.

If YOU were there...

For many years, your city has been ruled by a small group of rich men. They have generally been good leaders. They have built new buildings and protected the city from enemies. But now a new leader wants to let all free men help run the government. It won't matter whether they are rich or poor. Some people, however, worry about giving power to ordinary people.

What do you think of this new government?

BUILDING BACKGROUND The decision to change a city's government was not unusual in Greece. Many cities tried several forms of government before people were satisfied. To see how these changes came about, we can look at one city whose government changed many times—Athens.

Aristocrats and Tyrants Rule

Greece is the birthplace of **democracy**, a type of government in which people rule themselves. The word democracy comes from Greek words meaning "rule of the people." But Greek city-states didn't start as democracies, and not all became democratic.

Government in Athens QUICK FACTS

Oligarchy

Early Athens was governed by a small group of powerful aristocrats. This type of government is called an oligarchy. Oligarchy means "rule by a few."

Rule by a Few People

Even Athens, the city where democracy was born, began with a different kind of government. In early Athens, kings ruled the city-state. Later, a group of rich landowners, or **aristocrats** (uh-RIS-tuh-krats), took power. A government in which only a few people have power is called an **oligarchy** (AH-luh-gar-kee).

The aristocrats dominated Athenian society. As the richest men in town, they ran the city's economy. They also served as its generals and judges. Common people had little say in the government.

In the 600s BC a group of rebels tried to overthrow the aristocrats. They failed. Possibly as a result of their attempt, however, a man named Draco (DRAY-koh) created a new set of laws for Athens. These laws were very harsh. For example, Draco's laws made minor crimes such as loitering punishable by death.

The people of Athens thought Draco's laws were too strict. In the 590s BC a man named Solon (SOH-luhn) created a set of laws that were much less harsh and gave more rights to nonaristocrats. Under Solon's laws, all free men living in Athens became **citizens**, people who had the right to participate in government. But his efforts were not enough for the Athenians. They were ready to end the rule of the aristocracy.

The Rise of the Tyrants

Because the Athenians weren't pleased with the rule of the aristocrats, they wanted a new government. In 546 BC a noble named Peisistratus (py-SIS-truht-uhs) overthrew the oligarchy. He became the ruler of Athens. Peisistratus was called a **tyrant**, which meant a leader who held power through the use of force.

Today the word *tyrant* means a ruler who is harsh, but the word had a different meaning in ancient Greece. Athenian tyrants were usually good leaders. Tyrants were able to stay in power because they had strong armies and because the people supported them.

Peisistratus brought peace and prosperity to the city. He began new policies meant to unify the city. He created new festivals and built temples and monuments. During his rule, many improvements were made in Athens.

After Peisistratus died, his son took over as tyrant. Many aristocrats, however, were unhappy because their power was gone. Some of these aristocrats convinced a rival city-state to attack Athens. As a result of this invasion, the tyrants lost power and, for a short time, aristocrats returned to power in Athens.

READING CHECK Finding the Main Idea
What was a tyrant in ancient Greece?

FOCUS ON READING
How do Greek roots give you clues to the meaning of oligarchy?

THE IMPACT TODAY
Today very harsh laws or rules are called "draconian" after Draco.

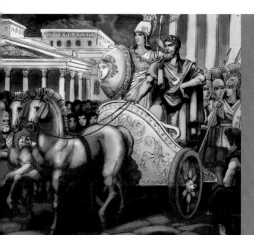
Tyranny
Peisistratus overthrew the oligarchy in 546 BC, and Athens became a tyranny. Tyranny means "rule by a tyrant"—a strong leader who has power.

Democracy
Around 500 BC Athens became a democracy. Democracy means "rule by the people." For the first time in history, a government was based on the votes of its free citizens.

Democracy in Action

Ancient Athens was the birthplace of democracy—the system of government in which the people rule themselves. Democracy was perhaps the greatest achievement of ancient Athens. In time, it became the Greeks' greatest gift to the world.

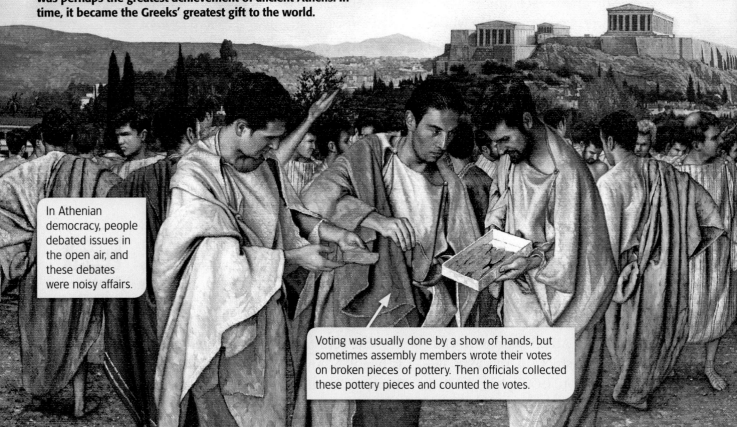

Only free male citizens of Athens were members of the assembly with the right to vote. Women, slaves, and foreigners could not participate.

In Athenian democracy, people debated issues in the open air, and these debates were noisy affairs.

Voting was usually done by a show of hands, but sometimes assembly members wrote their votes on broken pieces of pottery. Then officials collected these pottery pieces and counted the votes.

Athens Creates Democracy

Around 500 BC a new leader named Cleisthenes (KLYS-thuh-neez) gained power in Athens. Although he was a member of one of the most powerful families in Athens, Cleisthenes didn't want aristocrats to run the government. He thought they already had too much influence. By calling on the support of the people, Cleisthenes was able to overthrow the aristocracy once and for all. In its place, he established a completely new form of government.

Under Cleisthenes' leadership, Athens developed the world's first democracy. For this reason, he is sometimes called the father of democracy.

Democracy under Cleisthenes

Under Cleisthenes, all citizens in Athens had the right to participate in the assembly, or gathering of citizens, that created the city's laws. The assembly met outdoors on a hillside so that everyone could attend the meetings. During meetings, people stood before the crowd and gave speeches on political issues. Every citizen had the right to speak his opinion. In fact, the Athenians encouraged people to speak. They loved to hear speeches and debates. After the speeches were over, the assembly voted. Voting was usually done by a show of hands, but sometimes the Athenians used secret ballots.

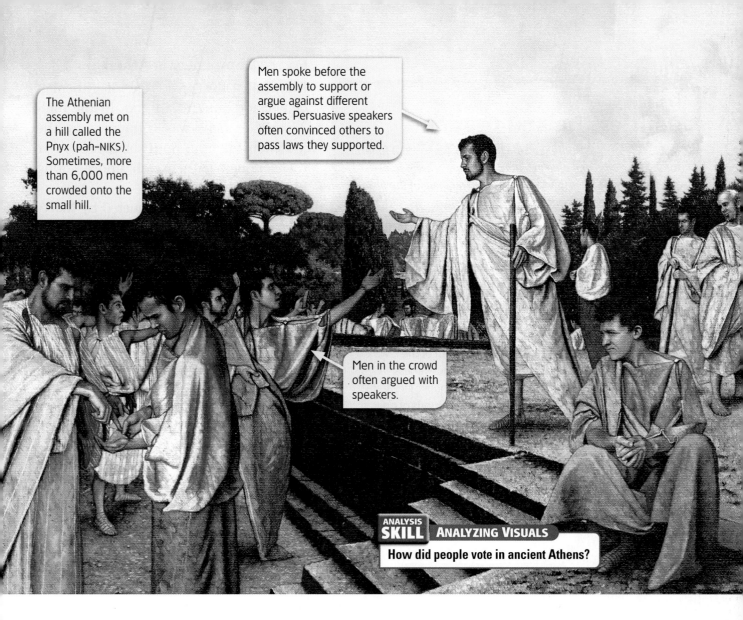

The Athenian assembly met on a hill called the Pnyx (pah-NIKS). Sometimes, more than 6,000 men crowded onto the small hill.

Men spoke before the assembly to support or argue against different issues. Persuasive speakers often convinced others to pass laws they supported.

Men in the crowd often argued with speakers.

ANALYSIS SKILL **ANALYZING VISUALS**

How did people vote in ancient Athens?

The number of people who voted in the assembly changed from day to day. For major decisions, however, the assembly needed about 6,000 people to vote. But it wasn't always easy to gather that many people together in one place.

According to one Greek writer, the government sent slaves to the market to round up more citizens if necessary. In one of the writer's plays, slaves walked through the market holding a long rope between them. The rope was covered in red dye and would mark the clothing of anyone it touched. Any citizen with red dye on his clothing had to go to the assembly meeting or pay a large fine.

Because the assembly was so large, it was sometimes difficult to make decisions. The Athenians therefore selected citizens to be city officials and to serve on a smaller council. These officials decided which laws the assembly should discuss. This helped the government run more smoothly.

Changes in Athenian Democracy

As time passed, citizens gained more powers. For example, they served on juries to decide court cases. Juries had anywhere from 200 to 6,000 people, although juries of about 500 people were much more common. Most juries had an odd number of members to prevent ties.

Like the ancient Greeks, we use juries to decide court cases. But our modern juries have only 12 people.

SPEECH
Pericles' Funeral Oration

In 430 BC Pericles addressed the people of Athens at a funeral for soldiers who had died in battle. In his speech, Pericles tried to comfort the Athenians by reminding them of the greatness of their government.

Pericles is praising the Athenians for creating a democracy.

"Our form of government does not enter into rivalry with the institutions of others. We do not copy our neighbors, but are an example to them. It is true that we are called a democracy, for the administration is in the hands of the many and not of the few . . . There is no exclusiveness [snobbery] in our public life, and . . . we are not suspicious of one another. . . . "

–Pericles, quoted in Thucydides, *The History of the Peloponnesian War*

Athenian government was open to all free men, not just a few.

ANALYSIS SKILL **ANALYZING PRIMARY SOURCES**

How do you think Pericles felt Athenian government compared to other cities' governments?

Athens remained a democracy for about 170 years. It reached its height under a brilliant elected leader named **Pericles** (PER-uh-kleez). He led the government from about 460 BC until his death in 429 BC.

Pericles encouraged the Athenians to take pride in their city. He believed that participating in government was just as important as defending Athens in war. To encourage people to participate in government, Pericles began to pay people who served in public offices or on juries. Pericles also encouraged the people of Athens to introduce democracy into other parts of Greece.

End of Democracy in Athens

Eventually, the great age of Athenian democracy came to an end. In the mid-330s BC Athens was conquered by the Macedonians from north of Greece. After the conquest, Athens fell under strong Macedonian influence.

Even after being conquered by Macedonia, Athens kept its democratic government. But it was a democracy with very limited powers. The Macedonian king ruled his country like a dictator, a ruler who held all the power. No one could make any decisions without his approval.

In Athens, the assembly still met to make laws, but it had to be careful not to upset the king. The Athenians didn't dare make any drastic changes to their laws without the king's consent. They weren't happy with this situation, but they feared the king's powerful army. Before long, though, the Athenians lost even this limited democracy. In the 320s BC a new king took over Greece and ended Athenian democracy forever.

READING CHECK **Summarizing** How were citizens involved in the government of Athens?

Ancient Democracy Differs from Modern Democracy

Like ancient Athens, the United States has a democratic government in which the people hold power. But our modern democracy is very different from the ancient Athenians' democracy.

Direct Democracy

All citizens in Athens could participate directly in the government. We call this form of government a direct democracy. It is called direct democracy because each person's decision directly affects the outcome of a vote. In Athens, citizens gathered together to discuss issues and vote on them. Each person's vote counted, and the majority ruled.

The United States is too large for direct democracy to work for the whole country. For example, it would be impossible for all citizens to gather in one place for a debate. Instead, the founders of the United States set up another kind of democracy.

Representative Democracy

The democracy created by the founders of the United States is a representative democracy, or republic. In this system, the citizens elect officials to represent them in the government. These elected officials then meet to make the country's laws and to enforce them. For example, Americans elect senators and representatives to Congress, the body that makes the country's laws. Americans don't vote on each law that Congress passes but trust their chosen representatives to vote for them.

READING CHECK Contrasting How are direct democracy and representative democracy different?

Democracy Then and Now

QUICK FACTS

In Athenian Direct Democracy…	In American Representative Democracy…
■ All citizens met as a group to debate and vote directly on every issue.	■ Citizens elect representatives to debate and vote on issues for them.
■ There was no separation of powers. Citizens created laws, enforced laws, and acted as judges.	■ There is a separation of powers. Citizens elect some people to create laws, others to enforce laws, and others to be judges.
■ Only free male citizens could vote. Women and slaves could not vote.	■ Men and women who are citizens have the right to vote.

SUMMARY AND PREVIEW In this section, you learned about the development and decline of democracy in Athens. You also learned how Athenian democracy influenced the government of the United States. In the next section, you will learn about the beliefs and culture of the ancient Greeks and how they affect our culture and literature today.

Section 2 Assessment

go.hrw.com
Online Quiz
KEYWORD: SQ6 HP9

Reviewing Ideas, Terms, and People HSS 6.4.2, 6.4.3

1. **a. Define** What are **aristocrats**?
   b. Contrast How were **oligarchy** and **tyranny** different?
2. **a. Describe** Describe the **democracy** created by Cleisthenes.
   b. Analyze How did **Pericles** change Athenian democracy?
3. **a. Identify** What type of democracy did Athens have?
   b. Develop In what situations would a representative democracy work better than a direct democracy?

Critical Thinking

4. **Compare and Contrast** Draw a chart like the one to the right. In each column, identify who had

power in each type of government. Then write a sentence explaining what role common people had in each government.

Oligarchy	Tyranny	Democracy

FOCUS ON WRITING

5. **Connecting Personalities and Governments** Think back to the personalities you assigned to natural features in Section 1. What if people with these same personalities were working to create a government? What kind would they create? Would they rule as tyrants or build a democracy? Write your thoughts in your notebook.

Greek Mythology and Literature

What You Will Learn...

Main Ideas

1. The Greeks created myths to explain the world.
2. Ancient Greek literature provides some of the world's greatest poems and stories.
3. Greek literature lives in and influences our world even today.

The Big Idea

The ancient Greeks created great myths and works of literature that influence the way we speak and write today.

Key Terms and People

mythology, *p. 269*
Homer, *p. 272*
Sappho, *p. 273*
Aesop, *p. 273*
fables, *p. 273*

HSS 6.4.4 Explain the significance of Greek mythology to the everyday life of people in the region and how Greek literature continues to permeate our literature and language today, drawing from Greek mythology and epics, such as Homer's *Iliad* and *Odyssey*, and from *Aesop's Fables*.

If YOU were there...

As a farmer in ancient Greece, your way of life depends on events in nature. The crops you grow need sunshine and rain, though thunder and lightning scare you. When you look up at the night sky, you wonder about the twinkling lights you see there. You know that at certain times of the year, the weather will turn cold and gray and plants will die. Then, a few months later, green plants will grow again.

How might you explain these natural events?

BUILDING BACKGROUND The Greeks lived in a time long before the development of science. To them, natural events like thunderstorms and changing seasons were mysterious. Today we can explain what causes these events. But to the Greeks, they seemed like the work of powerful gods.

Hephaestus

Hestia

Demeter

Poseidon

Dionysus

Myths Explain the World

The ancient Greeks believed in many gods. These gods were at the center of Greek **mythology**—a body of stories about gods and heroes that try to explain how the world works. Each story, or myth, explained natural or historical events.

Greek Gods

People today have scientific explanations for events like thunder, earthquakes, and volcanic eruptions. The ancient Greeks did not. They believed their gods caused these events to happen, and they created myths to explain the gods' actions.

Among the most important Greek gods were the ones in the picture below:

- Zeus, king of the gods
- Hera, queen of the gods
- Poseidon, god of the sea
- Hades, god of the underworld
- Demeter, goddess of agriculture
- Hestia, goddess of the hearth
- Athena, goddess of wisdom
- Apollo, god of the sun
- Artemis, goddess of the moon
- Ares, god of war
- Aphrodite, goddess of love
- Hephaestus, god of metalworking
- Dionysus, god of celebration, and
- Hermes, the messenger god

Olympian Gods

Zeus

Hermes

Athena

Ares

Apollo

Aphrodite

Hera

Artemis

Hades

ANALYSIS SKILL **ANALYZING VISUALS**

What can you see that indicates the Olympian gods have superhuman powers?

Gods and Mythology

The Greeks saw the work of the gods in events all around them. For example, the Greeks lived in an area where volcanic eruptions were common. To explain these eruptions, they told stories about the god Hephaestus (hi-FES-tuhs), who lived underground. The fire and lava that poured out of volcanoes, the Greeks said, came from the huge fires of the god's forge. At this forge he created weapons and armor for the other gods.

The Greeks did not think the gods spent all their time creating disasters, though. They also believed the gods caused daily events. For example, they believed the goddess of agriculture, Demeter (di-MEE-tuhr), created the seasons. According to Greek myth, Demeter had a daughter who was kidnapped by another god. The desperate goddess begged the god to let her daughter go, and eventually he agreed to let her return to her mother for six months every year. During the winter, Demeter is separated from her daughter and misses her. In her grief, she doesn't let plants grow. When her daughter comes home, the goddess is happy, and summer comes to Greece. To the Greeks, this story explained why winter came every year.

To keep the gods happy, the Greeks built great temples to them all around Greece. In return, however, they expected the gods to give them help when they needed it. For example, many Greeks in need of advice traveled to Delphi, a city in central Greece. There they spoke to the oracle, a female priest of Apollo to whom they thought the god gave answers. The oracle at Delphi was so respected that Greek leaders sometimes asked her for advice about how to rule their cities.

Theseus the Hero
According to legend, Athens had to send 14 people to Crete every year to be eaten by the Minotaur, a terrible monster. But Theseus, a hero from Athens, traveled to Crete and killed the Minotaur, freeing the people of Athens from this burden.

Let the Games Begin!

One way the ancient Greeks honored their gods was by holding sporting contests like the one shown on the vase. The largest took place every four years at Olympia, a city in southern Greece. Held in honor of Zeus, this event was called the Olympic Games. Athletes competed in footraces, chariot races, boxing, wrestling, and throwing events. Only men could compete. The Greeks held these games every four years for more than 1,000 years, until the AD 320s.

In modern times, people began to hold the Olympics again. The first modern Olympics took place in Athens in 1896. Since then, athletes from many nations have assembled in cities around the world to compete. Today the Olympics include 28 sports, and both men and women participate. They are still held every four years. In 2004 the Olympic Games once again returned to their birthplace, Greece.

ANALYSIS SKILL **ANALYZING INFORMATION**

How do you think the modern Olympics are similar to the ancient Games? How do you think they are different?

Heroes and Mythology

Not all Greek myths were about gods. Many told about the adventures of great heroes. Some of these heroes were real people, while others were not. The Greeks loved to tell the stories of heroes who had special abilities and faced terrible monsters. The people of each city had their favorite hero, usually someone from there.

The people of Athens, for example, told stories about the hero Theseus. According to legend, he traveled to Crete and killed the Minotaur, a terrible monster that was half human and half bull. People from northern Greece told myths about Jason and how he sailed across the seas in search of a great treasure, fighting enemies the whole way.

Perhaps the most famous of all Greek heroes was a man called Hercules. The myths explain how Hercules fought many monsters and performed nearly impossible tasks. For example, he fought and killed the hydra, a huge snake with nine heads and poisonous fangs. Every time Hercules cut off one of the monster's heads, two more heads grew in its place. In the end, Hercules had to burn the hydra's neck each time he cut off a head to keep a new head from growing. People from all parts of Greece enjoyed stories about Hercules and his great deeds.

READING CHECK **Finding Main Ideas** How did the Greeks use myths to explain the world around them?

Ancient Greek Literature

Because the Greeks loved myths and stories, it is no surprise that they created great works of literature. Early Greek writers produced long epic poems, romantic poetry, and some of the world's most famous stories.

Homer and Epic Poetry

Among the earliest Greek writings are two great epic poems, the *Iliad* and the *Odyssey*, by a poet named **Homer**. Like most epics, both poems describe the deeds of great heroes. The heroes in Homer's poems fought in the Trojan War. In this war, the Mycenaean Greeks fought the Trojans, people of the city called Troy.

The *Iliad* tells the story of the last years of the Trojan War. It focuses on the deeds of the Greeks, especially Achilles (uh-KIL-

eez), the greatest of all Greek warriors. It describes in great detail the battles between the Greeks and their Trojan enemies.

The *Odyssey* describes the challenges that the Greek hero Odysseus (oh-DI-see-uhs) faced on his way home from the war. For 10 years after the war ends, Odysseus tries to get home, but many obstacles stand in his way. He has to fight his way past terrible monsters, powerful magicians, and even angry gods.

Both the *Iliad* and the *Odyssey* are great tales of adventure. But to the Greeks Homer's poems were much more than just entertainment. They were central to the ancient Greek education system. People memorized long passages of the poems as part of their lessons. They admired Homer's poems and the heroes described in them as symbols of Greece's great history.

Homer's poems influenced later writers. They copied his writing styles and borrowed some of the stories and ideas he wrote about in his works. Homer's poems are considered some of the greatest literary works ever produced.

BIOGRAPHY

Homer
800s–700s BC

Historians know nothing about Homer, the greatest poet of the ancient world. Some don't think such a person ever lived. The ancient Greeks believed he had, though, and seven different cities claimed to be his birthplace. According to ancient legend, Homer was blind and recited the *Iliad* and the *Odyssey* aloud. It wasn't until much later that the poems were written down.

Making Predictions Why might scholars not be sure that Homer existed?

In Homer's *Odyssey*, the half woman and half bird Sirens sang sweet songs that made passing sailors forget everything and crash their ships. To trick the Sirens, Odysseus plugged his crew's ears with wax and had himself tied to his ship's mast.

Lyric Poetry

Other poets wrote poems that were often set to music. During a performance, the poet played a stringed instrument called a lyre while reading a poem. These poets were called lyric poets after their instrument, the lyre. Today, the words of songs are called lyrics after these ancient Greek poets.

Most poets in Greece were men, but the most famous lyric poet was a woman named **Sappho** (SAF-oh). Her poems were beautiful and emotional. Most of her poems were about love and relationships with her friends and family.

Fables

Other Greeks told stories to teach people important lessons. **Aesop** (EE-sahp), for example, is famous for his fables. **Fables** are short stories that teach the reader lessons about life or give advice on how to live.

In most of Aesop's fables, animals are the main characters. The animals talk and act like humans. One of Aesop's most famous stories is the tale of the ants and the grasshopper:

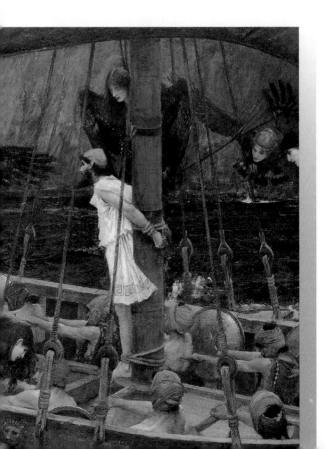

"The ants were spending a fine winter's day drying grain collected in the summertime. A Grasshopper, perishing [dying] with famine [hunger], passed by and earnestly [eagerly] begged for a little food. The Ants inquired [asked] of him, "Why did you not treasure up food during the summer?" He replied, "I had not leisure enough. I passed the days in singing." They then said in derision: "If you were foolish enough to sing all the summer, you must dance supperless to bed in the winter."

–Aesop, from "The Ants and the Grasshopper"

The lesson in this fable is that people shouldn't waste time instead of working. Those who do, Aesop says, will be sorry.

Another popular fable by Aesop, "The Tortoise and the Hare," teaches that it is better to work slowly and carefully than to hurry and make mistakes. "The Boy Who Cried Wolf" warns readers not to play pranks on others. Since we still read these fables, you may be familiar with them.

READING CHECK **Summarizing** Why did the Greeks tell fables?

Greek Literature Lives

The works of ancient Greek writers such as Homer, Sappho, and Aesop are still alive and popular today. In fact, Greek literature has influenced modern language, literature, and art. Did you know that some of the words you use and some of the stories you hear come from ancient Greece?

Language

Probably the most obvious way we see the influence of the Greeks is in our language. Many English words and expressions come from Greek mythology. For example, we call a long journey an "odyssey" after Odysseus, the wandering hero of Homer's poem. Something very large and powerful is called "titanic." This word comes from the Titans, a group of large and powerful gods in Greek myth.

Many places around the world today are also named after figures from Greek myths. For example, Athens is named for Athena, the goddess of wisdom. Africa's Atlas Mountains were named after a giant from Greek mythology who held up the sky. The name of the Aegean Sea comes from Aegeus, a legendary Greek king. Europe itself was named after a figure from Greek myth, the princess Europa. Even places in space bear names from mythology. For example, Jupiter's moon Io was named after a goddess's daughter.

Literature and the Arts

Greek myths have inspired artists for centuries. Great painters and sculptors have used gods and heroes as the subjects of their works. Writers have retold ancient stories, sometimes set in modern times. Moviemakers have also borrowed stories from ancient myths. Hercules, for example, has been the subject of dozens of films. These films range from early classics to a Walt Disney cartoon.

Mythological references are also common in today's popular culture. Many sports teams have adopted the names of powerful figures from myths, like Titans or

Greek Influence on Language

In Greek Literature and Mythology...	Today...
■ Achilles was a great warrior who was killed when an arrow struck his heel.	■ An "Achilles heel" is a person's weak spot.
■ Hercules was the strongest man on earth who completed 12 almost impossible tasks.	■ When a person has a really hard job to do it is called a "Herculean" task.
■ A fox wanted to eat some grapes but he couldn't reach the branch they were on, so he said, "Those grapes are probably sour anyway."	■ When people pretend they don't want something after they find out they can't have it, they are said to have "sour grapes."
■ King Midas was granted one wish by the god Dionysus, so he wished that everything he touched turned to gold.	■ A person who seems to get rich easily is said to have a "Midas touch."
■ Tantalus was punished for offending the gods. He had to stand up to his chin in water and he was always thirsty, but if he tried to drink the water it went away.	■ Something is "tantalizing" if you want it but it's just out of your reach.

Greek Names Today

The influence of Greek stories and culture can still be seen in names. Astronomers named one of Jupiter's moons Io (EYE-oh) after a woman from Greek mythology. Sports teams also use Greek names. This college mascot is dressed like a Trojan warrior.

Trojans. Businesses frequently use images or symbols from mythology in their advertising. Although people no longer believe in the Greek gods, mythological ideas can still be seen all around us.

READING CHECK Finding Main Ideas
How did Greek myths influence later language and art?

SUMMARY AND PREVIEW The myths, stories, and poems of ancient Greece have shaped how people today speak, read, and write. Like democracy, these myths, stories, and poems are part of ancient Greece's gift to the world. In the next chapter you will learn more about life and culture in ancient Greece.

Section 3 Assessment

go.hrw.com
Online Quiz
KEYWORD: SQ6 HP9

Reviewing Ideas, Terms, and People HSS 6.4.4

1. **a. Define** What is **mythology**?
   b. Summarize Why did the ancient Greeks create myths?
2. **a. Identify** What are **Homer**'s most famous works?
   b. Contrast How are **fables** different from myths?
3. **a. Recall** In what areas have Greek myths influenced our culture?
   b. Analyze Why do you think mythological references are popular with sports teams and businesses today?
   c. Evaluate Why do you think Greek literature has been so influential throughout history?

Critical Thinking

4. **Categorizing** Draw a chart like this one. List two characteristics of each type of Greek literature.

Epic Poetry	Lyric Poetry	Fables

FOCUS ON WRITING

5. **Putting Your Ideas Together** Look at your notes from the previous sections. Think about the personalities you gave physical features and government leaders. Now imagine that those personalities belonged to gods. What stories might be told about these gods? Write some ideas down.

ANCIENT GREECE **275**

The Epic Poetry of Homer

from the *Iliad*

as translated by Robert Fitzgerald

About the Reading *The* Iliad *describes one part of a ten-year war between the Greeks and the city of Troy. As the poem opens, the Greek hero Achilles (uh-KIL-eez) has left the battle to wait for help from the gods. When he learns that his best friend Patroclus is dead, however, Achilles springs back into action. In this passage, the angry Achilles sprints across the plain toward Troy—and Hector, the Trojan warrior who has killed his friend.*

AS YOU READ Look for words and actions that tell you Achilles is a hero.

Then toward the town with might and main
he ran magnificent, like a racing chariot horse
that holds its form at full stretch on the plain. ❶
So light-footed Achilles held the pace.
And aging Priam was the first to see him
sparkling on the plain, bright as that star
in autumn rising, whose unclouded rays
shine out amid a throng of stars at dusk—
the one they call Orion's dog, most brilliant... ❷
So pure and bright
the bronze gear blazed upon him as he ran.
The old man gave a cry. ❸ With both his hands
thrown up on high he struck his head, then
shouted, groaning, appealing to his dear son.
Unmoved, Lord Hector stood in the gateway,
resolute to fight Achilles.
        Stretching out his hands,
old Priam said, imploring him:
        "No, Hector!
... don't try to hold your ground against this man,
or soon you'll meet the shock of doom..."

The painting on this vase shows people fighting in the Trojan War.

from the *Odyssey*

About the Reading *The* Odyssey *takes place after the Trojan War has ended. It describes the adventures of another hero, Odysseus (oh-DIS-ee-uhs), as he makes his way home to his kingdom of Ithaca. His voyage is full of obstacles—including the two sea monsters described in this passage. The idea for these monsters probably came from an actual strait in the Mediterranean Sea, where a jagged cliff rose on one side and dangerous whirlpools churned on the other.*

AS YOU READ Try to picture the action in your mind.

GUIDED READING

WORD HELP

travail pain
dire gorge terrible throat
spume foam or froth
maelstrom whirlpool
blanched grew pale
anguish great suffering

          And all this time,
in travail, sobbing, gaining on the current,
we rowed into the strait—Scylla to port
and on our starboard beam Charybdis, dire
gorge of the salt sea tide. ❶ By heaven! when she
vomited, all the sea was like a cauldron
seething over intense fire, when the mixture
suddenly heaves and rises.

          The shot spume
soared to the landside heights, and fell like rain.
But when she swallowed the sea water down
we saw the funnel of the maelstrom, heard
the rock bellowing all around, and dark
sand raged on the bottom far below. ❷
My men all blanched against the gloom, our eyes
were fixed upon that yawning mouth in fear
of being devoured.

          Then Scylla made her strike,
whisking six of my best men from the ship.
I happened to glance aft at ship and oarsmen
and caught sight of their arms and legs, dangling
high overhead. Voices came down to me
in anguish, calling my name for the last time . . . ❸
               We rowed on.

The Rocks were now behind; Charybdis, too,
and Scylla dropped astern.

❶ Odysseus is the speaker. He is referring to himself and his crew.

Why might the crew be sobbing?

❷ Three times a day, the monster Charybdis (cuh-RIB-duhs) takes in water and then spits it out.

❸ Like many Greek monsters, Scylla (SIL-uh) is part human and part animal. She has the body of a woman, six heads with snake-like necks, and twelve feet.

CONNECTING LITERATURE TO HISTORY

1. **Comparing** Many Greek myths were about heroes who had special abilities. What heroic abilities or traits do Achilles, Hector, and Odysseus share?

2. **Analyzing** The Greeks used myths to explain the natural world. How does the *Odyssey* passage illustrate this?

Social Studies Skills

HSS Analysis HI 6 Students interpret basic indicators of economic performance and conduct cost-benefit analyses of economic and political issues.

| Analysis | Critical Thinking | Participation | Study |

Analyzing Costs and Benefits

Understand the Skill

Everything you do has both costs and benefits connected to it. *Benefits* are what you gain from something. *Costs* are what you give up to obtain benefits. For example, if you buy a video game, the benefits of your action include the game itself and the enjoyment of playing it. The most obvious cost is what you pay for the game. However, there are also costs that do not involve money. One of these costs is the time you spend playing the game. This is a cost because you give up something else, such as doing your homework or watching a TV show, when you choose to play the game.

The ability to analyze costs and benefits is a valuable life skill as well as a useful tool in the study of history. Weighing an action's benefits against its costs can help you decide whether or not to take it.

Learn the Skill

Analyzing the costs and benefits of historical events will help you to better understand and evaluate them. Follow these guidelines to do a cost-benefit analysis of an action or decision in history.

1 First determine what the action or decision was trying to accomplish. This step is needed in order to determine which of its effects were benefits and which were costs.

2 Then look for the positive or successful results of the action or decision. These are its benefits.

3 Consider the negative or unsuccessful effects of the action or decision. Also think about what positive things would have happened if it had *not* occurred. All these things are its costs.

4 Making a chart of the costs and benefits can be useful. By comparing the list of benefits to the list of costs you can better understand the action or decision and evaluate it.

For example, you learned in Chapter 9 that because of Greece's geography, the early Greeks settled near the sea. A cost-benefit analysis of their dependence on the sea might produce a chart like this one.

Benefits	Costs
Got food from sea	Would have paid more attention to agriculture than they did
Didn't have to depend on Greece's poor soil for food	
Became great shipbuilders and sailors	Had to rely on trade with other peoples for some food and other necessities
Became great traders and grew rich from trade	
Settled colonies throughout the region	

Based on this chart, one might conclude that the Greeks' choice of where to settle was a good one.

Practice and Apply the Skill

In 546 BC a noble named Peisistratus overthrew the oligarchy and ruled Athens as a tyrant. Use information from the chapter and the guidelines above to do a cost-benefit analysis of this action. Then write a paragraph explaining whether or not it was good for the people of Athens.

Standards Review

Visual Summary

Use the visual summary below to help you review the main ideas of the chapter.

QUICK FACTS

The early Greeks developed trading cultures and independent city-states.

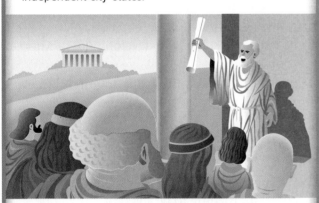

Athens had the world's first direct democracy.

The stories of Greek literature and mythology have influenced language and culture today.

Reviewing Vocabulary, Terms, and People

Unscramble each group of letters below to spell a term that matches the given definition.

1. **olpsi**—a Greek city-state

2. **iciznets**—people who have the right to participate in government

3. **ntaryt**—a person who rules alone, usually through military force

4. **comdeyacr**—rule by the people

5. **bleafs**—stories that teach lessons

6. **tsrarciotas**—rich landowners

7. **coiglhary**—rule by a few people

8. **siclalacs**—referring to a period of great achievements

Comprehension and Critical Thinking

SECTION 1 *(Pages 254–259)* **HSS** 6.4.1

9. **a. Describe** How did geography affect the development of the Greek city-states?

   b. Compare and Contrast What did the Minoans and Mycenaeans have in common? How were the two civilizations different?

   c. Elaborate How did the concept of the polis affect the growth of Greek colonies?

SECTION 2 *(Pages 262–267)* **HSS** 6.4.2, 6.4.3

10. **a. Identify** What roles did Draco, Solon, and Peisistratus play in the history of Greek government?

    b. Contrast The Greeks tried many forms of government before they created a democracy. How did these various forms of government differ?

    c. Evaluate Do you agree or disagree with this statement: "Representative democracy works better than direct democracy in large countries." Defend your answer.

11. a. Recall Who were some of the main gods of Greek mythology? Who were some of the main heroes?

b. Analyze What are some of the topics that appear in ancient Greek literature, such as the *Iliad* and the *Odyssey*?

c. Predict Do you think the language and literature of ancient Greece will play roles in Western civilization in years to come? Why or why not?

Reading Skills

Understanding Word Origins *Look at the list of Greek words and their meanings below. Then answer the questions that follow.*

archos (ruler)	*monos* (single)
bios (life)	*oligos* (few)
geo (earth)	*pente* (five)
micros (small)	*treis* (three)

12. Which of the following words means rule by a single person?

a. oligarchy   **c.** pentarchy

b. monarchy   **d.** triarchy

13. Which of the following words means the study of life?

a. biology   **c.** archaeology

b. geology   **d.** pentology

14. Is something that is *microscopic* very small or very large?

Using the Internet

go.hrw.com
KEYWORD: SQ6 WH9

15. Activity: Comparing Greek Governments Greek government had many forms: tyranny, oligarchy, direct democracy, and monarchy. Create a three-dimensional model, a drawing, or a diagram to illustrate what a person's life under each type of government might have looked like. Include information about the type of government you are representing.

Social Studies Skills

16. Analyzing Costs and Benefits Under Cleisthenes' leadership, Athens developed the world's first democracy. Create a chart comparing costs and benefits of this event. Then write a sentence explaining whether or not it was good for the people of Athens.

Cleisthenes' Leadership

Costs	Benefits

Reviewing Themes

17. Geography How do you think Greek society would have been different if Greece were a land-locked country?

18. Geography How did Crete's physical geography both help and hurt the development of Minoan civilization?

19. Politics Why was citizenship so important in Athens?

FOCUS ON WRITING

20. Writing Your Myth First, decide if your main character is going to be a god or if it will be a human who interacts with the gods. Think about the situations and decisions that your character will face, and how he or she will react to them.

Now it's time to write your myth down. Write a paragraph of seven to eight sentences about your character. You may want to include terrible monsters or heroes with great powers. Don't forget that a myth is supposed to explain something about the world.

Standards Assessment

DIRECTIONS: Read each question, and write the letter of the best response.

1

> ... that multitude of gleaming helms and bossed shields issued from the ships, with plated cuirasses [armor] and ashwood spears. Reflected glintings flashed to heaven, as the plain in all directions shone with glare of bronze and shook with trampling feet of men. Among them Prince Achilles armed. One heard his teeth grind hard together, and his eyes blazed out like licking fire, for unbearable pain had fixed upon his heart. Raging at Trojans, he buckled on the arms Hephaestus forged.

The content of this passage suggests that it was written by

A Homer.

B Zeus.

C Apollo.

D Cleisthenes.

2 What type of ancient Greek literature would *most* likely describe the deeds of a great hero?

A fable

B epic poem

C lyric poem

D oration

3 Which was the main cause for the independence of city-states in ancient Greece?

A the Greeks' location on the sea

B the threat of warlike neighbors to the north

C the geography of mountainous peninsulas

D the spread of Minoan culture

4 Athens was ruled by a single person under the type of government known as

A direct democracy.

B representative democracy.

C oligarchy.

D tyranny.

5 The citizens' assembly in ancient Athens was an example of

A trial by jury.

B rule by aristocrats.

C direct democracy.

D representative democracy.

Connecting with Past Learnings

6 Recently you learned about Hebrew history and beliefs. The ancient Hebrew and Greek civilizations shared all of the following characteristics *except*

A great written works.

B democratic governments.

C strong political leaders.

D influence on later civilizations.

7 You know that early towns in India were controlled by small groups of priests. Like ancient Greek government, this early Indian government was an example of

A oligarchy.

B tyranny.

C monarchy.

D democracy.

The Greek World

California Standards

History–Social Science

6.4 Students analyze the geographic, political, economic, religious, and social structures of the early civilizations of Ancient Greece.

Analysis Skills

HI 2 Students understand and distinguish cause, effect, sequence, and correlation in historical events, including long- and short-term causal relations.

English–Language Arts

Writing 6.2.2 Follow an organizational pattern appropriate to the type of composition.

Reading 6.2.2 Analyze text that uses the compare-and-contrast organizational pattern.

FOCUS ON WRITING

A Poem Ancient Greek poets often wrote poems in praise of great leaders, victorious military commanders, star athletes, and other famous people. As you read this chapter, you will learn about the accomplishments of Greek and Persian kings, generals, writers, thinkers, and scientists. As you read, you'll choose the one person you most admire and write a five-line poem praising that person.

CHAPTER EVENTS

c. 550 BC
Cyrus the Great founds the Persian Empire.

550 BC

WORLD EVENTS

c. 551 BC
Confucius is born in China.

HOLT

History's Impact

▶ **video series**
Watch the video to understand the impact of the Greek scholars.

What You Will Learn...

In this chapter you will learn that the ancient Greeks were both fierce fighters and great builders. The ruins shown in this photo are from the Parthenon, a beautiful temple built to celebrate a Greek victory in war.

431 BC
The Peloponnesian War begins.

334–323 BC
Alexander the Great builds his empire.

30 BC
Rome conquers Egypt, ending the Hellenistic Age.

450 BC   350 BC   250 BC   150 BC   50 BC

343 BC
The last Egyptian ruler of Egypt is overthrown.

c. 325 BC
The Mauryan Empire is founded in India.

c. 160 BC
The Maccabees regain Jewish independence.

THE GREEK WORLD   **283**

Reading Social Studies

by Kylene Beers

| Economics | Geography | Politics | Religion | Society and Culture | Science and Technology |

Focus on Themes In this chapter, you will learn about Persia's attempt to take over Greece. You will also read about two great Greek cities, Sparta and Athens, and how they both worked to protect Greece from this invader. Finally, you will discover how, even though another invader conquered Greece, Greek influence continued to spread. Without a doubt, you need to understand the **politics** of the time in order to understand the Greek world and its **society and culture**.

Comparing and Contrasting Historical Facts

Focus on Reading Comparing and contrasting is a good way to learn. That's one reason historians use comparison and contrast to explain people and events in history.

Understanding Comparison and Contrast To **compare** is to look for likenesses, or similarities. To **contrast** is to look for differences. Sometimes writers point out similarities and differences. Other times you have to look for them yourself. You can use a diagram like this one to keep track of similarities and differences as you read.

Additional reading support can be found in the

Reader and Study Guide

Greek Cities

Athens

Differences

- Democratic government
- Emphasis on many subjects in education
- Known as the home of artists, writers, and philosophers

Similarities

- Greek language and religion
- More rights for men than for women

Sparta

Differences

- Ruled by kings and officials
- Emphasis only on physical education
- Known for its powerful and disciplined army

Clues for Comparison-Contrast

Writers sometimes signal comparisons or contrasts with words like these:

Comparison—*similarly, like, in the same way, too*

Contrast—*however, unlike, but, while, although, in contrast*

You Try It!

The following passage is from the chapter you are getting ready to read. As you read the passage, look for word clues about similarities and differences.

Boys and Men in Athens

From a young age, Athenian boys from rich families worked to improve both their bodies and their minds. Like Spartan boys, Athenian boys had to learn to run, jump, and fight. But this training was not as harsh or as long as the training in Sparta.

From Chapter 10, pp. 294–295

Unlike Spartan men, Athenian men didn't have to devote their whole lives to the army. All men in Athens joined the army, but only for two years. They helped defend the city between the ages of 18 and 20. Older men only had to serve in the army in times of war.

In addition to their physical training, Athenian students, unlike the Spartans, also learned other skills. They learned to read, write, and count as well as sing and play musical instruments.

After you read the passage, answer the following questions.

1. What does the word *like* (line 3 of the passage) compare or contrast?

2. Which boys had harsher training, Athenian boys or Spartan boys? What comparison or contrast signal word helped you answer this question?

3. What other comparison or contrast words do you find in that passage? How do these words or phrases help you understand the passage?

4. Draw a diagram like the one on the previous page to compare educational opportunities for boys in Athens and Sparta.

Key Terms and People

Academic Vocabulary

Success in school is related to knowing academic vocabulary—the words that are frequently used in school assignments and discussions. In this chapter, you will learn the following academic words:

strategy (p. 288)
neutral (p. 306)

As you read Chapter 10, think about the organization of the ideas. Look for comparison and contrast signal words.

Greece and Persia

What You Will Learn...

Main Ideas

1. Persia became an empire under Cyrus the Great.
2. The Persian Empire grew stronger under Darius I.
3. The Persians fought Greece twice in the Persian Wars.

The Big Idea

Over time the Persians came to rule a great empire which eventually brought them into conflict with the Greeks.

Key Terms and People

Cyrus the Great, *p. 287*
cavalry, *p. 288*
Darius I, *p. 288*
Persian Wars, *p. 289*
Xerxes I, *p. 290*

HSS 6.4.5 Outline the founding, expansion, and political organization of the Persian Empire.

If YOU were there...

You're a great military leader and the ruler of a great empire. You control everything in the nations you've conquered. One of your advisers urges you to force conquered people to give up their customs. He thinks they should adopt your way of life. But another adviser disagrees. Let them keep their own ways, she says, and you'll earn their loyalty.

Whose advice do you take? Why?

BUILDING BACKGROUND Among the rulers who faced decisions like the one described above were the rulers of the Persian Empire. Created in 550 BC, the empire grew quickly. Within about 30 years, the Persians had conquered many peoples, and Persian rulers had to decide how these people would be treated.

Persia Becomes an Empire

While the Athenians were taking the first steps toward creating a democracy, a new power was rising in the East. This power, the Persian Empire, would one day attack Greece. But early in their history, the Persians were an unorganized nomadic people. It took the skills of leaders like Cyrus the Great and Darius I to change that situation. Under these leaders, the Persians created a huge empire, one of the mightiest of the ancient world.

Cyrus the Great

Early in their history, the Persians often fought other peoples of Southwest Asia. Sometimes they lost. In fact, they lost a fight to a people called the Medes (MEEDZ) and were ruled by them for about 150 years. In 550 BC, however, Cyrus II (SY-ruhs) led a Persian revolt against the Medes. His revolt was successful. Cyrus won independence for Persia and conquered the Medes. His victory marked the beginning of the Persian Empire.

The Persian Empire

GREECE
Athens
LYDIA
Sardis
ASIA MINOR
Mediterranean Sea
Black Sea
Caucasus Mts.
Caspian Sea
Aral Sea
Jaxartes River
HINDU KUSH
Euphrates R.
Tigris R.
Zagros Mts.
Ecbatana
Plateau of Iran
Susa
MESOPOTAMIA
Jerusalem
Memphis
EGYPT
Nile River
Red Sea
ARABIAN PENINSULA
Persian Gulf
Pasargadae
Persepolis
PERSIA
Arabian Sea

Persia under Cyrus, 559 BC
Conquered by Cyrus, 559–530 BC
Conquered by Cambyses, 530–522 BC
Conquered by Darius, 521–486 BC
Royal Road
⊛ Capital City

0   250   500 Miles
0   250   500 Kilometers

GEOGRAPHY SKILLS   **INTERPRETING MAPS**

1. **Region** Which Persian leader conquered the most territory?
2. **Movement** The Royal Road connected which two Persian cities?

BIOGRAPHY

Cyrus the Great
c. 585–c. 529 BC

One reason that Cyrus the Great was so successful as emperor was the way he treated conquered people. He didn't force people to adopt Persian customs, and he didn't mistreat them. For example, Cyrus allowed the conquered Babylonians to keep worshipping their own gods. He also allowed the Jews who had been Babylonian slaves to return to their homeland. Because of these acts, both the Babylonians and the Jews had great respect for Cyrus.

As you can see on the map, Cyrus conquered much of Southwest Asia, including nearly all of Asia Minor, during his rule. Included in this region were several Greek cities that Cyrus took over. He then marched south to conquer Mesopotamia.

Cyrus also added land to the east. He led his army into central Asia to the Jaxartes River, which we now call the Syr Darya. When he died around 529 BC, Cyrus ruled the largest empire the world had ever seen.

Cyrus let the people he conquered keep their own customs. He hoped this would make them less likely to rebel. He was right. Few people rebelled against Cyrus, and his empire remained strong. Because of his great successes, historians call him **Cyrus the Great**.

The Persian Army

Cyrus was successful in his conquests because his army was strong. It was strong because it was well organized and loyal.

Persia Under Darius

Sitting on a throne, the emperor Darius meets with an officer of his empire. Darius restored order to the Persian Empire and then expanded it. His army included royal guards like the two shown here.

Why do you think Darius appears larger than the official he is meeting with?

ACADEMIC
VOCABULARY
strategy
(STRA-tuh-jee)
a plan for fighting
a battle or war

At the heart of the Persian army were the Immortals, 10,000 soldiers chosen for their bravery and skill. In addition to the Immortals, the army had a powerful cavalry. A **cavalry** is a unit of soldiers who ride horses. Cyrus used his cavalry to charge at and shoot an enemy with arrows. This strategy weakened the enemy before the Immortals attacked. Together the cavalry and the Immortals could defeat almost any foe.

READING CHECK Finding Main Ideas
Who created the Persian Empire?

The Persian Empire Grows Stronger

Cyrus's son Cambyses continued to expand the Persian Empire after Cyrus died. For example, he conquered Egypt and added it to the empire. Soon afterward, though, a rebellion broke out in Persia. During this rebellion, Cambyses died. His death left Persia without a clear leader.

Within four years a young prince named **Darius I** (da-RY-uhs) claimed the throne and killed all his rivals for power. Once he was securely in control, Darius worked to restore order in Persia. He also improved Persian society and expanded the empire.

Political Organization

Darius organized the empire by dividing it into 20 provinces. Then he chose governors called satraps (SAY-traps) to rule the provinces for him. The satraps collected taxes for Darius, served as judges, and put down rebellions within their territories. Satraps had great power within their provinces, but Darius remained the empire's real ruler. His officials visited each province to make sure the satraps were loyal to Darius. He called himself king of kings to remind other rulers of his power.

Persian Society

After Darius restored order to the empire, he made many improvements to Persian society. For example, he built many roads.

Darius had roads built to connect various parts of the empire. Messengers used these roads to travel quickly throughout Persia. One road, called the Royal Road, was more than 1,700 miles long. Even Persia's enemies admired these roads and the Persian messenger system. For example, one Greek historian wrote:

> "Nothing mortal travels so fast as these Persian messengers . . . these men will not be hindered from accomplishing at their best speed the distance which they have to go, either by snow, or rain, or heat, or by the darkness of night."
>
> –Herodotus, from *History of the Persian Wars*

Darius also built a new capital for the empire. It was called Persepolis. Darius wanted his capital to reflect the glory of his empire, so he filled the city with beautiful works of art. For example, 3,000 carvings like the ones on the previous page line the city's walls. Statues throughout the city glittered with gold, silver, and precious jewels.

During Darius's rule a new religion arose in the Persian Empire as well. This religion, which was called Zoroastrianism (zawr-uh-WAS-tree-uh-nih-zuhm), taught that there were two forces fighting for control of the universe. One force was good, and the other was evil. Its priests urged people to help the side of good in its struggle. This religion remained popular in Persia for many centuries.

Persian Expansion

Like Cyrus, Darius wanted the Persian Empire to grow. In the east, he conquered the entire Indus Valley. He also tried to expand the empire westward into Europe. However, before Darius could move very far into Europe, he had to deal with a revolt in the empire.

READING CHECK **Summarizing** How did Darius I change Persia's political organization?

The Persians Fight Greece

In 499 BC several Greek cities in Asia Minor rebelled against Persian rule. To help their fellow Greeks, a few city-states in mainland Greece sent soldiers to join the fight against the Persians.

The Persians put down the revolt, but Darius was still angry with the Greeks. Although the cities that had rebelled were in Asia, Darius was enraged that other Greeks had given them aid. He swore to get revenge on the Greeks.

The Battle of Marathon

Nine years after the Greek cities rebelled, Darius invaded Greece. He and his army sailed to the plains of Marathon near Athens. This invasion began a series of wars between Persia and Greece that historians call the **Persian Wars**.

The Athenian army had only about 11,000 soldiers, while the Persians had about 15,000. However, the Greeks won the battle because they had better weapons and clever leaders.

The Persian Wars
This Greek vase shows a Persian soldier (at left) and a Greek soldier in a fight to the death. During the Persian Wars, the Greeks fiercely defended their homeland against massive invasions by the Persians.

With what kinds of weapons are the two soldiers fighting?

The Persian Wars

Legend:
- Persian Empire
- Rebellious Greek city-states
- Greek city-states allied against the Persians
- Neutral and pro-Persian city-states
- ★ Greek victory
- ★ Persian victory
- → Darius's fleet
- → Xerxes's army
- → Xerxes's fleet

Byzantium

Wreck of Darius's Fleet

Aegean Sea

Thermopylae ★

Plataea ★

Marathon ★

Athens

Salamis ★

Peloponnesus

N W E S

Sparta

Sardis

IONIA

ASIA MINOR

Rhodes

Mediterranean Sea

0   50   100 Miles
0   50   100 Kilometers

GEOGRAPHY SKILLS | **INTERPRETING MAPS**

1. **Location** Where in Greece were most of the allies against the Persians located?
2. **Movement** About how far did Xerxes's army have to march to reach Thermoplyae?

THE IMPACT TODAY

Athletes today re-create the Greek messenger's run in 26-mile races called marathons.

According to legend, a messenger ran from Marathon to Athens—a distance of just over 26 miles—to bring news of the great victory. After crying out "Rejoice! We conquer!" the exhausted runner fell to the ground and died.

The Second Invasion of Greece

Ten years after the Battle of Marathon, Darius's son **Xerxes I** (ZUHRK-seez) tried to conquer Greece again. In 480 BC the Persian army set out for Greece. This time they were joined by the Persian navy.

The Greeks prepared to defend their homeland. This time Sparta, a powerful city-state in southern Greece, joined with Athens. The Spartans had the strongest army

in Greece, so they went to fight the Persian army. Meanwhile, the Athenians sent their powerful navy to attack the Persian navy.

To slow the Persian army, the Spartans sent about 1,400 soldiers to Thermopylae (thuhr-MAH-puh-lee), a narrow mountain pass. The Persians had to cross through this pass to attack Greek cities. For three days, the small Greek force held off the Persian army. Then the Persians asked a traitorous Greek soldier to lead them through another pass. A large Persian force attacked the Spartans from behind. Surrounded, the brave Spartans and their allies fought to their deaths. After winning the battle, the Persians swept into Athens, attacking and burning the city.

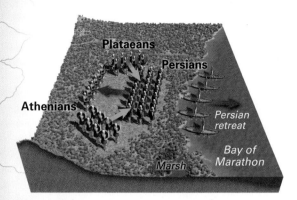

Marathon

At Marathon, the Greeks defeated a larger Persian force by luring the Persians into the middle of their forces. The Athenians then surrounded and defeated the Persians.

Salamis

At Salamis, the Greeks destroyed the Persian navy by attacking in a narrow strait where the Persian ships could not maneuver well.

Although the Persians won the battle in the pass, the Greeks quickly regained the upper hand. A few days after Athens was burned, the Athenians defeated the Persian navy through a clever plan. They led the larger Persian navy into the narrow straits of Salamis (SAH-luh-muhs). The Persians had so many ships that they couldn't steer well in the narrow strait. As a result, the smaller Athenian boats easily sank many Persian ships. Those ships that were not destroyed soon returned home.

Soon after the Battle of Salamis, an army of soldiers from all over Greece beat the Persians at Plataea (pluh-TEE-uh). This battle ended the Persian Wars. Defeated, the Persians left Greece.

For the Persians, this defeat was humiliating, but it was not a major blow. Their empire remained strong for more than a century after the war. For the Greeks, though, the defeat of the Persians was a triumph. They had saved their homeland.

READING CHECK **Analyzing** Why did Darius and Xerxes want to conquer Greece?

SUMMARY AND PREVIEW Athens and Sparta fought together against Persia. Their friendship didn't last long, though. In the next section, you will learn what happened when they became enemies.

Section 1 Assessment

go.hrw.com
Online Quiz
KEYWORD: SQ6 HP10

Reviewing Ideas, Terms, and People   HSS 6.4.5

1. **a. Describe** Describe the empire of **Cyrus the Great**.
   b. Make Generalizations Why did peoples conquered by Cyrus the Great seldom rebel?
2. **a. Identify** How did **Darius I** change Persia's political organization?
   b. Make Generalizations How did Persia's roads help improve the empire's organization?
3. **a. Explain** Why did Persia want to invade Greece?
   b. Predict How might the **Persian Wars** have ended if the Spartans had not slowed the Persians at Thermopylae?

Critical Thinking

4. **Categorizing** Draw a chart like the one below. In the first column, list the major battles of the Persian Wars. In the other columns, identify who fought in each battle, who won, and what happened as a result of each battle.

Battle	Armies	Winner	Result

FOCUS ON WRITING

5. **Taking Notes on Persian Leaders** Draw a table with three columns. In the first column, write the names of each leader mentioned in this section. In the second column, list each person's military accomplishments. In the third column, list any other accomplishments.

Sparta and Athens

If **YOU** were there...

Your father, a wandering trader, has decided it is time to settle down. He offers the family a choice between two cities. In one city, everyone wants to be athletic, tough, and strong. They're good at enduring hardships and following orders. The other city is different. There, you'd be admired if you could think deeply and speak persuasively, if you knew a lot about astronomy or history, or if you sang and played beautiful music.

Which city do you choose? Why?

BUILDING BACKGROUND Two of the greatest city-states in Greece were Sparta and Athens. Sparta, like the first city mentioned above, had a culture that valued physical strength and military might. The Athenian culture placed more value on the mind. However, both city-states had military strength, and they both played important roles in the defense of ancient Greece.

Spartans Build a Military Society

Spartan society was dominated by the military. According to Spartan tradition, their social system was created between 900 and 600 BC by a man named Lycurgus (ly-KUHR-guhs) after a slave revolt. To keep such a revolt from happening again, he increased the military's role in society. The Spartans believed that military power was the way to provide security and protection for their city. Daily life in Sparta reflected this belief.

Boys and Men in Sparta

Daily life in Sparta was dominated by the army. Even the lives of children reflected this domination. When a boy was born, government officials came to look at him. If he was not healthy, the baby was taken outside of the city and left to die. Healthy boys were trained from an early age to be soldiers.

Main Ideas

1. The Spartans built a military society to provide security and protection.
2. The Athenians admired the mind and the arts in addition to physical abilities.
3. Sparta and Athens fought over who should have power and influence in Greece.

The Big Idea

The two most powerful city-states in Greece, Sparta and Athens, had very different cultures and became bitter enemies in the 400s BC.

Key Terms and People

alliance, *p. 296*
Peloponnesian War, *p. 297*

HSS 6.4.6 Compare and contrast life in Athens and Sparta, with emphasis on their roles in the Persian and Peloponnesian Wars.

As part of their training, boys ran, jumped, swam, and threw javelins to increase their strength. They also learned to endure the hardships they would face as soldiers. For example, boys weren't given shoes or heavy clothes, even in winter. They also weren't given much food. Boys were allowed to steal food if they could, but if they were caught, they were whipped. At least one boy chose to die rather than admit to his theft:

"One youth, having stolen a fox and hidden it under his coat, allowed it to tear out his very bowels [organs] with its claws and teeth and died rather than betray his theft."

–Plutarch, from *Life of Lycurgus*

To this boy—and to most Spartan soldiers—courage and strength were more important than one's own safety.

Soldiers between the ages of 20 and 30 lived in army barracks and only occasionally visited their families. Spartan men stayed in the army until they turned 60.

The Spartans believed that the most important qualities of good soldiers were self-discipline and obedience. To reinforce self-discipline they required soldiers to live tough lives free from comforts. For example, the Spartans didn't have luxuries like soft furniture and expensive food. They thought such comforts made people weak. Even the Spartans' enemies admired their discipline and obedience.

Girls and Women in Sparta

Because Spartan men were often away at war, Spartan women had more rights than other Greek women. Some women owned land in Sparta and ran their households when their husbands were gone. Unlike women in other Greek cities, Spartan women didn't spend time spinning cloth or weaving. They thought of those tasks as the jobs of slaves, unsuitable for the wives and mothers of soldiers.

Life in Sparta QUICK FACTS

The Spartans valued discipline, obedience, and courage above all else. Spartan men learned these values at an early age, when they were trained to be soldiers. Spartan women were also expected to be strong, athletic, and disciplined.

The Life of a Spartan Soldier

Ages 7–12: Values training
Boys left home and got a basic education.

Ages 12–18: Physical training
Boys developed physical skills through exercise.

Ages 18–20: Military training
Men learned how to fight as part of the army.

Ages 20–30: Military service
Soldiers formed the body of the Spartan army.

Age 30: Full citizenship
Soldiers could participate in the assembly and move back home.

293

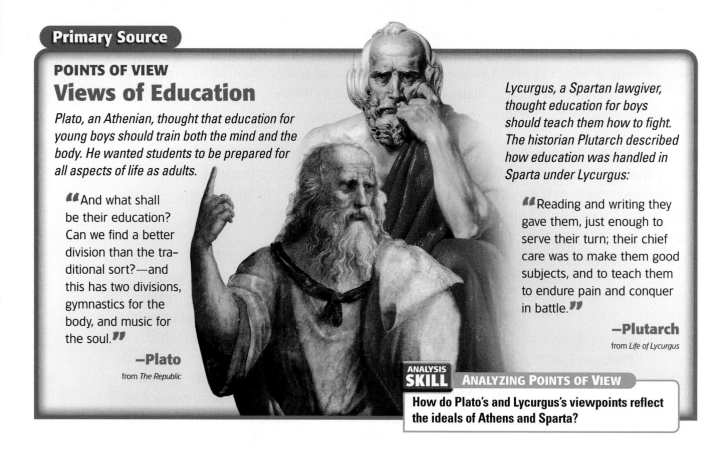

Primary Source

POINTS OF VIEW
Views of Education

Plato, an Athenian, thought that education for young boys should train both the mind and the body. He wanted students to be prepared for all aspects of life as adults.

❝ And what shall be their education? Can we find a better division than the traditional sort?—and this has two divisions, gymnastics for the body, and music for the soul. **❞**

—Plato
from *The Republic*

Lycurgus, a Spartan lawgiver, thought education for boys should teach them how to fight. The historian Plutarch described how education was handled in Sparta under Lycurgus:

❝ Reading and writing they gave them, just enough to serve their turn; their chief care was to make them good subjects, and to teach them to endure pain and conquer in battle. **❞**

—Plutarch
from *Life of Lycurgus*

ANALYSIS SKILL **ANALYZING POINTS OF VIEW**

How do Plato's and Lycurgus's viewpoints reflect the ideals of Athens and Sparta?

Spartan women also received physical training. Like the men, they learned how to run, jump, wrestle, and throw javelins. The Spartans believed this training would help women bear healthy children.

Government

Sparta was officially ruled by two kings who jointly led the army. But elected officials actually had more power than the kings. These officials ran Sparta's day-to-day activities. They also handled dealings between Sparta and other city-states.

Sparta's government was set up to control the city's helots (HEL-uhts), or slaves. These slaves grew all the city's crops and did many other jobs. Their lives were miserable, and they couldn't leave their land. Although slaves greatly outnumbered Spartan citizens, fear of the Spartan army kept them from rebelling.

FOCUS ON READING

How can the words **like** and **unlike** help you compare and contrast Athens and Sparta?

READING CHECK **Analyzing** What was the most important element of Spartan society?

Athenians Admire the Mind

Sparta's main rival in Greece was Athens. Like Sparta, Athens had been a leader in the Persian Wars and had a powerful army. But life in Athens was very different from life in Sparta. In addition to physical training, the Athenians valued education, clear thinking, and the arts.

Boys and Men in Athens

From a young age, Athenian boys from rich families worked to improve both their bodies and their minds. Like Spartan boys, Athenian boys had to learn to run, jump, and fight. But this training was not as harsh or as long as the training in Sparta.

Unlike Spartan men, Athenian men didn't have to devote their whole lives to the army. All men in Athens joined the army, but for only two years. They helped defend the city between the ages of 18 and 20. Older men only had to serve in the army in times of war.

In addition to their physical training, Athenian students, unlike the Spartans, also learned other skills. They learned to read, write, and count as well as sing and play musical instruments. Boys also learned about Greek history and legend. For example, they studied the *Iliad*, the *Odyssey*, and other works of Greek literature.

Boys from very rich families often continued their education with private tutors. These tutors taught their students about philosophy, geometry, astronomy, and other subjects. They also taught the boys how to be good public speakers. This training prepared boys for participation in the Athenian assembly.

Very few boys had the opportunity to receive this much education, however. Boys from poor families usually didn't get any education, although most of them could read and write at least a little. Most of the boys from poor families became farmers and grew food for the city's richer citizens. A few went to work with craftspeople to learn other trades.

Girls and Women in Athens

While many boys in Athens received good educations, girls didn't. In fact, girls got almost no education. Athenian men didn't think girls needed to be educated. A few girls were taught how to read and write at home by private tutors. However, most girls only learned household tasks like weaving and sewing.

Despite Athens's reputation for freedom and democracy, women there had fewer rights than women in many other city-states. Athenian women could not

- serve in any part of the city's government, including the assembly and juries,
- leave their homes, except on special occasions,
- buy anything or own property, or
- disobey their husbands or fathers.

In fact, women in Athens had almost no rights at all.

READING CHECK **Identifying Cause and Effect** Why did girls in Athens receive little education?

Life in Athens
QUICK FACTS

The Athenians valued education and the arts and believed that educated people made the best citizens.

- Boys from wealthy families were taught how to read, how to speak, and even how to think properly.
- Some boys were required to memorize long passages of plays or poems. Some had to commit both the *Iliad* and the *Odyssey* to memory.
- Very few girls, however, received educations.

The Peloponnesian War, c. 431–404 BC

Legend:
- Athens and allies
- Sparta and allies
- Neutral states
- ✦ Battle site

0 50 100 Miles
0 50 100 Kilometers

MACEDON

Sea of Marmara

PERSIAN EMPIRE

IONIA

Ionian Sea

Thebes · Athens
ATTICA

Peloponnesus
Sparta

SPARTA

Aegean Sea

Delos

Miletus

Segesta
Himera
Messana
Selinius
Locri
Rhegium
Catana
Sicily
Gela
Camarina
Syracuse

Mediterranean Sea

Rhodes

Crete

GEOGRAPHY SKILLS INTERPRETING MAPS

1. **Region** Most islands in the Aegean Sea were allied with which city?
2. **Movement** About how far did Athenian ships have to sail from Athens to invade Sicily?

Sparta and Athens Fight

As you learned earlier, Sparta and Athens worked together to win the Persian Wars. The Spartans fought most of the battles on land, and the Athenians fought at sea. After the war, the powerful Athenian fleet continued to protect Greece from the Persian navy. As a result, Athens had a great influence over much of Greece.

Athenian Power

After the Persian Wars ended in 480 BC, many city-states formed an **alliance**, or an agreement to work together. They wanted to punish the Persians for attacking Greece. They also agreed to help defend each other and to protect trade in the Aegean Sea. To pay for this defense, each city-state gave money to the alliance. Because the money was kept on the island of Delos, historians call the alliance the Delian League.

With its navy protecting the islands, Athens was the strongest member of the league. As a result, the Athenians began to treat other league members as their subjects. They refused to let members quit the league and forced more cities to join it. The Athenians even used the league's money to pay for buildings in Athens. Without even fighting, the Athenians made the Delian League an Athenian empire.

The Peloponnesian War

The Delian League was not the only alliance in Greece. After the Persian Wars, many cities in southern Greece, including Sparta, banded together as well. This alliance was called the Peloponnesian League after the peninsula on which the cities were located.

The growth of Athenian power worried many cities in the Peloponnesian League. Finally, to stop Athens's growth, Sparta declared war.

This declaration of war began the **Peloponnesian War**, a war between Athens and Sparta that threatened to tear all of Greece apart. In 431 BC the Spartan army marched north to Athens. They surrounded the city, waiting for the Athenians to come out and fight. But the Athenians stayed in the city, hoping that the Spartans would leave. Instead, the Spartans began to burn the crops in the fields around Athens. They hoped that Athens would run out of food and be forced to surrender.

The Spartans were in for a surprise. The Athenian navy escorted merchant ships to Athens, bringing plenty of food to the city. The navy also attacked Sparta's allies, forcing the Spartans to send troops to defend other Greek cities. At the same time, though, disease swept through Athens, killing thousands. For 10 years neither side could gain an advantage over the other. Eventually, they agreed to a truce. Athens kept its empire, and the Spartans went home.

A few years later, in 415 BC, Athens tried again to expand its empire. It sent its army and navy to conquer the island of Sicily. This effort backfired. The entire Athenian army was defeated by Sicilian allies of Sparta and taken prisoner. Even worse, these Sicilians also destroyed most of the Athenian navy.

Taking advantage of Athens's weakness, Sparta attacked Athens, and the war started up once more. Although the Athenians fought bravely, the Spartans won. They cut off the supply of food to Athens completely. In 404 BC, the people of Athens, starving and surrounded, surrendered. The Peloponnesian War was over, and Sparta was in control.

Fighting Among the City-States

With the defeat of Athens, Sparta became the most powerful city-state in Greece. For about 30 years, the Spartans controlled nearly all of Greece, until other city-states started to resent them. This resentment led to a period of war. Control of Greece shifted from city-state to city-state. The fighting went on for many years, which weakened Greece and left it open to attack from outside.

READING CHECK Identifying Cause and Effect
What happened after the Peloponnesian War?

SUMMARY AND PREVIEW In this section you read about conflicts between city-states for control of Greece. In the next section, you will learn what happened when all of Greece was conquered by a foreign power.

go.hrw.com

Section 2 Assessment

Online Quiz
KEYWORD: SQ6 HP10

Reviewing Ideas, Terms, and People   HSS 6.4.6

1. **a. Recall** How long did Spartan men stay in the army?
   b. Summarize How did the army affect life in Sparta?
2. **a. Identify** What skills did rich Athenian boys learn in school?
   b. Elaborate How might the government of Athens have influenced the growth of its educational system?
3. **a. Identify** Which city-state won the Peloponnesian War?
   b. Explain Why did many city-states form an **alliance** against Athens?

Critical Thinking

4. **Compare and Contrast** Draw a graphic organizer like the one shown here in your notebook. Use it to compare and contrast life in Sparta and Athens before the Peloponnesian War.

Military
Education
Women

Sparta   Athens

FOCUS ON WRITING

5. **Analyzing Greek Accomplishments** Think about the characteristics you would expect to be admired in Sparta and Athens. Write down some of these characteristics in your notebook. How do they relate to the Persian leaders you listed before?

Alexander the Great

What You Will Learn...

Main Ideas

1. Macedonia conquered Greece in the 300s BC.
2. Alexander the Great built an empire that united much of Europe, Asia, and Egypt.
3. The Hellenistic kingdoms formed from Alexander's empire blended Greek and other cultures.

The Big Idea

Alexander the Great built a huge empire and helped spread Greek culture into Egypt and Asia.

Key Terms and People

Philip II, *p. 298*
phalanx, *p. 299*
Alexander the Great, *p. 300*
Hellenistic, *p. 301*

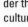 **HSS** 6.4.7 Trace the rise of Alexander the Great and the spread of Greek culture eastward and into Egypt.

If **YOU** were there...

You are a soldier in the most powerful army in the world. In just eight years, you and your fellow soldiers have conquered an enormous empire. Now your general wants to push farther into unknown lands in search of greater glory. But you're thousands of miles from home, and you haven't seen your family in years.

Do you agree to go on fighting? Why or why not?

BUILDING BACKGROUND The world's most powerful army in the 300s BC was from Macedonia, a kingdom just north of Greece. The Greeks had long dismissed the Macedonians as unimportant. They thought of the Macedonians as barbarians because they lived in small villages and spoke a strange form of the Greek language. But the Greeks underestimated the Macedonians, barbarians or not.

Macedonia Conquers Greece

In 359 BC **Philip II** became king of Macedonia. Philip spent the first year of his rule fighting off invaders who wanted to take over his kingdom. Once he defeated the invaders, he was ready to launch invasions of his own.

Philip's main target was Greece. The leaders of Athens, knowing they were the target of Philip's powerful army, called for all Greeks to join together. Few people responded.

As a result, the armies of Athens and its chief ally Thebes were easily defeated by the Macedonians. Having witnessed this defeat, the rest of the Greeks agreed to make Philip their leader.

Philip's Military Strength

Philip defeated the Greeks because he was a brilliant military leader. He borrowed and improved many of the strategies Greek armies used in battle. For example, Philip's soldiers, like the Greeks, fought as a phalanx (FAY-langks). A **phalanx** was a group of warriors who stood close together in a square. Each soldier held a spear pointed outward to fight off enemies. As soldiers in the front lines were killed, others stepped up from behind to fill their spots.

Philip improved upon the Greeks' idea. He gave his soldiers spears that were much longer than those of his opponents. This allowed his army to attack first in any battle. Philip also sent cavalry and archers into battle to support the phalanx.

After conquering Greece, Philip turned his attention to Persia. He planned to march east and conquer the Persian Empire, but he never made it. He was murdered in 336 BC while celebrating his daughter's wedding. When Philip died, his throne—and his plans—passed to his son, Alexander.

READING CHECK **Summarizing** How was Philip II able to conquer Greece?

Alexander Builds an Empire

When Philip died, the people in the Greek city of Thebes rebelled. They thought that the Macedonians would not have a leader strong enough to keep the kingdom together. They were wrong.

Controlling the Greeks

Although he was only 20 years old, Philip's son Alexander was as strong a leader as his father had been. He immediately went south to end the revolt in Thebes.

The Phalanx
With men holding 16-foot-long spears, a phalanx marches into battle.

Why were the soldiers' spears so long?

Within a year, Alexander had destroyed Thebes and enslaved the Theban people. He used Thebes as an example to other Greeks of what would happen if they turned against him. Then, confident that the Greeks would not rebel again, he set out to build an empire.

Alexander's efforts to build an empire made him one of the greatest conquerors in history. These efforts earned him the name **Alexander the Great**.

Building a New Empire

Like his father, Alexander was a brilliant commander. In 334 BC he attacked the Persians, whose army was much larger than his own. But Alexander's troops were well trained and ready for battle. They defeated the Persians time after time.

According to legend, Alexander visited a town called Gordium in Asia Minor while he was fighting the Persians. There he heard an ancient tale about a knot tied by an ancient king. The tale said that whoever untied the knot would rule all of Asia. According to the legend, Alexander pulled out his sword and cut right through the knot. Taking this as a good sign, he and his army set out again.

If you look at the map, you can follow the route Alexander took on his conquests. After defeating the Persians near the town of Issus, Alexander went to Egypt, which was part of the Persian Empire. The Persian governor had heard of his skill in battle. He surrendered without a fight in 332 BC and crowned Alexander pharaoh.

After a short stay in Egypt, Alexander set out again. Near the town of Gaugamela (gaw-guh-MEE-luh), he defeated the Persian army for the last time. After the battle, the Persian king fled. The king soon died, killed by one of his nobles. With the king's death, Alexander became the ruler of what had been the Persian Empire.

THE IMPACT TODAY

We still use the phrase "cutting the Gordian knot" to mean solving a difficult problem easily.

Marching Home

Still intent on building his empire, Alexander led his army through Central Asia. In 327 BC Alexander crossed the Indus River and wanted to push deeper into India. But his exhausted soldiers refused to go any farther. Disappointed, Alexander began the long march home.

Alexander left India in 325 BC, but he never made it back to Greece. In 323 BC, on his way back, Alexander visited the city of Babylon and got sick. He died a few days later at age 33. After he died, Alexander's body was taken to Egypt and buried in a golden coffin.

Alexander the Great's Empire, c. 323 BC

CAUCASUS MOUNTAINS

Aral Sea

Jaxartes River (Syr Darya)

Oxus River (Amu Darya)

Caspian Sea

Alexandria Eskhata

BACTRIA

HINDU KUSH

Alexander the Great

☆ Gaugamela 331 BC

Alexandropolis

Alexandria on the Caucasus
Kabul

Alexandria Nicaea

Alexandria Bucephala

Ecbatana

PARTHIA

Alexandria Areia

PERSIAN EMPIRE

Alexandria Arachoton (Kandahar)

Alexandria Opiana

Tigris River

Susa

Alexandria Opiana

Babylon

Euphrates River

Pasargadae

INDIA

Alexandria
Persepolis

Alexandria Carmana

Alexandria

Arabian Peninsula

Persian Gulf

Alexandria
Pattala

Arabian Sea

GEOGRAPHY SKILLS | **INTERPRETING MAPS**

1. **Movement** About how long was the route of Alexander from Pella to Babylon?
2. **Region** What bodies of water did Alexander cross?

Spreading Greek Culture

Alexander's empire was the largest the world had ever seen. An admirer of Greek culture, he worked to spread Greek influence throughout his empire by founding cities in the lands he conquered.

Alexander modeled his new cities after the cities of Greece. He named many of them Alexandria, after himself. He built temples and theaters like those in Greece. He then encouraged Greek settlers to move to the new cities. These settlers spoke Greek, which became common throughout the empire. In time, Greek art, literature, and science spread into surrounding lands.

Even as he supported the spread of Greek culture, however, Alexander encouraged conquered people to keep their own customs and traditions. As a result, a new blended culture developed in Alexander's empire. It combined elements of Persian, Egyptian, Syrian, and other cultures with Greek ideas. Because this new culture was not completely Greek, or Hellenic, historians call it **Hellenistic**, or Greek-like. It wasn't purely Greek, but it was heavily influenced by Greek ideas.

READING CHECK **Sequencing** What steps did Alexander take to create his empire?

Hellenistic Kingdoms

When Alexander died, he didn't have an obvious heir to take over his kingdom, and no one knew who was in power. With no clear direction, Alexander's generals fought for power. In the end, three powerful generals divided the empire among themselves. One became king of Macedonia and Greece, one ruled Syria, and the third claimed Egypt.

Hellenistic Macedonia

As you might expect, the kingdom of Macedonia and Greece was the most Greek of the three. However, it also had the weakest government. The Macedonian kings had to put down many revolts by the Greeks. Damaged by the revolts, Macedonia couldn't defend itself. Armies from Rome, a rising power from the Italian Peninsula, marched in and conquered Macedonia in the mid-100s BC.

Hellenistic Syria

Like the kings of Macedonia, the rulers of Syria faced many challenges. Their kingdom, which included most of the former Persian Empire, was home to many different peoples with many different customs.

Unhappy with Hellenistic rule, many of these people rebelled against their leaders. Weakened by years of fighting, the kingdom slowly broke apart. Finally in the 60s BC the Romans marched in and took over Syria.

Hellenistic Egypt

The rulers of Egypt encouraged the growth of Greek culture. They built the ancient world's largest library in the city of Alexandria. Also in Alexandria, they built the Museum, a place for scholars and artists to meet. Through their efforts, Alexandria became a great center of culture and learning. In the end, the Egyptian kingdom lasted longer than the other Hellenistic kingdoms. However, in 30 BC it too was conquered by Rome.

READING CHECK **Analyzing** Why were three kingdoms created from Alexander's empire?

SUMMARY AND PREVIEW Alexander the Great caused major political changes in Greece and the Hellenistic world. In the next section, you will learn about artistic and scientific advances that affected the lives of people in the same areas.

Section 3 Assessment

Reviewing Ideas, Terms, and People HSS 6.4.7

1. **Identify** What king conquered Greece in the 300s BC?
2. **a. Describe** What territories did **Alexander the Great** conquer?
   b. Interpret Why did Alexander destroy Thebes?
   c. Elaborate Why do you think Alexander named so many cities after himself?
3. **a. Recall** What three kingdoms were created out of Alexander's empire after his death?
   b. Explain Why were these kingdoms called **Hellenistic**?

Critical Thinking

4. **Finding the Main Idea** Draw a diagram like the one here. Use it to identify four major accomplishments of Alexander the Great.

Alexander the Great

FOCUS ON WRITING

5. **Evaluating Alexander** Add Alexander the Great to the table you created earlier. Remember that although Alexander was a military man, not all of his accomplishments were in battle.

Greek Achievements

If YOU were there...

Everyone in Athens has been talking about a philosopher and teacher named Socrates, so you decide to go and see him for yourself. You find him sitting under a tree, surrounded by his students. "Teach me about life," you say. But instead of answering, he asks you, "What is life?" You struggle to reply. He asks another question, and another. If he's such a great teacher, you wonder, shouldn't he have all the answers? Instead, all he seems to have are questions.

What do you think of Socrates?

BUILDING BACKGROUND Socrates was only one of the brilliant philosophers who lived in Athens in the 400s BC. The city was also home to some of the world's greatest artists and writers. In fact, all over Greece men and women made great advances in the arts and sciences. Their work inspired people for centuries.

The Arts

Among the most notable achievements of the ancient Greeks were those they made in the arts. These arts included sculpture, painting, architecture, and writings.

Statues and Paintings

The ancient Greeks were master artists. Their paintings and statues have been admired for hundreds of years. Examples of these works are still displayed in museums around the world.

What You Will Learn...

Main Ideas

1. The Greeks made great contributions to the arts.
2. The teachings of Socrates, Plato, and Aristotle are the basis of modern philosophy.
3. In science, the Greeks made key discoveries in math, medicine, and engineering.

The Big Idea

Ancient Greeks made lasting contributions in the arts, philosophy, and science.

Key Terms and People

Socrates, *p. 307*
Plato, *p. 307*
Aristotle, *p. 307*
reason, *p. 307*
Euclid, *p. 308*
Hippocrates, *p. 308*

Greek sculpture is admired for its realism, natural look, and details.

HSS 6.4.8 Describe the enduring contributions of important Greek figures in the arts and sciences (e.g., Hypatia, Socrates, Plato, Aristotle, Euclid, Thucydides).

Greek statues are so admired because the sculptors who made them tried to make them look perfect. They wanted their statues to show how beautiful people could be. To improve their art, these sculptors carefully studied the human body, especially how it looked when it was moving. Then, using what they had learned, they carved stone and marble statues. As a result, many Greek statues look as though they could come to life at any moment.

Greek painting is also admired for its realism and detail. For example, Greek artists painted detailed scenes on vases, pots, and other vessels. These vessels often show scenes from myths or athletic competitions. Many of the scenes were created using only two colors, black and red. Sometimes artists used black glaze to paint scenes on red vases. Other artists covered whole vases with glaze and then scraped parts away to let the red background show through.

Greek Architecture

If you went to Greece today, you would see the ruins of many ancient buildings. Old columns still hold up parts of broken roofs, and ancient carvings decorate fallen walls. These remains give us an idea of the beauty of ancient Greek buildings.

History Close-up

The Parthenon

The Parthenon was a beautiful temple to the goddess Athena, whom the people of Athens considered their protector. The temple, which stood on the Athenian acropolis, was built by Pericles and is still one of the most famous buildings in the world.

The carvings on the west side of the Parthenon show a contest between Athena and the god Poseidon to decide who would be honored in the city.

Once a year, the people of Athens held a great festival in honor of Athena. Part of the festival included a great procession that wound through the city.

The Greeks took great care in designing their buildings, especially their temples. Rows of tall columns surrounded the temples, making the temples look stately and inspiring. Greek designers were very careful when they measured these columns. They knew that columns standing in a long row often looked as though they curved in the middle. To prevent this optical illusion, they made their columns bulge slightly in the middle. As a result, Greek columns look perfectly straight.

Ancient Greek designers took such care because they wanted their buildings to reflect the greatness of their cities. The most impressive of all ancient Greek buildings was the Parthenon (PAHR-thuh-nahn) in Athens, pictured below. This temple to Athena was built in the 400s BC on the Athenian acropolis. It was designed to be magnificent not only outside, but inside as well. As you can see, the interior was decorated with carvings and columns.

New Forms of Writing

Sculpture, painting, and architecture were not the only Greek art forms. The Greeks also excelled at writing. In fact, Greek writers created many new writing forms, including drama and history.

Inside the Parthenon was a magnificent statue of Athena by the sculptor Phidias, whom many people considered the greatest sculptor in all of Greece.

The Parthenon's 46 columns are a type called Doric columns. These simple columns have no decoration at the top.

ANALYSIS SKILL **ANALYZING VISUALS**

Why do you think people are bringing animals and goods with them to the temple?

305

The Greeks created drama, or plays, as part of their religious ceremonies. Actors and singers performed scenes in honor of the gods and heroes. These plays became a popular form of entertainment, especially in Athens.

ACADEMIC VOCABULARY

neutral
unbiased, not favoring either side in a conflict

In the 400s BC Athenian writers created many of the greatest plays of the ancient world. Some writers produced tragedies, which described the hardships faced by Greek heroes. Among the best tragedy writers were Aeschylus (ES-kuh-luhs) and Sophocles (SAHF-uh-kleez). For example, Sophocles wrote about a Greek hero who mistakenly killed his own father. Other Greek dramatists focused on comedies, which made fun of people and ideas. One famous comedy writer was Aristophanes (ar-uh-STAHF-uh-neez). He used his comedy to make serious points about war, courts of law, and famous people.

The Greeks were also among the first people to write about history. They were interested in the lessons history could teach. One of the greatest of the Greek historians was Thucydides (thoo-SID-uh-deez). He wrote a history of the Peloponnesian War based in part on his experiences as an Athenian soldier. Even though he was from Athens, Thucydides tried to be **neutral** in his writing. He studied the war and tried to figure out what had caused it. He may have hoped the Greeks could learn from their mistakes and avoid similar wars in the future. Many later historians modeled their works after his.

READING CHECK **Summarizing** What were some forms of art found in ancient Greece?

Philosophy

The ancient Greeks worshipped gods and goddesses whose actions explained many of the mysteries of the world. But by around 500 BC a few people had begun to think about other explanations. We call these people philosophers. They believed in the power of the human mind to think, explain, and understand life.

Primary Source

BOOK
The Death of Socrates

In 399 BC Socrates was arrested and charged with corrupting the young people of Athens and ignoring religious traditions. He was sentenced to die by drinking poison. Socrates spent his last hours surrounded by his students. One of them, Plato, later described the event in detail.

Socrates himself does not protest against his sentence but willingly drinks the poison.

The students and friends who have visited Socrates, including the narrator, are much less calm than he is.

"Then raising the cup to his lips, quite readily and cheerfully he drank off the poison. And hitherto most of us had been able to control our sorrow; but now when we saw him drinking . . . my own tears were flowing fast; so that I covered my face and wept . . . Socrates alone retained his calmness: What is this strange outcry? he said . . . I have been told that a man should die in peace. Be quiet then, and have patience."

–Plato, from *Phaedo*

ANALYSIS SKILL ANALYZING PRIMARY SOURCES

How does Socrates tell his students to act when he drinks the poison?

Socrates

Among the greatest of these thinkers was a man named **Socrates** (SAHK-ruh-teez). He believed that people must never stop looking for knowledge.

Socrates was a teacher as well as a thinker. Today we call his type of teaching the Socratic method. He taught by asking questions. His questions were about human qualities such as love and courage. He would ask, "What is courage?" When people answered, he challenged their answers with more questions.

Socrates wanted to make people think and question their own beliefs. But he made people angry, even frightened. They accused him of questioning the authority of the gods. For these reasons, he was arrested and condemned to death. His friends and students watched him calmly accept his death. He took the poison he was given, drank it, and died.

Plato

Plato (PLAYT-oh) was a student of Socrates. Like Socrates, he was a teacher as well as a philosopher. Plato created a school, the Academy, to which students, philosophers, and scientists could come to discuss ideas.

Although Plato spent much of his time running the Academy, he also wrote many works. The most famous of these works was called *The Republic*. It describes Plato's idea of an ideal society. This society would be based on justice and fairness to everyone. To ensure this fairness, Plato argued, society should be run by philosophers. He thought that only they could understand what was best for everyone.

Aristotle

Perhaps the greatest Greek thinker was **Aristotle** (ar-uh-STAH-tuhl), Plato's student. He taught that people should live lives of moderation, or balance. For example,

people should not be greedy, but neither should they give away everything they own. Instead, people should find a balance between these two extremes.

Aristotle believed that moderation was based on **reason**, or clear and ordered thinking. He thought that people should use reason to govern their lives. In other words, people should think about their actions and how they will affect others.

Aristotle also made great advances in the field of logic, the process of making inferences. He argued that you could use facts you knew to figure out new facts. For example, if you know that Socrates lives in Athens and that Athens is in Greece, you can conclude that Socrates lives in Greece. Aristotle's ideas about logic helped inspire many later Greek scientists.

READING CHECK **Generalizing** What did ancient Greek philosophers like Socrates, Plato, and Aristotle want to find out?

Science

Aristotle's works inspired many Greek scientists. They began to look closely at the world to see how it worked.

Mathematics

Some Greeks spent their lives studying mathematics. One of these people was **Euclid** (YOO-kluhd). He was interested in geometry, the study of lines, angles, and shapes. In fact, many of the geometry rules we learn in school today come straight from Euclid's writings.

Other Greek mathematicians included a geographer who used mathematics to accurately calculate the size of the earth. Years later, in the AD 300s and 400s, a woman named Hypatia (hy-PAY-shuh) taught about mathematics and astronomy.

Medicine and Engineering

Not all Greek scientists studied numbers. Some studied other areas of science, such as medicine and engineering.

Greek doctors studied the human body to understand how it worked. In trying to cure diseases and keep people healthy, Greek doctors made many discoveries.

The greatest Greek doctor was **Hippocrates** (hip-AHK-ruh-teez). He wanted to figure out what caused diseases so he could better treat them. Hippocrates is better known today, though, for his ideas about how doctors should behave.

Greek engineers also made great discoveries. Some of the devices they invented are still used today. For example, farmers in many countries still use water screws to bring water to their fields. This device, which brings water from a lower level to a higher one, was invented by a Greek scientist named Archimedes (ahr-kuh-MEED-eez) in the 200s BC. Greek inventors could be playful as well as serious. For example, one inventor created mechanical toys like birds, puppets, and coin-operated machines.

READING CHECK **Summarizing** What advances did Greek scientists make in medicine?

SUMMARY AND PREVIEW Through their art, philosophy, and science, the Greeks have greatly influenced Western civilization. In the next chapter, you will learn about another group that has helped shape the Western world—the Romans.

Section 4 Assessment

Reviewing Ideas, Terms, and People **HSS** 6.4.8

1. **a. Identify** What two types of drama did the Greeks invent?
   b. Explain Why did Greek columns bulge in the middle?
   c. Draw Conclusions How did studying the human body help Greek artists make their statues look real?
2. **Describe** How did **Socrates** teach? What is this method of teaching called?
3. **a. Identify** In what fields did **Hippocrates** and **Euclid** make their greatest achievements?
   b. Make Inferences Why do some people call Greece the birthplace of the Western world?

Critical Thinking

4. **Summarizing** Draw a chart like the one here. Use it to list one contribution each person made to the arts and sciences.

Person	Contribution
Thucydides	
Socrates	
Plato	
Aristotle	
Euclid	
Hypatia	

FOCUS ON WRITING

5. **Taking Notes about Artists and Thinkers** Add the artists and thinkers from this section to your chart. Because these people were not military leaders, all of your notes will go in the third column of your chart.

Greek Philosophers—Socrates, Plato, and Aristotle

What would the world be like if no one believed in the importance of knowledge and truth?

When did they live? the 400s and 300s BC

Where did they live? Athens

What did they do? They thought. Socrates, Plato, and Aristotle thought about the world and searched for knowledge, wisdom, and truth. They created the Socratic method of learning, the first political science book, and a method of scientific reasoning.

Why are they important? In most of the ancient world, strong fighters won all the glory. But in Athens, great thinkers and wise men were honored. People listened to them and followed their advice. Even today, people admire the ideas of Socrates, Plato, and Aristotle. Their teachings are at the root of modern philosophy and science.

Making Inferences Do you think these philosophers would have been as influential if they had lived in a different city? Why or why not?

This drawing shows how one artist imagined Plato (left), Aristotle (center), and Socrates (right) to look.

KEY FACTS

How did Socrates, Plato, and Aristotle influence history?

- **Socrates** taught Plato.

- **Plato** taught Aristotle.

- **Aristotle** taught Alexander the Great, who helped spread Greek ideas through much of the world.

Social Studies Skills

Analysis	Critical Thinking	Participation	Study

Interpreting Charts and Tables

Understand the Skill

Charts present information visually to make it easier to understand. Different kinds of charts have different purposes. *Organizational charts* can show relationships among the parts of something. *Flowcharts* show steps in a process or cause-and-effect relationships. *Classification charts* group information so it can be easily compared. *Tables* are a type of classification chart that organize information into rows and columns for easy comparison. The ability to interpret charts helps you to analyze information and understand relationships.

Learn the Skill

Use these basic steps to interpret a chart:

1 Identify the type of chart and read its title in order to understand its purpose and subject.

2 Note the parts of the chart. Read the headings of rows and columns to determine the categories of information. Note any other labels that accompany the information in the chart. Look for any lines that connect its parts.

3 Study the chart's details. Look for relationships in the information it presents. In classification charts, analyze and compare all content in rows and columns. In flowcharts and organizational charts, read all labels and other information. Follow directional arrows or lines.

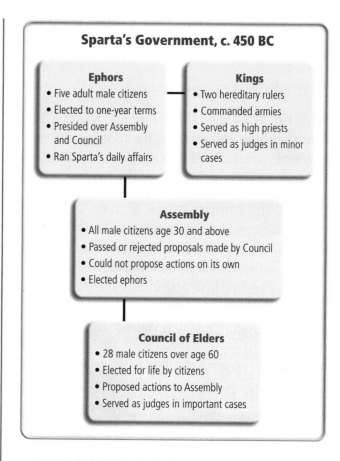

Sparta's Government, c. 450 BC

Ephors
- Five adult male citizens
- Elected to one-year terms
- Presided over Assembly and Council
- Ran Sparta's daily affairs

Kings
- Two hereditary rulers
- Commanded armies
- Served as high priests
- Served as judges in minor cases

Assembly
- All male citizens age 30 and above
- Passed or rejected proposals made by Council
- Could not propose actions on its own
- Elected ephors

Council of Elders
- 28 male citizens over age 60
- Elected for life by citizens
- Proposed actions to Assembly
- Served as judges in important cases

Practice and Apply the Skill

Apply the strategies here to interpret the chart above and answer the following questions.

1. What type of chart is this and what is its purpose?

2. In what ways were the ephors and the Assembly connected?

3. How did the roles of the Assembly and the Council of Elders differ?

4. What position in Spartan government had no direct relationship with the Assembly?

Standards Review

Visual Summary

Use the visual summary below to help you review the main ideas of the chapter.

QUICK FACTS

Sparta and Athens fought together to defeat Persia in the Persian Wars.

Spartan culture centered on the military, while Athenian culture emphasized government and the arts.

Alexander the Great built a huge empire and spread Greek culture.

The ancient Greeks made lasting contributions to architecture, philosophy, science, and many other fields.

Reviewing Vocabulary, Terms, and People

Choose one word from each word pair to correctly complete each sentence below.

1. A ruler named _____ created the Persian Empire. **(Cyrus the Great/Xerxes I)**

2. A _____ was a group of soldiers that stood in a square to fight. **(cavalry/phalanx)**

3. _____ built the largest empire the world had ever seen. **(Alexander the Great/Aristotle)**

4. The _____ War(s) pitted two city-states against each other. **(Persian/Peloponnesian)**

5. The philosopher _____ taught people by asking them questions. **(Darius/Socrates)**

6. The greatest medical scholar of ancient Greece was _____. **(Philip II/Hippocrates)**

7. Aristotle taught the importance of _____ in his writings. **(reason/alliance)**

8. _____ was a great mathematician. **(Plato/Euclid)**

Comprehension and Critical Thinking

SECTION 1 *(Pages 286–291)* **HSS** 6.4.5

9. **a. Identify** Who were Cyrus the Great, Darius I, and Xerxes I?

   b. Analyze How did the Greeks use strategy to defeat a larger fighting force?

   c. Elaborate What were some factors that led to the success of the Persian Empire?

SECTION 2 *(Pages 292–297)* **HSS** 6.4.6

10. **a. Describe** What was life like for Spartan women? for Athenian women?

   b. Compare and Contrast How was the education of Spartan boys different from the education of Athenian boys? What did the education of both groups have in common?

   c. Evaluate Do you agree or disagree with this statement: "The Athenians brought the Peloponnesian War on themselves." Defend your argument.

SECTION 3 *(Pages 298–302)* **HSS** 6.4.7

11. a. Describe How did Philip II improve the phalanx?

b. Analyze How did the cultures that Alexander conquered change after his death?

c. Predict How might history have been different if Alexander had not died so young?

SECTION 4 *(Pages 303–308)* **HSS** 6.4.8

12. a. Identify What is the Parthenon? For which goddess was it built?

b. Compare What did Socrates, Plato, and Aristotle have in common?

c. Evaluate Why do you think Greek accomplishments in the arts and sciences are still admired today?

Reviewing Themes

13. Politics Why did the Persians and the Greeks react differently to the end of the Persian Wars?

14. Politics How were the government and the army related in Sparta?

15. Society and Culture How were the roles of women different in Athens and Sparta?

Using the Internet

go.hrw.com
KEYWORD: SQ6 WH10

16. Activity: Writing a Dialogue While rulers such as Alexander and Cyrus fought to gain land, thinkers like Socrates may have questioned their methods. Enter the keyword activity. Write a dialogue between Socrates and a student on whether it was right to invade another country. Socrates should ask at least 10 questions to his student.

Social Studies Skills

17. Understanding Charts and Tables Create a chart in your notebook that identifies key Greek achievements in architecture, art, writing, philosophy, and science. Complete the chart with details from this chapter.

Reading Skills

18. Comparing and Contrasting Complete the chart below to compare and contrast two powerful leaders you studied in this chapter, Cyrus the Great and Alexander the Great.

Compare	List two characteristics that Cyrus and Alexander shared.
	a. _____
	b. _____

Contrast	How did Cyrus's and Alexander's backgrounds differ?	
	Cyrus	Alexander
	c. _____	d. _____
	What happened to their empires after they died?	
	Cyrus	Alexander
	e. _____	f. _____

FOCUS ON WRITING

19. Writing Your Poem Look back over your notes from this chapter. Ask yourself which of the accomplishments you noted are the most significant. Do you admire people for their ideas? their might? their leadership? their brilliance?

Choose one person whose accomplishments you admire. Look back through the chapter for more details about the person's accomplishments. Then write a poem in praise of your chosen figure. Your poem should be five lines long. The first line should identify the subject of the poem. The next three lines should note his or her accomplishments, and the last line should sum up why he or she is respected.

Standards Assessment

DIRECTIONS: Read each question and write the letter of the best response.

1

> The freedom which we enjoy in our government extends also to our ordinary life . . . Further, we provide plenty of means for the mind to refresh itself from business. We celebrate games and sacrifices all the year round . . . Where our rivals from their very cradles by a painful discipline seek after manliness . . . we live exactly as we please and yet are just as ready to encounter every legitimate danger.

The information in this passage suggests that the person who wrote it probably lived in

A Athens.

B Persia.

C Sparta.

D Troy.

2 The Athenians' main rivals were from

A Sparta.

B Rome.

C Macedonia.

D Persia.

3 Which people were the chief enemies of the Greeks in the 400s BC?

A the Romans

B the Persians

C the Egyptians

D the Macedonians

4 All of the following were Greek philosophers *except*

A Aristotle.

B Plato.

C Socrates.

D Zoroaster.

5 Hellenistic culture developed as a result of the activities of which person?

A Darius I

B Philip II

C Cyrus the Great

D Alexander the Great

Connecting with Past Learnings

6 Cyrus the Great and Alexander the Great both built huge empires. What other leader that you have studied in this course also created an empire?

A Moses

B Shi Huangdi

C Confucius

D Hatshepsut

7 In this chapter you have read about many great philosophers and thinkers. Which of the following people you have studied was *not* a philosopher or thinker?

A Socrates

B Ramses the Great

C Confucius

D Siddhartha Gautama

Assignment

Collect information and write an informative report on a topic related to the Hebrews or the ancient Greeks.

TIP **Narrowing a Topic**

Broad: Sparta

Less Broad: Women and Girls in Sparta

Focus Question: What was life like for women and girls in Sparta?

ELA Writing 6.2.3 Write Research Reports:
a. Pose relevant questions.
b. Support the main idea with information from multiple sources.
c. Include a bibliography.

Analysis Skill Students frame questions that can be answered by historical study and research.

A Social Studies Report

The purpose of a social studies report is to share information. Often, this information comes from research. You begin your research by asking questions about a subject.

1. Prewrite

Choosing a Subject

You could ask many questions about the unit you have just studied.

> • Why was Ruth an important person in the history of the Jewish religion?
> • What was the role of mythology in the lives of the ancient Greeks?
> • What were the most important accomplishments of Alexander the Great?

Jot down some topics that interested you. Then, brainstorm a list of questions about one or more of these topics. Make sure your questions are narrow and focused. Choose the question that seems most interesting.

Finding Historical Information

Use at least three sources besides your textbook to find information on your topic. Good sources include

- books, maps, magazines, newspapers
- television programs, movies, videos
- Internet sites, CD-ROMs, DVDs

Keep track of your sources of information by writing them in a notebook or on cards. Give each source a number as shown below.

Taking Notes

Take notes on important facts and details from your sources. Historical writing needs to be accurate. Carefully record all names, dates, and other information from sources. Copy any direct quotation word for word and enclose the words in quotation marks. Along with each note, include the number of its source and its page number.

Stating the Big Idea of Your Report

You can easily turn your original question into the big idea for your report. If your question changes a bit as you do your research, rewrite it before turning it into a statement. The big idea of a report is often, but not always, stated in the first paragraph.

Organizing Your Ideas and Information

Sort your notes into topics and subtopics. Put them in an order that is logical, that will make sense to your reader. We often use one of these ways to organize information:

- placing events and details in the order they happened
- grouping causes with their effects
- grouping information by category, usually in the order of least to most important

Here is a partial outline for a paper on Greek mythology.

> Big Idea: The ancient Greeks told myths to explain the world.
>
> I. Purpose of mythology in ancient Greece
>   A. Greeks' questions about the world around them
>   B. Greeks' use of myths for answers
> II. Myths about everyday events in the Greeks' lives
>   A. The myth of Hestia, goddess of the home
>   B. The myth of Hephaestus, god of crafts and fire
> III. Myths about the natural world of the Greeks
>   A. The myth of Apollo, god of the sun
>   B. The myth of Persephone, goddess of the seasons

TIP Statement or Question
Your big idea statement can be a statement of the point you want to make in your paper.

> The ancient Greeks used mythology to explain nature.

It can also be a question, similar to your original research question.

> How did the ancient Greeks use mythology to explain their lives?

TIP Making the Most of Your Outline If you write each of your topics and subtopics as a complete sentence, you can use those sentences to create your first draft.

2. Write

It is good to write a first draft fairly quickly, but it's also helpful to organize it as you go. Use the following framework as a guide.

A Writer's Framework

Introduction

- Start with a quotation or interesting historical detail.
- State the big idea of your report.
- Provide any historical background readers need in order to understand your big idea.

Body

- Present your information under at least three main ideas.
- Write at least one paragraph for each of these main ideas.
- Add supporting details, facts, or examples to each paragraph.

Conclusion

- Restate your main idea, using slightly different words.
- Close with a general comment about your topic or tell how the historical information in your report relates to later historical events.

Studying a Model

Here is a model of a social studies report. Study it to see how one student developed a social studies paper. The first and the concluding paragraphs are shown in full. The paragraphs in the body of the paper are summarized.

INTRODUCTORY PARAGRAPH

Attention grabber

Statement of Big Idea

The ancient Greeks faced many mysteries in their lives. How and why did people fall in love? What made rain fall and crops grow? What are the planets and stars, and where did they come from? Through the myths they told about their heroes, gods, and goddesses, the Greeks answered these questions. They used mythology to explain all things, from everyday events to forces of nature to the creation of the universe.

Body Paragraphs

The first body paragraph opens with a statement about how the Greeks used myths to explain their daily lives. Then two examples of those kinds of myths are given. The student summarizes myths about Aphrodite, goddess of love, and Hephaestus, god of crafts and fire.

In the next paragraph, the student shows how the Greeks used myths to explain the natural world. The example of such a story is Persephone and her relationship to the seasons.

The last paragraph in the body contains the student's final point, which is about creation myths. The two examples given for these myths are stories about Helios, god of the sun, and Artemis, goddess of the moon.

CONCLUDING PARAGRAPH

First two sentences restate the thesis

Last three sentences make a general comment about the topic, Greek myths.

The Greeks had a huge number of myths. They needed that many to explain all of the things that they did and saw. Besides explaining things, myths also gave the Greeks a feeling of power. By praying and sacrificing to the gods, they believed they could affect the world around them. All people want to have some control over their lives, and their mythology gave the Greeks that feeling of control.

Notice that each paragraph is organized in the same way as the entire paper. Each paragraph expresses a main idea and includes information to support that main idea. One big difference is that not every paragraph requires a conclusion. Only the last paragraph needs to end with a concluding statement.

3. Evaluate and Revise

It is important to evaluate your first draft before you begin to revise it. Follow the steps below to evaluate and revise your draft.

Evaluating and Revising an Informative Report

1. Does the introduction grab the readers' interest and state the big idea of your report?
2. Does the body of your report have at least three paragraphs that develop your big idea? Is the main idea in each paragraph clearly stated?
3. Have you included enough information to support each of your main ideas? Are all facts, details, and examples accurate? Are all of them clearly related to the main ideas they support?
4. Is the report clearly organized? Does it use chronological order, order of importance, or cause and effect?
5. Does the conclusion restate the big idea of your report? Does it end with a general comment about your topic?
6. Have you included at least three sources in your bibliography? Have you included all the sources you used and not any you did not use?

4. Proofread and Publish

Proofreading

To correct your report before sharing it, check the following:

- the spelling and capitalization of all proper names for specific people, places, things, and events
- punctuation marks around any direct quotation
- punctuation and capitalization in your bibliography

Publishing

Choose one or more of these ideas to share your report.

- Create a map to accompany your report. Use a specific color to highlight places and routes that are important in your report.
- File a copy of your report in your school's library for other students' reference. Include illustrations to go with the report.
- If your school has a Web site, you might post your report there. See if you can link to other sources on your topic.

> **TIP** Bibliography
>
> - Underline the titles of all books, television programs, and Web sites.
> - Use quotation marks around titles of articles and stories.

● Practice and Apply

Use the steps and strategies outlined in this workshop to research and write an informative report.

The Roman World

From a small town in Italy, Rome grew to become the center of one of the world's greatest empires. Like the Greeks, whom they admired, the Romans had a lasting influence on world history.

The legacy of Rome was great. The Romans made many huge advances in engineering and architecture, and they developed advanced systems of written laws and government. In the first century AD, a new religion called Christianity appeared and spread throughout the empire.

In the next three chapters, you will learn how Rome began, how it became an empire, and how Christianity became a central part of life in the Roman world.

Explore the Art

In this scene, a Roman tutor teaches two young students how to read. What does this scene suggest about life in ancient Rome?

The Roman Republic

California Standards

History–Social Science

6.7 Students analyze the geographic, political, economic, religious, and social structures during the development of Rome.

Analysis Skills

CS 3 Use maps to identify cultural features.

English–Language Arts

Speaking 6.2.1 Deliver narrative presentations.

Reading 6.2.4 Clarify an understanding of texts by creating outlines, logical notes, summaries, or reports.

FOCUS ON SPEAKING

A Legend The ancient Romans created many legends about their early history. They told of heroes and kings who performed great deeds to build and rule their city. As you read this chapter, look for people or events that could be the subjects of legends. When you finish studying this chapter, you will create and present a legend about one of the people or events that you have studied.

CHAPTER EVENTS

753 BC
According to legend, Rome is founded.

800 BC

WORLD EVENTS

c. 700 BC
The Assyrians conquer Israel.

History's Impact
▶ **video series**
Watch the video to understand the impact of Roman government on American government today.

What You Will Learn...

In this chapter you will learn about the history of the Roman Republic. The Roman Forum, the ruins of which are shown above, was a public meeting place at the heart of Rome.

c. 600 BC
The Etruscans take over Rome.

509 BC
The Roman Republic is founded.

264–146 BC
Rome and Carthage fight in the Punic Wars.

27 BC
Augustus becomes Rome's first emperor.

600 BC

490 BC
The Persians invade Greece.

334–323 BC
Alexander the Great builds his empire.

400 BC

c. 221–206 BC
The Qin dynasty rules China.

200 BC

BC 1 AD

321

Reading Social Studies

by Kylene Beers

Economics	Geography	Politics	Religion	Society and Culture	Science and Technology

Focus on Themes In this chapter, you will read about the Roman Republic, about how Rome's location and **geography** helped it become a major power in the ancient world. You will also read about the city's **politics** and discover how its three-pronged government affected all of society. Finally, you will read about the wars the Roman Republic fought as it expanded its boundaries. You will see how this growth led to problems that were difficult to solve.

Outlining and History

Focus on Reading How can you make sense of all the facts and ideas in a chapter? One way is to take notes in the form of an outline.

Outlining a Chapter Here is an example of a partial outline for Section 1 of this chapter. Compare the outline to the information on pages 324–327. Notice how the writer looked at the heads in the chapter to determine the main and supporting ideas.

Additional reading support can be found in the

Inter**active**

Reader and Study Guide

The writer picked up the first heading in the chapter (page 324) as the first main idea. She identified it with Roman numeral I.

Section 1, Geography and the Rise of Rome
I. The Geography of Italy
  A. Physical features—many types of features
    1. Mountain ranges
    2. Hills
    3. Rivers
  B. Climate—warm summers, mild winters
II. Rome's Legendary Origins
  A. Aeneas
    1. Trojan hero
    2. Sailed to Italy and founded city
  B. Romulus and Remus
    1. Twin brothers
    2. Founded city of Rome
      a. Romulus killed Remus
      b. City named for Romulus
      c. Rome's Early Kings

The writer saw two smaller heads under the bigger head on page 324 and listed them as A and B.

The writer identified two facts that supported II.A (the head on page 326). She listed them as numbers 1 and 2.

The writer decided it was important to note some individual facts under B.2. That's why she added a, b, and c.

Outlining a Few Paragraphs When you need to outline only a few paragraphs, you can use the same outline form. Just look for the main idea of each paragraph and give each one a Roman numeral. Supporting ideas within the paragraph can be listed with A, B, and so forth. You can use Arabic numbers for specific details and facts.

ELA Reading 6.2.4 Clarify an understanding of texts by creating outlines, logical notes, summaries, or reports.

You Try It!

Read the following passage from this chapter. Then fill in the blanks to complete the outline below.

Growth of Territory

Roman territory grew mainly in response to outside threats. In about 387 BC a people called the Gauls attacked Rome and took over the city. The Romans had to give the Gauls a huge amount of gold to leave the city.

From Chapter 11, pages 338–339

Inspired by the Gauls' victory, many of Rome's neighboring cities also decided to attack. With some difficulty, the Romans fought off these attacks. As Rome's attackers were defeated, the Romans took over their lands. As you can see on the map, the Romans soon controlled all of the Italian Peninsula except far northern Italy.

One reason for the Roman success was the organization of the army. Soldiers were organized in legions . . . This organization allowed the army to be very flexible.

Complete this outline based on the passage you just read.

I. Roman territory grew in response to outside threats.

   A. Gauls attacked Rome in 387 BC.
      1. Took over the city
      2. _____

   B. The Gauls' victory inspired other people to attack Rome.
      1. _____
      2. Romans took lands of defeated foes.
      3. _____

II. _____

   A. Soldiers were organized in legions.
   B. _____

Key Terms and People

Chapter 11

Section 1
Aeneas *(p. 326)*
Romulus and Remus *(p. 327)*
republic *(p. 328)*
dictators *(p. 328)*
Cincinnatus *(p. 328)*
plebeians *(p. 329)*
patricians *(p. 329)*

Section 2
magistrates *(p. 333)*
consuls *(p. 333)*
Roman Senate *(p. 333)*
veto *(p. 334)*
Latin *(p. 334)*
checks and balances *(p. 335)*
Forum *(p. 335)*

Section 3
legions *(p. 339)*
Punic Wars *(p. 339)*
Hannibal *(p. 340)*
Gaius Marius *(p. 342)*
Lucius Cornelius Sulla *(p. 343)*
Spartacus *(p. 343)*

Academic Vocabulary

Success in school is related to knowing academic vocabulary—the words that are frequently used in school assignments and discussions. In this chapter, you will learn the following academic words:

primary *(p. 333)*
purpose *(p. 342)*

As you read Chapter 11, identify the main ideas you would use in an outline of this chapter.

Geography and the Rise of Rome

What You Will Learn...

Main Ideas

1. The geography of Italy made land travel difficult but helped the Romans prosper.
2. Ancient historians were very interested in Rome's legendary history.
3. Once a monarchy, the Romans created a republic.

The Big Idea

Rome's location and government helped it become a major power in the ancient world.

Key Terms and People

Aeneas, *p. 326*
Romulus and Remus, *p. 327*
republic, *p. 328*
dictators, *p. 328*
Cincinnatus, *p. 328*
plebeians, *p. 329*
patricians, *p. 329*

HSS 6.7.1 Identify the location and describe the rise of the Roman Republic, including the importance of such mythical and historical figures as Aeneas, Romulus and Remus, Cincinnatus, Julius Caesar, and Cicero.

If YOU were there...

You are the ruler of a group of people looking for a site to build a new city. After talking with your advisors, you have narrowed your choice to two possible sites. Both locations have plenty of water and good soil for farming, but they are otherwise very different. One is on top of a tall rocky hill overlooking a shallow river. The other is on a wide open field right next to the sea.

Which site will you choose for your city? Why?

BUILDING BACKGROUND From a small town on the Tiber River, Rome grew into a mighty power. Rome's geography—its central location and good climate—were important factors in its success and growth. The city's rise as a military power began when the Romans went to war and conquered neighboring Italian tribes.

The Geography of Italy

Rome eventually became the center of one of the greatest civilizations of the ancient world. In fact, the people of Rome conquered many of the territories you have studied in this book, including Greece, Egypt, and Asia Minor.

Italy, where Rome was built, is a peninsula in southern Europe. If you look at the map, you can see that Italy looks like a high-heeled boot sticking out into the Mediterranean Sea.

Physical Features

Look at the map again to find Italy's two major mountain ranges. In the north are the Alps, Europe's highest mountains. Another range, the Apennines (A-puh-nynz), runs the length of the Italian Peninsula. This rugged land made it hard for ancient people to cross from one side of the peninsula to the other. In addition, some of Italy's mountains, such as Mount Vesuvius, are volcanic. Their eruptions could devastate Roman towns.

Italy: Physical

ALPS

L. Como

Garda

Gulf of Venice

Po River

Gulf of Genoa

Ligurian Sea

Arno River

Apennines

Italian Peninsula

Adriatic Sea

Tiber River

Rome

Mt. Vesuvius
4,190 ft.
(1,277 m)

40°N

Sardinia

Tyrrhenian Sea

10°E

15°E

Ionian Sea

Sicily

ELEVATION

Feet	Meters
6,560	2,000
1,640	500
656	200
(Sea level) 0	0 (Sea level)

0   75   150 Miles
0   75   150 Kilometers

Mountains cover much of the Italian Peninsula. These mountains are in the Alps in northern Italy.

Italy's fertile coastal plains have been settled for thousands of years.

GEOGRAPHY SKILLS | **INTERPRETING MAPS**

Place What mountain range runs down the length of the Italian Peninsula?

Not much of Italy is flat. Most of the land that isn't mountainous is covered with hills. Throughout history, people have built cities on these hills for defense. As a result, many of the ancient cities of Italy—including Rome—sat atop hills. Rome was built on seven hills.

Several rivers flow out of Italy's mountains. Because these rivers were a source of fresh water, people also built their cities near them. For example, Rome lies on the Tiber (TY-buhr) River.

Climate

Most of Italy, including the area around Rome, has warm, dry summers and mild, rainy winters. This climate is similar to that of southern California. Italy's mild climate allows people to grow a wide variety of crops. Grains, citrus fruits, grapes, and olives all grow well there. A plentiful food supply was one key factor in Rome's early growth.

READING CHECK **Drawing Conclusions**
How did Rome's location affect its early history?

Rome's Legendary Origins

Rome's early history is wrapped in mystery. No written records exist, and we have little evidence of the city's earliest days. All we have found are ancient ruins that suggest people lived in the area of Rome as early as the 800s BC. However, we know very little about how they lived.

Would it surprise you to think that the ancient Romans were as curious about their early history as we are today? Rome's leaders wanted their city to have a glorious past that would make the Roman people proud. Imagining that glorious past, they told legends, or stories, about great heroes and kings who built the city.

Aeneas

The Romans believed their history could be traced back to a great Trojan hero named **Aeneas** (i-NEE-uhs). When the Greeks destroyed Troy in the Trojan War, Aeneas fled with his followers. After a long and dangerous journey, he reached Italy. The story of this trip is told in the *Aeneid* (i-NEE-id), an epic poem written by a poet named Virgil (VUHR-juhl) around 20 BC.

According to the story, when Aeneas reached Italy, he found several groups of people living there. He formed an

Legendary Founding of Rome QUICK FACTS

Roman historians traced their city's history back to legendary figures such as Aeneas, Romulus, and Remus.

Aeneas
According to the *Aeneid*, Aeneas carried his father from the burning city of Troy and then searched for a new home for the Trojans. After traveling around the Mediterranean, Aeneas finally settled in Italy.

alliance with one of these groups, a people called the Latins. Together they fought the other people of Italy. After defeating these opponents, Aeneas married the daughter of the Latin king. Aeneas, his son, and their descendants became prominent rulers in Italy.

Romulus and Remus

Among the descendants of Aeneas were the founders of Rome. According to Roman legends, these founders were twin brothers named **Romulus** (RAHM-yuh-luhs) and **Remus** (REE-muhs). In the story, these boys led exciting lives. When they were babies, they were put in a basket and thrown into the Tiber River. They didn't drown, though, because a wolf rescued them. The wolf cared for the boys for many years. Eventually, a shepherd found the boys and adopted them.

After they grew up, Romulus and Remus decided to build a city to mark the spot where the wolf had rescued them. While they were planning the city, Remus mocked one of his brother's ideas. In a fit of anger, Romulus killed Remus. He then built the city and named it Rome after himself.

Rome's Early Kings

According to ancient historians, Romulus was the first king of Rome, taking the throne in 753 BC. Modern historians believe that Rome could have been founded within 50 years before or after that date.

Roman records list seven kings who ruled the city. Not all of them were Roman. Rome's last three kings were Etruscans (i-TRUHS-kuhnz), members of a people who lived north of Rome. The Etruscans, who had been influenced by Greek colonies in Italy, lived in Italy before Rome was founded.

The Etruscan kings made great contributions to Roman society. They built huge temples and Rome's first sewer. Many historians think that the Romans learned their alphabet and numbers from the Etruscans.

The last Roman king was said to have been a cruel man who had many people killed, including his own advisors. Finally, a group of nobles rose up against him. According to tradition, he was overthrown in 509 BC. The nobles, who no longer wanted kings, created a new government.

READING CHECK **Drawing Conclusions** Why did early Romans want to get rid of the monarchy?

Romulus and Remus
The Romans believed that the twins Romulus and Remus were descendants of Aeneas. In Roman legend, Romulus and Remus were rescued and raised by a wolf. Romulus later killed Remus and built the city of Rome.

The Early Republic

THE IMPACT TODAY

The government of the United States today is a republic.

The government the Romans created in 509 BC was a republic. In a **republic**, people elect leaders to govern them. Each year the Romans elected officials to rule the city. These officials had many powers but only stayed in power for one year. This system was supposed to keep any one person from becoming too powerful in the government.

But Rome was not a democracy. The city's elected officials nearly all came from a small group of wealthy and powerful men. These wealthy and powerful Romans held all the power, and other people had little to no say in how the republic was run.

Challenges from Outside

Shortly after the Romans created the republic, they found themselves at war. For about 50 years the Romans were at war with other peoples of the region. For the most part the Romans won these wars. But they lost several battles, and the wars destroyed many lives and much property.

During particularly difficult wars, the Romans chose **dictators**—rulers with almost absolute power—to lead the city. To keep them from abusing their power, dictators could only stay in power for six months. When that time was over, the dictator gave up his power.

One of Rome's famous dictators was **Cincinnatus** (sin-suh-NAT-uhs), who gained power in 458 BC. Although he was a farmer, the Romans chose him to defend the city against a powerful enemy that had defeated a large Roman army.

Cincinnatus quickly defeated the city's enemies. Immediately, he resigned as dictator and returned to his farm, long before his six-month term had run out.

The victory by Cincinnatus did not end Rome's troubles. Rome continued to fight its neighbors on and off for many years.

Italy, 500 BC

Romans
Etruscans
Greeks
Carthaginians

0   30   60 Miles
0   30   60 Kilometers

Ligurian Sea

Adriatic Sea

Rome

Tyrrhenian Sea

Mediterranean Sea

Ionian Sea

Carthage

GEOGRAPHY SKILLS   INTERPRETING MAPS

Location What group lived mostly north of Rome?

BIOGRAPHY

Cincinnatus
c. 519 BC–?

Cincinnatus is the most famous dictator from the early Roman Republic. Because he wasn't eager to hold on to his power, the Romans considered Cincinnatus an ideal leader. They admired his abilities and his loyalty to the republic. The early citizens of the United States admired the same qualities in their leaders. In fact, some people called George Washington the "American Cincinnatus" when he refused to run for a third term as president. The people of the state of Ohio also honored Cincinnatus by naming one of their major cities, Cincinnati, after him.

Challenges within Rome

Enemy armies weren't the only challenge facing Rome. Within the city, Roman society was divided into two groups. Many of Rome's **plebeians** (pli-BEE-uhnz), or common people, were calling for changes in the government. They wanted more of a say in how the city was run.

Rome was run by powerful nobles called **patricians** (puh-TRI-shuhnz). Only patricians could be elected to office, so they held all political power.

The plebeians were peasants, craftspeople, traders, and other workers. Some of these plebeians, especially traders, were as rich as patricians. Even though the plebeians outnumbered the patricians, they couldn't take part in the government.

In 494 BC the plebeians formed a council and elected their own officials, an act that frightened many patricians. They feared that Rome would fall apart if the two groups couldn't cooperate. The patricians decided that it was time to change the government.

READING CHECK **Contrasting** How were patricians and plebeians different?

QUICK FACTS

Roman Society

Patricians	Plebeians
■ Wealthy, powerful citizens	■ Common people
■ Nobles	■ Peasants, craftspeople, traders, other workers
■ Small minority of the population	■ Majority of the population
■ Once controlled all aspects of government	■ Gained right to participate in government
■ After 218 BC, not allowed to participate in trade or commerce	■ Only Romans who could be traders, so many became wealthy

SUMMARY AND PREVIEW In this section you read about the location and founding of Rome, its early rule by kings, and the creation of the city's republican government. In the next section you'll learn more about that government, its strengths and weaknesses, how it worked, and how it changed over time.

Section 1 Assessment

go.hrw.com
Online Quiz
KEYWORD: SQ6 HP11

Reviewing Ideas, Terms, and People **HSS** 6.7.1

1. **a. Describe** Where is Italy located?
   b. Explain How did mountains affect life in Italy?
   c. Predict How do you think Rome's location on the Mediterranean affected its history as it began to grow into a world power?
2. **a. Identify** What brothers supposedly founded the city of Rome?
   b. Summarize What role did **Aeneas** play in the founding of Rome?
3. **a. Describe** What type of government did the Romans create in 509 BC?
   b. Contrast How were **patricians** and **plebeians** different?

Critical Thinking

4. **Sequencing** Draw a diagram like the one below. Use it to identify the key events in the legendary history of the founding and growth of Rome.

FOCUS ON SPEAKING

5. **Gathering Background Ideas** In this section you read about several legends the Romans told about their own history. Look back at the text to get some ideas about what you might include in your own legend. Write some ideas in your notebook.

from the Aeneid

by Virgil

Translated by Robert Fitzgerald

About the Reading *Virgil wrote the* Aeneid *to record the glorious story of Rome's founding and to celebrate the Rome of his present. At the center of the poem stands the hero Aeneas, survivor of the Trojan War and son of the goddess Venus. After wandering for seven years, Aeneas finally reaches southern Italy—then known as Ausonia. Here, Aeneas's friend Ilioneus leads a group of representatives to visit a nearby Latin settlement.*

AS YOU READ **Try to identify each group's goals and desires.**

     Latinus
Called the Teucrians before him, saying
Tranquilly as they entered:
       "Sons of Dardanus—
You see, we know your city and your nation,
As all had heard you laid a westward course—
Tell me your purpose. ❶ What design or need
Has brought you through the dark blue sea so far
To our Ausonian coast? Either astray
Or driven by rough weather, such as sailors
Often endure at sea, you've broached the river,
Moored ship there. Now do not turn away
From hospitality here. Know that our Latins
Come of Saturn's race, that we are just—
Not by constraint or laws, but by our choice
And habit of our ancient god . . ."
Latinus then fell silent, and in turn
Ilioneus began:
       "Your majesty,
Most noble son of Faunus, no rough seas
Or black gale swept us to your coast, no star
Or clouded seamark put us off our course. ❷

Aeneas, from an Italian painting of the 1700s

We journey to your city by design
And general consent, driven as we are
From realms in other days greatest by far
The Sun looked down on, passing on his way
From heaven's far eastern height. ❸ Our line's from Jove,
In his paternity the sons of Dardanus
Exult, and highest progeny of Jove
Include our king himself—Trojan Aeneas,
Who sent us to your threshold . . . ❹
So long on the vast waters, now we ask
A modest settlement of the gods of home,
A strip of coast that will bring harm to no one,
Air and water, open and free to all . . .
Our quest was for your country. Dardanus
Had birth here, and Apollo calls us back,
Directing us by solemn oracles
To Tuscan Tiber . . . ❺ Here besides
Aeneus gives you from his richer years
These modest gifts, relics caught up and saved
From burning Troy . . ."
            Latinus heard
Ilioneus out, his countenance averted,
Sitting immobile, all attention, eyes
Downcast but turning here and there. The embroidered
Purple and the scepter of King Priam
Moved him less in his own kingliness
Than long thoughts on the marriage of his daughter,
As he turned over in his inmost mind
Old Faunus' prophecy.
            "This is the man,"
he thought, "foretold as coming from abroad
To be my son-in-law, by fate appointed,
Called to reign here with equal authority—
The man whose heirs will be brilliant in valor
And win the mastery of the world." ❻

GUIDED READING

WORD HELP

progeny offspring
threshold door
oracle person who gives advice
averted turned away
immobile unmoving

❸ Ilioneus explains that the Trojans have come to Italy "by design"—both on purpose and with help from the gods.

❹ Aeneas and Dardanus, the founder of Troy, were both believed to be descendants of Jove, the king of the gods.

❺ The Romans believed that Troy's founder Dardanus was born in Italy.

What does Ilioneus ask the king to give the Trojans?

❻ Virgil included this vision of Rome's great future to point out the city's greatness to his readers.

CONNECTING LITERATURE TO HISTORY

1. **Analyzing** Rome's leaders wanted their city to have a glorious past that would make the Roman people proud. What details in this passage would make Roman readers proud of their past?

2. **Drawing Conclusions** When Aeneas reached Italy, he formed an alliance with the Latins. Think about how Virgil portrays the Latins in this passage. What words or phrases would you use to describe them? Why might such people make good allies?

Government and Society

What You Will Learn...

Main Ideas

1. Roman government was made up of three parts that worked together to run the city.
2. Written laws helped keep order in Rome.
3. The Roman Forum was the heart of Roman society.

The Big Idea

Rome's tripartite government and written laws helped create a stable society.

Key Terms

magistrates, *p. 333*
consuls, *p. 333*
Roman Senate, *p. 333*
veto, *p. 334*
Latin, *p. 334*
checks and balances, *p. 335*
Forum, *p. 335*

HSS **6.7.2** Describe the government of the Roman Republic and its significance (e.g. written constitution and tripartite government, checks and balances, civic duty).

If YOU were there...

You have just been elected as a government official in Rome. Your duty is to represent the plebeians, the common people. You hold office for only one year, but you have one important power—you can stop laws from being passed. Now city leaders are proposing a law that will hurt the plebeians. If you stop the new law, it will hurt your future in politics. If you let it pass, it will hurt the people you are supposed to protect.

Will you let the new law pass? Why or why not?

BUILDING BACKGROUND Government in Rome was often a balancing act. Like the politician above, leaders had to make compromises and risk the anger of other officials to keep the people happy. To keep anyone from gaining too much power, the Roman government divided power among many different officials.

Roman Government

When the plebeians complained about Rome's government in the 400s BC, the city's leaders knew they had to do something. If the people stayed unhappy, they might rise up and overthrow the whole government.

To calm the angry plebeians, the patricians made some changes to Rome's government. For example, they created new offices that could only be held by plebeians. The people who held these offices protected the plebeians' rights and interests. Gradually, the distinctions between patricians and plebeians began to disappear, but that took a very long time.

As a result of the changes the patricians made, Rome developed a tripartite (try-PAHR-tyt) government, or a government with three parts. Each part had its own responsibilities and duties. To fulfill its duties, each part of the government had its own powers, rights, and privileges.

Magistrates

The first part of Rome's government was made up of elected officials, or **magistrates** (MA-juh-strayts). The two most powerful magistrates in Rome were called **consuls** (KAHN-suhlz). The consuls were elected each year to run the city and lead the army. There were two consuls so that no one person would be too powerful.

Below the consuls were other magistrates. Rome had many different types of magistrates. Each was elected for one year and had his own duties and powers. Some were judges. Others managed Rome's finances or organized games and festivals.

Senate

The second part of Rome's government was the Senate. The **Roman Senate** was a council of wealthy and powerful Romans that advised the city's leaders. It was originally created to advise Rome's kings. After the kings were gone, the Senate continued to meet to advise consuls.

Unlike magistrates, senators—members of the Senate—held office for life. By the time the republic was created, the Senate had 300 members. At first most senators were patricians, but as time passed many wealthy plebeians became senators as well. Because magistrates became senators after completing their terms in office, most didn't want to anger the Senate and risk their future jobs.

As time passed the Senate became more powerful. It gained influence over magistrates and took control of the city's finances. By 200 BC the Senate had great influence in Rome's government.

Assemblies and Tribunes

The third part of Rome's government, the part that protected the common people, had two branches. The first branch was made up of assemblies. Both patricians and plebeians took part in these assemblies. Their **primary** job was to elect the magistrates who ran the city of Rome.

FOCUS ON READING

If you were outlining the discussion on this page, what headings would you use?

ACADEMIC VOCABULARY

primary main, most important

Government of the Roman Republic

QUICK FACTS

Magistrates	Senate	Assemblies and Tribunes
■ Consuls led the government and army, judged court cases	■ Advised the consuls	■ Represented the common people, approved or rejected laws, declared war, elected magistrates
■ Served for one year	■ Served for life	■ Roman citizens could take part in assemblies all their adult lives, tribunes served for one year
■ Had power over all citizens, including other officials	■ Gained control of financial affairs	■ Could veto the decisions of consuls and other magistrates

Do as the Romans Do

The government of the Roman Republic was one of its greatest strengths. When the founders of the United States sat down to plan our government, they copied many elements of the Roman system. Like the Romans, we elect our leaders. Our government also has three branches—the president, Congress, and the federal court system. The powers of these branches are set forth in our Constitution, just like the Roman officials' powers were. Our government also has a system of checks and balances to prevent any one branch from becoming too strong. For example, Congress can refuse to give the president money to pay for programs. Like the Romans, Americans have a civic duty to participate in the government to help keep it as strong as it can be.

ANALYSIS SKILL **ANALYZING INFORMATION**

Why do you think the founders of the United States borrowed ideas from Roman government?

THE IMPACT TODAY

Like tribunes, the president of the United States has the power to veto actions by other government officials.

The second branch was made up of a group of elected officials called tribunes. Elected by the plebeians, tribunes had the ability to **veto** (VEE-toh), or prohibit, actions by other officials. Veto means "I forbid" in **Latin**, the Romans' language. This veto power made tribunes very powerful in Rome's government. To keep them from abusing their power, each tribune remained in office only one year.

Civic Duty

Rome's government would not have worked without the participation of the people. People participated in the government because they felt it was their civic duty, or their duty to the city. That civic duty included doing what they could to make sure the city prospered. For example,

they were expected to attend assembly meetings and to vote in elections. Voting in Rome was a complicated process, and not everyone was allowed to do it. Those who could, however, were expected to take part in all elections.

Wealthy and powerful citizens also felt it was their duty to hold public office to help run the city. In return for their time and commitment, these citizens were respected and admired by other Romans.

Checks and Balances

In addition to limiting terms of office, the Romans put other restrictions on their leaders' power. They did this by giving government officials the ability to restrict the powers of other officials. For example, one consul could block the actions of the other.

Laws proposed by the Senate had to be approved by magistrates and ratified by assemblies. We call these methods to balance power **checks and balances**. Checks and balances keep any one part of a government from becoming stronger or more influential than the others.

Checks and balances made Rome's government very complicated. Sometimes quarrels arose when officials had different ideas or opinions. When officials worked together, however, Rome's government was strong and efficient, as one Roman historian noted:

> "In unison [together] they are a match for any and all emergencies, the result being that it is impossible to find a constitution that is better constructed. For whenever some common external danger should come upon them and should compel [force] them to band together in counsel [thought] and in action, the power of their state becomes so great that nothing that is required is neglected [ignored]."
>
> –Polybius, from *The Constitution of the Roman Republic*

READING CHECK **Finding Main Ideas** What were the three parts of the Roman government?

Written Laws Keep Order

Rome's officials were responsible for making the city's laws and making sure that people followed them. At first these laws weren't written down. The only people who knew all the laws were the patricians who had made them.

Many people were unhappy with this situation. They did not want to be punished for breaking laws they didn't even know existed. As a result, they began to call for Rome's laws to be written down and made accessible to everybody.

Rome's first written law code was produced in 450 BC on 12 bronze tables, or tablets. These tables were displayed in the **Forum**, Rome's public meeting place. Because of how it was displayed, this code was called the Law of the Twelve Tables.

Over time, Rome's leaders passed many new laws. Throughout their history, though the Romans looked to the Law of the Twelve Tables as a symbol of Roman law and of their rights as Roman citizens.

READING CHECK **Making Inferences** Why did many people want a written law code?

Primary Source

HISTORIC DOCUMENT
Law of the Twelve Tables

The Law of the Twelve Tables governed many parts of Roman life. Some laws were written to protect the rights of all Romans. Others only protected the patricians. The laws listed here should give you an idea of the kinds of laws the tables included.

A Roman who did not appear before a government official when called or did not pay his debts could be arrested.

[from Table I] If anyone summons a man before the magistrate, he must go. If the man summoned does not go, let the one summoning him call the bystanders to witness and then take him by force.

[from Table III] One who has confessed a debt, or against whom judgment has been pronounced, shall have thirty days to pay it. After that forcible seizure of his person is allowed . . . unless he pays the amount of the judgment.

Women—even as adults—were legally considered to be children.

[from Table V] Females should remain in guardianship even when they have attained their majority.

No one in Rome could be executed without a trial.

[from Table IX] Putting to death of any man, whosoever he might be, unconvicted is forbidden.

–Law of the Twelve Tables, translated in *The Library of Original Sources* edited by Oliver J. Thatcher

ANALYSIS SKILL **ANALYZING PRIMARY SOURCES**

How are these laws similar to and different from our laws today?

The Roman Forum

The Forum was the center of life in ancient Rome. The city's most important temples and government buildings were located there, and Romans met there to talk about the issues of the day. The word *forum* means "public place."

The Roman Forum

The Roman Forum, the place where the Law of the Twelve Tables was kept, was the heart of the city of Rome. It was the site of important government buildings and temples. Government and religion were only part of what made the Forum so important, though. It was also a popular meeting place for Roman citizens. People met there to shop, chat, and gossip.

The Temple of Jupiter stood atop the Capitoline Hill, overlooking the Forum.

Important government records were stored in the Tabularium.

Roman citizens often wore togas, loose-fitting garments wrapped around the body. Togas were symbols of Roman citizenship.

Public officials often addressed people from this platform.

ANALYSIS SKILL **ANALYZING VISUALS**

What can you see in this illustration that indicates the Forum was an important place?

The Forum lay in the center of Rome, between two major hills. On one side was the Palatine (PA-luh-tyn) Hill, where Rome's richest people lived. Across the forum was the Capitoline (KA-pet-uhl-yn) Hill, where Rome's grandest temples stood. Because of this location, city leaders could often be found in or near the forum, mingling with the common people. These leaders used the Forum as a speaking area, delivering speeches to the crowds.

But the Forum also had attractions for people not interested in speeches. Various shops lined the open square, and fights between gladiators were sometimes held there. Public ceremonies were commonly held in the Forum as well. As a result, the forum was usually packed with people.

READING CHECK **Making Generalizations** How was the Forum the heart of Roman society?

SUMMARY AND PREVIEW In this section you read about the basic structure of Roman government. In the next section you'll see how that government changed as Rome's territory grew and its influence expanded.

The Senate met here in the curia, or Senate House.

Section 2 Assessment

go.hrw.com
Online Quiz
KEYWORD: SQ6 HP11

Reviewing Ideas, Terms, and People HSS 6.7.2

1. **a. Identify** Who were the **consuls**?
   b. Explain Why did the Romans create a system of **checks and balances**?
   c. Elaborate How do you think the **Roman Senate** gained power?
2. **a. Recall** What was Rome's first written law code called?
   b. Draw Conclusions Why did Romans want their laws written down?
3. **a. Describe** What kinds of activities took place in the Roman **Forum**?

Critical Thinking

4. **Analyzing Information** Draw a diagram like the one at right. In each oval, list the main powers of each part of Rome's government.

Magistrates

Senate

Assemblies and Tribunes

FOCUS ON SPEAKING

5. **Choosing a Topic** You've just read about Roman laws and government. Would anything related to these topics make good subjects for your legend? Write some ideas in your notebook.

THE ROMAN REPUBLIC **337**

The Late Republic

What You Will Learn...

Main Ideas

1. The late republic period saw the growth of territory and trade.
2. Through wars, Rome grew beyond Italy.
3. Several crises struck the republic in its later years.

The Big Idea

The later period of the Roman Republic was marked by wars of expansion and political crises.

Key Terms and People

legions, *p. 339*
Punic Wars, *p. 339*
Hannibal, *p. 340*
Gaius Marius, *p. 342*
Lucius Cornelius Sulla, *p. 343*
Spartacus, *p. 343*

HSS 6.7.3 Identify the location of and the political and geographic reasons for the growth of Roman territories and expansion of the empire, including how the empire fostered economic growth through the use of currency and trade routes.

If YOU were there...

You are a farmer in Italy during the Roman Republic. You are proud to be a Roman citizen, but times are hard. Rich landowners are buying farmland, and many farmers like you have lost their jobs. Some are moving to the city, but you've heard that there are not many jobs there, either. You've also heard that a famous general is raising an army to fight in Asia. That seems very far away, but it would mean good pay.

What might convince you to join the army?

BUILDING BACKGROUND The Roman army played a vital part in the expansion of the republic. Roman soldiers were well trained and defeated many of the city's enemies. As they did so, the Romans took over new lands. As the army conquered these new lands, traders moved in, seeking new products and markets that could make them rich.

Growth of Territory and Trade

After about 400 BC the Roman Republic grew quickly, both geographically and economically. Within 200 years the Roman army had conquered nearly all of Italy. Meanwhile Roman traders had begun to ship goods back and forth around the Mediterranean in search of new products and wealth.

Growth of Territory

Roman territory grew mainly in response to outside threats. In about 387 BC a people called the Gauls attacked Rome and took over the city. The Romans had to give the Gauls a huge amount of gold to leave the city.

Inspired by the Gauls' victory, many of Rome's neighboring cities also decided to attack. With some difficulty, the Romans fought off these attacks. As Rome's attackers were defeated, the Romans took over their lands. As you can see on the map, the Romans soon controlled all of the Italian Peninsula except far northern Italy.

One reason for the Roman success was the organization of the army. Soldiers were organized in **legions** (LEE-juhnz), or groups of up to 6,000 soldiers. Each legion was divided into centuries, or groups of 100 soldiers. This organization allowed the army to be very flexible. It could fight as a large group or as several small ones. This flexibility allowed the Romans to defeat most enemies.

Farming and Trade

Before Rome conquered Italy, most Romans were farmers. As the republic grew, many people left their farms for Rome. In place of these small farms, wealthy Romans built large farms in the countryside. These farms were worked by slaves who grew one or two crops. The owners of the farms didn't usually live on them. Instead, they stayed in Rome or other cities and let others run the farms for them.

Roman trade also expanded as the republic grew. Rome's farmers couldn't grow enough food to support the city's increasing population, so merchants brought food from other parts of the Mediterranean. These merchants also brought metal goods and slaves to Rome. To pay for these goods, the Romans made coins out of copper, silver, and other metals. Roman coins began to appear in markets all around the Mediterranean.

READING CHECK **Identifying Cause and Effect** Why did the Romans conquer their neighbors?

Rome Grows Beyond Italy

As Rome's power grew other countries came to see the Romans as a threat to their own power and declared war on them. In the end the Romans defeated their opponents, and Rome gained territory throughout the Mediterranean.

The Roman Republic, 509–270 BC

Roman lands in 509 BC
Roman lands in 270 BC

0   75   150 Miles
0   75   150 Kilometers

Ligurian Sea

Adriatic Sea

Rome

Tyrrhenian Sea

Ionian Sea

Mediterranean Sea

Carthage

N · S · E · W

GEOGRAPHY SKILLS **INTERPRETING MAPS**

Location What seas bordered Roman lands in 270 BC?

The Punic Wars

The fiercest of the wars Rome fought were the **Punic** (PYOO-nik) **Wars**, a series of wars against Carthage, a city in northern Africa. The word *Punic* means "Phoenician" in Latin. As you learned earlier in this book, the Phoenicians were an ancient civilization that had built the city of Carthage.

Rome and Carthage went to war three times between 264 and 146 BC. The wars began when Carthage sent its armies to Sicily, an island just southwest of Italy. In response, the Romans also sent an army to the island. Before long, war broke out between them. After almost 20 years of fighting, the Romans forced their enemies out and took control of Sicily.

In 218 BC Carthage tried to attack Rome itself. An army led by the brilliant general **Hannibal** set out for Rome. Although he forced the Romans right to the edge of defeat, Hannibal was never able to capture Rome itself. In the meantime, the Romans sent an army to attack Carthage. Hannibal rushed home to defend his city, but his troops were defeated at Zama (ZAY-muh) in the battle illustrated below.

By the 140s BC many senators had grown alarmed that Carthage was growing powerful again. They convinced Rome's consuls to declare war on Carthage, and once again the Romans sent an army to Africa and destroyed Carthage. After this victory, the Romans burned the city, killed most of its people, and sold the rest of the people into slavery. They also took control of northern Africa.

Rome Battles Carthage

During the Second Punic War, Hannibal invaded Italy, as you can see on the map. But Rome's leaders sent an army under their general Scipio (SIP-ee-oh) to attack Carthage itself, forcing Hannibal to return and defend his city. The two generals met at Zama, where Scipio defeated Hannibal's army in the last great battle of the Second Punic War.

Rome

Carthage

Carthage
Roman Republic
0   150   300 Miles
0   150   300 Kilometers

Battle of Zama, 202 BC
Hannibal's route
Scipio's route

The Romans had the advantage in cavalry, which helped them win the battle.

Some Roman soldiers blew trumpets and yelled to distract the war elephants.

Later Expansion

During the Punic Wars, Rome took control of Sicily, Corsica, Spain, and North Africa. As a result, Rome controlled most of the western Mediterranean region.

In the years that followed, Roman legions marched north and east as well. In the 120s Rome conquered the southern part of Gaul. By that time, Rome had also conquered Greece and parts of Asia.

Although the Romans took over Greece, they were greatly changed by the experience. We would normally expect the victor to change the conquered country. Instead, the Romans adopted ideas about literature, art, philosophy, religion, and education from the Greeks.

READING CHECK **Summarizing** How did the Romans gain territory?

BIOGRAPHY

Hannibal
247–183 BC

Many historians consider Hannibal to be one of the greatest generals of the ancient world. From an early age, he hated Rome. In 218 BC he began the Second Punic War by attacking one of Rome's allies in Spain. After the war he became the leader of Carthage, but later he was forced by the Romans to flee the city. He went to Asia and joined with a king fighting the Romans there. The king was defeated, and Hannibal killed himself so that he wouldn't become a Roman prisoner.

Hannibal's forces included about 80 war elephants.

The Romans left empty spaces between their soldiers so the elephants would do less damage.

ANALYSIS SKILL **ANALYZING VISUALS**

How did the Romans deal with Hannibal's war elephants?

341

The Roman Republic, 270–100 BC

ATLANTIC OCEAN

Bay of Biscay

GAUL

SPAIN

Po River

Ligurian Sea

Rome

Adriatic Sea

MACEDONIA

GREECE

Black Sea

Aegean Sea

ASIA MINOR

Strait of Gibraltar

Mediterranean

Tyrrhenian Sea

Carthage

Sea

Ionian Sea

AFRICA

| | Roman lands in 270 BC |
| | Roman lands in 100 BC |

0   150   300 Miles
0   150   300 Kilometers

N W E S

GEOGRAPHY SKILLS INTERPRETING MAPS

Place What new places did Rome add between 270 and 100 BC?

Crises Strike the Republic

As the Romans' territory grew, problems arose in the republic. Rich citizens were getting richer, and many leaders feared that violence would erupt between rich and poor.

Tiberius and Gaius Gracchus

Among the first leaders to address Rome's problems were brothers named Tiberius (ty-BIR-ee-uhs) and Gaius Gracchus (GY-uhs GRAK-uhs). Both served as tribunes.

Tiberius, who took office in 133 BC, wanted to create farms for poor Romans. The **purpose** of these farms was to keep the poor citizens happy and prevent rebellions. Tiberius wanted to create his farms on public land that wealthy citizens had illegally taken over. The public supported this idea, but the wealthy citizens opposed it. Conflict over the idea led to riots in the city, during which Tiberius was killed.

ACADEMIC VOCABULARY

purpose the reason something is done

A few years later Gaius also tried to create new farms. He also began to sell food cheaply to Rome's poor citizens. Like his brother, Gaius angered many powerful Romans and was killed for his ideas.

The violent deaths of the Gracchus brothers changed Roman politics. From that time on people saw violence as a political weapon. They often attacked leaders with whom they disagreed.

Marius and Sulla

In the late 100s BC another social change nearly led to the end of the republic. In 107 BC the Roman army desperately needed more troops. In response, a consul named **Gaius Marius** (MER-ee-uhs) encouraged poor people to join the army. Before, only people who owned property had been allowed to join. As a result of this change, thousands of poor and unemployed citizens joined Rome's army.

Because Marius was a good general, his troops were more loyal to him than they were to Rome. The army's support gave Marius great political power. Following his example, other ambitious politicians also sought their armies' support.

One such politician, **Lucius Cornelius Sulla** (LOO-shuhs kawr-NEEL-yuhs SUHL-uh), became consul in 88 BC. Sulla soon came into conflict with Marius, a conflict that led to a civil war in Rome. A civil war is a war between citizens of the same country. In the end Sulla defeated Marius. He later named himself dictator and used his power to punish his enemies.

Spartacus

Not long after Sulla died, another crisis arose to challenge Rome's leaders. Thousands of slaves led by a former gladiator, **Spartacus** (SPAHR-tuh-kuhs), rose up and demanded freedom.

Spartacus and his followers defeated an army sent to stop them and took over much of southern Italy. Eventually, though, Spartacus was killed in battle. Without his leadership, the revolt fell apart. Victorious, the Romans executed 6,000 rebellious

BIOGRAPHY

Lucius Cornelius Sulla
138–78 BC

Although the two eventually became enemies, Sulla learned much of what he knew about military affairs from Gaius Marius. He had been an assistant to Marius before he became consul. Sulla changed Rome's government forever when he became dictator, but he actually had many traditional ideas. For example, he believed the Senate should be the main ruling group in Rome, and he increased its power during his rule.

Analyzing Information Do you think Sulla was a traditional Roman leader? Why or why not?

slaves as an example to others who thought about rebelling. The rebellion was over, but the republic's problems were not.

READING CHECK **Predicting** How do you think Marius and Sulla influenced later leaders?

SUMMARY AND PREVIEW You have read about crises that arose in the late Roman Republic. These crises eventually led to changes in society, as you will see in the next chapter.

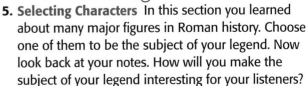

Section 3 Assessment

Reviewing Ideas, Terms, and People **HSS** 6.7.3

1. **a. Define** What was a Roman **legion**?
   b. Explain Why did the Romans decide to conquer all of Italy?
   c. Elaborate How did the growth of territory help increase Roman trade?
2. **a. Recall** Who fought in the **Punic Wars**?
   b. Summarize What led to the beginning of the Punic Wars?
   c. Elaborate Why do you think the Romans borrowed many ideas from Greek culture?
3. **a. Identify** Who was **Spartacus**?
   b. Explain How did the deaths of the Gracchus brothers change Roman politics?

Critical Thinking

4. **Summarizing** Draw an idea web like the one here. In each of the outer circles, list a crisis that faced Rome during the later period of the republic. Then list two facts about each crisis.

Crises

FOCUS ON SPEAKING

5. **Selecting Characters** In this section you learned about many major figures in Roman history. Choose one of them to be the subject of your legend. Now look back at your notes. How will you make the subject of your legend interesting for your listeners?

Social Studies Skills

Analysis | Critical Thinking | Participation | Study

Interpreting Culture Maps

Understand the Skill

A culture map is a special type of political map. As you know, physical maps show natural features, such as mountains and rivers. Political maps show the human features of an area, such as boundaries, cities, and roads. The human features shown on a culture map are cultural ones, such as the languages spoken or religions practiced in an area. Historians often use culture maps in their work. Therefore, being able to interpret them is important for understanding history.

Learn the Skill

The process for interpreting a culture map is similar to that for understanding any other map. Follow these guidelines.

1 Use map basics. Read the title to identify the subject. Note the labels, legend, and scale. Pay extra attention to special symbols for cultural features. Be sure you understand what these symbols represent.

2 Study the map as a whole. Note the location of the cultural symbols and features. Ask yourself how they relate to the rest of the map.

3 Connect the information on the map to any written information about the subject in the text.

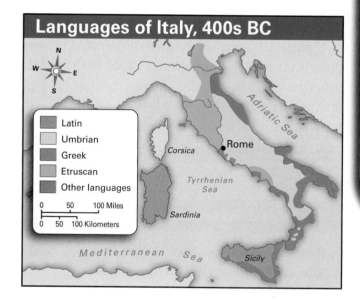

Languages of Italy, 400s BC

Legend:
- Latin
- Umbrian
- Greek
- Etruscan
- Other languages

0   50   100 Miles
0 50 100 Kilometers

Practice and Apply the Skill

Apply the guidelines to the map on this page and answer the following questions.

1. What makes this map a culture map?

2. What language was most widely spoken on the Italian Peninsula? What other language was widely spoken?

3. Where was Greek spoken? Why did the people there talk in Greek?

Visual Summary

Use the visual summary below to help you review the main ideas of the chapter.

QUICK FACTS

The Romans created many legends about their city's glorious history.

The early Romans set up a type of government called a republic.

The Roman Republic conquered lands in Italy and around the Mediterranean.

Reviewing Vocabulary, Terms, and People

Match each numbered definition with the correct lettered vocabulary term.

a. republic
b. plebeians
c. Spartacus
d. legions
e. Aeneas
f. consuls
g. Forum
h. dictator
i. veto
j. Roman Senate
k. patricians
l. primary

1. Rome's public meeting place
2. groups of about 6,000 soldiers
3. the legendary Trojan founder of Rome
4. main, most important
5. a government in which people elect leaders
6. a council that advised Rome's leaders
7. a leader with absolute power for six months
8. the common people of Rome
9. the two most powerful officials in Rome
10. leader of a slave rebellion
11. prohibit
12. noble, powerful Romans

Comprehension and Critical Thinking

SECTION 1 *(Pages 324–329)* **HSS** **6.7.1**

13. **a. Describe** What are two legends that describe Rome's founding? How are the two legends connected?

b. Compare and Contrast What roles did the plebeians and the patricians take in the early Roman government? In what other ways were the two groups different?

c. Predict How do you think Italy's geography and Rome's location would affect the spread of Rome's influence?

SECTION 2 *(Pages 332–337)* **HSS** 6.7.2

14. a. Describe What were the three parts of Rome's government?

b. Analyze How do checks and balances protect the rights of the people? How do written laws do the same thing?

c. Elaborate What are some places in modern society that serve purposes similar to those of the Roman Forum?

SECTION 3 *(Pages 338–343)* **HSS** 6.7.3

15. a. Identify What difficulties did Hannibal, Lucius Cornelius Sulla, and Spartacus cause for Rome?

b. Analyze How did Roman occupations, economics, and society change during the Late Republic?

c. Evaluate Some historians say that Rome and Carthage were destined to fight each other. Why do you think they say this?

Reviewing Themes

16. Politics Why did Roman magistrates only hold office for one year?

17. Geography How do you think Rome's location helped the Romans in their quest to conquer the entire Mediterranean region?

Using the Internet
go.hrw.com
KEYWORD: SQ6 WH11

18. Activity: Explaining Roman Society A key reason the Roman Republic fell was because the Roman people gave up on it. The army, once Rome's protector, let itself be turned against the Roman people. The Senate gave up on debate and compromise when it turned to political violence. Enter the keyword. Research the fall of the Roman Republic and create an exhibit for a local history museum. Make sure your exhibit contains information about key figures in the Roman military and government. Use words and pictures to explain the political, religious, and social structures that made Rome an empire and what caused its eventual downfall.

Reading Skills

19. Creating Outlines Look back at the discussion "Crises Strike the Republic" in the last section of this chapter. Prepare an outline that will help clarify the people, events, and ideas of this discussion. Before you prepare your outline, decide what your major headings will be. Then choose the details that will appear below each heading. Remember that most outlines follow this basic format:

> I. Main Idea
>   A. Supporting Idea
>   B. Supporting Idea
>   1. Detail
>   2. Detail
> II. Main Idea
>   A. Supporting Idea

Social Studies Skills

Using Culture Maps *Look back at the map of Italy in 500 BC that appears in Section 1 of this chapter. Use the map to answer the following questions.*

20. Which people controlled the most land on the Italian Peninsula?

21. Which peoples on this map had learned to sail across the sea? How can you tell?

22. What evidence on this map suggests that the Romans and the Etruscans had contact with each other?

FOCUS ON SPEAKING

23. Presenting Your Legend Now that you've chosen the subject for your legend, it's time to write and present it. As you write your legend, focus on exciting details that will bring the subject to life in your listeners' minds. Once you've finished writing, share your legend with the class. Try to make your legend exciting as you present it. Remember to alter the tone and volume of your voice to convey the appropriate mood.

Standards Assessment

DIRECTIONS: Read each question, and write the letter of the best response.

1 Use the map to answer the following question.

The order in which Rome expanded its control in the Mediterranean region is shown by which of the following sequences of letters?

A Y–W–X

B X–W–Y

C Y–X–W

D W–X–Y

2 Which was the *least* important reason for the growth of Rome's power and influence in the Mediterranean region?

A religion

B trade

C military organization

D wars and conquests

3 According to Roman legend, the city of Rome was founded by

A Latin peoples who moved to Italy from ancient Egypt.

B two men named Romulus and Remus who were raised by a wolf.

C the gods of Greece, who were looking for a new home.

D a Greek warrior named Achilles who had fled from the destruction of Troy.

4 Roman nobles were called

A patricians.

B plebeians.

C tribunes.

D magistrates.

5 Which of the following characteristics did *not* apply to Roman government?

A system of checks and balances

B sense of civic duty

C written code of laws

D equality of all people

Connecting with Past Learnings

6 You learned earlier in this course about other ancient peoples who, like the Romans, founded their civilizations along rivers. These peoples include all of the following *except* the

A Chinese.

B Egyptians.

C Sumerians.

D Hebrews.

7 Virgil's *Aeneid* is similar to what other piece of ancient literature that you've learned about in this course?

A the *Shiji*

B the *Book of the Dead*

C *The Odyssey*

D the *Bhagavad Gita*

The Roman Empire

California Standards

History–Social Science

6.7 Students analyze the geographic, political, economic, religious, and social structures during the development of Rome.

Analysis Skills

CS 2 Construct time lines of key events, people, and periods.

English–Language Arts

Writing 6.1.3 Use a variety of effective and coherent organizational patterns.

Reading 6.2.6 Determine the adequacy and appropriateness of the evidence for an author's conclusions.

FOCUS ON WRITING

Note Cards for a Screenplay You are a research assistant for a movie studio that is making a movie about the Roman Empire. Your job is to find out about the people, places, and events of the Roman Empire and report this information to a group of writers who will create a screenplay. As you read this chapter, look for descriptions of the people, places, and events of the Roman Empire.

CHAPTER EVENTS

44 BC
Julius Caesar is assassinated.

50 BC

WORLD EVENTS

47 BC
Cleopatra becomes sole queen of Egypt.

HOLT

History's Impact
▶ video series
Watch the video to understand the impact of ancient Rome on the world today.

What You Will Learn...

In this chapter you will learn how Rome changed from a republic into a vast empire that has had a lasting influence on the Western world. This photo shows the Roman Colosseum, a building that has influenced the design of stadiums and sporting facilities around the world.

27 BC
Augustus becomes Rome's first emperor.

4 BC
Herod the Great, king of Judea, dies.

AD 80
The first games are held in the Colosseum.

AD 60
Warrior queen Boudicca burns the city of London.

AD 122
Hadrian's Wall is begun in northern England.

AD 132
The Chinese invent the seismograph.

| BC 1 AD | AD 50 | AD 100 | AD 150 |

THE ROMAN EMPIRE **349**

Reading Social Studies

by Kylene Beers

Focus on Themes This chapter will describe the development of Rome as it grew from a republic into a strong and vast empire. First, you will learn about the **geographic** expansion of the empire under such powerful leaders as Julius Caesar, Marc Antony, and Augustus. You will also learn about how the Romans' many contributions to literature, language, law, and **science and technology** have shaped how people have lived since the days of Rome some 2,000 years ago.

Online Research

Focus on Reading Finding information on the World Wide Web can be easy. Just enter a word or two into a search engine and you will instantly find dozens—or hundreds—of sites full of information.

Evaluating Web Sites However, not all web sites have good or accurate information. How do you know which sites are the ones you want? You have to evaluate, or judge, the sites. You can use an evaluation form like the one below to evaluate a Web site.

Additional reading support can be found in the

Inter active

Reader and Study Guide

Evaluating Web-Based Resources

Name of site: _____ URL: _____ Date of access: _____

I. Evaluating the author of the site
   A. Who is the author? What are his or her qualifications?
   B. Is there a way to contact the author?

II. Evaluating the content of the site
   A. Is the site's topic related to the topic you are studying?
   B. Is there enough information at this site to help you?
   C. Is there too much information for you to read or understand?
   D. Does the site include pictures or illustrations to help you understand the information?
   E. Does the site discuss more than one point of view about the topic?
   F. Does the site express the author's opinions rather than facts?
   G. Does the site provide references for its information, including quotes?
   H. Are there links to other sites that have valuable information?

III. Evaluating the overall design and quality
   A. Is the site easy to navigate or to find information on?
   B. When was the site last updated?

IV. My overall impression
   Does this site have good information that will help me with my research?

You Try It!

Below is an example of an evaluation of a fictional Web site on Julius Caesar. Review the student's answers to the questions on the previous page and then answer the questions at the bottom of the page.

Web Site Evaluation

I. Evaluating the author
A. Author is listed as Klee O. Patra. She has read many books about Julius Caesar.
B. No information is listed for contacting the author.

II. Evaluating content of the site
A. Yes. It is about Julius Caesar.
B. There appears to be a lot of information about Julius Caesar.
C. No, it looks easy to understand.
D. There are some pictures, but most are from movies. There are no historical images.
E. No.
F. Yes, it is all about how she loves Caesar.
G. I can't find any references.
H. There are two links, but they are both dead.

III. Evaluating Overall Design and quality
A. No. It takes a long time to find any specific information. Also, the layout of the page is confusing.
B. It was last updated in July 1998.

Study the evaluation then answer the following questions.

1. What do you know about the author of this site? Based on the evaluation information, do you think she is qualified to write about Caesar?

2. Does the content of the site seem valuable and reliable? Why?

3. The site has not been updated for many years, but that may not be a major problem for a site about Julius Caesar. Why? When might recent updates be more important?

4. Overall, would you say this site would be helpful? Why or why not?

Key Terms and People

Chapter 12

Section 1
Cicero *(p. 352)*
orator *(p. 352)*
Julius Caesar *(p. 353)*
Pompey *(p. 353)*
Brutus *(p. 355)*
Marc Antony *(p. 355)*
Augustus *(p. 355)*
Cleopatra *(p. 356)*

Section 2
Hadrian *(p. 359)*
provinces *(p. 360)*
currency *(p. 360)*
Pax Romana *(p. 361)*
villas *(p. 362)*

Section 3
Galen *(p. 366)*
aqueduct *(p. 367)*
vault *(p. 367)*
Virgil *(p. 370)*
Ovid *(p. 370)*
satire *(p. 370)*
Romance languages *(p. 371)*
civil law *(p. 371)*

Academic Vocabulary
Success in school is related to knowing academic vocabulary— the words that are frequently used in school assignments and discussions. In this chapter, you will learn the following academic words:

agreement *(p. 353)*
effect *(p. 361)*

As you read Chapter 12, think about what topics would be interesting to research on the Web. If you do any research on the Web, remember to evaluate the site and its contents.

From Republic to Empire

What You Will Learn...

Main Ideas

1. Romans called for change in their government.
2. Julius Caesar rose to power and became the sole ruler of Rome.
3. Augustus became Rome's first emperor after defeating Caesar's killers and his own former allies.

The Big Idea

Julius Caesar and Augustus led Rome's transition from a republic to an empire.

Key Terms and People

Cicero, *p. 352*
orator, *p. 352*
Julius Caesar, *p. 353*
Pompey, *p. 353*
Brutus, *p. 355*
Marc Antony, *p. 355*
Augustus, *p. 355*
Cleopatra, *p. 356*

HSS **6.7.4** Discuss the influence of Julius Caesar and Augustus in Rome's transition from republic to empire.

If **YOU** were there...

You are a friend of a Roman Senator. Your friend is worried about the growing power of military men in Rome's government. Some other Senators want to take violent action to stop generals from taking over as dictators. Your friend wants your advice: Is violence justified to save the Roman Republic?

What advice will you give your friend?

BUILDING BACKGROUND By the first century BC, the government of the Roman Republic was in trouble. Politicians looked for ways to solve the problems. Philosophers offered ideas, too. In the end, however, the republic could not survive the great changes that were taking place in Rome.

The Call for Change

Rome in the 70s BC was a dangerous place. Politicians and generals went to war to increase their power even as political order broke down in Rome. Unemployed Romans rioted in the streets because they couldn't get enough food. All the while more and more people from all around the republic flooded into the city, further adding to the confusion.

Some Romans tried to stop the chaos in Rome's government. One such person was **Cicero** (SIS-uh-roh), a gifted philosopher and **orator**, or public speaker. In his speeches Cicero called on Romans to make Rome a better place. One way to do this, he argued, was to limit the power of generals. Cicero wanted the Romans to give more support to the Senate and to restore the checks and balances on government.

But Cicero was unsuccessful. Many Romans didn't agree with him. Others were too caught up in their own affairs to pay any attention. Rome's government did not change.

READING CHECK **Summarizing** What did Cicero want Romans to do?

Caesar's Rise to Power

As Cicero was calling on the Romans to take power away from the generals, a new group of generals was working to take over the government. The most powerful of these generals was **Julius Caesar** (JOOL-yuhs SEE-zuhr).

Caesar the General

Caesar was probably the greatest general in Roman history. Other Romans admired him for his bravery and skill in battle. At the same time, his soldiers respected him because he treated them well.

Between 58 and 50 BC Caesar conquered nearly all of Gaul—a region that included much of modern France, Germany, and northern Italy—and part of Britain. He wrote a description of this conquest, describing in great detail how he defeated each of the tribes he faced.

Here he describes how he defeated a group called the Menapii. Notice how he refers to himself as Caesar:

"Caesar, having divided his forces . . . and having hastily [quickly] constructed some bridges, enters their country in three divisions, burns their houses and villages, and gets possession of a large number of cattle and men. Constrained [forced] by these circumstances the Menapii send ambassadors to him for the purpose of suing [asking] for peace."

–Julius Caesar, from *The Gallic Wars*

Caesar's military successes made him a major figure in Roman politics. In addition to being a good leader, Caesar was an excellent speaker. He won many people to his side with his speeches in the forum.

Caesar also had powerful friends. Before he went to Gaul he made an **agreement** with two of the most powerful men in Rome, **Pompey** and Crassus. The three agreed to work together to fight against the Senate. Together, Caesar and his allies changed the course of Roman history.

ACADEMIC VOCABULARY

agreement a decision reached by two or more people or groups

Julius Caesar conquered Gaul and added it to the empire. This painting from the late 1800s shows a Frankish leader surrendering to Caesar by dropping his weapons at Caesar's feet.

Conflict with an Ally

At the end of the fighting in Gaul, Caesar was one of the most powerful men in the Roman Republic. He was so powerful that even his friends were jealous and afraid of him. This jealousy and fear changed Caesar's relationship with Pompey.

In 50 BC Pompey's allies in the Senate ordered Caesar to give up command of his armies and return to Rome. Caesar refused. He knew that Pompey was trying to take power away from him and would arrest him if he gave up his command. As a result, Caesar led his army into Italy. In 49 BC Caesar and his troops crossed the Rubicon River, the boundary between Gaul and Italy.

Because Roman law said that no general could enter Italy with his army, Pompey and the Senate considered Caesar's return to Italy a sign of war. Afraid that Caesar would attack him, Pompey and his allies fled Italy. They didn't think they had enough troops to defeat Caesar.

Caesar and his army chased Pompey's forces around the Mediterranean for a year. Eventually they drove Pompey into Egypt, where he was killed. There Caesar met Cleopatra, whom he made queen. As queen, Cleopatra became his new ally.

Conflict with the Senate

Finally, Caesar returned to Rome. When he got there, he forced the Senate to name him dictator for 10 years. Later this term was extended and Caesar became dictator for life.

Although Caesar wanted to improve Roman society, some people resented the way he had gained power. They feared that Caesar was trying to make himself the king of Rome. The Romans certainly didn't want a king.

Some Senators were especially angry with Caesar. On March 15—a date the Romans called the Ides of March—in 44 BC, a group of Senators attacked Caesar in the Senate house and stabbed him to death.

The Death of Julius Caesar

Caesar was stabbed to death on March 15, 44 BC. To the Romans, March 15 was called the Ides of March, and before Caesar was killed he was warned to "beware the Ides of March."

Among the attackers was a young Senator named **Brutus** (BROOT-uhs), who had been a friend and ally of Caesar's. Some Romans even believed that Brutus may have been Caesar's son but didn't know it. According to Roman historians, Caesar was shocked by Brutus's betrayal and stopped fighting against his attackers when he recognized him.

Rather than becoming heroes, Caesar's murderers were forced to flee for their lives. Rome was shocked by Caesar's murder, and many people were furious about it. He had been loved by many common people, and many of these people rioted after his death. From the chaos that followed Caesar's assassination, the Senate had to act quickly to restore order.

READING CHECK **Sequencing** What were the events that led to Caesar's gaining power in Rome?

Augustus the Emperor

Two leaders emerged to take control of Roman politics. One was Caesar's former assistant, **Marc Antony**. The other was Caesar's adopted son Octavian (ahk-TAY-vee-uhn), later called **Augustus** (aw-GUHS-tuhs).

Antony and Octavian

Antony and Octavian worked to punish the people who had killed Caesar. At Caesar's funeral, Antony delivered a famous speech that turned even more Romans against the killers. Shortly afterward, he and Octavian set out with an army to try to avenge Caesar's death.

Their army caught up to the killers near Philippi (FI-luh-py) in northern Greece. In 42 BC Antony and Octavian soundly defeated their opponents. After the battle the leaders of the plot to kill Caesar, including Brutus, killed themselves.

THE IMPACT TODAY

Some people today still use the name Brutus to refer to people who betray them.

Primary Source

POINTS OF VIEW
Views of Caesar

Some Senators admired Caesar and were horrified by his murder. The biographer Plutarch (PLOO-tahrk) described their reactions to the event.

❝So the affair began, and those who were not privy to the plot were filled with consternation [dismay] and horror at what was going on; they dared not fly, nor go to Caesar's help, nay, nor even utter a word.❞

—Plutarch
from *Life of Caesar*

The historian Suetonius (swe-TOH-nee-uhs) explained that other Senators thought Caesar deserved to be killed because his actions were threatening the republic.

❝He abused his power and was justly slain. For not only did he accept excessive honors, such as an uninterrupted consulship, the dictatorship for life, and the censorship of public morals . . . but he also allowed honors to be bestowed on him which were too great for mortal man.❞

—Suetonius
from *The Lives of the Caesars, The Deified Julius*

ANALYSIS SKILL **ANALYZING PRIMARY SOURCES**

How does Plutarch say people reacted to Caesar's death?

Cleopatra was a devoted ally of Julius Caesar and Marc Antony, but she didn't like Octavian. After the Battle of Actium, she feared that Octavian would arrest her and take over Egypt. Rather than see Octavian running her kingdom, Cleopatra chose to commit suicide. According to tradition, she poisoned herself with the venom of a deadly snake.

Drawing Conclusions Why do you think Cleopatra feared that Octavian would take over Egypt?

Octavian Becomes Emperor

After the Battle of Philippi, Octavian returned to Italy while Antony went east to fight Rome's enemies. In Turkey, Antony met **Cleopatra**, the queen of Egypt, and the two fell in love. Antony divorced his wife, Octavian's sister, to be with Cleopatra. Octavian saw this divorce as an insult to his sister and to himself.

Antony's behavior led to civil war in Rome. In 31 BC Octavian sent a fleet to attack Antony. Antony sailed out to meet it, and the two forces met just west of Greece in the Battle of Actium (AK-shee-uhm). Antony's fleet was defeated, but he escaped back to Egypt with Cleopatra. There the two committed suicide so they wouldn't be taken prisoner by Octavian.

With Antony's death, Octavian became Rome's sole ruler. Over the next few years he gained power. In 27 BC Octavian announced that he was giving up all his power to the Senate, but, in reality, he kept much power. He took the title *princeps* (PRIN-seps), or first citizen. The Senate gave him a new name—Augustus, which means "revered one." Modern historians consider the naming of Augustus to mark the end of the Roman Republic and the beginning of the Roman Empire.

READING CHECK **Summarizing** How did the Roman Republic become an empire?

SUMMARY AND PREVIEW In this section, you learned how Augustus gained power and made the Roman Republic into an empire. In the next section you'll learn what he and his successors did as the heads of that empire.

Section 1 Assessment

Reviewing Ideas, Terms, and People HSS 6.7.4

1. **a. Recall** Whom did **Cicero** want Romans to give power to?
   b. Explain Why did some Romans call for change in their government?
2. **a. Identify** Who killed **Julius Caesar**?
   b. Explain Why did many Senators consider Caesar a threat?
   c. Elaborate Why do you think Caesar wanted the title of dictator for life?
3. **a. Identify** Who took over Rome after Caesar's death?
   b. Summarize How did Octavian take power from **Marc Antony**?

Critical Thinking

4. **Sequencing** Draw a time line like the one shown here. Use it to identify key events in Rome's change from a republic to an empire.

FOCUS ON WRITING

5. **Taking Notes for a Screenplay** Create a chart with columns labeled "Characters," "Setting," and "Plot." In appropriate columns, write notes about people, events, and locations in this section that should appear in the movie.

Augustus

What would you do if you had great power?

When did he live? 63 BC–AD 14

Where did he live? Rome

What did he do? As the leader of Rome, Augustus made many improvements in the city. He created a fire department and a police force to protect the city's people. He built new aqueducts and repaired old ones to increase Rome's water supply. Augustus also worked on improving and expanding Rome's road network.

Why is he important? As Rome's first emperor, Augustus is one of the most significant figures in Roman history. Almost singlehandedly, he changed the nature of Roman government forever. But Augustus is also known for the great monuments he had built around Rome. He built a new forum that held statues, monuments, and a great temple to the god Mars. In writing about his life, Augustus wrote, "I found Rome a city of brick and left it a city of marble."

Identifying Points of View Why do you think many Romans greatly admired Augustus?

KEY EVENTS

45 BC Julius Caesar adopts Octavian as his son and heir.

44 BC Octavian moves to Rome when Caesar dies.

42 BC Octavian and Antony defeat Brutus.

31 BC Octavian defeats Antony.

27 BC Octavian takes the name Augustus and becomes emperor of Rome.

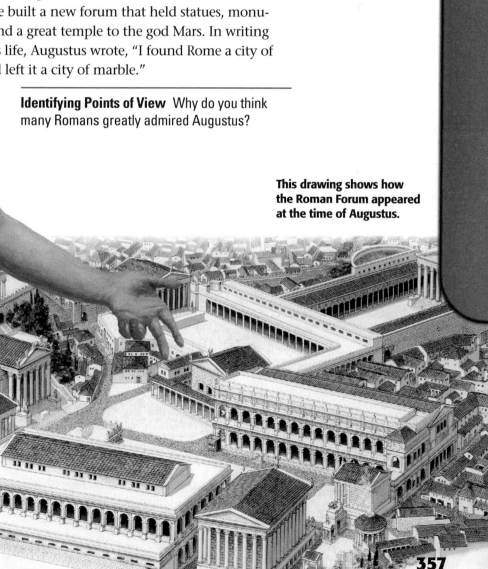

This drawing shows how the Roman Forum appeared at the time of Augustus.

A Vast Empire

What You Will Learn...

Main Ideas

1. The Roman Empire expanded to control the entire Mediterranean world.
2. Trade increased in Rome, both within the empire and with other people.
3. The Pax Romana was a period of peace and prosperity in the cities and the country.

The Big Idea

After Augustus became emperor, the Roman Empire grew politically and economically, and life improved for the Roman people.

Key Terms and People

Hadrian, *p. 359*
provinces, *p. 360*
currency, *p. 360*
Pax Romana, *p. 361*
villas, *p. 362*

HSS 6.7.3 Identify the location of and the political and geographic reasons for the growth of Roman territories and expansion of the empire, including how the empire fostered economic growth through the use of currency and trade routes.

If YOU were there...

You live in the Roman town of Londinium, in the Roman province of Britannia. Your people were conquered by the Roman army many years ago. Roman soldiers have mixed with your people, and many have settled down here. Many Britons in Londinium have adopted Roman customs. You live in a Roman-style house and eat from pottery made in Italy. Your cousins in the country live very differently, however. They still think of the Romans as invaders.

How do you like being part of the Roman Empire?

BUILDING BACKGROUND Since the days of the republic, Rome had grown steadily. The conquests of generals such as Julius Caesar and Pompey added more territory. Once Rome became an empire, its rulers continued to expand its power. Soldiers and settlers carried Roman culture to distant provinces such as Britannia, or Britain.

The Empire Expands

When Rome became an empire, it already controlled most of the Mediterranean world. Within about 150 years, though, the empire had grown even bigger. Augustus and the emperors who followed him pushed the boundaries of their empire, taking over huge chunks of Europe, Africa, and Asia. At its height Rome ruled one of the largest empires in all of world history.

Reasons for Expansion

Why did emperors add so much land to the empire? They had many reasons. One of these reasons was to control hostile neighbors. Some countries that shared borders with Rome were threatening Rome. To keep these countries from attacking the empire or its citizens, the Romans conquered them.

Not all of the territories the Romans conquered were political threats. Some were conquered for economic reasons. Many of these territories had vast supplies of gold, good farmlands, or other resources the Romans wanted. Other areas were conquered for another reason: Some emperors liked a good fight.

Expansion of Rome, 100 BC–AD 117

Roman Republic, 100 BC

Rome at Caesar's death, 44 BC

Empire at Augustus's death, AD 14

Greatest extent of empire, AD 117

0   200   400 Miles

0   200   400 Kilometers

North Sea

BRITAIN

ATLANTIC OCEAN

EUROPE

GAUL

ALPS

Rhine River

Danube River

SPAIN

Rome

Carthage

Mediterranean Sea

AFRICA

GREECE

Athens

Byzantium

ASIA MINOR

Black Sea

Caspian Sea

Euphrates River

Jerusalem

Alexandria

ASIA

EGYPT

Nile River

Red Sea

GEOGRAPHY SKILLS **INTERPRETING MAPS**

1. **Place** Where were the borders of the empire in AD 117?
2. **Location** Based on the map, why do you think the Romans called the Mediterranean "Our Sea"?

Directions of Expansion

As the map above shows, the Roman Empire grew after Augustus died. By the early 100s the Romans had taken over Gaul and much of central Europe.

By the time of the emperor **Hadrian**, the Romans had also conquered most of the island of Britain. The people of Britain, the Celts (KELTZ), had fought fiercely against the Roman army. Fearing attacks by barbarian invaders in the north, Hadrian built a huge wall across northern Britain. Hadrian's Wall marked the border between Roman and non-Roman territory.

In the east the empire stretched all the way into Mesopotamia. Other Asian territories the Romans ruled included Asia Minor and the eastern coast of the Mediterranean. All of the north African coast belonged to Rome as well, so the Romans controlled everything that bordered the Mediterranean. In fact, Roman control of the Mediterranean was so great that they called it *Mare Nostrum*, or "Our Sea."

READING CHECK **Drawing Conclusions**

Why did Roman emperors want to expand the empire?

Roman Trade Routes, AD 200

Legend:
- Roman Empire, c. AD 200
- Trade route
- Grains
- Olives/olive oil
- Grapes/wine
- Silk
- Spices
- Gold
- Iron

0   100   200 Miles
0   100   200 Kilometers

GEOGRAPHY SKILLS **INTERPRETING MAPS**

Movement What were some goods that traveled along Roman trade routes?

Trade Increases

As the empire grew, the Romans met many different peoples. In many cases these peoples had goods that the Romans wanted. Thinking that there would be a market for these products in Rome, merchants began to travel all over the empire, as you can see on the map.

People in the city of Rome needed raw materials that they couldn't produce themselves. Many of the materials could be found, though, in Rome's **provinces**, the areas outside of Italy that the Romans controlled. Traders brought metals, cloth, and food from the provinces to the city. They also brought more exotic goods, like spices from Asia and animals from Africa. In return the Romans sent goods made by artisans to the provinces. These goods included jewelry, glass, and clothing.

Some Roman traders also traveled beyond the empire's borders. They sailed as far as eastern Africa, India, and what is now Vietnam to find goods they couldn't get in the empire. Others traveled overland into Asia to meet merchants bringing goods from China on the Silk Road. Silk was especially popular in Rome. Wealthy Romans were willing to pay high prices for it.

To pay for their trade goods, Romans used **currency**, or money. They traded coins made of gold and silver for the items they wanted. These coins allowed the Romans to trade with people even if they had no items their trade partners wanted. Nearly everyone accepted Roman coins, which helped trade grow even more.

READING CHECK **Identifying Cause and Effect**
How did currency help Roman trade grow?

The Pax Romana

The first 200 years of the Roman Empire were a time of general peace and prosperity. Several characteristics, such as a stable government and an organized military, helped the empire to thrive and maintain peace during these years. There were no major wars or rebellions in the empire. We call this peaceful period the **Pax Romana**, or Roman Peace. It lasted until about AD 180.

During the Pax Romana the empire's population grew. Trade continued to increase, and many Romans became wealthy through this trade. One <u>effect</u> of these changes was an improvement in the quality of life for people living in Rome and in its provinces.

Life in Cities

During the Pax Romana many Romans lived in cities scattered throughout the empire. Some of these cities, like Alexandria in Egypt, were major centers of trade and had huge populations. Other cities, like Pompeii (pom-PAY) in Italy, had much smaller populations.

By far the largest city in the empire was, of course, Rome. Some historians think that Rome may have had more than a million residents at its height. Although many were wealthy, many were not, and that large population led to difficulties for many poorer residents. Many poor Romans lived in crowded, sometimes dangerous, apartment buildings.

ACADEMIC VOCABULARY
effect the result of an action or decision

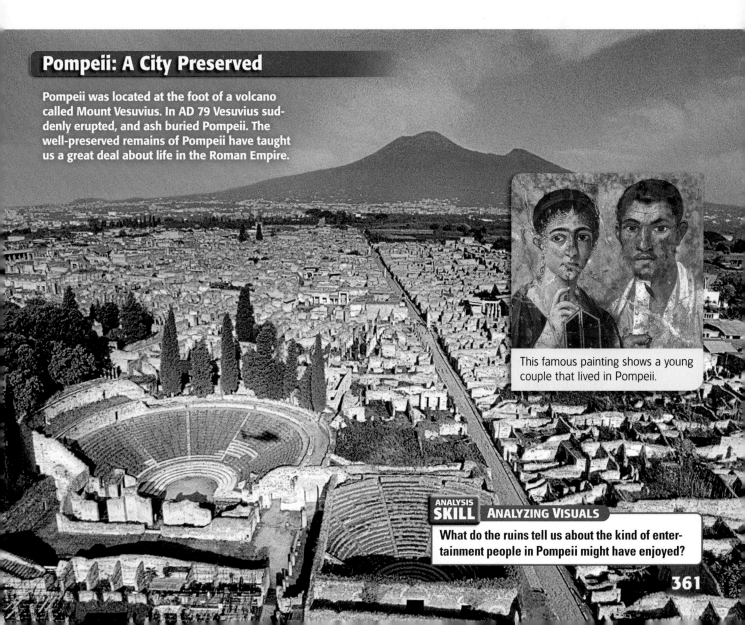

Pompeii: A City Preserved

Pompeii was located at the foot of a volcano called Mount Vesuvius. In AD 79 Vesuvius suddenly erupted, and ash buried Pompeii. The well-preserved remains of Pompeii have taught us a great deal about life in the Roman Empire.

This famous painting shows a young couple that lived in Pompeii.

ANALYSIS SKILL **ANALYZING VISUALS**

What do the ruins tell us about the kind of entertainment people in Pompeii might have enjoyed?

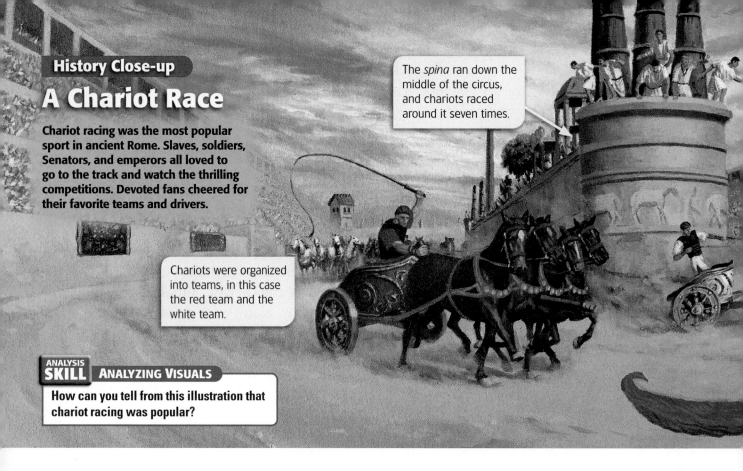

A Chariot Race

Chariot racing was the most popular sport in ancient Rome. Slaves, soldiers, Senators, and emperors all loved to go to the track and watch the thrilling competitions. Devoted fans cheered for their favorite teams and drivers.

The *spina* ran down the middle of the circus, and chariots raced around it seven times.

Chariots were organized into teams, in this case the red team and the white team.

ANALYSIS SKILL ANALYZING VISUALS

How can you tell from this illustration that chariot racing was popular?

Despite their poor living conditions, the people of Rome enjoyed many types of entertainment. They could go to comic plays, thrilling chariot races, or fierce gladiator fights. Those who wanted more peace and quiet could head for one of Rome's public baths. The huge bath complexes in Rome were more like spas or health clubs than bathtubs. At the bath people could swim, soak in a hot pool, or mingle with other Romans.

Romans looking for fun could also just tour the city. Rome was filled with beautiful temples and monuments built by city leaders. The Romans were proud of their city and took great pride in how it looked:

> "In great buildings as well as in other things the rest of the world has been outdone by us Romans. If, indeed, all the buildings in our City are considered . . . together in one vast mass, the united grandeur of them would lead one to imagine that we were describing another world, accumulated in a single spot."
> –Pliny the Elder, from *Natural History*

Life in the Country

When we think of life in the Roman Empire, we often think of a city. In truth, though, more people lived in the country than in the empire's cities. People outside of the cities had a very different way of life than city dwellers did.

In rural areas most people farmed. On their small farms they grew just enough food for themselves and their families. Many of these farmers spoke languages other than Latin. In fact, many people in the country didn't seem Roman at all. These people had kept many of their own customs and traditions when they were conquered by the Romans.

Scattered among the groups of farmers, though, were large farms and **villas**, or country homes belonging to rich Romans. Many people from the cities liked to have a house outside the city. They visited these homes when they wanted a break from the city crowds.

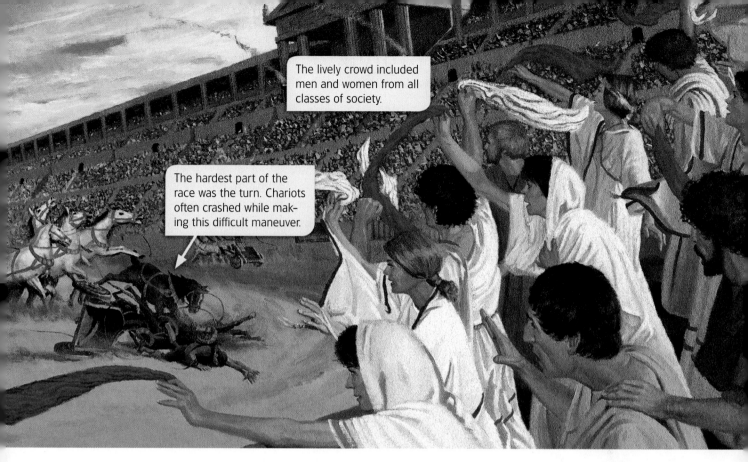

The lively crowd included men and women from all classes of society.

The hardest part of the race was the turn. Chariots often crashed while making this difficult maneuver.

At their villas, these wealthy Romans lived much like they did at home. They hosted huge, elaborate dinner parties where they served exotic foods. Some of the foods served at these parties sound very unusual to modern people. For example, Romans cooked and served peacocks, ostriches, jellyfish, and even mice!

These meals were often served by slaves who worked in the villas. Other slaves worked in the villa owners' fields. The sale of crops grown in these fields helped pay for the villa owners' extravagant expenses.

READING CHECK **Contrasting** How was life different in the country than in the city?

SUMMARY AND PREVIEW The Roman Empire grew and changed during its first 200 years. In the next section you will learn about the great advances made in art, engineering, and other fields.

Section 2 Assessment

go.hrw.com
Online Quiz
KEYWORD: SQ6 HP12

Reviewing Ideas, Terms, and People **HSS** 6.7.3

1. **a. Identify** What areas of the world did the Romans take over?
   b. Explain Why did **Hadrian** build a wall in northern Britain?
2. **a. Define** What were **provinces**?
   b. Summarize Why did trade increase as the Roman Empire expanded?
3. **a. Explain** Why is the period before AD 180 called the **Pax Romana**?
   b. Evaluate Would you have preferred to live in a Roman city or the country? Why?

Critical Thinking

4. **Contrasting** Draw two houses like these. In the house on the left, write two facts about life in a Roman city. In the house on the right, write two facts about life in the country.

City   Country

FOCUS ON WRITING

5. **Adding Details** Add information about additional characters to your chart. Under the "Setting" column, add information about life during the Pax Romana.

Roman Roads

The Romans are famous for their roads. They built a road network so large and well constructed that parts of it remain today, roughly 2,000 years later. Roads helped the Romans run their empire. Armies, travelers, messengers, and merchants all used the roads to get around. They stretched to every corner of the empire in a network so vast that people even today say that "all roads lead to Rome."

Roman roads stretched as far north as Scotland.

The Romans built about 50,000 miles of roads. That's enough to circle the earth—twice!

EUROPE

PYRENEES

ITALY

Rome

In the west, roads crisscrossed Spain.

Roman roads in the south connected different parts of northern Africa.

N
W   E
S

AFRICA

Paving stones

Drainage ditch

Curbstones

Sand, clay, and gravel

Stone chips

Gravel concrete

Roman roads were built to last. They were constructed of layers of sand, concrete, rock, and stone. Drainage ditches let water drain off, preventing water damage.

The roads were built by and for the military. The main purpose of the roads was to allow Rome's armies to travel quickly throughout the empire.

In the east, Roman roads stretched into Southwest Asia.

The Romans built tall "milestones" along their roads to mark distances. Just like modern highway signs, the markers told travelers how far it was to the next town.

GEOGRAPHY SKILLS | **INTERPRETING MAPS**

1. **Movement** Why did the Romans build their roads?
2. **Location** How does the map show that "all roads lead to Rome"?

Rome's Legacy

If YOU were there...

You live on a farm in Gaul but are visiting your older brother in town. You are amazed by the city's beautiful temples and towers. Another surprise is the water! At home you must draw up water from a well. But here, water bubbles out of fountains all over the city. It even runs through pipes in the public baths. One day your brother introduces you to the engineer who maintains the water system.

What questions will you ask the engineer?

BUILDING BACKGROUND Ideas of law and government spread widely. But those were not the Romans' only accomplishments. Roman scientists, engineers, artists, and writers also made contributions to life in Rome. Many of the ideas the Romans developed 2,000 years ago are still influential today.

Roman Science and Engineering

The Romans took a practical approach to their study of science and engineering. Unlike the Greeks, who studied the world just to know about it, the Romans were more concerned with finding knowledge that they could use to improve their lives.

Science

Roman scientists wanted to produce results that could benefit their society. For example, they studied the stars not just to know about them but to produce a calendar. They studied plants and animals to learn how to produce better crops and meat.

The practical Roman approach to science can also be seen in medicine. Most of the greatest doctors in the Roman Empire were Greek. One doctor in the empire was **Galen**, who lived in the AD 100s. He was a Greek surgeon who made many discoveries about the body. For example, Galen described the valves of the heart and noted differences between arteries and veins. For centuries, doctors based their ideas on Galen's teachings and writings.

What You Will Learn...

Main Ideas

1. The Romans looked for ways to use science and engineering to improve their lives.
2. Roman architecture and art were largely based on Greek ideas.
3. Roman literature and language have influenced how people write and speak.
4. Roman law serves as a model for modern law codes around the world.

The Big Idea

Many features of Roman culture were copied by later civilizations and continue to influence our lives today.

Key Terms and People

Galen, *p. 366*
aqueduct, *p. 367*
vault, *p. 367*
Virgil, *p. 370*
Ovid, *p. 370*
satire, *p. 370*
Romance languages, *p. 371*
civil law, *p. 371*

HSS 6.7.8 Discuss the legacies of Roman art and architecture, technology and science, literature, language, and law.

Engineering

The Romans' practical use of science can also be seen in their engineering. The Romans were great builders. Even today people walk along Roman roads and drive over Roman bridges built almost 2,000 years ago. How have these structures survived for so long?

The Romans developed some new building materials to help their structures last. The most important of these materials was cement. They made cement by mixing a mineral called lime with volcanic rock and ash. The resulting material dried to be very hard and watertight.

More important than the materials they used, though, were the designs the Romans had for their structures. For example, they built their roads in layers. Each layer was made of a different material. This layered construction made the road durable. Many Roman roads have not worn down even after centuries of traffic and exposure to wind and rain.

Another way the Romans created structures to last was by using arches. Because of its rounded shape, an arch can support much heavier weights than other shapes can. This strength has allowed arched structures such as Roman bridges to last until the present.

The Romans also used arches in their aqueducts (A-kwuh-duhkts). An **aqueduct** was a channel used to carry water from mountains into cities. When they crossed deep valleys, aqueducts were supported by rows of arches. The Romans' aqueducts were so well built that many still stand.

Roman builders also learned how to combine arches to create vaults. A **vault** is a set of arches that supports the roof of a building. The Romans used vaults to create huge, open areas within buildings. As a result, Roman buildings were much larger than anything that had come before.

READING CHECK **Summarizing** What were two ways the Romans built strong structures?

THE IMPACT TODAY

People still build aqueducts today. One of the largest carries water from northern to southern California.

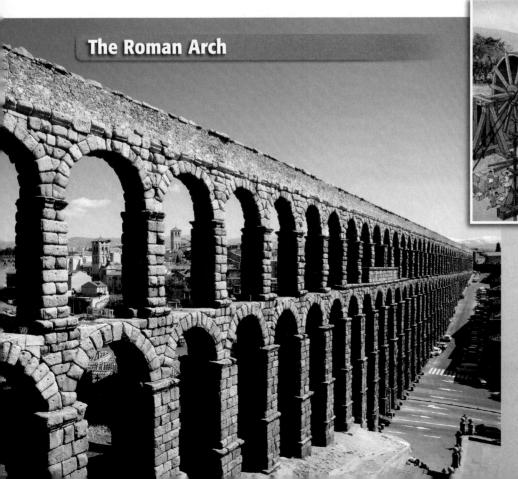

The Roman Arch

The Romans were the first people to make wide use of the arch. The photograph at left shows a Roman aqueduct supported by hundreds of arches. Above is a drawing showing how Roman engineers built their tall and strong arches.

How did the Romans support arches during their construction?

Architecture and Art

The Romans weren't only interested in practicality, though. They also admired beauty. Roman appreciation for beauty can be seen in their architecture and art. People still admire their magnificent buildings, statues, and paintings.

Architecture

Roman architecture was largely based on older Greek designs. Like the ancient Greeks, the Romans used columns to make their public buildings look stately and impressive. Also like the Greeks, the Romans covered many of their buildings with marble to make them more majestic.

But Roman engineering techniques allowed them to take architecture beyond what the Greeks had done. For example, the Roman vault let them build huge structures, much larger than anything the Greeks could build. One such Roman structure that used vaults was the Colosseum pictured below. It was built to hold fights between gladiators.

History Close-up

The Colosseum

The Colosseum was a huge arena in ancient Rome. The giant building was more than 150 feet tall and could seat about 50,000 people, who came to watch events like gladiator fights. The building's design was based on many arches and vaults, hallmarks of Roman engineering.

This modern sports stadium in Oakland, California, is known as the Coliseum after the building in ancient Rome.

The arches on the outside of the building were decorated with statues of Roman gods.

People entered the Colosseum through 80 arched entrances, each with its own number.

The Romans also used more domes in their architecture than the Greeks had. Domes were difficult to build and required a great deal of support. Once the Romans developed cement, they could provide that support. Many Roman structures are topped with huge domes, some of the largest ever built.

Art

The artists of the Roman Empire were known for their beautiful mosaics, paintings, and statues. Mosaics and paintings were used to decorate Roman buildings. Many Roman homes and businesses had elaborate mosaics built into their floors. The walls of these buildings were often covered with paintings. Most Roman paintings were frescoes. A fresco is a type of painting done on wet plaster.

Many Roman artists were particularly skilled at creating portraits, or pictures of people. When they made a portrait, artists tried to show their subject's personality. We can guess a great deal about individual Romans by studying their portraits.

THE IMPACT TODAY

Many public buildings in the United States are modeled after Roman designs.

Trap doors in the floor were opened to allow animals and gladiators to enter the arena.

By combining many arches, the Romans created long vaulted passageways for the crowd to walk through.

This is a vault, or combination of arches.

Underneath the floor was a system of animal cages, rooms, and tunnels.

ANALYSIS SKILL ANALYZING VISUALS

How does the modern sports stadium compare to the ancient Colosseum?

A Roman Fresco

A fresco is a type of painting in which paint is applied to wet plaster and then left to dry. Roman artists painted many beautiful frescoes like this one.

What activities can you see in this fresco?

FOCUS ON READING

What type of Web site would you use to research Roman sculpture?

Roman sculptors were also talented. They created some original works, but many Roman statues are actually copies of older Greek works. Roman sculptors studied what the Greeks had done and tried to re-create it in their own statues. Although their works are not original, we owe a great deal to these Roman artists. Many of the original Greek works they copied have been destroyed over time. Without the Roman copies, the world would know little about many Greek masterpieces.

READING CHECK Drawing Conclusions
Why did many Roman architects and artists base their work on earlier Greek works?

Literature and Language

Like Roman artists, Roman authors are greatly admired. In addition, the works they created and the language they used have shaped our language today.

Literature

The Romans admired good writers. Many emperors encouraged authors to write. As a result, Rome was home to many of the greatest authors of the ancient world. One such author was **Virgil**, who wrote a great epic about the founding of Rome, the *Aeneid*. Another was **Ovid** (AHV-uhd), who wrote poems about Roman mythology.

The Romans also excelled in other types of writing:

- **satire**, a style of writing that pokes fun at people or society
- history and speeches
- drama, both tragedies and comedies

Many of these works have served as models for hundreds of years and are still enjoyed today.

Language

Virgil, Ovid, and other poets wrote in Latin, the language of ancient Rome. The Roman Empire was huge, and it had two official languages. In the east, some people spoke Greek. People throughout the western Roman world wrote, conducted business, and kept records in Latin. This wide use of Latin helped tie people in various parts of the empire together.

After the Roman Empire ended, Latin developed into many different languages. Together, the languages that developed from Latin are called **Romance languages**. The main Romance languages are Italian, French, Spanish, Portuguese, and Romanian. They share many elements with each other and with Latin.

Over time, Latin also influenced other languages. For example, many Latin words entered non-Romance languages, including English. Words like *et cetera, circus,* and *veto* were all originally Latin terms. Latin words are also common in scientific terms and mottoes. For example, the motto of the United States is the Latin phrase *e pluribus unum* (ee PLOOHR-uh-buhs OO-nuhm), which means "out of many, one." Many legal terms also come from Latin.

READING CHECK **Finding the Main Idea** How did Roman literature and language influence later societies?

Law

Perhaps even more influential than Rome's artistic and literary traditions was its system of law. Roman law was enforced across much of Europe. After the empire fell apart, Roman laws continued to exist.

Over time, Roman law inspired a system called civil law. **Civil law** is a legal system based on a written code of laws, like the one created by the Romans.

Most countries in Europe today have civil law traditions. In the 1500s and 1600s, European explorers and colonists carried civil law around the world. As a result, some countries in Africa, Asia, and the Americas developed law codes as well.

READING CHECK **Summarizing** How are Roman legal ideas reflected in the modern world?

SUMMARY AND PREVIEW In this section you learned about many of Rome's contributions to the world and how they have influenced our society. In the next chapter you will learn about an even more influential development that changed life in Rome—Christianity.

Section 3 Assessment

go.hrw.com
Online Quiz
KEYWORD: SQ6 HP12

Reviewing Ideas, Terms, and People HSS 6.7.8

1. **a. Identify** What were **aqueducts** used for?
   b. Contrast How was the Romans' attitude toward science different from the Greeks'?
2. **a. Define** What is a **fresco**?
   b. Explain What influence did Greek art have on Roman art?
3. **a. Recall** What were three forms of writing in which the Romans excelled?
   b. Elaborate Why did Latin develop into different languages after the fall of the Roman Empire?
4. **Identify** What type of law is based on the Roman law code?

Critical Thinking

5. **Comparing and Contrasting** Draw a chart like this one. In the first column, list two ways Greek and Roman architecture were similar. In the other, list two ways they were different.

Similar	Different

FOCUS ON WRITING

6. **Completing Your Notes** Add some information on Roman achievements to your chart. For example, you might add a description of architecture under "Setting." Decide what details you will give to the movie studio.

Social Studies Skills

Analysis   **Critical Thinking**   **Participation**   **Study**

Interpreting Time Lines

Understand the Skill

A time line is a visual summary of important events that occurred during a period of history. It displays the events in the order in which they happened. It also shows how long after one event another event took place. In this way time lines allow you to see at a glance what happened and when. You can better see relationships between events and remember important dates when they are displayed on a time line.

Learn the Skill

Some time lines cover huge spans of time—sometimes even many centuries. Other time lines, such as the one on this page, cover much shorter periods of time.

Time lines can be arranged either vertically or horizontally. This time line is vertical. Its dates are read from top to bottom. Horizontal time lines are read from left to right.

Follow these steps to interpret a time line.

1 Read the time line's title. Note the range of years covered and the intervals of time into which it is divided.

2 Study the order of events on the time line. Note the length of time between events.

3 Note relationships. Ask yourself how an event relates to others on the time line. Look for cause-and-effect relationships and long-term developments.

Practice and Apply the Skill

Interpret the time line to answer the following questions.

1. What is the subject of this time line? What years does it cover?

2. How long did Octavian and Antony rule Rome together?

3. How long after dividing the empire did Antony ally with Cleopatra?

4. What steps did Octavian take to end his alliance with Antony and become emperor? When did he take them? How long did it take?

AUGUSTUS BECOMES EMPEROR

50 BC

44 BC Caesar becomes dictator and is murdered.

43 BC Octavian and Antony decide to rule Rome together.

42 BC Octavian and Antony divide Rome and rule separately.

40 BC

37 BC Antony allies with Cleopatra, queen of Egypt.

31 BC Octavian defeats Antony and Cleopatra in a naval battle near Greece.

30 BC Octavian conquers Egypt. Antony and Cleopatra avoid capture by killing themselves.

30 BC

27 BC Octavian becomes emperor and is renamed Augustus.

23 BC Augustus becomes ruler for life.

Visual Summary

Use the visual summary below to help you review the main ideas of the chapter.

QUICK FACTS

In 27 BC Rome became an empire. Emperors ruled with complete power, and Roman armies conquered new territories. As the empire reached its height, Roman art, architecture, and law flourished.

Reviewing Vocabulary, Terms, and People

Choose the letter of the answer that best completes each statement below.

1. The first emperor of Rome was
   - **a.** Galen.
   - **b.** Julius Caesar.
   - **c.** Augustus.
   - **d.** Marc Antony.

2. A region that lay outside the city of Rome but was controlled by the Romans was called a(n)
   - **a.** aqueduct.
   - **b.** province.
   - **c.** orator.
   - **d.** villa.

3. Another word for money is
   - **a.** currency.
   - **b.** province.
   - **c.** vault.
   - **d.** octavian.

4. The time of peace and prosperity that lasted for the first 200 years of the Roman Empire was the
   - **a.** Ovid.
   - **b.** Romance language.
   - **c.** civil law.
   - **d.** Pax Romana.

Comprehension and Critical Thinking

SECTION 1 *(Pages 352–356)* **HSS** 6.7.4

5. **a. Describe** What action did Cicero recommend? How were the goals of Julius Caesar, Pompey, and Crassus different from Cicero's?

   b. Analyze What were the most important events in the life of Julius Caesar? Which event best qualifies as a turning point in Caesar's life? Defend your choice.

   c. Elaborate How did personal relationships—between Marc Antony and Octavian, and between Marc Antony and Cleopatra—affect the history of the Roman Empire?

SECTION 2 *(Pages 358–363)* **HSS** 6.7.3

6. **a. Identify** What natural disaster has allowed us to learn more about Roman cities? What is the name of the main city affected by that disaster?

SECTION 2 (continued)

b. Make Inferences How do you think the size of the Roman Empire affected the popularity of Roman currency?

c. Evaluate For a poor resident of Rome, do you think the benefits of living in the city would have outweighed the problems? Why or why not?

SECTION 3 *(Pages 366–371)*   **HSS** 6.7.8

7. a. Describe What were the main Roman achievements in architecture? in literature and language?

b. Contrast How did the Roman attitude toward science compare to the traditional Greek attitude? What is an example of the Roman attitude?

c. Evaluate Of all the Romans' achievements, which do you think has affected the most people? Defend your answer.

Reviewing Themes

8. Geography Into what main areas did the Roman Empire expand during its early years?

9. Technology What Roman achievement in science or engineering do you think is most impressive? Why?

Reading Skills

Evaluating Web Sites *Each question below lists two types of Web sites you could use to answer the question. Decide which Web site is likely to be a more valuable and reliable source of information.*

10. What was Roman sculpture like?

a. a site describing someone's trip to Rome

b. a site by a university's art history department

11. What happened after Antony met Cleopatra?

a. a movie studio site for a movie about Cleopatra

b. an online encyclopedia

Social Studies Skills

12. Creating Time Lines Create a time line that shows the key events in the creation and expansion of the Roman Empire. First, look back through this chapter for key dates and events. Decide which of these dates you will include. Once you have completed your time line, compare it to those of your classmates to see if you have included different information.

70 BC   AD 180

Using the Internet

go.hrw.com
KEYWORD: SQ6 WH12

13. Activity: Researching Culture By studying art and culture, you can see into the thoughts and values of the people making up the society. Enter the keyword. Study the background on the Roman legal code and the artifacts provided. Then present an oral report with visual aids that explains what we learn about Rome by studying its art and legal institutions.

FOCUS ON WRITING

14. Creating Note Cards Now you're ready to prepare note cards for studio executives. Choose the most intriguing details from your chart to present on note cards labeled "Characters," "Setting," and "Plot." On each card write a one- to two-sentence description of a person, place, or event that could be featured in the screenplay. Then write another sentence that tells why you think the person, place, or event might be a good one to feature. Prepare six cards that you could give to a screenwriter to use.

Standards Assessment

DIRECTIONS: Read each question, and write the letter of the best response.

1 Use the time line to answer the following question.

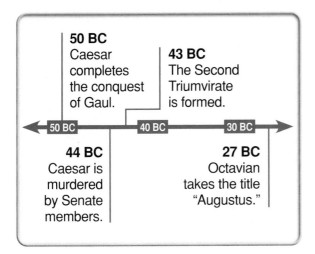

50 BC
Caesar completes the conquest of Gaul.

43 BC
The Second Triumvirate is formed.

50 BC — 40 BC — 30 BC

44 BC
Caesar is murdered by Senate members.

27 BC
Octavian takes the title "Augustus."

Most historians mark the end of the Roman Republic and the beginning of the Roman Empire as taking place in the year

A 50 BC.

B 44 BC.

C 43 BC.

D 27 BC.

2 Roman emperors conquered new lands for all of the following reasons *except*

A to end threats to Rome.

B because they enjoyed fighting.

C to gain resources.

D to defeat people of different religions.

3 Which Roman leader seized power from the Senate and became the dictator of the entire Roman Republic?

A Julius Caesar

B Hadrian

C Brutus

D Marc Antony

4 Roman traders

A refused to trade with people outside of the empire.

B tried to overthrow the emperor.

C carried goods between Rome and its provinces.

D made very little money.

5 Rome's contributions to the world include all of the following *except*

A techniques used to build strong bridges and other structures.

B the building of pyramids.

C the idea of civil law.

D the creation of great works of literature.

Connecting with Past Learnings

6 In Grade 5 you learned about George Washington's contributions as a military leader during the Revolution and as the nation's first president. Which person's contributions to Rome were *most* like those Washington made to the United States?

A Cicero

B Cleopatra

C Augustus

D Galen

7 Earlier in this course you learned about Homer, the poet who told about Greek myths and heroes. Which Roman's writing was *most* like Homer's poetry?

A Virgil

B Cicero

C Horace

D Pompey

Rome and Christianity

California Standards

History–Social Science

6.7 Students analyze the geographic, political, economic, religious, and social structures during the development of Rome.

Analysis Skills

HI 3 Explain the sources of historical continuity and how the combination of ideas and events explains the emergence of new patterns.

English–Language Arts

Writing 6.1.2a Engage the interest of the reader and state a clear purpose.

Reading 6.2.0 Read and understand grade-level-appropriate material.

FOCUS ON WRITING

Magazine Article You're a freelance writer who has been assigned to write a short magazine article about religion and early Christianity in the Roman Empire. As you read this chapter, identify main ideas and interesting details that you can use in your article.

CHAPTER EVENTS

c. 30 Jesus is crucified.

BC 1 AD

WORLD EVENTS

43 London is built as a Roman city.

HOLT

History's Impact
▶ video series
Watch the video to understand the impact of ancient Rome on the world today.

What You Will Learn...

In this chapter you will learn about the beginnings of Christianity in the Roman Empire. In this photo, members of one Christian church, the Roman Catholic Church, gather in Vatican City in Rome.

100s–200s
From time to time, Christians are persecuted in Rome.

309
Emperor Constantine ends the persecution of Christians.

381
Emperor Theodosius bans all non-Christian religions in Rome.

100   200   300   400

c. 65 According to tradition, Buddhism is introduced into China.

c. 250
The Maya Classical Age begins in Mexico.

320
The Gupta dynasty takes charge in India.

ROME AND CHRISTIANITY   **377**

Reading Social Studies

by Kylene Beers

| Economics | Geography | Politics | Religion | Society and Culture | Science and Technology |

Focus on Themes In this chapter, you will learn about the early beginnings of Christianity. You will read about the life and teachings of Jesus of Nazareth and about the Apostles who spread Jesus's teachings after his death. Later in the chapter, you will see how Christianity spread through the Roman Empire and became its official religion. Throughout the chapter, you will see how the Christian **religion** has shaped the **society and culture** of many people throughout history.

Questioning

Focus on Reading If you don't understand something your teacher says in class, how do you get an explanation? You ask a question. You can use the same method to improve your understanding while reading.

The W Questions The most basic questions you can ask about a historical text are who, what, when, and where—the W questions. Answering these questions will help you get to the very basics of what you need to learn from a passage.

Additional reading support can be found in the

Inter active

Reader and Study Guide

Who?
Augustine of Hippo, a Christian writer

What?
read works of classical philosophers

Growth of Territory

As Christianity spread through the Roman world, Christian writers read the works of classical philosophers. One such writer was Augustine of Hippo. He lived in Hippo, a town in northern Africa, in the late 300s and early 400s.

Where?
Hippo, a town in northern Africa

When?
the late 300s and early 400s

ELA **Reading 6.2.0** Read and understand grade-level-appropriate material.

You Try It!

Read the following passage, and then answer the questions below.

Christianity Spreads Quickly in Rome

From Chapter 13, Pages 392–393

Early Christians like Paul wanted to share their message about Jesus with the world. Because of their efforts, Christianity spread quickly in many Roman communities. But as it grew more popular, Christianity began to concern some Roman leaders. They looked for ways to put an end to this new religion.

Early Growth

The first Christians worked to spread Jesus's teachings only among Jews. But some early Christians, including Paul, wanted to introduce Christianity to non-Jews as well. As a result, Christianity began to spread in the Roman Empire. Within a hundred years after Jesus's death, historians estimate that thousands of Christians lived in the Roman Empire.

Answer the following questions about the passage above.

1. Who is this passage about?

2. What did they do?

3. When did they live?

4. Where did they live and work?

5. How can knowing the answers to these questions help you better understand what you've read?

Key Terms and People

Chapter 13

Section 1
Christianity *(p. 382)*
Jesus of Nazareth *(p. 382)*
Messiah *(p. 383)*
John the Baptist *(p. 383)*

Section 2
Bible *(p. 384)*
crucifixion *(p. 385)*
Resurrection *(p. 385)*
disciples *(p. 385)*
Apostles *(p. 387)*
Paul *(p. 387)*
saint *(p. 388)*

Section 3
martyrs *(p. 393)*
persecution *(p. 393)*
bishops *(p. 393)*
Eucharist *(p. 393)*
pope *(p. 394)*
Augustine of Hippo *(p. 394)*
Constantine *(p. 395)*

Academic Vocabulary

Success in school is related to knowing academic vocabulary—the words that are frequently used in school assignments and discussions. In this chapter, you will learn the following academic words:

ideals *(p. 388)*
classical *(p. 394)*

As you read Chapter 13, use the W questions as guides to help you clarify your understanding of the text.

Religion in the Roman Empire

What You Will Learn...

Main Ideas

1. The Romans allowed many religions to be practiced in their empire.
2. Jews and Romans clashed over religious and political ideas.
3. The roots of Christianity had appeared in Judea by the end of the first century BC.

The Big Idea

The Roman Empire accepted many religions, but it came into conflict with Judaism.

Key Terms and People

Christianity, *p. 382*
Jesus of Nazareth, *p. 382*
Messiah, *p. 383*
John the Baptist, *p. 383*

HSS 6.7.5 Trace the migration of Jews around the Mediterranean region and the effects of their conflict with the Romans, including the Romans' restrictions on their right to live in Jerusalem.

If YOU were there...

You are a Roman soldier stationed in one of the empire's many provinces. You are proud that you've helped bring Roman culture to this place far from the city of Rome. But one group of local people refuses to take part in official Roman holidays and rituals, saying it is against their beliefs. Other than that, they seem peaceful. Some soldiers think that this group is dangerous.

What will you do about this group?

BUILDING BACKGROUND As the Roman Empire expanded, it came to include people who spoke many different languages and followed many different religions. While Roman officials were generally tolerant of local religions and cultures, they did not allow anything—like the religion noted above—that might threaten their authority.

Romans Allow Many Religions

The Romans were a very religious people. To celebrate their religious beliefs, the Romans held many festivals in honor of their gods. Because of the empire's huge size and diverse population, the nature of these festivals varied widely from place to place.

As you have read, the Romans were a very practical people. This practicality also extended into their religious lives. The Romans didn't think that they could be sure which gods did or did not exist. To avoid offending any gods who did exist, the Romans prayed to a wide range of gods and goddesses. Many of the most popular gods in the Roman Empire were adopted from people the Romans had conquered.

Because of their ideas about religion, the Romans allowed people they conquered to keep their beliefs. In many cases these beliefs also spread among nearby Romans. As time passed the Romans built temples to the gods of these new religions, and knowledge of them spread throughout the empire.

For example, many Romans worshipped the Olympian gods of Greece. When the Romans conquered Greece they learned about Greek mythology. Before long, the Greek gods became the main gods of Rome as well. In the same way, many Romans also adopted gods from the Egyptians, Gauls, or Persians.

The only time the Romans banned a religion was when the rulers of Rome considered it a political problem. In these cases, government officials took steps to prevent problems. Sometimes they placed restrictions on when and where members of a religion could meet. One religion that some Roman leaders came to consider a political problem was Judaism.

READING CHECK Finding Main Ideas Why did the Romans forbid certain religions?

Jews and Romans Clash

Roman leaders considered Judaism to be a potential problem for two reasons. One reason was religious, the other political. Both reasons led to conflict between the Romans and the Jews of the empire.

Religious Conflict

Unlike the Romans, the Jews did not worship many gods. They believed that their God was the only god. Some Romans, though, thought the Jews were insulting Rome's gods by not praying to them.

Still, the Romans did not attempt to ban Judaism in the empire. They allowed the Jews to keep their religion and practice it as they pleased. It was not until later when political conflict arose with the Jews that the Romans decided to take action.

FOCUS ON READING

Before you read this discussion, look at the heads and subheads. Who is this paragraph about? What did they do?

The Romans built many temples to honor their many gods. Temples built to honor all the gods were called pantheons, and the most famous of these is the Pantheon in Rome, first built in the 20s BC. Its huge dome awes visitors even today.

381

Resistance to Rome

Unhappy with Roman rule, many Jews rebelled in the AD 60s but were defeated. Refusing to accept defeat, about 1,000 Jews locked themselves in a mountain fortress called Masada and held off the Romans for four years. In the end, these rebels killed themselves to avoid surrendering to the Romans.

The Roman general Titus captured Jerusalem in AD 70. To celebrate this victory, the Romans built this arch that shows Roman soldiers carrying a stolen menorah from Jerusalem's holy Second Temple.

Political Conflict

Political conflict arose because the Jews rebelled against Roman rule. Judea, the territory in which most Jews lived, had been conquered by Rome in 63 BC. Since then, many Jews had been unhappy with Roman rule. They wanted to be ruled only by Jews, not by outsiders. As a result, the Jews rebelled in the AD 60s. The rebellion was defeated, however, and the Jews were punished for their actions.

In the early 100s the Jews rebelled once more against the Romans. Tired of putting down Jewish revolts, the emperor Hadrian banned the practice of certain Jewish rituals. He thought this ban would cause people to give up Judaism and end their desire for independence.

Hadrian was wrong. His actions made the Jews even more upset with Roman rule. Once again they rebelled. This time Hadrian decided to end the rebellions in Jerusalem once and for all.

The Roman army crushed the Jews' revolt, destroyed the Jewish capital of Jerusalem, and forced all Jews to leave the city. Then the Romans built a new city on the ruins of Jerusalem and brought settlers from other parts of the empire to live there. Jews were forbidden to enter this new city more than once a year. Forced out of their ancient city, many Jews moved into other parts of the Roman world.

READING CHECK **Summarizing** Why did the Romans come to consider Judaism a threat?

The Roots of Christianity

Early in the first century AD, before the Jews' first rebellion against the Romans, what would become a new religion appeared in Judea. This religion began as one of the many Jewish sects, and later developed into **Christianity.** It was based on the life and teachings of the Jew **Jesus of Nazareth**. Christianity was rooted in Jewish ideas and traditions.

When the Romans took over Judea in 63 BC, many Jews thought the Messiah would soon appear. Prophets wandered throughout Judea, announcing that the Messiah was coming. The most famous of these prophets was **John the Baptist**. Inspired by the prophets' teachings, many Jews anxiously awaited the Messiah.

READING CHECK **Summarizing** Why were Jews waiting for the Messiah to arrive?

SUMMARY AND PREVIEW You just read about Jewish prophecies that foretold the coming of a Messiah. In the next section you'll learn what happened when a man many people believed to be that Messiah—Jesus—was born.

At the time that Jesus was born, there were several groups of Jews in Judea. The largest of these groups was very strict in how it practiced Judaism. Members of this group were particularly strict in obeying the laws of Moses. Jews believed that Moses had given them these laws to follow.

Many Jews followed the laws closely because Jewish prophets had said that a new leader would appear among the Jews. Many people thought this leader was more likely to appear if they were strict in their religious behavior.

According to the prophecies, the Jews' new leader would be a descendent of King David. When he came, he would restore the greatness of David's ancient kingdom, Israel. The prophets called this leader the **Messiah** (muh-SY-uh), which means "anointed" in Hebrew. In other words, the Jews believed that the Messiah would be chosen by God to lead them. However, no one knew when the Messiah would come.

go.hrw.com
Online Quiz
KEYWORD: SQ6 HP13

Section 1 Assessment

Reviewing Ideas, Terms, and People HSS 6.7.5

1. a. **Describe** What was the Roman attitude toward religion?
    b. **Explain** Why did the Romans ban some religions?
2. a. **Recall** What was a major religious difference between the Romans and the Jews?
    b. **Analyze** Why did the Romans destroy Jerusalem?
    c. **Elaborate** How do you think the spreading of Jews through the Roman world affected Jewish culture?
3. a. **Define** Who did Jews believe the **Messiah** was?
    b. **Make Inferences** How did the anticipation of the Messiah's arrival lead many Jews to follow laws strictly?

Critical Thinking

4. **Categorizing** Draw a graphic organizer like the one here. Use it to identify reasons the Romans might accept or forbid a religion.

FOCUS ON WRITING

5. **Taking Notes** Create a chart with columns labeled Main Ideas and Supporting Details. Then write two main ideas in your chart: "Romans allowed many religions" and "Jews and Romans differed over religion." Take notes about these ideas in the Supporting Details column.

ROME AND CHRISTIANITY   **383**

Origins of Christianity

What You Will Learn...

Main Ideas

1. In Christian belief, Jesus was the Messiah and the son of God.
2. Jesus taught about salvation, love for God, and kindness.
3. Jesus's followers, especially Paul, spread his teachings after his death.

The Big Idea

Christianity, based on the teachings of Jesus of Nazareth, spread quickly after his death.

Key Terms and People

Bible, p. 384
crucifixion, p. 385
Resurrection, p. 385
disciples, p. 385
Apostles, p. 387
Paul, p. 387
saint, p. 388

HSS 6.7.6 Note the origins of Christianity in the Jewish Messianic prophecies, the life and teachings of Jesus of Nazareth as described in the New Testament, and the contributions of St. Paul the Apostle to the definition and spread of Christian beliefs (e.g., belief in the Trinity, resurrection, salvation).

If YOU were there...

You are a fisher in Judea, bringing in the day's catch. As you reach the shore, you see a large crowd. They are listening to a man tell stories. A man in the crowd whispers to you that the speaker is a teacher with some new ideas about religion. You are eager to get your fish to the market, but you are also curious.

What might convince you to stay to listen?

BUILDING BACKGROUND In the first century AD, Judea was a province of the Roman Empire. Roman soldiers occupied the country, but the Jews living there held firmly to their own beliefs and customs. During that time, religious teachers could attract large followings among the people of Judea. One such teacher was Jesus of Nazareth.

The Life and Death of Jesus of Nazareth

Jesus of Nazareth, the man whom many people believe was the Jewish Messiah, lived at the beginning of the first century AD. Although Jesus was one of the most influential figures in world history, we know relatively little about his life. Most of what we know about Jesus is contained in the New Testament of the Christian **Bible**, the holy book of Christianity.

The Christian Bible is made up of two parts. The first part, the Old Testament, is largely the same as the Hebrew Bible. It tells the history and ideas of the Hebrew people. The second part, the New Testament, is an account of the life and teachings of Jesus and of the early history of Christianity.

The Birth of Jesus

According to the Bible, Jesus was born in a small town called Bethlehem (BETH-li-hem) at the end of the first century BC. In fact, in our dating system his birth marks the shift from BC to AD. Jesus's mother, Mary, was married to a carpenter named Joseph. But Christians believe God, not Joseph, was Jesus's father.

As a young man Jesus lived in the town of Nazareth and probably studied with Joseph to become a carpenter. Like many young Jewish men of the time, he also studied the laws and teachings of Judaism. By the time he was about 30, Jesus had begun to travel and teach. Stories of his teachings and actions from this time make up the beginning of the New Testament.

The Crucifixion

As a teacher, Jesus drew many followers with his ideas. But at the same time, his teachings challenged the authority of political and religious leaders. According to the Christian Bible, Roman authorities arrested Jesus while he was in Jerusalem in or around AD 30.

Shortly after his arrest, Jesus was tried and executed. He was killed by **crucifixion** (kroo-suh-FIK-shuhn), a type of execution in which a person was nailed to a cross. In fact, the word *crucifixion* comes from the Latin word for "cross." After he died Jesus's followers buried him.

The Resurrection

According to Christian beliefs, Jesus rose from the dead and vanished from his tomb three days after he was crucified. Christians refer to Jesus's rise from the dead as the **Resurrection** (re-suh-REK-shuhn).

Christians further believe that after the Resurrection, Jesus appeared to several groups of his **disciples** (di-SY-puhls), or followers. Jesus stayed with these disciples for the next 40 days, teaching them and giving them instructions about how to pass on his teachings. Then Jesus rose up into heaven.

Early Christians believed that the Resurrection was a sign that Jesus was the Messiah and the son of God. Some people began to call him Jesus Christ, from the Greek word for Messiah, *Christos*. It is from this word that the words *Christian* and *Christianity* eventually developed.

READING CHECK **Summarizing** What do Christians believe happened after Jesus died?

THE IMPACT TODAY

Because Jesus was crucified, the cross is an important symbol of Christianity today.

Jesus of Nazareth

The Bible says that Jesus was born in Bethlehem but grew up in Nazareth. This painting from about 1300 shows Jesus with his followers.

385

Christian Holidays

For centuries, Christians have honored key events in Jesus's life. Some of these events inspired holidays that Christians celebrate today.

The most sacred holiday for Christians is Easter, which is celebrated each spring. The exact date changes from year to year. Easter is a celebration of the Resurrection. Christians usually celebrate Easter by attending church services. Many people also celebrate by dyeing eggs because eggs are seen as a symbol of new life.

Another major Christian holiday is Christmas. It honors Jesus's birth and is celebrated every December 25. Although no one knows on what date Jesus was actually born, Christians have placed Christmas in December since the 200s. Today, people celebrate with church services and the exchange of gifts. Some, like people in this picture, reenact scenes of Jesus's birth.

ANALYSIS SKILL **ANALYZING INFORMATION**

Why do you think people celebrate events in Jesus's life?

Acts and Teachings

During his lifetime, Jesus traveled from village to village spreading his message among the Jewish people. As he traveled, he attracted many followers. These early followers later became the first Christians.

Miracles

According to the New Testament, many people became Jesus's followers after they saw him perform miracles. A miracle is an event that cannot normally be performed by a human. For example, the books of the New Testament tell how Jesus healed people who were sick or injured. One passage also describes how Jesus once fed an entire crowd with just a few loaves of bread and a few fish. Although there should not have been enough food for everyone, people ate their fill and had food to spare.

Parables

The Bible says that miracles drew followers to Jesus and convinced them that he was the son of God. Once Jesus had attracted followers, he began to teach them. One way he taught was through parables, stories that teach lessons about how to live. Parables are similar to fables, but they usually teach religious lessons. The New Testament includes many of Jesus's parables.

Through his parables, Jesus linked his teachings to people's everyday lives. The parables explained complicated ideas in ways that people could understand. For example, Jesus compared people who lived sinfully to a son who had left his home and family. Just as the son's father would joyfully welcome him home, Jesus said, God would forgive sinners who turned away from sin.

Jesus's Message

Much of Jesus's message was rooted in older Jewish traditions. For example, he emphasized two rules that were also in the Torah: love God and love other people.

Jesus expected his followers to love all people, not just friends or family. He encouraged his followers to be generous to the poor and the sick. He told people that they should even love their enemies. The way people treated others, Jesus said, showed how much they loved God.

Another important theme in Jesus's teachings was salvation, or the rescue of people from sin. Jesus taught that people who were saved from sin would enter the Kingdom of God when they died. Many of his teachings dealt with how people could reach the kingdom.

Over the many centuries since Jesus lived, people have interpreted his teachings in different ways. As a result, many different denominations of Christians have been developed. A denomination is a group of people who hold the same beliefs. Still, despite their differences, Christians around the world share some basic beliefs about Jesus and his importance to the world.

READING CHECK **Summarizing** Why did Jesus tell parables?

Jesus's Followers

Shortly after the Resurrection, the Bible says, Jesus's followers traveled throughout the Roman world telling about Jesus and his teachings. Among the people to pass on Jesus's teachings were 12 chosen disciples called **Apostles** (uh-PAHS-uhls), the writers of the Gospels (GAHS-puhlz), and a man named **Paul**.

The Apostles

The Apostles were 12 men whom Jesus chose to receive special teaching. During Jesus's lifetime they were among his closest followers and knew him very well. Jesus frequently sent the Apostles to spread his teachings. After the Resurrection, the Apostles continued this task.

One of the Apostles, Peter, became the leader of the group after Jesus died. Peter traveled to a few Roman cities and taught about Jesus in the Jewish communities there. Eventually he went to live in Rome, where he had much authority among Jesus's followers. In later years after the Christian Church was more organized, many people looked back to Peter as its first leader.

The Last Supper
This famous painting by Italian artist Leonardo da Vinci shows Jesus and his Apostles at the Last Supper. The Last Supper was the last meal they shared before Jesus was arrested. Later, the Apostles would spread Jesus's teachings.

Paul's Journeys

Legend:
First journey
Second journey
Third journey
Fourth journey

Rome

ITALY

Sicily

Malta

GREECE

Athens

Corinth

Crete

Mediterranean Sea

ASIA MINOR

Derbe

Antioch

Cyprus

SYRIA

Damascus

Jerusalem

EGYPT

GEOGRAPHY SKILLS **INTERPRETING MAPS**

Movement Where did Paul go on his fourth journey?

The Gospels

Some of Jesus's disciples wrote accounts of his life and teachings. These accounts are called the Gospels. Four Gospels are found in the New Testament of the Bible. They were written by men known as Matthew, Mark, Luke, and John. Both historians and religious scholars depend on the Gospels for information about Jesus's life.

Paul

Probably the most important figure in the spread of Christianity after Jesus's death was named Paul of Tarsus. He had never met Jesus, but Paul did more to spread Christian **ideals** than anyone else did. He was so influential that many people consider him an additional Apostle. After he died, Paul was named a **saint**, a person known and admired for his or her holiness.

ACADEMIC VOCABULARY

ideals ideas or goals that people try to live up to

Like most of Jesus's early followers, Paul was born Jewish. At first he didn't like Jesus's ideas, which he considered a threat to Judaism. For a time, Paul even worked to prevent the followers of Jesus from spreading their message.

According to the Bible, though, one day while Paul was traveling to Damascus he saw a blinding light and heard the voice of Jesus calling out to him. Soon afterward, Paul became a Christian.

After his conversion Paul traveled widely, spreading Christian teachings. As you can see on the map, he visited many of the major cities along the eastern coast of the Mediterranean on his journeys. In addition, he wrote long letters that he sent to communities throughout the Roman world. These letters helped explain and elaborate on Jesus's teachings.

LETTER
Paul's Letter to the Romans

In the late AD 50s Paul traveled to Corinth, a city in Greece. While there he wrote a letter to the people of Rome. In this letter he told the Romans that he planned to come to their city to deliver God's message. In the meantime, he told them, they should learn to live together peacefully.

"Let love be genuine; hate what is evil, hold fast to what is good; love one another with mutual affection; outdo one another in showing honor. Do not lag in zeal, be ardent [strong] in spirit, serve the Lord. Rejoice in hope, be patient in suffering, persevere in prayer. Contribute to the needs of the saints; extend hospitality to strangers.

Bless those who persecute you; bless and do not curse them. Rejoice with those who rejoice, weep with those who weep. Live in harmony with one another; do not be haughty, but associate with the lowly; do not claim to be wiser than you are. Do not repay anyone evil for evil, but take thought for what is noble in the sight of all. If it is possible, so far as it depends on you, live peaceably with all."

—Romans 12:9–18 NRSV

ANALYSIS SKILL **ANALYZING PRIMARY SOURCES**

How did Paul's letter express Jesus's teachings?

In his letters Paul wrote at length about the Resurrection and about salvation. He also mentioned ideas of the Trinity. The Trinity is a central Christian belief that God is made up of three persons—God the Father, Jesus the Son, and the Holy Spirit. But even though there are three persons, there is still only one God.

Both Jews and non-Jews were attracted to Christianity by Paul's teachings. In time, this helped the Christian Church break away from its Jewish roots.

READING CHECK **Drawing Conclusions** Why was Paul important to early Christianity?

SUMMARY AND PREVIEW By AD 100, Christianity had spread beyond Judea into many parts of the Roman world. As you will learn, the Christian Church would come to have a huge influence on Roman society.

Section 2 Assessment

go.hrw.com
Online Quiz
KEYWORD: SQ6 HP13

Reviewing Ideas, Terms, and People **HSS** 6.7.6

1. a. **Define** In Christian teachings, what was the **Resurrection**?
   b. **Elaborate** Why do you think Christians use the cross as a symbol of their religion?
2. a. **Identify** What did Jesus mean by salvation?
   b. **Explain** How have differing interpretations of Jesus's teachings affected Christianity?
3. a. **Recall** Who were the **Apostles**?
   b. **Summarize** How did **Saint Paul** influence early Christianity?

Critical Thinking

4. **Finding the Main Idea** Draw a graphic organizer like the one shown here. Use it to identify and describe some of Jesus's acts and teachings.

Acts and Teachings of Jesus of Nazareth

Miracles	Parables	Message

FOCUS ON WRITING

5. **Adding to Your Notes** Add two main ideas about the origins of Christianity to your notebook. What details support these main ideas?

from The Bible

The Sermon on the Mount

Matthew 5:1–16 New Revised Standard Version

About the Reading *The Bible says that Jesus attracted many followers. One day he led his followers onto a mountainside to preach a sermon, or religious speech, called the Sermon on the Mount. Jesus taught that people who love God will be blessed when they die. The sayings that Jesus used to express this message are called the Beatitudes (bee-A-tuh-toodz), because in Latin they all begin with the word* beati, *or blessed.*

AS YOU READ Note who Jesus says are blessed.

When Jesus saw the crowds, he went up the mountain; and after he sat down, his disciples came to him. Then he began to speak, and taught them, saying:

"Blessed are the poor in spirit, for theirs is the kingdom of heaven. ❶

"Blessed are those who mourn, for they will be comforted.

"Blessed are the meek, for they will inherit the earth.

"Blessed are those who hunger and thirst for righteousness, for they will be filled.

"Blessed are the merciful, for they will receive mercy.

"Blessed are the pure in heart, for they will see God.

"Blessed are the peacemakers, for they will be called children of God.

"Blessed are those who are persecuted for righteousness' sake, for theirs is the kingdom of heaven. ❷

"Blessed are you when people revile you and persecute you and utter all kinds of evil against you falsely on my account. Rejoice and be glad, for your reward is great in heaven, for in the same way they persecuted the prophets who were before you.

"You are the salt of the earth; but if salt has lost its taste, how can its saltiness be restored? It is no longer good for anything, but is thrown out and trampled under foot.

"You are the light of the world. A city built on a hill cannot be hid. No one after lighting a lamp puts it under the bushel basket, but on the lampstand, and it gives light to all in the house. In the same way, let your light shine before others, so that they may see your good works and give glory to your Father in heaven." ❸

The Parable of the Good Samaritan

Luke 10:29–37 New Revised Standard Version

About the Reading *In his teaching, Jesus used many parables, or stories intended to teach lessons about how people should live. One of his most famous parables is the story of the Good Samaritan. The Samaritans were a minority group living in what is now northern Israel. The parable of the Good Samaritan is Jesus's response to someone who asks what Jesus means when he says to love your neighbor.*

AS YOU READ Think about the lesson Jesus is trying to teach.

But wanting to justify himself, he asked Jesus, "And who is my neighbor?" Jesus replied, "A man was going down from Jerusalem to Jericho, and fell into the hands of robbers, who stripped him, beat him, and went away, leaving him half dead. Now by chance a priest was going down that road; and when he saw him, he passed by on the other side. So likewise a Levite, when he came to the place and saw him, passed by on the other side. But a Samaritan while traveling came near him; and when he saw him, he was moved with pity. He went to him and bandaged his wounds, having poured oil and wine on them. ❶ Then he put him on his own animal, brought him to an inn, and took care of him. The next day he took out two denarii, gave them to the innkeeper, and said, 'Take care of him; and when I come back, I will repay you whatever you spend.' Which of these three, do you think, was a neighbor to the man who fell into the hands of the robbers?" He said, "The one who showed him mercy." Jesus said to him, "Go and do likewise." ❷

GUIDED READING

WORD HELP

Levite (LEE-vyt) a member of the Hebrew priest class
denarii (di-NAR-ee-eye) Roman coins

❶ Oil and wine were used to clean cuts and wounds.

What does the Samaritan do after he cleans the traveler's wounds?

❷ *Which person did the man say was the traveler's neighbor?*

The Samaritans lived in the northern part of what is now Israel.

CONNECTING SACRED TEXTS TO HISTORY

1. **Analyzing** Jesus taught that people who loved God and lived good lives would achieve salvation. How do the Beatitudes support this teaching?

2. **Supporting a Point of View** Jesus also told people that they should be kind to everyone, even their enemies. How is the parable of the Good Samaritan an example of this?

The Early Christian World

If **YOU** were there...

You live in a town in Greece in the first century AD. Near your town are two places dedicated to the ancient Greek gods—a grove of sacred trees and a temple to the god Apollo. One day, two Christians come to your town talking about their religion. They urge people to give up their old gods and follow Christian ways. Some townspeople listen eagerly. Others, however, get angry.

What do you think the townspeople will do?

BUILDING BACKGROUND From its origins in Judea, Christianity began to spread quickly. Apostles such as Peter and Paul traveled throughout the eastern Mediterranean world, preaching and writing letters to local churches. They were welcomed in some places but met anger and hostility in others.

Christianity Spreads Quickly in Rome

Early Christians like Paul wanted to share their message about Jesus with the world. Because of their efforts, Christianity spread quickly in many Roman communities. But as it grew more popular, Christianity began to concern some Roman leaders. They looked for ways to put an end to this new religion.

Time Line

Early Christianity

BC 1 AD

c. 30
Jesus is crucified.

Early Growth

The first Christians worked to spread Jesus's teachings only among Jews. But some early Christians, including Paul, wanted to introduce Christianity to non-Jews as well. As a result, Christianity began to spread in the Roman Empire. Within a hundred years after Jesus's death, historians estimate that thousands of Christians lived in the Roman Empire.

As Christianity spread, Christians began to write down parts of Jesus's message, including the Gospels. They distributed copies of the Gospels and other writings to strengthen people's faith.

Persecution

From time to time, Christians trying to spread their beliefs faced challenges from local officials. Some of these officials even arrested and killed Christians who refused to worship Rome's gods. We call such people who suffer death for their religious beliefs **martyrs** (MAHR-tuhrz). Many leaders of the early Christians—including Peter and Paul—were killed for spreading Christian teachings. Even today, Christians honor them as martyrs and saints.

Most of Rome's emperors let Christians worship as they pleased. A few emperors in the 200s and 300s, though, feared that the Christians could cause unrest in the empire. To prevent such unrest, these emperors banned Christianity. This ban led to several periods of persecution (puhr-si-KYOO-shuhn) against Christians. **Persecution** means punishing a group because of its beliefs or differences.

Because their religion had been banned, Christians were often forced to meet in secret. To arrange their meetings, they used secret symbols to identify people who shared their beliefs. One of the most common symbols they used was a fish. The fish became a Christian symbol because the Greek word for fish begins with the same letters as the Greek words for *Jesus* and *Christ*.

THE IMPACT TODAY
The fish is still commonly used as a symbol of Christianity.

READING CHECK Identifying Cause and Effect
Why did the Romans begin persecuting Christians?

The Church Grows

Because the early church largely had to meet in secret, it didn't have any single leader to govern it. Instead, **bishops**, or local Christian leaders, led each Christian community. Most bishops lived in cities. They helped people understand and live by Christian teachings.

One of the bishops' most important duties was leading Christians in celebrating the Eucharist (YOO-kuh-ruhst). The **Eucharist** was the central ceremony of the Christian Church. It was created to honor the last supper Jesus shared with his Apostles. During the Eucharist, Christians ate bread and drank wine in memory of Jesus's death.

c. 250 Widespread persecution of Christians begins.

381 Roman emperor Theodosius I bans the practice of all religions except Christianity in the empire.

200 300 400

ANALYSIS SKILL **READING TIME LINES**
About how many years after Christianity began were other religions banned in Rome?

The Spread of Christianity, 300–400

BRITAIN
North Sea
EUROPE
ATLANTIC OCEAN
Tours
GAUL
Rhine River
Danube River
SPAIN
Toledo
Corsica
Rome
Sardinia
Carthage
Sicily
Crete
AFRICA
Mediterranean Sea
Black Sea
Constantinople
ASIA MINOR
Antioch
Cyprus
Jerusalem
Alexandria
EGYPT
Nile River
Red Sea

Christian areas, AD 300
Christian areas, AD 400
Boundary of Roman Empire, AD 395

0   250   500 Miles
0   250   500 Kilometers

GEOGRAPHY SKILLS INTERPRETING MAPS

Location What three continents had Christian areas by 400?

Growth of the Papacy

ACADEMIC VOCABULARY

classical
referring to the cultures of ancient Greece or Rome

By the late 100s Christians were looking to the bishops of large cities for guidance. These bishops had great influence, even over other bishops. The most honored of all the empire's bishops was the bishop of Rome, or the **pope**. The word *pope* comes from the Greek word for father. The pope was so honored in the Christian world largely because Peter, the leader of the Apostles and a key figure in the early church, had been the first bishop of Rome. Later popes were seen as his spiritual successors.

Gradually, the pope's influence grew and many people in the West came to see him as the head of the whole Christian Church. As the church grew, so did the influence of the papacy, the office of the pope.

New Teachings and Emperors

As Christianity spread through the Roman world, Christian writers read the works of **classical** philosophers. One such writer was **Augustine** (AW-guhs-teen) **of Hippo**. He lived in Hippo, a town in northern Africa, in the late 300s and early 400s. As a young man, Augustine studied the works of Plato. When he became a Christian, he applied Plato's ideas to Christian beliefs. Augustine taught that Christians should focus not on worldly goods but on God's plan for the world. His ideas helped shape Christian beliefs for hundreds of years.

At about the same time that Saint Augustine was writing, an event changed the standing of Christians in Rome. The emperor himself became a Christian.

The emperor who became a Christian was **Constantine** (KAHN-stuhn-teen). He came to power in 306 after fighting and defeating many rivals. According to legend, Constantine was preparing for battle against one of these rivals when he saw a cross in the sky. He thought that this vision meant he would win the battle if he converted to Christianity. Constantine did convert, and he won the battle. As a result of his victory he became the emperor of Rome.

As emperor, Constantine removed bans against the practice of Christianity. He also called together a council of Christian leaders from around the empire to clarify Christian teaching.

Almost 60 years after Constantine died, another emperor, Theodosius I (thee-uh-DOH-shuhs), banned all non-Christian religious practices in the Empire. Like Constantine, Theodosius was a Christian. As emperor, he called together Christian leaders to clarify church teachings. He wanted to be sure that all Christians believed the same things he did.

READING CHECK **Sequencing** How did Constantine and Theodosius influence Christianity?

BIOGRAPHY

Constantine
c. 280–337

Constantine grew up in the court of the Roman emperor. As a young man he became a general and led his army in many successful campaigns. After he converted to Christianity, Constantine came to believe that he had been successful all his life because he had God's favor. He built several great churches in the empire, including one in Jerusalem at the spot where Jesus was believed to have been buried. Throughout history Christians have considered him one of Rome's greatest emperors.

Drawing Conclusions Why do you think Constantine was so popular with Christians?

SUMMARY AND PREVIEW By the late 300s Christianity had become one of the most influential forces in the Roman world. Its influence provided security and stability for many people when the once mighty Roman Empire began to fall apart in the 400s.

Section 3 Assessment

go.hrw.com
Online Quiz
KEYWORD: SQ6 HP13

Reviewing Ideas, Terms, and People **HSS** 6.7.7

1. **a. Define** What is **persecution**?
   b. Summarize How did Paul change the way people spread Christianity?
   c. Elaborate Why do you think **martyrs** are admired?
2. **a. Identify** Who was Rome's first Christian emperor?
   b. Contrast How did **Constantine**'s policies toward Christianity differ from Theodosius's?
3. **a. Recall** What was the role of **bishops** in the early church?
   b. Explain Why did the **pope** have influence over many other bishops?

Critical Thinking

4. **Sequencing** Draw a diagram like the one below. In each box identify one step in the relationship between Christianity and the Roman Empire.

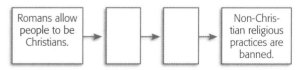

Romans allow people to be Christians. → □ → □ → Non-Christian religious practices are banned.

FOCUS ON WRITING

5. **Completing Your Chart** Finish your chart by adding two more main ideas and details that support them.

Social Studies Skills

| Analysis | Critical Thinking | Participation | Study |

Continuity and Change in History

Understand the Skill

A well-known saying claims that "the more things change, the more they stay the same." Nowhere does this observation apply more than to the study of history. Any look back over the past will show many changes—nations expanding or shrinking, empires rising and falling, changes in leadership, and people on the move, to name just a few.

The reasons for change have not changed, however. The same general forces have driven the actions of people and nations across time. These forces are the "threads" that run through history and give it continuity, or connectedness. They are the "sameness" in a world of constant change.

Learn the Skill

You can find the causes of all events of the past in one or more of these major forces or themes that run throughout history.

1 **Cooperation and Conflict:** Throughout time, people and groups have worked together to achieve goals. They have also opposed others who stood in the way of their goals.

2 **Cultural Invention and Interaction:** The values and ideas expressed in peoples' art, literature, customs, and religion have enriched the world. But the spread of cultures and their contact with other cultures has also sometimes produced conflict.

3 **Geography and Environment:** Physical environment and natural resources have shaped how people live. Efforts to gain or protect land and resources have been a major cause of cooperation and conflict in history.

4 **Science and Technology:** Technology, or the development and use of tools, has helped people make better use of their environment. Science has always changed people's lives also.

5 **Economic Opportunity:** From hunting and gathering to farming, manufacturing, and trade, people have tried to make the most of their resources. Hope for a better life is a main reason people have moved from one place to another.

6 **The Impact of Individuals:** Political, religious, military, business, and other leaders have been a major influence in history. The actions of many ordinary people have also shaped history.

7 **Nationalism and Imperialism:** Nationalism is the desire of a people to have their own country. Imperialism is the wish to control other peoples. Both have existed through history.

8 **Political and Social Systems:** People have always been part of groups—families, villages, nations, or religious groups, for example. The groups to which people belong affect how they relate to people around them. History is mostly the study of past interactions of people.

Practice and Apply the Skill

Check your understanding of the sources of continuity and change in history by answering the following questions.

1. How did relations between the Romans and the Jews show cultural interaction and conflict in history?

2. Identify three forces of history that are illustrated by the rise and spread of Christianity.

Visual Summary

Use the visual summary below to help you review the main ideas of the chapter.

QUICK FACTS

In the Roman Empire, people practiced many religions and worshipped many gods.

The teachings of Jesus of Nazareth inspired a new religion called Christianity.

After Jesus died, his followers spread Christianity throughout the Roman Empire.

Reviewing Vocabulary, Terms, and People

Match the "I" statement with the person or thing that might have made the statement.

a. Messiah   **f.** martyr

b. Constantine   **g.** pope

c. Apostle   **h.** Paul

d. Jesus of Nazareth   **i.** Augustine of Hippo

e. Bible   **j.** ideal

1. "I helped spread Christian teachings through the Mediterranean world through my journeys and letters."

2. "I died for my religious beliefs."

3. "My teachings became the foundations for Christianity."

4. "I was the first Christian emperor of Rome."

5. "I was a Christian writer who combined Plato's ideas with Christian teachings."

6. "I am an idea or goal that people try to live up to."

7. "I am the holy book of Christianity."

8. "I was the bishop of Rome who became the head of the Christian Church."

9. "I was a promised leader who was to appear among the Jews."

10. "I was one of Jesus's 12 chosen followers."

Comprehension and Critical Thinking

SECTION 1 *(Pages 380–383)*   **HSS** 6.7.5

11. **a. Identify** Who were Jesus of Nazareth and John the Baptist?

   b. Contrast How did the Romans' attitude toward religion differ from the Jews' attitude?

   c. Evaluate Why might a historian say that one ancient religion, Judaism, set the scene for a new religion, Christianity?

SECTION 2 *(Pages 384–389)* **HSS** 6.7.6

12. a. Describe According to the Bible, what were the crucifixion and Resurrection? What do Christians believe the Resurrection means?

b. Analyze Why do you think Jesus's teachings appealed to many people within the Roman Empire?

c. Evaluate Why is Saint Paul considered one of the most important people in the history of Christianity?

SECTION 3 *(Pages 392–395)* **HSS** 6.7.7

13. a. Describe What was the connection between the Apostle Peter and the papacy?

b. Compare and Contrast What did Roman emperors Constantine and Theodosius I have in common? How did their actions differ?

c. Predict Why do you think Christianity spread despite the fact that early Christians were often persecuted?

Reviewing Themes

14. Society and Culture How did early Christian leaders such as Paul help separate Christianity from Judaism?

15. Religion How do you think the early Christian Church would have been different if Paul had not converted to Christianity?

Social Studies Skills

16. Understanding Historical Continuity Christianity has been one of the forces that has most influenced the course of world history. Why has its influence been so great? Choose one of the following factors that help promote historical continuity. Then write a sentence explaining how that factor is related to Christianity's influence.

Cooperation and conflict	Economic opportunity
Cultural interaction	Impact of individuals
Geography and environment	Nationalism and imperialism
Science and technology	Political and social systems

Using the Internet

go.hrw.com
KEYWORD: SQ6 WH13

17. Activity: Creating Maps Within 400 years of Jesus's death, Christianity had grown from a small group of Jesus's disciples into the only religion practiced in the entire Roman Empire. Although 400 years sounds like a long time, to a historian it's practically the blink of an eye. What explains the rapid growth of Christianity? Enter the activity keyword. Then research the key figures, events, and factors in the spread of Christianity. Use what you learn to create an illustrated and annotated map of the spread of Christianity.

Reading Skills

Using Questions *Read the following passage and answer the questions that follow.*

> *"Women were among Jesus's earliest followers. From the beginning, Jewish women disciples, including Mary Magdalene, Joanna, and Susanna, had accompanied Jesus during his ministry and supported him out of their private means (Luke: 8:1–3). After the death of Jesus, women continued to play prominent roles in the early movement. Some scholars have even suggested that the majority of Christians in the first century may have been women."*
>
> –Karen L. King, from *Women in Ancient Christianity: The New Discoveries*

18. Who is this passage about?

19. When did they live?

20. What did they do that made them important?

FOCUS ON WRITING

21. Writing Your Article Now that you've taken notes on the main ideas and supporting details about early Christianity in the Roman Empire, you have the information you'll need to write your two- to three-paragraph magazine article. Write the article in chronological order and include a catchy title that describes the article. You might begin the article with a question or an intriguing fact to get your audience's attention.

Standards Assessment

DIRECTIONS: Read each question, and write the letter of the best response.

1

> The practice of any other religion but Christianity shall be against the law.
>
> All temples to the ancient gods shall be closed and become property of the Roman government.
>
> All festivals and other celebrations and gatherings in honor of the ancient gods shall be banned.

Which person would have been *most* likely to have issued a document like this one?

A Jesus of Nazareth

B Emperor Constantine

C Emperor Theodosius I

D Paul

2 Early Christianity grew out of the beliefs, practices, and values of which early people?

A Jews

B Greeks

C Chinese

D Egyptians

3 Which persons were *most* active in and responsible for spreading the Christian faith immediately after the death of Jesus?

A Constantine and Theodosius I

B Peter and Augustine

C Paul and Constantine

D Peter and Paul

4 Which statement about Jesus is *not* true?

A Some people believed Jesus was the Messiah that Jewish prophets had predicted.

B Some Roman leaders viewed Jesus as a threat to their power.

C Jesus led a rebellion of the Jews against the Romans.

D Jesus taught people to love God and to be kind to each other.

Connecting with Past Learnings

5 In Grade 5, you learned about religious leaders who explained Puritan beliefs through their writings, teaching, and preaching. All of the following made the same contribution to Christianity during Roman times *except*

A Augustine.

B Constantine.

C the Gospel writers.

D Paul.

6 The role of Jesus in Christianity is *most* like the role in earlier times of

A Moses among the ancient Hebrews.

B Hammurabi among the ancient Babylonians.

C Pericles among the ancient Greeks.

D Ramses among the ancient Egyptians.

Historical Problem and Solution

Assignment
Write about a problem the Romans faced and what their solution was or what you think would be a better solution.

History is the story of how individuals have solved political, economic, and social problems. Learning to write an effective problem-solution paper will be useful in school and in many other situations.

1. Prewrite

Identifying a Problem
Think of a problem the Romans faced. Look at the problem closely. What caused it? What were its effects? Here is an example.

Problem: The Gauls overran Rome.

Solution A: Pay the Gauls a huge ransom to leave Rome. [caused other cities to attack in the hope of getting similar ransoms]

Solution B: Attack other cities. [caused other cities to stop attacking Rome; let Rome gain power and wealth]

Finding a Solution and Proof
Compare the Roman solution to the problem to one they didn't try. Choose either the Roman solution or your own solution to write about. Your explanation should answer these questions.

- How does the solution address the cause of the problem?
- How does the solution fix the effects of the problem?

Use historical evidence to support what you say about the problem:

- facts, examples, or quotations
- comparisons with similar problems your readers know about

ELA Writing 6.2.2d Offer persuasive evidence to validate arguments and conclusions as needed.

2. Write
This framework can help you clearly explain the problem and its solution.

A Writer's Framework

Introduction	Body	Conclusion
■ Tell your reader what problem the Romans faced.	■ Explain the solution.	■ Summarize the problem and the solution.
■ Explain the causes and effects of the problem.	■ Connect the solution directly to the problem.	■ Discuss how well the solution deals with the problem.
■ State your purpose in presenting this problem and its solution.	■ Give supporting historical evidence and details that show how the solution deals with the problem.	

3. Evaluate and Revise

Evaluating

Now you'll want to evaluate your draft to see where you can improve your paper. Try using the following questions to decide what to revise.

Evaluation Questions for a Historical Problem and Solution

- Does your introduction state the problem clearly and describe it fully?
- Does the introduction give causes and effects of the problem?
- Do you clearly explain how the solution relates to the problem?
- Do you give supporting historical evidence showing how the solution deals with the problem?
- Do you conclude by summarizing the problem and the solution?

TIP **Problem-Solution Clue Words.** It's not enough simply to tell your reader what the problem and solution are. You need to show how they are related. Here is a list of words and phrases that will help you do so.

as a result	therefore
consequently	this led to
nevertheless	thus

Revising

Revise your draft to make what you say clear and convincing. You may need to

- Add historical facts, examples, quotations and other evidence to give your readers all the information they need to understand the problem and solution
- Reorganize paragraphs to present information in a clear, logical order
- Insert words like *thus, therefore,* and *as a result* to show how causes link to effects and how the solution deals with the problem

4. Proofread and Publish

Proofreading

To improve your paper before sharing it, check the following:

- spelling of all names, places, and other historical information, especially Latin words, because they can be tricky
- punctuation around linking words such as *so, thus,* and *in addition* that you use to connect causes with effects and solutions with problems

Publishing

Choose one or more of these ideas to share your report.

- Create a poster that Roman leaders might put up to announce how they will solve the problem.
- Hold a debate between teams of classmates who have chosen similar problems but different solutions. Have the rest of the class vote on whose solutions are best.

TIP **Seeing Your Paper as Others See It.** To you, your paper makes perfect sense. To others, it may not. Whenever possible, ask someone else to read your paper. Others can see flaws and errors that you never will see. Listen closely to questions and suggestions. Do your best to see the other person's point before defending what you have written.

● Practice and Apply

Use the steps and strategies outlined in this workshop to write a problem-solution paper.

Endings and Beginnings

Rome dominated the Mediterranean for hundreds of years and left a lasting imprint on the region's cultures. But problems within the empire and pressures from outside eventually combined to bring about the end of the vast Roman Empire.

Even as Rome fell apart, though, other civilizations began to flourish. To the east, the Byzantine Empire achieved fabulous wealth and was a center of Christianity. In the Americas, the Mayas reached the height of their civilization as the Roman Empire fell.

In the next two chapters, you will learn about the end of one great civilization and the beginnings of others.

Explore the Art

In this scene, the Byzantine princess Anna Comnena admires a mosaic in Hagia Sophia, a famous church in Constantinople. What features of Byzantine culture can you see?

The Fall of Rome

California Standards

History–Social Science

7.1 Students analyze the causes and effects of the vast expansion and ultimate disintegration of the Roman Empire.

Analysis Skills

HI 4 Recognize the role of chance, oversight, and error in history.

English–Language Arts

Speaking 7.1.6 Use speaking techniques, including voice modulation, inflection, tempo, enunciation, and eye contact, for effective presentations.

Reading 6.2.8 Note instances of unsupported inferences, fallacious reasoning, persuasion, and propaganda in text.

FOCUS ON SPEAKING

A Narrative Poem How do people remember great historical events like the fall of Rome? Sometimes it's because a poet created a poem to tell the story. As you read this chapter, you'll learn what happened to Rome as it became weak and lost its power. Then you'll write and present a short poem—8 to 10 lines—about this fascinating story.

CHAPTER EVENTS

200

WORLD EVENTS

220 The Han dynasty ends in China.

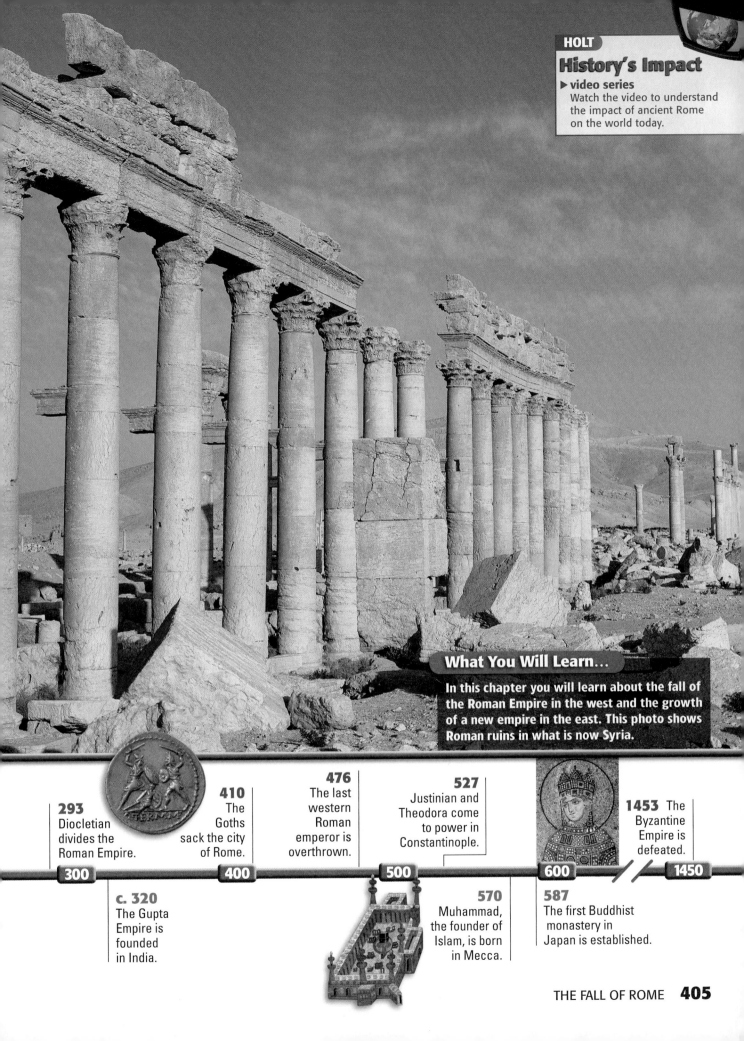

HOLT

History's Impact
▶ video series
Watch the video to understand the impact of ancient Rome on the world today.

What You Will Learn...

In this chapter you will learn about the fall of the Roman Empire in the west and the growth of a new empire in the east. This photo shows Roman ruins in what is now Syria.

293
Diocletian divides the Roman Empire.

410
The Goths sack the city of Rome.

476
The last western Roman emperor is overthrown.

527
Justinian and Theodora come to power in Constantinople.

1453 The Byzantine Empire is defeated.

300

400

500

600

1450

c. 320
The Gupta Empire is founded in India.

570
Muhammad, the founder of Islam, is born in Mecca.

587
The first Buddhist monastery in Japan is established.

THE FALL OF ROME **405**

Focus on Themes In this chapter, you will read about the fall of one of the great ancient civilizations—the Roman Empire. You will learn about problems that arose in its cities and about the invaders who attacked the weakened empire. You will read about the division of the empire into the western empire and the eastern empire and about the reasons for that division. You will see how **political** and **religious** practices differed in the two parts of the empire and learn what those differences meant.

Stereotypes and Bias in History

Focus on Reading Historians today try to be impartial in their writing. They don't let their personal feelings affect what they write.

Roman writers, however, didn't always feel the need to be impartial. Their writings were often colored by their pride in their city and their attitudes about other people, places, and ideas.

Identifying Stereotypes and Bias Two ways in which writing can be colored by the author's ideas are stereotypes and bias. A **stereotype** is a generalization about a whole group of people. **Bias** is an attitude that one group is superior to another. The examples below can help you identify stereotypes and bias in the things you read.

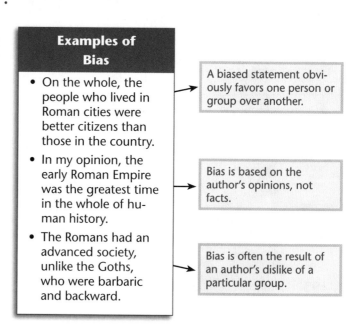

Stereotypes suggest that all members of a group act, think, or feel the same.

Stereotypes can often hurt or offend members of a group.

Some stereotypes encourage the reader to think about a group in a certain way.

Examples of Stereotypes

- All Roman citizens were honest, hardworking, trustworthy, and loyal to their emperors.
- German barbarians were rude, disgusting people who didn't smell very good.
- The lower classes in Rome didn't care about politics and shouldn't have been able to vote.

Examples of Bias

- On the whole, the people who lived in Roman cities were better citizens than those in the country.
- In my opinion, the early Roman Empire was the greatest time in the whole of human history.
- The Romans had an advanced society, unlike the Goths, who were barbaric and backward.

A biased statement obviously favors one person or group over another.

Bias is based on the author's opinions, not facts.

Bias is often the result of an author's dislike of a particular group.

Additional reading support can be found in the

Inter active

Reader and Study Guide

ELA Reading 6.2.8 Note instances of unsupported inferences, fallacious reasoning, persuasion, and propaganda in text.

You Try It!

The following passage is from a Roman history. It describes a former Roman citizen that has chosen to live among the Scythians, a group the Romans considered barbarians. As you read the passage, look for examples of stereotypes and bias.

Romans and Scythians

He considered his new life among the Scythians better than his old life among the Romans, and the reasons he gave were as follows: "After war the Scythians live in inactivity, enjoying what they have got, and not at all, or very little, harassed. The Romans, on the other hand, are in the first place very liable to perish in war . . . But the condition of the subjects in time of peace is far more grievous than the evils of war, for the exaction of taxes is very severe, and unprincipled men inflict injuries on others, because the laws are practically not valid against all classes . . .

In reply to this attack on the Empire . . . I said . . . The Romans treat their servants better than the king of the Scythians treats his subjects. They deal with them as fathers or teachers . . . They are not allowed, like the Scythians, to inflict death upon them.

—Priscus, from Fragmenta Historicorum Graecorum, translated by J. B. Bury

Answer the following questions about the passage you just read.

1. Is the man whom the author describes biased in favor of Roman or Scythian society? How can you tell?

2. Is the author himself biased in favor of one society? How can you tell?

3. What stereotypes about Rome and Roman citizens does the former Roman citizen express?

4. What stereotypes about the Scythians does the author express? What stereotypes about the Romans does he express? Are these stereotypes positive or negative?

Key Terms and People

Chapter 14

Section 1
Diocletian *(p. 409)*
Clovis *(p. 411)*
Attila *(p. 411)*
corruption *(p. 412)*

Section 2
Justinian *(p. 414)*
Theodora *(p. 415)*
Byzantine Empire *(p. 416)*
mosaics *(p. 417)*

Academic Vocabulary

Success in school is related to knowing academic vocabulary—the words that are frequently used in school assignments and discussions. In this chapter, you will learn the following academic word:

cause *(p. 412)*

As you read **Chapter 14,** notice examples of Roman bias against other groups and peoples.

Fall of the Western Roman Empire

Main Ideas

1. Many problems threatened the Roman Empire, leading one emperor to divide it in half.
2. Barbarians invaded Rome in the 300s and 400s.
3. Many factors contributed to Rome's fall.

The Big Idea

Problems from both inside and outside caused the Roman Empire to split and the western half to collapse.

Key Terms and People

Diocletian, *p. 409*
Clovis, *p. 411*
Attila, *p. 411*
corruption, *p. 412*

HSS 7.1.2 Discuss the geographic borders of the empire at its height and the factors that threatened its territorial cohesion.

If YOU were there...

You are a former Roman soldier who has settled on lands in Gaul. In the last few months, groups of barbarians have been raiding local towns and burning farms. The commander of the local army garrison is an old friend, but he says he is short of loyal soldiers. Many troops have been called back to Rome. You don't know when the next raid will come.

How will you defend your lands?

BUILDING BACKGROUND Though the Roman Empire remained large and powerful, it faced serious threats from both outside and inside. Beyond the borders of the empire, many different groups of people were on the move. They threatened the peace in Rome's provinces—and eventually attacked the heart of the empire itself.

Problems Threaten the Empire

At its height the Roman Empire included all the land around the Mediterranean Sea. The empire in the early 100s stretched from Britain south to Egypt, and from the Atlantic Ocean all the way to the Persian Gulf.

But the empire did not stay that large for long. By the end of the 100s emperors had given up some of the land the Roman army had conquered. These emperors feared that the empire had become too large to defend or govern efficiently. As later rulers discovered, these emperors were right.

Problems in the Empire

Even as emperors were giving up territory, new threats to the empire were appearing. Tribes of Germanic warriors, whom the Romans called barbarians, attacked Rome's northern borders. At the same time, Persian armies invaded in the east. The Romans defended themselves for 200 years, but only at great cost.

The Romans struggled with problems within the empire as well. As frontier areas were abandoned because they were too dangerous, Germanic tribes moved in. To help produce more food, the Romans even invited Germanic farmers to grow crops on Roman lands. These farmers often came from the same tribes that threatened Rome's borders. Over time, whole German communities had moved into the empire. They chose their own leaders and largely ignored the emperors, which caused problems for the Romans.

Other internal problems also threatened Rome's survival. Disease swept through the empire, killing many people. The government increased taxes to pay for the defense of the empire. Desperate, the Romans looked for a strong emperor to solve their problems.

Division of the Empire

The emperor the Romans were looking for was **Diocletian** (dy-uh-KLEE-shuhn), who took power in the late 200s. Convinced that the empire was too big for one person to rule, Diocletian divided the empire. He ruled the eastern half of the empire and named a co-emperor to rule the west.

Not long after Diocletian left power, Emperor Constantine (KAHN-stuhn-teen) reunited the two halves of the Roman Empire for a short time. Constantine also moved the empire's capital to the east into what is now Turkey. He built a grand new capital city there. It was called Constantinople (KAHN-stant-uhn-oh-puhl), which means "the city of Constantine." Although the empire was still called the Roman Empire, Rome was no longer the real seat of power. Power had moved to the east.

READING CHECK Identifying Cause and Effect
Why did Diocletian divide the Roman Empire in two?

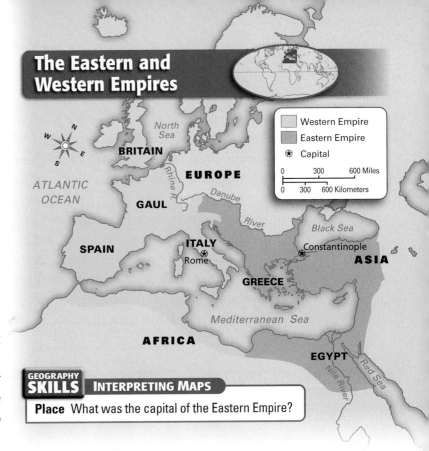

The Eastern and Western Empires

Western Empire
Eastern Empire
★ Capital

0   300   600 Miles
0   300   600 Kilometers

North Sea
BRITAIN
EUROPE
ATLANTIC OCEAN
Rhine R.
GAUL
Danube
River
SPAIN
ITALY
Rome
Black Sea
Constantinople
ASIA
GREECE
Mediterranean Sea
AFRICA
EGYPT
Nile River
Red Sea

GEOGRAPHY SKILLS INTERPRETING MAPS

Place What was the capital of the Eastern Empire?

Barbarians Invade Rome

Not long after Constantine moved Rome's capital, German barbarians—people the Romans considered uncivilized—from the north began to raid the Roman Empire. As you have already read, barbarian tribes had settled along the empire's northern border in the 200s. For more than 100 years these tribes mostly stayed out of Roman territory. Late in the 300s, though, the barbarians began raiding deep into the heart of the empire.

Early Invasions

The source of these raids was a new group of people who moved into Europe. Called the Huns, they were fierce warriors from Central Asia.

As you can see on the map on the next page, the Huns invaded southeastern Europe. From there they launched raids on nearby kingdoms. Among the victims of these raids were several groups of people called the Goths.

FOCUS ON READING

How is the Roman attitude toward the Germans both a bias and a stereotype?

THE IMPACT TODAY

Constantinople is now called Istanbul. It is Turkey's largest city and a thriving economic center.

The Goths could not defeat the Huns in battle. As the Huns continued to raid their territories, the Goths fled. Trapped between the Huns and Rome, they had nowhere to go but into Roman territory.

Rome's leaders were afraid that the Goths would destroy Roman land and property. To stop this destruction, the emperors fought to keep the Goths out of Roman lands. In the east the armies were largely successful. They forced the Goths to move farther west. As a result, however, the western armies were defeated by the Goths, who moved into Roman territory.

The Sack of Rome

The Romans fought desperately to keep the Goths away from Rome. They also paid the Goths not to attack them. For many years this strategy worked. In 408, however, the Romans stopped making payments. This made the Goths furious. Despite the Romans' best efforts to defend their city, the Goths sacked, or destroyed, Rome in 410.

The destruction of Rome absolutely devastated the Romans. No one had attacked their city in nearly 800 years. For the first time, many Romans began to feel afraid for the safety of their empire.

Invasions of the Roman Empire, 340–500

Western Roman Empire
Eastern Roman Empire

0   200   400 Miles
0   200   400 Kilometers

GEOGRAPHY SKILLS | **INTERPRETING MAPS**

Location Which group invaded Italy before moving on to Spain?

The Empire in Chaos

Unfortunately for Rome, the city's fall to the Goths in 410 wasn't the end of the invasions. The Gothic victory served as an example for other barbarian groups to invade the western half of the empire.

In the early 400s the Vandals invaded Spain. Then they crossed into northern Africa and destroyed Roman settlements there. As they passed through Roman areas, the Vandals destroyed nearly everything in their path. At about the same time, the Angles, Saxons, and Jutes invaded Britain, and the Franks invaded Gaul.

By the 480s a Frankish king named **Clovis** had built a huge kingdom in Gaul. Clovis, a Christian, was one of the most powerful of all the German kings.

Meanwhile, the Huns, under a new leader named **Attila** (AT-uhl-uh), raided Roman territory in the east. Attila was a brilliant leader and a very scary enemy. Here is one description that shows why he was so terrifying.

" He was a man born into the world to shake the nations, the scourge of all lands, who in some way terrified all mankind by the dreadful rumors noised abroad concerning him. "

–Jordanes, from *History of the Goths*

THE IMPACT TODAY

We still use the word *vandal* today to describe someone who destroys property.

The Goths and Huns were just two of the groups that invaded the Roman Empire. In this illustration, a Goth warrior is shown on the right, and a Hun is shown on the left. These invaders also battled each other, as Huns attacked Goths and fought for territory and riches.

Key Events in Roman History

264–146 BC
Rome battles Carthage during the Punic Wars.

27 BC
The Roman Republic becomes the Roman Empire.

500 BC

BC 1 AD

c. 509 BC
Rome sets up a republic.

AD 117
The Roman Empire reaches its height.

Attila led the Huns in raids against Constantinople, Greece, Gaul, and parts of northern Italy. But because he was told that diseases ran wild in southern Italy, he decided not to go south to Rome.

ACADEMIC VOCABULARY

cause the reason something happens

The End of the Western Empire

Rome needed strong leaders to survive these constant attacks, but the emperors of the 400s were weak. As attacks on Rome's borders increased, military leaders took power away from the emperors. By the 450s military leaders ruled Rome.

Unfortunately for Rome, most of these military leaders were too busy fighting among themselves to protect the empire. Barbarian leaders took advantage of this situation and invaded Rome. In 476 a barbarian general overthrew the last emperor in Rome and named himself king of Italy. Many historians consider this event the end of the western Roman Empire.

READING CHECK **Analyzing** Why did Rome fall to barbarians in the 400s?

Factors in Rome's Fall

Barbarian invasions are often considered the **cause** of Rome's decline. In truth, they were only one of several causes.

One cause of Rome's decline was the vast size of the empire. In some ways, Rome had simply grown too big to govern. Communication among various parts of the empire was difficult, even in peaceful times. During times of conflict it became even more difficult.

Political crises also contributed to the decline. By the 400s **corruption**, the decay of people's values, had become widespread in Rome's government. Corrupt officials used threats and bribery to achieve their goals, often ignoring the needs of Roman citizens. Because of officials like these, Rome's government was no longer as efficient as it had been in the past.

In the face of this corruption, many wealthy citizens fled the city of Rome to their country estates. This action created a series of causes and effects that further weakened the empire.

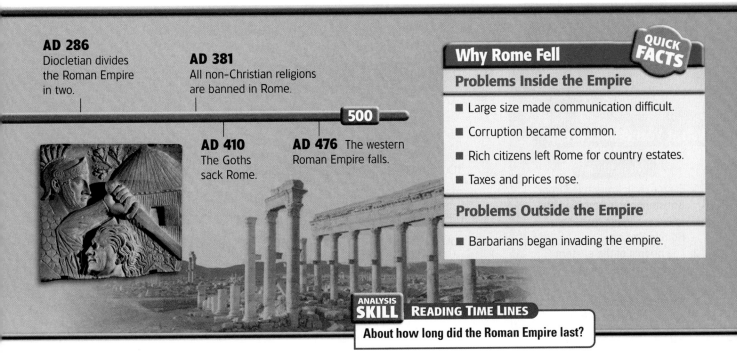

AD 286 Diocletian divides the Roman Empire in two.

AD 381 All non-Christian religions are banned in Rome.

500

AD 410 The Goths sack Rome.

AD 476 The western Roman Empire falls.

QUICK FACTS

Why Rome Fell

Problems Inside the Empire

- Large size made communication difficult.
- Corruption became common.
- Rich citizens left Rome for country estates.
- Taxes and prices rose.

Problems Outside the Empire

- Barbarians began invading the empire.

ANALYSIS SKILL **READING TIME LINES**

About how long did the Roman Empire last?

Outside Rome, many landowners used slaves or serfs to work on their lands. To protect their estates and their wealth, many landowners created their own armies. Ambitious landowners used these personal armies to overthrow emperors and take power for themselves.

As wealthy citizens abandoned Rome and other cities, city life became more difficult for those who remained. Rome's population decreased, and schools closed. At the same time taxes and prices soared, leaving more and more Romans poor. By the end of the 400s Rome was no longer the city it had once been. As it changed, the empire slowly collapsed around it.

READING CHECK Finding Main Ideas How did corruption alter Roman society in the 400s?

SUMMARY AND PREVIEW By the early 500s Rome no longer ruled western Europe. But as you will read in the next section, the empire in the east continued to prosper for several hundred years.

Section 1 Assessment

go.hrw.com
Online Quiz
KEYWORD: SQ6 HP14

Reviewing Ideas, Terms, and People **HSS** 7.1.2

1. **a. Recall** Where did Constantine move Rome's capital?
   b. Explain Why did **Diocletian** divide the empire in two?
2. **a. Identify** Who was **Attila**?
   b. Summarize Why did the Goths move into the Roman Empire in the 300s?
   c. Elaborate Why do you think the sack of Rome was so devastating?
3. **a. Describe** What kinds of problems did Rome's size cause for its emperors?
   b. Make Generalizations How did **corruption** weaken Rome in the 400s?

Critical Thinking

4. **Drawing Conclusions** Draw a word web like the one shown on the right. In each of the outer circles, list a factor that helped lead to the fall of the western Roman Empire. You may add more circles if needed.

   Fall of the Western Roman Empire

 FOCUS ON SPEAKING

5. **Adding Details** Make a list of the most important events that led to the fall of the western Roman Empire. Then circle the events you will mention in your poem.

The Byzantine Empire

What You Will Learn...

Main Ideas

1. Eastern emperors ruled from Constantinople and tried but failed to reunite the whole Roman Empire.
2. The people of the eastern empire created a new society that was very different from society in the west.
3. Byzantine Christianity was different from religion in the west.

The Big Idea

The Roman Empire split into two parts, and the eastern Roman Empire prospered for hundreds of years after the western empire fell.

Key Terms and People

Justinian, *p. 414*
Theodora, *p. 415*
Byzantine Empire, *p. 416*
mosaics, *p. 417*

HSS 7.1.3 Describe the establishment by Constantine of the new capital in Constantinople and the development of the Byzantine Empire, with an emphasis on the consequences of the development of two distinct European civilizations, Eastern Orthodox and Roman Catholic, and their two distinct views on church-state relations.

If YOU were there...

You are a trader visiting Constantinople. You have traveled to many cities but have never seen anything so magnificent. The city has huge palaces and stadiums for horse races. In the city center you enter a church and stop, speechless with amazement. Above you is a vast, gold dome lit by hundreds of candles.

How does the city make you feel about its rulers?

BUILDING BACKGROUND Even before the western empire fell to the Goths, power had begun to shift to the richer, more stable east. The people of the eastern empire considered themselves Romans, but their culture was very different from that of Rome itself.

Emperors Rule from Constantinople

Constantinople was built on the site of an ancient Greek trading city called Byzantium (buh-ZAN-shuhm). It lay near both the Black Sea and the Mediterranean Sea. This location between two seas protected the city from attack and let the city control trade between Europe and Asia. Constantinople was in an ideal place to grow in wealth and power.

Justinian

After Rome fell in 476, the emperors of the eastern Roman Empire dreamed of taking it back and reuniting the old Roman Empire. For **Justinian** (juh-STIN-ee-uhn), an emperor who ruled from 527 to 565, reuniting the empire was a passion. He couldn't live with a Roman Empire that didn't include the city of Rome, so he sent his army to retake Italy. In the end this army conquered not only Italy but also much land around the Mediterranean.

Justinian's other passions were the law and the church. He ordered officials to examine all of Rome's laws and remove any out-of-date or unchristian laws. He then organized all the laws

The Byzantine Empire, 1025

EUROPE

Rome

ITALY

Adriatic Sea

Danube River

Black Sea

Constantinople

ASIA

GREECE

Aegean Sea

ASIA MINOR

Ionian Sea

Athens

Antioch

Euphrates River

Tigris River

SYRIA

Mediterranean Sea

Crete

Cyprus

Byzantine Empire

0   150   300 Miles
0   150   300 Kilometers

GEOGRAPHY SKILLS **INTERPRETING MAPS**

Location Where was Constantinople?

into a legal system called Justinian's Code. By simplifying Roman law, this code helped guarantee fair treatment for all.

Despite his achievements, Justinian made many enemies. Two groups of these enemies joined together and tried to overthrow him in 532. These groups led riots in the streets and set fire to buildings. Scared for his life, Justinian prepared to leave Constantinople.

Justinian was stopped from leaving by his wife, **Theodora** (thee-uh-DOHR-uh). She convinced Justinian to stay in the city. Smart and powerful, Theodora helped her husband rule effectively. With her advice, he found a way to end the riots. Justinian's soldiers killed all the rioters—some 30,000 people—and saved the emperor's throne.

The Empire after Justinian

After the death of Justinian in 565, the eastern empire began to decline. Faced with invasions by barbarians, Persians, and Muslims, later emperors lost all the

City walls

Harbor

Forum

Hippodrome

Hagia Sophia

Imperial Palace

Constantinople was strategically located where Europe and Asia meet. As a result, the city was in a perfect location to control trade routes between the two continents.

land Justinian had gained. The eastern empire remained a major power for several hundred years, but it never regained its former strength.

The eastern empire's struggles finally ended nearly 900 years after the death of Justinian. In 1453 a group called the Ottoman Turks captured Constantinople. With this defeat the 1,000-year history of the eastern Roman Empire came to an end.

READING CHECK **Drawing Conclusions**
Why did Justinian reorganize Roman law?

A New Society

In many ways Justinian was the last Roman emperor of the eastern empire. After he died, non-Roman influences took hold throughout the empire. People began to speak Greek, the language of the eastern empire, rather than Latin. Scholars studied Greek, not Roman, philosophy. Gradually, the empire lost its ties to the old Roman Empire, and a new society developed.

The people who lived in this society never stopped thinking of themselves as Romans. But modern historians have given their society a new name. They call the society that developed in the eastern Roman Empire after the west fell the **Byzantine** (BI-zuhn-teen) **Empire**, named after the Greek town of Byzantium.

Outside Influence

One reason eastern and western Roman society was different was the Byzantines' interaction with other groups. This interaction was largely a result of trade. Because Constantinople's location was ideal for trading between Europe and Asia, it became the greatest trading city in Europe.

Merchants from all around Europe, Asia, and Africa traveled to Constantinople to trade. Over time Byzantine society began to reflect these outside influences as well as its Roman and Greek roots.

Government

The forms of government that developed in the eastern and western empires also created differences. Byzantine emperors had

History Close-up

The Glory of Constantinople

Constantinople was a crossroads for traders, a center of Christianity, and the capital of an empire. It was a magnificent city filled with great buildings, palaces, and churches. The city's rulers led processions, or ceremonial walks, to show their wealth and power.

This procession went from the church to the royal palace. The procession showed the power and importance of the emperor as head of the church.

more power than western emperors did. They liked to show off their great power. For example, people could not stand while they were in the presence of the eastern emperor. They had to crawl on their hands and knees to talk to him.

The power of an eastern emperor was greater, in part, because the emperor was considered the head of the church as well as the political ruler. The Byzantines thought the emperor had been chosen by God to lead both the empire and the church. In the west the emperor was limited to political power. Popes and bishops were the leaders of the church.

READING CHECK Contrasting What were two ways in which eastern and western Roman society were different?

Byzantine Christianity

Just as it was in the west, Christianity was central to the Byzantines' lives. From the beginning, nearly everyone who lived in the Byzantine Empire was Christian.

To show their devotion to God and the Christian church Byzantine artists created beautiful works of religious art. Among the grandest works were **mosaics**, pictures made with pieces of colored stone or glass. Some mosaics sparkled with gold, silver, and jewels.

The procession began at Hagia Sophia, the Byzantines' famous church.

Citizens and visitors crowded the square to see the royal rulers pass by.

ANALYSIS SKILL ANALYZING VISUALS
Where did the procession begin and end?

417

The Western Roman and Byzantine Empires

In the Western Roman Empire . . .

- Popes and bishops led the church, and the emperor led the government.
- Latin was the main language.

In the Byzantine Empire . . .

- Emperors led the church and the government.
- Greek was the main language.

THE IMPACT TODAY

The Orthodox Church is still the main religion in Russia, Greece, and other parts of eastern Europe.

Even more magnificent than their mosaics were Byzantine churches, especially Hagia Sophia (HAH-juh soh-FEE-uh). Built by Justinian in the 530s, its huge domes rose high above Constantinople. According to legend, when Justinian saw the church he exclaimed in delight

"Glory to God who has judged me worthy of accomplishing such a work as this! O Solomon, I have outdone you!"

–Justinian, quoted in *The Story of the Building of the Church of Santa Sophia*

As time passed, people in the east and west began to interpret and practice some elements of Christianity differently. For example, eastern priests could get married, while priests in the west could not. Religious services were performed in Greek in the east. In the west they were held in Latin.

For hundreds of years, church leaders from the east and west worked together peacefully despite their differences. However, the differences between their ideas continued to grow. In time the differences led to divisions within the Christian Church. In the 1000s the split between east and west became official. Eastern Christians formed what became known as the Orthodox Church. As a result, eastern and western Europe were divided by religion.

READING CHECK Contrasting What led to a split in the Christian Church?

SUMMARY AND PREVIEW The Roman Empire and the Christian Church both divided into two parts. As Christianity became a major force in the Byzantine Empire, a civilization across the world was reaching its height. You will read about this civilization—the Maya—in the next chapter.

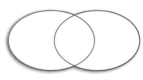

Section 2 Assessment

go.hrw.com
Online Quiz
KEYWORD: SQ6 HP14

Reviewing Ideas, Terms, and People HSS 7.1.3

1. **a. Describe** Where was Constantinople located?
   b. Summarize What were two of **Justinian**'s major accomplishments?
   c. Elaborate What do you think **Theodora**'s role in the government says about women in the eastern empire?

2. **a. Identify** What was one major difference between the powers of emperors in the east and the west?
   b. Explain How did contact with other cultures help change the **Byzantine Empire**?

3. **a. Define** What is a **mosaic**?
   b. Make Generalizations What led to the creation of two different Christian societies in Europe?

Critical Thinking

4. **Comparing and Contrasting** Draw a Venn diagram like the one shown here. In the left oval describe the western Roman Empire. In the right oval describe the eastern empire. Where the ovals overlap, list features the two had in common.

FOCUS ON SPEAKING

5. **Organizing Dates** Add key events from Byzantine history to the list you made in the last section. Once you have your list complete, arrange the events on your list in the order they happened.

Justinian and Theodora

How would you rebuild a fallen empire?

When did they live? Justinian, 483–565; Theodora, c. 500–548

Where did they live? Constantinople

What did they do? As Byzantine emperor, Justinian reconquered parts of the fallen western empire and simplified Roman laws. He also ordered the building of many beautiful public buildings and churches, including Hagia Sophia.

Why are they important?

Justinian and Theodora worked together to restore the power, beauty, and strength of the Roman Empire. They made Constantinople into a grand capital city and the center of a strong empire. While Justinian tried to reconquer the west, Theodora helped create laws to aid women and children and to end government corruption.

Evaluating Which of Justinian and Theodora's accomplishments do you find most impressive? Why?

KEY EVENTS

- **525** Justinian and Theodora are married.

- **527** Justinian becomes emperor and names Theodora empress.

- **532** Theodora persuades Justinian not to flee Constantinople during riots.

- **534** Justinian's Code is produced.

- **534–565** Justinian's armies reconquer parts of the Roman Empire, from North Africa to Italy to Spain.

Hagia Sophia rises high above Istanbul, Turkey, the city once called Constantinople.

Social Studies Skills

Analysis	Critical Thinking	Participation	Study

Chance, Error, and Oversight in History

Understand the Skill

History is nothing more than what people thought and did in the past, and the people of the past were just as human as people today. Like us, they occasionally forgot or overlooked things. They made mistakes in their decisions or judgments. Unexpected things happened that they couldn't control. Sometimes, these oversights, errors, and just plain luck shaped history.

Learn the Skill

This chapter notes several examples of the role of error, chance, and oversight in history.

1 **Error:** The Gothic chief Alaric offered peace with Rome in return for land and supplies for his people. Rome's leaders paid for many years, but then they stopped. Stopping the payments was a mistake, because Alaric attacked and looted Rome in 410. For the first time in 800 years, Rome fell to an outside invader.

2 **Chance:** In 452 Attila the Hun attacked northern Italy. After several victories, however, he halted his invasion and turned back. Southern Italy was suffering from a plague, and Attila did not want to risk weakening his army by entering the region. If not for this chance occurrence, Rome might have been conquered again.

3 **Oversight:** Emperor Justinian's subjects failed to appreciate his wife's importance. Theodora was a commoner, so they gave her little respect. When they launched a revolt in 532, Justinian was ready to flee. However, Theodora gave a powerful speech about the rewards of risking one's life for a great cause. Her speech inspired Justinian's supporters to attack and defeat the rebels.

Practice and Apply the Skill

As you read in the chapter, military leaders ruled the western empire by the 450s. Analyze the reasons for this development. Write a paragraph to explain how chance, error, or oversight influenced this shift in power in Rome.

Visual Summary

Use the visual summary below to help you review the main ideas of the chapter.

Western Roman Empire
Eastern Roman Empire

The eastern Byzantine Empire remained after the Roman Empire fell and was an important center of Christianity and trade.

Barbarian invasions and internal problems caused the split and collapse of the Roman Empire.

Reviewing Vocabulary, Terms, and People

Unscramble each group of letters below to spell a term that matches the given definition.

1. **anzbtinye**—name given to the eastern half of the Roman Empire
2. **latcodeiin**—emperor who divided the Roman Empire into two parts
3. **zticeins**—people who had the right to participate in Rome's government
4. **ohtradoe**—empress of the Byzantine Empire
5. **rcotponiur**—the decay of people's values
6. **smiacso**—pictures made from pieces of colorful glass or stone
7. **vlsioc**—powerful Frankish king
8. **tatali**—leader of the Huns who invaded Rome in the 400s
9. **njiasunti**—Byzantine emperor who tried to reunite the entire Roman Empire

Comprehension and Critical Thinking

SECTION 1 *(Pages 408–413)* **HSS** 7.1.2

10. **a. Identify** Who were the Huns? Who were the Goths?

    b. Compare and Contrast What did Diocletian and Constantine have in common? How did their actions differ?

    c. Evaluate Of all the causes for the fall of the western Roman Empire, which, if any, could have been prevented? Explain your answer.

SECTION 2 *(Pages 414–418)* **HSS** 7.1.3

11. **a. Identify** Who were Justinian and Theodora, and what did they accomplish?

    b. Contrast In what ways was the Byzantine Empire different from the western Roman Empire?

    c. Elaborate Would Constantinople have been an exciting place to visit in the 500s? Why or why not?

Social Studies Skills

Recognizing Chance, Oversight, and Error in History *Answer the following questions about the role of chance, oversight, or error in history.*

12. Would you consider the decision by Rome's leaders to stop paying Alaric and the Goths an error in judgment? Why or why not?

13. Attila planned to lead the Huns in an attack on the eastern Roman Empire in 453, but he died of a nosebleed the night of his wedding that year. How might history have been different if Attila had not happened to die?

14. How might the revolt against Justinian in 532 have been caused by an oversight on his part? What might he have done to prevent the revolt?

Using the Internet

go.hrw.com
KEYWORD: SQ6 WH14

15. Activity: Summarizing Most law students are required to learn about Justinian's Code because it had such a strong influence on modern law. Enter the keyword. Then create a chart like the one below that summarizes the ways in which Justinian's Code influences modern issues such as the rights and responsibilities of individuals. Explain how values such as an individual's right to equality before the law influenced the world. You may be asked to present your summaries to the class.

Justinian's Code	Modern Issues

Reviewing Themes

16. Politics How did weak government and ineffective leaders help lead to the end of the western Roman Empire?

17. Religion Do you agree or disagree with this statement: By the 1000s, Europe was divided into two distinct Christian societies. Why or why not?

Reading Skills

Understanding Bias and Stereotypes *The passage below is taken from a Roman historian's description of Attila, the leader of the Huns. Read the passage and then answer the questions that follow.*

> "A lavish meal, served on silver trenchers, was prepared for us and the other barbarians, but Attila just had some meat on a wooden platter, for this was one aspect of his self-discipline. For instance, gold or silver cups were presented to the other diners, but his own goblet was made of wood. His clothes, too, were simple, and no trouble was taken except to have them clean. The sword that hung by his side, the clasps of his barbarian shoes and the bridle of his horse were all free from gold, precious stones or other valuable decorations affected by the other Scythians ... As twilight came on torches were lit, and two barbarians entered before Attila to sing some songs they had composed, telling of his victories and valour in war. The guests paid close attention to them, and some were delighted with the songs, others excited at being reminded of the wars, but others broke down and wept if their bodies were weakened by age and their warrior spirits forced to remain inactive."
>
> –Priscus, quoted in *Eyewitness to History*, edited by John Carey

18. What does the word *barbarian* suggest that Priscus thought of Attila and his allies? What do you think he expected the Huns to be like?

19. How does Priscus think the Huns view war? How can you tell?

20. Does Priscus appear to have let his opinions color his description of Attila? Why or why not?

FOCUS ON SPEAKING

21. Presenting a Narrative Poem Look back over the details and events you listed while reading this chapter. Choose five or six of these events to include in your poem. Write your poem. In the first one or two lines, introduce the subject. Write five or six more lines, each about one event that occurred during Rome's decline. Then write one or two lines about the importance of the fall of Rome. Once you have finished writing, present your poem. Practice altering your voice and the rhythm of your words to make your poem more interesting to listeners.

Standards Assessment

DIRECTIONS: Read each question, and write the letter of the best response.

1

> - Empire is ruled by all-powerful emperors.
> - Emperors are both religious leaders and political leaders.
> - Women have significant roles in government.
> - Greek, Egyptian, and Muslim cultural influences shape society.
> - People practice the Orthodox Christian religion.
> - People identify themselves as Romans.

The six characteristics listed above describe

A the eastern Roman Empire.

B the western Roman Empire.

C both the eastern and western empires.

D neither the eastern nor the western empire.

2 Byzantine artists were known *especially* for creating colorful

A statues.

B mosaics.

C frescoes.

D pottery.

3 Which of the following was *not* a reason for the fall of the Roman Empire?

A the empire's vast size

B corruption in Roman government

C pressure on the Goths from the Huns

D the influence of Greek government

4 The eastern Roman Empire is also known as the

A Holy Roman Empire.

B Eastern Orthodox Empire.

C Ottoman Empire.

D Byzantine Empire.

5 In 410 the city of Rome was destroyed for the first time in 800 years by the army of a foreign people called the

A Huns.

B Vandals.

C Goths.

D Franks.

Connecting with Past Learnings

6 Constantine unified the entire Roman Empire and introduced a new religion into the Roman government. Which leader that you learned about earlier in this course is known for his similar accomplishments?

A Asoka

B Hammurabi

C Alexander

D Piankhi

7 Earlier in this course you learned that the Persians threatened Greek civilization for a time. All of the following peoples played a similar role in Roman history *except* the

A Byzantines.

B Goths.

C Vandals.

D Huns.

CHAPTER 15

12,000 BC–AD 1000

The Early Americas

California Standards

History–Social Science

7.7 Students compare and contrast the geographic, political, economic, religious, and social structures of the Meso-American and Andean civilizations.

Analysis Skill

HR 3 Distinguish relevant from irrelevant, essential from incidental, and verifiable from unverifiable information.

English–Language Arts

Writing 7.1.2 Support all statements and claims with anecdotes, descriptions, facts and statistics, and specific examples.

Reading 7.2.6 Assess the adequacy, accuracy, and appropriateness of the author's evidence.

 FOCUS ON WRITING

A Travel Brochure Each year, millions of people visit the places you'll read about in this chapter. Try your hand at writing part of a brochure for a historical tour of the early Americas. As you read, you'll discover spots you won't want to miss.

CHAPTER EVENTS

c. 12,000–10,000 BC
The first people arrive in the Americas.

12,000 BC

WORLD EVENTS

c. 5000 BC
Irrigation is used in Mesopotamia and Egypt.

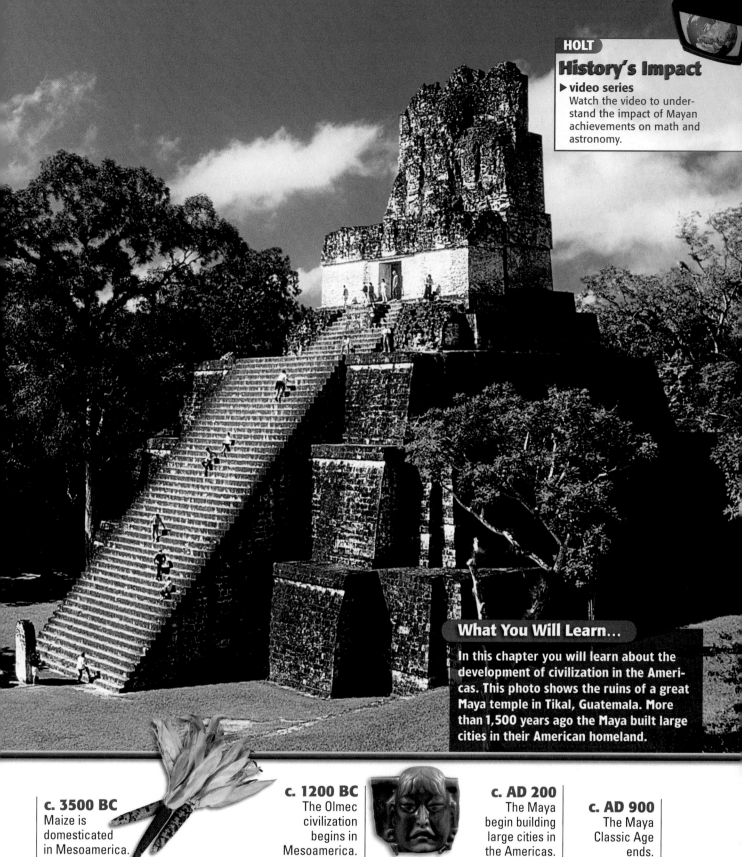

What You Will Learn...

In this chapter you will learn about the development of civilization in the Americas. This photo shows the ruins of a great Maya temple in Tikal, Guatemala. More than 1,500 years ago the Maya built large cities in their American homeland.

c. 3500 BC
Maize is domesticated in Mesoamerica.

c. 1200 BC
The Olmec civilization begins in Mesoamerica.

c. AD 200
The Maya begin building large cities in the Americas.

c. AD 900
The Maya Classic Age ends.

3000 BC	2000 BC	1000 BC	BC 1 AD	AD 1000

c. 3000 BC
Egyptians begin to write using hieroglyphics.

c. 500 BC
Athens develops the world's first democracy.

AD 476
The Roman Empire falls.

THE EARLY AMERICAS **425**

Focus on Themes In this chapter, you will read about the development of civilizations in Mesoamerica, which is in the southern part of North America, and in the Andes, which is in South America. As you read about the Olmec and Maya in Mesoamerica and Chavín in South America, you will see how the **geography** of the areas affected their way of life. You will learn that these ancient civilizations made interesting advancements in **science and technology**.

Analyzing Historical Information

Focus on Reading History books are full of information. As you read, you are confronted with names, dates, places, terms, and descriptions on every page. Because you're faced with so much information, you don't want to have to deal with unimportant or untrue material in a history book.

Identifying Relevant and Essential Information Information in a history book should be relevant, or related to the topic you're studying. It should also be essential, or necessary, to understanding that topic. Anything that is not relevant or essential distracts from the important material you are studying.

The passage below comes from an encyclopedia, but some irrelevant and nonessential information has been added so that you can learn to identify it.

The Maya

The first sentence of the paragraph expresses the main idea. Anything that does not support this idea is nonessential.

This paragraph discusses Maya communication. Any other topics are irrelevant.

Who They Were Maya were an American Indian people who developed a magnificent civilization in Mesoamerica, which is the southern part of North America. They built their largest cities between AD 250 and 900. Today, many people travel to Central America to see Maya ruins.

Communication The Maya developed an advanced form of writing that used many symbols. Our writing system uses 26 letters. They recorded information on large stone monuments. Some early civilizations drew pictures on cave walls. The Maya also made books of paper made from the fig tree bark. Fig trees need a lot of light.

The last sentence does not support the main idea and is nonessential.

The needs of fig trees have nothing to do with Maya communication. This sentence is irrelevant.

Portions of this text and the one on the next page were taken from the 2004 World Book Online Reference Center.

Additional reading support can be found in the

Inter active

Reader and Study Guide

HSS Analysis HR 3 Distinguish relevant from irrelevant information.
ELA 7.2.6 Assess the adequacy, accuracy, and appropriateness of the author's evidence.

You Try It!

The following passage has some sentences that aren't important, necessary, or relevant. Read the passage and identify those sentences.

The Maya Way of Life

Religion The Maya believed in many gods and goddesses. More than 160 gods and goddesses are named in a single Maya manuscript. Among the gods they worshipped were a corn god, a rain god, a sun god, and a moon goddess. The early Greeks also worshipped many gods and goddesses.

Family and Social Structure Whole families of Maya—including parents, children, and grandparents—lived together. Not many houses today could hold all those people. Each family member had tasks to do. Men and boys, for example, worked in the fields. Very few people are farmers today. Women and older girls made clothes and meals for the rest of the family. Now most people buy their clothes.

After you read the passage, answer the following questions.

1. Which sentence in the first paragraph is irrelevant to the topic? How can you tell?

2. Which three sentences in the second paragraph are not essential to learning about the Maya? Do those sentences belong in this passage?

Key Terms and People

Chapter 15

Section 1
Mesoamerica *(p. 428)*
maize *(p. 431)*

Section 2
obsidian *(p. 434)*
Pacal *(p. 436)*

Section 3
observatories *(p. 442)*
Popol Vuh *(p. 443)*

Academic Vocabulary

Success in school is related to knowing academic vocabulary—the words that are frequently used in school assignments and discussions. In this chapter, you will learn the following academic words:

rebel *(p. 438)*
aspects *(p. 441)*

As you read **Chapter 15**, notice how the writers have left out information that is not essential or relevant to what you are reading.

Geography and Early Cultures

Main Ideas

1. The geography of the Americas is varied with a wide range of landforms.
2. The first people to arrive in the Americas were hunter-gatherers.
3. The development of farming led to early settlements in the Americas.

The Big Idea

The landforms and climate of the Americas affected farming and the development of early cultures.

Key Terms

Mesoamerica, *p. 428*
maize, *p. 431*

HSS **7.7.1** Study the locations, landforms, and climates of Mexico, Central America, and South America and their effects on Mayan, Aztec, and Incan economies, trade, and development of urban societies.

If **YOU** were there...

You are a hunter-gatherer in North America. All of your life you have been moving south, following herds of animals. This year you have found a place where the climate is warmer and there are more kinds of plants to eat. Some people say this would be a good place to stay and make a permanent home. But others think you need to keep moving.

Do you think your people should keep going or settle down in this new place? Why?

BUILDING BACKGROUND The first people to arrive in the Americas were hunter-gatherers. Their ability to find food greatly depended on the geography of this new land.

Geography of the Americas

Two continents—North America and South America—make up the region we call the Americas. These two continents have a wide range of landforms and climates.

The northern continent, North America, has high mountains, desert plateaus, grassy plains, and forests. Look at the map to find the location of some of these physical features. In the northern part of the continent, the climate is cold and icy. Temperatures get warmer toward the south.

In the southern part of North America lies Mesoamerica. **Mesoamerica** is a region that includes the southern part of what is now Mexico and parts of the northern countries of Central America. Steamy rain forests cover some of this region. In some places, volcanoes rise above the forest. Their activity over the years has made the surrounding soil very fertile. Fertile mountain valleys, rivers, and a warm climate make Mesoamerica good for farming. In fact, the first farmers in the Americas domesticated plants in Mesoamerica.

The Americas: Physical

160° W 140° W

ARCTIC OCEAN

BROOKS RANGE

Greenland

Baffin Island

Bering Strait

Bering Sea

Gulf of Alaska

Aleutian Islands

Hudson Bay

Labrador Sea

60° N

NORTH AMERICA

ROCKY MOUNTAINS

GREAT PLAINS

APPALACHIAN MTS.

ATLANTIC OCEAN

40° N

PACIFIC OCEAN

In North America, long mountain ranges run from north to south, and rolling plains occupy the heart of the continent.

Tropic of Cancer

Hawaiian Islands

Gulf of Mexico

Mesoamerica

Yucatán Peninsula

West Indies

Mesoamerica has large areas of rain forest and a warm climate that is good for farming.

Area of Inset Map

Caribbean Sea

In South America, the Andes Mountains run along the western edge of the continent, and the Amazon Basin dominates the east.

Equator 0°

AMAZON BASIN

SOUTH AMERICA

ANDES MOUNTAINS

BRAZILIAN HIGHLANDS

Mesoamerica

SIERRA MADRE OCCIDENTAL

SIERRA MADRE ORIENTAL

Gulf of Mexico

Cape Catoche

Cozumel

Mesoamerica

Pico de Orizaba 18,700 ft. (5,700 m)

Yucatán Peninsula

20° N

Oaxaca Plateau

Isthmus of Tehuantepec

SIERRA MADRE DEL SUR

Gulf of Tehuantepec

Gulf of Honduras

PACIFIC OCEAN

Atacama Desert

20° S

Tropic of Capricorn

PAMPAS

ELEVATION

Feet	Meters
13,120	4,000
6,560	2,000
1,640	500
656	200
(Sea level) 0	0 (Sea level)

40° S

0   750   1,500 Miles

0   750   1,500 Kilometers

0   200   400 Miles

0   200   400 Kilometers

100° W   90° W

Strait of Magellan

Tierra del Fuego

80° W   60° W   40° W

Cape Horn

GEOGRAPHY SKILLS   **INTERPRETING MAPS**

1. **Location** Describe the relative location of Mesoamerica.
2. **Place** What is the name of the large peninsula in eastern Mesoamerica?

Like North America, South America has many different kinds of landforms. The towering Andes Mountains run along the western shore of the continent. There, a narrow desert sits on the edge of rich fishing waters in the Pacific Ocean. East of the Andes lies the Amazon region—a huge, hot, and wet rain forest. The mighty Amazon River drains this region. As you will see, the geography of the Americas played an important role in the development of early societies there.

READING CHECK **Comparing** What kinds of landforms and climates do North and South America have in common?

The First People Arrive

No one is sure how the first people got to the Americas or when they arrived. Most historians think they came to North America from Asia by 12,000 BC. They probably walked across a land bridge that crossed the Bering Strait. A land bridge may have formed there during the ice ages when ocean levels dropped and exposed land.

Most scientists accept the theory of the land bridge to explain how the first people came to the Americas. But some scientists today are challenging that theory. They think the first Americans may have arrived even earlier—perhaps by sea.

Regardless of how they arrived, the first people to arrive in the Americas were hunter-gatherers. They hunted herds of large animals that wandered the land. These animals, including bison and huge woolly mammoths, provided their main food source. Early people also gathered fruits, nuts, and wild grains to eat. Early people didn't settle in one place very long, because they were always looking for food.

Eventually, some early people began to settle down. They formed small settlements on the coasts of North and South America, where they fished and gathered food. As populations grew, people started to experiment with seeds.

READING CHECK **Drawing Inferences** How do you think the geography of the Americas affected early peoples' search for food?

Migration to the Americas

ASIA

BERINGIA

Bering Strait

ARCTIC OCEAN

NORTH AMERICA

ATLANTIC OCEAN

Gulf of Mexico

PACIFIC OCEAN

SOUTH AMERICA

Possible land route
Possible sea route
Glacier
Sea ice

0   750   1,500 Miles
0   750   1,500 Kilometers

GEOGRAPHY SKILLS **INTERPRETING MAPS**

1. **Place** According to the map, from which continent did the first Americans come?
2. **Movement** The coastal route runs along which American coast—east or west?

Farming and Settlement

From their experiments with seeds, people eventually learned to farm. Farming allowed people to stop following animal herds and settle permanently in one place.

First Farming Settlements

The first permanent farming settlements in the Americas appeared in Mesoamerica. This region had rich soils, warm temperatures, and plenty of rain. By 3500 BC people in Mesoamerica were growing **maize** (MAYZ), or corn. Later they learned to grow beans and squash. By growing these foods, settlements could support larger populations. More advanced societies grew, and people began to focus on activities such as building, trade, art, and organized religion. Eventually, settlements developed into towns and cities.

The Olmec

The Olmec (OHL-mek) formed the first urban civilization in Mesoamerica around 1200 BC. Most Olmec lived in small villages, but some lived in larger towns. These towns were religious and government centers with temples and plazas. Impressive sculptures and buildings mark the Olmec as the first complex civilization in the Americas. They built the first pyramids in the Americas. They also made sculptures of huge stone heads. Each head probably represented a different Olmec ruler. Other sculptures, such as jaguars, probably represented Olmec gods.

Other factors that may mark the Olmec as a complex civilization are writing and scientific study. Some researchers think the Olmec may have developed the first writing system in the Americas. Scientists recently found an Olmec artifact with symbols that might be an early form of writing. The Olmec may have also had a calendar.

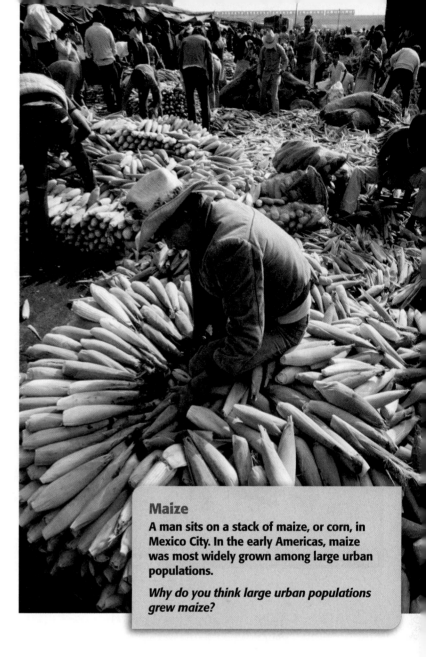

Maize

A man sits on a stack of maize, or corn, in Mexico City. In the early Americas, maize was most widely grown among large urban populations.

Why do you think large urban populations grew maize?

The Olmec civilization also had a large trading network. Villages traded with each other and with other peoples farther away. The Olmec may have even established a string of trading colonies along the Pacific coast. Through trade the Olmec got valuable goods such as the stones they used for building and sculpture.

Olmec civilization ended around 400 BC. By then trade had spread Olmec influence around Mesoamerica. Later peoples were able to build on their achievements. Some later peoples in Mesoamerica also followed some Olmec traditions.

POINTS OF VIEW
Views of Writing

Scientists have discovered an Olmec roller used for printing symbols. It may be evidence of the earliest writing system in the Americas. Some people don't believe the Olmec had a written language. Scientists disagree on what defines a written language. Some scientists think written language must include symbols that stand for sounds—not just for images.

"Even if you have symbols—like a light bulb in a cartoon—that's not writing.**"**

–**David Grove,**
Professor Emeritus of Anthropology,
University of Illinois Urbana–Champaign

Other scientists think a system of symbols is a form of written communication. The symbols do not have to represent sound or spoken language. These scientists think written communication is the same thing as written language.

"We're not arguing that we have phonetics (sounds). But we say we do have logographs (symbols representing words), and we're arguing the Maya copied this. We have a system here that goes back to the Olmec.**"**

–**Mary E. D. Pohl,**
Professor of Anthropology, Florida State University

ANALYSIS SKILL **ANALYZING POINTS OF VIEW**

Why might it be hard to define written language?

Farming and the Growth of Other Civilizations

Early civilizations also developed in other parts of the Americas. As in Mesoamerica, people in North and South America formed civilizations after they domesticated plants and learned how to farm.

About the time Mesoamericans started growing maize, South Americans in the Andes started growing potatoes. Later, maize farming spread south into the Andes from Mesoamerica. By about 2000 BC, South Americans were growing maize and beans as well as potatoes.

A number of small civilizations developed in South America, but the first major civilization began in the Andes. It is known as the Chavín (chah-VEEN) culture, and it lasted from about 900 to 200 BC. Its city was a major religious and trading center. The Chavín culture is known for its woven textiles, carved stone monuments, and pottery shaped like animals and humans.

Several hundred years after farming began in South America, maize farming also spread north from Mesoamerica. People began growing maize in what is now the southwestern United States. The dry climate made farming difficult there, so people learned to choose fertile soils and use river water to irrigate their crops. Eventually maize became an important crop to people in the region. It was the main food of people in hundreds of small villages.

FOCUS ON READING

What is the purpose of this paragraph? Are any sentences irrelevant?

This Native American legend reveals the importance of maize, or corn:

"The breaths of the corn maidens blew rain-clouds from their homes in the Summer-land, and when the rains had passed away green corn plants grew everywhere the grains had been planted."

—Zuni legend, quoted in *Kingdoms of Gold, Kingdoms of Jade* by Brian Fagan

The development of farming was important in the growth of civilizations all over the Americas. As with other peoples you have studied, a steady food supply led to population growth. Farming also encouraged people to establish permanent villages and cities.

READING CHECK Finding Main Ideas How did farming influence settlement patterns in the Americas?

SUMMARY AND PREVIEW You have learned that geography affected settlement and farming in the Americas. Early civilizations, such as the Olmec and Chavín, developed there. In Section 2 you will learn about a later civilization influenced by the Olmec—the Maya.

Early Civilizations in the Americas

NORTH AMERICA

ATLANTIC OCEAN

Gulf of Mexico

Caribbean Sea

PACIFIC OCEAN

ANDES

SOUTH AMERICA

ANDES

Olmec, 1200–400 BC
Chavín, 900–200 BC

0   200   400 Miles
0   200   400 Kilometers

GEOGRAPHY SKILLS **INTERPRETING MAPS**

Location Which early civilization was located in Mesoamerica?

Section 1 Assessment

Reviewing Ideas, Terms, and People **HSS** 7.7.1

1. **a. Recall** Where is **Mesoamerica**?
   b. Explain In what ways is the geography of Mesoamerica good for agriculture?
2. **a. Identify** What landform do most scientists think the first people crossed to reach America?
   b. Make Inferences Why do you think scientists aren't sure how the first people came to the Americas?
3. **a. Identify** What was the first crop domesticated in Mesoamerica?
   b. Predict How might the Olmec civilization have influenced later civilizations in Mesoamerica?

Critical Thinking

4. **Sequencing** Draw the graphic organizer below. Use it to show how the development of maize farming laid the foundation for cultural advances.

   Maize Farming → ☐ → ☐ → ☐

FOCUS ON WRITING

5. **Taking Notes about Early Settlements in the Americas** Note where people first settled in the Americas. What sites would show how early hunter-gatherers and farmers lived? What geographical features are important to mention?

The Maya

If YOU were there...

You live in a village in the lowlands of Mesoamerica. Your family members have always been weavers, and now your aunts are teaching you to weave cloth from the cotton grown by nearby farmers. Traders from other areas often pass through your village. They tell wonderful stories about strange animals and sights they see in their travels. After talking to the traders who buy your cloth, you begin to think about becoming a trader, too.

Why might you want to become a trader?

BUILDING BACKGROUND Through trade, people get resources unavailable in their own natural environment. The natural environment, or geography, of Mesoamerica affected how a people called the Maya lived.

Geography Affects Early Maya

The Maya (MY-uh) civilization developed in Mesoamerica. Early Maya lived in the lowlands of this region beginning around 1000 BC. Thick forests covered most of the land, so the Maya had to clear wooded areas for farmland. Like earlier Mesoamericans, the Maya grew maize and other crops.

Although the thick forests made farming hard, they provided valuable resources. Forest animals such as deer and monkeys were a source of food. In addition, trees and other plants made good building materials. For example, the Maya used wood poles and vines, along with mud, to build their houses.

The early Maya lived in small villages. Eventually these villages started trading with one another. They traded goods such as cloth and **obsidian**, a sharp, glasslike volcanic rock, that came from different parts of Mesoamerica. As trade helped support larger populations, villages grew. By about AD 200 the Maya were building large cities in the Americas.

READING CHECK Finding Main Ideas What were two ways in which the early Maya relied on their physical environment?

Maya Classic Age

The Maya civilization reached its height between about AD 250 and 900. Historians call this period of Maya history the Classic Age. During the Classic Age, Maya civilization spread to the Yucatán Peninsula and grew to include more than 40 cities of 5,000 to 50,000 people each.

Trade

Maya cities in the highlands traded with those in the lowlands. In this way people all over Maya territory got things that they didn't have nearby.

Look at the trade routes on the map to see the goods that were available in different areas of Mesoamerica. For example, the warm lowlands were good for growing cotton, rubber trees, and cacao (kuh-KOW) beans, the source of chocolate. Cacao beans had great value. Chocolate was known as the food of rulers and of the gods. The Maya even used cacao beans as money.

Lowland crops didn't grow well in the cool highlands. Instead, the highlands had valuable stones such as jade and obsidian. People carried these and other products along Maya trade routes.

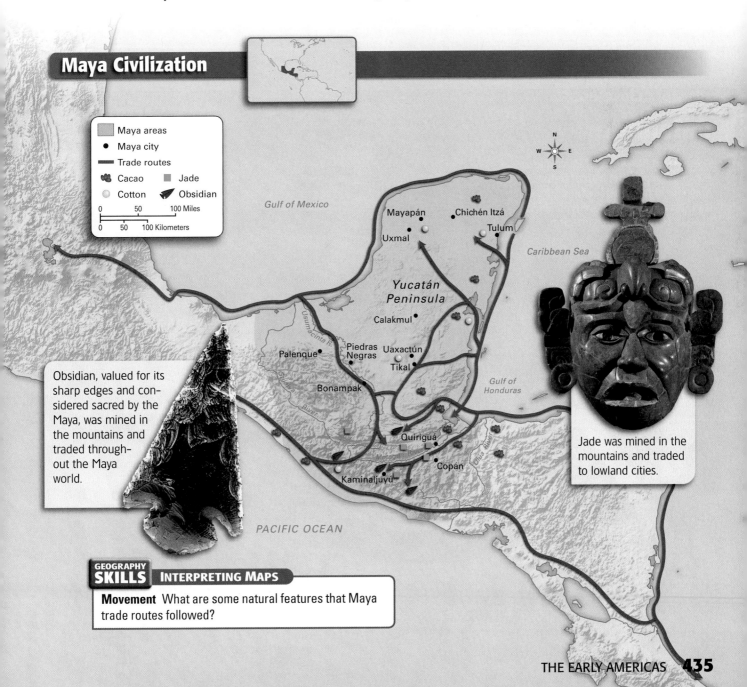

Maya Civilization

Obsidian, valued for its sharp edges and considered sacred by the Maya, was mined in the mountains and traded throughout the Maya world.

Jade was mined in the mountains and traded to lowland cities.

GEOGRAPHY SKILLS INTERPRETING MAPS

Movement What are some natural features that Maya trade routes followed?

Cities

Maya cities had many grand buildings, including large stone pyramids, temples, and palaces. Some of these buildings honored local Maya kings. For example, in the city of Palenque (pah-LENG-kay), a temple honored the king **Pacal** (puh-KAHL). Pacal had the temple built to record his achievements as a ruler. Maya artists decorated temples and palaces with carvings and colorful paintings.

In addition to temples and palaces, the Maya also built structures to improve life in their cities. For example, builders paved large plazas for public gatherings, and they built canals to control the flow of water through their cities. Farmers shaped nearby hillsides into flat terraces so they could grow crops on them.

Most Maya cities also had a special ball court. People played or watched a type of ball game in these large stone arenas. Using only their heads, shoulders, or hips, players tried to bounce a heavy, hard rubber ball through a stone ring above their heads. Players weren't allowed to use their hands or feet. The winners were awarded jewels and clothing. The losers were sometimes killed. This ball game was one that the Maya had picked up from Olmec traditions.

History Close-up

Palenque

The ancient Maya city of Palenque was a major power on the border between the Maya highlands and lowlands. Its great temples and plazas were typical of the Classic Age of Maya civilization.

Flat terraces made more land usable for farming.

Priests led religious ceremonies from the tops of temples.

The Maya cities were really city-states. Each had its own government and its own king. No single ruler united the many cities into one empire.

Warfare

Conflicts between cities often led to fighting. Maya cities usually battled each other to gain power and land. For example, the city of Tikal (tee-KAHL) fought many battles with its rival Calakmul (kah-lahk-MOOL). Both cities wanted to control a smaller city that lay between them. Power shifted back and forth between the two larger cities for years.

Maya warfare was bloody. Warriors fought hand-to-hand using spears, flint knives, and wooden clubs. The Maya often captured enemy prisoners and killed them in religious ceremonies as a sacrifice to their gods. They burned enemy towns and villages. Warfare probably tore up the land and destroyed crops. Maya warfare was so destructive that some scholars think it may have contributed to the end of the Maya civilization.

READING CHECK **Summarizing** What were two ways Maya cities interacted with each other?

Maya temples were shaped like mountains, which the Maya considered sacred because they allowed people to approach the gods.

BIOGRAPHY

Pacal
603–683

Pacal became king of the Maya city of Palenque when he was just 12 years old. As king, Pacal led many important community events, such as religious dances and public meetings. When he died he was buried at the bottom of the pyramid-shaped Temple of the Inscriptions.

Maya buildings were covered with stucco and painted in bright colors.

ANALYSIS SKILL **ANALYZING VISUALS**

In what ways might Palenque's setting have helped the city? In what ways might it have hurt the city?

THE EARLY AMERICAS **437**

Maya Civilization Declines

THE IMPACT TODAY

Many Maya still live in villages throughout Meso-america. Others have moved to big cities.

Maya civilization began to collapse in the 900s. People stopped building temples and other structures. They left the cities and moved back to the countryside. What caused this collapse? Historians aren't sure, but they do have some theories.

One theory says that increased warfare brought about the end of the Maya Classic Age. A related theory is that, as cities grew, perhaps the Maya could not grow enough food to feed everyone. Growing the same crops year after year might have left the soil too weak for farming. As a result, competition between cities for land may have increased. This competition could have led to even more warfare than before. Increased warfare would have destroyed more crops and made farming more difficult.

Another possible cause of the decline of Maya civilization is the demands Maya kings made on their people. Kings forced people to build huge temples or farm for them. Maybe people didn't want to work for the kings. They might have **rebelled** or left the cities because of these demands.

ACADEMIC VOCABULARY

rebel to fight against authority

Some historians also think climate might have played a role in the collapse of Maya civilization. Scientists have learned that the region suffered from a long dry period and droughts for about 150 years. This dry period took place about the time the Maya moved away from their cities. A drier climate and droughts would have made it hard to grow enough food to feed everyone in the cities.

Most researchers agree that there was probably no single event that caused the end of the Classic Age. More likely, a mix of several factors led to the decline of the Maya civilization.

READING CHECK **Drawing Inferences** Why do you think scientists aren't sure what caused the end of Maya civilization?

SUMMARY AND PREVIEW You have learned that the Maya built a great civilization, but it collapsed for what were probably several reasons. In Section 3 you will learn more about what Maya life and society was like at its height.

Section 2 Assessment

go.hrw.com
Online Quiz
KEYWORD: SQ6 HP15

Reviewing Ideas, Terms, and People   HSS 7.7.1, 7.7.3

1. **a. Recall** What resources did the Maya get from the forest?
   b. Make Inferences How might the Maya have used **obsidian**?
2. **a. Identify** Who was an important king of Palenque?
   b. Make Generalizations Why did Maya cities fight each other?
3. **a. Describe** What happened to Maya civilization in the 900s?
   b. Analyze In what way did growth of cities, warfare, and drought possibly affect Maya civilization?
   c. Elaborate What might scientists study to find out about the end of Maya civilization?

Critical Thinking

4. **Identifying Cause and Effect** Draw a diagram like the one to the right. Use it to show four possible causes for the decline of the Classic Age in Maya civilization.

Decline of Maya Civilization

FOCUS ON WRITING

5. **Gathering Information about the Maya** Much of the tour would likely be devoted to the Maya. Use the maps and pictures in this chapter to help you choose which places to write about. What areas and features of each site would you point out? What would you say about the history of these different places?

Maya Life and Society

If YOU were there...

You are a Maya farmer, growing corn on a farm near the city. Often you enter the city to join the crowd at a religious ceremony. You watch the king and his priests, standing at the top of a tall pyramid. They wear capes of brightly colored feathers and many heavy gold ornaments that glitter like the sun. As the king offers a sacrifice to the gods, a ray of sun strikes the pyramid.

How do these ceremonies make you feel about your king?

> **BUILDING BACKGROUND** Fancy clothes and important responsibilities showed the role kings and priests played in Maya society. The roles people played determined what their daily life was like.

Roles in Maya Society

Maya society had a complex class structure. As you might expect, life for the upper social classes differed greatly from life for the lower classes.

Upper Class

The upper class of Maya society included different groups of people. The king held the highest position in society. Priests, warriors, and merchants were also part of the upper class.

What You Will Learn...

Main Ideas

1. Roles in Maya society were based on a complex class structure.
2. Religion in Maya society was often bloody.
3. The Maya made achievements in art, science, math, and writing.

The Big Idea

People played different roles in Maya society, but together they made great achievements in art, science, math, and writing.

Key Terms

observatories, *p. 442*
Popol Vuh, *p. 443*

HSS 7.7.2 Study the roles of people in each society, including class structures, family life, warfare, religious beliefs and practices, and slavery.

7.7.4 Describe the artistic and oral traditions and architecture in the three civilizations.

7.7.5 Describe the Meso-American achievements in astronomy and mathematics, including the development of the calendar and the Meso-American knowledge of seasonal changes to the civilizations' agricultural systems.

Maya society had a rigid class structure.

An attendant brings gifts to two Maya rulers.

THE EARLY AMERICAS **439**

The Maya believed their rulers were related to the gods. For this reason, rulers were often involved in religious ceremonies. They also led battles. As the richest people in Maya society, rulers had beautiful clothing and jewelry. Kings wore huge feather headdresses and capes of cotton, jaguar skins, and feathers.

Priests were usually born into their role in Maya society. They led religious ceremonies. They were also the most educated people. Priests used their knowledge of astronomy and math to plan the best times for religious ceremonies.

Professional warriors fought battles against other Maya cities. In battle, these warriors wore animal headdresses, jade jewelry, and jaguar-skin capes. They painted their bodies red and black.

Merchants directed trade among the cities. They organized the transportation and distribution of goods. They also supervised the people who carried goods between cities. Together, the members of the upper class controlled the politics, religion, and economy in Maya society.

Lower Classes

Although the upper classes had the most power, most Maya belonged to the lower classes as farming families. These Maya lived in small houses outside the cities. Girls learned from their mothers how to cook, make yarn, and weave. Women cared for children. Men crafted household tools such as knives. They had to provide food for their family, so they also spent a lot of time hunting and farming. They kept small gardens next to their houses and worked together to farm larger fields.

Farmers had to give some of their crops to their rulers. Lower-class Maya also had to "pay" their rulers with goods such as cloth and salt. They had to work on building temples, palaces, and other buildings.

They also had to serve in the army during times of war. If captured in battle, a lower-class man usually became a slave.

Slaves held the lowest position in society. Orphans, slaves' children, and people who owed money also became slaves. Slaves had to carry trade goods between cities. They also served upper-class Maya by working as farmers or household servants.

The lower class supported the upper class with food and labor, but the upper class also helped the lower class. For example, upper-class Maya led the religious ceremonies that were vital to daily life for all classes of society.

READING CHECK **Identifying Cause and Effect**
How might one become a slave in Maya society?

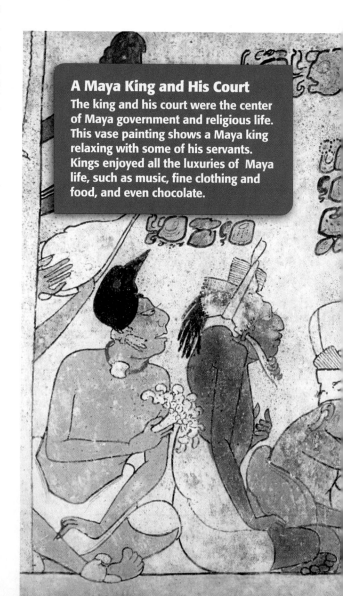

A Maya King and His Court
The king and his court were the center of Maya government and religious life. This vase painting shows a Maya king relaxing with some of his servants. Kings enjoyed all the luxuries of Maya life, such as music, fine clothing and food, and even chocolate.

Religion

The Maya worshipped many gods related to different **aspects** of their daily life. The most important god was the creator. This god would take many different forms. Others included a sun god, moon goddess, and maize god. The Maya believed their kings communicated with the gods.

According to Maya beliefs, the gods could be helpful or harmful, so people tried to please the gods to get their help. The Maya believed their gods needed blood to prevent disasters or the end of the world. Every person offered blood to the gods by piercing their tongue or skin. The Maya sometimes held special ceremonies to give blood at events such as births, weddings, and funerals.

On special occasions the Maya believed they needed extra amounts of blood. On these occasions they made human sacrifices to their gods. They usually used prisoners captured in battle for this ritual. A priest would offer human hearts to stone carvings of gods. These sacrifices usually took place at a temple.

READING CHECK **Generalizing** Why did the Maya want to please their gods?

Achievements

The Maya's many artistic and architectural skills are reflected in their sculpture and in their temples. Maya achievements also included discoveries in science and math, as well as developments in writing.

ACADEMIC
VOCABULARY

aspects parts

The king is gazing at this mirror, which the Maya believed held magical powers.

A bodyguard stands behind the king.

These vases held a chocolate drink, a favorite of Maya nobles.

The fly whisk in the king's hand is a symbol of authority.

ANALYSIS SKILL **ANALYZING VISUALS**

What about the king indicates he is an important person?

441

Art and Architecture

Some of the best-known Maya art is their sculpture and their jade and gold jewelry. They carved stone sculptures of kings or gods for their cities.

Maya cities showed the talent of their architects and builders. The Maya built cities without using metal tools. They didn't even have wheeled vehicles to carry supplies. Instead, workers used obsidian tools to cut limestone into blocks. Then, to move the giant blocks, workers rolled them over logs and lifted them with ropes. It took many workers to build Maya cities, perhaps the most recognizable Maya achievement.

Science and Math

Maya achievements in science and math were just as important as their achievements in art and architecture. The Maya built **observatories**, or buildings to study astronomy, so their priests could study the stars. Maya astronomers figured out that a year is about 365 days long. They also learned about the cycles of the moon and how to predict eclipses.

Partly based on their discoveries in astronomy, the Maya developed calendars. They had a religious calendar to plan religious events. The Maya used a different calendar for agriculture. It had symbols for different months tied to farming activities such as planting or harvesting. These activities matched changes in the seasons. The Maya calendar was more accurate than the calendar used in Europe at that time.

To go along with their calendars, the Maya created a number system that included some new concepts in math. For example, the Maya were among the first people with a symbol for zero. The Maya used their number system to record important dates in their history.

Writing and Oral Traditions

The Maya also developed a writing system. It was similar to Egyptian hieroglyphics. Symbols represented both objects and sounds. The Maya created records, especially about achievements of their kings, by carving symbols into large stone tablets. They also wrote in bark-paper books.

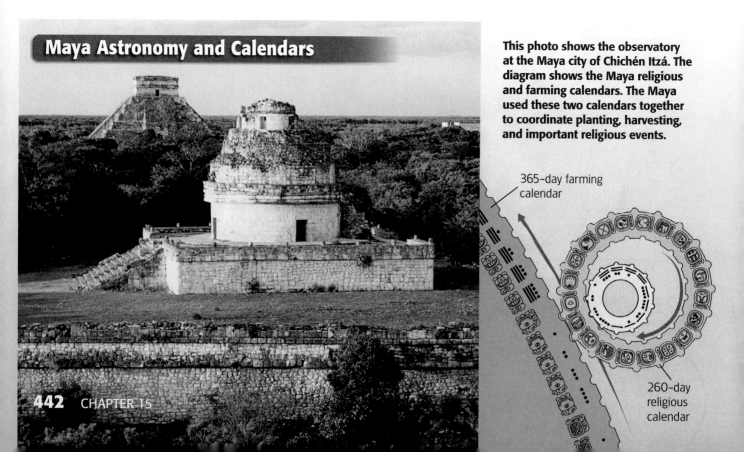

Maya Astronomy and Calendars

This photo shows the observatory at the Maya city of Chichén Itzá. The diagram shows the Maya religious and farming calendars. The Maya used these two calendars together to coordinate planting, harvesting, and important religious events.

365-day farming calendar

260-day religious calendar

ART
A Maya Carving

This carving comes from the palace at Yaxchilán (yahsh-chee-LAHN). The Maya recorded historical events on carvings like this one. Historians can now translate most Maya writing. They study the pictures and writings to learn about events in Maya history.

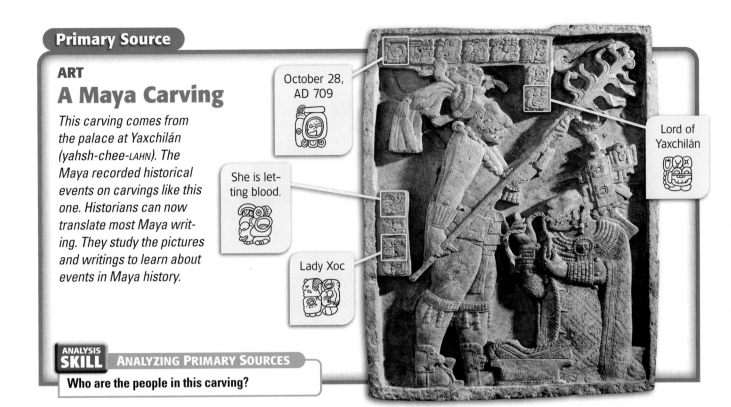

October 28, AD 709

She is letting blood.

Lady Xoc

Lord of Yaxchilán

ANALYSIS SKILL **ANALYZING PRIMARY SOURCES**
Who are the people in this carving?

Stories and poetry got passed down orally from one generation to the next. After the Spanish arrived, Maya legends and history were written in a book called the **Popol Vuh** (poh-pohl VOO). This book provides valuable information about the Maya.

READING CHECK **Analyzing** What activities did the Maya calendar regulate?

SUMMARY The Maya had a complex social structure. They also made great achievements in art and learning. The Maya left behind many records of their culture, society, and history. By studying these records, archaeologists and historians may be able to learn more about the achievements of the Maya.

Section 3 Assessment

Reviewing Ideas and Terms **HSS** 7.7.2, 7.7.4, 7.7.5

1. **a. Identify** Who were members of the upper class in Maya society?
   b. Explain In what ways did lower-class Maya support upper-class Maya?
2. **a. Describe** What did the Maya do to try to please their gods?
   b. Explain Why did the Maya practice human sacrifice?
3. **a. Recall** What did the Maya study from **observatories**?
   b. Rank What do you think was the most impressive Maya achievement?

Critical Thinking

4. **Analyzing Information** Draw a diagram like the one to the right. Use it to identify some major achievements of the Maya.

   Writing system
   Achievements

FOCUS ON WRITING

5. **Identifying Key Details about Maya Culture** Some sites might have displays of Maya art and tools. There could even be scenes and live performances of how the Maya lived. Make a list of what the people on the tour might see of Maya culture.

from the
Popol Vuh

translated by Dennis Tedlock

About the Reading *In the language of the Maya,* Popol Vuh *means "Council Book." This work contains both the myths and the history of a group of Maya. It was first used by Maya kings and lords to help them govern their people. Today, the* Popol Vuh *helps modern readers understand how the Maya lived and what they believed. The following myth, for example, tells us how the gods tried to create people several times before they eventually succeeded.*

AS YOU READ Pay close attention to the behavior of the creator-gods.

Again there comes an experiment with the human work, the human design, by the Maker, Modeler, Bearer, Begetter:

"It must simply be tried again. The time for the planting and dawning is nearing. For this we must make a provider and nurturer. ❶ How else can we be invoked and remembered on the face of the earth? We have already made our first try at our work and design, but it turned out that they didn't keep our days, nor did they glorify us."

"So now let's try to make a giver of praise, giver of respect, provider, nurturer," they said.

So then comes the building and working with earth and mud. They made a body, but it didn't look good to them. It was just separating, just crumbling, just loosening, just softening, just disintegrating, and just dissolving. ❷ Its head wouldn't turn, either. Its face was just lopsided, its face was just twisted. It couldn't look around. It talked at first, but senselessly. It was quickly dissolving in the water.

"It won't last," the mason and sculptor said then. "It seems to be dwindling away, so let it just dwindle. It can't walk and it can't multiply, so let it be merely a thought," they said.

So then they dismantled, again they brought down their work and design. Again they talked:

"What is there for us to make that would turn out well, that would succeed in keeping our days and praying to us?" they said. Then they planned again . . .

GUIDED READING

WORD HELP

disintegrating breaking apart
mason one who works with stone or brick
dismantled took apart

❶ Why do the gods wish to make human beings?

❷ What do the gods use to make the body? What happens to it?

ELA Reading 7.3.2 Identify events that advance the plot and determine how each event explains past or present action(s) or foreshadows future action(s).

The creator-gods try again. This time, they produce a group of wooden creatures called "manikins." They came into being, they multiplied, they had daughters, they had sons, these manikins, woodcarvings. But there was nothing in their hearts and nothing in their minds, no memory of their mason and builder. They just went and walked wherever they wanted. They did not remember the Heart of Sky. ❸

Monkeys were common subjects in Maya carvings.

And so they fell, just an experiment and just a cutout for humankind.

They were not competent, nor did they speak before the builder and sculptor who made them and brought them forth, and so they were killed, done in by a flood:

There came a rain of resin from the sky.

There came the one named Gouger of Faces: he gouged out their eyeballs.

There came Sudden Bloodletter: he snapped off their heads.

There came Crunching Jaguar: he ate their flesh.

There came Tearing Jaguar: he tore them open.

They were pounded down to the bones and tendons, smashed and pulverized even to the bones . . . ❹

Such was the scattering of the human work, the human design. The people were ground down, overthrown. The mouths and faces of all of them were destroyed and crushed. And it used to be said that the monkeys in the forests today are a sign of this. They were left as a sign because wood alone was used for their flesh by the builder and sculptor.

❺ And so this is why monkeys look like people: they are a sign of a previous human work, human design—mere manikins, mere woodcarvings.

GUIDED READING

WORD HELP

competent capable; fit
resin a gooey substance that comes from trees
pulverized crushed

❸ The Heart of Sky is the father-god of the Maya.

❹ *In your own words, explain what happened to the creatures.*

❺ *This myth explains the origin, or beginning, of what animal?*

CONNECTING LITERATURE TO HISTORY

1. **Evaluating** According to Maya beliefs, the gods could be helpful or harmful, so people tried to please the gods to get their help. Are the gods in this myth helpful or harmful? Explain your answer.

2. **Analyzing** By studying Maya records, archaeologists are learning about the achievements of the Maya. What have you learned about the Maya by reading this "record" of their life and society?

Accepting Social Responsibility

Understand the Skill

"No man is an island entire of itself; every man is a piece of the continent, a part of the main." The great English poet John Donne made this observation almost 400 years ago. It is a famous quotation that remains as true today as when Donne wrote it. It means that no one exists alone. We are all members of society—"a part of the main."

Donne's poem continues, "If a clod be washed away by the sea, Europe is the less." This was Donne's way of saying that a society's strength depends on the contributions of its members. They must be willing to fulfill their roles in that society and to do what is best for it.

Learn the Skill

As a member of society, you have obligations to the people around you. The most obvious obligation is to do nothing that might harm society. This duty can range from small things, such as not littering, to large things, such as not committing a crime.

In addition, you have a duty to participate in society. At the very least, this means using the rights and responsibilities of citizenship. These responsibilities include being informed about important issues in your school, community, and country. Later, when you are older, they will also include serving on juries and voting in elections.

Another level of social responsibility and participation is becoming involved in change to benefit society. It goes beyond just being informed about issues to trying to do something about them. Before you take this important step, however, here are some points to consider.

➊ Few changes that benefit society will have everyone's support. Some people always want things to stay the same. They may get upset or treat you badly if you work for change. You must be prepared for this possibility if you decide to take action.

➋ Sometimes efforts to improve things involve opposing laws or rules that you believe need to be changed. No matter how just your cause is, if you break laws or rules, you must be willing to accept the consequences of your behavior.

➌ Remember that violence is *never* an acceptable method for change. People who use force in seeking change are not behaving in a socially responsible manner, even if their cause is good.

Practice and Apply the Skill

Review the "If You Were There" scene in Section 3. Imagine yourself as that Maya farmer. You respect your king as the leader of your city and its army. War is very important in your culture. Your city is at war nearly all the time, and you feel this fighting is hurting your society. Farming is difficult because farmers must spend so much time in the army. In addition, enemy attacks destroy the crops farmers are able to grow. Food shortages are common.

1. If you did something to try to end the warfare, in what ways might that benefit your society?

2. Why might some people oppose your efforts?

3. What might the consequences be for you if you refuse to fight?

4. If you were this Maya farmer, what would you do? Explain your answer.

Visual Summary

Use the visual summary below to help you review the main ideas of the chapter.

QUICK FACTS

People arrived in the Americas sometime before 10,000 BC.

By 2500 BC people in Mesoamerica had domesticated maize.

The Maya built cities in the Americas during their Classic Age.

The Maya civilization eventually collapsed, but no one knows why.

Reviewing Vocabulary, Terms, and People

Imagine that these terms from the chapter are correct answers to six items in a crossword puzzle. Write the six clues for the answers. Then make the puzzle with some answers written down and some across.

1. Mesoamerica
2. Pacal
3. obsidian
4. observatories
5. maize
6. Popol Vuh

Comprehension and Critical Thinking

SECTION 1 *(Pages 428–433)* **HSS** 7.7.1

7. a. Identify What plants did early farmers in Mesoamerica grow for food? What plants did farmers grow in South America?

b. Make Inferences What do Olmec towns, sculptures, and other items tell us about Olmec society?

c. Evaluate Evaluate this statement: "Global temperature change had a big impact on the history of the Americas."

SECTION 2 *(Pages 434–438)* **HSS** 7.7.1, 7.7.3

8. a. Recall What were two important trade goods for the early Maya?

b. Analyze Why did the Maya civilization decline?

c. Elaborate For which people in Maya society was life probably pleasant and secure? For which people was life less pleasant or secure?

SECTION 3 *(Pages 439–443)* **HSS** 7.7.2, 7.7.4, 7.7.5

9. a. Describe What are some things that happened during Maya religious ceremonies?

b. Contrast How did daily life for the upper and lower classes of Maya society differ?

c. Evaluate Of the Maya's many achievements, which do you think is the most important? Why?

THE EARLY AMERICAS **447**

Reviewing Themes

10. Science and Technology Do you agree or disagree with this statement: "The Maya were clever and talented because they built their cities without the help of metal tools or wheeled vehicles." Why?

11. Geography How did geography play a role in the Maya economy?

Using the Internet

go.hrw.com
KEYWORD: SQ6 WH15

12. Activity: Understanding Maya Math The ancient Maya invented a number system that helped them construct buildings and keep track of their agriculture and commerce. Number glyphs are mostly simple dots and lines. The Maya also used head glyphs, which are more intricate drawings for numbers. Enter the activity keyword. Then visit the Web sites and complete some math problems using Maya numbers.

Reading and Analysis Skills

Analyzing Information In each of the following passages, one underlined selection is irrelevant or nonessential to the meaning of the sentence, or it cannot be verified as true. Identify the irrelevant, nonessential, or unverifiable selection in each sentence.

13. Pacal was greatly honored by the Maya. He was very tall. The Maya built a great temple to record his achievements.

14. Ball games were popular in Maya cities. Players could not use their hands or feet to touch the ball. The Maya would not enjoy modern basketball very much.

15. Chocolate was valuable in Maya society. Only rulers and gods could have chocolate. Today, many people enjoy chocolate every day.

16. The Maya developed an accurate calendar system. They knew that a year had 365 days. The ancient Romans also had a calendar. The Maya calendar used symbols to represent months.

17. Mesoamerica is largely covered by rain forests. Many kinds of plants and animals live in rain forests. The people of Mesoamerica probably liked to watch monkeys playing in the trees.

Social Studies Skills

18. Accepting Responsibility and Consequences Organize your class into groups. Choose one member of your group to represent the ruler of a Maya city. The rest of the group will be his or her advisers. As a group, decide how you will behave toward other cities. Will you go to war, or will you trade? Once you have made your decisions, declare your intentions to other cities. Ask the representatives of those cities how they will respond to your action. As a class, discuss the consequences of the actions you have chosen to take.

FOCUS ON WRITING

19. Writing Your Brochure Travel brochures often feature exciting descriptions of tours. Use your notes to help you write such a description for a historical tour of the ancient Americas.

Choose sites from the most ancient ones to the Maya cities. For each site, write several sentences about the people who lived there. You might tell how they came to live there or how an object there played a part in their lives.

Most travel brochures show lots of pictures. What pictures would you choose to go with what you've written?

Standards Assessment

DIRECTIONS: Read each question, and write the letter of the best response.

1 Use the map to answer the following question.

Which of the areas on the map shows the location of the Maya civilization?

A J

B K

C L

D M

2 Mesoamerica contains all of the following geographic features *except*

A mountains.

B rain forests.

C deserts.

D rivers.

3 Which word *best* describes the Maya civilization during its Classic Age?

A peaceful

B religious

C united

D democratic

4 Despite their accomplishments, the Maya did *not* have

A a reliable calendar.

B wheeled vehicles.

C a writing system.

D knowledge of mathematics.

5 Which class of people held the lowest position in Maya society?

A priests

B farmers

C slaves

D merchants

Connecting with Past Learnings

6 In this chapter you read that Maya civilization during the Classic Age included independent city-states. What other civilization that you have studied was organized into city-states?

A ancient Greece

B ancient Persia

C Han China

D the Roman Empire

7 The Maya believed their rulers were related to the gods. What other ancient civilization believed the same thing?

A Jews

B Indians

C Phoenicians

D Egyptians

Persuasion and Historical Issues

Assignment

Write an essay stating your opinion on this topic or another historical topic of your choice: All great empires are likely to end in the same way the Roman and Maya empires did.

> **TIP** **Fact vs. Opinion** A fact is a statement that can be proved true. Facts include
> - measurements
> - dates
> - locations
> - definitions
>
> An opinion is a statement of a personal belief. Opinions often include judgmental words and phrases such as *better, should,* and *think.*

ELA **Writing 6.2.5** Write persuasive compositions.

The study of history raises questions, or issues, that can be argued from both sides. Effective persuasive writing supports a point of view with evidence.

1. Prewrite

Taking a Position

Do you think all great empires will follow the same course as the Romans and Maya, or could an empire take a different course? Write a sentence that states your position, or opinion about, this topic or another topic.

Supporting Your Position

To convince your audience to agree with your position, you will need reasons and evidence. **Reasons** tell *why* a writer has a particular point of view. **Evidence** backs up, or helps prove, the reasons. Evidence includes facts, examples, and opinions of experts, like historians. You can find this evidence in this textbook or other books recommended by your teacher.

Organizing Reasons and Evidence

Try to present your reasons and evidence in order of importance, so that you can end with your most convincing points. Use transitions such as *mainly, last,* and *most important* to emphasize ideas.

2. Write

This framework can help you state your position clearly and present convincing reasons and evidence.

A Writer's Framework

Introduction
- Introduce the topic by using a surprising fact, quotation, or comparison to get your reader's attention.
- Identify at least two differing positions on this topic.
- State your own position on the topic.

Body
- Present at least two reasons to support your position.
- Support each reason with evidence (facts, examples, expert opinions).
- Organize your reasons and evidence in order of importance with your most convincing reason last.

Conclusion
- Restate your position.
- Summarize your supporting reasons and evidence.
- Project your position into history by using it to predict the course of current and future events.

3. Evaluate and Revise

Evaluating

Use the following questions to evaluate your draft and find ways to make your paper more convincing.

Evaluation Questions for a Persuasive Essay

- Does your introduction include an opinion statement that clearly states your position?
- Have you given at least two reasons to support your position?
- Do you provide convincing evidence to back up your reasons?

- Are your reasons and evidence organized by order of importance, ending with the most important?
- Does your conclusion restate your position and summarize your reasons and evidence? Do you apply your opinion to future history?

Revising

Strengthen your argument with loaded words. Loaded words are words with strong positive or negative connotations.

- Positive—leader
- Negative—tyrant, despot
- Neutral—ruler, emperor

Loaded words can add powerful emotional appeals to your reader's feelings and help convince them to agree with your opinion.

4. Proofread and Publish

Proofreading

Keep the following guidelines in mind as you reread your paper.

- Wherever you have added, deleted, or changed anything, make sure your revision fits in smoothly and does not introduce any errors.
- Double-check names, dates, and other factual information.

Publishing

Team up with one of your classmates who has taken the same position you have. Combine your evidence to create the most powerful argument you can. Challenge a team that has taken an opposing view to a debate. Ask the rest of the class for feedback: Which argument was more convincing? What were the strengths and weaknesses of each position?

Practice and Apply

Use the steps and strategies outlined in this workshop to write a persuasive composition.

TIP **Using a Computer to Check Spelling in History Papers** Whenever you can, use a spell-checker program to help you catch careless errors. However, keep in mind that it will not solve all your spelling problems.

- It will not catch misspellings that correctly spell other words, such as *their, they're,* and *there,* or *an* instead of *and.*
- It will highlight but not give the preferred spelling for many proper names.
- It cannot be relied upon for correct capitalization.

References

The Declaration of Independence

In Congress, July 4, 1776
The unanimous Declaration of the thirteen united States of America,

When in the Course of human events, it becomes necessary for one people to dissolve the political bands which have connected them with another, and to assume among the Powers of the earth, the separate and equal station to which the Laws of Nature and of Nature's God entitle them, a decent respect to the opinions of mankind requires that they should declare the causes which **impel** them to the separation.

We hold these truths to be self-evident, that all men are created equal, that they are **endowed** by their Creator with certain unalienable Rights, that among these are Life, Liberty, and the pursuit of Happiness. That to secure these rights, Governments are instituted among Men, deriving their just powers from the consent of the governed, That whenever any Form of Government becomes destructive of these ends, it is the Right of the People to alter or to abolish it, and to institute new Government, laying its foundation on such principles and organizing its powers in such form, as to them shall seem most likely to effect their Safety and Happiness. Prudence, indeed, will dictate that Governments long established should not be changed for light and transient causes; and accordingly all experience hath shown, that mankind are more disposed to suffer, while evils are sufferable, than to right themselves by abolishing the forms to which they are accustomed. But when a long train of abuses and **usurpations**, pursuing invariably the same Object **evinces** a design to reduce them under absolute **Despotism**, it is their right, it is their duty, to throw off such Government, and to provide new Guards for their future security.—Such has been the patient sufferance of these Colonies; and such is now the necessity which constrains them to alter their former Systems of Government. The history of the present King of Great Britain is a history of repeated injuries and usurpations, all having in direct object the establishment of an absolute **Tyranny** over these States. To prove this, let Facts be submitted to a **candid** world.

He has refused his Assent to Laws, the most wholesome and necessary for the public good.

He has forbidden his Governors to pass Laws of immediate and pressing importance, unless suspended in their operation till his Assent should be obtained; and when so suspended, he has utterly neglected to attend to them.

Vocabulary

impel force

endowed provided

usurpations wrongful seizures of power

evinces clearly displays

despotism unlimited power

tyranny oppressive power exerted by a government or ruler

candid fair

He has refused to pass other Laws for the accommodation of large districts of people, unless those people would **relinquish** the right of Representation in the Legislature, a right **inestimable** to them and **formidable** to tyrants only.

He has called together legislative bodies at places unusual, uncomfortable, and distant from the depository of their Public Records, for the sole purpose of fatiguing them into compliance with his measures.

He has dissolved Representative Houses repeatedly, for opposing with manly firmness his invasions on the rights of the people.

He has refused for a long time, after such dissolutions, to cause others to be elected; whereby the Legislative Powers, incapable of **Annihilation**, have returned to the People at large for their exercise; the State remaining in the mean time exposed to all the dangers of invasion from without, and **convulsions** within.

He has endeavored to prevent the population of these States; for that purpose obstructing the Laws of **Naturalization of Foreigners**; refusing to pass others to encourage their migration hither, and raising the conditions of new **Appropriations of Lands**.

He has obstructed the Administration of Justice, by refusing his Assent to Laws for establishing Judiciary Powers.

He has made Judges dependent on his Will alone, for the **tenure** of their offices, and the amount and payment of their salaries.

He has erected **a multitude of** New Offices, and sent hither swarms of Officers to harass our people, and eat out their substance.

He has kept among us, in times of peace, Standing Armies without the Consent of our legislature.

He has affected to render the Military independent of and superior to the Civil Power.

He has combined with others to subject us to a jurisdiction foreign to our constitution, and unacknowledged by our laws; giving his Assent to their Acts of pretended legislation:

For **quartering** large bodies of armed troops among us:

For protecting them, by a mock Trial, from Punishment for any Murders which they should commit on the Inhabitants of these States:

For cutting off our Trade with all parts of the world:

For imposing taxes on us without our Consent:

For depriving us in many cases, of the benefits of Trial by Jury:

Vocabulary

relinquish release, yield

inestimable priceless

formidable causing dread

annihilation destruction

convulsions violent disturbances

naturalization of foreigners the process by which foreign-born persons become citizens

appropriations of lands setting aside land for settlement

tenure term

a multitude of many

quartering lodging, housing

Vocabulary

arbitrary not based on law

render make

abdicated given up

foreign mercenaries soldiers hired to fight for a country not their own

perfidy violation of trust

insurrections rebellions

petitioned for redress asked formally for a correction of wrongs

unwarrantable jurisdiction unjustified authority

magnanimity generous spirit

conjured urgently called upon

consanguinity common ancestry

acquiesce consent to

For transporting us beyond Seas to be tried for pretended offences:

For abolishing the free System of English Laws in a neighboring Province, establishing therein an **Arbitrary** government, and enlarging its Boundaries so as to **render** it at once an example and fit instrument for introducing the same absolute rule into these Colonies:

For taking away our Charters, abolishing our most valuable Laws, and altering fundamentally the Forms of our Governments:

For suspending our own Legislature, and declaring themselves invested with Power to legislate for us in all cases whatsoever.

He has **abdicated** Government here, by declaring us out of his Protection and waging War against us.

He has plundered our seas, ravaged our Coasts, burnt our towns, and destroyed the lives of our people.

He is at this time transporting large armies of **foreign mercenaries** to complete the works of death, desolation and tyranny, already begun with circumstances of Cruelty & **perfidy** scarcely paralleled in the most barbarous ages, and totally unworthy the Head of a civilized nation.

He has constrained our fellow Citizens taken Captive on the high Seas to bear Arms against their Country, to become the executioners of their friends and Brethren, or to fall themselves by their Hands.

He has excited domestic **insurrections** amongst us, and has endeavored to bring on the inhabitants of our frontiers, the merciless Indian Savages, whose known rule of warfare, is an undistinguished destruction of all ages, sexes and conditions.

In every stage of these Oppressions We have **Petitioned for Redress** in the most humble terms: Our repeated Petitions have been answered only by repeated injury. A Prince, whose character is thus marked by every act which may define a Tyrant, is unfit to be the ruler of a free People.

Nor have We been wanting in attention to our British brethren. We have warned them from time to time of attempts by their legislature to extend an **unwarrantable jurisdiction** over us. We have reminded them of the circumstances of our emigration and settlement here. We have appealed to their native justice and **magnanimity**, and we have **conjured** them by the ties of our common kindred to disavow these usurpations, which, would inevitably interrupt our connections and correspondence. They too have been deaf to the voice of justice and of **consanguinity**. We must, therefore, **acquiesce** in the necessity, which denounces our Separation, and hold them, as we hold the rest of mankind, Enemies in War, in Peace Friends.

We, therefore, the Representatives of the united States of America, in General Congress, Assembled, appealing to the Supreme Judge of the world for the **rectitude** of our intentions, do, in the Name, and by Authority of the good People of these Colonies, solemnly publish and declare, That these United Colonies are, and of Right ought to be Free and Independent States; that they are Absolved from all Allegiance to the British Crown, and that all political connection between them and the State of Great Britain, is and ought to be totally dissolved; and that as Free and Independent States, they have full Power to levy War, conclude Peace, contract Alliances, establish Commerce, and to do all other Acts and Things which Independent States may of right do. And for the support of this Declaration, with a firm reliance on the Protection of Divine Providence, we mutually pledge to each other our Lives, our Fortunes and our sacred Honor.

John Hancock

Button Gwinnett

Lyman Hall

George Walton

William Hooper

Joseph Hewes

John Penn

Edward Rutledge

Thomas Heyward, Jr.

Thomas Lynch, Jr.

Arthur Middleton

Samuel Chase

William Paca

Thomas Stone

Charles Carroll
  of Carrollton

George Wythe

Richard Henry Lee

Thomas Jefferson

Benjamin Harrison

Thomas Nelson, Jr.

Francis Lightfoot Lee

Carter Braxton

Robert Morris

Benjamin Rush

Benjamin Franklin

John Morton

George Clymer

James Smith

George Taylor

James Wilson

George Ross

Caesar Rodney

George Read

Thomas McKean

William Floyd

Philip Livingston

Francis Lewis

Lewis Morris

Richard Stockton

John Witherspoon

Francis Hopkinson

John Hart

Abraham Clark

Josiah Bartlett

William Whipple

Samuel Adams

John Adams

Robert Treat Paine

Elbridge Gerry

Stephen Hopkins

William Ellery

Roger Sherman

Samuel Huntington

William Williams

Oliver Wolcott

Matthew Thornton

The Constitution of the United States

Preamble

We the People of the United States, in Order to form a more perfect Union, establish Justice, insure domestic Tranquility, provide for the common defense, promote the general Welfare, and secure the Blessings of Liberty to ourselves and our Posterity, do ordain and establish this Constitution for the United States of America.

Article I | The Legislature

Section 1. | Congress

All legislative Powers herein granted shall be vested in a Congress of the United States, which shall consist of a Senate and House of Representatives.

Section 2. | The House of Representatives

1. Elections The House of Representatives shall be composed of Members chosen every second Year by the People of the several States, and the Electors in each State shall have the Qualifications requisite for Electors of the most numerous Branch of the State Legislature.

2. Qualifications No Person shall be a Representative who shall not have attained to the Age of twenty five Years, and been seven Years a Citizen of the United States, and who shall not, when elected, be an Inhabitant of that State in which he shall be chosen.

3. Number of Representatives Representatives and direct Taxes shall be apportioned among the several States which may be included within this Union, according to their respective Numbers, which shall be determined by adding to the whole Number of free Persons, including **those bound to Service**[1] for a Term of Years, and excluding Indians not taxed, three fifths of **all other Persons**.[2] The actual **Enumeration**[3] shall be made within three Years after the first Meeting of the Congress of the United States, and within every subsequent Term of ten Years, in such Manner as they shall by Law direct. The Number of Representatives shall not exceed one for every

Note: The parts of the Constitution that have been lined through are no longer in force or no longer apply because of later amendments. The titles of the sections and articles are added for easier reference.

Legislative Branch

Article I explains how the legislative branch, called Congress, is organized. The chief purpose of the legislative branch is to make laws. Congress is made up of the Senate and the House of Representatives.

The House of Representatives

The number of members each state has in the House is based on the population of the individual state. In 1929 Congress permanently fixed the size of the House at 435 members.

Vocabulary

[1] **those bound to Service** indentured servants

[2] **all other Persons** slaves

[3] **Enumeration** census or official population count

thirty Thousand, but each State shall have at Least one Representative; and until such enumeration shall be made, the State of New Hampshire shall be entitled to choose three, Massachoosetts eight, Rhode-Island and Providence Plantations one, Connecticut five, New-York six, New Jersey four, Pennsylvania eight, Delaware one, Maryland six, Virginia ten, North Carolina five, South Carolina five, and Georgia three.

4. Vacancies When vacancies happen in the Representation from any State, the Executive Authority thereof shall issue Writs of Election to fill such Vacancies.

5. Officers and Impeachment The House of Representatives shall choose their Speaker and other Officers; and shall have the sole Power of impeachment.

Section 3. The Senate

1. Number of Senators The Senate of the United States shall be composed of two Senators from each State, chosen by the Legislature thereof, for six Years; and each Senator shall have one Vote.

2. Classifying Terms Immediately after they shall be assembled in Consequence of the first Election, they shall be divided as equally as may be into three Classes. The Seats of the Senators of the first Class shall be vacated at the Expiration of the second Year, of the second Class at the Expiration of the fourth Year, and of the third Class at the Expiration of the sixth Year, so that one third may be chosen every second Year; and if Vacancies happen by Resignation, or otherwise, during the Recess of the Legislature of any State, the Executive thereof may make temporary Appointments until the next Meeting of the Legislature, which shall then fill such Vacancies.

3. Qualifications No Person shall be a Senator who shall not have attained to the Age of thirty Years, and been nine Years a Citizen of the United States, and who shall not, when elected, be an Inhabitant of that State for which he shall be chosen.

4. Role of Vice-President The Vice President of the United States shall be President of the Senate, but shall have no Vote, unless they be equally divided.

5. Officers The Senate shall choose their other Officers, and also a President **pro tempore**,[4] in the Absence of the Vice President, or when he shall exercise the Office of President of the United States.

6. Impeachment Trials The Senate shall have the sole Power to try all **Impeachments**.[5] When sitting for that Purpose, they shall be on Oath or Affirmation. When the President of the United States is tried, the Chief Justice shall preside: And no Person shall be convicted without the Concurrence of two thirds of the Members present.

7. Punishment for Impeachment Judgment in Cases of Impeachment shall not extend further than to removal from Office, and disqualification to hold

The Vice President

The only duty that the Constitution assigns to the vice president is to preside over meetings of the Senate. Modern presidents have usually given their vice presidents more responsibilities.

Vocabulary

[4] **pro tempore** temporarily

[5] **Impeachments** official accusations of federal wrongdoing

and enjoy any Office of honor, Trust or Profit under the United States: but the Party convicted shall nevertheless be liable and subject to Indictment, Trial, Judgment and Punishment, according to Law.

Section 4.   Congressional Elections

1. Regulations   The Times, Places and Manner of holding Elections for Senators and Representatives, shall be prescribed in each State by the Legislature thereof; but the Congress may at any time by Law make or alter such Regulations, except as to the Places of choosing Senators.

2. Sessions   ~~The Congress shall assemble at least once in every Year, and such Meeting shall be on the first Monday in December, unless they shall by Law appoint a different Day.~~

Section 5.   Rules/Procedures

1. Quorum   Each House shall be the Judge of the Elections, Returns and Qualifications of its own Members, and a Majority of each shall constitute a **Quorum**[6] to do Business; but a smaller Number may **adjourn**[7] from day to day, and may be authorized to compel the Attendance of absent Members, in such Manner, and under such Penalties as each House may provide.

2. Rules and Conduct   Each House may determine the Rules of its Proceedings, punish its Members for disorderly Behaviour, and, with the Concurrence of two thirds, expel a Member.

3. Records   Each House shall keep a Journal of its Proceedings, and from time to time publish the same, excepting such Parts as may in their Judgment require Secrecy; and the Yeas and Nays of the Members of either House on any question shall, at the Desire of one fifth of those Present, be entered on the Journal.

4. Adjournment   Neither House, during the Session of Congress, shall, without the Consent of the other, adjourn for more than three days, nor to any other Place than that in which the two Houses shall be sitting.

Section 6.   Payment

1. Salary   The Senators and Representatives shall receive a Compensation for their Services, to be ascertained by Law, and paid out of the Treasury of the United States. They shall in all Cases, except Treason, Felony and Breach of the Peace, be privileged from Arrest during their Attendance at the Session of their respective Houses, and in going to and returning from the same; and for any Speech or Debate in either House, they shall not be questioned in any other Place.

2. Restrictions   No Senator or Representative shall, during the Time for which he was elected, be appointed to any civil Office under the Authority of the United States, which shall have been created, or the **Emoluments**[8]

Vocabulary

[6] **Quorum** the minimum number of people needed to conduct business

[7] **adjourn** to stop indefinitely

[8] **Emoluments** salary

whereof shall have been increased during such time; and no Person holding any Office under the United States, shall be a Member of either House during his **Continuance**[9] in Office.

Section 7. How a Bill Becomes a Law

1. Tax Bills All **Bills**[10] for raising Revenue shall originate in the House of Representatives; but the Senate may propose or concur with Amendments as on other Bills.

2. Lawmaking Every Bill which shall have passed the House of Representatives and the Senate, shall, before it become a Law, be presented to the President of the United States: If he approve he shall sign it, but if not he shall return it, with his Objections to that House in which it shall have originated, who shall enter the Objections at large on their Journal, and proceed to reconsider it. If after such Reconsideration two thirds of that House shall agree to pass the Bill, it shall be sent, together with the Objections, to the other House, by which it shall likewise be reconsidered, and if approved by two thirds of that House, it shall become a Law. But in all such Cases the Votes of both Houses shall be determined by yeas and Nays, and the Names of the Persons voting for and against the Bill shall be entered on the Journal of each House respectively. If any Bill shall not be returned by the President within ten Days (Sundays excepted) after it shall have been presented to him, the Same shall be a Law, in like Manner as if he had signed it, unless the Congress by their Adjournment prevent its Return, in which Case it shall not be a Law.

3. Role of the President Every Order, Resolution, or Vote to which the Concurrence of the Senate and House of Representatives may be necessary (except on a question of Adjournment) shall be presented to the President of the United States; and before the Same shall take Effect, shall be approved by him, or being disapproved by him, shall be repassed by two thirds of the Senate and House of Representatives, according to the Rules and Limitations prescribed in the Case of a Bill.

Section 8. Powers Granted to Congress

1. Taxation The Congress shall have Power To lay and collect Taxes, **Duties**,[11] **Imposts**[12] and **Excises**,[13] to pay the Debts and provide for the common Defense and general Welfare of the United States; but all Duties, Imposts and Excises shall be uniform throughout the United States;

2. Credit To borrow Money on the credit of the United States;

3. Commerce To regulate Commerce with foreign Nations, and among the several States, and with the Indian Tribes;

4. Naturalization and Bankruptcy To establish an uniform **Rule of Naturalization**,[14] and uniform Laws on the subject of Bankruptcies throughout the United States;

Vocabulary

[9] **Continuance** term

[10] **Bills** proposed laws

[11] **Duties** tariffs

[12] **Imposts** taxes

[13] **Excises** internal taxes on the manufacture, sale, or consumption of a commodity

[14] **Rule of Naturalization** a law by which a foreign-born person becomes a citizen

THE CONSTITUTION

5. Money To coin Money, regulate the Value thereof, and of foreign Coin, and fix the Standard of Weights and Measures;

6. Counterfeiting To provide for the Punishment of counterfeiting the **Securities**[15] and current Coin of the United States;

7. Post Office To establish Post Offices and post Roads;

8. Patents and Copyrights To promote the Progress of Science and useful Arts, by securing for limited Times to Authors and Inventors the exclusive Right to their respective Writings and Discoveries;

9. Courts To constitute Tribunals inferior to the supreme Court;

10. International Law To define and punish Piracies and Felonies committed on the high Seas, and Offences against the Law of Nations;

11. War To declare War, grant **Letters of Marque and Reprisal**,[16] and make Rules concerning Captures on Land and Water;

12. Army To raise and support Armies, but no Appropriation of Money to that Use shall be for a longer Term than two Years;

13. Navy To provide and maintain a Navy;

14. Regulation of the Military To make Rules for the Government and Regulation of the land and naval Forces;

15. Militia To provide for calling forth the Militia to execute the Laws of the Union, suppress Insurrections and repel Invasions;

16. Regulation of the Militia To provide for organizing, arming, and disciplining, the Militia, and for governing such Part of them as may be employed in the Service of the United States, reserving to the States respectively, the Appointment of the Officers, and the Authority of training the Militia according to the discipline prescribed by Congress;

17. District of Columbia To exercise exclusive Legislation in all Cases whatsoever, over such District (not exceeding ten Miles square) as may, by Cession of particular States, and the Acceptance of Congress, become the Seat of the Government of the United States, and to exercise like Authority over all Places purchased by the Consent of the Legislature of the State in which the Same shall be, for the Erection of Forts, Magazines, Arsenals, dock-Yards, and other needful Buildings;—And

The Elastic Clause

The framers of the Constitution wanted a national government that was strong enough to be effective. This section lists the powers given to Congress. The last portion of Section 8 contains the so-called elastic clause.

18. Necessary and Proper Clause To make all Laws which shall be necessary and proper for carrying into Execution the foregoing Powers, and all other Powers vested by this Constitution in the Government of the United States, or in any Department or Officer thereof.

Section 9. Powers Denied Congress

1. Slave Trade The Migration or Importation of such Persons as any of the States now existing shall think proper to admit, shall not be prohibited by the Congress prior to the Year one thousand eight hundred and eight, but a Tax or duty may be imposed on such Importation, not exceeding ten dollars for each Person.

2. Habeas Corpus The Privilege of the **Writ of Habeas Corpus**[17] shall not be suspended, unless when in Cases of Rebellion or Invasion the public Safety may require it.

3. Illegal Punishment No **Bill of Attainder**[18] or **ex post facto Law**[19] shall be passed.

4. Direct Taxes No **Capitation**,[20] or other direct, Tax shall be laid, unless in Proportion to the Census or enumeration herein before directed to be taken.

5. Export Taxes No Tax or Duty shall be laid on Articles exported from any State.

6. No Favorites No Preference shall be given by any Regulation of Commerce or Revenue to the Ports of one State over those of another; nor shall Vessels bound to, or from, one State, be obliged to enter, clear, or pay Duties in another.

7. Public Money No Money shall be drawn from the Treasury, but in Consequence of Appropriations made by Law; and a regular Statement and Account of the Receipts and Expenditures of all public Money shall be published from time to time.

8. Titles of Nobility No Title of Nobility shall be granted by the United States: And no Person holding any Office of Profit or Trust under them, shall, without the Consent of the Congress, accept of any present, Emolument, Office, or Title, of any kind whatever, from any King, Prince, or foreign State.

Section 10. Powers Denied the States

1. Restrictions No State shall enter into any Treaty, Alliance, or Confederation; grant Letters of Marque and Reprisal; coin Money; emit Bills of Credit; make any Thing but gold and silver Coin a Tender in Payment of Debts; pass any Bill of Attainder, ex post facto Law, or Law impairing the Obligation of Contracts, or grant any Title of Nobility.

2. Import and Export Taxes No State shall, without the Consent of the Congress, lay any Imposts or Duties on Imports or Exports, except what may be absolutely necessary for executing it's inspection Laws: and the net Produce of all Duties and Imposts, laid by any State on Imports or Exports, shall be for the Use of the Treasury of the United States; and all such Laws shall be subject to the Revision and Control of the Congress.

3. Peacetime and War Restraints No State shall, without the Consent of Congress, lay any Duty of Tonnage, keep Troops, or Ships of War in time of Peace, enter into any Agreement or Compact with another State, or with a foreign Power, or engage in War, unless actually invaded, or in such imminent Danger as will not admit of delay.

Vocabulary

[17] **Writ of Habeas Corpus** a court order that requires the government to bring a prisoner to court and explain why he or she is being held

[18] **Bill of Attainder** a law declaring that a person is guilty of a particular crime

[19] **ex post facto Law** a law that is made effective prior to the date that it was passed and therefore punishes people for acts that were not illegal at the time

[20] **Capitation** a direct uniform tax imposed on each head, or person

Article II | The Executive

Section 1. | The Presidency

1. Terms of Office The executive Power shall be vested in a President of the United States of America. He shall hold his Office during the Term of four Years, and, together with the Vice President, chosen for the same Term, be elected, as follows:

2. Electoral College Each State shall appoint, in such Manner as the Legislature thereof may direct, a Number of Electors, equal to the whole Number of Senators and Representatives to which the State may be entitled in the Congress: but no Senator or Representative, or Person holding an Office of Trust or Profit under the United States, shall be appointed an Elector.

3. Former Method of Electing President The Electors shall meet in their respective States, and vote by Ballot for two Persons, of whom one at least shall not be an Inhabitant of the same State with themselves. And they shall make a List of all the Persons voted for, and of the Number of Votes for each; which List they shall sign and certify, and transmit sealed to the Seat of the Government of the United States, directed to the President of the Senate. The President of the Senate shall, in the Presence of the Senate and House of Representatives, open all the Certificates, and the Votes shall then be counted. The Person having the greatest Number of Votes shall be the President, if such Number be a Majority of the whole Number of Electors appointed; and if there be more than one who have such Majority, and have an equal Number of Votes, then the House of Representatives shall immediately choose by Ballot one of them for President; and if no Person have a Majority, then from the five highest on the List the said House shall in like Manner choose the President. But in choosing the President, the Votes shall be taken by States, the Representation from each State having one Vote; A quorum for this purpose shall consist of a Member or Members from two thirds of the States, and a Majority of all the States shall be necessary to a Choice. In every Case, after the Choice of the President, the Person having the greatest Number of Votes of the Electors shall be the Vice President. But if there should remain two or more who have equal Votes, the Senate shall choose from them by Ballot the Vice President.

4. Election Day The Congress may determine the Time of choosing the Electors, and the Day on which they shall give their Votes; which Day shall be the same throughout the United States.

5. Qualifications No Person except a natural born Citizen, or a Citizen of the United States, at the time of the Adoption of this Constitution, shall be eligible to the Office of President; neither shall any Person be eligible to

---

THE CONSTITUTION

Executive Branch

The president is the chief of the executive branch. It is the job of the president to enforce the laws. The framers wanted the president's and vice president's terms of office and manner of selection to be different from those of members of Congress. They decided on four-year terms, but they had a difficult time agreeing on how to select the president and vice president. The framers finally set up an electoral system, which varies greatly from our electoral process today.

Presidential Elections

In 1845 Congress set the Tuesday following the first Monday in November of every fourth year as the general election date for selecting presidential electors.

that Office who shall not have attained to the Age of thirty five Years, and been fourteen Years a Resident within the United States.

6. Succession In Case of the Removal of the President from Office, or of his Death, Resignation, or Inability to discharge the Powers and Duties of the said Office, the Same shall devolve on the Vice President, and the Congress may by Law provide for the Case of Removal, Death, Resignation or Inability, both of the President and Vice President, declaring what Officer shall then act as President, and such Officer shall act accordingly, until the Disability be removed, or a President shall be elected.

7. Salary The President shall, at stated Times, receive for his Services, a Compensation, which shall neither be increased nor diminished during the Period for which he shall have been elected, and he shall not receive within that Period any other Emolument from the United States, or any of them.

8. Oath of Office Before he enter on the Execution of his Office, he shall take the following Oath or Affirmation:—"I do solemnly swear (or affirm) that I will faithfully execute the Office of President of the United States, and will to the best of my Ability, preserve, protect and defend the Constitution of the United States."

Section 2. Powers of Presidency

1. Military Powers The President shall be Commander in Chief of the Army and Navy of the United States, and of the Militia of the several States, when called into the actual Service of the United States; he may require the Opinion, in writing, of the principal Officer in each of the executive Departments, upon any Subject relating to the Duties of their respective Offices, and he shall have Power to grant **Reprieves**[21] and **Pardons**[22] for Offences against the United States, except in Cases of Impeachment.

2. Treaties and Appointments He shall have Power, by and with the Advice and Consent of the Senate, to make Treaties, provided two thirds of the Senators present concur; and he shall nominate, and by and with the Advice and Consent of the Senate, shall appoint Ambassadors, other public Ministers and Consuls, Judges of the supreme Court, and all other Officers of the United States, whose Appointments are not herein otherwise provided for, and which shall be established by Law: but the Congress may by Law vest the Appointment of such inferior Officers, as they think proper, in the President alone, in the Courts of Law, or in the Heads of Departments.

3. Vacancies The President shall have Power to fill up all Vacancies that may happen during the Recess of the Senate, by granting Commissions which shall expire at the End of their next Session.

Presidential Salary

In 1999 Congress voted to set future presidents' salaries at $400,000 per year. The president also receives an annual expense account. The president must pay taxes only on the salary.

Commander in Chief

Today the president is in charge of the army, navy, air force, marines, and coast guard. Only Congress, however, can decide if the United States will declare war.

Appointments

Most of the president's appointments to office must be approved by the Senate.

Vocabulary

[21] **Reprieves** delays of punishment

[22] **Pardons** releases from the legal penalties associated with a crime

Section 3. Presidential Duties

He shall from time to time give to the Congress Information of the State of the Union, and recommend to their Consideration such Measures as he shall judge necessary and expedient; he may, on extraordinary Occasions, convene both Houses, or either of them, and in Case of Disagreement between them, with Respect to the Time of Adjournment, he may adjourn them to such Time as he shall think proper; he shall receive Ambassadors and other public Ministers; he shall take Care that the Laws be faithfully executed, and shall Commission all the Officers of the United States.

Section 4. Impeachment

The President, Vice President and all civil Officers of the United States, shall be removed from Office on Impeachment for, and Conviction of, Treason, Bribery, or other high Crimes and Misdemeanors.

Article III The Judiciary

Section 1. Federal Courts and Judges

The judicial Power of the United States shall be vested in one supreme Court, and in such inferior Courts as the Congress may from time to time ordain and establish. The Judges, both of the supreme and inferior Courts, shall hold their Offices during good Behavior, and shall, at stated Times, receive for their Services a Compensation, which shall not be diminished during their Continuance in Office.

Section 2. Authority of the Courts

1. General Authority The judicial Power shall extend to all Cases, in Law and Equity, arising under this Constitution, the Laws of the United States, and Treaties made, or which shall be made, under their Authority;—to all Cases affecting Ambassadors, other public Ministers and Consuls;—to all Cases of admiralty and maritime Jurisdiction;—to Controversies to which the United States shall be a Party;—to Controversies between two or more States ~~—between a State and Citizens of another State;~~ —between Citizens of different States;—between Citizens of the same State claiming Lands under Grants of different States, ~~and between a State, or the Citizens thereof, and foreign States, Citizens or Subjects.~~

2. Supreme Authority In all Cases affecting Ambassadors, other public Ministers and Consuls, and those in which a State shall be Party, the supreme Court shall have original Jurisdiction. In all the other Cases before mentioned, the supreme Court shall have appellate Jurisdiction, both as to Law and Fact, with such Exceptions, and under such Regulations as the Congress shall make.

The State of the Union

Every year the president presents to Congress a State of the Union message. In this message, the president introduces and explains a legislative plan for the coming year.

Judicial Branch

The Articles of Confederation did not set up a federal court system. One of the first points that the framers of the Constitution agreed upon was to set up a national judiciary. In the Judiciary Act of 1789, Congress provided for the establishment of lower courts, such as district courts, circuit courts of appeals, and various other federal courts. The judicial system provides a check on the legislative branch: It can declare a law unconstitutional.

3. Trial by Jury The Trial of all Crimes, except in Cases of Impeachment, shall be by Jury; and such Trial shall be held in the State where the said Crimes shall have been committed; but when not committed within any State, the Trial shall be at such Place or Places as the Congress may by Law have directed.

Section 3. Treason

1. Definition Treason against the United States, shall consist only in levying War against them, or in adhering to their Enemies, giving them Aid and Comfort. No Person shall be convicted of Treason unless on the Testimony of two Witnesses to the same overt Act, or on Confession in open Court.

2. Punishment The Congress shall have Power to declare the Punishment of Treason, but no Attainder of Treason shall work **Corruption of Blood**,[23] or Forfeiture except during the Life of the Person attainted.

Article IV Relations among States

Section 1. State Acts and Records

Full Faith and Credit shall be given in each State to the public Acts, Records, and judicial Proceedings of every other State. And the Congress may by general Laws prescribe the Manner in which such Acts, Records and Proceedings shall be proved, and the Effect thereof.

Section 2. Rights of Citizens

1. Citizenship The Citizens of each State shall be entitled to all Privileges and Immunities of Citizens in the several States.

2. Extradition A Person charged in any State with Treason, Felony, or other Crime, who shall flee from Justice, and be found in another State, shall on Demand of the executive Authority of the State from which he fled, be delivered up, to be removed to the State having Jurisdiction of the Crime.

3. Fugitive Slaves No Person held to Service or Labour in one State, under the Laws thereof, escaping into another, shall, in Consequence of any Law or Regulation therein, be discharged from such Service or Labour, but shall be delivered up on Claim of the Party to whom such Service or Labour may be due.

Section 3. New States

1. Admission New States may be admitted by the Congress into this Union; but no new State shall be formed or erected within the Jurisdiction of any other State; nor any State be formed by the Junction of two or more States, or Parts of States, without the Consent of the Legislatures of the States concerned as well as of the Congress.

Vocabulary

[23] **Corruption of Blood** punishing the family of a person convicted of treason

The States

States must honor the laws, records, and court decisions of other states. A person cannot escape a legal obligation by moving from one state to another.

2. Congressional Authority The Congress shall have Power to dispose of and make all needful Rules and Regulations respecting the Territory or other Property belonging to the United States; and nothing in this Constitution shall be so construed as to Prejudice any Claims of the United States, or of any particular State.

Section 4. Guarantees to the States

The United States shall guarantee to every State in this Union a Republican Form of Government, and shall protect each of them against Invasion; and on Application of the Legislature, or of the Executive (when the Legislature cannot be convened), against domestic Violence.

Article V Amending the Constitution

The Congress, whenever two thirds of both Houses shall deem it necessary, shall propose Amendments to this Constitution, or, on the Application of the Legislatures of two thirds of the several States, shall call a Convention for proposing Amendments, which, in either Case, shall be valid to all Intents and Purposes, as Part of this Constitution, when ratified by the Legislatures of three fourths of the several States, or by Conventions in three fourths thereof, as the one or the other Mode of Ratification may be proposed by the Congress; Provided that no Amendment which may be made prior to the Year One thousand eight hundred and eight shall in any Manner affect the first and fourth Clauses in the Ninth Section of the first Article; and that no State, without its Consent, shall be deprived of its equal Suffrage in the Senate.

Article VI Supremacy of National Government

All Debts contracted and Engagements entered into, before the Adoption of this Constitution, shall be as valid against the United States under this Constitution, as under the Confederation.

This Constitution, and the Laws of the United States which shall be made in Pursuance thereof; and all Treaties made, or which shall be made, under the Authority of the United States, shall be the supreme Law of the Land; and the Judges in every State shall be bound thereby, any Thing in the Constitution or Laws of any State to the Contrary notwithstanding.

The Senators and Representatives before mentioned, and the Members of the several State Legislatures, and all executive and judicial Officers, both of the United States and of the several States, shall be bound by Oath or Affirmation, to support this Constitution; but no religious Test shall ever be required as a Qualification to any Office or public Trust under the United States.

National Supremacy

One of the biggest problems facing the delegates to the Constitutional Convention was the question of what would happen if a state law and a federal law conflicted. Which law would be followed? Who would decide? The second clause of Article VI answers those questions. When a federal law and a state law disagree, the federal law overrides the state law. The Constitution and other federal laws are the "supreme Law of the Land." This clause is often called the supremacy clause.

Article VII Ratification

The Ratification of the Conventions of nine States, shall be sufficient for the Establishment of this Constitution between the States so ratifying the Same.

Done in Convention by the Unanimous Consent of the States present the Seventeenth Day of September in the Year of our Lord one thousand seven hundred and Eighty seven and of the Independence of the United States of America the Twelfth In witness whereof We have hereunto subscribed our Names,

> *George Washington—*
> President and deputy from Virginia

Delaware

George Read
Gunning Bedford Jr.
John Dickinson
Richard Bassett
Jacob Broom

Maryland

James McHenry
Daniel of
   St. Thomas Jenifer
Daniel Carroll

Virginia

John Blair
James Madison Jr.

North Carolina

William Blount
Richard Dobbs Spaight
Hugh Williamson

South Carolina

John Rutledge
Charles Cotesworth
   Pinckney
Charles Pinckney
Pierce Butler

Georgia

William Few
Abraham Baldwin

New Hampshire

John Langdon
Nicholas Gilman

Massachusetts

Nathaniel Gorham
Rufus King

Connecticut

William Samuel Johnson
Roger Sherman

New York

Alexander Hamilton

New Jersey

William Livingston
David Brearley
William Paterson
Jonathan Dayton

Pennsylvania

Benjamin Franklin
Thomas Mifflin
Robert Morris
George Clymer
Thomas FitzSimons
Jared Ingersoll
James Wilson
Gouverneur Morris

Attest:
William Jackson,
Secretary

Ratification

The Articles of Confederation called for all 13 states to approve any revision to the Articles. The Constitution required that 9 out of the 13 states would be needed to ratify the Constitution. The first state to ratify was Delaware, on December 7, 1787. Almost two-and-a-half years later, on May 29, 1790, Rhode Island became the last state to ratify the Constitution.

Bill of Rights

One of the conditions set by several states for ratifying the Constitution was the inclusion of a bill of rights. Many people feared that a stronger central government might take away basic rights of the people that had been guaranteed in state constitutions.

Vocabulary

[24] **quartered** housed

[25] **Warrants** written orders authorizing a person to make an arrest, a seizure, or a search

[26] **infamous** disgraceful

[27] **indictment** the act of charging with a crime

[28] **ascertained** found out

Rights of the Accused

The Fifth, Sixth, and Seventh Amendments describe the procedures that courts must follow when trying people accused of crimes.

Trials

The Sixth Amendment makes several guarantees, including a prompt trial and a trial by a jury chosen from the state and district in which the crime was committed.

Constitutional Amendments

Note: The first 10 amendments to the Constitution were ratified on December 15, 1791, and form what is known as the Bill of Rights.

Amendments 1–10. The Bill of Rights

Amendment I

Congress shall make no law respecting an establishment of religion, or prohibiting the free exercise thereof; or abridging the freedom of speech, or of the press; or the right of the people peaceably to assemble, and to petition the Government for a redress of grievances.

Amendment II

A well regulated Militia, being necessary to the security of a free State, the right of the people to keep and bear Arms, shall not be infringed.

Amendment III

No Soldier shall, in time of peace be **quartered**[24] in any house, without the consent of the Owner, nor in time of war, but in a manner to be prescribed by law.

Amendment IV

The right of the people to be secure in their persons, houses, papers, and effects, against unreasonable searches and seizures, shall not be violated, and no **Warrants**[25] shall issue, but upon probable cause, supported by Oath or affirmation, and particularly describing the place to be searched, and the persons or things to be seized.

Amendment V

No person shall be held to answer for a capital, or otherwise **infamous**[26] crime, unless on a presentment or **indictment**[27] of a Grand Jury, except in cases arising in the land or naval forces, or in the Militia, when in actual service in time of War or public danger; nor shall any person be subject for the same offence to be twice put in jeopardy of life or limb; nor shall be compelled in any criminal case to be a witness against himself, nor be deprived of life, liberty, or property, without due process of law; nor shall private property be taken for public use, without just compensation.

Amendment VI

In all criminal prosecutions, the accused shall enjoy the right to a speedy and public trial, by an impartial jury of the State and district wherein the crime shall have been committed, which district shall have been previously **ascertained**[28] by law, and to be informed of the nature and cause of the accusation; to be confronted with the witnesses against him; to have compulsory process for obtaining witnesses in his favor, and to have the Assistance of Counsel for his defence.

Amendment VII

In suits at common law, where the value in controversy shall exceed twenty dollars, the right of trial by jury shall be preserved, and no fact tried by a jury, shall be otherwise reexamined in any Court of the United States, than according to the rules of the common law.

Amendment VIII

Excessive bail shall not be required, nor excessive fines imposed, nor cruel and unusual punishments inflicted.

Amendment IX

The enumeration in the Constitution, of certain rights, shall not be construed to deny or disparage others retained by the people.

Amendment X

The powers not delegated to the United States by the Constitution, nor prohibited by it to the States, are reserved to the States respectively, or to the people.

Amendments 11–27

Amendment XI

Passed by Congress March 4, 1794. Ratified February 7, 1795.

The Judicial power of the United States shall not be **construed**[29] to extend to any suit in law or equity, commenced or prosecuted against one of the United States by Citizens of another State, or by Citizens or Subjects of any Foreign State.

Amendment XII

Passed by Congress December 9, 1803. Ratified June 15, 1804.

The Electors shall meet in their respective states and vote by ballot for President and Vice-President, one of whom, at least, shall not be an inhabitant of the same state with themselves; they shall name in their ballots the person voted for as President, and in distinct ballots the person voted for as Vice-President, and they shall make distinct lists of all persons voted for as President, and of all persons voted for as Vice-President, and of the number of votes for each, which lists they shall sign and certify, and transmit sealed to the seat of the government of the United States, directed to the President of the Senate;—the President of the Senate shall, in the presence of the Senate and House of Representatives, open all the certificates and the votes shall then be counted;—The person having the greatest number of votes for President, shall be the President, if such number be a majority of the whole number of Electors appointed; and if no person have such majority, then from the persons having the highest numbers not exceeding three on the list of those voted for as President, the House of Representatives shall choose immediately, by ballot, the President. But in choosing the

Vocabulary

[29] **construed** explained or interpreted

President and Vice President

The Twelfth Amendment changed the election procedure for president and vice president.

President, the votes shall be taken by states, the representation from each state having one vote; a quorum for this purpose shall consist of a member or members from two-thirds of the states, and a majority of all the states shall be necessary to a choice. ~~And if the House of Representatives shall not choose a President whenever the right of choice shall devolve upon them, before the fourth day of March next following, then the Vice-President shall act as President, as in case of the death or other constitutional disability of the President.~~—The person having the greatest number of votes as Vice-President, shall be the Vice-President, if such number be a majority of the whole number of Electors appointed, and if no person have a majority, then from the two highest numbers on the list, the Senate shall choose the Vice-President; a quorum for the purpose shall consist of two-thirds of the whole number of Senators, and a majority of the whole number shall be necessary to a choice. But no person constitutionally ineligible to the office of President shall be eligible to that of Vice-President of the United States.

Amendment XIII

Passed by Congress January 31, 1865. Ratified December 6, 1865.

1. Slavery Banned Neither slavery nor **involuntary servitude,**[30] except as a punishment for crime whereof the party shall have been duly convicted, shall exist within the United States, or any place subject to their jurisdiction.

2. Enforcement Congress shall have power to enforce this article by appropriate legislation.

Amendment XIV

Passed by Congress June 13, 1866. Ratified July 9, 1868.

1. Citizenship Defined All persons born or naturalized in the United States, and subject to the jurisdiction thereof, are citizens of the United States and of the State wherein they reside. No State shall make or enforce any law which shall abridge the privileges or immunities of citizens of the United States; nor shall any State deprive any person of life, liberty, or property, without due process of law; nor deny to any person within its jurisdiction the equal protection of the laws.

2. Voting Rights Representatives shall be apportioned among the several States according to their respective numbers, counting the whole number of persons in each State, ~~excluding Indians not taxed~~. But when the right to vote at any election for the choice of electors for President and Vice-President of the United States, Representatives in Congress, the Executive and Judicial officers of a State, or the members of the Legislature thereof, is denied to any of the ~~male~~ inhabitants of such State, ~~being twenty-one years of age~~, and citizens of the United States, or in any way abridged, except for participation in rebellion, or other crime, the basis of representation therein shall be reduced in the proportion which the number of such ~~male~~ citizens shall bear to the whole number of ~~male~~ citizens ~~twenty-one years of age~~ in such State.

Vocabulary

[30] **involuntary servitude** being forced to work against one's will

Abolishing Slavery

Although some slaves had been freed during the Civil War, slavery was not abolished until the Thirteenth Amendment took effect.

Protecting the Rights of Citizens

In 1833 the Supreme Court ruled that the Bill of Rights limited the federal government but not the state governments. This ruling was interpreted to mean that states were able to keep African Americans from becoming state citizens and keep the Bill of Rights from protecting them. The Fourteenth Amendment defines citizenship and prevents states from interfering in the rights of citizens of the United States.

3. Rebels Banned from Government   No person shall be a Senator or Representative in Congress, or elector of President and Vice-President, or hold any office, civil or military, under the United States, or under any State, who, having previously taken an oath, as a member of Congress, or as an officer of the United States, or as a member of any State legislature, or as an executive or judicial officer of any State, to support the Constitution of the United States, shall have engaged in insurrection or rebellion against the same, or given aid or comfort to the enemies thereof. But Congress may by a vote of two-thirds of each House, remove such disability.

4. Payment of Debts   The validity of the public debt of the United States, authorized by law, including debts incurred for payment of pensions and bounties for services in suppressing insurrection or rebellion, shall not be questioned. But neither the United States nor any State shall assume or pay any debt or obligation incurred in aid of insurrection or rebellion against the United States, ~~or any claim for the loss or emancipation of any slave~~; but all such debts, obligations and claims shall be held illegal and void.

5. Enforcement   The Congress shall have the power to enforce, by appropriate legislation, the provisions of this article.

Amendment XV

Passed by Congress February 26, 1869. Ratified February 3, 1870.

1. Voting Rights   The right of citizens of the United States to vote shall not be denied or abridged by the United States or by any State on account of race, color, or previous condition of servitude.

2. Enforcement   The Congress shall have the power to enforce this article by appropriate legislation.

Amendment XVI

Passed by Congress July 2, 1909. Ratified February 3, 1913.

The Congress shall have power to lay and collect taxes on incomes, from whatever source derived, without apportionment among the several States, and without regard to any census or enumeration.

Amendment XVII

Passed by Congress May 13, 1912. Ratified April 8, 1913.

1. Senators Elected by Citizens   The Senate of the United States shall be composed of two Senators from each State, elected by the people thereof, for six years; and each Senator shall have one vote. The electors in each State shall have the qualifications requisite for electors of the most numerous branch of the State legislatures.

2. Vacancies   When vacancies happen in the representation of any State in the Senate, the executive authority of such State shall issue writs of election to fill such vacancies: *Provided*, That the legislature of any State may empower the executive thereof to make temporary appointments until the people fill the vacancies by election as the legislature may direct.

3. Future Elections ~~This amendment shall not be so construed as to affect the election or term of any Senator chosen before it becomes valid as part of the Constitution.~~

Amendment XVIII

Passed by Congress December 18, 1917. Ratified January 16, 1919. Repealed by Amendment XXI.

1. Liquor Banned ~~After one year from the ratification of this article the manufacture, sale, or transportation of intoxicating liquors within, the importation thereof into, or the exportation thereof from the United States and all territory subject to the jurisdiction thereof for beverage purposes is hereby prohibited.~~

2. Enforcement ~~The Congress and the several States shall have concurrent power to enforce this article by appropriate legislation.~~

3. Ratification ~~This article shall be inoperative unless it shall have been ratified as an amendment to the Constitution by the legislatures of the several States, as provided in the Constitution, within seven years from the date of the submission hereof to the States by the Congress.~~

Amendment XIX

Passed by Congress June 4, 1919. Ratified August 18, 1920.

1. Voting Rights The right of citizens of the United States to vote shall not be denied or abridged by the United States or by any State on account of sex.

2. Enforcement Congress shall have power to enforce this article by appropriate legislation.

Amendment XX

Passed by Congress March 2, 1932. Ratified January 23, 1933.

1. Presidential Terms The terms of the President and the Vice President shall end at noon on the 20th day of January, and the terms of Senators and Representatives at noon on the 3d day of January, of the years in which such terms would have ended if this article had not been ratified; and the terms of their successors shall then begin.

2. Meeting of Congress The Congress shall assemble at least once in every year, and such meeting shall begin at noon on the 3d day of January, unless they shall by law appoint a different day.

3. Succession of Vice President If, at the time fixed for the beginning of the term of the President, the President elect shall have died, the Vice President elect shall become President. If a President shall not have been chosen before the time fixed for the beginning of his term, or if the President elect

Prohibition

Although many people believed that the Eighteenth Amendment was good for the health and welfare of the American people, it was repealed 14 years later.

Women's Suffrage

Abigail Adams and others were disappointed that the Declaration of Independence and the Constitution did not specifically include women. It took many years and much campaigning before suffrage for women was finally achieved.

Taking Office

In the original Constitution, a newly elected president and Congress did not take office until March 4, which was four months after the November election. The officials who were leaving office were called lame ducks because they had little influence during those four months. The Twentieth Amendment changed the date that the new president and Congress take office. Members of Congress now take office during the first week of January, and the president takes office on January 20.

shall have failed to qualify, then the Vice President elect shall act as President until a President shall have qualified; and the Congress may by law provide for the case wherein neither a President elect nor a Vice President shall have qualified, declaring who shall then act as President, or the manner in which one who is to act shall be selected, and such person shall act accordingly until a President or Vice President shall have qualified.

4. Succession by Vote of Congress The Congress may by law provide for the case of the death of any of the persons from whom the House of Representatives may choose a President whenever the right of choice shall have devolved upon them, and for the case of the death of any of the persons from whom the Senate may choose a Vice President whenever the right of choice shall have devolved upon them.

5. Ratification ~~Sections 1 and 2 shall take effect on the 15th day of October following the ratification of this article.~~

6. Ratification ~~This article shall be inoperative unless it shall have been ratified as an amendment to the Constitution by the legislatures of three-fourths of the several States within seven years from the date of its submission.~~

Amendment XXI

Passed by Congress February 20, 1933. Ratified December 5, 1933.

1. 18th Amendment Repealed The eighteenth article of amendment to the Constitution of the United States is hereby repealed.

2. Liquor Allowed by Law The transportation or importation into any State, Territory, or Possession of the United States for delivery or use therein of intoxicating liquors, in violation of the laws thereof, is hereby prohibited.

3. Ratification ~~This article shall be inoperative unless it shall have been ratified as an amendment to the Constitution by conventions in the several States, as provided in the Constitution, within seven years from the date of the submission hereof to the States by the Congress.~~

Amendment XXII

Passed by Congress March 21, 1947. Ratified February 27, 1951.

1. Term Limits No person shall be elected to the office of the President more than twice, and no person who has held the office of President, or acted as President, for more than two years of a term to which some other person was elected President shall be elected to the office of President more than once. ~~But this Article shall not apply to any person holding the office of President when this Article was proposed by Congress, and shall not prevent any person who may be holding the office of President, or acting as President, during the term within which this Article becomes operative from holding the office of President or acting as President during the remainder of such term.~~

2. Ratification ~~This article shall be inoperative unless it shall have been ratified as an amendment to the Constitution by the legislatures of three-fourths of the several States within seven years from the date of its submission to the States by the Congress.~~

Amendment XXIII

Passed by Congress June 16, 1960. Ratified March 29, 1961.

1. District of Columbia Represented The District constituting the seat of Government of the United States shall appoint in such manner as Congress may direct:

A number of electors of President and Vice President equal to the whole number of Senators and Representatives in Congress to which the District would be entitled if it were a State, but in no event more than the least populous State; they shall be in addition to those appointed by the States, but they shall be considered, for the purposes of the election of President and Vice President, to be electors appointed by a State; and they shall meet in the District and perform such duties as provided by the twelfth article of amendment.

2. Enforcement The Congress shall have power to enforce this article by appropriate legislation.

Amendment XXIV

Passed by Congress August 27, 1962. Ratified January 23, 1964.

1. Voting Rights The right of citizens of the United States to vote in any primary or other election for President or Vice President, for electors for President or Vice President, or for Senator or Representative in Congress, shall not be denied or abridged by the United States or any State by reason of failure to pay poll tax or other tax.

2. Enforcement The Congress shall have power to enforce this article by appropriate legislation.

Amendment XXV

Passed by Congress July 6, 1965. Ratified February 10, 1967.

1. Sucession of Vice President In case of the removal of the President from office or of his death or resignation, the Vice President shall become President.

2. Vacancy of Vice President Whenever there is a vacancy in the office of the Vice President, the President shall nominate a Vice President who shall take office upon confirmation by a majority vote of both Houses of Congress.

3. Written Declaration Whenever the President transmits to the President pro tempore of the Senate and the Speaker of the House of Representatives his written declaration that he is unable to discharge the powers and duties of his office, and until he transmits to them a written declara-

---

Voting Rights

Until the ratification of the Twenty-third Amendment, the people of Washington, D.C., could not vote in presidential elections.

Presidential Disability

The illness of President Eisenhower in the 1950s and the assassination of President Kennedy in 1963 were the events behind the Twenty-fifth Amendment. The Constitution did not provide a clear-cut method for a vice president to take over for a disabled president or upon the death of a president. This amendment provides for filling the office of the vice president if a vacancy occurs, and it provides a way for the vice president—or someone else in the line of succession—to take over if the president is unable to perform the duties of that office.

tion to the contrary, such powers and duties shall be discharged by the Vice President as Acting President.

4. Removing the President Whenever the Vice President and a majority of either the principal officers of the executive departments or of such other body as Congress may by law provide, transmit to the President pro tempore of the Senate and the Speaker of the House of Representatives their written declaration that the President is unable to discharge the powers and duties of his office, the Vice President shall immediately assume the powers and duties of the office as Acting President.

Thereafter, when the President transmits to the President pro tempore of the Senate and the Speaker of the House of Representatives his written declaration that no inability exists, he shall resume the powers and duties of his office unless the Vice President and a majority of either the principal officers of the executive department or of such other body as Congress may by law provide, transmit within four days to the President pro tempore of the Senate and the Speaker of the House of Representatives their written declaration that the President is unable to discharge the powers and duties of his office. Thereupon Congress shall decide the issue, assembling within forty-eight hours for that purpose if not in session. If the Congress, within twenty-one days after receipt of the latter written declaration, or, if Congress is not in session, within twenty-one days after Congress is required to assemble, determines by two-thirds vote of both Houses that the President is unable to discharge the powers and duties of his office, the Vice President shall continue to discharge the same as Acting President; otherwise, the President shall resume the powers and duties of his office.

Amendment XXVI

Passed by Congress March 23, 1971. Ratified July 1, 1971.

1. Voting Rights The right of citizens of the United States, who are eighteen years of age or older, to vote shall not be denied or abridged by the United States or by any State on account of age.

2. Enforcement The Congress shall have power to enforce this article by appropriate legislation.

Amendment XXVII

Originally proposed September 25, 1789. Ratified May 7, 1992.

No law, varying the compensation for the services of the Senators and Representatives, shall take effect, until an election of representatives shall have intervened.

Expanded Suffrage

The Voting Rights Act of 1970 tried to set the voting age at 18. However, the Supreme Court ruled that the act set the voting age for national elections only, not for state or local elections. The Twenty-sixth Amendment gave 18-year-old citizens the right to vote in all elections.

World: Political

ATLAS

ARCTIC OCEAN

Greenland
(DENMARK)

ALASKA
(U.S.)

60°N

Godthåb

ICELAND

Ar

CANADA

Aleutian Islands

Vancouver   Winnipeg

40°N

NORTH
AMERICA

Chicago   Ottawa   Montreal
Toronto

UNITED
STATES

Washington,   New York City
D.C.

ATLANTIC
OCEAN

Rabat
Casablanca

MOROCCO

Los Angeles

Houston

Bermuda
(U.K.)

WESTERN
SAHARA
(Sovereignty
Disputed)

Tropic of Cancer

MEXICO

20°N

Mexico
City

MAURITANIA

Nouakchott

HAWAII
(U.S.)

CAPE VERDE   Dakar   SENEGAL

Bamako   BUF

GAMBIA

GUINEA-BISSAU   GUINEA

Caracas

VENEZUELA   GUYANA

SIERRA   G
LEONE   CÔTE
D'IVOI

Georgetown   SURINAME

LIBERIA

0°   Equator

PACIFIC

Bogotá   Paramaribo   FRENCH GUIANA
(FRANCE)

N

KIRIBATI

OCEAN

COLOMBIA

Quito

W   E

Galápagos
Islands
(ECUADOR)

ECUADOR

S

SAMOA   American
Samoa

PERU

SOUTH
AMERICA

Lima

BRAZIL

Brasília

20°S

TONGA

BOLIVIA
La Paz
Sucre

Rio de Janeiro

Tropic of Capricorn

PARAGUAY

São Paulo

ATLANTIC

CHILE

Asunción

OCEAN

	Boundaries
⊛	National capitals
•	Other cities

0   500   1,000 Miles

0   500 1,000 Kilometers

Projection: Mollweide

URUGUAY

Santiago   Buenos
Aires   Montevideo

ARGENTINA

40°S

Falkland
Islands
(U.K.)

South
Georgia
(U.K.)

South Sandwich
Islands

60°S

160°W   140°W   120°W   100°W   80°W   60°   40°W   20°W

Antarctic Circle

90°W   80°W

70°W

FLORIDA
(U.S.)

Nassau

Tropic of Cancer   60°W

0   200   400 Miles

BAHAMAS

ATLANTIC   OCEAN

20°N

0   200   400 Kilometers

Projection: Mercator

Havana

Turks and Caicos Is.
(U.K.)

GULF OF
MEXICO

CUBA

Cayman Is.
(U.K.)

HAITI   DOMINICAN
REPUBLIC

Virgin Islands
(U.S. and U.K.)

1

MEXICO   BELIZE

Port-au-Prince

Santo

Puerto Rico
(U.S.)

2

Belmopan

JAMAICA

Domingo

Guadeloupe (FRANCE)

3

GUATEMALA   HONDURAS

Kingston

CARIBBEAN   SEA

Martinique (FRANCE)

4

6

Guatemala City   Tegucigalpa

San Salvador

NICARAGUA

Netherlands
Antilles
(NETHERLANDS)

5

7

EL SALVADOR   Managua

Aruba
(NETHERLANDS)

N

COSTA RICA

Panama

Port-of-
Spain

W   E

City

TRINIDAD AND
TOBAGO

S

San José

10°N

PANAMA

VENEZUELA

PACIFIC   OCEAN

COLOMBIA

GUYANA

90°W

COUNTRY	CAPITAL
1 Antigua and Barbuda	St. Johns
2 St. Kitts and Nevis	Basseterre
3 Dominica	Roseau
4 St. Lucia	Castries
5 St. Vincent and the Grenadines	Kingstown
6 Barbados	Bridgetown
7 Grenada	St. George's

R26 ATLAS

	COUNTRY	CAPITAL
1	Czech Republic	Prague
2	Slovakia	Bratislava
3	Slovenia	Ljubljana
4	Croatia	Zagreb
5	Bosnia and Herzegovina	Sarajevo
6	Macedonia	Skopje
7	Serbia and Montenegro	Belgrade
8	Lithuania	Vilnius
9	Latvia	Riga
10	Estonia	Tallinn

North America: Physical

ASIA

EUROPE

ARCTIC OCEAN

+ North Pole

POLAR ICE PACK

St. Lawrence Island

Bering Sea

Nunivak Island

Bering Strait

BROOKS RANGE

Queen Elizabeth Islands

Greenland

Denmark Strait

Beaufort Sea

Banks Island

Ellesmere Island

Baffin Bay

Cape Farewell

Arctic Circle

Mt. McKinley 20,320 ft. (6,194 m)

ALASKA RANGE

Yukon River

YUKON PLATEAU

Victoria Island

Baffin Island

Davis Strait

Labrador Sea

Kodiak Island

Gulf of Alaska

Great Bear Lake

Southampton Island

Hudson Strait

Alexander Archipelago

Queen Charlotte Islands

Peace River

Great Slave Lake

Coats Island

Mansel Island

Hudson Bay

Anticosti Island

Newfoundland

PACIFIC OCEAN

Vancouver Island

Mackenzie River

Athabasca River

Lake Athabasca

CANADIAN

Nelson River

Lake Winnipeg

SHIELD

Prince Edward Island

Gulf of St. Lawrence

Cape Breton Island

Mount Rainier 14,410 ft. (4,392 m)

CASCADE RANGE

ROCKY

Saskatchewan River

St. Lawrence River

Cape Mendocino

Columbia River

GREAT

MOUNTAINS

Missouri River

Lake Superior

L. Michigan

Lake Huron

Lake Ontario

Lake Erie

APPALACHIAN

Cape Cod

Long Island

ATLANTIC OCEAN

COAST

SIERRA NEVADA

GREAT BASIN

DEATH VALLEY

CENTRAL VALLEY

BLACK HILLS

PLAINS

Platte River

INTERIOR PLAINS

Ohio River

MOUNTAINS

Cumberland R.

PIEDMONT

Cape Hatteras

Bermuda

Mount Whitney 14,494 ft. (4,418 m)

COLORADO PLATEAU

RANGES

MOUNTAINS

OZARK PLATEAU

Arkansas River

Red River

Mississippi River

Tennessee River

ATLANTIC COASTAL PLAIN

Guadalupe Island

BAJA CALIFORNIA

Rio Grande

Brazos River

GULF COASTAL PLAIN

Mississippi River

FLORIDA PENINSULA

Cape Canaveral

Tropic of Cancer

SIERRA MADRE OCCIDENTAL

Gulf of California

Gulf of Mexico

Florida Keys

Straits of Florida

Bahamas

SIERRA MADRE ORIENTAL

Popocatépetl 17,887 ft. (5,452 m)

YUCATÁN PENINSULA

Cuba

Jamaica

Greater Antilles

Hispaniola

Puerto Rico

Lesser Antilles

SIERRA MADRE DEL SUR

Caribbean Sea

Trinidad

CENTRAL AMERICA

Lake Nicaragua

ISTHMUS OF PANAMA

SOUTH AMERICA

0° Equator

ELEVATION

Feet	Meters
13,120	4,000
6,560	2,000
1,640	500
656	200
(Sea level) 0	0 (Sea level)
Below sea level	Below sea level

Ice cap

0 300 600 Miles

0 300 600 Kilometers

Projection: Azimuthal Equal Area

N
W   E
S

North America: Political

ARCTIC OCEAN

+North Pole

EUROPE

ASIA

ATLAS

ICELAND

Greenland (DENMARK)

ALASKA (U.S.)

Anchorage

Juneau

CANADA

Edmonton

Calgary

Vancouver

Seattle

Portland

Winnipeg

Minneapolis

Milwaukee   Detroit

Chicago   Cleveland

Columbus

Indianapolis   St. Louis

San Francisco   San Jose

Salt Lake City

Denver   Kansas City

UNITED STATES

Los Angeles   San Diego   Tijuana

Phoenix

Memphis

Atlanta   Birmingham

Dallas

Austin   San Antonio

Houston   New Orleans

Monterrey

MEXICO

Guadalajara   Mexico City

Puebla   Mérida

Belmopan   BELIZE

GUATEMALA   HONDURAS

Guatemala City   Tegucigalpa

San Salvador   NICARAGUA

EL SALVADOR   Managua

San José

COSTA RICA   PANAMA   Panama City

Ottawa   Toronto

Montreal   Quebec

Boston   Cape Cod

New York City

Philadelphia

Baltimore   Washington, D.C.

Norfolk

Cape Hatteras

Jacksonville

Cape Canaveral

Miami   THE BAHAMAS   Nassau

Havana   CUBA   HAITI

JAMAICA   Kingston   Port-au-Prince

DOMINICAN REPUBLIC   Santo Domingo

San Juan   Puerto Rico (U.S.)

ATLANTIC OCEAN

Bermuda (U.K.)

PACIFIC OCEAN

SOUTH AMERICA

Legend

- Boundaries
- ⊛ National capitals
- • Other cities

0   300   600 Miles

0   300   600 Kilometers

Projection: Azimuthal Equal Area

South America: Physical

CENTRAL
AMERICA

Caribbean Sea

Panama
Canal

Gulf
of
Panama

Margarita
Island

Tobago

Trinidad

Orinoco River
Delta

LLANOS

Meta
River

Orinoco River

Angel Falls

GUIANA

HIGHLANDS

Devil's Island
Cape Orange

ATLANTIC
OCEAN

Mount Tolima
18,425 ft.
(5,616 m)

Malpelo
Island

Orinoco River

Rio
Negro

Amazon
River Delta

Amazon River

Galápagos
Islands

Equator

Mount Chimborazo
20,561 ft.
(6,267 m)

Caqueta
River

Japurá
River

Amazon

River

AMAZON
BASIN

Equator 0°

Gulf of Guayaquil

Marañón River

Juruá

River

Amazon
River

Ucayali River

Purus

Tapajós River

Tocantins
River

Xingu River

River

Madeira

River

River

Parnaíba River

BRAZILIAN

HIGHLANDS

Mount Huascarán
22,205 ft.
(6,768 m)

PACIFIC

OCEAN

ANDES

Mamoré

River

MATO GROSSO
PLATEAU

Araguaia

River

São Francisco River

ANDES

Ancohuma Peak
20,958 ft.
(6,388 m)

ATACAMA DESERT

Lake
Poopó

CHACO

Paraguay
River

BRAZILIAN
PLATEAU

Tropic of Capricorn

Tropic of Capricorn

San Ambrosio
Island

San Félix Island

Salado

River

Uruguay River

Juan Fernández
Islands

Mount Aconcagua
22,834 ft.
(6,960 m)

PAMPAS

Salado River

Río de la Plata

ATLANTIC

OCEAN

Colorado
River

Gulf of San Matías

PATAGONIA

Chiloé
Island

Chonos
Archipelago

Gulf of
San Jorge

Cape Tres Puntas

Bahía
Grande

Strait of
Magellan

Falkland
Islands

South
Georgia
Islands

Tierra del
Fuego

Cape Horn

ELEVATION

Feet		Meters
13,120		4,000
6,560		2,000
1,640		500
656		200
(Sea level) 0		0 (Sea level)
Below sea level		Below sea level

0 — 250 — 500 Miles

0 — 250 — 500 Kilometers

Projection: Azimuthal Equal Area

South America: Political

CENTRAL
AMERICA

Caribbean Sea

Barranquilla
Cartagena

Caracas

VENEZUELA

Medellín

Bogotá

COLOMBIA

Cali

Lake
Maracaibo

Orinoco River

Georgetown
Paramaribo

GUYANA

Cayenne

SURINAME   FRENCH
GUIANA
(FRANCE)

ATLANTIC
OCEAN

Malpelo
Island
(COLOMBIA)

Quito

ECUADOR

Guayaquil

Galápagos
Islands
(ECUADOR)

Equator

Río Negro

Amazon

Amazon River

Belém

PERU

Marañón River

Ucayali River

Trujillo

Callao   Lima

Lake
Titicaca

Arequipa

La Paz

BOLIVIA

Sucre

Lake
Poopó

BRAZIL

Brasília

São Francisco River

Recife

Salvador

Belo Horizonte

PACIFIC
OCEAN

PARAGUAY

Paraguay River

Asunción

Campinas

São Paulo

Rio de Janeiro

Tropic of Capricorn

San Ambrosio
Island
(CHILE)

San Félix Island
(CHILE)

Curitiba

Paraná River

Uruguay River

Pôrto Alegre

CHILE

Juan Fernández
Islands
(CHILE)

Córdoba

Valparaíso
Santiago

Rosario

Buenos Aires

ARGENTINA

URUGUAY

Montevideo

Río de la Plata

ATLANTIC
OCEAN

Boundaries

⊛ National capitals
• Other cities

0   250   500 Miles

0   250   500 Kilometers

Projection: Azimuthal Equal Area

Strait of
Magellan

Falkland
Islands (U.K.)

Tierra del
Fuego

South Georgia
Island
(U.K.)

Europe: Physical

ELEVATION

Feet	Meters
13,120	4,000
6,560	2,000
1,640	500
656	200
(Sea level) 0	0 (Sea level)
Below sea level	Below sea level

Ice cap

300 Miles

300 Kilometers

0   150

0   150   300

Projection: Azimuthal Equal Area

ASIA

URAL MOUNTAINS

NORTHERN EUROPEAN PLAIN

CAUCASUS MTS.

Mt. Elbrus 15,642 m 18,510 ft.

Caspian Sea

SOUTHWEST ASIA

Barents Sea

KOLA PENINSULA

White Sea

Lake Onega

Lake Ladoga

Rybinsk Reservoir

Pechora River

Kama River

Dvina River

North River

Volga River

Don River

Dnipro River

Sea of Azov

CRIMEAN PENINSULA

Black Sea

North Cape

ARCTIC OCEAN

KJØLEN MOUNTAINS

BALTIC PLAINS

Gulf of Finland

Gulf of Bothnia

Lake Vänern

Lake Vättern

Daugava River

Dnister River

CARPATHIAN MTS.

TRANSYLVANIAN ALPS

Nistru River

BALKAN PENINSULA

Sea of Marmara

Aegean Sea

Rhodes

Crete

30°E

Norwegian Sea

Baltic Sea

Vistula River

Oder River

Elba River

Danube River

DINARIC ALPS

Adriatic Sea

APENNINES

Tiber River

Sea

Malta

Sicily

Tyrrhenian Sea

20°E

Skagerrak

Kattegat

North Sea

Rhine River

ALPS

Lake Geneva

Mont Blanc 15,781 ft. 14,810 m

Po River

Corsica

Sardinia

Balearic Islands

Mediterranean Sea

AFRICA

Shetland Islands

Orkney Islands

PENNINES

Hebrides

British Isles

Irish Sea

Thames River

English Channel

Seine River

Loire River

Garonne River

Bay of Biscay

PYRENEES

IBERIAN PENINSULA

Douro River

Tagus River

Guadiana River

Guadalquivir River

Ebro River

Strait of Gibraltar

Faeroe Islands

Iceland

ATLANTIC OCEAN

Arctic Circle

Cape Finisterre

Cape

N E S W

R32 ATLAS

Europe: Political

Boundaries
⊛ National capitals
• Other cities

150   300 Miles
150   300 Kilometers

Projection: Azimuthal Equal Area

ASIA

URAL MOUNTAINS

RUSSIA

Nizhny Novgorod

Ural River

Volga River

Caspian Sea

SOUTHWEST ASIA

Moscow

Don River

Black Sea

St. Petersburg

White Sea

Barents Sea

North Cape

Gulf of Finland

FINLAND

Helsinki

ESTONIA
Tallinn

LATVIA
Riga

LITHUANIA
Vilnius

RUSSIA

BELARUS
Minsk

Kiev

UKRAINE

MOLDOVA
Chișinău

Dnieper River

Bucharest

ROMANIA

BULGARIA
Sofia

Danube River

MACEDONIA
Skopje

GREECE
Athens

Aegean Sea

Rhodes

Crete

SWEDEN

Stockholm

Göteborg

Gulf of Bothnia

Baltic Sea

POLAND
Warsaw

Krakow

CZECH REPUBLIC
Prague

SLOVAKIA
Bratislava

HUNGARY
Budapest

Vienna

AUSTRIA

Zagreb

CROATIA

SLOVENIA
Ljubljana

BOSNIA AND HERZEGOVINA
Sarajevo

SERBIA AND MONTENEGRO
Belgrade

ALBANIA
Tiranë

Adriatic Sea

ARCTIC OCEAN

NORWAY
Oslo

Bergen

DENMARK
Copenhagen

Hamburg

GERMANY
Berlin
Dresden

Cologne
Bonn

Elbe River

Munich

LIECHTENSTEIN
Vaduz

SWITZERLAND
Bern

Milan

SAN MARINO

ITALY
Rome

VATICAN CITY

Naples

Sicily

MALTA
Valletta

North Sea

Shetland Islands

Faeroe Islands (DENMARK)

ICELAND
Reykjavik

SCOTLAND
Edinburgh

NORTHERN IRELAND
Belfast

IRELAND
Dublin

UNITED KINGDOM

WALES
Liverpool

ENGLAND
London

NETHERLANDS
Amsterdam
The Hague

BELGIUM
Brussels

LUXEMBOURG
Luxembourg

FRANCE
Paris

Lyon

Marseille

Rhône River

MONACO
Monaco

Corsica (FRANCE)

Sardinia (ITALY)

PYRENEES

ANDORRA
Andorra la Vella

Barcelona

Balearic Islands (SPAIN)

Mediterranean Sea

AFRICA

British Isles

English Channel

Channel Islands (U.K.)

Bay of Biscay

SPAIN
Madrid
Valencia
Seville

Gibraltar (U.K.)

Strait of Gibraltar

PORTUGAL
Lisbon

Tagus River

ATLANTIC OCEAN

Arctic Circle

N E W S

Asia: Physical

ELEVATION

Feet	Meters
13,120	4,000
6,560	2,000
1,640	500
656	200
0 (Sea level)	0 (Sea level)
Below sea level	Below sea level

Ice cap

0   250   500   750 Miles
0   250   500   750 Kilometers

Projection: Azimuthal Equal Area

N   E   W   S

EUROPE

AFRICA

AUSTRALIA

PACIFIC OCEAN

INDIAN OCEAN

North Pole

Arctic Circle

Tropic of Cancer

Equator

Aleutian Islands

KAMCHATKA PENINSULA

Bering Sea

Sea of Okhotsk

CENTRAL RANGE

KOLYMA MTS.

CHERSKY RANGE

VERKHOYANSKY RANGE

STANOVOY MOUNTAINS

YABLONOV RANGE

Amur River

Aldan River

Lena River

SIBERIA

CENTRAL SIBERIAN PLATEAU

Sakhalin Island

Kuril Islands

Hokkaido

Honshu

Shikoku

Kyushu

Sea of Japan (East Sea)

Korean Strait

Ryukyu Islands

Okinawa

East China Sea

Yellow Sea

North China Plain

GREATER KHINGAN RANGE

MONGOLIAN PLATEAU

GOBI

Yellow River

Huang He

QIN LING

Yangtze

Si River

South China Sea

Hainan

BOREA HILLS

Taiwan

Luzon Strait

Luzon

Philippines

Mindanao

Celebes Sea

MADKE MOUNTAINS

New Guinea

Arafura Sea

Banda Sea

Celebes

Moluccas

Borneo

Java Sea

Bangka

Sumatra

Mentawai Islands

Java

MALAY PENINSULA

Gulf of Thailand

INDOCHINA PENINSULA

Chao Phraya River

Mekong River

Gulf of Tonkin

Irrawaddy River

Andaman Sea

Andaman Islands

Nicobar Islands

Bay of Bengal

Sri Lanka

Maldives

Lakshadweep Islands

Arabian Sea

Socotra Island

Gulf of Aden

Red Sea

RUB' AL-KHALI

AN-NAFUD

SINAI PENINSULA

SYRIAN DESERT

Euphrates River

Tigris River

Persian Gulf

ZAGROS MTS.

Gulf of Oman

Strait of Hormuz

ANATOLIAN PLATEAU

Mount Ararat 16,945 ft. (5,165 m)

CAUCASUS MTS.

Cyprus

Mediterranean Sea

Black Sea

Bosporus

Sea of Azov

Caspian Sea

USTYURT PLATEAU

Ural River

GREAT SALT DESERT

KARA KUM

Amu Darya

KYZYL KUM

TURAN LOWLAND

Syr Darya

HINDU KUSH

Suleiman Range

THAR DESERT

INDO-GANGETIC PLAIN

Indus River

Ganges River

DECCAN PLATEAU

Godavari

EASTERN GHATS

WESTERN GHATS

Brahmaputra River

HIMALAYAS

Mount Everest 29,035 ft. (8,850 m)

PLATEAU OF TIBET

KUNLUN MOUNTAINS

TARIM BASIN

TAKLIMAKAN DESERT

TIAN SHAN

Balqash Lake

KAZAKH UPLANDS

ALTAY MOUNTAINS

SAYAN MOUNTAINS

Irtysh River

Ishim River

Ural River

Tobol River

Ob River

WEST SIBERIAN PLAIN

URAL MOUNTAINS

Yenisey River

Lower Tunguska River

Angara River

TAYMYR PENINSULA

North Land

Franz Josef Land

Novaya Zemlya

Kara Sea

Barents Sea

Laptev Sea

Wrangel Island

New Siberian Islands

Asia: Political

Boundaries
⊛ National capitals
• Other cities

Boundaries
National capitals
Other cities

750 Miles
250 500 750 Kilometers

Projection: Two-Point Equidistant

PACIFIC OCEAN

New Guinea

AUSTRALIA

EAST TIMOR

Arafura Sea

Aleutian Islands

Bering Sea

Sea of Okhotsk

Sakhalin Island

Kuril Islands (RUSSIA)

JAPAN
Sapporo
Tokyo
Yokohama
Osaka
Nagoya
Kyoto
Hiroshima
Nagasaki

Vladivostok

NORTH KOREA
P'yongyang
SOUTH KOREA
Seoul
Pusan

Ryukyu Islands (JAPAN)
East China Sea
Yellow Sea

Shanghai
Qingdao
Dalian
Beijing
Great Wall of China
Fushun
Changchun
Harbin

TAIWAN
Taipei

Hong Kong
Macao
Guangzhou

PHILIPPINES
Manila

Celebes Sea

INDONESIA
Ujung Pandang
Surabaya
Semarang
Jakarta
Bandung

BRUNEI
Bandar Seri Begawan

MALAYSIA
Kuala Lumpur
SINGAPORE
Singapore

Medan

Tropic of Cancer

VIETNAM
Ho Chi Minh City
Hanoi
Hainan (CHINA)
South China Sea
Luzon Strait

CAMBODIA
Phnom Penh

LAOS
Vientiane
THAILAND
Bangkok
Gulf of Thailand

Wuhan
Nanjing
Xi'an
Chongqing
Chengdu
Huang He (Yellow River)
Jiang (Yangtze)

MYANMAR (BURMA)
Yangon (Rangoon)
Mandalay

Andaman Sea
Andaman Islands (INDIA)

YAKUTSK

Irkutsk

MONGOLIA
Ulaanbaatar

CHINA

Lena River
Angara River
Yenisey River
Lake Baykal

RUSSIA
Novosibirsk
Omsk
Chelyabinsk
Yekaterinburg

Ob River
Irtysh River
Lake Balkhash

KAZAKHSTAN
Astana
Almaty

URAL MOUNTAINS

KYRGYZSTAN
Bishkek

TAJIKISTAN
Dushanbe

UZBEKISTAN
Tashkent

TURKMENISTAN
Ashgabat

Moscow

Caspian Sea

AFGHANISTAN
Kabul

Mashhad

PAKISTAN
Islamabad
Lahore
Faisalabad
Karachi

IRAN
Tehran
Isfahan
Shiraz
Tabriz

NEPAL
Kathmandu
BHUTAN
Thimphu
BANGLADESH
Dhaka
Chittagong

Delhi
New Delhi
Jaipur
Ahmadabad
Bhopal
Nagpur
Kolkata (Calcutta)

INDIA
Hyderabad
Mumbai (Bombay)
Bangalore
Chennai (Madras)

Nu River
Brahmaputra River
Ganges River

Bay of Bengal

SRI LANKA
Colombo

MALDIVES
Male

Lakshadweep Islands (INDIA)

Nicobar Islands (INDIA)

Arabian Sea

INDIAN OCEAN

OMAN
Masqat (Muscat)

UNITED ARAB EMIRATES
Abu Dhabi

QATAR
Doha

BAHRAIN
Manama

KUWAIT
Kuwait City

SAUDI ARABIA
Riyadh
Mecca
Jidda

IRAQ
Baghdad
Basra
Mosul

Persian Gulf
Tigris River
Euphrates River

GEORGIA
T'bilisi
ARMENIA
Yerevan
AZERBAIJAN
Baku

TURKEY
Ankara
Istanbul
Izmir

Black Sea

CYPRUS
Nicosia

SYRIA
Damascus
Aleppo

LEBANON
Beirut

ISRAEL
Tel Aviv
Jerusalem

JORDAN
Amman

YEMEN
Sanaa

Gulf of Aden

Red Sea

Socotra (YEMEN)

Mediterranean Sea

EUROPE

RUSSIA

AFRICA

Equator

Arctic Circle

North Pole

Barents Sea
Kara Sea
Laptev Sea
Kazakhstan

Africa: Physical

EUROPE

SOUTHWEST
ASIA

Azores

Madeira
Islands

Strait of
Gibraltar

ATLAS MOUNTAINS

Mediterranean Sea

Gulf of
Sidra

Suez Canal

Persian Gulf

Canary
Islands

QATTARA
DEPRESSION

Tropic of Cancer

Cape
Blanc

EL DJOUF

S A H A R A

AHAGGAR
MOUNTAINS

AIR MTS.

TIBESTI
MOUNTAINS

LIBYAN DESERT

Lake
Nasser

Nile River

NUBIAN
DESERT

Red Sea

Cape Verde
Islands

Cape
Verde

Senegal R.

Niger River

S A H E L

S U D A N

CHAD
BASIN

Lake
Chad

Gulf of Aden

FOUTA
DJALLON

White Volta R.

Black Volta R.

Benue River

SUDAN
BASIN

Blue Nile

White Nile

ETHIOPIAN
HIGHLANDS

HORN OF AFRICA

SOMALI
PENINSULA

Cape
Palmas

Lake
Volta

Gulf of
Guinea

ADAMAWA MTS.

Ubangi River

Congo River

CONGO
BASIN

Lake
Albert

Lake
Edward

Lake
Turkana

RIFT VALLEY

Mount Kenya
17,058 ft.
(5,199 m)

Equator

Cape
Lopez

Kasai River

CAMEROON MT.

WESTERN RIFT VALLEY

Lake
Kivu

SERENGETI
PLAIN

EASTERN RIFT VALLEY

MASAI
STEPPE

Mount Kilimanjaro
19,340 ft.
(5,895 m)

Zanzibar

INDIAN
OCEAN

Seychelles

Ascension

ATLANTIC
OCEAN

Cuanza River

Lake
Tanganyika

Lake
Mweru

Lake Rukwa

Lake Malawi
(Nyasa)

Cape Delgado

Comoro
Islands

Lake
Kariba

Zambezi River

Mozambique Channel

Madagascar

Mauritius

Réunion

Tropic of Capricorn

NAMIB DESERT

Okavango
Delta

Victoria
Falls

KALAHARI BASIN

KALAHARI
DESERT

Limpopo River

Orange River

Vaal River

GREAT
KARROO

DRAKENSBERG MOUNTAINS

Cape of
Good Hope

ELEVATION

Feet	Meters
13.120	4,000
6,560	2,000
1,640	500
656	200
(Sea level) 0	0 (Sea level)
Below sea level	Below sea level

0   250   500 Miles

0   250   500 Kilometers

Projection: Azimuthal Equal Area

Africa: Political

EUROPE

SOUTHWEST
ASIA

Azores
(PORTUGAL)

Madeira
(PORTUGAL)

Strait of
Gibraltar

Algiers Tunis

Casablanca Rabat

MOROCCO

TUNISIA

Tripoli

Mediterranean Sea

Alexandria

Giza Cairo

Suez Canal

Canary Islands
(SPAIN)

El Aaiún

WESTERN
SAHARA
(Claimed by
Morocco)

ALGERIA

LIBYA

EGYPT

Lake
Nasser

Tropic of Cancer

**CAPE
VERDE**

Praia

MAURITANIA

Nouakchott

MALI

Niger River

SENEGAL

Dakar

GAMBIA

Banjul

Bissau

**GUINEA
BISSAU**

Bamako

GUINEA

Conakry

Freetown

SIERRA LEONE

Monrovia

LIBERIA

Abidjan

**BURKINA
FASO**

Ouagadougou

**CÔTE
D'IVOIRE**

Yamoussoukro

GHANA

Accra

Niamey

NIGER

BENIN

TOGO

Lomé

NIGERIA

Abuja

Lagos

Porto-
Novo

CHAD

N'Djamena

Lake
Chad

Khartoum

SUDAN

River White Nile

Blue Nile

ERITREA

Asmara

DJIBOUTI

Djibouti

Red Sea

Gulf of Aden

ETHIOPIA

Addis Ababa

SOMALIA

Mogadishu

CAMEROON

Malabo

Yaoundé

Bangui

**CENTRAL AFRICAN
REPUBLIC**

EQUATORIAL GUINEA

SÃO TOMÉ AND PRÍNCIPE

São Tomé

Gulf of
Guinea

Libreville

**REPUBLIC
OF THE
CONGO**

GABON

Brazzaville

CABINDA
(ANGOLA)

Kinshasa

Kisangani

Congo River

**DEMOCRATIC
REPUBLIC
OF THE CONGO**

UGANDA

Kampala

RWANDA

Kigali

Bujumbura

BURUNDI

Lake
Victoria

KENYA

Nairobi

Mombasa

Pemba
Zanzibar

**INDIAN
OCEAN**

Victoria

SEYCHELLES

TANZANIA

Dodoma

Lake
Tanganyika

Dar es Salaam

Luanda

ANGOLA

Lubumbashi

Lake Malawi
(Nyasa)

COMOROS

Moroni

MALAWI

Lilongwe

ZAMBIA

Lusaka

Zambezi River

Harare

ZIMBABWE

Bulawayo

MOZAMBIQUE

Antananarivo

MADAGASCAR

MAURITIUS

Port Louis

Réunion
(FRANCE)

St. Helena
(U.K.)

*ATLANTIC
OCEAN*

Equator

0° Equator 0°

NAMIBIA

Windhoek

BOTSWANA

Gaborone

Pretoria

Johannesburg

Bloemfontein

Maputo

Mbabane

SWAZILAND

Maseru

LESOTHO

Orange River

SOUTH AFRICA

Cape Town

Tropic of Capricorn

N W E S

Legend

- Boundaries
- ⊛ National capitals
- • Other cities

0   250   500 Miles

0   250   500 Kilometers

Projection: Azimuthal Equal Area

Gazetteer

A

Aegean Sea (ee-JEE-uhn) a sea east of Greece; the sea provided Greeks with a source of food and a means of trading with other peoples (p. 255)

Africa the second-largest continent (p. R36)

Akkad (A-kad) (33°N, 44°E) a city along the Euphrates River near modern Baghdad; started by Akkadian emperor Sargon in 2300s BC (p. 63)

Aksum (AHK-soom) an ancient state in southeast Nubia on the Red Sea, in what are now Ethiopia and Eritrea; through trade, Aksum became the most powerful state in the region (p. 131)

Alexandria (31°N, 30°E) a city in Egypt, named after Alexander the Great (p. 300)

Alps a mountain range extending across south-central Europe (p. R32)

Amazon River a river east of the Andes in South America; it flows through a rain forest and into the Atlantic Ocean (p. R30)

Americas the two continents of North America and South America (p. 429)

Andes Mountains a mountain range along the west coast of South America (p. R30)

Antarctica the ice-covered continent at the South Pole (p. R26–27)

Asia the world's largest continent, bounded by the Arctic, Pacific, and Indian oceans (p. R34)

Asia Minor a large peninsula in west Asia, between the Black Sea and the Mediterranean Sea, forming modern Turkey (p. 258)

Athens (38°N, 24°E) an ancient city and modern capital of Greece; the world's first democracy developed in Athens around 500 BC (p. 258)

Australia an island continent between the South Pacific and Indian oceans (p. R27)

B

Babylon (32°N, 45°E) an ancient city on the lower Euphrates River in modern central Iraq (p. 63)

Bering Strait a 55-mile-wide body of water between Alaska and Siberia; location of possible land bridge connecting Asia and the Americas during the Ice Ages (p. R28)

Bethlehem (BETH-li-hem) (32°N, 35°E) a town in Judea; traditionally regarded as the birthplace of Jesus (p. 385)

Black Sea a sea between southeast Europe and Asia, north of Asia Minor (p. R32)

Byzantine Empire the eastern part of the Roman Empire that developed non-Roman influences (p. 415)

C

Calakmul (kah-lahk-MOOL) an ancient Maya city; fought battles against its rival city, Tikal (p. 435)

Canaan (KAY-nuhn) a region in what is now Israel near the coast of the Mediterranean Sea; according to the Bible, Abraham settled in Canaan and his Hebrew descendants lived there for many years (p. 227)

Carthage (KAHR-thij) (37°N, 10°E) a key trade center built by the Phoenicians on the northern coast of Africa; it became one of the most powerful cities in the Mediterranean (p. 79)

Central America the part of North America between Mexico and South America; parts of the northern countries of Central America make up the area known as Mesoamerica (p. R28)

Chang Jiang (or Yangzi River) a river that cuts through central China, flowing from the mountains of Tibet to the Pacific Ocean (p. 183)

China a country located east of India and the
Ganges River; a series of dynasties built
China into a world power (p. 183)

Constantinople (KAHN-stant-uhn-oh-puhl)
(42°N, 76°E) the capital of the Byzantine
Empire, located in modern Turkey between
the Black Sea and Mediterranean Sea (p. 415)

Crete an island in the Mediterranean Sea,
south of Greece; a civilization formed there
around 2000 BC (p. 255)

Damascus (34°N, 36°E) an ancient city and
the modern capital of Syria; important in
the spread of Christianity (p. 388)

Dead Sea a salty lake on the boundary
between Israel and Jordan; 2,000-year-old
scrolls discovered near there help scholars
learn about the history of the Jews (p. 230)

Delhi (29°N, 77°E) historic city and capital of modern India; it was ruled by the
Gupta dynasty (p. 170)

Delphi an ancient city in central Greece;
Greeks traveled here to get advice from an
oracle of Apollo (p. 270)

Egypt a country in northeast Africa and location of the mouth of the Nile River; ancient
Egypt was famous for its temples, pyramids,
art, and cultural achievements, such as an
early writing system (p. R37)

Euphrates River a river that flows mainly
through Iraq and empties into the Persian
Gulf; silt from the Euphrates helped form
the Fertile Crescent in Mesopotamia (p. 57)

Europe a continent of many peninsulas
located between Asia and the Atlantic
Ocean (p. R32)

Fertile Crescent a large arc of rich farmland
between the Persian Gulf and the
Mediterranean Sea (p. 57)

Gaul an ancient region in Western Europe,
consisting mainly of parts of modern
France and Belgium; the Frankish king,
Clovis, built a kingdom in Gaul (p. 410)

Gaya (25°N, 85°E) a town in India; according to legend, Siddhartha Gautama found
enlightenment in Gaya (p. 160)

Gibraltar, Strait of (ji-BRAHL-ter) a strait, or narrow sea passage, between Spain and Moroc-
co, connecting the Mediterranean Sea and
the Atlantic Ocean (p. R32)

Giza (30°N, 31°E) an Egyptian city and the
site of large pyramids, including the Great
Pyramid of Khufu (p. 98)

Gobi (GOH-bee) a desert covering much of
northern China; the Gobi helped isolate
China from its neighbors (p. R34)

Greece a country in southern Europe with
mountains, rugged coastlines and scenic
islands; the country is called the birthplace
of democracy (p. R33)

Harappa (huh-RA-puh) a city that thrived
between 2300 and 1700 BC in the Indus
Valley, in what is now Pakistan (p. 147)

Himalayas a mountain range on the northern
Indian border; they are the highest mountains in the world (p. R34)

Huang He (Yellow River) a river that stretches
nearly 3,000 miles across China; it is sometimes called "China's Sorrow" (p. 183)

India a country and subcontinent in south
Asia; India was home to one of the world's
oldest civilizations (p. R35)

Indus Valley a river valley in modern Pakistan
where one of the earliest civilizations began
(p. 145)

GAZETTEER

Ionian Sea (eye-OH-nee-uhn) a sea west of Greece (p. 255)

Israel a country between the Mediterranean Sea and Jordan; it was the kingdom of the ancient Hebrews (p. 230)

Italy a country in southern Europe located on a peninsula in the Mediterranean; it was the center of the Roman Empire (p. R33)

J–K

Jerusalem (32°N, 35°E) a city established as the capital of Israel around 960–1000 BC (p. 230)

Judah (JOO-duh) one of the two kingdoms created when Israel was divided; the people in Judah came to be called Jews (p. 230)

Kerma (KAR-muh) a city on the Nile in the kingdom of Kush; it was captured by Egypt, forcing the Kushites to move their capital to Napata (p. 89)

Kish a city-state in Sumer that became powerful around 3500 BC (p. 63)

Kush the first great kingdom in Africa's interior; at times Kush ruled Egypt and at other times was ruled by Egypt (p. 123)

M

Macedonia a small kingdom located west of the Black Sea and north of the Aegean Sea; Macedonians conquered Greece in the 300s BC (p. 296)

Marathon an ancient city in Greece; it was the site of a battle in which the Greeks defeated the Persians (p. 290)

Mediterranean Sea a large sea surrounded by Europe, Africa, and Asia; it played a vital role in the development of civilizations and trade in the region (p. R32, R34)

Memphis (30°N, 31°E) an ancient Egyptian capital city at the southern tip of the Nile Delta; built around 3100 BC, it was the political and cultural center of Egypt for centuries (p. 89)

Meröe (MER-oh-wee) an ancient capital of Kush, located on the east bank of the Nile (p. 123)

Mesoamerica a region that includes the southern part of modern Mexico and part of northern Central America; the first permanent farming settlements in the Americas developed in Mesoamerica (p. 429)

Mesopotamia (mes-uh-puh-TAY-mee-uh) the region in southwest Asia between the Tigris and Euphrates rivers; it was the site of some of the world's earliest civilizations (p. 57)

Mohenjo Daro (mo-HEN-joh DAR-oh) (27°N, 68°E) an ancient city of the Harappan civilization, located in modern Pakistan (p. 147)

Mount Sinai according to the Bible, the mountain in Egypt where God gave Moses the stone tablets containing the Ten Commandments (p. 227)

Mycenae (my-SEE-nee) an ancient Greek city; the site of a strong fortress built by the Mycenaeans (p. 257)

N

Napata an ancient city on the Nile in Egypt; it was the capital of Kush in the 700s and 600s BC (p. 123)

Nile the longest river in the world; it flows from central Africa to the Mediterranean Sea and was vital to the development of civilizations in Egypt and Kush (p. R36)

Nineveh (37°N, 43°E) an ancient capital of Assyria, located on the Tigris River (p. 76)

North America a large continent in the northern and western hemispheres, bordered on the west by the Pacific Ocean and on the east by the Atlantic Ocean (p. R28)

Nubia a region in northeast Africa on the Nile, south of Egypt; the kingdom of Kush developed in Nubia (p. 123)

P

Palenque (pah-LENG-kay) (18°N, 92°W) an ancient Maya city in what is now southern Mexico (p. 435)

Persepolis (30ºN, 53ºE) the ancient capital of Persia, located in modern Iran (p. 287)

Persia an ancient empire in Southwest Asia in what is now Iran; it was one of the most powerful empires of the ancient world (p. 287)

Persian Gulf (PER-suhn) a body of water located between the Arabian Peninsula and the Zagros Mountains in Iran; the Tigris and Euphrates rivers empty into the gulf, (p. R34)

Phoenicia (fi-NI-shuh) an ancient country that was a strip of land at the western end of the Fertile Crescent, along the Mediterranean Sea; Phoenicians were some of the leading traders of the ancient world (p. 79)

Plateau of Tibet a high plateau in central Asia, mostly in Tibet and China (p. R34)

Pompeii (pom-PAY) (41ºN, 14ºE) an ancient city in the Roman Empire; the city was buried in a volcanic eruption in AD 79 (p. 361)

Q–S

Qinling Shandi (CHIN-LING shahn-DEE) a mountain range that extends east from the Plateau of Tibet; it separates northern and southern China (p. 183)

Rome (42ºN, 13ºE) a city in Italy near the Mediterranean Sea; it became the center of the Roman Empire, which controlled most of the lands around the Mediterranean (p. 325)

Silk Road an ancient trade route from China through Central Asia to the Mediterranean (p. 210)

South America a large continent in the southern and western hemispheres, bordered on the west by the Pacific Ocean and on the East by the Atlantic Ocean (p. R30)

Sparta (37ºN, 22ºE) an ancient city in Greece; its society was dominated by the military (p. 290)

Sumer (SOO-muhr) the region in southern Mesopotamia where the world's first civilization developed (p. 63)

T

Tanzania a country in East Africa; fossils from the earliest humans were discovered there (p. R37)

Thebes (38ºN, 23ºE) an ancient Greek city destroyed by Alexander (p. 89)

Tiber River a river that flows out of Italy's mountains; Rome was built on the Tiber (p. 325)

Tigris River a river that flows mainly through modern Iraq; silt from the Tigris and Euphrates formed the Fertile Crescent, where the world's first farming civilizations developed (p. 57)

Tikal (tee-KAHL) (17ºN, 90ºW) a major Maya city in modern Guatemala (p. 435)

Troy (40ºN, 26ºE) an ancient city in what is now Turkey; according to Greek legend and literature, it was the site of the Trojan War (p. 257)

Turkey a country occupying Asia Minor and a southeast portion of the Balkan Peninsula (p. R35)

U–Z

Ur a city in ancient Sumer, located on the Euphrates River near the Persian Gulf; it was one of the largest cities of ancient Mesopotamia (p. 63)

Uruk a city in ancient Sumer, located on the Euphrates River; Uruk and Ur fought for dominance around 3500–2500 BC (p. 63)

Xi'an (34ºN, 109ºE) a city in western China; Emperor Shi Huangdi built a capital city in Xianyang (now Xi'an) and it remained the capital for hundreds of years (p. R35)

Yucatán Peninsula a peninsula in southeast Mexico; many Maya cities were located on the Yucatán Peninsula (p. R28)

Ancient Civilizations

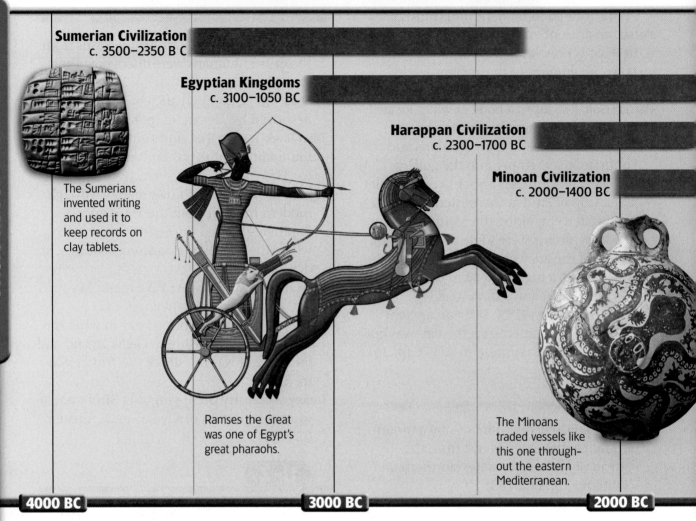

Sumerian Civilization
c. 3500–2350 B C

The Sumerians invented writing and used it to keep records on clay tablets.

Egyptian Kingdoms
c. 3100–1050 BC

Harappan Civilization
c. 2300–1700 BC

Minoan Civilization
c. 2000–1400 BC

Ramses the Great was one of Egypt's great pharaohs.

The Minoans traded vessels like this one throughout the eastern Mediterranean.

| 4000 BC | 3000 BC | 2000 BC |

Important Dates

c. 4000–3000 BC The first cities are founded in Sumer.

c. 3500 BC The Sumerians invent writing.

c. 3500 BC Maize (corn) is domesticated in Mesoamerica.

c. 3200 BC The Sumerians invent the wheel.

c. 3100 BC Upper Egypt and Lower Egypt are united.

c. 2500 BC The Great Pyramid of Khufu is built in Egypt.

c. 2350 BC The first empire is created in Mesopotamia.

c. 1750 BC The earliest known set of written laws is issued by Hammurabi.

c. 1250 BC Hinduism begins to develop.

c. 1100 BC The Phoenicians create an alphabet.

c. 1050 BC Saul becomes the first King of Israel.

c. 500 BC Buddhism begins to develop.

c. 500 BC Athens becomes the world's first democracy.

c. 140 BC Confucianism becomes China's official government philosophy.

c. 100 BC The Silk Road connects China and Southwest Asia.

27 BC The Roman Empire begins.

c. AD 30 Christianity begins to develop.

c. AD 200 The Maya build large cities in Mesoamerica.

c. AD 320 The Gupta dynasty begins in India.

AD 476 The western Roman Empire falls.

Shang dynasty artisans created beautiful bronze objects.

Shang Dynasty
c. 1500–1050 BC

Roman civilization grew to dominate the entire Mediterranean region.

Olmec Civilization
c. 1200–400 BC

The Greek World
c. 750–330 BC

The ancient Greeks made great advances in sculpture, art, and literature.

The Roman World
c. 509 BC–AD 476

Han Dynasty
c. 206 BC–AD 220

Gupta Dynasty
c. AD 320–550

1000 BC

BC 1 AD

Important People

Sargon (c. 2350 BC) was a king of Akkad, a land north of Sumer. He created a powerful army and used it to build the world's first empire.

Hammurabi (ruled c. 1792–1750 BC) founded the Babylonian Empire and issued the first known written code of laws.

Queen Hatshepsut (ruled c. 1503–1482 BC) was a ruler of Egypt who expanded trade routes.

Siddhartha Gautama (c. 563–483 BC) was an Indian prince who became known as the Buddha. His teachings became the foundation for Buddhism.

Confucius (c. 551–479 BC) was a Chinese philosopher and teacher. His teachings, known as Confucianism, became a major philosophy in China.

Alexander the Great (c. 356–323 BC) built one of

the largest empires in the ancient world and spread Greek culture throughout his empire.

Pericles (c. 495–429 BC) was an Athenian orator and politician. During his 30-year rule, Athenian democracy reached its height.

Shi Huangdi (c. 259–210 BC), the first Qin emperor, united China for the first time and built what would become the Great Wall of China.

Augustus (c. 63 BC–AD 14) was Rome's first emperor. During his reign Rome entered the Pax Romana.

Jesus of Nazareth (c. AD 1–30) was one of the most influential people in history. His life and teachings were the basis for Christianity.

Medieval to Early Modern Times

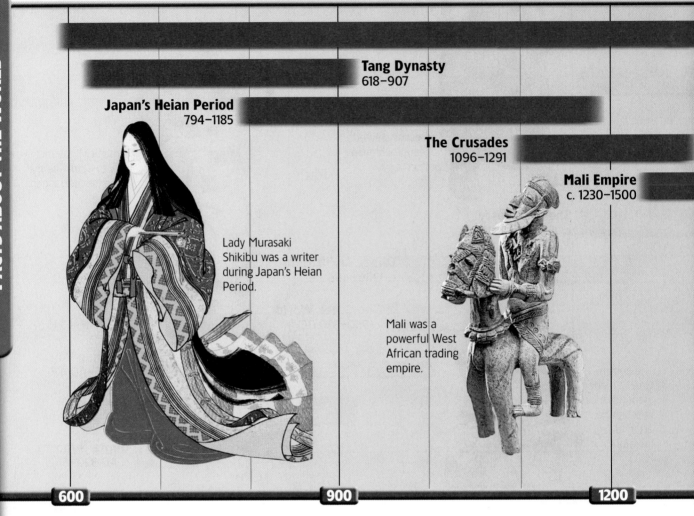

Tang Dynasty
618–907

Japan's Heian Period
794–1185

The Crusades
1096–1291

Mali Empire
c. 1230–1500

Lady Murasaki Shikibu was a writer during Japan's Heian Period.

Mali was a powerful West African trading empire.

600   900   1200

Important Dates

476 The western Roman Empire falls.

534 The Byzantine emperor Justinian creates a unified code of laws.

581 The Sui dynasty reunites China.

622 Muhammad leaves Mecca for Medina.

711 The Moors invade Spain.

800 Pope Leo III crowns Charlemagne Emperor of the Romans.

1066 William the Conqueror leads the Norman invasion of Britain.

1192 The first shogun takes power in Japan.

1215 A group of nobles forces King John to sign Magna Carta.

1324 Mansa Musa leaves Mali on a hajj to Mecca.

1347–1351 The Black Death strikes Europe.

1453 The Ottoman Turks capture Constantinople.

1492 Christopher Columbus sails to the Americas.

1517 Martin Luther posts his Ninety-Five Theses.

1521 Hernán Cortés conquers the Aztec Empire.

1533 Francisco Pizarro conquers the Inca Empire.

1545–1563 The Council of Trent meets to reform Catholic teachings.

1588 England defeats the Spanish Armada.

1633 Galileo is put on trial for promoting ideas that go against the Catholic Church.

1776 The American colonies declare independence from Great Britain.

1789 The French Revolution begins when a mob storms the Bastille in Paris.

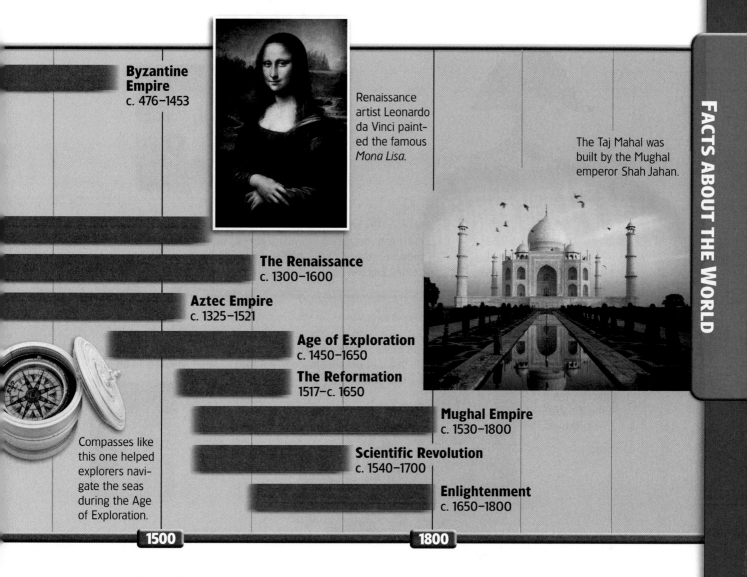

Byzantine Empire c. 476–1453

Renaissance artist Leonardo da Vinci painted the famous *Mona Lisa.*

The Taj Mahal was built by the Mughal emperor Shah Jahan.

The Renaissance c. 1300–1600

Aztec Empire c. 1325–1521

Age of Exploration c. 1450–1650

The Reformation 1517–c. 1650

Mughal Empire c. 1530–1800

Scientific Revolution c. 1540–1700

Compasses like this one helped explorers navigate the seas during the Age of Exploration.

Enlightenment c. 1650–1800

1500

1800

Important People

Muhammad (c. 570–632) was the founder of Islam. He spread Islam's teachings to the people of Arabia. His teachings make up the Qur'an.

Charlemagne (742–814) was a Frankish king who ruled most of what is now France and Germany. He helped promote Christianity in western Europe.

Lady Murasaki Shikibu (c. 1000) was a court lady during Japan's Heian Period. She wrote *The Tale of Genji,* considered by some to be the world's first novel.

Kublai Khan (1215–1294) was a Mongol ruler who completed the conquest of China and founded the Yuan dynasty.

Mansa Musa (c. 1300) was the ruler of the Mali Empire at the height of its wealth and power. He helped spread Islam throughout West Africa.

Johann Gutenberg (c. 1390–1468) was a German inventor who invented a method of printing with moveable type.

Christopher Columbus (1451–1506) was an Italian navigator who sailed to the Americas for Spain searching for a route to Asia.

Leonardo da Vinci (1452–1519) painted the *Mona Lisa,* one of the world's most admired paintings.

Sir Isaac Newton (1642–1727) was one of the most influential scientists in history. He proposed a law of gravity to explain the movement of objects.

The Modern World

Napoleon

1804
Politics
Napoleon is crowned emperor of France.

1829
Politics Greece wins independence from the Ottoman Empire.

1850s–1890
Society and Culture
Artists portray ordinary people and events realistically during the Realism movement.

1800

1875

1823
Politics
The Monroe Doctrine makes the United States the dominant power in the Western Hemisphere.

1830s
Science and Technology
The Industrial Revolution transforms life in Great Britain and soon spreads to other countries.

1871
Politics Otto von Bismarck founds the German Empire.

Otto von Bismarck

Events and People

Politics

1790s Toussaint-L'Ouverture successfully leads a rebellion of slaves against French rule in Haiti.

1811 Simon Bolívar helps Venezuela fight for its independence from Spain, influencing independence movements in Bolivia, Colombia, and Ecuador.

1837 Queen Victoria begins her 63-year reign in the United Kingdom.

1868 Tokugawa Keiki resigns as the last shogun of Japan.

1916 Jeanette Rankin becomes the first woman elected to the United States House of Representatives.

1933 Mohandas Gandhi begins a 21-day hunger strike as a non-violent protest against British rule in India.

1949 Mao Zedong transforms China into a Communist nation.

1994 Nelson Mandela is elected the first black president of South Africa after many years of struggling against apartheid.

Science and Technology

1856 Henry Bessemer develops a method for converting iron into steel.

1886 Josephine Cochran receives a patent for the first workable dishwasher.

1903 Orville and Wilbur Wright complete the first controlled aircraft flight.

Israeli flag

1948
Politics
The country of Israel is established.

1989
Politics Communist control collapses in Bulgaria, Czechoslovakia, East Germany, Hungary, Poland, and Romania.

1950

2025

1939–1945
Politics World War II is fought in Europe, North Africa, and Asia between the Axis powers and Allies.

1957
Science and Technology The Soviet Union launches the satellite Sputnik 1, beginning the space race.

Sputnik 1

1983
Society and Culture The Internet becomes available to the general public.

2001
Politics Terrorists attack the World Trade Center in New York City and the Pentagon in Washington, D.C. on September 11, 2001.

1905 Albert Einstein introduces the theory of relativity.

1911 Marie Curie wins the Nobel Prize in chemistry for discovering several radioactive elements including radium.

1925 George Washington Carver publishes a book on how to find industrial uses for agricultural products.

1969 Neil Armstrong becomes the first person to walk on the moon.

1996 Ian Wilmut clones a mammal, Dolly the sheep.

Society and Culture

1824 Louis Braille introduces a reading system for the blind.

1848 Karl Marx and Friedrich Engels introduce *The Communist Manifesto.*

1880 Pyotr Ilyich Tchaikovsky pens the *1812 Overture* to commemorate Russia's victory over Napoleon in 1812.

1921 Pablo Picasso paints *The Three Musicians,* one of the most renowned cubist works.

1937 Zora Neale Hurston writes *Their Eyes Were Watching God.*

1997 J. K. Rowling publishes the first Harry Potter book.

2004 Lance Armstrong wins a record 6th Tour de France bicycle race.

Biographical Dictionary

A

Abraham Biblical figure, according to the Bible, God led Abraham to Canaan, and Abraham's descendants became the Jewish people. (p. 226)

Aeneas (i-NEE-uhs) (c. 2500s BC) Legendary Roman hero, the Romans traced their history back to Aeneas. Aeneas was a Trojan hero who left Troy after the Trojan War, eventually settling in Italy. (p. 326)

Aesop (EE-sahp) (before 400 BC) Ancient Greek storyteller, he was famous for his fables— short stories that teach important lessons about life. (p. 273)

Alexander the Great (c. 356–323 BC) Macedonian ruler, he was one of the greatest military commanders in history. The son of Philip II, Alexander conquered large areas of Asia and parts of Europe and Africa and spread Greek culture throughout his empire. (p. 300)

Antony, Marc (c. 82–30 BC) Roman general, he fought against Octavian after the death of Julius Caesar. Antony was allies with Cleopatra of Egypt, but was defeated by Octavian at the Battle of Actium in 31 BC. (p. 355)

Aristotle (ar-uh-STAH-tuhl) (384–322 BC) Greek philosopher, he was a student of Plato. Aristotle taught that people should live lives of moderation and use reason in their lives. (pp. 307, 309)

Asoka (uh-SOH-kuh) (ruled 270–232 BC) Ruler of the Mauryan Empire, he extended his control over most of India and promoted the spread of Buddhism. (pp. 163, 166)

Attila (AT-uhl-uh) (c. 406–453) Leader of the Huns, he led invasions of Constantinople, Greece, Gaul, and northern Italy and was greatly feared by the Romans. (p. 411)

Augustine of Hippo (AW-guhs-teen) (c. 300s–400s) Christian writer who taught that Christians should focus not on worldly goods but on God's plan for the world; his ideas helped shape Christian beliefs. (p. 394)

Augustus (aw-GUHS-tuhs) (63 BC–AD 14) First Roman emperor, he was originally named Octavian. He was the great-nephew of Julius Caesar and gained control of Rome after defeating Marc Antony in battle. As emperor, Augustus built many monuments and a new forum. (pp. 355, 357)

B

Buddha (BOO-duh) (c. 563–483 BC) Founder of Buddhism, he was originally an Indian prince named Siddhartha Gautama. He founded the Buddhist religion after a long spiritual journey through India. (p. 157)

Augustus

Caesar, Julius (JOOL-yuhs SEE-zuhr) (100–44 BC) Roman general, he was one of the greatest military leaders in history. Caesar conquered most of Gaul and was named dictator for life, but was later murdered by a group of senators. (p. 353)

Chandragupta II (kuhn-druh-GOOP-tuh) (300s–400s) Gupta emperor, he ruled India during the height of Gupta power. (p. 164)

Chandragupta Maurya (kuhn-druh-GOOP-tuh mour-yuh) (late 300s BC) Mauryan ruler, he founded the Mauryan Empire in northern India. (p. 162)

Cicero (SIS-uh-roh) (106–43 BC) Roman orator and philosopher, he tried to limit the power of Rome's generals and give control of the government back to the Senate. (p. 352)

Cincinnatus (sin-suh-NAT-uhs) (born c. 519) Roman dictator, he was chosen by the Romans to defend their lands from attack. Later, he willingly gave up power and was considered an ideal leader by the Romans. (p. 329)

Cleopatra (69–30 BC) Egyptian queen, she became a devoted ally of Julius Caesar and Marc Antony. After Antony was defeated by Octavian, she committed suicide. (p. 356)

Clovis (c. 466–511) King of the Franks, he was a Christian leader who was one of the most powerful rulers of the Germanic barbarians. (p. 411)

Confucius (551–479 BC) Chinese philosopher, he was the most influential teacher in Chinese history. His teachings, called Confucianism, focused on morality, family, society, and government. (p. 191)

Constantine (KAHN-stuhn-teen) (c. 280–337) Roman emperor, he was the first Roman emperor to become a Christian. Constantine moved the empire's capital from Rome to Constantinople and removed bans on Christianity. (p. 395)

Cyrus the Great (SY-ruhs) (c. 585–529 BC) Persian emperor, he created the Persian Empire by conquering most of Southwest Asia. (p. 287)

Daniel Biblical figure, according to the Hebrew Bible, he was a prophet who was thrown into a lions' den after angering the king. Daniel survived because of his faith in God. (p. 235)

Darius I (da-RY-uhs) (550–486 BC) Persian emperor, he restored order to the Persian Empire after a period of rebellion. Darius I built roads and made other improvements to Persian society. (p. 288)

David (c. 1000 BC) King of Israel, he defeated the Philistines and established the capital in Jerusalem as a governmental and religious center. (p. 229)

Diocletian (dy-uh-KLEE-shuhn) (c. 245–c. 316) Roman emperor, he divided the Roman Empire into eastern and western halves. (p. 409)

Confucius

Euclid (YOO-kluhd) (c. 300 BC) Greek mathematician, he was one of the greatest mathematicians in history. Euclid is famous for his contributions to the field of geometry. (p. 308)

Ezana (AY-zah-nah) (c. 300s) Aksumite ruler, he destroyed Meroë and took over the kingdom of Kush around AD 350. (p. 131)

Galen (129–c. 199) Greek surgeon of the Roman Empire, he described heart valves and studied arteries and veins. (p. 366)

Gilgamesh (c. 3000 BC) King of Uruk, a city-state in Sumer, he became a legendary figure in Sumerian literature. (p. 63)

Hadrian (76–138) Roman emperor, he conquered most of Britain and built a huge wall across the northern part of the island to keep barbarian invaders from the north out of Roman territory. (p. 359)

Hammurabi (ruled c. 1792–1750 BC), Baylonian ruler, he was a brilliant military leader who brought all of Mesopotamia into the Babylonian Empire. Hammurabi is known for a unified code of 282 laws, the earliest known set of written laws, that was produced during his reign. (p. 75)

Hannibal (247–183 BC) Carthaginian general, he was one of the greatest generals of the ancient world. Hannibal invaded Italy during the Second Punic War but was eventually defeated by Scipio at the Battle of Zama. (p. 341)

Hatshepsut (ruled c. 1503–1482 BC) Egyptian queen, she worked to increase trade with places outside of Egypt and ordered many impressive monuments and temples built during her reign. (pp. 102, 103)

Hippocrates (hip-AHK-ruh-teez) (c. 460–c. 377 BC) Greek doctor, he is regarded as the father of medicine. Hippocrates tried to find out what caused diseases and is known today for his ideas on how doctors should conduct themselves. (p. 308)

Homer (800s–700s BC) Greek poet, he wrote the *Iliad* and the *Odyssey*, two famous Greek epic poems. They describe the deeds of heroes during and after the Trojan War. (p. 272)

Homer

Hypatia (hy-PAY-shuh) (c. 370–415) Greek mathematician and astronomer, she made important contributions to science. (p. 308)

Iceman (c. 3300 BC) Stone Age traveler, he was found in the Alps in 1991. Scientists have learned a great deal about Stone Age people from his clothing and tools. (p. 35)

Jesus of Nazareth (c. AD 1–30) Founder of Christianity, he taught about kindness and love for God. His teachings spread throughout the Roman Empire and the world. (p. 382)

John the Baptist (c. 1st Century AD) Biblical figure, according to the Bible, he was a prophet who announced that the Messiah was coming. (p. 383)

Justinian (juh-STIN-ee-uhn) (c. 483–565) Byzantine emperor, he reunited the Roman Empire, simplified Roman laws with Justinian's Code, and ordered Hagia Sophia built. (pp. 414, 419)

Khufu (KOO-foo) (ruled 2500s BC) Egyptian pharaoh, he ruled during Egypt's Old Kingdom and is known for the many monuments built to honor him. (p. 94)

Laozi (LOWD-zuh) (c. 500s or 400s BC) Chinese philosopher, he was the most famous Daoist teacher. Laozi is credited with writing *The Way and Its Power*, Daoism's basic text. (p. 192)

Marius, Gaius (GY-uhs MER-ee-uhs) (157–86 BC) Roman consul, he was a popular general who encouraged the unemployed poor to join the Roman army. (p. 342)

Menes (MEE-neez) (c. 3100 BC) Legendary Egyptian ruler, he unified the kingdoms of Upper and Lower Egypt and built the new capital city of Memphis. (p. 91)

Moses (c. 1200s BC) Biblical figure, according to the Bible, he led the Hebrew people out of Egypt and back to Canaan in the Exodus. During this journey, Moses received the Ten Commandments from God. (p. 227)

Naomi (nay-OH-mee) Bibilical figure, according to the Bible, she had a strong faith in God. (p. 231)

Ruth and Naomi

BIOGRAPHICAL DICTIONARY

Nebuchadnezzar (neb-uh-kuhd-NEZ-uhr) (ruled 605–561 BC) Chaldean king, he rebuilt Babylon into a beautiful city, which featured the famed Hanging Gardens. (p. 77)

Noah (no-uh) Biblical figure, according to the Bible, God told Noah to build an ark, or great ship, to survive a great flood of the earth. (p. 238)

Ovid (ahv-uhd) (43 BC–AD 17) Roman poet and author, he was one of the greatest authors of the ancient world and wrote poems on Roman mythology. (p. 370)

Pacal (puh-KAHL) (603–683) Maya king of Palenque, he had a temple built in the city to record his achievements. (p. 437)

Paul (c. AD 10–67) One of the most important figures in the spread of Christianity, he worked to spread Jesus's teachings and wrote letters that explained key ideas of Christianity. (p. 387)

Pericles (PER-uh-kleez) (495–429 BC) Athenian leader, he encouraged the spread of democracy and led Athens when the city was at its height. (p. 266)

Philip II (ruled 359–336 BC) Macedonian king, he was a brilliant military leader who defeated the Greeks. Alexander the Great was his son. (p. 298)

Piankhi (PYANG-kee) (c. 751–716 BC) Ruler of Kush, he was one of Kush's most successful military leaders. His army captured all of Egypt. (p. 125)

Plato (PLAYT-oh) (428–389 BC) Greek philosopher, he was a student of Socrates. Plato started a school in Athens called the Academy and wrote *The Republic*, which describes an ideal society run by philosophers. (pp. 307, 309)

Pompey (106–48 BC) Roman general, he was an ally of Caesar but later the two went to war and Pompey was defeated in Egypt. (p. 353)

Ramses the Great (RAM-seez) (late 1300s and early 1200s BC) Egyptian pharaoh, he expanded the kingdom and built lasting temples at Karnak, Luxor, and Abu Simbel. Ramses the Great is often considered one of Egypt's greatest rulers. (pp. 103, 107)

Romulus and Remus (c. 753 BC) Legendary figures in Roman history, they built a city that eventually became Rome. (p. 327)

Ruth Biblical figure, according to the Bible, she left her family to care for her mother-in-law, Naomi. Ruth is an example of a model of devotion. (p. 231)

Sappho (SAF-oh) (c. 610–580 BC) Greek poet, she was one of the most famous lyric poets of Greece. (p. 273)

Sargon (c. 2300 BC) King of Akkad, a land north of Sumer, he built the world's first empire after defeating Sumer and northern Mesopotamia. (p. 63)

Shanakhdakheto (shah-nahk-dah-KEE-toh) (ruled 170–150 BC) Ruler of Kush, historians think she was the first woman to rule Kush. Her tomb is one of the largest pyramids in Meroë. (p. 129)

Shi Huangdi (SHEE hwahng-dee) (259–210 BC) Ruler of China, he united China for the first time. He built roads and canals and began the Great Wall of China. Shi Huangdi also imposed a standard system of laws, money, weights, and writing system in China. (pp. 194, 199)

Sima Qian (c. 145–190 BC) a Chinese historian, wrote a history of all the dynasties through the Han. His style became the model for later writings. (p. 204)

Socrates (SAHK-ruh-teez) (470–399 BC) Greek philosopher, his teaching style was based on asking questions. He wanted people to question their own beliefs. Socrates was arrested and condemned to death for challenging authority. (pp. 307, 309)

Solomon (SAHL-uh-muhn) (ruled c. 965–930 BC) King of Israel, he formed alliances with nearby kingdoms and built a temple to God in Jerusalem. (p. 229)

Spartacus (SPAHR-tuh-kuhs) (c. 73 BC) Former Roman gladiator, he led a slave revolt against Rome. (p. 343)

Sulla, Lucius Cornelius (LOO-shuhs kawr-NEEL-yuhs SUHL-uh) (138–78 BC) Roman consul, he battled Gaius Marius in a civil war. (p. 343)

Theodora (thee-uh-DOHR-uh) (c. 500–548) Wife of the Byzantine emperor Justinian, she was a smart and powerful woman who helped him rule effectively. (p. 419)

Thucydides (c. 400s BC) Greek historian, he was a former Athenian soldier who wrote a history of the Peloponnesian War based on his experiences. He tried to be impartial and study the causes and effects of war in hopes that future Greeks would not repeat their mistakes. (p. 306)

Tutankhamen (too-tang-KAHM-uhn) (c. 1300 BC) Egyptian pharaoh, he died while still a young king. The discovery of his tomb in 1922 has taught archaeologists much about Egyptian culture. (p. 113)

Xerxes I (ZUHRK-seez) (519–465 BC) Persian ruler, he tried to conquer Greece during the Persian Wars but was defeated. (p. 290)

Yohanan ben Zaccai (yoh-HAN-uhn ben ZAK-ay-y) (c. AD 70) Jewish teacher, he built a school near Jerusalem where he trained rabbis to carry on the Jewish religion after the Temple had been destroyed by the Romans. (p. 242)

Zealots (ZE-luhts) (AD 66–73) a group of Jews who rebelled against Roman rule (p. 240)

Justinian and Theodora

BIOGRAPHICAL DICTIONARY

English and Spanish Glossary

MARK	AS IN	RESPELLING	EXAMPLE
a	alphabet	a	*AL-fuh-bet
ā	Asia	ay	AY-zhuh
ä	cart, top	ah	KAHRT, TAHP
e	let, ten	e	LET, TEN
ē	even, leaf	ee	EE-vuhn, LEEF
i	it, tip, British	i	IT, TIP, BRIT-ish
ī	site, buy, Ohio	y	SYT, BY, oh-HY-oh
	iris	eye	EYE-ris
k	card	k	KAHRD
ō	over, rainbow	oh	OH-vuhr, RAYN-boh
ủ	book, wood	ooh	BOOHK, WOOHD
ò	all, orchid	aw	AWL, AWR-kid
òi	foil, coin	oy	FOYL, KOYN
aủ	out	ow	OWT
ə	cup, butter	uh	KUHP, BUHT-uhr
ü	rule, food	oo	ROOL, FOOD
yü	few	yoo	FYOO
zh	vision	zh	VIZH-uhn

*A syllable printed in small capital letters receives heavier emphasis than the other syllable(s) in a word.

Phonetic Respelling and Pronunciation Guide

Many of the key terms in this textbook have been respelled to help you pronounce them. The letter combinations used in the respelling throughout the narrative are explained in the following phonetic respelling and pronunciation guide. The guide is adapted from *Merriam-Webster's Collegiate Dictionary, Eleventh Edition; Merriam-Webster's Biographical Dictionary;* and *Merriam-Webster's Geographical Dictionary.*

A

acropolis (uh-KRAH-puh-luhs) a high hill upon which a Greek fortress was built (p. 258)
acrópolis colina elevada sobre la que se construyó una fortaleza griega (pág. 258)

acupuncture (AK-yoo-punk-cher) the Chinese practice of inserting fine needles through the skin at specific points to cure disease or relieve pain (p. 205)
acupuntura práctica china que consiste en insertar pequeñas agujas en la piel en puntos específicos para curar enfermedades o aliviar el dolor (pág. 205)

afterlife life after death (p. 96)
la otra vida vida después de la muerte (pág. 96)

agriculture farming (p. 42)
agricultura cultivo de la tierra (pág. 42)

alliance an agreement to work together (p. 296)
alianza acuerdo de colaboración (pág. 296)

alloy a mixture of two or more metals (p. 170)
aleación mezcla de dos o más metales (pág. 170)

alphabet a set of letters that can be combined to form words (p. 79)
alfabeto conjunto de letras que pueden combinarse para formar palabras (pág. 79)

ancestor a relative who lived in the past (p. 28)
antepasado pariente que vivió hace muchos años (pág. 28)

Apostles (uh-PAHS-uhls) the 12 chosen disciples of Jesus who spread his teachings (p. 387)
apóstoles los 12 discípulos elegidos por Jesucristo que difundieron sus enseñanzas (pág. 387)

aqueduct a raised channel used to carry water (p. 367)

acueducto canal elevado que se utiliza para el transporte de agua (pág. 367)

archaeology (ar-kee-AH-luh-jee) the study of the past based on what people left behind (p. 7)

arqueología estudio del pasado a través de los objetos que dejaron las personas tras desaparecer (pág. 7)

architecture the science of building (p. 70)

arquitectura ciencia de la construcción (pág. 70)

aristocrat (uh-RIS-tuh-krat) a rich landowner or noble (p. 263)

aristócrata propietario de tierras o noble rico (pág. 263)

artifact an object created and used by humans (p. 10)

artefacto objeto creado y usado por los humanos (pág. 10)

astronomy the study of stars and planets (p. 171)

astronomía estudio de las estrellas y los planetas (pág. 171)

B

Bible the holy book of Judaism and Christianity. The Hebrew Bible is also part of the Christian Bible, where it is called the Old Testament. The Christian Bible includes the Old Testament and the New Testament. (p. 384)

Biblia libro sagrado del judaísmo y el cristianismo. La Biblia hebrea también forma parte de la Biblia cristiana, en donde se conoce como el Viejo Testamento. La Biblia cristiana incluye el Viejo Testamento y el Nuevo Testamento. (pág. 384)

bishops local leaders in the early Christian church (p. 393)

obispos líderes regionales en los comienzos de la iglesia cristiana (pág. 393)

Buddhism a religion based on the teachings of the Buddha that developed in India in the 500s BC (p. 158)

budismo religión basada en las enseñanzas de Buda, originada en la India en el siglo VI a. C. (pág. 158)

Byzantine Empire the society that developed in the eastern Roman Empire after the fall of the western Roman Empire (p. 416)

Imperio bizantino sociedad que surgió en el Imperio romano de oriente tras la caída del Imperio romano de occidente (pág. 416)

C

canal a human-made waterway (p. 58)

canal vía de agua hecha por el ser humano (pág. 58)

caste system the division of Indian society into groups based on rank, wealth, or occupation (p. 151)

sistema de castas división de la sociedad india en grupos basados en la clase social, el nivel económico o la profesión (pág. 151)

cataracts rapids along a river, such as those along the Nile in Egypt (p. 89)

rápidos fuertes corrientes a lo largo de un río, como las del Nilo en Egipto (pág. 89)

cavalry a group of soldiers who ride on horses (p. 288)

caballería grupo de soldados a caballo (pág. 288)

chariot a wheeled, horse-drawn cart used in battle (p. 76)

cuadriga carro tirado por caballos usado en las batallas (pág. 76)

checks and balances a system that balances the distribution of power in a government (p. 335)

pesos y contrapesos sistema creado para equilibrar la distribución del poder en un gobierno (pág. 335)

ENGLISH AND SPANISH GLOSSARY

Christianity a religion based on the teachings of Jesus of Nazareth that developed in Judea at the beginning of the first century AD (p. 382)

cristianismo religión basada en las enseñanzas de Jesús de Nazaret que se desarrolló en Judea a comienzos del siglo I d. C. (pág. 382)

citizen a person who has the right to participate in government (p. 263)

ciudadano persona que tiene el derecho de participar en el gobierno (pág. 263)

city-state a political unit consisting of a city and its surrounding countryside (p. 62)

ciudad estado unidad política formada por una ciudad y los campos que la rodean (pág. 62)

civil law a legal system based on a written code of laws (p. 371)

derecho civil sistema jurídico basado en un código de leyes escritas (pág. 371)

classical referring to the cultures of ancient Greece or Rome (p. 394)

clásica referente a las culturas de la Antigua Grecia y la Antigua Roma (pág. 394)

climate the average weather conditions in a certain area over a long period of time (p. 12)

clima condiciones del tiempo medias de una zona específica durante un largo período de tiempo (pág. 12)

Confucianism a philosophy based on the ideas of Confucius that focuses on morality, family order, social harmony, and government (p. 191)

confucianismo filosofía basada en las ideas de Confucio que se basa en la moralidad, el orden familiar, la armonía social y el gobierno (pág. 191)

consuls (KAHN-suhlz) the two most powerful officials in Rome (p. 333)

cónsules los dos funcionarios más poderosos en Roma (pág. 333)

corruption the decay of people's values (p. 412)

corrupción decadencia de los valores de las personas (pág. 412)

crucifixion (kroo-suh-FIK-shuhn) a type of execution in which a person was nailed to a cross (p. 385)

crucifixión tipo de ejecución en la que se clavaba a una persona en una cruz (pág. 385)

culture the knowledge, beliefs, customs, and values of a group of people (p. 7)

cultura el conocimiento, las creencias, las costumbres y los valores de un grupo de personas (pág. 7)

cuneiform (kyoo-NEE-uh-fohrm) the world's first system of writing; developed in Sumer (p. 67)

cuneiforme primer sistema de escritura del mundo; desarrollado en Sumeria (pág. 67)

currency money (p. 360)

moneda dinero (pág. 360)

D

Daoism (DOW-ih-zum) a philosophy that developed in China and stressed the belief that one should live in harmony with the Dao, the guiding force of all reality (p. 192)

taoismo filosofía que se desarrolló en China y que enfatizaba la creencia de que se debe vivir en armonía con el Tao, la fuerza que guía toda la realidad (pág. 192)

Dead Sea Scrolls writings about Jewish beliefs created about 2,000 years ago (p. 236)

manuscritos del mar Muerto escritos sobre las creencias judías, redactados hace unos 2,000 años (pág. 236)

delta a triangle-shaped area of land made from soil deposited by a river (p. 89)

delta zona de tierra de forma triangular creada a partir de los sedimentos que deposita un río (pág. 89)

democracy a type of government in which people rule themselves (p. 262)
  democracia tipo de gobierno en el que el pueblo se gobierna a sí mismo (pág. 262)

Diaspora (dy-AS-pruh) the scattering of the Jews outside of Judah after the Babylonian Captivity (p. 230)
  diáspora la dispersión de los judíos desde Judá tras el cautiverio en Babilonia (pág. 230)

dictator a ruler who has almost absolute power (p. 328)
  dictador gobernante que tiene poder casi absoluto (pág. 328)

diffusion the spread of ideas from one culture to another (p. 211)
  difusión traspaso de ideas de una cultura a otra (pág. 211)

disciples (di-SY-puhls) followers (p. 385)
  discípulos seguidores (pág. 385)

division of labor an arrangement in which each worker specializes in a particular task or job (p. 58)
  división del trabajo organización mediante la que cada trabajador se especializa en un trabajo o tarea en particular (pág. 58)

domestication the process of changing plants or animals to make them more useful to humans (p. 41)
  domesticación proceso en el que se modifican los animales o las plantas para que sean más útiles para los humanos (pág. 41)

dynasty a series of rulers from the same family (p. 91)
  dinastía serie de gobernantes pertenecientes a la misma familia (pág. 91)

E

ebony a dark, heavy wood (p. 124)
  ébano madera oscura y pesada (pág. 124)

elite (AY-leet) people of wealth and power (p. 97)
  élite personas ricas y poderosas (pág. 97)

empire land with different territories and peoples under a single rule (p. 63)
  imperio zona que reúne varios territorios y pueblos bajo un mismo gobierno (pág. 63)

engineering the application of scientific knowledge for practical purposes (p. 98)
  ingeniería aplicación del conocimiento científico para fines prácticos (pág. 98)

environment all the living and nonliving things that affect life in an area (p. 13)
  medio ambiente todos los seres vivos y elementos inertes que afectan la vida de un área (pág. 13)

epics long poems that tell the stories of heroes (p. 68)
  poemas épicos poemas largos que narran hazañas de héroes (pág. 68)

ethics moral values (p. 191)
  ética valores morales (pág. 191)

Eucharist the central ceremony of the Christian church, honoring the last supper that Jesus shared with his Apostles before he died (p. 393)
  Eucaristía ceremonia principal de la iglesia cristiana que conmemora la última cena que Jesús compartió con sus apóstoles antes de morir (pág. 393)

Exodus the journey of the Hebrews, led by Moses, from Egypt to Canaan after they were freed from slavery (p. 227)
  Éxodo viaje de los hebreos, guiados por Moisés, desde Egipto hasta Canaán después de su liberación de la esclavitud (pág. 227)

exports items sent to other regions for trade (p. 128)
  exportaciones productos enviados a otras regiones para el intercambio comercial (pág. 128)

ENGLISH AND SPANISH GLOSSARY

F

fable a short story that teaches a lesson about life or gives advice on how to live (p. 273)
fábula relato breve que presenta una enseñanza u ofrece algún consejo sobre la vida (pág. 273)

fasting going without food for a period of time (p. 157)
ayunar dejar de comer durante un período de tiempo (pág. 157)

Fertile Crescent an area of rich farmland in Southwest Asia where the first civilizations began (p. 57)
Media Luna de las tierras fértiles zona de ricas tierras de cultivo situada en el sudoeste de Asia, en la que comenzaron las primeras civilizaciones (pág. 57)

forum a Roman public meeting place (p. 335)
foro lugar público de reuniones en Roma (pág. 335)

fossil a part or imprint of something that was once alive (p. 10)
fósil parte o huella de un ser vivo ya desaparecido (pág. 10)

G

geography the study of Earth's physical and cultural features (p. 12)
geografía estudio de las características físicas y culturales de la Tierra (pág. 12)

Great Wall a barrier made of walls across China's northern frontier (p. 197)
Gran Muralla barrera formada por muros situada a lo largo de la frontera norte de China (pág. 197)

H

Hammurabi's Code a set of 282 laws governing daily life in Babylon; the earliest known collection of written laws (p. 75)
Código de Hammurabi conjunto de 282 leyes que regían la vida cotidiana en Babilonia; la primera colección de leyes escritas conocida (pág. 75)

Hellenistic Greek-like; heavily influenced by Greek ideas (p. 301)
helenístico al estilo griego; muy influido por las ideas de la Grecia clásica (pág. 301)

hieroglyphics (hy-ruh-GLIH-fiks) the ancient Egyptian writing system that used picture symbols (p. 108)
jeroglíficos sistema de escritura del antiguo Egipto, en el cual se usaban símbolos ilustrados (pág. 108)

High Holy Days the two most sacred days of Jewish religious observance—Rosh Hashanah and Yom Kippur (p. 245)
Supremos Días Santos los dos días más sagrados de la práctica religiosa judía: Rosh Hashaná y Yom Kippur (pág. 245)

Hindu-Arabic numerals the number system we use today; it was created by Indian scholars during the Gupta dynasty (p. 170)
numerales indoarábigos sistema numérico que usamos hoy en día; fue creado por estudiosos de la India durante la dinastía Gupta (pág. 170)

Hinduism the main religion of India; it teaches that everything is part of a universal spirit called Brahman (p. 153)
hinduismo religión principal de la India; sus enseñanzas dicen que todo forma parte de un espíritu universal llamado Brahman (pág. 153)

history the study of the past (p. 6)
historia estudio del pasado (pág. 6)

hominid an early ancestor of humans (p. 28)
homínido antepasado primitivo de los humanos (pág. 28)

hunter-gatherers people who hunt animals and gather wild plants, seeds, fruits, and nuts to survive (p. 33)
cazadores y recolectores personas que cazan animales y recolectan plantas, semillas, frutas y nueces para sobrevivir (pág. 33)

ice ages long periods of freezing weather (p. 36)
eras glaciales largos períodos de clima helado (pág. 36)

imports goods brought in from other regions (p. 128)
importaciones bienes que se introducen en un país procedentes de otras regiones (pág. 128)

inoculation (i-nah-kyuh-LAY-shuhn) injecting a person with a small dose of a virus to help build up defenses to a disease (p. 170)
inoculación acto de inyectar una pequeña dosis de un virus a una persona para ayudarla a crear defensas contra una enfermedad (pág. 170)

irrigation a way of supplying water to an area of land (p. 58)
irrigación método para suministrar agua a un terreno (pág. 58)

ivory a white material made from elephant tusks (p. 124)
marfil material de color blanco procedente de los colmillos de los elefantes (pág. 124)

jade a hard gemstone often used in jewelry (p. 185)
jade piedra preciosa de gran dureza que se suele utilizar en joyería (pág. 185)

Jainism an Indian religion based on the teachings of Mahavira that teaches all life is sacred (p. 155)
jainismo religión de la India basada en las enseñanzas de Mahavira, que proclama que toda forma de vida es sagrada (pág. 155)

Judaism (JOO-dee-i-zuhm) the religion of the Hebrews (practiced by Jews today); it is the world's oldest monotheistic religion (p. 232)
judaísmo religión de los hebreos (practicada por los judíos hoy en día); es la religión monoteísta más antigua del mundo (pág. 232)

K

karma in Buddhism and Hinduism, the effects that good or bad actions have on a person's soul (p. 154)
karma en el budismo y el hinduismo, los efectos que las buenas o malas acciones producen en el alma de una persona (pág. 154)

L

land bridge a strip of land connecting two continents (p. 36)
puente de tierra franja de tierra que conecta dos continentes (pág. 36)

landforms the natural features of the land's surface (p. 12)
accidentes geográficos características naturales de la superficie terrestre (pág. 12)

Latin the language of the Romans (p. 334)
latín idioma de los romanos (pág. 334)

Legalism the Chinese belief that people were bad by nature and needed to be controlled (p. 192)
legalismo creencia china de que las personas eran malas por naturaleza y debían ser controladas (pág. 192)

legion (LEE-juhn) a group of up to 6,000 Roman soldiers (p. 339)
legión grupo que podía incluir hasta 6,000 soldados romanos (pág. 339)

lord a person of high rank who owned land but owed loyalty to his king (p. 189)
señor feudal persona de alto nivel social que poseía tierras y debía lealtad al rey (pág. 189)

M

magistrate (MA-juh-strayt) an elected official in Rome (p. 333)
magistrado funcionario electo en Roma (pág. 333)

maize (MAYS) corn (p. 431)
maíz cereal conocido también como elote o choclo (pág. 431)

martyr a person who dies for his or her beliefs (p. 393)
mártir persona que muere por sus creencias (pág. 393)

meditation deep continued thought that focuses the mind on spiritual ideas (p. 157)
meditación reflexión profunda y continua, durante la cual la persona se concentra en ideas espirituales (pág. 157)

megalith a huge stone monument (p. 42)
megalito enorme monumento de piedra (pág. 42)

merchant a trader (p. 128)
mercader comerciante (pág. 128)

Mesoamerica a region that includes the southern part of what is now Mexico and parts of northern Central America (p. 428)
Mesoamérica región que incluye la zona sur del México actual y zonas del norte de Centroamérica (pág. 428)

Mesolithic Era the middle part of the Stone Age; marked by the creation of smaller and more complex tools (p. 38)
Mesolítico período central de la Edad de Piedra, caracterizado por la creación de herramientas más pequeñas y complejas (pág. 38)

Messiah (muh-SY-uh) in Judaism, a new leader that would appear among the Jews and restore the greatness of ancient Israel (p. 383)
Mesías en el judaísmo, nuevo líder que aparecería entre los judíos y restablecería la grandeza del antiguo Israel (pág. 383)

metallurgy (MET-uhl-uhr-jee) the science of working with metals (p. 170)
metalurgia ciencia de trabajar los metales (pág. 170)

Middle Kingdom the period of Egyptian history from about 2050 to 1750 BC and marked by order and stability (p. 102)
Reino Medio período de la historia de Egipto que abarca aproximadamente del 2050 al 1750 a. C. y que se caracterizó por el orden y la estabilidad (pág. 102)

migrate to move to a new place (p. 36)
migrar desplazarse a otro lugar (pág. 36)

missionary someone who works to spread religious beliefs (p. 160)
misionero alguien que trabaja para difundir sus creencias religiosas (pág. 160)

monarch (MAH-nark) a ruler of a kingdom or empire (p. 74)
monarca gobernante de un reino o imperio (pág. 74)

monotheism the belief in only one God (p. 232)

monoteísmo creencia en un solo Dios (pág. 232)

monsoon a seasonal wind pattern that causes wet and dry seasons (p. 145)

monzón viento estacional cíclico que causa estaciones húmedas y secas (pág. 145)

mosaic a picture made with pieces of colored stone or glass (p. 417)

mosaico dibujo hecho con trozos de piedra o cristal de colores (pág. 417)

mummy a specially treated body wrapped in cloth for preservation (p. 96)

momia cadáver especialmente tratado y envuelto en tela para su conservación (pág. 96)

mythology stories about gods and heroes that try to explain how the world works (p. 269)

mitología relatos sobre dioses y héroes que tratan de explicar cómo funciona el mundo (pág. 269)

N

Neolithic Era the New Stone Age; when people learned to make fire and tools such as saws and drills (p. 41)

Neolítico Nueva Edad de Piedra; el ser humano aprendió a producir fuego y a fabricar herramientas como sierras y taladros manuales (pág. 41)

New Kingdom the period from about 1550 to 1050 BC in Egyptian history when Egypt reached the height of its power and glory (p. 102)

Reino Nuevo período de la historia egipcia que abarca aproximadamente desde el 1550 hasta el 1050 a. C., en el que Egipto alcanzó la cima de su poder y su gloria (pág. 102)

nirvana (nir-vah-nuh) in Buddhism, a state of perfect peace (p. 158)

nirvana en el budismo, estado de paz perfecta (pág. 158)

noble a rich and powerful person (p. 94)

noble persona rica y poderosa (pág. 94)

nonviolence the avoidance of violent actions (p. 155)

no violencia rechazo de las acciones violentas (pág. 155)

O

obelisk (AH-buh-lisk) a tall, pointed, four-sided pillar in ancient Egypt (p. 110)

obelisco pilar alto, de cuatro caras y acabado en punta, propio del antiguo Egipto (pág. 110)

observatory a building used to study astronomy (p. 442)

observatorio edificio usado para estudiar la astronomía (pág. 442)

obsidian a sharp, glasslike volcanic rock (p. 434)

obsidiana roca volcánica cortante y parecida al vidrio (pág. 434)

Old Kingdom the period from about 2700 to 2200 BC in Egyptian history that began shortly after Egypt was unified (p. 93)

Reino Antiguo período de la historia egipcia que abarca aproximadamente del 2700 hasta el 2200 a. C. y comenzó poco después de la unificación de Egipto (pág. 93)

oligarchy (AH-luh-gar-kee) a government in which only a few people have power (p. 263)

oligarquía gobierno en el que sólo unas pocas personas tienen el poder (pág. 263)

oracle a prediction by a wise person, or a person who makes a prediction (p. 186)

oráculo predicción de un sabio o de alguien que hace profecías (pág. 186)

ENGLISH AND SPANISH GLOSSARY

orator a public speaker (p. 352)
　orador persona que habla en público (pág. 352)

P

Paleolithic Era (pay-lee-uh-LI-thik) the first part of the Stone Age; when people first used stone tools (p. 31)
　Paleolítico primera parte de la Edad de Piedra; cuando el ser humano usó herramientas de piedra por primera vez (pág. 31)

papyrus (puh-PY-ruhs) a long-lasting, paper-like material made from reeds that the ancient Egyptians used to write on (p. 108)
　papiro material duradero hecho de juncos, similar al papel, que los antiguos egipcios utilizaban para escribir (pág. 108)

Passover a holiday in which Jews remember the Exodus (p. 245)
　Pascua judía festividad en la que los judíos recuerdan el Éxodo (pág. 245)

patricians (puh-TRI-shunz) the nobility in Roman society (p. 329)
　patricios nobles de la sociedad romana (pág. 329)

Pax Romana Roman Peace; a period of general peace and prosperity in the Roman Empire that lasted from 27 BC to AD 180 (p. 361)
　Pax Romana Paz Romana; período de paz y prosperidad generales en el Imperio romano que duró del 27 a. C. al 180 d. C. (pág. 361)

peasant a farmer with a small farm (p. 189)
　campesino agricultor dueño de una pequeña granja (pág. 189)

Peloponnesian War a war between Athens and Sparta in the 400s BC (p. 297)
　guerra del Peloponeso guerra entre Atenas y Esparta en el siglo V a. C. (pág. 297)

persecution (puhr-si-KYOO-shuhn) the punishment of a group because of its beliefs or differences (p. 393)
　persecución castigo a un grupo debido a sus creencias o diferencias (pág. 393)

Persian Wars a series of wars between Persia and Greece in the 400s BC (p. 289)
　guerras persas serie de guerras entre Persia y Grecia en el siglo V a. C. (pág. 289)

phalanx (FAY-langks) a group of Greek warriors who stood close together in a square formation (p. 299)
　falange grupo de guerreros griegos que se mantenían unidos en formación compacta y cuadrada (pág. 299)

pharaoh (FEHR-oh) the title used by the rulers of Egypt (p. 91)
　faraón título usado por los gobernantes de Egipto (pág. 91)

pictograph a picture symbol (p. 68)
　pictograma símbolo ilustrado (pág. 68)

plebeians (pli-BEE-uhnz) the common people of ancient Rome (p. 329)
　plebeyos gente común de la antigua Roma (pág. 329)

polis (PAH-luhs) the Greek word for a city-state (p. 258)
　polis palabra griega para designar una ciudad estado (pág. 258)

polytheism the worship of many gods (p. 64)
　politeísmo culto a varios dioses (pág. 64)

pope the bishop of Rome and the head of the Roman Catholic Church (p. 394)
　Papa obispo de Roma y cabeza de la Iglesia católica romana (pág. 394)

Popol Vuh (poh-pohl VOO) a book containing Maya legends and history (p. 443)
　Popol Vuh libro que contiene las leyendas y la historia de los mayas (pág. 443)

prehistory the time before there was writing (p. 28)
　prehistoria período anterior a la existencia de la escritura (pág. 28)

priest a person who performs religious ceremonies (p. 65)
    sacerdote persona que lleva a cabo ceremonias religiosas (pág. 65)

primary source an account of an event by someone who took part in or witnessed the event (p. 10)
    fuente primaria relato de un hecho por parte de alguien que participó o presenció el hecho (pág. 10)

prophet someone who is said to receive messages from God to be taught to others (p. 235)
    profeta alguien del que se cree que recibe mensajes de Dios para transmitírselos a los demás (pág. 235)

provinces areas outside of Italy that the Romans controlled (p. 360)
    provincias zonas fuera de Italia que controlaban los romanos (pág. 360)

Punic Wars a series of wars between Rome and Carthage in the 200s and 100s BC (p. 339)
    guerras púnicas sucesión de guerras entre Roma y Cartago en los siglos III y II a. C. (pág. 339)

pyramid a huge triangular tomb built by the Egyptians and other peoples (p. 98)
    pirámide tumba triangular y gigantesca construida por los egipcios y otros pueblos (pág. 98)

Q, R

rabbi (RAB-y) a Jewish religious leader and teacher (p. 242)
    rabino líder y maestro religioso judío (pág. 242)

reason clear and ordered thinking (p. 307)
    razón pensamiento claro y ordenado (pág. 307)

region an area with one or more features that make it different from surrounding areas (p. 15)
    región zona con una o varias características que la diferencian de las zonas que la rodean (pág. 15)

reincarnation a Hindu and Buddhist belief that souls are born and reborn many times, each time into a new body (p. 153)
    reencarnación creencia hindú y budista de que las almas nacen y renacen muchas veces, siempre en un cuerpo nuevo (pág. 153)

republic a political system in which people elect leaders to govern them (p. 328)
    república sistema político en el que el pueblo elige a los líderes que lo gobernarán (pág. 328)

resources the materials found on Earth that people need and value (p. 16)
    recursos materiales de la Tierra que las personas necesitan y valoran (pág. 16)

Resurrection in Christianity, Jesus's rise from the dead (p. 385)
    Resurrección en el cristianismo, la vuelta a la vida de Jesús (pág. 385)

Roman Senate a council of wealthy and powerful citizens who advised Rome's leaders (p. 333)
    Senado romano consejo de ciudadanos ricos y poderosos que aconsejaba a los gobernantes de Roma (pág. 333)

Romance languages languages that developed from Latin, such as Italian, French, Spanish, Portuguese, and Romanian (p. 371)
    lenguas romances lenguas que surgieron del latín, como el italiano, el francés, el español, el portugués y el rumano (pág. 371)

Rosetta Stone a huge stone slab inscribed with hieroglyphics, Greek, and a later form of Egyptian that allowed historians to understand Egyptian writing (p. 109)
piedra Roseta gran losa de piedra en la que aparecen inscripciones en jeroglíficos, en griego y en una forma tardía del idioma egipcio que permitió a los historiadores descifrar la escritura egipcia (pág. 109)

rural a countryside area (p. 62)
rural zona del campo (pág. 62)

S

saint a person known and admired for his or her holiness (p. 388)
santo persona conocida y admirada por su santidad (pág. 388)

Sanskrit the most important language of ancient India (p. 149)
sánscrito el idioma más importante de la antigua India (pág. 149)

satire a style of writing that pokes fun at people or society (p. 370)
sátira estilo de escritura que hace burla de las personas o de la sociedad (pág. 370)

scribe a writer (p. 68)
escriba escritor (pág. 68)

secondary source information gathered by someone who did not take part in or witness an event (p. 10)
fuente secundaria información recopilada por alguien que no participó ni presenció un hecho (pág. 10)

seismograph a device that measures the strength of an earthquake (p. 204)
sismógrafo aparato que mide la fuerza de un terremoto (pág. 204)

silk a soft, light, and highly valued fabric developed in China (p. 209)
seda tejido suave, ligero y muy apreciado que se originó en China (pág. 209)

Silk Road a network of trade routes that stretched across Asia from China to the Mediterranean Sea (p. 209)
Ruta de la Seda red de rutas comerciales que se extendían a lo largo de Asia desde China hasta el mar Mediterráneo (pág. 209)

silt a mixture of fertile soil and tiny rocks that can make land ideal for farming (p. 57)
cieno mezcla de tierra fértil y piedrecitas que pueden crear un terreno ideal para el cultivo (pág. 57)

social hierarchy the division of society by rank or class (p. 65)
jerarquía social división de la sociedad en clases o niveles (pág. 65)

society a community of people who share a common culture (p. 33)
sociedad comunidad de personas que comparten la misma cultura (pág. 33)

sphinx (sfinks) an imaginary creature with a human head and the body of a lion that was often shown on Egyptian statues (p. 110)
esfinge criatura imaginaria con cabeza humana y cuerpo de león que aparecía representada a menudo en las estatuas egipcias (pág. 110)

subcontinent a large landmass that is smaller than a continent, such as India (p. 144)
subcontinente gran masa de tierra menor que un continente, como la India (pág. 144)

sundial a device that uses the position of shadows cast by the sun to tell the time of day (p. 204)
reloj de sol dispositivo que utiliza la posición de las sombras que proyecta el sol para indicar las horas del día (pág. 204)

surplus more of something than is needed (p. 58)
excedente cantidad que supera lo que se necesita (pág. 58)

synagogue (si-nuh-gawg) a Jewish house of worship (p. 234)
sinagoga lugar de culto judío (pág. 234)

Talmud (TAHL-moohd) a set of commentaries, stories, and folklore that explains Jewish law (p. 236)
Talmud conjunto de comentarios, relatos y folklore que explican la ley judía (pág. 236)

Ten Commandments in the Bible, a code of moral laws given to Moses by God (p. 228)
los Diez Mandamientos en la Biblia, código de leyes morales que Dios le entregó a Moisés (pág. 228)

tool an object that has been modified to help a person accomplish a task (p. 30)
herramienta objeto que ha sido modificado para ayudar a una persona a realizar una tarea (pág. 30)

Torah the most sacred text of Judaism (p. 234)
Torá el texto más sagrado del judaísmo (pág. 234)

trade network a system of people in different lands who trade goods back and forth (p. 128)
red comercial sistema de personas en diferentes lugares que comercian productos entre sí (pág. 128)

trade route a path followed by traders (p. 102)
ruta comercial itinerario seguido por los comerciantes (pág. 102)

tyrant an ancient Greek leader who held power through the use of force (p. 263)
tirano gobernante de la antigua Grecia que mantenía el poder mediante el uso de la fuerza (pág. 263)

urban a city area (p. 62)
urbano zona de ciudad (pág. 62)

vault a set of arches that supports the roof of a building (p. 367)
bóveda conjunto de arcos que sostienen el tejado de un edificio (pág. 367)

veto (VEE-toh) to reject or prohibit actions and laws of other government officials (p. 334)
vetar rechazar o prohibir acciones y leyes de otros funcionarios del gobierno (pág. 334)

villa a country home or estate (p. 362)
villa finca o casa de campo (pág. 362)

wheelbarrow a single-wheeled cart (p. 209)
carretilla carrito de una sola rueda (pág. 209)

X, Y, Z

Zealots (ZE-luhts) radical Jews who supported rebellion against the Romans (p. 240)
zelotes judíos radicales que apoyaron la rebelión contra los romanos (pág. 240)

ziggurat a pyramid-shaped temple in Sumer (p. 70)
zigurat templo sumerio en forma de pirámide (pág. 70)

ENGLISH AND SPANISH GLOSSARY

Index

Credits and Acknowledgments

Illustrations and Photo Credits

Staff Credits

The people who contributed to **Holt California Social Studies: World History, Ancient Civilizations** are listed below. They represent editorial, design, intellectual property resources, production, emedia, and permissions.

Lissa B. Anderson, Melanie Baccus, Charles Becker, Jessica Bega, Ed Blake, Gillian Brody, Shirley Cantrell, Erin Cornett, Rose Degollado, Chase Edmond, Mescal Evler, Rhonda Fariss, Marsh Flournoy, Leanna Ford, Bob Fullilove, Matthew Gierhart, Janet Harrington, Rhonda Haynes, Rob Hrechko, Wilonda Ieans, Cathy Jenevein, Kadonna Knape, Cathy Kuhles, Debbie Lofland, Bob McClellan, Joe Melomo, Richard Metzger, Andrew Miles, Cynthia Munoz, Karl Pallmeyer, Chanda Pearmon, Jarred Prejean, Shelly Ramos, Désirée Reid, Curtis Riker, Marleis Roberts, Diana Rodriguez, Gene Rumann, Annette Saunders, Jenny Schaeffer, Kay Selke, Ken Shepardson, Michele Shukers, Chris Smith, Christine Stanford, Elaine Tate, Jeannie Taylor, Joni Wackwitz, Ken Whiteside